NEW CENTURY
COMMENTARY

General Editors

RONALD E. CLEMENTS	MATTHEW BLACK
(Old Testament)	(New Testament)

1 and 2 KINGS

VOLUME II

THE NEW CENTURY BIBLE COMMENTARIES

EXODUS (J. P. Hyatt)
LEVITICUS AND NUMBERS (N. H. Snaith)*
DEUTERONOMY (A. D. H. Mayes)
JOSHUA, JUDGES, AND RUTH (John Gray)*
1 AND 2 KINGS (Gwilym H. Jones)
1 AND 2 CHRONICLES (H. G. Williamson)
EZRA, NEHEMIAH, AND ESTHER (D. J. Clines)
JOB (H. H. Rowley)
PSALMS Volumes 1 and 2 (A. A. Anderson)
ISAIAH 1-39 (R. E. Clements)
ISAIAH 40-66 (R. N. Whybray)
EZEKIEL (John W. Wevers)
THE GOSPEL OF MATTHEW (David Hill)
THE GOSPEL OF MARK (Hugh Anderson)
THE GOSPEL OF LUKE (E. Earle Ellis)
THE GOSPEL OF JOHN (Barnabas Lindars)
THE ACTS OF THE APOSTLES (William Neil)
ROMANS (Matthew Black)
1 and 2 CORINTHIANS (F. F. Bruce)
GALATIANS (Donald Guthrie)
EPHESIANS (C. Leslie Mitton)
PHILIPPIANS (Ralph P. Martin)
COLOSSIANS AND PHILEMON (Ralph P. Martin)
PASTORAL EPISTLES (A. T. Hanson)
1 and 2 THESSALONIANS (I. Howard Marshall)
1 PETER (Ernest Best)
JOHANNINE EPISTLES (K. Grayston)
JAMES, JUDE and 2 PETER (E. M. Sidebottom)
THE BOOK OF REVELATION (G. R. Beasley-Murray)

*Not yet available in paperback
Other titles are in preparation

NEW CENTURY BIBLE COMMENTARY

Based on the Revised Standard Version

1 and 2 KINGS

VOLUME II
1 Kings 17:1–2 Kings 25:30

GWILYM H. JONES

WM. B. EERDMANS PUBL. CO., GRAND RAPIDS

MARSHALL, MORGAN & SCOTT PUBL. LTD., LONDON

Library of Congress Cataloging in Publication Data

Jones, Gwilym H. (Gwilym Henry), 1930-
1 and 2 Kings.

(New century Bible commentary)
Bibliography: p. xiv
Includes indexes.
Contents: v. 1 Kings, 1-16:34 — v. 2. 1 Kings,
17:1-2 Kings, 25:30.
1. Bible. O.T. Kings — Commentaries. I. Title.
II. Title: One and Two Kings. III. Series.
BS1335.3.J66 1984   222'.507   84-21074

ISBN 0-8028-0019-X (pbk. : v. 1.)
ISBN 0-8028-0040-8 (pbk. : v. 2.)

CONTENTS

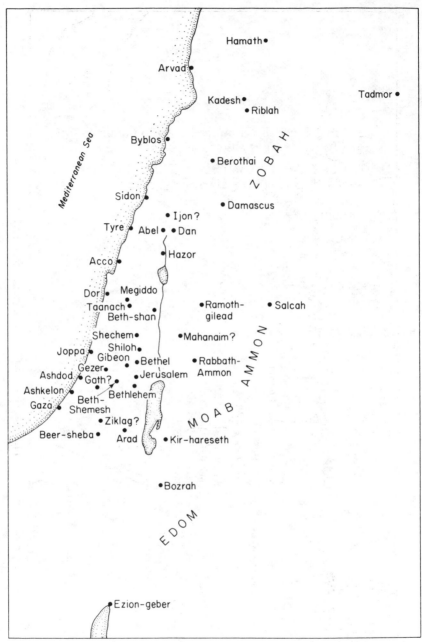

Syro-Palestine at the time of David and Solomon

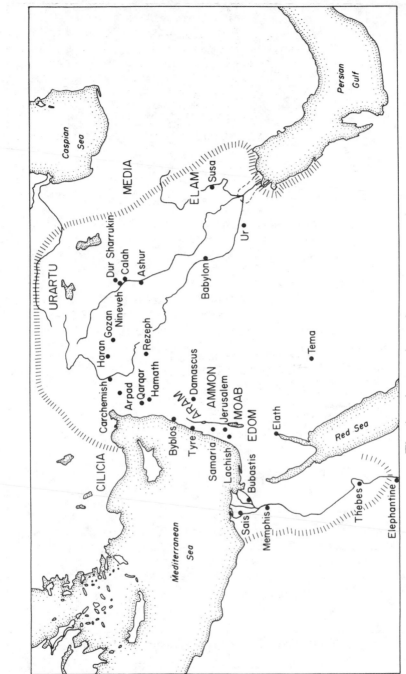

The Assyrian empire at its greatest expansion

COMMENTARY

on

1 and 2 Kings

1 Kings 17:1–2 Kings 25:30

3. FROM THE REIGN OF AHAB TO THE REVOLT OF JEHU
I Kg. 17:1–2 Kg. 10:36

The stereotyped and formal account of the reigns of the kings of
Judah and Israel found in I Kg. 15:1–16:34 gives way to a
completely different genre in I Kg. 17ff. This new section is dominated by two cycles of prophetical narratives, the first connected
with Elijah (I Kg. 17:1–2 Kg. 1:18) and the other connected with
Elisha (2 Kg. 2:1–10:36). See further, Introduction, pp. 64ff. Not
all the material contained in these prophetical cycles is of the same
character or of equal significance. As already noted, there are
personal anecdotes, which exaggerate the miraculous and have
distinctly legendary characteristics. But, included with these, are
narratives recording the participation of the prophets in the political
and social affairs of Israel and its rulers. These narratives are
important for assessing the impact of social and religious developments on the life of Israel during this time; they are also significant
for estimating the contribution made by the prophetic movement.
Elijah's interference with Ahab's religious (I Kg. 18) and social (I
Kg. 21) policies is significant in that it represents a standpoint that
reached its culmination in the revolt of Jehu. Similarly, Elisha's
participation in the events surrounding the *coup d'état* of both Hazael
(2 Kg. 8:7–15) and Jehu (2 Kg. 9:1–6) is of considerable
significance.

Nevertheless, the period is not covered simply by prophetical
narratives; interspersed with them in this section are accounts of
events in the form of historical narrative, some of which have
undoubtedly drawn upon historical records or annals. It is to this
category that the accounts of the Syrian wars (I Kg. 20:22), the war
against Moab (2 Kg. 3), the siege of Samaria (2 Kg. 6:24–7:20) and
the revolt of Jehu (2 Kg. 9:1–10:14) must be ascribed.

(a) Elijah and his time
17:1–2 Kg. 1:18

Elijah's activities are placed in the period of Ahab (875–854 BC) and
his successor Ahaziah (854–853 BC). Very little is known about him
personally, since the narratives do not even mention the name of
his father, and the reference to him as 'Elijah the Tishbite, of Tishbe
in Gilead' (17:1) is problematic (see below). Any attempt to assess
his work and contribution will have to take into account literary

and form-critical studies of the narratives; the legendary anecdotes
can be dismissed and a measure of redaction has to be recognized.

What then, if anything, is known of the historical Elijah? (see
Smend, *VTS* 28 [1975], pp. 167–84). He is presented in chapters
18–19 and 2 Kg. 1 as the defender of Yahwism against the cult of
Baal, and against the social evils of the king (1 Kg. 21). In contrast
to an earlier sceptical attitude towards their historical value (as
expressed, for instance, by Gunkel, *Elias*, pp. 3ff.), there is at
present a tendency to accept that the narratives contain a tradition
that is essentially reliable. Whilst admitting that it is more important
to enquire about the meaning of the narratives than about the actual
course of events (as suggested by Würthwein, *ZThK* 59 [1962], p.
138), it is now appreciated that the narratives are concerned with
the activities of a real person, who can only be understood against
the background of the northern kingdom at a particular time (Steck,
Überlieferung, p. 135). Phoenicia was once again exerting its
influence on Israelite affairs, and the prophet is presented as an
opponent of the religious syncretism that accommodated the Tyrian
Baal. This is the theme of chapters 18–19; likewise 2 Kg. 1 is critical
of the king's acknowledgement of Baal-zebub the god of Ekron.
The prophet's name, Elijah ('Yahweh is God'), epitomises his
mission, which was to show that 'the LORD, he is God' (1 Kg.
18:39).

Admittedly the presentation of Elijah has exaggerated and perhaps
over-dramatized the clash between the prophet and the reigning
monarch. Our knowledge of conditions in Ahab's reign does not
point to a crisis of the dimension described in 1 Kg. 18 (Fohrer,
Elia, pp. 53ff.). A deterioration after Ahab's death led to Jehu's
revolt, and because the Elijah traditions were compiled by the Elisha
circle in the aftermath of that revolt, the crisis that led to it
influenced their presentation of Elijah's work (cf. Smend, *VT* 25
[1975], pp. 537ff.). Nevertheless, an admission that the picture has
been exaggerated does not justify the conclusion that Elijah's
mission is completely fictitious and has nothing to do with the
historical Elijah (cf. Smend, *VTS* 28 [1975], pp. 173ff.). On the
contrary, Elijah presented his challenge to Israel during a time when
the cult of the Phoenician Baal was making an impact that was later
to develop to more critical dimensions.

(i) *Incidents during a drought* **17:1–24**
After an introductory notice of the drought (v. 1), three incidents
follow: the feeding of Elijah at the brook of Cherith (vv. 2–6), the
widow of Zarephath (vv. 7–16) and the resuscitation of a child (vv.
17–24). The latter incident is not necessarily connected with the

drought, and seems to be independent of the first two episodes; but it is bound to its present context because it is often assumed that the child was the widow of Zarephath's son and that the incidents belong together. The historical reliability of these accounts is in question since they clearly have the characteristics of prophetic wonder legends (Hentschel, *Die Elijaerzählungen*, pp. 93ff.). Moreover, the similarity between them and incidents in the Elisha cycle (cf. 2 Kg. 4:1–7; 4:18–37) is taken as an indication that they did not belong originally to the Elijah cycle (Steck, *op. cit.*, p. 19; cf. Dietrich, *Prophetie*, pp. 122ff.). Nevertheless, these anecdotes had been connected to 1 Kg. 17:1 and chapter 18 at an earlier stage than their incorporation in the books of Kings (cf. Dietrich, *op. cit.*, p. 123).

1. **Elijah**: Because the name means 'Yah is God', which is also the theme of the Mount Carmel scene (1 Kg. 18:39), there must be some connection between the prophet's name and his mission. The contention that Elijah was a fictitious figure devised to represent a programme can be dismissed (Smend,*VTS* 28 [1975], p. 177); it seems reasonable to accept that his name was a 'confessional name' (Noth, *Personennamen*, pp. 140ff.), which may not have been the prophet's original name but one give later in view of his work (Bronner, *Elijah and Elisha*, pp. 22ff.). **the Tishbite, of Tishbe in Gilead**: *RSV*'s **of Tishbe** is obtained from the Gk. in preference to the irregular form of MT for 'of the settlers' (which is preferred by Gray, p. 377). Another possibility that has been suggested is to emend the text slightly to give 'from Jabesh Gilead' (cf. Glueck, *River Jordan*, p. 170); but this is unacceptable in view of the many other references to Elijah as the Tishbite (cf. 1 Kg. 21:17, 28; 2 Kg. 1:3, 8; 9:36). The difficulty is that **of Tishbe** is, on the one hand, tautologous; on the other hand, it is questionable if the text intends to suggest that he was a Tishbite living elsewhere. Moreover, the exact location of Tishbe is unknown, and there is no confirmation of its traditional identification with *Listib* (*BHH III*, cols. 1973f.). **neither dew nor rain these years**: The length of the drought is not mentioned, although Josephus (*Ant.* VIII.13.2), on the evidence of Menander, refers to a drought that lasted a year. Lk. 4:25 gives a figure of three and a half years; a drought extending to a full three and a half years would have devastating effects (see Fichtner, p. 265), and the figure of three and a half is rather suspect in that it was half a sabbatical (Montgomery, p. 293). Possibly the figure denotes one full year and smaller parts of two other years. The natural sequence to the introduction of the drought in this verse is 18:1; although it has been frequently contended that the original beginning to the drought narratives has been extracted and

replaced by the present version, it is probable that the basic content
of 17:1 is pre-deuteronomistic (cf. Smend, *VT* 25 [1975], p. 534).

2–6. The first anecdote, which relates how Elijah was mira-
culously fed by the brook of Cherith, has been joined to its present
context by its introduction, **and the word of the LORD came to
him**. This introduction has also brought with it a secondary addition
in v. 5*a*, **so he went and did according to the word of the LORD**,
which makes a clear division between vv. 3–4 and vv. 5*b*–6. The
original narrative was probably short and factual, and is preserved
in vv. 5*b*–6; but because of the later 'word of God' concept an
extension became necessary in vv. 3–4 (Dietrich, *op. cit.*, pp. 122ff.;
Smend, *op. cit.*, pp. 528ff.; Kuhl, *ZAW* 64 [1952], pp. 1–11; Timm,
op. cit., p. 57).

3. Depart from here and turn eastward: Although Elijah may
have originated from east of Jordan, he had obviously addressed
Ahab in Samaria, and was then advised to depart again eastwards
out of the area that was under Ahab's jurisdiction. **hide yourself**:
This is a stronger word than 'he dwelt', which occurs in the original
account in v. 5*b*; it is intended to convey the impression that Elijah
was not acceptable in the court after his declaration in v. 1. A more
drastic, and an unnecessary, course is to place 1 Kg. 19:2–14 in
front of chapter 17 and to interpret **hide yourself** as a measure made
necessary by Jezebel's action against the prophets. **by the brook
Cherith**: The meaning of **Cherith** is 'cutting', and the wadi has
been variously interpreted as a stream in the Damascus area (Šanda
I, p. 419, which is totally unnecessary), with *Wadi Qilt* (which is
unsuitable because it is west of the Jordan) and with *Wadi Yabis*
(which flows into the Jordan from the east). One of the many
tributaries running into the Jordan from the east would be most
suitable here (*BHH II*, col. 1014).

4. the ravens: the Heb. *'ōreḇîm*, 'ravens', is often read as *'arāḇîm*,
'Arabs', although there is no authoritative support for this (Skinner,
p. 224). Gray (p. 378) defends this emended reading on the ground
that it provides a good parallel for the Phoenician woman in the
following anecdote. It has also been contended that textual emendation is unnecessary because 'ravens' was used as a name for the
black Arabs of the Jordan valley (Seale, *ExpT* 68 [1956–7], p. 28;
Wenham, *ExpT* 68 [1956–7], p. 121). However, the fact that the
narratives contain such a high miraculous content, may be taken as
a strong argument against rationalisation and for the retention of
the original rendering (Fohrer, *op. cit.*, p. 9; cf. Timm, *op. cit.*, p.
55).

5. As noted above, v. 5*a* is taken as a secondary addition, but v.
5*b* provides the beginning of the original anecdote.

6. bread and meat in the morning, and bread and meat in the evening: Luc. reads 'bread in the morning and meat in the evening', and this has been favoured by some commentators because it repeats the provision made in Exod. 16:8, 12. Whether intentional or not, the Elijah narratives provide many parallels with the Mosaic tradition; in the present instance the emphasis of both traditions is on miraculous provision by God (cf. Fohrer, *op. cit.*, p. 55).

7–16. The account of Elijah's sojourn in Zarephath and of the miraculous provision of food for him there has many similarities with the previous section. After a short statement in v. 7 defining the occasion (cf. v. 1), it is stated that the word of God to the prophet was the prime mover (cf. v. 8 and also v. 16b). The course of the action in v. 10 is a repetition of what had been commanded by God (cf. above, the relation between vv. 3–4 and vv. 5b–6). God's command to feed the prophet features in this narrative (v. 9b), as it does in the previous one (v. 4b). The motif of fulfilled prophecy appears in this section too (cf. vv. 14 and 16b), and also the fulfilment of the prophet's word (cf. vv. 13a and 15a) (Dietrich, *op. cit.*, pp. 124ff.; Smend, *op. cit.*, pp. 528ff.). Basically the narratives in vv. 5b–6 and in vv. 10–15 have the same structure and belong to the same genre (see also Hentschel, *op. cit.*, pp. 95ff.).

Miracle-working of the kind described here has its parallels in most religions and in hagiology in general (cf. Guillaume, *Divination*, p. 401; Rofé, *JBL* 89 [1970], pp. 427–40). The miraculous element has to be recognized, and any attempt to find a factual cause, such as the suggestion that the widow's generosity became contagious (Gray, p. 381), is unnecessary when dealing with this genre.

7. Although this verse appears as a conclusion to the first anecdote in *RSV*, it is preferable to take it as an introduction to the Zarephath anecdote, as in *BHS* and *NIV* (against Timm, *op. cit.*, p. 55). Like v. 1 it provides an occasion for the miracle that follows, and the opening phrase, **after a while the brook dried up**, gives a reason for the prophet's movement to a new area.

9. Arise, go: The original anecdote beginning in v. 10 has again received an addition in the form of a command given to the prophet as a divine word. **Zarephath, which belongs to Sidon**: As Cherith to the east of the Jordan was out of Ahab's jurisdiction, so also **Zarephath** near the coast in Sidon fell outside his territory. **Zarephath** is to be identified with Sarepta (Lk. 4:26) to the south of Sidon; its name has been preserved in the modern *Sarafand*.

10. a widow was there gathering sticks: The prophet is directed to a widow from whom help could not be expected; this sets the stage once again for the extraordinary. The Heb. verb for gathering is derived from the root *qšš*, which is also used of 'chaff, stubble';

the widow was probably gathering dry material which had fallen from a plant. The prophet's double request in vv. 10*b*, 11 serves to emphasize the hopelessness of the situation in order to prepare the way for the miraculous. He was asking for **a little water** in a time of severe drought, and for **a morsel of bread** from a widow who was struggling to feed herself and her son.

12. the LORD your God: The woman, although a Sidonian and a heathen, answers in the name of Elijah's God. **nothing baked**: The Heb. *mā'ôg* is connected with the root meaning to bake a cake on dried dung (cf. Ezek. 4:12); hence *RSV* translates as **nothing baked**. Other possibilities are to connect the Heb. with an Arab. root meaning 'to be cooked', thus getting 'round cake' or 'cake' (cf. Gray, p. 379) or with an Arab. root denoting the place where one turns for sustenance (*K-B*), thus giving 'sustenance' (*NEB*) or 'bread' (*NIV*). Whatever its derivation, the meaning of the word is clear; the woman did not have what the prophet had asked, or, as interpreted by the Syr. and Targ., she did not have anything. **a jar**: The reference here is to fairly large earthenware jars (cf. Gen. 24:14; Jg. 7:16; 1 Kg. 18:34). The **cruse** (*NEB*, 'flask'; *NIV*, 'jug') denotes a smaller flask which could be easily carried (cf. 1 Sam. 26:11ff.; Honeyman, *PEQ* 71 [1939], pp. 81–9). **and my son**: There is no need to read the plural with the Gk., which probably understood 'household' in v. 15 to mean that she had more than one son.

13. first make me a little cake . . . afterward make for yourself and your son: As noted by Thenius (p. 219), this was a test of her faith and self-renunciation.

14. Beginning with the usual messenger formula, **thus says the LORD God of Israel**, this verse introduces God's statement that the jar and the cruse shall not fail during the period of the drought. The messenger formula is probably secondary, since this particular form is found mostly in the book of Jeremiah and is ascribed by Dietrich (*op. cit.*, p. 124) to DtrP. Moreover, there are signs that v. 14*b* is also a secondary addition; it speaks of God in the 3rd person, introduces the rain motif into an anecdote that is really concerned with an unfailing supply of meal and oil, and seems to have been composed in order to give a base for the fulfilment of prophecy theme in v. 16*b* (cf. Smend, *VT* 25 [1975], p. 533).

15. and her household: There is no need to follow the suggestion to read 'her son' for **her household**, which probably refers to her family and servants. One of the reasons for separating vv. 17–24 from vv. 7–16 is that, whereas the widow of Zarephath was poor, the 'mistress of the house' was a woman of property, having a house with an upper chamber. The retention of **her household** in v. 15, and its interpretation as referring to family and servants, may also mean that this widow too was a woman of means (cf. Montgomery, p. 295).

16. according to the word of the LORD which he spoke by Elijah: This reference to fulfilling the word of God is a deuteronomistic addition, which may be attributed to DtrP (cf. Dietrich, *op. cit.*, pp. 88, 124).

17–24. This section contains an independent wonder narrative, which is not directly linked with the drought presupposed in the previous anecdotes and which also stands apart structurally from the remainder of the chapter. But the present linkage in v. 17, 'after this', connects these verses to the previous sections, and because of this it is assumed, but not stated, that the 'mistress of the house' is the same as the widow of Zarephath in vv. 7–16. It must be noted, however, that the introductory instruction given through the word of God (cf. vv. 2, 8) is absent from this narrative, and 'the word of the LORD' is only acknowledged in a secondary addition at the very end (v. 24*b*; cf. Smend, *op. cit.*, p. 531). Furthermore, Elijah the Tishbite of v. 1 is now called 'man of God', a title that is only applied to him elsewhere in 2 Kg. 1:9ff. (see Timm, *op. cit.*, p. 59). For the similarity between this narrative and sections in Exodus, see Schmitt, *VT* 24 [1974], pp. 466ff.

A similar incident appears in the Elisha cycle (2 Kg. 4:8–37), but with marked differences in structure and content (see further, Hentschel, *op. cit.*, pp. 188ff.; Schmitt, *Elisa*, pp. 93–9). Dependence on 2 Kg. 4:8–37 seems probable; this abbreviated form of a narrative that did not belong originally to the Elijah tradition has been secondarily added to it from the Elisha cycle (for another view, see Kilian, *BZ* 10 [1966], pp. 49ff. and for a full analysis of both sections, see Schmitt, *BZ* 19 [1975], pp. 1–25; *VT* 24 [1974], pp. 454–74). Because the event was attached to the narrative about the widow of Zarephath, the introductory 'word of God' theme was probably considered superfluous; it was, however, added at the end by the redactors who also inserted vv. 2 and 8.

Variations in the vocabulary of the narrative have also to be noted. 'Son' in vv. 17*a*, 18, 19*a*, 23*b* is replaced by 'child' in vv. 21*a*, 23*a*; 'woman' in vv. 17*a*, 24*a* has become 'mother' in v. 23*a*. On such bases it has been contended that the original kernel of the narrative can be traced in vv. 19*b*, 21*a*, 22*b*, 23*a* (Hentschel, *op. cit.*, p. 193).

17. mistress of the house: This title for the woman is not necessarily incongruous with the description of the widow of Zarephath (see above on v. 15), and need not be emended, as suggested by Klostermann (p. 364), to give 'in the upper chamber of the house'. **there was no breath left in him**: It is a debatable point whether the meaning of this phrase is that the child had died (Mitchell, *VT*

11 [1961], pp. 177–87), although it is presupposed elsewhere in the narrative that this was the case; cf. the use of the verb for dying in vv. 18, 20 and the concept of the soul departing from the body in vv. 21, 22.

18. What have you against me?: cf. also Jg. 11:12; 2 Sam. 16:10; 19:22; 2 Kg. 3:13; 2 Chr. 35:21; it also occurs in the *NT*; see Mk. 1:24; Mt. 8:29; Jn. 2:4. Literally the question asked is 'what have I and you (in common)?', which means 'why do you interfere in my affairs?'; cf. *NEB*, 'what made you interfere?'. **You have come to bring my sin to remembrance**: *NEB*, 'bring my sins to light'. The idea here is that the very presence of the 'man of God' has revealed some obscure or forgotten sin: because of the incompatibility between God and sin, God's presence, through his representative, has made punishment inevitable; hence **the death of my son**. This verse ascribes to the general view of the *OT* that sickness and death come as punishment for sin. The verb is adequately rendered by 'bring to light' and it is unnecessary to think of it as a more formal registering of sin before God (as by Montgomery, p. 295).

19. carried him in to the upper chamber: There is more to this action than a pure matter of hygiene (as suggested by Gray, p. 382). In 2 Kg. 4:33 it is stressed that only the prophet and the child were in the room when Elisha revived the Shunammite's son; Elijah's action here may also imply that resuscitation occurred in private.

20. This verse belongs to the elaboration of the original kernel, according to the suggestion made by Hentschel (see above).

21. Then he stretched himself upon the child three times: Although the same verb for stretching over is not used in 2 Kg. 4:34ff., the action is identical (cf. also the revival of Eutychus in Ac. 20:10). In the more detailed description of 2 Kg. 4 the prophet is seen stretching over the child, mouth to mouth, eyes to eyes and hands to hands. Parallels are found elsewhere, especially in Babylonian texts, which also refer to eyes, mouth, head, hands and feet being matched against each other (see Hentschel, *op. cit.*, pp. 193ff. for reference to Babylonian cuneiform texts). The suggestion is that strength from the healthy body is transferred to the corresponding infirm organs of the sick body. The action thus belongs to the field of contactual magic (Gray, p. 382), and Elijah is acting like a witch-doctor (Martin-Achard, *Death to Life*, p. 59). The Gk. 'he breathed into the boy', although easier to understand because it implies something similar to a kiss-of-life, is obviously a guess at the meaning of the Heb. and is unacceptable. **let this child's soul come in to him again**: The soul's departure from the body occurred at death. But because the *OT* has a different concept from ours of the demarcation between life and death, it is not easy to determine if the child had actually died. 'Death' was regarded as a weak form of life, and there seems to have been a prolonged existence that is called 'death', but from which revival seems possible. Within a certain period (cf. Jn. 11), provided that the body was not buried and the soul had not descended to Sheol, body and soul could be brought together again and the person resuscitated. There is no need to regard the child's revival as a challenge to the Baal myths, which claimed that he and other deities could revive the dead (as has been argued by Bronner, *Elijah and Elisha*, pp. 86–122).

22. According to Hentschel's reconstruction of the original narrative (see above), v. 22*a*, stating that God listened to Elijah's plea, is an addition to the original kernel (cf. also the Gk.). **and he revived**: As the word 'death' can denote physical weakness rather than actual death, the verb *ḥāyāh* can mean **revived** rather than 'lived' (implying previous death). See Johnson, *Prophecy*, pp. 89ff.

24. The woman's response falls into two parts. Initially she claims that **now I know that you are a man of God**, an acknowledgement that was probably carried over with the original narrative from the Elisha tradition, the home of the 'man of God' concept. The second part, **and that the word of the LORD is in your mouth**, is a redactional addition that brings the third anecdote into line with the general presentation of chapter 17, namely the inspiration of Elijah's miraculous activities by the word of God (Smend, *op. cit.*, p. 531).

(ii) Elijah on Mount Carmel 18:1–46

Although the present account of Elijah's contest with the prophets of Baal on Mount Carmel gives the impression of being a smoothly running, continuous narrative, different elements seem to have been combined together to form this chapter. An analysis of these elements results in their separation, which renders the argument for the original unity of the chapter (as by Gunkel, *Elias*, pp. 9–13; cf. Eissfeldt, *Der Gott Karmel*, pp. 32–55) an impossible proposition. Elijah's relationship with Ahab is the basic material in some sections, especially vv. 1–20, 41–46; but Ahab is conspicuously absent from the Mount Carmel scene in vv. 21–40. The drought in 1 Kg. 17:1 and the return of rain is taken to be the background for the whole event; allusions to the drought are made in vv. 1–2, 5–6 and to the coming of rain in vv. 41–46. On the other hand, not only is the drought theme absent from other sections, but there are incidents presupposing ample water (cf. vv. 33–35, 38). The Mount Carmel scene, lacking as it does any reference to the clash between prophet and king, and having no allusion to the drought, can be isolated from the remainder of the chapter (Timm, *Die Dynastie*, pp. 60–87).

The separation of the ordeal on Carmel from other surrounding material is basic to any understanding of the chapter and its growth. According to Alt (*Kleine Schriften II*, pp. 135ff.) this narrative in vv. 17–40, with its culmination in securing fire upon the sacrifice, is one of the two strands of tradition brought together in the chapter; the other is Elijah's encounter with Obadiah (vv. 2b–16), which reaches its culmination in vv. 41–46 with the securing of rain. Fohrer (*Elia*, pp. 34–6; cf. Fichtner, p. 264) finds that three independent traditions have been combined in this chapter, for he separates Elijah's encounter with Obadiah in vv. 2b–16 from his clash with Ahab and makes it an independent tradition; he further suggests that the encounter with Ahab and its climax (vv. 1–2a, 16–17, 41–46), which was intended to prove Yahweh's control over rain, is to be located near Jezreel rather than on Carmel.

In attempting to trace the nature and extent of the material available and how it was subsequently used in the composition of the chapter, the first step is to define more closely the Carmel ordeal and its limits. Although Elijah's encounter with Ahab is concluded in v. 16, thus suggesting that the Carmel ordeal begins at v. 17, it has to be admitted that the real beginning of the Carmel scene is delayed until v. 21 (as proposed by Würthwein, *ZThK* 59 [1962], pp. 131–44). Verses 17ff. are best regarded as the completion of the Elijah-Ahab encounter, and vv. 19ff. as transition verses composed to tie the Carmel ordeal with Elijah's clash with Ahab. To decide on the original termination of the Carmel narrative is also difficult. Its present ending with the slaying of the prophets of Baal in v. 40, although fitting as a conclusion, is not a necessary and integral part of the ordeal between Elijah and the prophets; the aim was to humiliate the prophets, not to kill them. Verse 40 can be taken as a later composition intended to complement the killing of the prophets by Jezebel in v. 13 (Würthwein, *ibid.*) and possibly betraying some influence on the present narrative by the subsequent revolt of Jehu. Smend (*VT* 25 [1975], pp. 538ff.) finds a close parallel in content and form between 1 Kg. 18:19ff., 40 and the narrative about Jehu in 2 Kg. 10, which again suggests that in its present form the narrative has received some accretions, possibly from the Elisha circle, after Jehu had killed the prophets of Baal.

Basically, therefore, the original Carmel ordeal is to be found in vv. 21–39, with additions in vv. 19–20, 40, but there remains the question of further accretions in the course of transmission. One element that must be considered in this connection is the pouring of water upon the altar, including the making of a trench (v. 32b), pouring the water in it three times (vv. 33b–35) and the sequel in v. 38b. As will be noted below, there is much disagreement about the significance of the water-pouring ceremony in these verses.

Possibly an ancient rain-making rite is being described here; the description was deliberately inserted into the Carmel scene in order to connect it more closely with the drought and return of rain theme to which it has by now become subservient (Tromp, *Bib* 56 [1975], pp. 480–502). Another indication of accretions to the text is to be found in the doublets present in the narrative (cf. Smend, *op. cit.*, pp. 526ff.). The building of an altar is reported twice, in v. 30*b* and in vv. 31–32*a*, the former being more original (see below); there are also two versions of Elijah's prayer in v. 36*b* and in v. 37, the former being a secondary variation of the latter (see below). In the section from v. 30 to v. 39 the following verses constituted the original narrative: 30, 33*a*, 36*a*, 37, 38*a*, 39.

The original Carmel narrative, which belonged to the Elijah tradition transmitted through the Elisha circle, has been integrated into the Elijah cycle on the one hand by giving it an introduction in vv. 19–20 which binds it more closely with Elijah's clash with Ahab, and on the other hand by inserting a rain-making rite to bind it to the drought cycle. In considering the nature of the material with which it has been integrated, the encounter between Elijah and Obadiah (vv. 2*b*–16) and the return of rain (vv. 41–46) call for attention. Undoubtedly the encounter with Obadiah can be treated as an independent tradition that has been inserted into the text at the point of Elijah's clash with Ahab, due to an affinity of theme (see Fohrer, *ibid.*). Verses 41–46 are more problematic, but it seems that the account of the return of the rain, with the introduction for the first time of Elijah's servant, had at one time existed independently (cf. Alt, *op. cit.*, p. 136; Smend, *op. cit.*, p. 536) but was added to the drought cycle as a fitting conclusion to it. When the Carmel scene was inserted into the drought cycle, transition verses (vv. 41–42) had to be composed, but the fusion is not entirely successful (cf. below, and see Tromp, *op. cit.*, pp. 490ff.). In the original drought cycle stood 1 Kg. 17:1; 18:1*a*–2*a*, 17–18, 43–46, but to this was added vv. 2*b*–16 together with the Carmel scene and its accompanying transition verses. The present narrative gives an unmistakable impression of unity because it has a dominating theme, namely the drought and Yahweh's control over rain. All else, including the Carmel narrative, has been made subservient to this main theme (Ap-Thomas, *PEQ* 92 [1960], p. 155; Tromp, *op. cit.*, pp. 494ff.). Moreover, this unity probably belonged to the narrative in its pre-deuteronomistic version, so that the deuteronomistic redactors had before them a drought cycle, including the Carmel scene, and reaching a climax in the giving of rain (cf. Eissfeldt, *op. cit.*, pp. 32ff.). The deuteronomistic redactors made a few additions, such as the reference to the word of God in v. 1, the phrase 'before whom I stand' in v. 15, the allusion to the commandments in v. 18*b* and probably the doublets in vv. 31–32*b* and in v. 36*b* (Fohrer, *op. cit.*, pp. 53ff.; Smend, *op. cit.*, pp. 526ff.).

1. This verse, with its statement that **the word of the LORD came to Elijah**, must be connected with 1 Kg. 17:2, 8 and attributed to the deuteronomistic redactor. Nevertheless, the verse as a whole takes up the drought theme from 1 Kg. 17:1, and **the third year** connects naturally with the 'three years' of the previous announcement. On the length of the period of drought, see above on 17:1, with the probability that **in the third year** denotes the beginning of the year and does not necessarily imply a three year drought. **show yourself to Ahab**: After announcing in chapter 17 that Yahweh was bringing the drought, Elijah had gone into hiding; but now, with the announcement that the drought was coming to an end, he is to appear again. A persecution of the prophet figures prominently in the following section on Obadiah (vv. 2–16), and is attributed by Fohrer (*op. cit.*, pp. 36ff.) to the circle that was responsible for the collecting of chapters 17–19 (cf. also 17:2–6; 18:10f., 13; 19:1–3*a*, 13*b*–14).

2. Whilst the first half of this verse is a continuation of the drought narrative of v. 1, its second half introduces the Obadiah narrative which proceeds in vv. 3ff.

3. **Obadiah**: The name, meaning 'the servant of Yahweh', may have been an assumed one, as probably was the case with Elijah (see in 17:1). **who was over the household**: For this office, see on 1 Kg. 4:6. Verses 3*b*–4 relate in passing Obadiah's action when Jezebel was killing the prophets, and the same incident figures again in v. 13. Fohrer (*op. cit.*, pp. 36ff.) has questioned the reliability of the persecution of the prophets theme, thus casting doubt on the unity of the Obadiah section. The theme occurs in vv. 3*b*–4, 10–11, 13, which are all regarded by him as secondary. As noted below, the deletion of vv. 10–11 is not justifiable; but vv. 3*b*–4 and 13, with their persecution theme, may be secondary material originating from a later date and seeking indirectly to justify the revolt of Jehu (Herrmann, *Heilserwartungen*, pp. 19ff.; Steck, *Überlieferung*, pp. 11–13). The Obadiah section may have been preserved in tradition simply as a record of Elijah's dealings with the king's court, where he found both hostility and reverence.

4. **hid them by fifties in a cave**: The Heb. 'hid them fifty in a cave' is obscure, but the Targ. and v. 13 understand the meaning to be that he hid them **by fifties**; this is also understood by Luc., which reads 'two caves'. Gray's proposal (p. 386) to read 'by fives' is unnecessary. Montgomery (p. 298), taking cave to be generic,

proposes 'in the cave-region' and refers to the chalk formation of the Mount Carmel area, where two thousand caves have been counted.

5–6. Ahab's plan of action to find grass near springs of water in order to preserve the animals connects the Obadiah narrative with the period of the drought. The only reference to the circumstances of Obadiah's encounter with Elijah are to be found in vv. 5–6, and indirectly in v. 15, which presupposes v. 1. Consequently, Herrmann (*ibid.*) deletes these verses as secondary accretions, which have been attached to the original narrative in vv. 7–14 in order to bind it to the drought cycle. His proposal, however, is impracticable, since it brings the narrative to an abrupt conclusion without providing an answer from Elijah to Obadiah's unwillingness to tell Ahab (and is thus rightly rejected by Steck, *op. cit.*, p. 12). It is more reasonable to accept that the Obadiah narrative was an independent tradition with the drought as its background; for that reason it became attached at this particular point to the drought cycle. **Go through the land**: The Heb. literally reads 'Go into the land', but the Gk. would suggest 'Come, let us traverse the land' (Gray, p. 386; Orlinsky, *JBL* 59 [1940], pp. 514–17). *NEB* has 'Let us go through the land'. **not lose some of the animals**: *NIV*'s 'any of our animals' and *NEB*'s 'none of our cattle' (cf. Luc.) give a better meaning than *RSV*, which renders the Heb. too literally.

7. **Obadiah recognized him**: It is assumed that Obadiah had not met the prophet previously, but **recognized him** possibly because of the hairy mantle that he was wearing (cf. also 2 Kg. 1:8).

8–9. Obadiah was unwilling to accept Elijah's commission to announce to Ahab, **Behold, Elijah is here**. The reason which he gives, that Ahab would kill him, is reported three times (vv. 9, 12, 14, with the Heb. using the same verb in vv. 12, 14); despite the repetition, the reason is not clarified, and no clue is given at first why Ahab should kill Obadiah, especially in view of the statement in v. 10 that the king had conducted a wide search for the prophet. An explanation is offered in v. 12, where it is stated that Obadiah assumed that Elijah would disappear and that he himself would become the victim of the king's rage. Whether Obadiah sincerely thought that he would be killed, or else produced an excuse in order to save Elijah from Ahab (cf. Montgomery, p. 299), is not clear.

10–11. The commission given by Elijah in v. 8 is repeated twice by Obadiah in his reply (cf. vv. 11 and 14). If Fohrer's suggestion (see above, on v. 3) that all references to the persecution of the prophets are to be deleted is followed, then vv. 10–11 are rejected, and v. 9 is followed immediately by v. 12. Against Fohrer's proposal, however, it must be noted that Ahab's search for Elijah, described in v. 10, is essential to the structure of the narrative and provides the background for the assumption in v. 12 that Obadiah would be killed. **he would take an oath of the kingdom or nation, that they had not found you:** The reference to other kingdoms in this verse is scarcely a hyperbole for the whole of Israel (as suggested by Benzinger, p. 109); more probably the meaning is that the search for Elijah had extended to some of Israel's near neighbours. Montgomery (p. 299) refers to other examples of such adjurations and their accompanying execrations.

12. the Spirit of the LORD will carry you: In the prophetical narratives the prophet or man of God is described as being possessed by **the Spirit of the LORD**, which enabled him to achieve the extraordinary. In this case it is thought that he will be suddenly transported out of sight (cf. 2 Kg. 3:12; 8:3; 11:1; 43:5, all using the verb *nāśʾā*, 'to lift up', which also occurs here). For other expressions to denote possession by the spirit, see Jg. 6:34; 11:29; 14:6, 29. Attempts to rationalize the experience by equating it here with power to perform exceptional acts, or with sagacity to avoid capture, unavoidably diminish the idea of abnormality, or rather supra-normality, associated with the spirit.

13. cf. on vv. 3*b*–4. It is accepted here that the tradition preserved in vv. 3*b*–4 and 13 comes from a later period and serves as propaganda that seeks to justify the blood purge of Jehu.

14. The deletion of v. 13 makes v. 14, which is a repetition of v. 11, unnecessary. Whilst retaining vv. 10–11 (see above), it is suggested that vv. 13–14 can be omitted; a more compact Obadiah episode thus appears in vv. 3*b*, 5–12, 15–16.

15. the LORD of hosts: This is the first occurrence in Kings of a title found five times in the book (cf. 19:10, 14; 2 Kg. 3:14, 19:31), all of them, as it happens, in prophetical utterances. Unquestionably the term, in its early occurrences, denoted that Yahweh was the God of Israel's armies (cf. 1 Sam. 17:45), and the translation 'the sustainer of the armies' (Obermann, *JBL* 68 [1949], pp. 309–14) can be justified. It is more difficult, however, to define the exact meaning of the term, and the changes through which it has passed, after its separation from a military context. A number of interpretations have been proposed, each with some support from *OT* texts, such as that the hosts were other gods regarded as subordinate to the God of Israel (Maag, *SThU* 20 [1950], pp. 75–100), or that the term refers to the all-powerful and irresistible God (Wambacq, *Yahwe Sᵉbaʾôt*), or that it indicates God's royal majesty (Ross, *VT* 17 [1967], pp. 76–92). None of these interpretations is convincing as a complete explanation of the term, because it appears that, after the term had lost its original basic meaning, it attracted to itself a number of different concepts. It is reasonable to suggest that the term refers basically to the notion of God as King (see further, Mettinger, *SPDS*, pp. 117ff.). **before whom I stand**: This is a typically deuteronomistic phrase (Dt. 4:10; 10:8; cf. Jer. 7:10; 15:19; 35:19), and may thus be regarded as a deuteronomistic annotation (cf. Fohrer, *op. cit.*, p. 53; Smend, *op. cit.*, p. 534) which is also found in 1 Kg. 17:1; 2 Kg. 3:14. The phrase is variously translated **before whom I stand**, 'whom I serve' (2 Kg. 3:14; *NIV*) or 'whose servant I am' (*NEB*), and probably serves to designate the prophet as God's servant rather than proof that he functioned in the cult (as argued by Haldar, *Associations*, p. 111, on the ground that the verb *'āmaḏ*, 'to stand', is also used of a priest).

17. The drought narrative is continued in vv. 17–18*b*, and Ahab's meeting with Elijah is a sequel to v. 2*a* rather than v. 16, which concludes the intrusion in vv. 2*b*–16. **you troubler of Israel**: *K-B* gives the meaning of the verb *'āḵar* as 'taboo, cast out from (social) intercourse', and it is used specifically of the disability caused by breaking the taboo in the case of Achan (Jos. 6:18; 7:25) and of Jonathan (1 Sam. 14:29). The meaning here, however, is more general, and the implication is that Elijah had brought upon Israel the wrath of Baal and so had caused disorder and injury to its life. Fohrer's translation 'bewitched' (*op. cit.*, p. 13) is rightly rejected (Gray, p. 392; cf. Timm, *op. cit.*, pp. 61ff.).

18. In turning the tables completely upon the king, Elijah accuses him and his family of bringing trouble upon Israel, **because you have forsaken the commandments of the LORD**. The typically deuteronomistic reference to **the commandments** is avoided by the Gk., which reads 'you have forsaken the Lord your God'. Most probably Elijah's accusation finished with the phrase 'your father's house', and the remainder is a deuteronomistic addition. **and followed the Baals**: See on 1 Kg. 16:31–32. The plural is used deliberately to refer to the various local manifestations of the Canaanite fertility god known as Baal, 'lord'.

19–20. As noted above, these verses are considered to be transition verses composed to connect the following Mount Carmel ordeal with the drought theme of the previous verses. **Mount Carmel**: The choice of Carmel for the ordeal was not accidental, for by moving so near to the Phoenician border Elijah was really challenging Jezebel. Until *c.* 1000 BC Carmel stood outside the boundary of Israel, and David's attempt to introduce Yahweh-worship into the area probably failed and Carmel still remained under Phoenician influence and was a noted centre for worshipping the Tyrian Baal (cf. Alt, *Kleine Schriften II*, pp. 140–2; Eissfeldt, *op. cit.*, p. 24; Aharoni, *Fest. Galling*, pp. 1–7). A Gk. inscription dated *c.* AD 200, and probably belonging to a sanctuary on Mount Carmel reads '*To*

Zeus Karmēlos Hēliopoleitēs', and thus identifies the deity with the mountain deity Hadad, who had many local manifestations on the mountains along the coast of the Eastern Mediterranean (cf. Avi-Yonah, *IEJ* 2 [1952], pp. 118ff.; Galling, *Fest. Alt*, pp. 105–25; Timm, *op. cit.*, pp. 87–101). Classical writers also refer to a sanctuary on Mount Carmel (Ap-Thomas, *op. cit.*, p. 146; Timm, *op. cit.*, pp. 88ff.). Although the site cannot be exactly identified, it is probable that a sanctuary existed here in pre-Israelite times and that it was the 'holy mountain' (*Ros Qds*) listed after Acco in the Palestinian list of Thutmose III (Montgomery, p. 300). Šanda (I, p. 431) accepted its identification with *el-Muhraka* 'the place of burning' (Friedman, *Ephem. Carmel.* 22 [1971], pp. 95–104).

Closely related to the choice of Mount Carmel is the identity of the **Baal** worshipped there. Taking the divine name *Karmelos* from the Gk. inscription as a starting point, it has been argued that the deity worshipped at Carmel was a local deity known by the name Carmel, and later identified with Zeus Heliopolis (Baalbek); cf. Alt, *op. cit.*, p. 135. Against this identification it has been argued that it was a more significant contest than a local one with Baal Carmel; it was a contest for the right to be the national God of Israel (Ap-Thomas, *op. cit.*, p. 149). If the Carmel deity is identified with Zeus, the contest was obviously of more than local significance, for he was the high god who had control over thunder, lightning and rain. The god of Jezebel's home, Tyre, was called Melqart, 'king of the city', who was identified in the Gk. period with Herakles. Tyre depended on maritime trade, and so its god had control over natural forces, such as the sea and the waters, and it has been argued that it was this deity that was worshipped at Carmel (cf. de Vaux, *BMB* 5 [1941], p. 8). Also worshipped in Tyre was Baal Shamem, 'lord of heaven', who was 'the Baal' as distinct from local deities; in Syrian lands he was regarded as the supreme deity, who in the Ras Shamra texts is identified with Hadad and in later times with Zeus (Eissfeldt, *ZAW* 57 [1939], pp. 20ff.; *Der Gott Karmel*, p. 23). Obviously an exact identification of the Carmel deity is by now impossible. The deity of the local shrine was probably known as 'Baal Carmel', who, because of the Phoenician connections known at the time, was a local manifestation of one of the Tyrian deities. Whether Baal Carmel was identified with Melqart or with Baal Shamem is immaterial, for it seems that all Phoenician and Palestinian mountain gods were in the last analysis weather or sky gods (cf. Galling, *Fest. Alt*, p. 121). What is important is that in the eyes of the Israelites a deity who had control over the natural order exercised the same function as the Canaanite Hadad and so presented a challenge to Yahweh's sovereignty in the land (cf. also

Mulder, *Ba'al*, pp. 27–9). The issue to be settled by the Mount Carmel contest was which god was to be worshipped in Israel (Rowley, *Men of God*, p. 45). As noted by Eakin (*JBL* 84 [1965], pp. 407–14) what was previously a *Kulturkampf* between seminomads and settled farmers became, from Elijah onwards, a conflict that was based on the incompatibility of Yahwism and Baalism. **prophets of Baal**: The Heb. uses the same word (*nābî'*) for the prophets of Baal as for Elijah himself, and it is by now clear that prophecy was not unique to Israel. Seers or visionaries were known in Mesopotamia, the *mahhu* being ecstatics and the *bārū* having the function of declaring the will of the deity (Haldar, *op. cit.*, pp. 1–28). Prophecy was witnessed by Wen-amon in Byblos *c.* 1100 BC (*ANET*, pp. 25–9), Zakir, king of Hamath (*c.* 800 BC), received an oracle through prophets (Herrmann, *VTS* 9 [1963], p. 47) and remarkable evidence of the possible antecedents of *OT* prophecy has been obtained from the Mari documents dated in the eighteenth century BC (Noth, *Laws*, pp. 183ff.; Malamat, *VTS* 15 [1966], pp. 214–19). Because the similarities, especially in the case of the early ecstatic prophets of Israel, are so evident, it is difficult to arrive at an exact definition of the distinctive element of *OT* prophecy. Whereas some of the *OT* ecstatic prophets resorted to imitative magic, like their Semitic counterparts, so too the seers and prophets known from outside Israel, exactly like the *OT* prophets, claimed to be recipients of oracles from the deity (see further, Malamat, *ibid.*). **prophets of Asherah**: Because these prophets are not mentioned in the subsequent narrative, it has been proposed to delete the reference to them from this verse (cf. *BHS*). In view of the fact that Ahab's father-in-law, Ithobaal, was a priest of Astarte (see on 1 Kg. 16:31), it is understandable that Baal and Astarte are named together in reference to Jezebel's deities. This is a transition verse, and the phrase need not be deleted.

21. How long will you go limping with different opinions? Elijah may have been using a popular saying, whose meaning is unmistakable because of its connection with v. 21*b*; but there is disagreement about the exact terms of reference, and the following proposals have been made. (i) **For with different opinions** the Gk. has 'on the knees', thus suggesting 'going lame on both joints' (Skinner, p. 231). (ii) The word translated opinions (Heb. *se'ippîm*) may have some connection with *sā'îp*, 'twig, bough', and the phrase may mean 'hobbling on two crutches', seeking help from both Yahweh and Baal (cf. *K-B*; Fohrer, *op. cit.*, p. 45). (iii) Accepting the connection with a twig, which branches off the trunk, it is possible to render as 'hobbling between two forks', as at a cross-roads. (iv) de Vaux (*op. cit.*, pp. 9–11), noticing that the word for limping (*pose'hîm*) is used for a ritual dance in v. 26, suggests that Elijah's question may have a reference to cultic rites. (v) The translation of *RSV* is based on the suggestion that *se'ippîm* may have been the same word as *śe'ippîm*, 'thoughts', which is used in Job 4:13; 20:2. This latter suggestion gives an adequate explanation of the question and its implied reference to the people's impossible position in trying to combine Baalism with Yahwism. **follow him; but if Baal, then follow him**: For the use of the term following God and its application to the following of other gods, cf. Helfmeyer, *Die Nachfolge*, pp. 130–82.

22. I, even I only, am left: cf. also 19:14, below. This is obviously an exaggeration in view of the statement in vv. 4 and 13 that a hundred prophets had been hidden and of the evidence in later chapters that other prophets existed. The explanation probably is that he was standing on his own for this present contest (cf. Steck, *op. cit.*, p. 19), although admittedly the dramatic element is prominent here.

23. Let two bulls be given to us: The preparations outlined in this verse can be construed to suggest that two separate altars were being prepared; the bulls were to be laid out by each party **on the wood**, but with **no fire**, and the contestants were to appeal in turn to their respective god. De Vaux (*op. cit.*, p. 7) was of the opinion that there were two sanctuaries in the locality, the Yahweh one at *el-Muḥraka*, and the Baal sanctuary towards the north-westerly end of Mount Carmel. Possibly both the Phoenician and Israelite sanctuaries were not in regular use and a certain amount of rebuilding was necessary (cf. vv. 26, 30). **let them choose one bull for themselves**: As Rowley points out (*op. cit.*, p. 47), Elijah, because of his confidence, accepted every handicap and encouraged his opponents to take the first choice of animal and to call first upon their god. He thus eliminated all possible excuse that the animal was unacceptable, and took the risk of granting them the first appeal.

24. the God who answers by fire, he is God: The test in the original form of the Carmel ordeal was the ability to produce fire, and not rain (against Ap-Thomas, *op. cit.*, pp. 151ff.). Rain belongs to a later redaction of the narrative when it was integrated with the drought cycle (see above; cf. Tromp, *op. cit.*, p. 495).

25–26. All preparations on both sides were undertaken by the prophets themselves, without any mention of priests. Despite the preference in Israel for a Levite to act as priest (Jg. 17:12), Elijah's action is by no means unique (cf. 1 Sam. 7:9, 17). **but put no fire to it**: This is a natural prohibition if it is accepted that the sign desired was fire upon the altar. Those who accept that rain was the expected sign have to accept the more difficult and fanciful explana-

tion that fire was not applied to the altar lest it should dry up the
rain (Ap-Thomas, *op. cit.*, p. 152, following Frazer, *The Golden
Bough III*, pp. 248ff.). **And they limped about the altar which
they had made**: The limp in this case was some form of limping
dance that was part of the ritual around the altar. Ritual dances
have been observed elsewhere, and some of them specifically in
connection with rain-making ceremonies. Ancient Arabs circumam-
bulated the Ka'ba stone in Mecca, as modern Palestinian Arabs
dance and leap with bended knees, with the object of producing
rain (Patai, *HUCA* 14 [1939], p. 255). However, such dances were
not necessarily connected with rain-making, but were an inducement to the deity to **answer us**. De Vaux (*op. cit.*, pp. 10f.) refers
to the dance of Tyrian sailors in honour of Herakles (to be identified
perhaps with Melqart) described by Heliodorus, who says that they
sometimes bent their knees to perform their dance. Presumably the
sailors were not seeking rain. A relief in Rome also shows dancers
making contortions of their body and bending their legs in front of
images, with spectators clapping their hands. A Phoenician shrine
was also dedicated to 'Baal of the Dance'. The reference is, therefore, to a ritual dance, which may have been characteristic of the
worship of Melqart, but not used specifically for a rain-producing
ritual.

27. for he is a god: This is a satirical statement, and need not
be deleted with Luc., which was obviously trying to avoid such a
confession from the mouth of the prophet. **either he is musing**:
The allusion to 'meditation' is preferable here to 'conversation'
(which is suggested by the Vsns.). Such a reference is not an absur-
dity (as suggested by Montgomery, p. 302), for, as noted by de
Vaux (*op. cit.*, pp. 13ff.), the Tyrian Herakles is described as 'the
philosopher', who through his wisdom had invented the purple
dye and shipping, and to whom science and astronomy were also
attributed. Ezek. 28 may also contain a reference to the inventive
wisdom of Melqart. **or he has gone aside**: The absence of this
phrase from Luc. has led to the suggestion that it is an erroneous
repetition of the former phrase. Driver too (*Mélanges Bibliques*, pp.
67ff.) omits the phrase, but interprets the former one differently.
Many commentators, however, follow the interpretation of the
Targum that it is an euphemism for going to relieve himself: Rashi
makes the meaning clear by combining it with the following reference to going on a journey and renders 'going to the privy'. *NEB*
has 'or engaged'. The Gk. suggests 'he is busy' (so *NIV*), implying
that he was too occupied to listen to the prophets (Rowley, *op. cit.*,
pp. 51f.). **or he is on a journey**: De Vaux (*op. cit.*, p. 15) refers to
Gk. sources telling of the journey of the Tyrian Herakles to Libya,

and to the establishment of Tyrian colonies in the Mediterranean, which possibly implies that Melqart was journeying with the merchants and colonists. **or perhaps he is asleep and must be awakened**: cf. Ps. 44:23. Parallels to this concept are found elsewhere: Egyptian texts refer to the gods awakening every morning (Erman, *Literature*, p. 12), and the Tyrians kept a festival in the spring for awakening Herakles (cf. de Vaux, *op. cit.*, p. 17). Gray (pp. 398ff.) is right in thinking of this occasion on Carmel as an *ad hoc* attempt to arouse Baal, although it has to be admitted that the concept is derived from the ritual of awakening the deity from the sleep of death to a new life in the New Year (cf. Jagersma, *VT* 25 [1975], pp. 674–6). For a contrast, see Ps. 121:4. The point of this verse is to emphasize the humanity of Baal; he is no god and is unable to act (cf. Preuss, *Verspottung*, p. 87). This meaning is clear without imposing upon each element in the verse an interpretation that is based on specific reference to a vegetation deity (as proposed by Hayman, *JNES* 10 [1951], pp. 57–8).

28. and cut themselves after their custom with swords and lances: The interpreters who claim that the Carmel contest was concerned with securing rain find further support in the voluntary maiming of the prophets, for the blood that **gushed out upon them** represents the rain (Patai, *op. cit.*, p. 255; Ap-Thomas, *op. cit.*, p. 153). But self-laceration was widely practised (see Rowley, *op. cit.*, p. 54 for examples from classical literature), and in no way demands such an interpretation. An example in an Akkad. text going back to at least 1300 BC bears remarkable similarity to the present case in that it connects the sprinkling of blood with ecstasy; in this particular example self-laceration is connected with burial rites (Roberts, *JBL* 89 [1970], pp. 76–7). In the Mount Carmel scene this rite was a more intense attempt to draw the deity's attention and to recommend themselves to him (cf. Rowley, *ibid.*).

29. they raved on: Although the Heb. uses the word for prophesying (*hitnabbēʾ*) here, *RSV*'s **raved** is a correct translation of it (cf. *NEB*, 'they raved and ranted', which is better than *NIV*'s 'frantic prophesying'). It is a verb that is used of unreasonable actions and even of madness (1 Sam. 18:10; cf. 2 Kg. 9:11; Jer. 29:26). The prophets of Baal do not prophesy in the present context, but were engaged in frenzied behaviour. **until the time of the offering of the oblation**: The main daily service was in the evening (Num. 28:3ff.; Exod. 29:38ff.), which is described as 'between the evenings' and further defined as around 'the ninth hour' (Josephus, *Ant.* XIV.4.3), or three o'clock. The term *minḥāh*, 'oblation', means a gift, and although confined later to vegetable offerings, there are instances, such as this verse, where it must refer to the sacrifice of animals (de Vaux, *Ancient Israel*, pp. 430ff.).

30. The two accounts of Elijah's altar in vv. 30–32, one alluding to the repair of an altar that had been thrown down (v. 30*b*), and the other suggesting that **he built an altar** (vv. 31–32*a*), are different in style and interest. Whilst the former is brief and to the point, the latter is verbose and theologically orientated. Although some give priority to vv. 31–32*a* and regard v. 30*b* as a summary of it (Burney, p. 225), or a dogmatic gloss to it (Montgomery, p. 304; Würthwein, *op. cit.*, p. 133), it seems more reasonable to regard v. 30*b* as the original text and the remainder as secondary (cf. Tromp, *op. cit.*, p. 492). Whether the doublet is to be ascribed to the deuteronomistic redactor (as suggested above, p. 311) is debatable, for the presence of another sanctuary outside Jerusalem was against the deuteronomic principle. However, it can be conceded that the redactor accepted the received tradition of v. 30*b*, possibly because it was an altar that was in any case destroyed (see v. 38*a*; cf. Steck, *op. cit.*, p. 17), and then attempted in vv. 31–32*a* to set it in a theological perspective. On the possibility of an Israelite altar in the Mount Carmel region, see above on v. 23.

31. Elijah took twelve stones: The twelve stones naturally connect this deuteronomistic extension with the concept of Israel as a twelve-tribe confederacy. According to Friedman (*op. cit.*, pp. 95–103), Elijah is presented as a new Joshua, who had raised twelve stones at Gilgal (Jos. 4) as a testimony 'that the hand of Yahweh is mighty' and 'that you may fear Yahweh'. Others find a closer connection with the stones of Exod. 24:4, which witness to the covenant (Carlson, *VT* 19 [1969], p. 427), and think of Elijah as a new Moses rather than a new Joshua (cf. Fohrer, *op. cit.*, pp. 55ff.). It is not impossible that both are in the redactor's mind, for Exod. 24 and Jos. 4 emphasize the amphictyony, and likewise the reference here to **Israel shall be your name**, which is a quotation from Gen. 35:10, is also distinctly amphictyonic. The redactor's theological interest in the relationship between God and the amphictyony serves to bring out Yahweh's exclusive rights over the nation (cf. Tromp, *op. cit.*, p. 499). It is questionable if the intrusion in vv. 31–32*a* is intended as an aetiology of a megalithic monument of twelve stones or of a topographical feature looking like molten stones (Friedman, *ibid.*; Gray, p. 402).

32. And he made a trench . . . as great as would contain two measures of seed: The measurement given for the trench has caused problems. It has been suggested that it is a surface measurement, i.e. the extent of the land to be sown with two seahs of corn (cf. the Mishnah; it was approximately 1568 sq. metres; see Montgomery, p.

304), and that the trench encircled this area. This is obviously too extensive a measurement for a trench that was filled with four jars of water. Taking this reference together with the stones, which are connected with Exod. 20:25; 24:4, it has been suggested that we are dealing here with a sacred precinct and that the sprinkling of water was an act of ceremonial cleansing (see Junker, *TThZ* 69 [1960], pp. 65–74). It is more reasonable to accept Gray's suggestion (p. 400) that this was an act of imitative magic, where the seed was put in a trench and soaked with water to cause it to sprout.

33a. The preparation of the animal described here, which follows the instructions given in v. 23, and has a much briefer parallel in v. 26, belongs to the original narrative.

33b–35. Elijah's action in filling four jars with water and pouring the contents three times **on the burnt offering and on the wood** has been interpreted as a piece of rain-making ritual and described as imitative or sympathetic magic. Pouring water, it is claimed, was the most common form of rain-making (cf. Patai, *op. cit.*, p. 256), to which several parallels are found, including a Persian water-pouring festival (Ap-Thomas, *op. cit.*, p. 153). The four jars have been taken to symbolize the four winds (Patai, *ibid.*), possibly indicating the four directions of the land where rain was desired (Gray, p. 401). The multiplication of four by three again gives the number twelve, possibly referring to the twelve tribes of Israel and certainly making use of the lucky number three (Ap-Thomas, *ibid.*). On the other hand the interpretation of the water pouring as imitative or sympathetic magic for securing rain has been rejected. It may be that the prophet was simply loading the dice against himself (Rowley, *op. cit.*, p. 56) and giving a sure guarantee against fraud (Gray, p. 400). The analysis of this chapter outlined above (pp. 309) accommodates the view that these two verses reflect an old water-securing ritual, which has been deliberately connected with Elijah by the editors, who wished to join the Carmel episode to the drought cycle. It can be conceded that Elijah did not use sympathetic magic on Carmel, since rain-making did not feature in the Carmel contest; it is this secondary addition that has imposed such an interpretation on the contest and ascribed rain-making to Elijah.

36. at the time of the offering of the oblation: See on v. 29. As noted above (p. 311), the first version of Elijah's prayer is secondary. It is similar in style to the verbose strand noted already in vv. 31–32*b* and in vv. 33*b*–35; the formula **let it be known this day that thou art God in Israel** anticipates v. 37. The mention of **thy word** is foreign to the Mount Carmel narrative and goes back to v. 1; this, according to Tromp (*op. cit.*, p. 493), confirms the suggestion that this verse was one of the number composed by the editor who inserted the Carmel narrative into the drought cycle. Admittedly there are differences between the two prayers; the first, by employing the impersonal **let it be known**, admits the possibility of the prophets of Baal acknowledging Yahweh, but the second has the specific wish **that this people** (i.e. Israel) **may know**. This does not mean that the first is basic (as suggested by Seebass, *ZThK* 70 [1973], p. 133); on the contrary, the aim of the contest was to win for Yahweh acclamation as sovereign by the people of Israel. The effect on the prophets of Baal, and their subsequent annihilation in v. 38, are foreign to the purpose of the contest.

37. **Answer me, O LORD, answer me**: The repetition of words from v. 26 binds this verse more closely than v. 36 to the remainder of the narrative.

38. **the fire of the LORD fell**: No adequate explanation of what happened in reply to Elijah's prayer has been proposed. One line of interpretation attributes the fire to trickery or to a concealed manipulation by Elijah. Hitzig (*Geschichte*, p. 176) proposed that he poured inflammable naphtha instead of water on the altar, and a parallel in 2 Mac. 1:29ff. has been noted. The naphtha was ignited by the direct rays of the sun or by a curved metal mirror held by Elijah (cf. Kennett, *Essays*, pp. 103ff.). Apart from the supposition that Elijah was not very scrupulous, this interpretation rests on the assumption on the one hand that such means could be hidden from the four hundred and fifty prophets of Baal, who were observing closely what was happening, and on the other that these prophets did not have knowledge, like Elijah, of the properties of naphtha which was available in the neighbourhood (see further, Rowley, *op. cit.*, pp. 56ff.). Another line of interpretation is to take **the fire of the LORD** to be lightning, which by miraculous coincidence struck at the right time (the close of Elijah's prayer) and the right place (the altar on Mount Carmel). Whilst those who favour this interpretation think of lightning as inaugurating the rainy period (Ap-Thomas, pp. 151ff.), those who reject it point to the fact that until v. 44 it was a cloudless sky, which does not produce lightning (Rowley, *op. cit.*, p. 58). Of course, if the Carmel ordeal was originally separate from the end of the drought theme, the latter objection is not valid, but the remarkable coincidence of time and place remains. Whilst accepting on the one hand that the response may have come through some natural phenomenon, which cannot be explained, and on the other that the narrative cannot be dismissed as a fabrication, like some of the miracle stories in the Elisha cycle, Rowley (*ibid.*) expresses the opinion that something remarkable must have happened here. The phrase used here, **the fire of the LORD** (cf. Num. 16:35; Lev. 9:24; 10:2), is to be compared with

'the fire of God from heaven' (Job 1:16) and 'fire from heaven' (2 Kg. 1:10, 12; 1 Chr. 21:26; 2 Chr. 7:1). In many such cases there is a distinction between the fire and God himself, but in the present verse, as in Num. 11:1, 3, it is implied that God himself is present in the fire (cf. Hentschel, *Die Elijaerzählungen*, pp. 170ff.). This text, therefore, has to be understood in conjunction with *OT* descriptions of theophany, where fire is a manifestation of God's presence (Jeremias, *Theophanie*, passim; Morgenstern, *Fire upon the Altar*, pp. 25ff.; Miller, *CBQ* 27 [1965], pp. 256–61). The statement that the fire **consumed the burnt offering** is understandable, but doubts have been expressed about the remainder of the verse. The issue of the Mount Carmel contest was the ability to provide fire on the altar, and the destruction of the altar itself is out of place. Of course, its destruction would be desirable from the deuteronomistic standpoint, and so some assume that vv. 38*b* and 31–32*a* come from the same hand (Steck, *op. cit.*, p. 17). The view taken here is that the editors who combined the Carmel episode with the drought theme had also to refer to the destruction of the altar, because they wished to include a reference to the fire licking up **the water that was in the trench**.

39. The LORD, he is God: The people's response is not simply an echo of the prophet's name, but recalls the basic issue of the Mount Carmel scene as expressed in vv. 21, 24. Verse 39, containing the decision made as to who is God, marks the end of the ordeal on Mount Carmel (Würthwein, *op. cit.*, p. 134; Jepsen, *Fest. Albright*, p. 302). This polemical and didactic narrative is not without a basis in the prophet's preaching (Preuss, *op. cit.*, p. 94).

40. As noted above (p. 311), this verse is regarded as a secondary addition, which not merely complements the killing of prophets of Jezebel, but also recalls the beginning of the narrative in v. 19. As has been noted, v. 40 does complete the curve of the narrative (cf. Galling, *op. cit.*, p. 122), but, like the transition composition in vv. 19–20, it too is secondary. It is hardly conceivable that the killing of the prophets is connected with the bringing of rain (cf. Ap-Thomas, *op. cit.*, p. 154, with a reference to 2 Sam. 21:8ff.). An argument that is often brought in favour of retaining v. 40 is that the execution of the vanquished is the natural conclusion of an ordeal (Fohrer, *op. cit.*, p. 13; Tromp, *op. cit.*, p. 494). It reflects a sound legal custom (cf. Exod. 21:24ff.), and may be connected with the execution of the ban (Dt. 7:16ff., 26; 13:13ff.). It has to be realized, however, that in the ancient tradition behind the Mount Carmel ordeal lies an account of how an issue that is clearly and simply set out was settled. Accretions to it, such as the acknowledgement of God by the prophets (v. 36), the destruction of the altar

(v. 38*b*) and the killing of the prophets (v. 40), introduce elements that are foreign to the main theme. Pressing for the retention of v. 40 in order to maintain fully the practice of ordeal also imposes on the simple narrative a secondary pattern. It further poses the question whether or not 'ordeal' is the correct term for describing the Carmel incident, and leads to a search for other terminology, such as 'decision narrative' (van den Born, p. 108, and favoured by Tromp, *op. cit.*, p. 497), which expresses more satisfactorily the intention of the original form. **to the brook Kishon**: The *Nahr el-Muqatta'* stood in the plain below Mount Carmel, and the massacre has been traditionally associated with *Tell el-Qasis* (Gray, p. 402). A feasible motive for removing the massacre away from Mount Carmel is found in a desire not to desecrate the site itself. A more fanciful reason is found in the course of the Kishon, which ran out in the direction of Phoenicia, and so took away the blood where it belonged (cf. Šanda I, p. 441; Montgomery, p. 306).

41. With this verse the chapter returns to the drought and return of rain theme, but because of its fusion with the Carmel episode some of the references in vv. 41ff. are unclear. **Go up** in this verse would suggest that Ahab too was down at the Kishon, and is now commanded to return to Carmel. Moreover, in v. 42 Elijah goes up to the top of Carmel, and then in v. 43 commands **his servant** to **Go up**. A possible solution is that the true conclusion of the drought saga is to be found in vv. 43–46, and that vv. 41–42 represent a not altogether successful attempt to provide a transition from the Carmel scene to the drought saga. An even better solution is to regard vv. 41–42 and vv. 43–46 as variant conclusions, with the shorter one presenting the first version and the longer one a second version (cf. Tromp, *op. cit.*, p. 491). **Go up, eat and drink**: Once the drought saga is separated from the Carmel scene, **go up** can mean 'go home'. The crisis is over, and Ahab is encouraged to resume a normal pattern of life. **sound of the rushing of rain**: This has been variously explained as a thunderclap (cf. Ap-Thomas, *op. cit.*, p. 152, with reference to Jer. 10:13), the rising west wind (Gray, p. 403), or, more appropriately, the imminent arrival of rain being vivid and real in the prophet's consciousness.

42. In the final scene of the drought saga, according to this first version of the conclusion, Elijah, after Ahab's return home, is presented as going up to Mount Carmel, where **he bowed himself down upon the earth and put his face between his knees**. The prophet's posture, squatting with his head between his knees, has been variously explained as an indication of humiliation and mourning pending the coming of the rain (Jirku, *ZDMG* 103 [1953], p. 372), as a piece of imitative magic whereby the prophet makes

himself like a cloud in order to draw a rain-cloud up from the sea
(Ap-Thomas, *op. cit.*, p. 154), or an act of concentration and ecstatic
absorption in which he presumably saw nothing but rain (cf.
Montgomery, p. 306). More appropriately, this posture in concluding the narrative intends to present Elijah in humble submission
and prayer before God (cf. Rowley, *op. cit.*, pp. 61ff.); but what
was originally a prayer of submission became, after the addition of
the second version in vv. 43–46, a prayer asking for rain.

43. The second conclusion introduces Elijah's **servant**, who has
not played any part in the remainder of the chapter; this is often
presented as a strong argument for separating the Carmel incident,
where the servant's help would have been expected, from the
drought saga. **Go again seven times**: This refers probably to a total
of seven; the Gk. adds a sentence stating that the lad went seven
times.

44. The prophet saw in the **little cloud** that was **rising out of the
sea** (the Mediterranean) a sure sign that rain was on its way. For
the concept that rain arose out of the sea, cf. Am. 5:8; 9:6. The
prophet acted on the sign and commanded Ahab to **go down**
(obviously to Jezreel, v. 45) **lest the rain stop you**, i.e. before the
heavy rains made the road impassable. It was a long journey of
some 25km.

**46. and he girded up his loins and ran before Ahab to the
entrance of Jezreel**: Elijah's action in outrunning Ahab to Jezreel
is attributed to an ecstatic experience of being under **the hand of
the LORD**. The feat was not impossible, especially when certain
contributory factors are considered, such as the fact that runners
travelled cross-country whilst chariots travelled along tracks, and
the fact that the coming of heavy rain after a period of drought
brought obstacles for a chariot (cf. Gray, pp. 404ff.; Montgomery,
pp. 306ff.). The motive for Elijah's action is not clear, but the
suggestion that he simulated a cloud moving eastwards in order to
secure rain over the plain of Jezreel (Ap-Thomas, *op. cit.*, p. 155)
can be dismissed. His journey to Jezreel was probably due to a
combination of his wish to be there in person to present the challenge of his God's achievement to Jezebel and of his desire to share
in the popular response in Jezreel to the coming of rain (Gray,
ibid.).

(iii) A visit to Horeb, the mountain of God **19:1–21**
A redactor composed vv. 1–3*a* in order to connect the visit of Elijah
to Horeb with the preceding events at Carmel. Despite the sound
psychological principle in placing Elijah's depression as a reaction
to the remarkable experience of Mount Carmel, it is doubtful if the

events of the Elijah cycle followed each other chronologically. Indeed the placement of chapters 18 and 19 in their present order may be attributed to a literary technique of contrast (Fohrer, *Elia*, p. 20), and some further thematic links between them have been observed (cf. Carslon, *VT* 19 [1969], pp. 416ff.). But it is not feasible to base an argument on a point of biographical sequence, either for retaining chapter 19 in the position allocated to it by the author of vv. 1–3a or for relocating it before chapter 17 (as, for example, by Jepsen, *Nabi*, p. 63).

Three originally independent traditions have been brought together in chapter 19. In vv. 3b–6 lies a tradition about Elijah's sojourn in the desert not far from Beersheba. This legendary material, with its reference to Elijah's retreat and to an extraordinary means of food provision, bears similarity to the anecdote in 1 Kg. 17:2–6. A tradition about Elijah's sojourn near Beersheba was probably in existence; the reason for placing it at this particular point in the tradition is that it facilitated his subsequent visit to Horeb, which is the keystone in the final presentation of the narrative.

The Horeb tradition in vv. 7–18 constitutes three elements: a transition section in vv. 7–8, the Horeb revelation in vv. 9–14 and the instructions to Elijah in vv. 15–18. As seen from the clear treatment of Würthwein (*Fest. Davies*, pp. 152ff.), it is difficult to resolve satisfactorily two interrelated questions, namely the lack of order in vv. 9–14 and the relationship of these verses to vv. 15–18. The narrative begins in vv. 9–10; it is interrupted by the description of a theophany in vv. 11–13a, and then, when it proceeds in vv. 13b–14, there is an almost identical repetition of vv. 9b–10. One widely accepted solution to the disorder of the text is the deletion of vv. 9b–10 as a gloss (Smend, *VT* 25 [1975], p. 531; cf. Wellhausen, *Composition*, p. 280) and the retention of the theophany scene. Würthwein, however, presents a convincing case for deleting the theophany scene in vv. 11–13a and for regarding vv. 13b–14 as a resumption made necessary by the interpolation of vv. 11–13a. His argument for regarding vv. 13b–14 as a resumption is based on the principle that a narrative is often resumed after an interpolation by repeating sentences or part of sentences from the section standing before the interpolation (Kuhl, *ZAW* 64 [1952], pp. 1–11). Würthwein thus finds in vv. 15–18 the real point of the narrative and so retains them. The original kernel, which is found in vv. 9–10, 15–18, belongs to the crisis in Elisha's day that found its culmination in the revolt of Jehu and attributes to Elijah an interpretation of that crisis as God's punishment for Israel's unfaithfulness together with a message of punishment (v. 17) and of promise (v. 18). In the eyes of the Elisha circle Elijah was a second Moses,

and so his message of punishment and promise was linked with the
mountain of God, Horeb. The view taken here is that vv. 7–8 were
composed by the compilers who attached the theophany of vv.
11–14 to the original kernel in order to locate it at Horeb; by
repeating elements from vv. 3b–6 they combined it with the Beersheba tradition which provided a suitable half-way stage between
Israel and Horeb (on vv. 7–8, see further, Fohrer, *op. cit.*, pp. 38ff.;
Steck, *Überlieferung*, pp. 24–6; Timm, *Die Dynastie*, pp. 104ff.).
Other attempts have been made to analyse these verses according
to the patterns of legal procedure (Steck, *op. cit.*, pp. 120ff.), audience ritual (Seybold, *EvTh* 33 [1973], pp. 8ff.) or a dialogue with
God (von Nordheim, *Bib* 59 [1978], pp. 153–73).

The third element in the chapter is the call of Elisha (vv. 19–21),
which has been separated from the remainder of the chapter and
thought to have belonged to the Elisha cycle (Alt, *ZAW* 32 [1912],
pp. 123–5; Timm, *op. cit.*, pp. 110–11). But the call of Elisha is
obviously linked with the instructions in vv. 15b–16 to anoint the
prophet with the two kings named. Although the close link with vv.
15b–16 can be taken as an argument for their deletion as secondary
(Hentschel, *Die Elijaerzählungen*, pp. 33–60), this is unnecessary in
view of the observations made above on the origin of the chapter.
It is unnecessary to separate vv. 19–21 on the grounds that they
have originated from the Elisha circle, for the contention here is
that the chapter as a whole, including the instructions to Elijah in
vv. 15–18, is derived from that same circle.

1. how he had slain all the prophets with the sword: The
secondary character of the link in vv. 1–3a is well illustrated by the
fact that it is based on the secondary addition in 18:40 (see above).
Furthermore, it introduces a change in the main participants in the
conflict; whereas chapters 17–18 present Elijah and Ahab as the
main figures, this section, by bringing Jezebel to the fore, reflects
a later situation, when Jezebel exercised her authority as queen-
mother (cf. Steck, *op. cit.*, pp. 20–1; Hentschel, *op. cit.*, pp. 65ff.).
Some elements in the linking verses are at variance with both
preceding and following chapters. Whereas Elijah challenges Ahab
in 18:7–18, he is now said to be afraid of Jezebel (v. 3a); again
Jezebel the persecutor of v. 2 has disappeared altogether from vv.
3b–18, where it is a case of persecution by the 'people of Israel' (see
vv. 10, 14).

2. Jezebel's message to Elijah is introduced by an additional
sentence in Luc., 'As surely as you are Elijah and I am Jezebel'
(Burney, p. 229) or 'If you are Elijah, I am Jezebel' (so Gray, pp.
406ff.). Commentators are divided about the value of Luc. here;
some accept it as a genuine saying (Burney, *ibid.*; Fohrer, *op. cit.*,

p. 17; Fichtner, p. 278), which had been accidentally omitted from
MT because it was possibly preceded by 'saying', like the following
phrase, and was lost (Eissfeldt, *VTS* 16 [1967], pp. 65–70; *BibOr*
28 [1971], p. 127). Others find it difficult to explain how such a
powerful saying could be omitted from MT (Montgomery, pp.
316ff.). If accepted, it may be taken with the following phrase, thus
strengthening the oath (as in Burney's translation); or else rendered
separately (as by Gray) and presenting the issue in a nutshell, 'you
are Elijah ('Yahweh is my God') and I am Jezebel ('Where is the
Prince [Baal])?', thus presenting the conflict as that between the
representative of Yahweh and the representative of Baal. **may the
gods do to me**: It is doubtful if Jezebel was pressing the universalistic claims of her god, as suggested by Gray, who translates 'may
god do to me'.

   3. The first half of the verse concludes the introductory section.
For **Then he was afraid** (*wayyīrā'*) of *RSV*, MT reads 'and he saw'
(*wayyar'*), which represents an early attempt to avoid the reference
to Elijah being afraid of Jezebel and the apparent discrepancy
between this Elijah and the Elijah of chapter 18. *RSV*'s reading has
the support of MSS and Vsns.

   Verse 3*b* introduces an independent narrative about Elijah's
sojourn in the wilderness near Beersheba, and is not therefore a
continuation of vv. 1–3*a*. The previous verses do not mention the
servant of v. 3*b*, but give the impression that Elijah fled alone from
before Jezebel. Moreover, the statement in v. 3*a* that he went **for
his life** stands in contrast to his prayer in v. 4 asking God to
take away my life, although it may be possible to reconcile them.
However, v. 3*b* is to be separated from v. 3*a* and the introductory
composition in vv. 1–3*a* from the narrative in vv. 3*b*–6. **and came to
Beersheba, which belongs to Judah**: This reference to **Beersheba**
suggests a date before 722 BC when the distinction between north
and south was important; the further description of it as belonging
to Judah indicates a northern origin for the Elijah traditions. Since
the narrative in vv. 3*b*–6 is legendary in character, it is irrelevant
to ask whether Elijah actually went as far as Beersheba. Perhaps the
name Beersheba had become symbolic of a flight to a lonely place
in the desert (cf. Gen. 21, where Gunkel, *Elias*, p. 22, finds a
parallel to this narrative; but the parallelism is very slight; cf. Steck,
op. cit., p. 27), and Elijah's name had become attached to it in
popular tradition. The legend suited the present context because it
took Elijah some way towards his ultimate destination, Horeb.

   4. under a broom tree: *NEB*, 'a broom-brush'. This shrub,
which grows to a height of over three metres, is plentiful in the
Sinai, Petra and Dead Sea areas; its botanical name is *Retama roetam*,

but it is also known as *Genista roetam*. For the wish **take away my life**, cf. Num. 11:15. There is a close connection between Num. 11 and early prophetic circles (Noth, *ÜSt*, pp. 141ff.), which makes it possible that Elijah, in saying **I am no better than my fathers**, is referring to earlier prophets. Possibly too the legend connected here with Elijah may have had an earlier history within prophetic circles.

5. behold, an angel touched him: The **angel** of this verse is further defined in v. 7 as 'the angel of the LORD'. Although the word *mal'āk̲* is used of ordinary messengers (Jg. 11:12; 2 Sam. 3:12f.; 1 Kg. 20:2ff.), it is obvious that here as in Gen. 16:7 (which uses the fuller form 'the angel of the LORD') the term denotes a messenger from God.

6. The provisions brought to the prophet are similar, but not identical, to those mentioned in 1 Kg. 17:4–6. Both this verse and the anecdote of 17:4–6 use the same motif of a miraculous feeding (as is recognised by Bronner, *Elijah and Elisha*, p. 83, although it is unnecessary to follow her suggestion of classifying them as polemic against Baal myths); both can be classified as legendary anecdotes. **a cake baked on hot stones**: Round and flat cakes were baked on stones heated in fire, cf. Isa. 6:6, where the word translated here as hot stones denotes 'burning coal'.

7–8. These verses recording a second visit by the angel repeat some phrases from vv. 5–6: although **an angel** (v. 5) has now become **the angel of the LORD** (v. 7), he still **touched him** (vv. 5, 7); the phrase **arise and eat** occurs in both sections (vv. 5, 7) and also **he ate and drank** (vv. 6, 8). But the meal described in v. 6 is not mentioned in vv. 7–8, which concentrate on the prophet's journey to Horeb. Fohrer (*op. cit.*, pp. 38ff.) finds in vv. 3b–8 the combination of two different versions of the same narrative, one being older than the other. The view taken here is that the independent tradition preserved in vv. 3b–6 has been deliberately extended in vv. 7–8 in order to accommodate the journey from Beersheba to Horeb and thus provide an introduction to the Horeb narrative. These transition verses carefully repeat elements from vv. 5–6 and also introduce the journey to Horeb; they are thus to be read with vv. 9–18. **else the journey will be too great for you**: The introduction of a journey in v. 7b is alien to the narrative in vv. 3b–6, which only envisage Elijah going on a day's journey from Beersheba to the wilderness. **and went in the strength of that food forty days and forty nights**: This is the first of several elements in the theophany narrative that are parallel to the account of Moses at Horeb. For a reference to forty days and forty nights see Exod. 24:18; 34:28. **to Horeb the mount of God**: Horeb is the name used in the Elohistic and deuteronomistic traditions of the Pentateuch for the holy mountain,

which is called Sinai in the Yahwistic and priestly tradition (see, for
example, Exod. 3:1; 17:6; 33:6; Dt. 1:2, 6, 19; 4:10, 15). For the
designation of Horeb as **the mount of God**, cf. Exod. 3:1; 4:27;
11:5; 24:13, which are again mostly Elohistic. It was at this mountain that Moses received his call, and it is obvious that in Hebrew
tradition the names Horeb and Sinai refer to the same mountain,
although originally perhaps Horeb designated the region in which
Sinai stood. Traditionally this mountain has been equated with *Jebel
Musa* in the southern massif of the Sinai peninsula, but over the
years several other identifications have been proposed, some locating
Sinai at Kadesh-barnea, *el-Qudeirat* (Hyatt, *Exodus*, pp. 203–7), or
some other site in the northern part of the Sinai desert (Gray, *VT*
[1954], pp. 148–54), or even near Midian (Gese, *Fest. Rost.*, pp.
81–94). See further, Davies, *VT* [1972], pp. 152–63 and *Wilderness*,
pp. 63–9. Whichever site is favoured and whatever the evidence for
pilgrimages to Sinai from an early period (cf. Noth, *PJB* [1940],
pp. 5ff.), the analysis of 1 Kg. 19 presented here treats Elijah's visit
to Horeb as a secondary addition originating from the Elisha circle.

9. And there he came to a cave and lodged there: Elijah's stay
in a cave in the wilderness belongs to the original tradition in which
he receives his new commission (vv. 15–18). But the reference to
'the entrance of the cave' in v. 13 echoes deliberately, although not
using identical words, the hiding of Moses in a cleft rock (Exod.
33:22). See also Carlson, *VT* 19 [1969], p. 432. **the word of the
LORD came to him**: On the importance of the concept of the divine
word in the final version of the Elijah narrative, see above, p. 309;
cf. Smend, *VT* [1975], p. 528. The following **and he said**, which
is not usual after **the word of the LORD**, suggests that the text has
been revised at a later date. Possibly the original referred to God's
voice as in v. 13 (so Würthwein, *op. cit.*, p. 162). Verses 9b–10 are
repeated word for word in vv. 13b–14, which is taken as an indication that one version is out of place and causes disorder in the
narrative. Many follow Wellhausen (*Composition*, p. 280) and delete
vv. 9b–11a; see Steck, *op. cit.*, pp. 20ff. and Timm, *op. cit.*, p. 105.
The view taken here, following Würthwein (*op. cit.*, pp. 152ff.), is
that vv. 13b–14 are secondary and have been inserted as part of a
literary device to continue the narrative after the interpolation in
vv. 11b–13. **I have been very jealous for the LORD, the God of
hosts**: The verb *qānā'*, 'to be jealous for', refers to zeal and devotion,
and can be applied to both God (Exod. 20:5) and man (2 Kg.
10:16). The suggestion that the verb is used deliberately to echo the
reference to the jealous God (*'ēl qannā'*, Exod. 20:5; 24:14; Dt.
4:24; 5:9; 6:15) in the Horeb-Sinai tradition (Carlson, *op. cit.*, p.
432), strives too much for parallelism with the Horeb tradition.

forsaken thy covenant, thrown down thy altars and slain thy prophets with the sword: These proofs of Israel's despicable behaviour reflect what is said elsewhere in the Elijah tradition: for **forsaken thy covenant** ('forsaken thee' in the Gk.), cf. 18:18*b*; for **thrown down thy altars**, cf. 18:30; for **slain thy prophets with the sword**, cf. 18:13; and for **I, even I only am left**, cf. 18:22. The words attributed here to Elijah point to a later reflection on the tradition, as is demonstrated by the fact that **the people of Israel** are now the guilty party. In 18:18 the offender was the king and his father's house, in 18:13 and 19:1 it was Jezebel, but here it is Israel that stands accused (Steck, *op. cit.*, pp. 23ff.; Frank, *CBQ* [1963], pp. 410–14).

11–12. The theophany interpolation which continues in v. 13 is now introduced. **Go forth, and stand up on the mount**: This is probably equivalent to the statement in v. 13 that he 'went out and stood at the entrance of the cave'. **And behold, the LORD passed by**: cf. Exod. 33:19, on which this reference is obviously based. The three elements of vv. 11*b*–12, wind, earthquake and fire, represent the upheaval of nature which is associated with the Sinai theophany (cf. Exod. 19:9ff.; 10:18ff.; Dt. 4:9ff.; 5:24ff.) as well as other references to theophany in the *OT* (cf. Jg. 5:4ff.; Hab. 3:3ff.; Ps. 18:12; 68:8); see further, Jeremias, *Theophanie*, pp. 100ff. On this occasion a negative statement follows each of these references—**but the Lord was not in** any of them. The various interpretations of these negatives have been classified by Jeremias (*op. cit.*, pp. 113ff.) into three main types: the natural or aesthetic interpretation, which sees in theophany a picture or an expression of God's majesty; the moralising interpretation, which finds in the negatives a message telling Elijah to fight with inner weapons; the spiritualizing interpretation, which sees in the description the power of God, which scorns man's self-defence. These interpretations, however, are to be rejected, and, as shown by Würthwein (*op. cit.*, pp. 152ff.), other more recent ones are equally unsatisfactory. Jeremias' own suggestion (*op. cit.*, p. 115) that the negatives contain a polemic against those who saw a connection between God and the destructive forces of nature is rejected because such a polemic is not made clear, and also because later descriptions of theophany retain these destructive elements. Even Steck's (*op. cit.*, p. 118) modification of Jeremias and his definition of the contrast as that between the deities of nature and Yahweh manifesting himself in his word to the prophets is not entirely satisfactory. Stamm (*Fest. Vriezen*, p. 334) attempts too complicated a solution by seeking to establish an inner connection between the negatives of vv. 11*b*–12 and the commission of Elijah in vv. 15–16; the three elements correspond to the three anointings, and the sound of a gentle breeze to the seven thousand of v. 18. Würthwein, because he takes vv. 11–13 as a secondary addition associating Elijah with Moses, is not pressed to interpret the negatives in combination with the remainder of the chapter. They are best interpreted in relation to the prophet Elijah himself; beginning with the contention that the theophany was a cultic event, Würthwein maintains that the negatives declare that God is not present in what is seen or heard, but in what Yahweh says to his prophet (Würthwein, *op. cit.*, pp. 163ff.). **a still small voice**: *NEB*, 'a low murmuring sound'; *NIV*, 'a gentle whisper' (cf. Burney, p. 231, 'the sound of a light whisper'). Carlson (*op. cit.*, p. 435) draws attention to a number of texts (Gen. 3:8; Jg. 4:5; 2 Sam. 5:24) which illustrate the importance of the concept of God's voice in Israelite religion. Nevertheless, the allusion and the exact meaning of the phrase used here is far from certain. Stamm's suggestion (*ibid.*) that the inner connection with vv. 14–18 indicates that the still small voice is to be identified with the remnant of seven thousand can be discarded on the ground that it offers too fanciful an interpretation. Jeremias' explanation of it as a reference to God's presence in the cult is based on a parallel in the Qumran scrolls (4QS1 39:24; see Strugnell, *VTS* 7 [1960], pp. 322–3) and provides a good base for a satisfactory interpretation. The point made is that Yahweh, as the prophet hears him when receiving his word, is the same as when he is present in the cult; he speaks not in outward symbols, but through his presence in his living word (cf. Steck, *ibid.*; Würthwein, *op. cit.*, p. 165). Such an interpretation is preferred to the attempt to find in the phrase the climax of a series of cosmic events and to translate it as 'A roaring and thunderous voice' (as by Lust, *VT* 25 [1975], pp. 110–15).

13. Elijah's reaction in wrapping **his face in his mantle** is similar to the arrangement made for Moses in Exod. 33:20–22 so that he would not see the face of God. This again confirms the link between the two accounts of theophany and the suggestion that Elijah is being presented as a second Moses. In vv. 13*b*–14 the narrative is resumed after the interpolation by repeating parts of vv. 9*b*–10 (see above, p. 327).

15–16. These verses continue the narrative interrupted at v. 10, and it is in their words that the real message of the narrative lies. The situation presupposed is that of a later period than Elijah's days; Israel's life was under serious threat from both external and internal forces, the former in the guise of the Syrian wars and the latter emanating from the influence of foreign cults and the elimination of the prophets (cf. v. 10). The reply contains a threefold message: (a) the crisis must be seen as God's punishment on Israel (cf. v. 17); (b) the process of judgment is set in motion by Elijah, for he is to anoint the agents, Hazael, Jehu and Elisha (vv. 15–16); the teaching of the Elisha circle in a time of crisis is given authority by connecting it with Elijah, whose own authority is validated by the comparison with Moses in the theophany interpolation (see further, Würthwein, *op. cit.*, pp. 162ff.); (c) despite the depressing situation, the prophet is not alone, for there are seven thousand who do not worship Baal (v. 18). **return on your way to the wilderness of Damascus**: The reference to **the wilderness of Damascus** causes some difficulty, since Elijah was not expected to anoint Hazael, Jehu and Elisha in the wilderness. It must be regarded as a gloss (cf. Würthwein, *op. cit.*, p. 161), which was inserted because of the necessity of bringing Elijah back from his travels; it is omitted from the Hexaplaric version of the Gk. The area in mind is the edge of the desert to the east of the Lake of Galilee, which is called *al-Leja* (Šanda I, p. 449; Gray, p. 411), and is a well-known refuge. Gray suggests that this passage may have given the Qumran sect the name 'wilderness of Damascus' for the place of their retreat. Elijah's new commission refers to three anointings. The first is the anointing of **Hazael to be king over Syria**. For the circumstances surrounding Hazael's rise to the throne, see on 2 Kg. 8:7–15, where the prophet Elisha designated Hazael as king of Syria, but did not anoint him. According to 2 Kg. 9:1ff. Elisha did not personally anoint **Jehu the son of Nimshi . . . to be king over Israel**, but he was indirectly responsible for the act. Although vv. 19–21 describe the call of Elisha, who according to 2 Kg. 2:9–18 was the acknowledged successor of Elijah, no account is given of anointing him **to be prophet in your place**. As a matter of fact this is the only example in the *OT* of a prophet appointing his successor, and the question does arise whether this isolated example is a further attempt to portray Elijah on the model of Moses, who appointed Joshua as his successor (see further, Carroll, *VT* 19 [1969], pp. 400–14). Gray (*ibid.*) suggests that since anointing was a rite for setting apart there is no need to interpret the verb literally in the present context; the intention is simply to claim that the authorization of the three persons named was Elijah's responsibility and thus to legitimize the events of a later period. Elisha's home is given as **Abel-meholah**; see on 1 Kg. 4:12, where various identifications are mentioned, and Zobel, *ZDPV* 82 [1966], pp. 83–108, where it is identified with *Tell abū ṣuṣ*.

17. Precise information about the events behind this verse is not given; it is obvious, however, that events over a period of time have been telescoped here. Jehu's revolt and its accompanying slaughter preceded the reign of Hazael and the Syrian wars with Israel, and so this verse relates to the period between the revolt of Jehu and the death of Hazael in 801 BC (Unger, *Israel and the Aramaeans*, pp. 75–82). In the account of the revolt of Jehu there is no reference to a slaughter instigated by the prophet, although Elisha was probably held responsible for setting in motion the sequence of events recorded in 2 Kg. 9 (cf. Šanda I, p. 451). The pronouncement of judgment found in this verse is in essence the interpretation given by the Elisha circle to the events of their own time.

18. The promise in this verse, which asserts, contrary to his own fears in v. 10, that Elijah is not alone, is the climax of the narrative. Despite the chastisements that are brought upon it, Israel will survive because it has a number who have not worshipped Baal. As von Rad observes (*Theology II*, p. 21), this verse strikes a new note in Israel's story by introducing the doctrine of the remnant. It is a doctrine that combines in itself a message of judgment and of survival. The suggestion that v. 18a contains an independent eschatological, political oracle (Reiser, *ThZ* 9 [1953], p. 338) is doubtful. **Yet I will leave seven thousand in Israel**: The number given is a round number and is a multiple of seven, the perfect number. **all the knees that have not bowed to Baal**: The phrase is used here, as elsewhere (cf. 1 Kg. 8:54; 2 Kg. 1:13), of worship and obeisance, and need not refer to a specific form of dance that was performed in the worship of Baal (as suggested by de Vaux, *BMB* 5 [1941], pp. 9–11 and favoured by Gray, p. 413). **and every mouth that has not kissed him**: This symbol of adoration and allegiance means more than throwing a kiss with the hand (as suggested in Job 31:27). Kissing an image, or at least the stand on which it stood, was usual practice (cf. Hos. 13:2).

19. The final section of the chapter provides an appendix to the narrative reaching its climax in v. 18 by relating how Elisha was called by Elijah. The Elisha circle, in emphasizing the importance of Elijah, were by implication legitimizing the work of Elisha. Because Elisha is given prominence in the final section, it has been contended that it belongs originally to the Elisha cycle rather than the Elijah cycle. The view taken here is that it need not be separated from the remainder of the chapter, since the preceding narrative as well as vv. 19–21 serves the interests of the Elisha circle. **he departed from there**: In its present context this report is joined to the Horeb narrative, and **there** in this case must refer to Horeb. This was not its original reference, however; but once the redactional link is removed the section is without a beginning (cf. Schmitt, *Elisa*, p. 102). **Elisha the son of Shaphat**: The prophet's name means 'God is salvation'; another example of it has been discovered on a seventh-century BC seal from Amman (see Gray, p. 412). **ploughing,**

with twelve yokes of oxen before him: Teams of oxen, with a plough attached to each pair and a driver in charge, worked in rows along a field (see Montgomery, p. 315). This may be an indication that Elisha came from a fairly prosperous background. **cast his mantle upon him**: The hairy mantle is mentioned elsewhere (cf. 2 Kg. 1:8; 2:8, 13f.; Zech. 13:4) and was probably the distinctive clothing of a prophet, or at least of some type of prophet. The suggestion that the mantle was made from the skin of a sacrificial animal, and was thus a means of close communion with God, is doubtful (cf. Johnson, *Cultic Prophet*, p. 28). Nevertheless, the mantle, through its contact with a person's body, possessed the power of its owner. Gray (p. 413) gives examples from Assyrian rituals, the Mari descriptions of prophets and Greek graffiti from a Phoenician tomb, to illustrate the power attached to the mantle, and suggests that the origin of the miraculous power of Elijah's mantle may have been derived from the reference to David cutting off the skirt of Saul's mantle, which signified that he had power over him. Noting that Elisha is called by Elijah to follow him, von Rad (*Theology II*, pp. 56ff., 71) is of the opinion that this narrative gives a genuine reflection of the tradition within the prophetic guilds.

20. Go back again, for what have I done to you?: *NEB*, 'what have I done to prevent you?'. The meaning is not clear. No indication is given that Elisha was being rebuked because he had not realized the demands of his call by Elijah (as suggested by Fohrer, *op. cit.*, p. 22). *NEB* accepts the explanation that the call does not interfere with a man's natural affection towards his family. More probably the meaning is 'Go, but realise what I have done to you', and therefore come back to me (Skinner, p. 243; Gray, p. 413).

21. Elisha took the **yoke of oxen**, presumably those that he himself had been using, and boiled their flesh with the yokes. His action is usually taken to be symbolical, for the slaughter of the animals and the destruction of their gear is a sign of complete break with his former life (Skinner, *ibid.*; Gray, *ibid.*). **and gave it to the people, and they ate**: Elisha's sacrifice was a thank-offering for his call, and it appears that his neighbours had been invited to join him on the occasion. **he went after Elijah, and ministered unto him**: Moses too had a servant, Joshua (Exod. 24:13), and in both cases they are disciples who are trained by the master in order to succeed him. Whether this is historically correct is a debatable point.

(iv) The Syrian Wars **20:1–43**
The two sections giving an account of Israel's wars with Damascus (1 Kg. 20:1–43; 22:1–38) are different in character and content from

the Elijah cycle. Elijah is not even mentioned, for the chief character is 'the king of Israel', who is only occasionally identified with Ahab (cf. 20:2, 13, 14, 34; 22:20).

The rise in Syria on Israel's north-eastern border of a kingdom that is named in biblical and extra-biblical sources as Damascus or Aram (Mazar, *BA* 25 [1962], pp. 109ff.; Malamat, *POTT*, pp. 143ff.) was a significant development for Israelite history during the ninth century BC. The political contacts of this new power are well illustrated by the discovery in Aleppo of Benhadad I's Milqart stele (*ANET*, p. 501; *DOTT*, pp. 139–41); with the increase of its power and influence this kingdom constituted a threat even to Israel's very existence. Naturally, the most vulnerable areas were the Israelite held territories to the east of the Jordan, and several events in this period, when considered in the context of this Syrian threat, are to be understood as political moves to ward off the danger. Omri sealed an alliance with Phoenicia by marrying his son Ahab to the Tyrian princess Jezebel, and he secured an alliance with Judah by marrying his daughter, or probably his grand-daughter, Athaliah to the Judaean royal family (on the problem of Athaliah, see Katzenstein, *IEJ* 5 [1955], pp. 194–7; Miller, *JBL* 85 [1966], p. 454).

The course of events during this period is obscure, and the crux is whether the tension developed into war during the reign of Ahab as indicated by 20:2–43 and 22:1–38. Acceptance of the biblical tradition leads to the difficulty of giving an exact date to the events. One possibility is to date them towards the end of Ahab's days and to interpret the aggression of Benhadad II (Hadadeser of Aram) as an attempt to secure his rear before Shalmaneser III (859–829 BC) attacked Syria following his notable successes in the Euphrates basin in 858 and 857–855 BC (Mazar, *op. cit.*, pp. 106ff.). A peace-treaty (20:26–34) was effected to meet the threat from Assyria and in anticipation of the coalition that fought Shalmaneser at Qarqar in 853 BC. Another possible solution is to date the wars in the early period of Ahab's reign, thus allowing more time for the mellowing of relationships in preparation for the alliance formed before 853 BC (Bright, *History*, p. 223). Another possibility is to date the first war in Ahab's early days, and the second war as Ahab's move to settle an old grievance after the collapse of the confederacy against Assyria in 853 BC (Yeivin, *WHJP*, pp. 142ff.).

Nevertheless, the reliability of the biblical tradition is suspect for several reasons. References to Ahab are surprisingly few, and in several of its occurrences the king's name is unnecessary because of the presence of the title 'the king of Israel'; this may suggest that the proper name was added to suit the present context. Moreover,

because the phrase 'the king of Israel' is so characteristic of the
Elisha cycle, a link is established between these narratives and the
Elisha tradition (Burney, pp. 207–15). Also under discussion is
whether the picture presented of the Omride dynasty is consistent
with what is known generally about the period (Miller, *op. cit.*,
p. 443). The Omride kings were energetic and successful; they
ruled Moab (cf. the Mesha inscription), exerted influence over other
peoples (1 Kg. 18:10), built cities (1 Kg. 15:24; 22:39; cf. Yadin,
BA 23 [1960], pp. 62–8), and sent a strong military contingent to
the battle of Qarqar (*ANET*, pp. 279, 320–1). For a full survey of
extra-biblical information about the dynasty of Omri and of recent
research on the period, see Timm, *Die Dynastie*, pp. 157–303. The
achievements of the Omride dynasty are difficult to explain if Israel
was under Syrian oppression and Ahab a vassal of Syria. In this
connection too it must be asked if Syria did oppress Israel for the
long period extending from the reign of Ahab to the reign of Joash
(Miller, *op. cit.*, p. 454), and if an alliance with Syria in 853 BC
is feasible in the context of this long period of harassment. The
circumstances surrounding Ahab's death also present a problem.
Whilst 1 Kg. 22:34–38 describe how Ahab was wounded in the
battlefield and died in his chariot facing the Syrians, the note in
22:40 states that he 'slept with his fathers', a phrase that is only
used of kings who died a natural death (Hölscher, *Eucharisterion*,
p. 185; Alfrink, *OSt* 2 [1943], pp. 106–18).

Consequently, the three battle-accounts in 1 Kg. 20:1–43; 22:1–38
are dated in the dynasty of Jehu rather than at the end of the
Omride dynasty, with the king waging the battle being identified
either with Joash (so Jepsen, *AfO* 14 [1942], pp. 154–8, followed
by Whitley, *VT* 2 [1952], pp. 137–52); or, more convincingly, with
Jehoahaz (Miller, *op. cit.*, pp. 441–54; *ZAW* 80 [1968], pp. 337–42),
and Benhadad with the Syrian king of 2 Kg. 13:3, 24–25. Miller
has attempted a detailed reconstruction of the history from these
accounts of the Syrian wars. He begins with the incorrect identification of the king in 2 Kg. 13:14 with Joash and corrects it to
Jehoahaz, who was king when Elisha died and the one who defeated
Benhadad three times. It was during Jehoahaz's reign that Benhadad
ascended the throne (2 Kg. 13:3, 24–25), and the three defeats of
Benhadad by Jehoahaz are the ones recorded in 1 Kg. 20:1–43;
22:1–38. Because his father Jehu had lost the city of Ramoth-gilead
and the whole district to Syria (2 Kg. 10:32–33), the son initiated
a campaign to restore them, but the present account of the campaign
has been overshadowed by the reminiscence of an earlier campaign
by Jehoram and Ahaziah (2 Kg. 8:28–9:28). It is further suggested
that originally the narratives did not name the kings, but that, when

they found circulation in Judah after the fall of Samaria, the king of Judah was identified with Jehoshaphat, who was remembered as a king who brought prosperity to Judah. The identification of the king of Judah with Jehoshaphat inevitably meant that the king of Israel was to be identified as his contemporary.

Evidence of the origin of the present form of the narratives in prophetical circles is obvious in the role assumed by the prophets in the course of events. Before they appeared in their present form, these narratives may have belonged to a larger collection giving an account of Israel's victories, but they acquired an emphasis on the part played by prophets from the prophetic circles in which they were transmitted. Such a reconstruction of their transmission dismisses the possibility that they were derived from the so-called 'history of Ahab', which presented a favourable account of his reign (cf. Fohrer, *Introduction*, p. 232). The indications are that these sections were added to the deuteronomistic history after its main outline and its basic formulae had been established; their addition is probably to be attributed to a second or later redactor. The tradition contained in these chapters had been associated with Ahab in pre-deuteronomistic times, and is therefore not the result of deuteronomistic dogma (as suggested by Whitley, *ibid.*).

1. **Benhadad the king of Syria**: The problem of identifying Benhadad, the Syrian king, has been variously resolved. The appearance of the name Benhadad in different periods and with reference to several Syrian kings lends support to the suggestion that Benhadad was a throne-name rather than a proper name (cf. Albright, *BASOR* 87 [1942], p. 28). Assuming that the Syrian king involved with Baasha and Asa in 1 Kg. 15:18–19 was Benhadad I, it is then accepted that the king on the Syrian throne in the time of Ahab was Benhadad II, known in Assyrian inscriptions as Adadidri (= Hadadezer); so Malamat, *op. cit.*, pp. 143ff.; Mazar, *op. cit.*, p. 106. However, it is not necessary to assume that Hadadezer was known by the throne-name Benhadad, if the events of this chapter are dated in the time of Jehoahaz, for the Syrian monarch succeeding Hazael was called Benhadad (Miller, *JBL* 85 [1966], p. 454). **thirty-two kings were with him**: The total of **thirty-two** includes more than the heads of satellite states, which, according to the Zakir inscription (*ANET*, p. 501), amounted to ten, of which seven are listed. The figure need not be disputed (see Montgomery, p. 320), for it probably includes not only kings and heads of state but also tribal princes and chieftains (cf. Mazar, *op. cit.*, p. 108), for Damascus was the natural centre to which the tribes of the North Arabian desert were drawn and around which some of them settled (so Jepsen, *op. cit.*, pp. 157f.). **and he went up and besieged**

Samaria: Benhadad, as was characteristic of a new ruler, acted to assert his authority by demonstrating to his vassals that he was going to maintain the policy of his predecessor. Yadin (*Bib* 36 [1955], p. 338) finds a parallel in Sennacherib's invasion of Palestine (2 Kg. 18), and according to Miller (*ZAW* 80 [1968], pp. 338f.) Benhadad took three steps to assert his authority soon after he succeeded Hazael to the throne.

2–3. Ahab king of Israel: As noted above, the name **Ahab** is probably an addition here. Benhadad's message was intended to give **the king of Israel** an indication that he was pursuing the line taken by his predecessor of keeping him in vassalage. By noting that the king's **silver, gold, fairest wives** (the Gk. omits **fairest**) **and children** are his, Benhadad was confirming that the Israelite king was his vassal.

4. The Israelite king interpreted Benhadad's message as a demand for verbal submission and so responded by acknowledging that he **and all that I have** belonged to Benhadad, who is fittingly called **my lord, O King** (*NEB*, 'my lord king'). The king's assertion that **I am yours** need not mean that he offered to surrender his person to Benhadad, but that the latter declined and demanded his family as hostages (as suggested by Gray, pp. 422ff.). The preliminary soundings demanded no more than verbal acknowledgement.

5–6. Benhadad's second message clarifies his intention. Admittedly it is not easy to formulate the contrast between his two demands, and some have changed the text slightly in v. 7 in order to find a second demand for the Israelite king's wife and children as hostages (see below). A contrast is achieved, however, by accepting that a demand for acknowledgement implied that Benhadad could confiscate property or take the king's family as hostages, if his demands for tribute were not met. Although his demand for submission is not to be interpreted literally as a request for the king's property and family to be delivered to Benhadad (v. 5), acknowledging him by the Israelite king meant that such a request could in certain circumstances be made effective. Benhadad's second measure, introducing his practical measures to assert his authority, means that the Syrian king is not content with verbal submission. He will send his officers to inspect the property of the king and his officials **and lay hands on whatever pleases them**. *RSV* here follows the Vsns. in rejecting the Heb. 'you'; but the Heb. can be retained and rendered 'everything you prize' (*NEB*) or 'everything you value' (*NIV*). This second demand meant that they would virtually take possession of the city.

7. The crux of the issue between the king of Israel and Benhadad is contained in the phrase **I did not refuse him**. This verse can be rendered differently on the basis of the Gk. to mean that he has now sent for the king's wives and children, despite the fact that when he sent previously for silver and gold he was not refused (see Montgomery, pp. 320ff.). According to the interpretation offered under vv. 5, 6, what is stated is that the Israelite king **did not refuse him** when Benhadad sent for submission and its implied commitment; but since he had acknowledged Benhadad and presumably paid his tribute, further action could not be justified, and must therefore, be interpreted as **seeking trouble** (*NEB*, 'picking a quarrel').

8–9. After obtaining advice from **all the elders and all the people** (the latter are not mentioned in v. 7), the king of Israel sent his reply to Benhadad. Whilst confirming his response to the first demand, his answer to the second demand is an uncompromising refusal, **this thing I cannot do.**

10. Benhadad's next message contains a threat of war against the city of Samaria. The vow formula, **The gods do so to me, and more also,** is the same as in 1 Kg. 19:2. There has been some uncertainty about the meaning of the threat, **if the dust of Samaria shall suffice for handfuls for all the people who follow me.** Samaria is threatened with total devastation, for Benhadad's army is so numerous that it will be able to carry away the dust of Samaria in handfuls. This is obviously an exaggerated boast, as in 2 Sam. 17:13. The Gk. read the Heb. *šeʿālîm*, 'handfuls', as *šûʿālîm*, 'foxes', thus suggesting that there would be enough earth left in which foxes could burrow. But the Gk. misses the point.

11. The reply sent to Benhadad, which is very concise in Heb., was probably a proverbial saying. **Let not him that girds on his armour boast himself as he that puts it off** means that it is time enough to boast when a war has been won and the armour discarded. For putting on armour, see 1 Sam. 17:39 and for putting it off see Isa. 45:1. In the context the reference must be to arming and disarming, and not to putting on a girdle in the morning and removing it at night (as suggested by Gray, p. 423). Luc. takes the first verb to mean 'being lame' (cf. Rabbinic Heb.) and the second as its antithesis; this is the basis of *NEB*'s rendering 'The lame must not think himself a match for the nimble'.

12. as he was drinking with the kings in the booths: The Heb. *sukkōt* is understood to refer to field bivouacs (Gray, *ibid.*) or shacks erected for the royal party (Montgomery, p. 322), although the word is only rarely used (cf. also 2 Sam. 11:11) instead of the more common word for tents. Yadin (*Bib* 36 [1955], pp. 332–51) takes it to be the proper name Succoth, and claims that both David (2 Sam. 11) and Benhadad had set up camp at Succoth in the Jordan valley;

the Gk. also takes it as a place-name in v. 16. The placing of the army at such a strategic point near the mouth of the Jabbok, thus giving him protection and at the same time keeping him within striking distance of Israel, Ammon and other capitals in the south, indicates that Benhadad at the beginning of his reign tried to assert his authority over all the southern provinces (Miller, *ZAW* 80 [1968], p. 338). **Take your positions**: The Heb. has a single verb here, *sîm*, 'set on', which has a technical use as elsewhere (cf. 1 Sam. 15:2; Ezek. 23:24) and can be rendered as 'Attack'! (Montgomery, p. 322; Gray, p. 415; cf. *NEB, NIV*).

13. Each of the reports of victories over the Syrians in 1 Kg. 20; 22 gives an account of prophetic intervention, cf. vv. 35ff. and 22:7ff. Although these sections have been called interpolations from a prophetic source, they are now integrated so well into the narrative that they cannot be separated from it. It is, therefore, more reasonable to suggest that accounts of victories over Syria, when taken over by prophetic circles, were rewritten by them from a prophetic standpoint, which gave the prophets a key role in securing the successes. Such a role was closely attached to the ideal of these prophetic circles, namely the prophet Elisha, and it was in association with the Elisha traditions that these narrative reports were transmitted (Miller, *JBL* 85 [1966], p. 446). **a prophet**: The prophet of this narrative, who is unnamed (cf. v. 22), is probably to be identified with 'the man of God' of v. 28. An unnamed prophet, designated as 'a certain man of the sons of the prophets', appears also in v. 35. But in chapter 22 the otherwise unknown prophets, Zedekiah and Micaiah, have been given names; there is, however, no basis for the identification of the unknown prophet of chapter 20 with Micaiah of chapter 22, as was proposed by Josephus (*Ant.* VIII.14.5). The prophet's message here as in v. 28 is a favourable one and, using the formula of the holy war war tradition **I will give it into your hand**, promises victory (cf. von Rad, *Der heilige Krieg*, pp. 7ff.). Connected with the holy war formula here and in v. 28 is the phrase **and you shall know that I am the LORD**, which again is a stereotyped formula recurring some sixty times in the book of Ezekiel (Zimmerli, *Fest. Robert*, pp. 154–64).

14. By the servants of the governors of the districts: The fact that such instructions concerning strategy constitute an integral part of the narrative (cf. vv. 15, 17, 19) is a clear indication that the prophetic section is not an interpolation but rather that the whole account has been rewritten by the prophetic circle. The soldiers mentioned here were literally 'the young men of the governors of the provinces'. **The governors of the districts** may correspond to the district prefects of the Solomonic administration (cf. 1 Kg.

2:7ff.), but in addition to their duties as fiscal officers they have now acquired the task of providing the king with a quota of warriors in time of emergency. The term **servants** ('young men', Heb. *ne'ārîm*; cf. the military term *na'aruna* in Egypt, de Vaux, *Ancient Israel*, p. 221) may refer to young unmarried men who were used as shock troops or commandos (cf. the analogous 'young knights' or 'squires' known from Arabic sources; Montgomery, p. 323). *RSV*'s **Who shall begin the battle?** (cf. *K-B*; and *NIV*, 'start') is rendered 'draw up the battle line' in *NEB* and 'clinch the fighting' by Gray (p. 419). It was the commandos who began the fighting and put the Syrians to flight; only afterwards did the king and his army go out to finish the battle (see vv. 20–21).

15. he mustered: The Heb. *pāqad* means 'to review, take stock' (cf. *K-B*), and for this they had to be mustered or called up. The commandos were a select group of **two hundred and thirty two**, but **all the people of Israel** could hardly be included in the figure of **seven thousand**. The Gk. adds as a qualification that only 'the men of substance' are meant; these were the men of property who were expected to take up arms.

16. they went out: Gray (p. 425) suggests that the correct meaning here is that 'they emerged to view' from an ambush. They left Samaria early in the morning and took up their positions **at noon. in the booths**: The Gk. reads 'in Succoth' here; see above on v. 12.

17. And Benhadad sent out scouts and they reported to him: The Heb. merely states 'and Benhadad sent and they reported to him'. Luc. has 'and they sent', presumably presupposing the report of outposts. The name of Benhadad may be mistaken as a subject, and the singular verb, 'and one sent' may simply mean 'and word was sent to Benhadad' (*NEB*).

18. The small band of commandos gave Benhadad the impression that the Israelites could be captured **alive**, whatever their intention.

19. and the army which followed them: This addendum is out of place, for the army, although probably following the commandos, was not engaged in fighting until it went into action later on under Benhadad's leadership (see v. 21). *BHS* transposes it after 'the Syrians fled' in v. 20, but it is best omitted altogether. Although some textual disarrangement is obvious in vv. 19–21, a satisfactory reading is obtained by a very slight rearrangement of the text to give the following sequence: vv. 19, 20*a*, 21, 20*b* (cf. Šanda I, pp. 479ff.).

20. escaped on a horse with horsemen: The Heb. here is awkward and states literally that he escaped 'on a horse and horsemen'. *RSV* conveys the meaning by taking the conjunction 'and' to mean 'with'; cf. *NEB*, 'on horseback with some of the cavalry'.

21. and captured the horses and chariots: *RSV* rightly follows the Gk. in reading **captured** in preference to MT 'smote'. By seizing the abandoned horses and chariots they were able to pursue the Syrians who were fleeing on foot.

22. This verse is usually taken with the account of the first campaign, which is taken to run to v. 22 (Montgomery, p. 323; Gray, p. 425) or even to v. 25 (Miller, *ZAW* 80 [1968], p. 338). However, vv. 22 and 23–25 give an account of preliminary preparations for the second campaign, one side being encouraged by a prophet and the other making changes in its military tactics. Thus the second campaign is covered by vv. 22–34. **the prophet**: He is still unnamed, but is presumably the same person as is mentioned in v. 13. **in the spring**: The Heb. has 'at the turn of the year', which in this case does not refer to the autumnal new year, but to the opening of the season for military expeditions, which began in the spring (cf. 2 Sam. 11:1). According to Miller's reconstruction (*op. cit.*, p. 341) the two campaigns were separated by less than a year, the first occurring in 805 BC and the second in 804 BC (or, if a different chronological reckoning is accepted, in 806 and 805 BC respectively).

23. The Syrian post-mortem on the first campaign showed them that **their gods are gods of the hills, and so they were stronger than we** . The rendering of *'elōhîm* by the plural **gods** is surely correct, since the Syrians ascribed a number of deities to Israel in accordance with general practice. The Gk. deliberately avoided the plurality by reading 'A mountain-god is the God of Israel'. In referring to the hills the Syrians made a correct assessment of the situation, for they were probably attacked in a different place on the Wadi Far'a, where the hilly terrain forced the Syrians to abandon their chariots (cf. Yadin, *op. cit.*, p. 340). Consequently, the Syrians propose a change of manoeuvres, **let us fight against them in the plains**.

24. Another change effected by the Syrians was to **remove the kings, each from his post, and put commanders in their places**. This record, it has been claimed (cf. Mazar, *op. cit.*, pp. 108–9), is historically trustworthy because it refers to structural changes made in the Aram-Damascus empire between 855 and 853 BC. A loose confederation of satellite kingdoms became a united empire, and the kings of these kingdoms were replaced by governors of districts under the leadership of Benhadad. It is doubtful, however, if such important structural and administrative changes are presupposed in this section and if they could have been accomplished in the short period of a winter rest between two campaigns. It is preferable to interpret the changes described in this verse as an *ad hoc* modification of military tactics. Benhadad's first campaign had been aimed at impressing upon the provinces of the south his intention of keeping them in subjection; he therefore assembled a vast army of satellite kings and their vassals at Succoth. His second campaign, which was directed more specifically at Israel, was to be a military engagement under the leadership of **commanders**. The Heb. *paḥôṯ*, translated **commanders** in *RSV* and 'officers' in *NEB*, is an Assyr. word denoting 'lord of a province'; it need not refer to fiscal district officers, but to regular officers of the army (Gray, p. 427; Rüterswörden, *Die Beamten*, p. 161).

26. As was predicted by the prophet in v. 24, Benhadad renewed his military activities against Israel **in the spring** and opened his second campaign by going **up to Aphek**. The location of **Aphek** is uncertain because a number of places mentioned in the *OT* bear this name; some of them are unsuitable in the present context and can be dismissed from the discussion (cf. Gray, p. 428). It is usual to identify it with *al-Fik*, east of the lake of Tiberias and on the direct route from Damascus to Israel (cf. Aharoni, *Land*, p. 67). But, because it is inconceivable that the Israelites would have moved so far north and set themselves in a direct line of attack by Syrians descending from the mountains, preference has been shown recently to the identification with the village of *Faqqua* on Mount Gilboa (cf. Miller, *op. cit.*, p. 339, following Tolkowsky, *JPOS* 2 [1922], pp. 145–58). Whereas the Syrians would go down to al-Fik, they would have to cross the Jordan and go up to Faqqua.

27. and were provisioned: A verb from the root *kûl*, 'to provision', is well attested (cf. 1 Kg. 4:7; 5:7; 17:4, 9), but it has been suggested that in this instance it is a military term connected with a similar root in Syr. and Arab. meaning 'were counted'; cf. *NEB*, 'formed into companies'. **like two little flocks of goats**: The Heb. *ḥaśîp*, 'little flock', is not found elsewhere, but this is the meaning given in all the Vsns.

28. The **man of God** is unnamed, and may possibly be identified with the prophet of vv. 13, 22. The oracle delivered by the prophet is in classical style, progressing from the opening formula **Thus says the LORD** to give a reason for (introduced by *ya'an*, 'because') the main pronouncement at the end of the verse, **therefore I will give**. On the phrase **and you shall know that I am the LORD**, see above on v. 13.

29. they encamped opposite one another seven days: The delay of **seven days**, the perfect number, is explained by Gray (*ibid.*) as a deliberate waiting period, during which omens were sought from the gods assuring the armies of their intervention in the battle. The

account given here is clearly derived from popular tradition with its
fictional and highly exaggerated figures, battle being waged **on the
seventh day**, the number slain being **a hundred thousand foot
soldiers,** and those killed by the falling wall in Aphek being **twenty-
seven thousand men** (v. 30). Even allowing that **smote** is to be
taken in its wider meaning of 'defeating' rather than 'killing', the
figures are enormous, especially when it is remembered that the
total Syrian contingent at Qarqar was only twenty-thousand (Gray,
p. 429).

30. and the wall fell: Although the number killed has been
exaggerated, the reference to a falling wall may be genuine, for the
undermining of city walls was practised, as is testified by the use of
machines for the purpose by Sennacherib (cf. Šanda I, p. 482). **the
inner-chamber in the city**: lit. 'a room within a room' (cf. 1 Kg.
22:52; 2 Kg. 9:2). This gives a suitable meaning, and there is no
need to find a reference here to an underground house (with Josephus, *Ant.* VIII.14.4) or to moving through the vaults of the fortress
from one chamber to another (Šanda, *ibid.*; Montgomery, p. 324).

31. sackcloth on our loins: Wearing sackcloth, a coarse black
material, around the loins was a traditional sign of mourning, fast
and penitence (cf. de Vaux, *Ancient Israel*, p. 59). **ropes upon our
heads**: This sign of captivity or subjection is only found here in the
OT. Although the general meaning is clear from the context, the
exact terms of reference are not specified, and the custom has
variously been interpreted as a sign of willingness to act as porter
to the victor (Šanda I, p. 483), a Syrian manner of supplication
(Josephus, *ibid.*), or simply a sign of poverty in that only the rope
of the Bedouin head-dress is worn (Kittel, p. 169).

32. He is my brother: Addressing each other as brothers is
common among kings; cf. Hiram and Solomon in 1 Kg. 9:13, and
also the Amarna tablets, where the kings mutually use this form of
address (so Montgomery, p. 324). This is preferable to *NEB*'s 'my
royal cousin'.

33. were watching for an omen: For this verb cf. Gen. 30:27.
Benhadad's men were observing carefully how the Israelite king
responded in order to obtain some indication of the king's mood
and likely course of action. **they quickly took it up from him**: The
verb used here is found nowhere else. One suggested meaning based
on the Arab. is 'to take a decision' (*K-B*), and the sentence is
rendered 'they were quick to take it as a definite decision' (Gray,
pp. 426ff.). *RSV* (as also *NEB* and *NIV*) suggests that they were
quick to pick up the word **brother** from the reply and to repeat it.
Whichever rendering is adopted, the Heb. consonants are divided
in accordance with MSS and Vsns. rather than with MT (see *BHS*).

and caused him to come up into the chariot: This is a symbolic
act of acceptance, whereby Benhadad's status as equal is acknowledged. It stands in contrast to what may have been Benhadad's
symbolic act of submission, whereby he placed his shoulder to the
wheel of the king's chariot (so Šanda I, p. 484; Gray, p. 430, with
reference to a description of this practice in an Aramaic inscription).

**34. The cities which my father took from your father I will
restore:** If the 'king of Israel' is identified with Ahab, it must be
assumed that Syria put pressure on Israel in the days of Omri, seized
territories from him and established bazaars in Samaria (Mazar, *op.
cit.*, p. 106; Yeivin, *WHJP*, p. 138). But there is no evidence of
such pressure in the time of Omri; the only possibility is that
reference is made to a loss in the time of Baasha, who, although
not an ancestor of Ahab, may have been referred to as 'father'
(Montgomery, p. 325). Accepting the annalistic note in 1 Kg. 13:25,
it has been suggested that Joash recovered from Benhadad cities
which his father Jehoahaz had lost to Hazael, thus identifying 'the
king of Israel' with Joash (so Gray, p. 430). Miller (*JBL* 85 [1966],
pp. 442ff.) is not satisfied that it was Jehoahaz who lost Israelite
territory to Hazael, for elsewhere in Kings such loss is said to have
occurred in the time of Jehu (2 Kg. 10:32–33, with which 1 Kg.
13:24–25 is to be compared). Consequently, the restoration of cities
in this verse is taken to refer to the return to Jehoahaz of cities lost
by Jehu his father. **establish bazaars for yourself in Damascus:**
There are other examples of the practice of establishing trading
quarters for merchants in large cities; cf. Neh. 13:16; see further,
Mazar, *ibid.*; Yeivin, *ibid.* They were colonies of merchants (cf.
Elat, *WHJP*, pp. 184ff.). **I will let you go on these terms:** The
Heb. literally says 'on the covenant or agreement' (*berît*). The
meaning is clear: the Israelite king is willing to release Benhadad
on agreement to restore the cities of Israel. It is unnecessary to
emend the text and to presuppose an idiom that has an Ugaritic
parallel in order to read 'I shall release you from the vassal-treaty'
(Gray, pp. 427, 431; see further van der Woude, *ZAW* 76 [1964],
pp. 188–91; Driver, *ZAW* 78 [1966], pp. 1–4).

35–43. The similarity of the lion incident in vv. 35ff. to the
prophetic legend in 1 Kg. 13:20–25 casts doubt on the historical
reliability of this narrative. The 'word of the LORD' features here
as in 1 Kg. 13:20; the unwillingness to obey the divine word in
v. 35 is to be compared with 13:21; the declaration of punishment
and its fulfilment in v. 36 is paralleled in 13:21–24. The narrative
is usually classified as a parable in action (Lindblom, *Prophecy*,
pp. 52ff.), but the legendary element is unmistakable here. Whitelam (*Just King*, pp. 167–70) accepts the definition 'acted parable',

but adds the suggestion that it is a literary construction composed to show that the king, whilst above the law, was subject to divine justice.

The prophetic circle from which this tradition was derived was critical of the king's leniency towards Benhadad of Syria, and the narrative in this respect preserves a genuine tradition of a reaction among the prophets. During the course of its transmission, however, this tradition acquired other elements. Not only was a popular legendary element added in vv. 35ff., but the judgment pronounced on the king in v. 42 anticipates the more severe judgment of chapter 21 and the report of its fulfilment in chapter 22. Moreover, deuteronomistic influence is seen in the change from a simple declaration that the one holding a captive was responsible for him (v. 39) to the concept in v. 42 that is so characteristic of the holy war tradition, namely that the captive was devoted to destruction by God.

35. of the sons of the prophets: This is the first reference to the prophetical guilds which play such a prominent role in the prophetic tradition, especially that associated with Elisha. 'Son' is a term used to denote a member of the prophetic guild or association which is designated by the plural **sons of the prophets** (cf. 2 Kg. 2:3, 5, 6, 15; 5:22; 6:1; 9:1), and the head or leader is called 'father' (cf. 1 Kg. 13:11ff. (Haldar, *Associations*, pp. 135ff.; Williams, *JBL* 85 [1966], pp. 344–8). The frequent use of the term **the sons of the prophets** in connection with Elisha gives some support to the contention that it refers to a particular prophetic movement that appeared in the period of the Omride dynasty and then disappeared after the days of Elisha (cf. Porter, *JTS* 32 [1981], pp. 423–9). **at the command of the LORD:** Heb. 'at the word of God'.

36. Judgment is announced formally **Because** (*ya'an*) . . . **behold** (*hinnēh*); cf. also v. 42 and 1 Kg. 13:21 for the same formal statement.

38. disguising himself with a bandage over his eyes: The Heb. '*ep̄ēr*, 'bandage', is not found elsewhere. The Gk. and Targ. 'bandage' or 'covering' is supported by the Akkad. *apāru*, 'to provide with a head covering' (Burney, p. 241; Cohen, *Hapaxlegomena*, p. 131), and there is no need to emend to '*ēp̄er*, 'ashes', with the Vulg. and Syr. The **bandage**, although used primarily as a disguise (see below, v. 41), added authenticity to the prophet's story that he had only recently returned from the battlefield.

39. The case presented to the king is that of a breach of contractual agreement for which the law demanded restitution; cf. Exod. 22:7ff., 10–13 (so Gray, p. 433, followed by Whitelam, *op. cit.*, p. 168). The compensation demanded here is excessive, for **a talent of silver** is reckoned to be equivalent to three thousand shekels, whilst the average price of a slave would be thirty shekels. The case is fictitious and would be so recognized if presented to the king. This adds some support to Whitelam's contention (*op. cit.*, pp. 169ff.) that this case is a literary creation to demonstrate the point that if such a punishment followed the breach of a legal contract, how much more the penalty for breaking the sacral law of the ban (cf. v. 42). Whether fictitious or not it presents the king as commander of the levy being responsible for jurisdiction (cf. Macholz, *ZAW* 84 [1972], pp. 173ff.).

40. So shall your judgment be: A confirmation of the judgment by the king is part of the plot of the narrative; it prepares the way for the announcement of a judgment upon the king himself. Cf. also 2 Sam. 12:7.

41. and the king of Israel recognized him as one of the prophets: On the basis of this and other passages in the *OT* (Ezek. 9:4; Zech. 13:6; Isa. 44:5) it has been suggested that the prophets had marked themselves as a sign of their profession. Although the sign was sometimes placed on the hand or on the chest (Isa. 44:5; Zech. 13:6), it could also be a cross on the forehead (Ezek. 9:4). The latter may well have been what the king saw on this occasion after the prophet had removed his bandage.

42. For the formula used to announce judgment, see above under v. 36. **the man whom I had devoted to destruction**: The Heb. literally reads 'the man of my ban'; cf. Isa. 34:5. He was a man whom God had put under the ban, and had thus devoted to destruction. Anything that was placed under the ban in warfare was sacrosanct and had to be destroyed (cf. Dt. 7:2; 20:16). Unwillingness to exercise the ban brought curse and punishment on the offender (cf. Jos. 7).

(v) Naboth's Vineyard 21:1–29

Chapter 21, which relates how Jezebel plotted to kill Naboth so that Ahab could take possession of his vineyard and finishes with Elijah's condemnation of Ahab and Jezebel, gives the impression of being a continuation of the Elijah narrative in 1 Kg. 17–19. In the Gk. it is read immediately after chapter 19. Its position in MT ties it more closely to the account of Ahab's Syrian wars, for the oracle in 21:19 is fulfilled in 22:38. However, the present close connection between this chapter and either the Elijah tradition or the history of Ahab is questionable (see further, Hentschel, *Die Elijaerzählungen*, pp. 20–35), and it is possible that what was originally an independent tradition has been secondarily embedded in the Elijah-Ahab complex. Once the Naboth narrative is separated from the other Elijah narratives, questions of origin and date have to be considered;

some consider it to be early and reflecting an earlier stage of legendary development than the Elijah legends of 1 Kg. 17–19 (Jepsen, *Nabi*, pp. 70–2; cf. Fohrer, *Elia*, pp. 41–2); others take it to be the work of a literary artist who wrote a historical novelette about an event that had taken place long before his time (Miller, *VT* 17 [1967], pp. 311ff.).

Another tradition about the death of Naboth appears in 2 Kg. 9:24–26, and thus the account in 1 Kg. 21 can only be evaluated after considering the respective reliability of the two traditions. A comparison of the two accounts naturally establishes that there are some fundamental differences between them. Naboth's murder may have occurred in the reign of Jehoram, not Ahab, according to one possible interpretation of 2 Kg. 9, which also adds a mention of the death of his sons too. Moreover, Elijah is not so directly involved in 2 Kg. 9, nor is Jezebel connected specifically with the murder. Admittedly the fragmentary character of the account in 2 Kg. 9 in contrast to the full account of 1 Kg. 21 can be construed as an indication that the latter is more dependable (Andersen, *JBL* 85 [1966], pp. 46–57), but there is more weight in the argument that the absence of legendary elements from the more objective account of 2 Kg. 9 claims for it priority for historical accuracy (cf. Miller, *op. cit.*, p. 309). The implications of accepting the reliability of the account in 2 Kg. 9 are significant for our analysis of 1 Kg. 21, for it is implied that Naboth was not murdered in the reign of Ahab, and that the involvement of Elijah, and possibly of Jezebel too, can be dismissed from the narrative. Consequently, some explanation must be found for the origin and development of the Naboth narrative in 1 Kg. 21.

The analyses of 1 Kg. 21, which attempt to decide the extent of the original narrative and to trace the stages at which accretions were made to it, are too numerous to be listed. For a full survey, see Bohlen, *Der Fall Nabot*, pp. 13ff.; cf. also Timm, *Die Dynastie*, pp. 111–18; Würthwein, *ZThK* 75 [1978], pp. 375ff. A few instances can be noted. Miller (*op. cit.*, pp. 312ff.) regards vv. 1–19a as original, and vv. 19b–29 as coming in different stages from the hands of redactors. Fohrer (*op. cit.*, p. 43) defines the original tradition as vv. 1–9; 11–20a, Hentschel (*op. cit.*, pp. 14ff.) as vv. 1–20b, 23, 27ff., 29, with vv. 20b–22, 24–26 as deuteronomistic additions, and Bohlen (*op. cit.*, pp. 90ff.) as vv. 1b–9, 11–16, with a series of fragments in vv. 17a–29. But Steck (*Überlieferung*, p. 43) reduces the kernel to the scene between Ahab and Elijah in vv. 17–18a, 19–20aba (see further, the comments of Würthwein, *op. cit.*, pp. 375–82). A consensus or a compromise cannot be extracted from such a variety of opinions.

The view taken here is that Naboth was murdered in the reign of Ahab and that the translation of 2 Kg. 9:25–26 does not demand the placing of the event in the reign of Joram (as argued by Miller, *op. cit.*, p. 308). The original tradition was very brief and only alluded to the clash between Elijah and Ahab because the latter had murdered Naboth and taken his property; it is found basically in vv. 18–19*a*, 20 (with the exception perhaps of v. 18*b*). But the tradition has been given the form of a prophetic declaration introduced by the 'word of the LORD', which indicates that even the earlier form of the tradition exists only in a much later mould. The basic tradition was extensively re-worked in prophetic and deuteronomistic circles, and the form that ultimately emerged is due to successive steps of development and interpretation that occurred during the transmission of the narrative.

An early modification of the tradition had extended the clash between Ahab and Elijah to include the prominent part ascribed to Jezebel in the present narrative. As noted above, Jezebel is not mentioned in 2 Kg. 9:24–26, and is only indirectly mentioned in the background in v. 22. According to the narrative in 1 Kg. 21, however, Jezebel is held responsible for the plan to take possession of Naboth's vineyard and for the plot to kill him. This aspect of the tradition must be a reflection of the enmity that arose towards Jezebel in prophetical circles, especially during the period when she was in power as queen-mother; this enmity persisted within these circles as a justification for the purge of Jehu. It was within these circles that the tradition contained in vv. 1–16 was composed with much skill and artistry. At a later stage (580–500 BC, according to Bohlen, *op. cit.*, pp. 318–19) the redactor responsible for the fulfilment of prophecy theme in Kings added the prophecy about Jezebel in v. 23 (Timm, *op. cit.*, pp. 126–36).

Before the Jezebel element had been brought to conclusion, the deuteronomistic redactors had made an addition in vv. 21–22, 24, which, as Miller (*op. cit.*, p. 317) rightly points out, brings the deuteronomistic account of the fall of the Omride dynasty into line with the two preceding dynasties, those of Jeroboam and Baasha. Verse 24 contains the same stereotyped prediction as 1 Kg. 14:11; 16:4. Although there are differences between the threat against the Omride dynasty and its fulfilment in the time of Jehu, there are sufficient similarities for Miller (*op. cit.*, pp. 322ff.) to conclude that the condemnation of the house of Omri, like that of the previous two dynasties in the north, was based on the charismatic-dynastic controversy.

Two other additions were made by the deuteronomistic circles. Verses 25–26 emphasize the unsurpassed evil of Ahab and can be

compared with the deuteronomistic comment in I Kg. 16:33. This
comment was added at this point in order to implicate Ahab and
Jezebel in the evil of that period. Bohlen (*op. cit.*, pp. 318–19)
attributes these verses to DtrN. Verses 27–29 were also added by
the deuteronomistic redactor (with Miller, *op. cit.*, p. 313, against
Bohlen, *ibid.*, who attributes them to a post-deuteronomistic hand).
In the case of the dynasties of Jeroboam and Baasha disaster fell on
the second king of the dynasty (on Nadab and Elah); in other words,
it happened as soon as the dynastic principle had become evident.
But Ahab, the second king of the Omride dynasty, escaped disaster,
according to the deuteronomistic record (cf. I Kg. 22:39, 40), and
it is suggested that vv. 27–29 were compiled by the deuteronomistic
redactor to explain why the fulfilment of that threat was postponed
until the time of Joram.

   The deuteronomistic redactor possibly did not know of the tradition in I Kg. 22, based on an incorrect identification, that Ahab
died a violent death. When this identification was made, and the
Syrian war narratives were connected with Ahab and joined to the
Elijah complex, a further link was added by inserting a prophecy
in v. 19*b*, which was fulfilled in I Kg. 22:38. Licking Naboth's
blood introduces a point that is not found in 2 Kg., and is possibly
a development of a deuteronomistic prediction in 9:34. Verse 19*b*
is attributed to DtrP (Dietrich, *Prophetie*, pp. 27ff.). Possibly v.
18*b*, if it is taken to be an attempt to locate the vineyard in Samaria,
must also be regarded as a late gloss (cf. Miller, *op. cit.*, p. 313).

   1. Now: The Heb. has 'and after these things', which is rendered
in *NIV* as 'Some time later'. The Gk. omits the phrase and reads
chapter 21 after chapter 19; probably, therefore, the words were
added to the Heb. (cf. I Kg. 17:17) when the chapter was placed
between chapters 20 and 22. **Naboth**: The name is to be connected
with the Arab. *nabata*, 'to sprout, to grow' (Noth, *Personennamen*,
p. 221), and may denote 'offspring'. **had a vineyard in Jezreel**: The
Gk. reads 'a certain vineyard' (followed by Gray, p. 436), but omits
in Jezreel, probably regarding it as tautologous after the description
of Naboth as **the Jezreelite**. But **in Jezreel** must be retained,
because it is intended to denote the location of the vineyard,
although there is considerable uncertainty about its site (see survey
in Timm, *op. cit.*, pp. 118–21). The prediction in v. 19*b*, taken with
its fulfilment in I Kg. 22:38, and possibly also with v. 18*b*, clearly
thinks of Samaria as the location, which may be interpreted as
confirmation that the reference to Jezreel here is secondary (cf.
Bohlen, *op. cit.*, pp. 51ff.; Seebass, *VT* 24 [1974], p. 478). However,
in the analysis proposed above, v. 19*b* and its fulfilment in I Kg.
22:38 are taken to be later intrusions into the narrative; thus the

location in v. 1 can be retained as original. **Jezreel**, which is usually identified with *Zer'in*, gave its name to the plain of Esdraelon and controlled the access to that plain from the east. It was an important base in the days of the Omride dynasty, possibly because it was the home of the Omrides, but definitely because it was used as a base against Damascus (Napier, *VT* 9 [1959], pp. 366–78). **beside the palace of Ahab**: This is the first occurrence in Kings of the Heb. *hēkāl* to denote a palace; the word is of Sumerian origin, from *ê-gallu*, 'the great house', and is used to refer to the Temple (see 1 Kg. 6:3). **king of Samaria**: This short title stands in contrast to the more specific 'king of Israel, who is in Samaria' (or *NIV*, 'who rules in Samaria') in v. 18. The title occurs without a proper name in 2 Kg. 1:3. The northern province was known as Samaria in Assyrian records (see Bohlen, *op. cit.*, p. 310), and this title belongs to the period of Assyrian expansion to the west. Gray (p. 438) finds in the title a reflection of the situation in which the crown possession of Samaria was the basis of power for the house of Omri.

2. No sinister motive can be detected in Ahab's proposal to Naboth; he was making a fair bid for property that he wanted because it was adjacent to the palace by offering either an exchange for **a better vineyard** or to give Naboth **its value in money**. It was a business proposition similar to his father's transaction when he bought Samaria (see 1 Kg. 16:24). Ugaritic literature provides evidence of both customs, the exchange of property and the offering of a purchase price (Andersen, *op. cit.*, p. 49).

3. The LORD forbid that I should give you the inheritance of my fathers: Naboth's refusal is based on a religious conviction that God as proprietor of the land of Israel had given it as an **inheritance** to his people. God also protected the rights of tenants, who held land in trust from him. The importance of possessing an inheritance in the land is seen in Num. 27:1–11; 36:1–12 (see further on these passages, Bohlen, *op. cit.*, pp. 320ff.; cf. Horst, *Fest. Rudolph*, pp. 134ff.). It is not clear, however, whether Lev. 25:23 is to be taken as an absolute prohibition of all land selling, for it is known that this was practised in Israel as elsewhere (Bohlen, *op. cit.*, pp. 335ff.). Comparison with the custom of land possession at Ugarit and Mari shows that Israel had made more pronounced the religious motive in what appears to have been common practice. Land possession was granted to certain classes or individuals (cf. Ugaritic literature; Gray, p. 439), probably to freemen or fully enfranchised citizens (Bohlen, *op. cit.*, p. 330). The transfer of such land was under strict control. The Mari documents show that fictitious adoptions were the only way to avoid these prohibitions, and Ugaritic deeds often stipulate that property was to remain perpetually in family possession. This seems to have been a West-Semitic pattern, and is different from the freedom enjoyed in this respect in Mesopotamia (cf. Andersen, *ibid.*). Naboth, by involving the name of God, faithfully represents the non-secular motivation attached to the practice in Israel (Timm, *op. cit.*, pp. 121-6).

4. Ahab went into his house vexed and sullen: These words imply that Ahab accepted Naboth's decision; if the one having possession was unwilling to sell or exchange his vineyard, he could not be forced to vacate it. Although Ahab is condemned for his religious policy, it appears from the names of his sons that he was still a Yahweh worshipper; probably too his respect for Naboth's decision is based on the latter's adjuration in the name of Yahweh. But Andersen (*op. cit.*, p. 50) reads too much into the text when he interprets the omission of reference to the oath in Ahab's version of Naboth's words in vv. 4 and 7 as an attempt by the king to conceal from Jezebel that he was a secret believer in Israel's God.

5. With repetition of material from previous verses, it is now shown how, once the position is made clear to her, **Jezebel his wife** takes the initiative; the decision to confiscate the vineyard for Ahab (v. 7) and the plan to stage a trial against Naboth (vv. 8-10) are attributed to the queen. Because the part played by Jezebel is such an integral element in the narrative, these verses are not to be separated from the remainder; they belong to the artistic composition in vv. 1-16 that forms an expansion of the Naboth tradition (see above, p. 351).

7. Do you now govern Israel?: Although Jezebel's reply may be construed as a word of positive encouragement or as a sarcastic statement, it is best rendered as an interrogative; cf. also *NEB*, 'Are you or are you not king in Israel?'; *NIV*, 'Is this how you act as king over Israel?'. Behind Jezebel's question, it is assumed, lies a different conception of kingship and its rights and prerogatives. The despotic attitude in the suggestion that the king is to exercise his authority and to take Naboth's vineyard belongs to Jezebel's foreign environment (Gressmann, *Geschichtsschreibung*, pp. 271ff.). The baalistic nature-cult displays a different attitude towards the land in regarding it simply as an object for barter in the struggle for trade and power (cf. Bohlen, *op. cit.*, p. 17; Kraus, *Kirche im Volk* 2 [1949], p. 157). Canaanite agrarian law accepted that the king had control over the land of which he was the proprietor, and Jezebel, as a Phoenician princess, took it for granted that kingship implied absolute power (Baltzer, *Wort und Dienst* 8 [1965], pp. 82-4; Macholz, *ZAW* 84 [1972], pp. 175ff.). **I will give you the vineyard**: Andersen (*op. cit.*, p. 50) finds a parallel in Ugarit for the queen's assumption of power. She had wealth, including ownership of land,

and foreign protégés, who enjoyed her protection and paid her dues. Jezebel's statement that she would give Ahab the vineyard implies that she had power to effect the transaction and to give it official ratification.

8. she wrote letters in Ahab's name: The Heb. plural may simply designate the singular, implying that Jezebel only wrote one letter (cf. Isa. 37:14; see Šanda I, p. 462; *NEB*, 'wrote a letter'); she did not write **to the elders and the nobles** individually but sent a letter to them as a body. Andersen (*ibid.*) retains the plural, maintaining that she also sent legal documents (cf. Dt. 24:3, where *sēp̱er*, 'letter', means a commercial document) that would be needed in the case against Naboth. **And sealed them with his seal**: A scribe writing in the name of a correspondent sealed the communication with the sender's seal. As noted by Gray (p. 440), many of these seals in clay or wax, and signifying royal authority, have been discovered in archaeological excavations. Andersen (*ibid.*) finds that the seal in this case did not belong to Ahab personally, but was the state seal or dynastic seal used on juridicial documents for which the king acted officially as witness or agent. Such an explanation supports the contention that Jezebel sent to the elders official documents which incriminated Naboth and secured for Jezebel the desired sentence. **the elders and the nobles**: The **elders** of Jezreel are mentioned again in 2 Kg. 10:1. The **nobles** (*NEB*, 'notables'), or freeborn, are mentioned here for the first time in the *OT*; but they appear again in Jer. 27:20; 39:6. They were probably a rank of gentry that developed around the kingship. Entrusting justice to such a group is not entirely in keeping with Dt. 16:18, unless it is argued that the judges and officers of justice in Jezreel are included in the two terms used here. According to v. 13 the people were also present, which may suggest that it was communal justice. If the Omrides originated from Jezreel, it goes without saying that Ahab had considerable influence on local officials and gentry. **who dwelt with Naboth in his city**: According to *RSV*, these men were like Naboth residents of Jezreel. The Heb. verb *yāšab̠*, which also means 'to sit', can be used to refer to the presiding of judges or government officials (cf. Isa. 28:6; Am. 6:3; Ps. 9:7); if this is the meaning, Naboth was one of the men reponsible for law and order in Jezreel, as is brought out by *NEB* 'who sat in council with him' (also v. 11; cf. Burney, pp. 244ff.).

9. Proclaim a fast: The king had power to proclaim a fast (cf. 2 Chr. 20:3; Jon. 3:5, 7–9; see also Welten, *EvTh* 33 [1973], p. 23; Timm, *op. cit.*, p. 122), but it is a matter of conjecture what pretext was used in this case. Because the Naboth incident occurs within the Elijah complex, it has been suggested that the fast was initiated

in response to the great drought of I Kg. 17:1. But it is also possible
that 'proclaiming a fast' is used in the present context as a technical
term for suspending all business in order to call the court into
session (Andersen, *op. cit.*, p. 56); it has to be admitted, however,
that such usage of the term is without parallel. **set Naboth on high
among the people**: Naboth was not placed in the position of a
defendant at court, who usually stood (cf. I Kg. 3:16), whilst the
court officials sat. Andersen (*ibid.*) finds an analogy in the procedure
and posture in Ru. 4:1, which describes a transaction of business
during which both parties were seated. Naboth was given a front
seat because the assembly's business concerned him. There is,
however, more to Naboth's seating on this occasion; placing him 'at
the head of the people' may denote a civic position of prominence,
especially in the juridicial sphere (cf. Bartlett, *VT* 19 [1969], pp.
1–10). By placing Naboth in a position of honour, possibly as
president of the council or as judge of the juridical assembly (cf.
Job 29:25), his alleged crime appears more serious. *NEB*, 'give
Naboth the seat of honour among the people'; *NIV*, 'seat Naboth
in a prominent place among the people'.

10. Some (e.g. Fohrer, *op. cit.*, p. 43) omit v. 10, because it is
unlikely that instructions regarding the scoundrels would be sent in
a written communication from Jezebel. The verse can, however, be
retained; possibly the official correspondence only contained a legal
document, the other instructions being carried by word of mouth.
set two base fellows opposite him: *NEB*, 'two scoundrels'. This
is correct legal procedure, since two witnesses were necessary to
secure a conviction (see Dt. 17:6; 19:15). The Heb. 'sons of Belial'
is translated as **base fellows**, because 'Belial' probably means
'worthlessness' (*BDB*; cf. *K-B*), despite many other suggested deriv-
ations, such as connecting it with Belili, the goddess of the underworld, or with a root meaning 'engulfing ruin' (Burney, pp. 245ff.;
Thomas, *Casey Memorial*, pp. 11–19). **You have cursed God and
the king**: *RSV*'s translation accepts that the verb 'blessed' in the
Heb. is an euphemism for 'cursed'; cursing God and king was
so objectionable that it was not directly mentioned (for a similar
substitution see Job 1:11; 2:5, 9; Ps. 10:3). Blasphemy was punishable by death (Lev. 24:10–16), and cursing the ruler was also
regarded as an act of blasphemy, for he was God's chosen representative (cf. Exod. 22:28). If this interpretation is accepted, Naboth was
to be accused of blasphemy, and those present at his trial represented the 'cultic' community (so Bohlen, *op. cit.*, p. 378). There
is, however, much in favour of the attempt to link Naboth's alleged
crime more directly with the question of the ownership of the
vineyard. Andersen (*op. cit.*, pp. 51ff.) contends that Jezebel's

forged case was that Ahab was the real owner of the vineyard, since
Naboth had promised to sell it, but had later withdrawn from his
agreement. Jezebel produced a sealed statement from Ahab (cf. v.
8) confirming that Naboth had promised to sell, or else a prepared
deed of sale, and two witnesses who were ready to testify to the
promise. Naboth's words of refusal to Ahab were thus completely
distorted, and were said to be an assent to sell. His words were
reported either as an invocation of God's blessing on the new owner,
'blessing God and king', or else as a promissory oath, 'May I be
cursed by God if I do not sell my vineyard'. Withdrawing from
such an agreement rendered the blessing or the promissory oath
invalid, perhaps as an act of cursing God and therefore punishable.
Andersen claims that his interpretation provides a valid reason for
Ahab's seizure of the vineyard; he also finds that parallels from
Alalakh show that a breach of promise was punished by a fine or
by forfeiture of the property to the prospective buyer, together with
the mutilation or death of the offender. **take him out and stone
him to death**: Not only was blasphemy punishable by death but
also a breach of agreement, according to the Alalakh parallel.
Stoning always happened outside the city to avoid ritual uncleanness
(Lev. 24:14; Num. 15:36). Although the death of Naboth's sons is
not mentioned in this narrative, it has been contended, on the basis
of 2 Kg. 9:26 and by reference to the case of Achan in Jos. 7:22ff.,
that Naboth's family was completely wiped out (Gray, p. 441).

11-13. These verses, repeating the content of the preceding
section and stating that all happened according to Jezebel's plan,
are abbreviated in the Gk., which is followed by many commentators
(Montgomery, p. 334). Abbreviation is unnecessary, since it is
customary in narrative sections to repeat; a proposed plan and a
notice of its effective fulfilment are obvious cases for such treatment.
For a word by word comparison, see table in Bohlen, *op. cit.*, pp.
65f.

14. Then they sent to Jezebel: The last subject given to a verb
lies as far back as the 'two base fellows' of v. 13a; but it is not to
be assumed that they were responsible for the actions mentioned in
vv. 13b-14a. The council or court was responsible for the stoning
in v. 13b, and probably official messengers were sent to Jezebel by
the elders and nobles (v. 14a). The task of the scoundrels had been
completed when they acted as witnesses.

15-16. The impression given in these verses is that the events
recorded happened in immediate succession without any delay.
Jezebel takes the initiative in v. 15, and it is assumed that news of
Naboth's death reached her the same day. Ahab too acted promptly

(v. 16), and probably took possession of the vineyard the following day (cf. Šanda I p. 464).

17. Then the word of the LORD came: As noted in the analysis above (p. 351), the basic Naboth tradition of vv. 18–19*a*, 20 has been worked over in prophetic circles; in this verse it has been set within the framework of 'the word of God' theme, which is also found in 1 Kg. 17:2, 8; 18:1.

18. who is in Samaria: The implication here is that Elijah is to **go down to meet Ahab** in Samaria (cf. *NEB*), unless locating Ahab in Samaria is deliberately avoided, either by rendering it as 'who rules in Samaria' (*NIV*) or by deleting it as a gloss (with Benzinger, p. 115; see further, Bohlen, *op. cit.*, pp. 76ff.). On the other hand, it is possible that Elijah encountered Ahab **in Samaria**, but that v. 18*b* locating Naboth's vineyard in Samaria is a gloss, which deliberately contradicts v. 1 and seeks to show that the prediction of v. 19*b* was literally fulfilled when the dogs licked Ahab's blood by the pool of Samaria (22:38).

19. The impression given by this verse is that it has been constructed according to the standard for presenting a prophetic announcement of judgment, moving from the accusation in v. 19*a* to the actual announcement in v. 19*b*. Consequently, many commentators accept the whole verse and defend the originality of v. 19*b* (Montgomery, p. 332; Gray, p. 442; cf. Seebass, *op. cit.*, p. 482). The view taken here is that v. 19*b* has been added to the text after the mistaken identification of Ahab as the king who was murdered in Samaria; thus v. 19*b* and 22:38 link the Syrian wars with the Elijah-Ahab tradition (see below, on 22:38; cf. Miller, *VT* 17 [1967], pp. 312ff.; Schmitt, *Elisa*, p. 122). In the deuteronomistic version of the Naboth tradition, before the addition of v. 19*b*, the encounter with Ahab is continued in v. 20. **Have you killed, and also taken possession?**: As Gray (p. 442) rightly points out, Ahab is accused of breaking two of the laws contained in the Decalogue and regarded as basic in Israelite society, namely, murder and coveting (or forcibly appropriating) property. Despite the leading role of Jezebel in vv. 1–16, Ahab is here held responsible for what happened. The original tradition was concerned with Ahab and the future of his dynasty; Jezebel's part became more prominent with the writing of the narrative in vv. 1–16. **In the place**: Whereas the narrative locates Naboth's vineyard in Jezreel (v. 1), **the place** in this verse (cf. v. 18*b* and 22:38) obviously refers to Samaria. The tradition preserved in 2 Kg. 9 locates the death of Joram at Jezreel in the plot of ground that belonged to Naboth. The death of a king in Samaria (1 Kg. 22), and the identification of that king with Ahab, has clearly influenced some verses in this chapter. **your own blood**: The emphasis of the Heb. on the fact that it was Ahab's own blood is conveyed in *NIV* by 'your blood—yes, yours'.

20. Ahab's question, **Have you found me, O my enemy?**, and Elijah's curt reply, **I have found you**, in v. 20*a* are separated by some commentators from v. 20*b*, which belongs, with vv. 21–29, to the later redactional accretions to this chapter (Montgomery, p. 332; Seebass, *op. cit.*, pp. 482ff.). Omitting v. 19*b* as a later addition, it is proposed here to take vv. 18, 19*a* and 20 together as constituting the basic account of Elijah's encounter with Ahab. Verse 20*b* was later expanded when vv. 21ff., 24 were added. **you have sold yourself to do what is evil**: The Gk. versions have some additions here: the first addition gives 'sold yourself to no purpose', and the second, following 2 Kg. 17:17, reads at the end 'provoking him to anger'. Burney (p. 249) dismisses the first as an addition but welcomes the second.

21–22. These verses do not continue Elijah's words in v. 20, but contain words which would more naturally be attributed to God. Their intention is to bring the destruction of the Ahab dynasty into line with the fate of **the house of Jeroboam and the house of Baasha**. Verse 21 in parts picks up a formula from 1 Kg. 14:10; 16:23, and v. 24 repeats 1 Kg. 14:11; 16:4. A deuteronomistic redactor was responsible for the addition of these verses, and they are not post-deuteronomistic glosses as suggested by Seebass (*op. cit.*, p. 483).

23. Steck (*op. cit.*, pp. 41ff.) rightly connects this verse with vv. 1–16, with which it shares an interest in the part played by Jezebel; vv. 17–10 ignore Jezebel and make Ahab solely responsible for the death of Naboth. The prominence of Jezebel in the affair has necessitated the inclusion of a judgment on her as well as on Ahab. Although the words of judgment in this verse are not directly attributed to Elijah, they are to be taken as a continuation of his pronouncement. Undoubtedly the prediction here reflects the fate of Jezebel as described in 2 Kg. 9:36ff. **within the bounds of Jezreel**: MT has 'by the wall (or rampart) of Jezreel', the Heb. *ḥēl* being similar in meaning to an Arab. cognate denoting 'what is round about'. Although MT has the support of LXX and Luc., some Heb. MSS, the Syr., Targ. and Vulg. all take *ḥēl* as *ḥēleq*, 'portion, territory', which is used in 2 Kg. 9:36. Of course these Vsns. may have changed the text here in order to achieve harmony between the two sections. Driver (*JBL* 55 [1936], p. 109) accepted MT and connected *ḥēl* with the Arab. *ḥiyāl*, 'by', which is preferred to Gray's 'round about Jezreel' (p. 443), which is based on another Arab. root and pictures the dogs carrying off pieces of flesh around the town to eat them.

24. As noted above (p. 351), this verse is to be read as a continuation of the words against Ahab in vv. 21–22. Admittedly they do not harmonize completely; whereas Ahab is addressed in the second person in vv. 21–22, this verse contains a statement about him in the third person. Nevertheless, comparison with the parallel in 1 Kg. 14:10ff. shows that v. 24 belongs to v. 21, and comparison with the parallel in 1 Kg. 16:3ff. shows that v. 24 belongs also to v. 22.

25–26. These verses, which bring together the names of Ahab and Jezebel for condemnation, are probably intended as a summary conclusion to the section (cf. Seebass, *ibid.*). Because they are deuteronomistic in tone and recall other phrases composed by the deuteronomistic redactor (cf. 1 Kg. 16:33), it is correct to describe them as the editor's summary remarks on the religious policy of Ahab (Weinfeld, *Deuteronomy*, p. 18); they refer to more than the particular incident reported in this chapter.

27–29. These verses form a deuteronomistic appendix to explain why, despite the severe words of judgment spoken against him, Ahab continued to reign until he died peacefully (see below, on 22.40) and his two sons reigned after him for some fourteen years. The reason given is that **when Ahab heard those words** (the words of condemnation in vv. 21–22, 24), he humbled himself and secured a postponement of judgment. Both the ideology and vocabulary of these verses are truly deuteronomistic; the phrases **humbled himself before me** and **I will not bring evil** stand out as typical of deuteronomistic style. There is no reason for regarding these verses as post-deuteronomistic additions (Bohlen, *op. cit.*, pp. 318–19), nor for ascribing them specifically to the Chronicler (Jepsen, *Die Quellen*, pp. 27–8); they are well and truly deuteronomistic (Weinfeld, *op. cit.*, p. 24).

(vi) Continuation of the Syrian Wars **22:1–38**
As already noted (see above, pp. 336ff.), 1 Kg. 22:1–38 are a continuation of the account begun in chapter 20 of the wars between Israel and Syria, and make the total number of campaigns into three. LXX does not separate the three campaigns from each other, but reads chapter 22 immediately after chapter 20, an arrangement that receives confirmation from the opening sentence of chapter 22 which picks up the Syrian narrative. As noted by Miller (*JBL* 85 [1966], p. 444), the three campaigns of chapters 20 and 22 fittingly fulfill Elisha's prophecy of three victories over Syria (2 Kg. 13:14–19).

Recent studies (for a survey, see de Vries, *Prophet against Prophet*, pp. 4–10) have highlighted the complexity of the problems with which this chapter is fraught: the historicity of the campaign against Ramoth-gilead and the question of its date; defining the nature of

the chapter, with some tension between the description of it as a
prophetic legend and the view that it is a political battle account;
the inconsistencies within the narrative, leading to suggestions that
it originated in the north, but was touched-up in the south or else
that two prophetical narratives have been combined.

With regard to the historical background, it is accepted here that
basically the chapter is a continuation of chapter 20, and gives an
account of the third campaign of Jehoahaz against the Syrians. The
reconstruction of the period which has been proposed by Miller
(*JBL* 85 [1966], pp. 441–54; *ZAW* 80 [1968], pp. 337–42),
combined with his reasons for not accepting an earlier identification
of the king with Joash, deals convincingly with the biblical data
and sets the Syrian wars in a suitable historical context. The third
campaign is set in the year of Jehoahaz's death (799 BC; see Table,
p. 28, as against Miller's proposed 801 BC). The case has not been
undermined by the more recent claim that the only possible cand-
idate for the role of 'king of Israel' in this chapter is Jehoram ben
Ahab, his Judaean ally being Ahaziah (as argued by de Vries, *op.
cit.*, pp. 93ff., whose main argument concerning the phrase 'slept
with his fathers' is adequately met in Miller's reconstruction).

Undoubtedly reminiscences of two different battles at Ramoth-
gilead have been combined in this chapter (cf. Whitley, *VT* 2 [1952],
p. 149; Miller, *ZAW* 80 [1968], pp. 340ff.; *JBL* 85 [1966],
pp. 444ff.). One battle, which is introduced in v. 3 as an attempt
to restore Ramoth-gilead, must be connected with Jehoahaz, whose
father Jehu had lost all Gilead to Syria (2 Kg. 10:32–33); details
about this battle have now been lost due to the combination of
reminiscences in chapter 22. Presumably Jehoahaz was again
successful in his third campaign; in view of the suggestion of his
peaceful death in 2 Kg. 13:9, it is unnecessary to assume that he
died in battle (Miller, *ZAW* 80 [1968], p. 341, finding Jehoahaz's
death in 22:29–36). Engaged in the second battle, which now dominates the account in chapter 22, were Jehoram of Israel and Ahaziah
of Judah, who were on guard at Ramoth (and not restoring it) and
were assassinated by Jehu (2 Kg. 8:28–9:28). Jehoram's death, and
the licking of his blood (v. 38), has now overshadowed the whole
report (see further, Miller, *VT* 17 [1967], pp. 307–24).

Additional material about Jehoshaphat has been introduced into
the narrative, with the glorification of the Judaean king suggesting
a Judaean source (cf. Jepsen, *Nabi*, p. 89). Instead of accepting that
the whole of chapter 22 originated from Judah, it is more reasonable
to follow Miller's suggestion (*JBL* 85 [1966], pp. 447ff.) that this
chapter, and the account of the Moabite campaign in 2 Kg. 3:4–27,
were modified in Judaean circles, which had identified the king of

Judah with Jehoshaphat. From these circles too came the emphasis on Jehoshaphat's piety, which is expressed in similar form and language in the two sections (cf. 1 Kg. 22:4, 5, 7; 2 Kg. 3:7, 11).

Unquestionably, the prophetic tradition in the present narrative is not homogeneous. Würthwein (*Fest. Rost*, pp. 245–54) finds that the original prophetic story about the testing of Micaiah's words (vv. 5–9, 13–17, 18, 26–28) was later annotated by a group sponsoring Zedekiah as the true prophet because he was led by the spirit (vv. 10–12, 24–25), only to be further annotated by an opposing group suggesting that it was a lying spirit (vv. 19–22). De Vries (*op. cit.*, pp. 25ff.) presents a different analysis, finding a narrative A in vv. 2b–4a, 4bb–9, 15–18, 26–37 and a narrative B in vv. 10–12a, 14, 19, 20aa, 20b–25. Accepting that the prophetic tradition can no longer be separated from the battle narrative, the view taken here is that the reason for the complexity in the prophetic tradition is to be sought in the original connection between its two strands and the mixed reminiscences of two battles at Ramoth-gilead. Jehoahaz's campaign, like his former one in chapter 20, was undertaken with approval from the prophets and was accompanied by a promise of success (cf. 22:6, 10–12 with 20:13–14, 22, 28). On the other hand, the death of Jehoram on the plot of ground belonging to Naboth (2 Kg. 13:21–26) had drawn to itself pronouncements of judgment (cf. 2 Kg. 13:26); possibly Micaiah's negative message (22:17) had become attached to the Jehoram tradition. When the prophetic circle came to join these traditions together and to combine them with the presentation of Jehoshaphat, they worked them together into a single narrative portraying the clash between true and false prophets. To bring these traditions together the prophetic circle composed some linking passages, most notably vv. 7–9, 13, 18, 24–28, and possibly inserted an existing piece of prophetic tradition, which is now found in vv. 19–23.

At present the prophetic material and the battle narrative cannot be separated from each other, for neither of them can stand independently to give a meaningful sequence (cf. Seebass, *VT* 21 [1971], pp. 380–3). Basically chapter 22, like chapter 20, was intended to give an account of another Israelite victory over the Syrians, but that victory has disappeared from the present version of the chapter because the account was fused with the report of another battle at Ramoth-gilead. Both reminiscences had a prophetic element in them, and the fusion of those two transformed the initial battle report into an account of a conflict between prophets.

1. For three years: This linking verse has taken the wars of chapter 20 as the basis of its reckoning. Israel's leniency towards Benhadad may have contributed to the softening of relations

between the two countries. This link makes it clear that the
campaign against Syria presented here is a continuation of the
struggle recorded in chapter 20; it is the third campaign in a series
of three.

2. The first half of this verse, picking up **the third year** from
the previous verse and referring to **Jehoshaphat**, is also secondary
(Würthwein, *op. cit.*, pp. 245ff.; de Vries, *op. cit.*, p. 25). The
identification of the king of Judah with Jehoshaphat occurred in
southern circles (Miller, *JBL* 85 [1966], p. 447), for Jehoshaphat,
whose son Jehoram had married the daughter of Ahab (2 Kg. 8:6ff.),
was revered and remembered in the south because of his alliance
with the king of Israel. The reconstruction favoured above gives a
later date for the battle at Ramoth-gilead. The historicity of the
material in vv. 2*b*–4 has again been questioned by Würthwein
(*ibid.*), who finds legendary motifs in the characterisation of the
king of Israel in these verses and also in vv. 29–37. Basically,
however, vv. 2*b*–4 have preserved a reliable historical tradition in
their emphasis on two elements, namely, that it was a military
exercise aimed at releasing Ramoth-gilead from Syrian hands and
also that it was initiated by Israel.

3. Ramoth-gilead is to be identified with *Tell Ramith*, which, it
has been claimed, was founded by Solomon (see on 1 Kg. 4:13).
Gray (p. 448) favours a more easterly location at *Husn 'Ajlūn*. The
real battle-ground between Syria and Israel was the territory east of
the Jordan, and one of the most frequently contested centres was
Ramoth-gilead, a border city between Aram and Israel (see Tadmor,
IEJ 12 [1962], pp. 114–19). Jehu lost all the land of Gilead to the
Syrians (2 Kg. 10:32–33), and the claim here **that Ramoth-gilead
belongs to us** indicates that this is an introduction to the battle
waged by Jehoahaz to re-capture what had been lost (Miller, *JBL*
85 [1966], p. 445). The reason for taking the initiative against Syria
at this time was that Adad-nirari's armies were on the march against
Damascus (Miller, *ZAW* 80 [1968], p. 341).

4. Will you go with me to battle at Ramoth-gilead?: Since Judah
had no interest in Ramoth-gilead, it has been suggested that it was
a vassal of Israel, and thus had no choice in the matter (cf.
Benzinger, p. 123); another possibility is that it was a free alliance
of which Judah was a weaker member (Gray, p. 449). **I am as you
are**: Jehoshaphat's reply is given in a slightly different form in 2
Chr. 18:3. An identical reply is again given by Jehoshaphat in 2
Kg. 3:7; it may be that the Heb. version of the present verse has
been influenced by 2 Kg. 3:7 (cf. de Vries, *op. cit.*, pp. 21ff.).

5. Inquire first for the word of the LORD: *NEB*, 'let us seek
counsel from the LORD'. Seeking divine counsel by means of an

oracle before going out to battle was common practice; cf. 1 Sam.
23:1ff. and also the consultation of seers and astrologers by Zakir
of Hamath (Montgomery, p. 337). Following the pattern of the
previous battles against Syria, it is probable that a prophetic declaration was included at this point in the narrative and that it was a
favourable one. Verse 5, with its attribution of the initiative to
Jehoshaphat, probably came from the Judaean circle, which
presented their king as more pious than his Israelite contemporary
(cf. 2 Kg. 3:7, 11; Miller, *JBL* 85 [1966], pp. 444ff.). Jehoshaphat
now seems to be retreating from his statement in v. 4.

6. The Israelite king's consultation with the prophets belonged
to the original tradition of the third campaign against Syria. The
number **four hundred** is an exaggeration, and has been influenced
by the figures four hundred and fifty and four hundred in 1 Kg.
18:19. **shall I forbear?**: or, better, 'shall I desist?' (*NEB*) or 'shall
I refrain?' (*NIV*). **the LORD will give it into the hand of the king**:
The favourable message that Syria will be conquered is identical
with that given in connection with the two earlier campaigns against
Syria (see 1 Kg. 20:13, 28). The account of the consultation with
the prophets is completed in vv. 10–12.

**7. Is there not here another prophet of the LORD of whom we
may inquire?**: The similar Jehoshaphat tradition in 2 Kg. 3 does
not contain a request for further consultation with another prophet.
The view taken here is that the second request, as indeed the whole
of vv. 7–9, has been inserted in order to present the prophet Micaiah
and the conflict between him and the other prophets. Gray (p. 449)
finds here a clash between two concepts of prophecy, an Israelite
concept, taking the prophets as agents of imitative magic, and a
concept represented by Jehoshaphat, who implies that the prophet
was an instrument of divine revelation. But it must be asked if the
conflict between true and false prophets claiming to be speaking in
the name of Yahweh had emerged in the days of the bitter clash
between Yahweh prophets and the prophets of Baal. It may be that
the conflict known in later times was imposed on the narrative in
the process of conflating two different traditions; the similarity to
the conflict in Jer. 27–29 cannot be missed.

8. Micaiah the son of Imlah: Although the name **Micaiah**
appears in Jg. 17:1, 4; Jer. 36:11, 13 and on a seal (Montgomery,
p. 344), the prophet **Micaiah the son of Imlah** is known only from
this chapter and its parallel in 2 Chr. 18. **but I hate him, for he
never prophesies good concerning me, but evil**: The conflict
between Micaiah and the prophets is defined in exactly the same
terms as used in later prophetic works; the false prophets are *Heil-
spropheten*, who speak favourable and pleasing words, but true

prophets, who are *Unheilspropheten*, speak words of judgment and woe that are not pleasing. Micaiah in the present form of the narrative appears as a woe prophet, who **never prophesies good**; the other prophets with their favourable speech are by implication false. De Vries (*op. cit.*, p. 38) finds the clash to be basically one between the interests of Israel and the personal interests of its political leaders.

9. an officer: The title *sārîs* is found elsewhere of the highest official in the kingdom (cf. Gen. 37:36; 2 Kg. 18:17; 20:18). Here it probably refers to an officer of a lower rank, who is designated as a 'messenger' in v. 13.

10. Now the king of Israel and Jehoshaphat the king of Judah were sitting on their thrones: Verses 10–12 continue the account of the favourable message given by the prophets, and the only addition here is the unnecessary name **Jehoshaphat. at the threshing floor at the entrance of the gate of Samaria**: The specific placing of the threshing floor at the city gate has caused some dispute with regard to this passage. Although the word *gōren*, **threshing floor**, is associated with threshing or winnowing in most of its occurrences (de Vries, *op. cit.*, pp. 22ff.), there are instances where it may denote an empty space with a rock or earth floor (cf. Jg. 6:37–40), which was not used specifically for an agricultural purpose (cf. 2 Sam. 6:6; Gen. 50:10). This, and a parallel usage in Ugaritic, supports the contention that the meaning of *gōren* here is an open public place at the gate of the city rather than a threshing floor (Gray, p. 450; *PEQ* 85 [1953], pp. 118–23). **were prophesying before them**: No details of their prophetic activity are given, but some commentators assume that some form of ecstatic rites were performed in the presence of the kings in the open space (so Šanda, I, p. 493). But it is not necessary to presuppose the performance of such rites; the verb may simply denote the function of prophesying (cf. vv. 8, 18; Jer. 26:20; Ezek. 37:10).

11. Zedekiah the son of Chenaanah: Nothing else is known of this Zedekiah, who is explicitly identified by giving the name of his father (cf. also of Micaiah in v. 8). It is assumed that he belonged to the group of prophets standing before the kings, but that he emerged from their midst in order to confirm the group's message by means of a symbolic act. **made for himself horns of iron**: The symbols of strength and invincibility used by Zedekiah, and the message pronounced, **With these you shall push the Syrians until they are destroyed**, are reminiscent of the oracle about Joseph in Dt. 33:17. Although the prophets declare their message in the presence of two kings, there is no inconsistency (against de Vries, *op. cit.*, pp. 27ff.) in the use of the singular, **you shall push**, for the question asked at the consultation was formulated in the singular (presumably by the Israelite king), and also answered with the singular 'Go up' (v. 6).

12. The group again confirms Zedekiah's action by stating that the king of Israel and his ally are to **go up to Ramoth-gilead and triumph**, and they confirm the promise of v. 6.

13. The conflation of the Micaiah tradition with the Zedekiah tradition and the presentation of the whole as a conflict between true and false prophecy, which began in vv. 7–9, is continued in vv. 13ff. The original Micaiah tradition, in so far as it can be reconstructed, recounted how Micaiah, when consulted about the outcome of a battle, possibly by Jehoram before he fought at Ramoth-gilead, declared an unexpected and unpopular message (vv. 14, 17). Micaiah's original oracle has by now been reset in a new context, and is connected on the one hand with the conflict with Zedekiah (by means of the linking vv. 13, 15–16, 18) and on the other hand with the tradition of a vision revealing how the prophets had been led by a deceiving spirit (vv. 19–23). **the messenger**: The fact that the 'officer' of v. 9 has by now become a **messenger** has been taken as an indication that two narratives have been combined (so de Vries, *op. cit.*, p. 28). But this is not necessarily the case; the officer may have been a junior one who was sent on an errand, or else the officer given the task sent a messenger to seek Micaiah. **speak favourably**: As the contrast between true and false prophecy is developed, it is emphasized that the true prophet declares the will of God and refuses to be enticed to give a more favourable message.

14. In this verse, which is taken as an introduction to the oracle in v. 17, the prophet states a general principle—he only speaks **what the LORD says to me** (significantly using the imperfect, according to Šanda I, p. 494). When he introduces his specific message for this particular occasion, he declares **I saw**, using the perfect tense.

15–16. Both question and answer in these verses repeat earlier material; cf. vv. 6, 12. Again, in order to bring out the contrast between true and false, Micaiah is presented as declaring initially the same message as the false prophets, which was recognized by the king as a hollow and non-genuine utterance (v. 16). The king demands that he be told **nothing but the truth in the name of the LORD**. Verses 15–16, because they interrupt the sequence of vv. 14 and 17, contain additional material composed to enhance the conflict theme.

17. It is in this verse that the true reply of Micaiah is contained, and it clearly declares that, when Israel goes up to battle, its leader will be lost (referring of course to the death of the Israelite king,

who is identified as Jehoram above, p. 361). The prophet's vision, as well as the divine oracle following it, is in poetic form, despite the irregularity of the metre. **as sheep that have no shepherd**: cf. Zech. 13:7, where the same figure for the king is used. **to his home in peace**: This refers presumably to the end of the war.

18. This verse refers back to v. 8, and belongs to the passages that link the Micaiah prophecy to the Zedekiah tradition.

19. The report of the vision in vv. 19–23 may have existed independently in prophetic circles, and conveys some of the thinking among the prophets on the question of false prophecy and its origin. Although it was originally independent of the Micaiah tradition, it has now been worked into this presentation of the clash between Micaiah and the prophets represented by Zedekiah. This vision has been integrated so closely with the present context that some correspondence is observed between it and the scene described in vv. 10–12, although it is easy to press the parallelism too far (as is done, for example, by de Vries, *op. cit.*, pp. 43ff.). The vision is similar in some ways to other parts of the *OT*, especially to the heavenly court scene in the prologue of Job (chapters 1–2), and again to the call-vision in Isa. 6 and Ezek. 1, with particularly close parallelism to the former (Zimmerli, *Ezechiel*, pp. 18–21; Habel, *ZAW* 77 [1965], pp. 297–323; de Vries, *op. cit.*, p. 44). **I saw the LORD sitting on his throne**: cf. Isa. 6. The dispute with false prophets is more prominent in the works of Judaean prophets, and it is possible that the conflict theme of this chapter was derived, like the presentation of Jehoshaphat, from Judaean circles. The vision of **the LORD sitting on his throne**, common to this chapter and Isa. 6, may be another indication of Judaean influence. The concept of the divine throne is also found in Canaanite mythology as preserved in the Ras Shamra texts (Gray, p. 451). **and all the host of heaven**: Although the term has various meanings in the *OT*, there can be no mistake about its usage here. It does not refer, as elsewhere, to astral deities that were introduced with the Baalim and Ashtoreth (2 Kg. 21:5; 23:4), nor to the stars serving as God's innumerable armies (Gen. 2:1; Ps. 33:6; Isa. 34:4; 45:12; Jer. 33:22), but rather to the heavenly beings or angels that act as God's servants (cf. Ps. 103:21). The close parallel to the heavenly court found in Ugaritic mythology is sufficient evidence that it is not a late concept (see further, Whybray, *Counsellor*, pp. 49ff.). The argument that the concept has been introduced here to provide a counterpart to the group of prophets in Samaria (de Vries, *op. cit.*, p. 44) is not convincing.

20. Who will entice Ahab?: or perhaps 'deceive', as in Ezek. 14:9; Jer. 20:7, which also refer to God deceiving a prophet. Evil had not at this stage been given a semi-independent existence in the form of the devil or Satan, as was to happen later. Therefore, God was conceived as the originator of everything, and no difficulty was felt in making him responsible for deceiving the prophet here nor for permitting Job to be tested by Satan (Job 1). **and fall at Ramoth-gilead**: There is some ambiguity in the Heb., which may be rendered as in *RSV*, or else as in *NEB*, 'fall on Ramoth-gilead', i.e. attack it.

21. Then a spirit came forward: The Heb. has a definite article, '*the* spirit', which may be taken as generic and translated 'a spirit', despite the argument that the article cannot be ignored and must refer to 'the spirit of revelation' (de Vries, *op. cit.*, p. 45). There are no textual or theological grounds for identifying 'the spirit' with a demon or with Satan, as has been conjectured. Gray (pp. 452ff.) correctly interprets it as a reference to the divinely inspired spirit of prophecy, which, because it was an extension of the divine personality, was personified. As becomes obvious in v. 22, it is this spirit that inspires the prophets to lie. There is a close parallelism here with Isa. 6:6, where one of the seraphim flies out towards the prophet.

22. will be a lying spirit in the mouth of all his prophets: The prophets will be inspired to prophesy, but it will be a false prophecy. Thus, the spirit will be a lying spirit (Klopfenstein, *Die Lüge*, p. 96). Divine influence thus lies behind false prophecy, for it is God's own plan in order to destroy the king. Similarly it was God who sent an evil spirit upon Saul to torment him (cf. 1 Sam. 16:14ff.). **You are to entice him**: God gives the spirit his consent to proceed with his plan, as he gives Satan permission to torment Job (Job 1:12; 2:6).

23. Micaiah's account of his vision is concluded in v. 22, and thus v. 23 appears to be the prophet's own comment on the scene. **Now therefore** are words which mark the transition from situation to consequence (so de Vries, *ibid.*), and lead on to an interpretation of the situation that falls into two parts—firstly, that the prophets speak through this **lying spirit**, and secondly that God intends evil against the king (translating with *NEB* and *NIV* 'has decreed disaster for you').

24. Zedekiah, the son of Chenaanah, when he **struck Micaiah on the cheek** was performing a second symbolic action to demonstrate his anger and frustration; cf. the acts of violence taken against Jeremiah (Jer. 37:15). **How did the Spirit of the LORD go from me to speak to you?**: Zedekiah's question is based on his belief that he had been speaking the truth when he prophesied to Ahab, but he does not understand how the same spirit could now say to Micaiah that Zedekiah has been speaking falsehood. The Heb. idiom, **how**

did (*'ē zeh*) followed by a verb, is not found elsewhere. 2 Chr. 18:23 has 'Which way did the Spirit of the LORD go from me to speak to you?' (supplying *hadderek*); cf. also 1 Kg. 13:12. This is accepted by Gray (p. 446) and *NIV*. Codex Vaticanus, which according to Burney (p. 255) preserves the original and superior text, omits the verb **go** and reads 'What kind of spirit of the LORD spoke to you?' But, the variants in the Gk. and in Chronicles are possibly attempts to cope with a difficult Heb. text and so testify to the originality of the Heb. (cf. de Vries, *op. cit.*, p. 16).

25. Behold, you shall see: The phrase is ambiguous in the Heb. *NEB*'s 'that you will see' makes it a direct reply to v. 24, suggesting that the question concerning genuine revelation will be settled. This is preferable to inserting 'it' after **you shall see** and explaining it as 'the evil consequence' (de Vries, *op. cit.*, p. 47). **on that day**: Despite the frequent use of this phrase as an eschatological technical term to refer to the Day of Yahweh, it does not have that meaning here, but is used simply as a temporal adverb (Munch, *Bajjôm Hāhū'*, p. 10). **when you go into an inner chamber**: The Heb. has 'chamber in chamber', which probably refers to **an inner chamber** as in *RSV*, rather than to running 'from one chamber to another' (as by Gray, pp. 446, 453); cf. also 1 Kg. 20:30.

26. Seize Micaiah: Like Jeremiah, the prophet was taken into custody, cf. Jer. 36:26; 38:5. The two responsible for him were **Amon the governor of the city** (cf. Jg. 9:30; 2 Kg. 10:1; 23:8) and **Joash the king's son**. The **governor of the city** is known elsewhere and was obviously a person holding royal authority over the city to which he was assigned (Avigad, *IEJ* 26 [1976], pp. 178–82; Rüterswörden, *Die Beamten*, pp. 66–8). Joash is an otherwise unknown son of Ahab, and it has been suggested that **the king's son** in this instance (as in Jer. 36:26; 38:6; 2 Chr. 28:7) is a title denoting an office; he was not a high-ranking official, but was specifically connected with prisoners and was similar to a police officer. A Palestinian seal and a stamp from a signet-ring confirm that it was an official title. Originally the officer may have been chosen from among the king's sons (de Vaux, *Ancient Israel*, pp. 119ff.).

27. scant fare of bread and water: *NEB*, 'prison diet of bread and water'. The Heb. has 'bread of affliction and water of affliction' (cf. Isa. 30:20), which is a term for prison food. **until I come in peace**: *NEB*, 'until I come home in safety' (cf. Gray, p. 454). Returning safely is the meaning here, rather than returning in peace (cf. Eisenbeis, *Die Wurzel šlm*, pp. 116–20).

28. The final words, **Hear, all you peoples!**, are not found in Chronicles, LXX nor Luc. and appear in the margin in *NEB*. The

same words appear in Mic. 1:2, and it is suggested that they have
been inserted here in an attempt to identify Micaiah with Micah
(Ball, *JTS* 28 [1977], pp. 90–4).

29–38. It is in the battle account of these verses that the battle
of Ramoth-gilead in the reign of Jehoram has become superimposed
over the battle in the reign of Jehoahaz (Miller, *ZAW* 80 [1968],
pp. 340f.; *VT* 17 [1967], pp. 314ff.) and coloured the whole presentation. The connection between this account and the report of Jehoram's death at the time of Jehu's rebellion (2 Kg. 8:28–29; 9:14–15)
is well established: in both cases the 'king of Israel' was wounded
in a battle with the Syrians; in both cases he died from a shot with
an arrow as he was riding in his chariot, and died in his chariot; in
both cases the ally, the king of Judah, was close at hand; both
deaths fulfilled a prophecy that the dogs would lick the blood of
the king concerned (Miller, *VT* 17 [1967], p. 315). It is, therefore,
accepted that the identification of the kings with Ahab and Jehoshaphat is secondary, and that basically this is an account of Jehoram's
death. Since details are not given elsewhere about the death of
Jehoahaz, it is difficult to establish Miller's contention (*ZAW* 80
[1968], p. 341) that it was Jehoahaz who went to battle disguised,
was shot and then propped up in his chariot until the evening
(vv. 29–36), but that it was Jehoram's blood that was licked (v. 38).

30. I will disguise myself and go into battle: The king of Israel
by discarding his royal attire was disguising himself; if a different
etymology is accepted, he was 'girding himself for battle' (Malamat,
Fest. Gaster, p. 278). The motive for his action is not clear. There
is probably more to it than his wish to acclaim the Judaean king as
the head of the combined armies; but it was not a trick to mix the
identity of the two kings as is suggested by the Gk. (see below). It
may be that the Israelite king was trying to escape fate; as noted by
Gray (p. 454), Mesopotamian kings also refrained from wearing their
usual clothes on some occasions in order to avoid evil influences. **you
wear your robes**: The Gk. reads 'my robes', which is accepted by
Gray (p. 447). But this changes the character of the action and
makes it into an act of treachery. The Gk., according to Burney
(p. 256), has accepted an easy but false correction, and is to be
rejected (de Vries, *op. cit.*, p. 17). *NEB* (cf. *NIV*) conveys the
meaning of MT well, 'but you shall wear your royal robes'.

31. had commanded the thirty-two captains of his chariots: 2
Chr. 18:30 omits the figure **thirty-two**, which is obviously an intrusion from 1 Kg. 20:1, where reference is made to thirty-two kings.

32. and Jehoshaphat cried out: There is no need to suppose that
he cried out in prayer, as suggested by Chronicles and the Gk., nor
that he raised a battle-cry (Montgomery, p. 340), from which he

was recognised. The context suggests that he was crying out in protest against his mistaken identity as the Israelite king (cf. de Vries, *op. cit.*, p. 48).

34–35. a certain man drew his bow at a venture: *NEB* (cf. *NIV*), 'drew his bow at random'. The Heb. has 'in his simplicity'; this means that he could not give a reason for shooting in a particular direction (cf. 2 Sam. 15:11; Gen. 20:5, 6). **between the scale armour and the breastplate: scale armour,** of which examples have been discovered in Egypt, Nuzi, Ugarit and Lachish (Montgomery, p. 340; Gray, p. 454), was a mobile apron-like covering to protect the lower abdomen and thighs. The Heb. *debāqîm* means 'joinery, attachment', and there is no need to find here a reference to 'arm-pits' as in the Targ. of Jer. 38:12. **carry me out of the battle, for I am wounded**: There is a discrepancy between this order and the statement in v. 35 that he remained **propped up in his chariot facing the Syrians.** A possible explanation is that the king requested that he be taken out of the main line of the battle to the side lines, where he was to remain to encourage his men and to boost their morale. Gray (*ibid.*) offers a more plausible understanding of the situation: the king requested to be taken away from the battle, but because of the press of the chariots, it was impossible for **the driver of his chariot** to turn back; he therefore had to remain in his chariot and died from loss of blood.

37. So the king died: The Gk., followed by Montgomery (p. 341) and Gray (p. 447), reads this phrase as part of the cry in v. 36—'for the king is dead'—and then takes the following verb in the plural, 'and they came to Samaria'. **and they buried the king in Samaria**: cf. 1 Kg. 16:28; 2 Kg. 10:35.

38. And they washed the chariot by the pool of Samaria, and the dogs licked up his blood: This is intended as a fulfilment of the prophecy in 1 Kg. 21:19, which is problematic and may have been inserted in chapter 21 on the basis of the mistaken connection between this violent death and Ahab, instead of his son Jehoram (Miller, *VT* 17 [1967], pp. 314ff.). A different version of the prophecy in 2 Kg. 9:25f. envisages the casting of the dead king's body on the plot of ground belonging to Naboth. The **pool of Samaria** has not been identified, but Gray (pp. 455ff.) thinks it unlikely that the reference is to one of the city's water cisterns; the word for pool (*berēkāh*) may refer to an area outside the city walls for washing clothes and watering animals. **and the harlots washed themselves in it**: This sentence, which is not included in 21:19, is problematic. The Heb. for 'and the prostitutes washed' is ambiguous. It is possible to take it as a parenthesis (Skinner, p. 269) referring to the pool of Samaria, and to render 'where the prostitutes bathed' (*NIV*). If it does not stand in parenthesis, the sentence must mean that the prostitutes washed themselves in the pool to which the king's blood had been drained, or else that they literally washed themselves in the king's blood (which is more specific in the Gk. 'in the blood'). This may refer to a superstitious and obscene practice, which must be understood against the background of the connection between blood and life, and between the king and fert-ility (Gray, p. 455). To support the latter connection it has been suggested that 'dogs' in the present context were professional male prostitutes (cf. Dt. 23:18). Another interpretation, accepted by some of the Vsns., is that 'they washed his armour' in the pool, reading *zain*, 'military equipment' (found in Rabbinic Heb. and Arm.) for *zōnôṯ*, 'prostitutes'. This is accepted by Gray (p. 448), despite Burney's rejection (pp. 258ff.) on the grounds that *zain* is never used for a weapon in biblical Heb. and that the verb *rāḥaz* for washing never refers to inanimate objects. It is preferred, therefore, to retain the difficult MT which is admittedly a later accretion, and to accept that prostitutes deliberately bathed in the pool because of the superstition connected with the king's blood.

(vii) Summary notices relating to Ahab, Jehoshaphat and Ahaziah **22:39-53 (MT 39-54)**
The deuteronomistic notices assembled together in this section contain: the usual concluding formula for the reign of Ahab (vv. 39-40), an account of the reign of Jehoshaphat of Judah within the regular deuteronomistic formulae, and including material relating to his reign drawn from Judaean annals (vv. 41-50; MT. 41-51), and the introductory formula for the reign of Ahaziah (vv. 51-53; MT. 52-54). See further, Hoffmann, *Reform*, pp. 82-4.

39-40. The account of Ahab's reign, which began in 1 Kg. 16:29-34, is only now brought to conclusion. **and the ivory house which he built**: The panelling and furniture of the royal palace in Samaria were inlaid with ivory. 'Houses of ivory' and 'beds of ivory' are elsewhere connected with the period of Jeroboam II (cf. Am. 3:15; 6:4). Large numbers of ivories have been discovered in Samaria, many of them panels with carved Phoenician motifs and early Heb. letters inscribed on their backs. Many of them have suffered damage in the destruction of 722 BC, but it is probable that some belonged to the time of Ahab (Ackroyd, *AOTS*, p. 345; Crowfoot, *Early Ivories*, pp. 1-2). There was an extensive use of ivory for decoration during this period (Montgomery, pp. 341ff.; Gray, p. 456). **and all the cities that he built**: Although the OT refers only to the building of Jericho (1 Kg. 16:34), it is probable that Ahab was engaged on a more extensive programme of rebuilding and fortifying cities. Omri's work on Samaria was continued by his son, and the large stable complex at Megiddo may also be assigned to Ahab (Schofield, *AOTS*, p. 323). Other building projects are also said to be Ahab's work (Yeivin, *WHJP*, pp. 140ff.). **So Ahab slept with his fathers**: This deuteronomistic phrase referring to Ahab's peaceful death indicates that the account of his death in the previous verses was unknown to the deuteronomistic historian. This supports the contention that the connection of that tradition with Ahab belonged to a later stage in the transmission of the narrative complex.

41. in the fourth year of Ahab king of Israel: For the problems of dating Jehoshaphat's reign and finding a satisfactory solution to the synchronisms for this period, see above, pp. 23f. According to this note he came to the throne in 872 BC; but this has to be reconciled with a note in the Gk. at 1 Kg. 16:28 that he came to the throne in Omri's eleventh year, with Jehoshaphat's chronology in v. 51, which dates Ahaziah's succession 'in the seventeenth year of Jehoshaphat', and with 1 Kg. 16:29, which gives the total of Ahab's reign as twenty-two years. The dates proposed for Ahab are 875–854 BC (see Table, p. 28).

42. was thirty-five years old when he began to reign: This is the first time for the king's age at the beginning of his reign to be noted; the detail is lacking in 15:24, although it is usual to provide such information about the kings of Judah (cf. 2 Kg. 8:17, 28; 14:1; 15:1, etc.). **Azubah the daughter of Shilhi**: Because of the status of the queen-mother in Judah, the mother's name is always recorded. **Azubah** is not known elsewhere, and there is no certainty about the derivation of the name and whether it is to be rendered 'abandoned, divorced' (Noth, *Personennamen*, p. 231) or derived from the Arab. for 'sweet' (Šanda I, p. 502) or from the Ugar. for 'prepared' (Montgomery, p. 347).

43. He walked in all the way of Asa his father: Details of the commendable works of Asa are given in 1 Kg. 15:11ff., but the phrase **yet the high places were not taken away** appears also in 15:14.

44. made peace with the king of Israel: Although the king is not named, the alliance mentioned is obviously the one between Jehoshaphat and Ahab. A close relationship between north and south became essential in view of the threat from Syria, and later of course from Assyria. Jehoshaphat's alliance with Ahab was sealed by his son Jehoram's marriage to Athaliah, Ahab's daughter (see on 2 Kg. 8:18, 26ff.); a more specific statement in 2 Chr. 18:1 alludes to the marriage alliance.

45. and how he warred: Although the formula concluding Asa's reign (1 Kg. 15:23) refers to 'his might', it does not mention his wars. The Gk. omits the phrase from this formula relating to Jehoshaphat.

46. the male cult prostitutes: See on 1 Kg. 14:24. It is also recorded in 1 Kg. 15:12 that Asa removed these from the land. The account of Jehoshaphat's reign in 2 Chr. presents this king as one of the most important monarchs in the Chronicler's view, and it is not unlikely that the Chronicler depended on sources other than what is recorded in Kings (see Williamson, *Chronicles*, pp. 277–303). In addition to the brief notice of his reforms in this verse, the Chronicler reports a judicial reform undertaken by Jehoshaphat (2 Chr. 19:4–11, with a doublet in 2 Chr. 17:7–9). Although it has been argued that the account in Chronicles is a reliable one (Albright, *Fest. Marx*, pp. 61–82), the most that can be said with certainty is that the tribal system of justice gave way eventually to a system under the jurisdiction of the king (Williamson, *op. cit.*, pp. 287–9; Macholz, *ZAW* 84 [1972], 1972, pp. 314–40), and that it is reasonable to attribute such a reform to Jehoshaphat.

47. Verses 47–48 provide evidence that Edom was subject to Judah in the time of Jehoshaphat, who attempted to revive trade in the Red Sea area, following the example of his ancestor Solomon. It was in the reign of Jehoram that the Edomites finally broke away and established a kingdom (2 Kg. 8:20–22). The meaning of v. 47 and its connection with v. 48 is not clear; a slight emendation of the text, coupled with a change in verse division, would give 'Now there was no king in Edom; and the deputy of king Jehoshaphat made . . .' (Burney, p. 260), or 'There was no king in Edom, only a viceroy of Jehoshaphat; he built . . .' (*NEB*).

48. ships of Tarshish: See on 1 Kg. 10:22. **to Ophir for gold**: See on 1 Kg. 9:28. **the ships were wrecked at Ezion-geber**: On **Ezion-geber**, see 1 Kg. 9:26. It is not stated how the ships were wrecked, and in an entirely different version, the action is attributed to divine penalty in 2 Chr. 20:35–37 (Williamson, *op. cit.*, pp. 302–3). It can be assumed here that Jehoshaphat made an attempt to renovate the ships used by Solomon, but because they proved unseaworthy they could not be taken out of the port at Ezion-geber (Donner, *IJH*, p. 392).

49. Ahaziah the son of Ahab said: Strengthening the Judaean hold on Edom and attempting to revive trade at Ezion-geber must have occurred towards the end of the reign of Jehoshaphat. The two kingdoms joined together to withstand the threat from Syria. Israel occupied the northern part of Moab, and Judah, by exerting its influence in Edom, gave Israel support, and also cut Syria's access to the Red Sea. Thus the Moabite war of independence, recorded in 2 Kg. 3:4–27, was waged against three allies, Israel, Judah and Edom. **but Jehoshaphat was not willing**: Jehoshaphat's refusal is to be interpreted as an attempt to maintain economic independence. Of course the northern kingdom, because of its closer ties with Phoenicia, could provide better ships and more efficient sailors. But Jehoshaphat was not willing to allow Israel access to his domain.

50. in the city of David his father: Burial in Jerusalem is mentioned in connection with the previous kings of Judah (cf. 1 Kg. 15:8, 24).

51. Ahaziah: An introduction to Ahaziah's reign is given in vv. 51–53, but the account of his reign is not concluded until 2 Kg. 1:17–18. **in the seventeenth year of Jehoshaphat**: The Gk. here reads 'twenty-fourth', obviously attempting to adjust this reckoning to the statement of 2 Kg. 1:17 that Jehoram followed Ahaziah in the second year of Jehoram son of Jehoshaphat, who had died after a reign of twenty-five years (see above, on v. 42). As seen from the Table, p. 28, the reckoning of MT is accepted and Ahaziah's reign is assigned to the two years 854–853 BC.

52. and walked in the way of his mother: This addition to the standard formula makes Ahaziah to follow in the steps of Jezebel as well as those of Jeroboam the son of Nebat.

53. provoked the LORD, the God of Israel, to anger: cf. 1 Kg. 16:13, 26.

(viii) Elijah and Ahaziah 2 Kg. 1:1–18

A division between the two books of Kings is not found in Hebrew MSS nor in the early printed editions, but has originated from LXX (see above, p. 2). The first verse of 2 Kg. obviously belongs to the annalistic material in 1 Kg. 22:51–53, and the content of chapter 1 belongs to the Elijah narratives in 1 Kg. 17–19, 21.

The Elijah narrative has been inserted within a deuteronomistic framework, which contains an introduction (1 Kg. 22:51–2 Kg. 1:1) and a conclusion (2 Kg. 1:17–18) to Ahaziah's reign. The narrative itself begins at 2 Kg. 1:2, but there is some uncertainty about its conclusion. There can be no question about the deuteronomistic character of the note in v. 17a; the fulfilment of prophecy theme is ascribed by Dietrich (*Prophetie*, p. 125) to DtrP. But, because the narrative itself is without conclusion, the first phrase of v. 17, 'so he died', is best regarded as part of the narrative and not a deuteronomistic addition (Steck, *EvTh* 27 [1967], p. 547; cf. Koch, *Growth*, p. 184).

An examination of the narrative itself displays two elements: one strand is concerned with Elijah's encounter with Ahaziah because

he had consulted the god of Ekron (vv. 2–8), and the other describes
Elijah's dealings with the military personnel sent to seek him
(vv. 9–16). Among the reasons for considering vv. 2–17a as a
combination of two independent narratives are: the picture of Elijah
is different, for in the one he declares a message to the king, but
in the other he annihilates his opponents; the scene is entirely
different, for Elijah is said in vv. 9–16 to be 'on top of a hill'; Elijah
the Tishbite of vv. 2–8 has become 'man of God' in vv. 9–16; it is
unclear why Ahaziah, who had already received Elijah's word
through messengers (v. 6), should now wish to consult him through
military personnel. This evidence warrants the conclusion that to
the original narrative in vv. 2–8, 17aa (cf. Fohrer, *Elia*, p. 43;
Dietrich, *ibid.*) a later addition (vv. 9–16) was made.

Other matters need further clarification, especially the origin of
this addition, its growth and development, and also the date of its
acceptance into the Elijah tradition. It is not difficult to establish a
link between the addition and the Elisha tradition. Whereas the title
'man of God' is only rarely used of Elijah (see on 1 Kg. 17:18, 24),
it is the normal title for Elisha (see 2 Kg. 2; 5; 6; 7 *passim*). In the
two narratives which apply the term to Elijah (the resuscitation of
the boy, 1 Kg. 17:17–24, and the annihilation of the captains here)
the prophet displays extraordinary and miraculous power, which
characterizes the narratives as legends. On at least two occasions in
the Elisha narratives too, the man of God executes destruction on
mockers or opponents, as is done by Elijah here (cf. 2 Kg. 2:23–25;
5:20–27). It is therefore natural to conclude that vv. 9–16 contain
legendary material that has been inserted into the Elisha narrative
under the influence of the Elisha tradition (Fohrer, *ibid.*; Koch, *op.
cit.*, p. 188). Despite the claim that 'the man of God' element was
a very late addition to the Elisha narrative (Schmitt, *Elisa*,
pp. 85–9), it can be asserted that the addition in vv. 9–16 originated
from the circle of Elisha's followers and became attached to the
Elijah complex in pre-deuteronomistic times. Whether it was added
as a single unit is not certain; Hentschel (*Die Elijaerzählungen*,
pp. 11ff.) has made a strong case for separating two stages here—vv.
9, 15–16, which give a simple account of a single episode, were
added first, and later vv. 10–14, which came from a younger hand;
but both stages are pre-deuteronomistic.

1. After the death of Ahab, Moab rebelled against Israel: A
similar record appears in 2 Kg. 3:5, from which this note may have
been borrowed (Noth, *ÜSt*, p. 83). This short statement and the
account of Jehoram's activities in 2 Kg. 3:4ff. have to be seen
in relation to the Mesha inscription (*DOTT*, pp. 195ff.; *ANET*,
pp. 320ff.). During the reign of Omri and his descendants Israel

had occupied Moab, until 'Israel perished utterly for ever' (inscription); the length of this period covered Omri's 'days and half the days of his son, forty years'. This latter statement need not imply that Moab's revolt occurred in the time of Ahab, thus contradicting the *OT* (as accepted in *DOTT*, *ibid.*); it can be translated 'and half the days of his sons' (Herrmann, *History*, p. 219), which brings the uprising of Moab to the last year of Ahaziah (Wallis, *ZDPV* 81 [1965], pp. 180–6; Schmitt, *op. cit.*, pp. 63–7). The evidence of 2 Kg. 1:1; 3:5 that there was a Moabite uprising after Ahab's death can be taken as correct, and also that in response to this uprising in the year of Ahaziah's death Jehoram moved into Moab. Israel's supremacy did not last long, for Moab was able to regain its territory in the last years of the Omride dynasty.

2. the lattice in his upper chamber in Samaria: The palace in Samaria had an upper storey, which was more extensive than the roof-chamber of 2 Kg. 4:10; the translation 'roof chamber' offered here in *NEB* is thus inadequate. As was common in North Syrian buildings, the second floor had open platforms or balconies, and a house of this character was known as *bīt hillāni*, 'house of windows'. The word used for lattice (Heb. *śebākāh*), which appears also in the description of ornamental net-work in the Temple in 1 Kg. 7:7ff., denotes a wooden screen to admit air but to exclude the strong glare of the sun (Gray, p. 463). **Baal-zebub**: This is the only reference in the *OT* to this particular cult. **zebub** means 'flies', which is supported by *Baal-muion*, 'lord of flies', in the Gk. and Josephus (*Ant.* IX.2.1). Abundant parallels of 'fly-gods' are available in classical and patristic literature, Herakles being known as Zeus Apomuios (see reference in Montgomery, p. 349). Because of their power over flies, these deities could send or retract plagues and diseases, and the increased activity of flies in high summer probably indicated that they were essentially sun-gods (Kittel, p. 182). On the evidence of the best textual tradition of the *NT*, 'Baal-zebul' is read in Mt. 10:25; 12:24; Mk. 3:22; Lk. 11:15ff. in preference to the variant form 'Baal-zebub'; many have preferred the same form here. Gray (p. 463) finds support for this in the use of *zebūl*, 'prince', as a common epithet for the Canaanite Baal in the Ras Shamra texts, and explains 'zebub' as a parody by the orthodox on the original *zebūl* (*BHH I*, cols., pp. 175ff.). There is no need to translate as 'the Flame' on the basis of Ugar. and to connect this particular deity with fire-motif (as proposed by Fensham, *ZAW* 79 [1967], pp. 361–4). **the god of Ekron**: Ekron is identified with *Khirbet el-Muqannaʿ*, a few kilometers south-east of ʿAqir, a name which bears resemblance to the Heb. **Ekron**.

3. the angel of the LORD: God is usually represented as speaking

directly to Elijah, and only rarely is the messenger or angel introduced (cf. on 1 Kg. 19:5ff.). The single messenger is virtually
indistinguishable from God himself (Johnson, *The One and the
Many*, pp. 29ff.), and although the Heb. uses the same word for
the messengers sent by Ahaziah, the concept of God's messenger is
different. Gray (pp. 463ff.) finds in the use of the term a reflection
of the theology of the Pentateuchal source E, which originated from
northern Israel about this time. But Koch (*op. cit.*, p. 187) takes it
to be a post-exilic expansion, for only at that time was there an
intermediary between God and his prophets. The rarity of the
appearance of the messenger in the Elijah-Elisha narratives adds
support to Koch's suggestion. **Is it because there is no God in
Israel?**: This question is repeated in vv. 6 and 16, but with slight
variations. **that you are going** has become 'you are sending' in v.
6, but there is no corresponding verb in the short form of v. 16.
Moreover, the changed position of the question in v. 16 may be a
conscious variation and an indication of the elaborated style of the
narrative (Koch, *op. cit.*, pp. 184ff.).

4. The crucial statement of the narrative is found in the prophetic
message contained in this verse. But again there is a difference
between the formulation of the message here and in v.16, where it
is given the form of a 'because/therefore' statement. The latter form
is thought to be an expansion of the original (cf. Hentschel, *op. cit.*,
p. 13).

5–7. The narrative continues with a dialogue between the king
and his messenger, in which Elijah's message is repeated (v. 6).
Ahaziah's final query was **What kind of man was he?**, where the
Heb. uses the word *mišpāṭ*, 'law, order' in the sense of 'description'
or 'manner' (cf. Jg. 13:12).

8. He wore a garment of haircloth: This statement, which is
very brief in Heb., is capable of two interpretations. A more literal
rendering would be 'a hairy man'; so the Gk., Vulg., *EVV* and
NEB; this probably means that he had long hair and a beard. A
more free rendering of the text applies the description to Elijah's
clothing rather than his personal appearance—'a man with garment
of hair' (*NIV*). Gray's description of it as a rough, shaggy cloak
(p. 464) is nearer the mark than Koch's 'fur coat' (*op. cit.*, p. 188).
In support of this latter kind of interpretation, reference can be
made to the importance attached to Elijah's mantle (1 Kg. 19:19; 2
Kg. 2:8, 13ff.), and to later allusions implying that such a garment
was one of the prophetic insignia (Zech. 13:4; Mt. 3:4). Moreover,
a suggestion that this kind of mantle was worn as a sign of austerity
is obtained from its use as an ascetic costume by Muslim Sufis (cf.
Joüon, *Bib* 16 [1935], pp. 74ff.). It may be that the intention of

wearing this garment, which was so typical of nomadic life, was to protest against the luxury of higher culture (Lindblom, *Prophecy*, pp. 66ff.). **a girdle of leather**: No other reference is made to the leather girdle in the *OT*. It was worn by John the Baptist (Mt. 3:4), probably in imitation of Elijah, who was the forerunner of the Messiah (Mal. 4:5); John wore it deliberately to signify his status.

9. Elijah's dealings with the captains come in a section that is clearly an addition. To the reasons already given for regarding vv. 9–16 as a later appendix, possibly added in more than one stage, may be added the fact that the king remains nameless in these verses. **a captain of fifty men**: The rank given is that of a professional soldier who had attained some distinction. Montgomery (p. 350) identifies the term with *rab ḥanšā* an honourable title in Akkad. cf. also Isa. 3:3. **who was sitting on top of a hill**: In the previous section Elijah had met the messengers on the road not far from Samaria and then disappeared. Locating him in these verses **sitting** on the top of an unnamed hill may again be a pointer to an independent, secondary tradition, despite Gray's claim (*ibid.*) that there were hills about seven miles to the west of Samaria on the way to Ekron. **O man of God**: As noted above, the title **man of God** is characteristic of the Elisha tradition and is rarely found in the Elijah narratives. The title is found in sections which depict Elisha as the possessor of extraordinary powers, and in which his actions display the character of wonder-works and miracles (Schmitt, *op. cit.*, pp. 85–9). The actions attributed to Elijah in these verses share the same characteristics, and denote that this secondary addition is derived from legendary material.

11–12. The encounter of the second captain with the man of God follows the same course, and its conclusion is identical. The incident is recorded in almost identical words, allowing for minor variations. *RSV* correctly follows the Gk. in reading he went up (*wayya'al*) as in vv. 9, 13 for MT's 'he answered' (*wayya'an*). The king's command is given more formally this time, as is conveyed by *RSV*'s rendering **this is the king's order** (lit. 'thus says the king'), and it is more urgent, **Come down quickly**. Both variations contribute to the rising crescendo of the narrative (cf. Koch, *op. cit.*, p. 185). **the fire of God came down**: Many MSS and the Gk. omit **God** and so read, like v. 10, 'fire came down'. **God** may have been deliberately inserted to produce a word-play on 'man of God' (*'îš 'elōhîm*) in 'fire of God' (*'ēš 'elōhîm*).

13. the captain of a third fifty: MT relates **third** to **fifty**, but Luc., Vulg. and Targ. read 'the third captain of fifty', as in v. 13*b*; cf. also v. 11. LXX omits the word, and the Syr. reads it as 'for the third time'. The climax of the narrative is reached by showing how the third captain adopted a different approach and achieved a different result. His plea, **let my life be precious in your sight**, is repeated for emphasis.

15. the angel of the LORD: The angel appears in this section again, as it did in the first (v. 3). As noted above, vv. 15ff., if read after v. 9, can be taken as the first stage of the insertion in vv. 9–16. At first it was only stated that Elijah was approached by a captain of fifty; he was commanded to go with him and to repeat his message in person to the king.

16. The prophetic word in this verse displays the essential form of an announcement of disaster. After the introductory messenger formula, **Thus says the LORD**, the message itself falls into two parts—firstly, the accusation, or reason for disaster, introduced by **because** (*ya'an*), and secondly, the announcement, or declaration of disaster, introduced by **therefore** (*lākēn*). See Westermann, *Basic Forms*, pp. 129ff.

17–18. The deuteronomistic formula has been combined with the conclusion of the preceding narrative. As noted above, the opening phrase **so he died** is taken to have been the original conclusion of the narrative, but the following phrase, **according to the word of the LORD, which Elijah had spoken**, is a deuteronomistic addition to it. The standard concluding formula for a north Israelite king in vv. 17*b*–18 has a note synchronising the accession of his successor with the reign of the Judaean king, which contradicts the information in 2 Kg. 3:1 and is omitted from the Codex Vaticanus. The reckoning in 2 Kg. 3:1 can be accepted as the correct version; it is probable that MT, because of the lack of dating in chapter 2, has added this note originating from an independent chronological scheme. If it is recognized as such there is no need to attempt to reconcile it with 3:1 by suggesting the co-regency of Jehoshaphat and Jehoram in Judah.

(b) Elisha and his time
2:1–8:29

As noted above (pp. 68ff.), any analysis of this section relating to Elisha and his time has to recognize the variety of the material included in it. Narratives, such as the section immediately following and recording the revolt of Jehu (9:1–10:27), and those noting Elisha's involvement in Syrian affairs (5:1–23; 8:7–15; 13:14–21) contain a core of reliable historical information. Others, especially war-narratives (3:1ff.; 6:24ff.; cf. 1 Kg. 20:22), may have been based on historical reminiscences; however, incorrect historical alignment forbids their classification as 'historical narratives', and makes the term 'legend' more appropriate. Some at least of the miracle stories are of doubtful reliability, as there are indications that they did not belong originally to the Elisha tradition, but were secondarily added to it (Rofé, *JBL* 89 [1970], pp. 427–40.)

Such studies have serious and inevitable implications for any attempt to picture 'the historical Elisha' (cf. Schmitt, *op. cit.*, pp. 189ff.). Elisha, the son of Shaphat, who came originally from Abel-mehola, is correctly envisaged as the leader of a prophetical guild, which was centred upon Gilgal near Jericho. The members of the guild probably married and were engaged in secular occupations; they had a house at which they assembled, but it was in no way a 'monastery', for the leader Elisha had a private dwelling in Samaria. Elisha's connection with Elijah is doubtful, and the portrayal of him as his successor may be a later projection.

Elisha, like other ecstatic persons, performed miraculous acts, which may be regarded as semi-magical. The Gilgal tradition portrayed Elisha in this way, as did the narratives recording his involvement in Syrian affairs. He could be correctly described as 'a man of God', and it is likely that some popular traditions about an unnamed ecstatic became attached to the Elisha tradition.

Because Elisha and his prophetical guild were the champions of true Yahwism, it is not surprising that he was critical of the Omrides, and supported Jehu's revolution and later Jehu's dynasty. Despite his support of this dynasty, and the appropriateness of the title 'the chariots of Israel and its horsemen' for the man who played such a leading role in Israel's activities against Syria, Schmitt denies the presence of the charismatic king ideal or of the holy war ideology in the work and thought of Elisha.

Elisha died in the first years of the reign of Joash, soon after 800 BC, and it is likely that the tradition siting his grave in the neighbourhood of Gilgal is reliable.

(i) Elisha succeeds Elijah 2:1–25

Elisha, after being designated by Elijah as his successor when he cast his mantle upon him, had become Elijah's follower and servant (1 Kg. 19:19–21). No allusion is made in the present narrative to the account in 1 Kg. 19, which was probably an independent tradition whose credibility is in doubt (see above, p. 328). The account of Elijah's translation and the acknowledgement of Elisha as his successor fittingly provides an introduction to the Elisha cycle of narratives to which it naturally belongs. In its present position, however, the narrative has been inserted within the deuteronomistic scheme between two notes about the accession of Jehoram (2 Kg.

1:17–18 and 3:1–3), which may be interpreted as an indication that it is a later addition (Eissfeldt, p. 544).

The narrative in chapter 2 is not a literary unit, and its various strands can be separated. Firstly, two different traditions have been combined in the report of Elijah's translation, one stating that he was taken in a whirlwind (v. 1, and repeated in v. 11*b*), and the other concentrating on the separation of the prophets by a chariot and horses (v. 11*a*). Obviously v. 1*a*, which contains the first reference to the whirlwind, is a redactional link (Galling, *ZThK* 53 [1956], p. 129; Schmitt, *Elisa*, p. 102). But opinions vary as to which of the two traditions is the original. Galling (*op. cit.*, pp. 141ff.) argues that the reference to chariot and horses is secondary, as is the reference in v. 12 to Elisha seeing it and crying out. According to his reconstruction, the original narrative stated that Elijah went up to heaven in a whirlwind and that Elisha saw him no more (vv. 11*b* and 12*ad*, with the remainder, vv. 11*a* and 12*abc*, being an insertion). Schmitt (*ibid.*) takes the opposite view and contends that the reference to the whirlwind in v. 11*b*, as well as in v. 1*a*, is an addition. The original report described a chariot and horses separating the prophets and contained a statement that Elisha saw Elijah no more (vv. 11*a*, 12*ad*); in a later redaction, v. 12*abc* was added together with v. 11*b*. As will become clear from the comments below on individual verses, Schmitt's analysis is favoured.

Secondly, vv. 2–6 differ in many ways from their context. The reasons for separating them noted by Schmitt (*op. cit.*, pp. 104ff.) are: whereas vv. 9, 10 refer to Elijah's translation with a passive verb ('I am taken'), vv. 2–6 refer to God taking him away (vv. 3, 5); in the narrative of vv. 1–15 the name Yahweh is used only in vv. 2–6 (v. 14*a* being dubious, as is noted below); vv. 2–6 are formal and repetitive, and if they are omitted it can be seen that vv. 1*b* and 7 link naturally. To accommodate the insertion, which Schmitt (*op. cit.*, pp. 126ff.) connects with the so-called 'Yahweh-revision' of the Elisha narratives, the phrase 'who were at Jericho' has been added to v. 15. Even if Schmitt's argument for a 'Yahweh-revision' dated in the sixth century is rejected, it can be accepted that vv. 2–6 belong to a later revision or expansion of the original kernel and that its presence has heightened the miraculous element.

Thirdly, vv. 16–18 did not originally conclude the narrative in vv. 1–15, but were appended later (Gunkel, *Elisa*, pp. 13ff.; Galling, *op. cit.*, p. 142). Whereas fifty 'sons of the prophets' accompanied Elijah and Elisha, according to the narrative (cf. v. 7), the appendix mentions 'fifty strong men' (v. 16). Furthermore, the desire to seek confirmation of Elijah's translation and the cynicism shown by the instigators of the search for the prophet do not provide a fitting climax to the narrative.

Fourthly, the two anecdotes reported in vv. 19–24 were originally independent narratives. Like the account of Elisha's designation as Elijah's successor, they were connected with Jericho, which may explain their attachment. Verse I refers to Gilgal, the sanctuary of the Jericho district, and although vv. 16–18 are dismissed as secondary, Schmitt (*op. cit.*, p. 107) retains the phrase 'and he stayed at Jericho' in v. 18*ab* as a conclusion to the narrative of Elijah's successor. Both anecdotes, it is claimed, belong to the same area.

Through these revisions and expansions the original account of Elisha's designation as Elijah's successor after the latter's departure has acquired greater emphasis on the miraculous. Separation of the prophets by a chariot and horses has become a translation in a whirlwind; the suspense of the translation event has been increased by the addition of vv. 2–6, and the emphasis has been shifted somewhat from the succession of Elisha to the translation of Elijah. The miraculous element of the event was but confirmed by the vain search for the prophet, which has been acquired as a later appendix, and again by the attachment of two independent anecdotes about the miraculous power of Elisha.

1. **Now, when the LORD was about to take Elijah up to heaven by a whirlwind**: The **Now, when** at the beginning is an indication that this sentence, like many others of similar structure, was added by a redactor to weld together two sections. Any suggestion as to how the narrative began before the substitution of this redactional device, such as Galling's 'Elijah and Elisha lived in Gilgal' (*op. cit.*, p. 129), is mere guesswork. The tradition preserved here and in v. 11*b* that Elijah was taken up **to heaven by a whirlwind**, as noted above, is regarded as secondary. **Elijah and Elisha were on their way from Gilgal**: Usually **Gilgal** refers to the sanctuary between Jericho and the Jordan mentioned in Jos. 4:19ff.; 5:9ff. But the statement in v. 2 that 'they went down to Bethel' causes a problem, which can be solved either by identifying Gilgal with *Jiljulieh* between Bethel and Shiloh (first suggested by Thenius, p. 270), or with a location west near *Kefr Tult* (with Šanda II, p. 10), or else by reading the verb as 'they went' (with the Gk.) instead of 'they went down', or again by suggesting that 'went down' reflects the author's geographical standpoint (Montgomery, pp. 353ff.). If the suggestion that vv. 2–6 are a later expansion is accepted, the identification of Gilgal with the sanctuary near Jericho (now located near *Khirbet el-Mafjar*; see Muilenburg, *BASOR* 140 [1955], pp. 11ff.) can be retained and the awkwardness of the verb in v. 2 attributed to this fact.

2. **Tarry here**: This command is repeated in vv. 4, 6, and by repeating in each case Elisha's stubborn refusal to obey the impression is given that he had some mysterious premonition of what was to happen; this increases the suspense and the mysterious character of the event. **for the LORD has sent me**: As noted above, reference to Yahweh is restricted to vv. 2–6, where it is found eight times, three of which appear in the statement that **the LORD has sent** Elijah on his journey. **they went down to Bethel**: See above, on v. 1.

3. **the sons of the prophets who were in Bethel**: On **the sons of the prophets**, see on 1 Kg. 20:35. As a major northern shrine, Bethel was probably a centre for a numerous community of prophets, cf. also 1 Kg. 13:11ff. **the LORD will take away your master**: This phrase, which is repeated in v. 5, attributes Elijah's departure to Yahweh's action; but the passive expression 'I am taken' (vv. 9, 10) does not specifically connect his departure with divine action. Moreover, he is taken **from over you** (lit. 'from over your head') in vv. 3, 5, but simply 'from you' in vv. 9, 10. Although these are only slight differences, the agreement between vv. 3 and 5 over against vv. 9 and 10 gives weight to the argument that different strands can be traced here.

4–5. These verses repeat vv. 2–3, only that the location now is **Jericho**. The fact that Jericho itself was not a cultic centre does not present an unsurmountable difficulty; it can be assumed that the prophets of these verses were attached to the sanctuary at Gilgal, which stood between Jericho and the Jordan (see on v. 1) Gilgal was an important sanctuary in early Israel, more especially because of the connection between it and the tradition of the conquest (Kraus, *Worship*, pp. 152–65; *VT* 1 [1951], pp. 181ff.). Although known as the prophets of Jericho, which gave its name to the district, they were in fact the prophets of Gilgal (Gray, p. 474; Schmitt, *op. cit.*, p. 156); possibly the basic tradition behind vv. 1–15, as well as some later appendices in vv. 19–25, originated from the Gilgal shrine.

6. This verse again is a repetition of vv. 2 and 4. But the third location is not a sanctuary to which the prophetic community was attached, but a more general geographical location—**to the Jordan**.

7. As noted above, Schmitt regards this verse as the original continuation of v. 1*b*. Thus, the **fifty men of the sons of the prophets** were obviously from the sanctuary at Gilgal.

8. **Elijah took his mantle**: cf. 1 Kg. 19:19 and 2 Kg. 1:8. **and the water was parted to the one side and to the other, till the two of them could go over on dry ground**: In the cultic celebrations at Gilgal the central place was taken by the Exodus from Egypt and

the conquest of Canaan, two themes which were easily linked by associating the crossing of the sea with the crossing of the Jordan. The former had clearly coloured the account of the latter in Jos. 3–5 (especially 4:22–24), and had drawn an unmistakable analogy between crossing the Jordan and the Exodus (Kraus, *ibid.*). This tradition was so firmly established in Gilgal that it also influenced the prophetical tradition associated with the sanctuary, and once again an analogy is drawn between the crossing of the Jordan by Elijah and Elisha and the crossing of the sea; cf. especially Exod. 14:21–22.

9. Yahweh is no longer mentioned, and Elijah himself seems to be assuming responsibility for what eventually materializes between him and Elisha. This is clearly brought out in his invitation **Ask what I shall do for you. let me inherit a double share of your spirit**: According to the regulation in Dt. 21:17 on the rights of the firstborn, the eldest son was to receive a 'double portion' of everything belonging to his father, and was thus given a share that was double the inheritance of any of the other sons. He did not receive two-thirds of the inheritance, as is suggested by the use of the phrase in conjunction with the third part in Zech. 13:8. Elisha is asking that he be granted special privileges as his master's successor, possibly as the leader of a community of prophets (cf. Carroll, *VT* 19 [1969], p. 400). On the privileges of the firstborn, see Mayes, *Deuteronomy*, p. 304.

10. Elijah lays down a condition for the granting of Elisha's request; it will be granted **if you see me as I am being taken**. This is not to be interpreted as a semi-magical sign, which will lead to the automatic transfer of Elijah's spirit to Elisha. What Elijah implies is that Elisha's status as successor depends on his ability to see and comprehend the spiritual world. If he possesses the ability of a visionary to penetrate into the heavenly world, his request will be granted; if he cannot demonstrate that he has that ability, his request will not be granted (cf. Haag, *TThZ* 78 [1969], pp. 23ff.).

11. a chariot of fire and horses separated the two of them: The secondary linking of the chariot of fire in v. 11*a* and the storm in v. 11*b* must not be taken as a clue to the meaning of the chariot and horses, as is done for example in the interpretation that finds in them a vivid comparison with the visible progress of the sirocco. Nor again is the origin of the vision to be sought in the title of Elijah in v. 12*a* (as is done by Gray, p. 476), for the connection between the title and the narrative may be secondary (see below). The horse has cultic and mythical associations, and often appears as the animal representing the sun-god (cf. 2 Kg. 23:11). It is possible that the Elijah-Elisha tradition borrowed motifs from local solar mythology (Kittel, pp. 188ff.), and took chariot and horses to stand for the deity. Israel's own tradition too explains the concept found here, for fire is frequently found in descriptions of theophany as one of the manifestations of God's presence (see under 1 Kg. 18:38). Basically Elisha's designation as Elijah's successor is connected with 'theophany', and when Elisha emerged from the experience he is acknowledged as a person having the ability mentioned under v. 10. Although the fire as a symbol of God's presence was derived from Israel's own tradition, in this particular case its connection with a chariot and horses reflects the use of local mythology. This verse only states that the chariot and horses **separated the two of them**, and it does not give any suggestion that Elijah was carried to heaven in the horse-drawn chariot. However, this figures in later tradition about Elijah (cf. Sir. 48:9). The present narrative is not concerned with details of Elijah's translation to heaven, but rather with the fact that Elisha saw the symbol of God's presence, and thus met the condition laid down in v. 10. This is the meaning of v. 11a, and this justifies the view that v. 11b is a later addition.

12. And Elisha saw it: This must refer back to the taking up of Elijah in v. 11b, and is to be regarded as secondary. In the reconstructions of Galling and Schmitt outlined above, there is an agreement with regard to v. 12a, namely that v. 12ad belonged to the original version, but that v. 12aabc came in with later revision. **My father, my father! the chariots of Israel and its horsemen!**: The Gk. and Vulg. read the singular 'horseman', presumably referring to Elijah as the charioteer. There is much in favour of reading the Heb. as 'horses' rather than 'horsemen' (Montgomery, p. 354). The meaning of the phrase is uncertain. Galling (*op. cit.*, p. 129), who considers this phrase together with the reference to chariots in v. 11acd to be an intrusion, thinks that it can only refer to the chariot and horses taking Elijah up to heaven. But, if the phrase is an addition to the original in v. 11a, its presence calls for further investigation. Many commentators favour a spiritualizing interpretation; seeing the chariot and horses gave Elisha the occasion to comment that Elijah was Israel's chariot and horses, for he was a representative of the invisible forces that were Israel's true defence (cf. Burney, p. 265; Montgomery, p. 354). Schmitt correctly takes as his starting-point the use of the same phrase in 2 Kg. 13:14 to refer to Elisha and also rightly connects with this phrase the theme of 2 Kg. 6:15b–17, which clarifies the concept, although it does not use this particular expression. Elisha's participation in the Syrian wars justifies the application of the phrase to him; but it is not appropriate in referring to Elijah. Moreover, the phrase in 13:14 is traditio-historically older than its use in 2:12 (cf. Carlson, *VT* 20 [1970], p. 388). Schmitt (*op. cit.*, p. 104) suggests that the phrase was borrowed from the Elisha tradition of 13:14, and was connected to the reference to chariot and horses here in v. 11*a* in order to join together more firmly the various Elisha traditions. Nevertheless, it is a misfit in its new context. **and rent them in two pieces**: Rending the clothes, as elsewhere in the *OT* (cf. Gen. 37:34; Lev. 10:6; 21:10; 1 Sam. 4:12; 2 Sam. 1:2), is a sign of sorrow and mourning.

13–14. The concrete evidence that Elisha was able to communicate with the spiritual world, and was therefore the true successor of Elijah is provided when he re-enacts Elijah's miraculous splitting of the waters (cf. v. 8). Many of the phrases in these two verses repeat v. 8, **he took the mantle . . . and struck the water . . . the water was parted to the one side and to the other**. Elisha's invocation, **Where is the LORD, the God of Elijah?** is followed by two words (*'aphû'*) which are difficult to render. In MT they are attached to the following sentence, which may be translated 'and when he also had smitten' (*EVV*). Another possibility is to attach them to the question for emphasis, 'Where is the LORD, the God of Elijah, even he?' (Gray, p. 473), but this is not entirely satisfactory (cf. Burney, p. 266). The Vulg. and Symmachus understood *'ap hû'* as *'ēpô'*, 'now'; cf. *NIV*, 'Where now is the LORD, the God of Elijah?' Luc. omits the words, which are so similar in Heb. to the name 'Elijah' that they could have been a mistaken repetition of the prophet's name; consequently no attempt has been made to represent them in *RSV* or *NEB*.

15. Elisha's action brought recognition from the community of prophets at Jericho that **the spirit of Elijah rests on Elisha**, which is an affirmation of the main point of the narrative (cf. vv. 9, 10), and so provides a fitting conclusion. **who were at Jericho**: This phrase is superfluous, since the reference is obviously to the fifty men of v. 7, who, according to the original version, followed Elijah from Gilgal. But the last named town of the insertion in vv. 2–6 is Jericho, and this has influenced the present version of this verse.

16–18. Because of the differences between this section and the preceding narrative, vv. 16–18 are considered to be secondary additions and were not originally the conclusion of the narrative in vv. 1–15. Schmitt (*op. cit.*, pp. 105ff.) lists three reasons for regarding these verses as secondary: (i) the fifty prophets of v. 7 represent the total number of men accompanying Elijah and Elisha, but the strong men of v. 16 are additional; (ii) vv. 1–15 are concerned with the spirit of Elijah, but vv. 16–18 with the spirit of Yahweh; (iii) a section that displays the disbelief of the prophets is not a fitting conclusion to the narrative, despite its final confirmation departure. The **fifty strong men** were able-bodied men who could endure a long and arduous search for the prophet in the mountains. Montgomery's description of them as 'fifty athletes of the guild' (p. 354) is incorrect in assuming that they were members of the prophetical community; they were **with your servants** and not of them. **the Spirit of the LORD**: It is obvious from the context that **the Spirit** is identified with the whirlwind (cf. Gen. 1:2), and is not in this instance an allusion to prophetic ecstasy carrying the prophet in a semi-conscious state to some lonely place. The concept of the spirit as an external, physical force differs from the idea of vv. 9, 15, where the spirit is an indwelling, spiritual force. **till he was ashamed**: This phrase in its three occurrences (2 Kg. 2:17; 8:11; Jg. 3:25) can be rendered as 'beyond measure' (cf. Schmitt, *op. cit.*, p. 202; *K-B*).

19–22. The first of the two appended anecdotes relates how Elisha purified the foul waters of a city, which, because of the close connection with v. 18, is identified with Jericho. Originally this must have been an independent tradition, but the connection with Jericho is probably correct and suggests that the tradition has been derived from the sanctuary at Gilgal. Gray (p. 477) finds for the original tradition in these verses a firm historical basis in the move to rebuild Jericho under Ahab (1 Kg. 16:34); in the locality, it became attached to the person of Elisha.

19. but the water is bad: The spring is usually identified with the *'Ain es-Sultan* near Jericho, which in Christian tradition is recognised as Elisha's spring. Gray (*ibid.*) refers to recent researches in the area which suggest that some springs cause sterility because the water is in contact with radio-active geographical strata (cf. Blake, *PEQ* 99 [1967], pp. 86–97). It is further suggested that sudden contamination, or cleansing, of the water was due to geological shifts in the area. According to Jos. 6:26, Joshua cursed the site at Jericho; but it is possible that some geological shift caused the dereliction of the city, and that this gave rise to the tradition of Joshua's curse. **and the land is unfruitful**: The Heb. verb used here (*mᵉšakkelet̲*) refers normally to miscarriages, which implies that the phrase refers to the inhabitants of the land. Luc. omits **the land**, and thus has 'the water is bad and causes miscarriages'. It is not impossible to retain **the land**, and to refer the curse to its inhabitants, 'the country is troubled with miscarriages' (*NEB*; cf. Schmitt, *op. cit.*, p. 202). Alternatively, Ma,l,. 3:11 provides an instance (albeit the only one) of the use of the verb 'miscarry' as referring to an unfruitful vine, and on that basis it is possible that this verse too refers to the land being unfruitful; cf. *NIV*, 'the land unproductive'.

20. Bring me a new bowl, and put salt in it: The use of salt, which

undoubtedly possessed hygienic qualities (Montgomery, p. 355), is
not to be understood simply as an act of cleansing, nor was it a case
of testing the water for infection (Blake, *ibid.*). Gray (p. 478) rightly
connects this act of purifying the water by means of salt with the
act of sowing a destroyed city with salt. Basically salt was used in
a ritual of separation; when a destroyed city was sown with salt it
was separated from common use and from its past (Honeyman, *VT*
3 [1953], pp. 192–5). Such separation lies also behind the custom
of using salt with sacrifice (Lev. 2:13; Num. 18:19; Ezek. 43:24)
and of rubbing a new-born child with salt (Ezek. 16:4). In this case
Jericho was separated by means of salt from the curse of Joshua,
and was made habitable once again. The demand for **a new bowl**
also indicates that a ritual was to be performed; there are many
examples of using the new, in other words the uncontaminated or
the unimpaired, in ritual (cf. 1 Kg. 11:29; Jg. 16:11; 1 Sam. 6:7;
2 Sam. 6:3).

21. I have made this water wholesome: *NEB*, 'I purify this
water'. The Heb. *rāpā'* normally means 'to heal'. Gray's translation
'I have refertilized this water' (pp. 477ff.) is strained, despite his
appeal to a similar usage of the verb in Gen. 20:17 and in the Ras
Shamra texts.

23–25. The second anecdote, like the preceding one and others
in 2 Kg. 4:1–7, 38–41; 6:1–7, emphasizes the miraculous power
possessed by Elisha. In its present version this narrative attributes
Elisha's action to the power of God, for the curse is made **in the
name of the LORD** (v. 24; cf. also 'this is what the LORD says' in
v. 21). The point of narrating this anecdote is not clear; as Gray
comments (p. 479), it cannot have a serious point and it does
no credit to the prophet. Montgomery (p. 355) classifies it as a
Bubenmärchen, which aimed, by frightening youngsters, to win
reverence for the elders.

23. went up to Bethel: Although the fact that Bethel is the only
place named in the anecdote lends support to the assumption that
the incident happened in the vicinity of Bethel, there is no basis for
this in the narrative itself. Schmitt (*op. cit.*, pp. 180ff.) argues that
this section too is a Gilgal tradition, and that the incident happened
as the prophet was leaving Jericho on his journey to Bethel. **Go up**:
If Elisha was near Bethel and was jeered at by boys from the city,
there seems to be little sense in their encouragement, **Go up**, unless
it is rendered as 'get along with you' (*NEB*). If on the other hand
the prophet had only set out from Jericho and was jeered by Jericho
youths, there is meaning in saying **go up**, which is understood as
'Go away from our city' (cf. Schmitt, *ibid.*). **baldhead**: This does
not refer to natural baldness, which would not be visible in any case

since the head would be covered. It is usually interpreted as denoting
the custom among prophets of wearing a tonsure (Lindblom,
Prophecy, p. 68). Elisha was recognised as a prophet from the mantle
he was wearing, and the derision of the boys shows that they took
it for granted that as a prophet he had this particular hair-style.

24. he cursed them in the name of the LORD: Without this
phrase, which may be taken as a later accretion, vv. 23–25 give a
popular legend about a prophet being jeered at and, by coincidence,
she-bears coming out of the woods and devastating the mocking
youngsters. A tradition grew around the legend, and it was claimed
that the she-bears appeared as a result of the prophet's curse. This
tradition, unworthy as it is, has found its way into the present
version of the narrative. **two she-bears came out of the woods**:
The bear was probably a common wild animal in ancient Palestine,
and is mentioned in an early account of a huntsman's experiences
(see Montgomery, p. 356). In later times they were confined to the
wilder parts like the Hermon massif and Lebanon. **and tore forty-
two of the boys**: This phrase again is an indication of the legendary
character of the narrative. Giving an exact figure betrays the attempt
to give the legend real credibility; but the figure **forty-two** was
probably a conventional one, and was significantly an ill-fated
number (cf. 2 Kg. 10:14; Rev. 11:2; 13:5).

25. This note about Elisha's itinerary intends to give the anecdote
a suitable conclusion, and probably names the places which were
known to be associated with the prophet. For his connection with
Mount Carmel, see 2 Kg. 4:25, and with Samaria, see 2 Kg. 5.

(ii) Israel and its allies wage war against Moab 3:1–27
The deuteronomistic introduction to the reign of Jehoram of Israel
(vv. 1–3), including a synchronisation with the reign of Jehoshaphat
of Judah (in contradiction to 1:17), is followed by an account of
Jehoram's war against Mesha king of Moab in which he was supported by the Judaean Jehoshaphat and the king of Edom (vv.
4–27).

The historical narrative in vv. 4–27 gives the impression of being
a smooth unit, recording how, during the initial stages of the
campaign against Moab, the kings decided to seek a divine oracle
through Elisha, and how after receiving a favourable oracle they
fought successfully against Moab. However, a closer analysis of the
narrative provides sufficient grounds for questioning its unity.
Elisha is introduced abruptly in v. 11, and no explanation of his
presence with the kings is given, nor is it said whence he came on
the scene. His disappearance after delivering his message in vv. 18ff.
is even more abrupt. Schmitt (*Elisa*, pp. 32ff.) finds it significant too

that the verses relating to Elisha are rich in theological terms which are completely absent from the remainder of the narrative. Noting especially the use of the name 'Yahweh', it can be seen that the name occurs ten times in the Elisha section (vv. 9–20), whilst it is not even mentioned in the remaining verses. Moreover, there is a discrepancy between the outcome of the war with Moab as envisaged by Elisha and what actually occurred in the war narrative. Elisha promised an unqualified victory in vv. 18–19, and although his words were fulfilled in the conquest of Moab by Israel (vv. 24–25), the Israelites finally withdrew from Moab (v. 27). Added to this again is the fact that the water motif is treated differently in the two sections; in the Elisha tradition the stream-bed was filled with water for the practical purpose of supplying the army and its accompanying beasts (see vv. 9b, 17), but in the war narrative the whole country was filled with water to create an illusion for the Moabites that there had been loss of blood in the opposite camp (cf. vv. 22–23).

The case for the composite character of the narrative cannot be refuted despite the attempts to regard it as a unit derived from a prophetic source (Bernhardt, *Fest. Jepsen*, pp. 11–22). But there is no agreement on the exact demarcation of its strands. Schmitt (*ibid.*) rightly rejects the complicated reconstruction of Glueck (*HUCA* 11 [1936], p. 150; cf. also Liver, *PEQ* 99 [1967], p. 27) with its separation of an original war-narrative in vv. 4–9, 16, 17ac, 21, 24ab, 26b–27 from a later Elisha revision in vv. 10–16a, 17, 20, 22f., 24aa, and allowing for a deuteronomistic revision in vv. 18ff., 24b, 25aab. Schmitt adopts the simpler solution of Jepsen (*Nabi*, p. 79), who separates the Elisha section in vv. 9–20 from the remainder, but he modifies his division slightly by reading the reference to the coming of water from Edom in v. 20 with the continuation of the war-narrative in vv. 21–27; the Elisha revision is thus confined to vv. 9–19.

Schmitt's division offers a sound basis for appreciating the character of the prophetic revision of an original war-narrative. The account of Israel's war against Moab in vv. 4–9a, 20–27 is a popular tradition, free from theological motives and containing a typically legendary element in the motif of the water appearing as blood. The Elisha intrusion in vv. 9b–19 gives the revised narrative a distinctly theological tone; by introducing theological phrases, making frequent use of the name Yahweh and subscribing to the view that Israel's victory is given by God, the narrative now becomes theologically motivated. Of course the Elisha section does not stand independently; it is a revision of the original tradition and is very closely tied to it through its reference to the same event and the

same king, and by including in v. 19 the content of v. 24. Nevertheless, the conclusion in v. 27 is not reflected in the Elisha section,
which leads Schmitt to suggest that the author of the prophetic
section had not fully understood the meaning of v. 27. As noted
above, the water motif has also been given a different interpretation
in the Elisha section.

Of particular interest in the Elisha section is the favourable attitude towards Jehoshaphat, king of Judah (especially vv. 12, 14), in
contrast to the negative judgment of the Israelite king (v. 13). As
in the previous accounts of victory in 1 Kg. 20; 22, there is a
tendency to designate the Israelite king simply as 'the king of Israel',
but to identify the Judaean king, and again to ascribe victory to the
prophets. A legitimate conclusion is that the narratives about the
prophets of the north had been through Judaean hands and had
been suitably modified (cf. Gray, p. 481; Miller, *JBL* 85 [1966],
pp. 446ff.). The affinity between 2 Kg. 3:4-27 and 1 Kg. 22 is
noted in Schweizer's detailed textual and form-critical analysis of
chapter 3 (*Elischa*, pp. 32ff.), but his conclusion that chapter 3 is
the original form is not acceptable. For a summary of recent discussion of this chapter, see Timm, *Die Dynastie*, pp. 171-80.

1. In the eighteenth year of Jehoshaphat: This chronological
note contradicts 2 Kg. 1:17, and a comparison of the Gk. and Heb.
texts adds further to the confusion. An easy solution is to assume
that Jehoram of Judah was co-regent with his father Jehoshaphat,
who had withdrawn from public life some time before his death,
thus allowing Jehoram to assume responsibility for state affairs
(Gray, p. 481). It is more reasonable to accept that different chronological sources were used, and that some of the reigns have been
exaggerated. Uniformity is not therefore to be expected. The years
given to Jehoshaphat in the Table (p. 28) are 874-850 BC, and
Jehoram's accession to the Israelite throne occurred in 853 BC. **in
Samaria**: This is omitted from the Gk., which inserts the material
relating to Jehoram in vv. 1-3 immediately after 2 Kg. 1:18. Verses
1-3 seem to be a continuation of 1:18, and the sequence has been
broken by the insertion of chapter 2.

2. he put away the pillar of Baal which his father had made:
The Gk. and Vulg., in reading 'pillars' for **pillar**, give the impression
that Jehoram launched a widespread attack on the Baal cult introduced by Ahab. But this is unlikely in view of the presence of
Jezebel on the scene and her power as queen-mother; the evidence
of 2 Kg. 10:26f. that **the pillar of Baal** was still in the temple of
Baal has also to be taken into consideration. However, the main
point, that Jehoram was not **like his father and mother**, is confirmed
by the fact that Jehu in 2 Kg. 10:18 refers only to the sin of Ahab,

excluding mention of his sons (Šanda II, p. 18). There is, therefore, no reason for accepting the reading of the Gk. 'his brother' for **his father**. The **pillar** (*maṣṣēbāh*) was probably a 'stele' or 'statue', which bore the image and inscription of the deity. Gray (p. 481) translates 'stele', Montgomery (p. 358) 'Baal-image', and *NEB* 'the sacred pillar of Baal'. Aramaic steles bearing inscriptions and reliefs of the deity are known from other areas (cf. Dhorme, *L'évolution religieuse*, pp. 161ff.; Cooke, *Inscriptions*, pp. 61f., 103).

3. he clung to the sin of Jeroboam: The singular of the Heb. is preferable to the plural 'sins' found in the Gk.

4. Mesha king of Moab: The Gk. *Mōsa*, suggesting the Heb. *mōšāʿ*, 'deliverance', is to some extent supported by the Mesha inscription, where the king dwells on the word 'salvation' and states that Chemosh 'saved me from all the kings' (ll.3-4; *DOTT*, p. 196). Although there may be a connection with this root, the spelling of MT has the support of analogous names such as Medad and Methar (Šanda II, p. 18). **was a sheep-breeder**: The translation 'sheep-breeder' (cf. *NEB*) is based on the connection between the Heb. *nōqēd* and the Arab. 'naqadun', a breed of small sheep, which Burney (p. 268) describes as ugly in appearance but valued for their wool. Amos is also called a *nōqēd* (Am. 1:1). The application of the term *rb nqdm* to the chief priest (*rb khnm*) at Ras Shamra (Gordon, *Textbook* II, text 62, ll. 54ff.) has led to the suggestion that it is a sacral term connected with the Akkad. verb 'naqadu', 'to probe' (especially the liver in augury) and denoting a hepatoscopist (cf. Bič, *VT* I [1951], pp. 293-5). Gray (pp. 484-5) accepts the translation 'hepatoscopist', adding the comment that Mesha, who also sacrificed his eldest son (v. 27), may well have gained a reputation as an augurer and also that the reference to sheep in v. 4*b* is probably an addition due to a later understanding of *nōqēd* as 'sheep-breeder'. This interpretation of the word is not without difficulties. Although there is some uncertainty about the meaning of the Akkad. 'naqadu', the Akkad. 'naqidum' is used in the sense of 'shepherd' (see von Soden, *Handwörterbuch*, p. 744), as also is the Ugaritic 'nqd' (Gordon, *Textbook* III, no. 1694, p. 447). For these reasons, and because of the hypothetical nature of the suggestion that v. 4*b* is an addition, the usual interpretation of the term as 'sheep-breeder' is preferred to the more recent 'hepatoscopist' (Schmitt, *op. cit.*, p. 203; Schweizer, *op. cit.*, p. 21; Murtonen, *VT* 2 [1952], pp. 170f.; Segert, *VTS* 16 [1967], pp. 279-83). **he had to deliver annually**: The Heb. uses a frequentative verb, 'he used to deliver', suggesting regular payments; this meaning is brought out by the Targ., which adds 'year by year', rendered by *RSV* as 'annually' and by *NEB* as 'regularly'. *RSV*'s understanding of the tribute as constituting **a hundred thousand lambs and the wool of a hundred thousand rams** correctly renders the Heb. idiom which places **wool** as an accusative denoting manner of payment at the end of the sentence. Other renderings are possible. Gray (p. 482ff.) takes the word **wool** to define the rams as being at their first shearing, and favours the translation 'shearling rams', thus making the tribute to be a payment of lambs and rams, and noting that mention is made of a tribute in sheep in Isa. 16:1. Another possibility is to refer the **wool** at the end of the verse to both clauses, and, like *NEB*, to define the payment as 'the wool of a hundred thousand lambs and a hundred thousand rams'. The latter is preferred.

5. when Ahab died, the king of Moab rebelled: On the apparent discrepancy between this statement and the dating of the rebellion in the reign of Ahab by the Moabite inscription, together with a possible solution, see on 2 Kg. 1:1.

7. Jehoshaphat king of Judah: In other instances (vv. 11, 12, 14), but not here, the Gk. reads **the king of Judah** and omits the name **Jehoshaphat**. Gray (p. 485) favours the vaguer mode of reference as being characteristic of narrative style; precise reference belongs to archival data. **I am as you are, my people as your people, my horses as your horses**: This is a repetition of what Jehoshaphat said to the king of Israel before the Ramoth-gilead campaign (1 Kg. 22:4). In this instance, however, a positive reply by the Judaean king, **I will go**, gives a clear conclusion to the negotiations between the two kings (cf. Schweizer, *op. cit.*, pp. 33ff.).

8. By the way of the wilderness of Edom: According to Mesha's inscription, the Moabite king had captured some key fortifications to the north of the river Arnon, *Wadi Mojib*, and a penetration into Moab from this direction was impossible. Likewise Moab was well protected to the south by the Brook Zered, *Wadi el-Hesa*. The route taken by the allies, therefore, took them out to the east of Moab and enabled them to enter from **the wilderness of Edom**, namely, the marshes to the east of that country. This detour to the east explains the 'circuitous march of seven days' in v. 9, the water coming 'from the direction of Edom' (v. 20) and the rising sun shining on the waters in v. 22 (Šanda II, p. 19; Gray, p. 485).

9. and the king of Edom: 1 Kg. 22:47 states categorically that Edom did not have a king; at a later date, when it revolted against Judah, it set up a king of its own (cf. 2 Kg. 8:20ff.). Despite the use of the title **king**, this verse must refer to a viceregent, who was a vassal of the king of Judah. His inferiority to the others is possibly reflected in Mesha's decision to attempt to breach 'opposite the king of Edom' (v. 26). The **circuitous march of seven days** is not

defined, but can be accounted for by the explanation given above
under v. 8. **there was no water for the army or for the beasts**: As
noted above, the part of the narrative which connects the filling of
the stream-bed with water to provide for the army and its beasts
belongs to the prophetic revision of the original (cf. also vv. 16–17).
Schmitt (*op. cit.*, pp. 204–5) breaks off the original narrative after
the words **seven days**, and finds its continuation in v. 20.

10. **the LORD has called these three kings**: The suggestion that
God has led out the armies to their destruction is similar to the
concept found in 1 Kg. 22:20 that he has enticed the prophets to
give a false message. Although it is not stated that Jehoram had
consulted prophets on this occasion, it is suggested in v. 13 that he
would most naturally resort to the prophets acknowledged by his
parents, and indeed may have already done so before setting out on
his campaign.

11. **Is there no prophet of the LORD here?**: The favourable
attitude towards Jehoshaphat in the prophetic revision of these
narratives confirms that the tradition about the prophets of the north
had been through Judaean hands (see above, p. 392). A contrast is
shown between the despairing words of Jehoram in v. 10 and the
determination of the Judaean king **to inquire of the LORD**, which
is a technical phrase for seeking a divine oracle. Jehoshaphat appears
as the champion of true Yahwism in his demand for **a prophet of
the LORD**, a role which is also attributed to him in 1 Kg. 22:5ff.
who poured water on the hands of Elijah: Elisha is designated as
Elijah's servant. The custom of washing hands before and after
eating is well attested; pouring water over the hands on such occasions was a gesture of respect shown by a servant to his master or
by a host to his guest.

12. **The word of the LORD is with him**: This comment about
Elisha again reflects favourably upon Jehoshaphat, and may be
attributed with other similar elements in the narrative to the Judaean
revision of the prophetic tradition. **went down to him**: The presence
of Elisha near a wadi (cf. v. 16), and the positioning of the kings
on high ground being understood, indicate that the verb **went down**
is to be taken literally here (cf. Šanda II, p. 20; Gray, p. 487).
Schmitt's contention (*op. cit.*, p. 174) that the Heb. verb merely
means 'to go, to arrive' is unnecessary in the present context. Unlike
1 Kg. 22:9, the prophet is not brought to the kings.

13. **What have I to do with you?**: cf. *NIV*, 'What do we have
to do with each other?' For this phrase, cf. 1 Kg. 17:18. *NEB*'s
rendering 'Why do you come to me?' loses some of the force of the
original. **Go to the prophets of your father and the prophets of
your mother**: Although the last phrase is omitted from the Gk., it

receives confirmation from 1 Kg. 18:19, from where it may have
been derived. Elisha, like Elijah before him, shows utter contempt
for the Baal prophets, and his words to the king are full of sarcasm.
No: The use of the negative on its own without an accompanying
phrase to complement it is found elsewhere (2 Kg. 4:16; 1 Sam.
2:24; Ru. 1:13) and denotes deprecation (Burney, p. 269). Jehoram
does not wish to consult the prophets acknowledged by his parents
because he clearly recognizes that it is Yahweh who has acted to
give him and his allies **into the hand of Moab**. Repetition of words
from v. 10 gives an indication that these verses are a secondary
insertion (cf. Kuhl, *ZAW* 64 [1952], pp. 1–11).

14. were it not that I have regard for Jehoshaphat: The pro-
Jehoshaphat theme developed by the Judaean revisers reaches its
climax in the assertion attributed to Elisha, that it is only out of
respect for the Judaean king that he is willing to participate in the
affair.

15. bring me a minstrel: Music used by dervishes to induce
excitement and ecstasy was a common phenomenon (cf. Lucian, *De
Dea Syra* 43, with a reference to pipers and flute-players inducing
frenzy; (Haldar, *Associations*, pp. 183f.; Oesterley, *The Sacred
Dance*, p. 116), and is not unknown in the *OT* (cf. 1 Sam. 10:5ff.).
The reference to Elisha's dependence on such a stimulant is an
ancient and genuine tradition, which places Elisha firmly in the
category of ecstatic prophets. **the power of the LORD came upon
him**: This phrase, with its possible reference to either the minstrel
or the prophet, is not as ambiguous as it appears (cf. Schweizer,
op. cit., p. 29), and can only refer to Elisha. **The power of the
LORD** (lit. 'the hand of the LORD') is used to indicate the special
possession of the prophets by God's power (cf. 1 Kg. 18:46); since
no outward signs are mentioned in this connection, it must refer to
the divine revelation that follows.

16. I will make: The use of an infinitive absolute in Heb. (cf.
also the oracles in 2 Kg. 4:43; 5:10) conveys the rush of the divine
oracle, and means literally 'A making of this dry stream-bed full of
pools!' (cf. Burney, pp. 269ff.). The imperative of other *EVV* (cf.
the Gk.), 'Make', implies human activity, with the possibility that
the army on Elisha's instructions was to dig pools or trenches in the
valley to trap the flood water that was soon to come. Gray (p. 487),
accepting that this is a correct interpretation of the circumstances,
thinks that this was the obvious expedient of tapping the water-
table. The rendering of the infinitive absolute by the finite verb, **I
will make**, as in *RSV*, or impersonally, 'pools will form', as in
NEB, does not allow for human co-operation, which, according to
another possible interpretation of the passage, cannot be allowed,

because the phenomenon described in vv. 22, 23 is produced by the sun shining on natural pools and not on artificially made trenches (Burney, p. 270). The rendering of the infinitive absolute as an emphatic and explosive statement, rather than an imperative, is to be preferred (Schmitt, *op. cit.*, p. 205), whatever details of procedure are envisaged. The abrupt form of the oracle in v. 16 denotes its originality as part of the prophetic revision, and, despite the possible discrepancy between filling the valley with pools in v. 16 and filling the whole valley with water (v. 17), this verse is not a secondary addition to the original oracle preserved in v. 17 (as argued by Reiser, *ThZ* 9 [1953], pp. 323–35). The main discrepancy here lies between vv. 16–17 and vv. 20ff., with the former being part of the prophetic revision of the original narrative preserved in the latter section. **this dry stream-bed**: The Heb. *nāḥāl* is variously rendered as 'valley' (*NIV*; Montgomery, p. 351), 'wadi' (Gray, p. 483) or 'ravine' (*NEB*). Several clues in the text facilitate the identification of the valley; it was on Moab's frontier (v. 21), and its water flowed from the direction of Edom (v. 20). It was probably the *Wadi el-Hesa*, which formed a boundary between Edom and Moab and was at times coloured by a red sandstone (Šanda II, p. 21; Glueck, *op. cit.*, pp. 148ff.).

17. **You shall not see wind or rain**: Elisha predicted what is usually called a cloud-burst or *sayl*. As noted by Gray (p. 487), had the army been placed on the western escarpment of Edom, it would have experienced the prevailing west wind and its accompanying rainfall. Since it was encamped in the eastern marshland, it was sheltered from the wind and only experienced a flood from a remote rainstorm. At this particular time of the year (the autumn, before the commencement of the winter rains, according to Šanda II, p. 19), such rainstorms may have been usual; but Elisha's prediction of a sudden and heavy rainfall gives it the character of a miracle. **your cattle, and your beasts**: Luc. reads 'your army' for **your cattle** (in Heb. *maḥᵉnēḵem* for *miqnēḵem*) as in v. 9, which has been accepted by many older commentators (such as Klostermann, p. 399, and Kittel, p. 194). Recent commentators and translators, viewing Luc. as an attempt to correct the Heb. to achieve consistency between this verse and v. 9, accept that the more difficult MT is the original. Possibly a distinction is to be drawn between **cattle**, the army's food supply, and **beasts**, the luggage animals (Šanda II, p. 21).

18–19. These two verses belong together; v. 18 contains a general statement that **he will . . . give the Moabites into your hands**, and v. 19, based on v. 25 in the original narrative, gives a more detailed account of the conquest of Moab. Whereas v. 17 contains a divine

oracle, introduced by 'thus says the LORD', vv. 18–19 refer to the
Lord in the 3rd person and are not a continuation of v. 17. These
two verses must contain Elisha's own comment on the oracle in
v. 17 and an exposition of it; it is characteristic of prophetical
revelation that a divine oracle is often combined with the prophet's
commentary to bring out its meaning (Schweizer, *op. cit.*, p. 31).
This extension of the divine oracle contains two elements—a
prophetical comment (v. 18) and an elaboration which connects it
more closely to the original narrative (v. 19; cf. v. 25). **and every
choice city**: This phrase is absent from one MS and the Gk. and is
obviously a doublet of the preceding phrase.

20. The original narrative, which has been interrupted by the
insertion in vv. 9*b*–19, is now continued. The note of time in this
verse presumably refers to the morning following the seven days
circuitous march of v. 9. **the time of offering the sacrifice** in the
morning was at the break of dawn (cf. Mishnah, *Tamid* 3:2); it is
to be distinguished from the daily offering of 1 Kg. 18:29, which
was celebrated in the late afternoon or early evening. **water came
from the direction of Edom, till the country was filled with water**:
The reference to Edom is not superfluous and an insertion to provide
a deliberate word-play on 'red (*'aḏummîm*) in v. 22 (as suggested by
Montgomery, p. 362); in view of the location of the forces (see
above, on v. 8) this is a correct description. The waters filled the
country, and were not confined to the stream-bed and its pools as
in vv. 16–17; but there is no need to relate this statement to the
prophetical insertion by claiming that the water was trapped in the
trenches described in those verses (as by Gray, p. 488). The *sayl*
often produced a heavy and devastating flood (Montgomery, *ibid.*).

21. were called out: This is a technical term for calling to arms.
The youngest age at which young men were called to military service
is defined by Gray (p. 489) as about eleven or twelve years old. **and
were drawn up at the frontier**: The scene is located on the frontier
between Edom and Moab, and more specifically to the south-east
of Moab (cf. v. 8).

22. The Moabites saw the water opposite them as red as blood:
That the rising sun shining on the water gave it the appearance of
blood is not improbable in this area. As noted under v. 16, the
waters of the *Wadi el-Hesa* were at times coloured by red sandstone.
Mirages have often been experienced in this region too, especially
in the desert of the Dead Sea area (Šanda II, p. 22).

23. This is blood; the kings have surely fought one another:
Although reasons were at hand for the appearance of water as blood,
the interpretation offered by the Moabites seems absurd. Among
the attempts to excuse them for their conclusion can be listed: the

fact that they did not know of the cloudburst, or that it was not the water itself, but, combined with it, the confused movement of men and animals that gave them the impression of hostilities, or again that the similarity of the water to blood was taken as a favourable omen (Gray, p. 489). Whatever the reason for the deception of the Moabites, and whether the tradition was derived from a credible source or from the narrator's view of the events, the content of v. 23 is inserted in the narrative to emphasize that the Moabites made a false move for which they suffered heavy defeat. **have surely fought one another**: This is the correct rendering of the Heb. $\d{h}\bar{a}rab$, which generally means 'to be devastated'; but in this case is a denominative verb from $\d{h}ereb$, 'sword' (Burney, pp. 270ff.).

24. The change of subject that occurs twice in the last half of this verse must be noted—**till they fled** (the Moabites) **before them** (the Israelites); **and they went forward** (the Israelites). The Heb. for **slaughtering the Moabites as they went** is impossible, and this generally accepted translation is obtained from the Gk.

25. and they overthrew the cities: As noted by Gray (p. 488), over sixty Iron Age settlements have been discovered in Moab, although it is likely that the country's defences were more fully organised after the date of Mesha's revolt. In the present campaign it appears that once the border fortresses had been conquered, the allied armies could march unhindered to the capital (cf. van Zyl, *The Moabites*, pp. 61ff.). **till only its stones were left in Kir-hareseth**: *NEB*, 'until only in Kir-hareseth were any buildings left standing'. *RSV*'s translation, like the Heb. original, is clumsy. The simplest solution is to emend the text slightly by reading '$^{a}b\bar{a}neyh\bar{a}$, 'its stones', as $l^{e}badd\bar{a}h$, 'only', thus translating 'until only Kir-hareseth remained' (cf. *BHS*; Schmitt, *op. cit.*, p. 206). This slight change is preferred to the more complicated emendations proposed by Burney (pp. 271f.) and Gray (p. 484). **Kir-hareseth**: The Vsns., because they did not recognize it as a proper name, offer various translations (see Montgomery, p. 366). Undoubtedly the reference here is to Moab's capital, also called Kir-haraseth, in Isa. 16:7, Kir-heres in Isa. 16:11; Jer. 48:31, and Kir Moab in Isa. 15:1. **Kir-haraseth**, probably meaning 'strong city', is usually identified with Kerak ('the fortress') as was done by the Targ. of Isaiah and Jeremiah. Kerak was an impregnable fortress controlling the route from north to south in the direction of the Red Sea (*BHH II*, col. 952).

26. opposite the king of Edom: *NEB*, 'through to the king of Aram'. Two possible ways of dealing with this text are reflected in the translations offered by *RSV* and *NEB*. (i) *NEB*'s supposition is that Mesha attempted to break out to reach an ally, presumably Damascus (Aram), and not Edom, which was in alliance with Israel

and Judah. In favour of this interpretation it can be noted that the
Latin reads 'Aram' for **Edom**, and that the king of Damascus, being
hostile to Israel and holding Ramoth-gilead, would be a natural ally
to seek. cf. Gray (p. 484) and Montgomery (p. 363). (ii) Behind
RSV lies the suggestion that he was attempting to make a breach
'opposite' or 'against' the king of Edom, the weakest partner in the
triple alliance (see on v. 9). In favour of this interpretation is the
total absence of Aram from the context, as well as its distance from
the scene of battle. It is more likely that Moab's plan of action was
to concentrate its efforts against the most vulnerable of the allies
(cf. Schmitt, *op. cit.*, p. 206; van Zyl, *op. cit.*, p. 142).

27. **and offered him for a burnt offering upon the wall**: The
offering of the firstborn on the wall of the besieged city was intended
to pacify Chemosh, the Moabite deity, because the disasters that
befell Moab were attributed to his anger, 'for Chemosh was angry
with his land' (*Mesha Inscription l.5*). Sacrifice of this kind in circumstances of extreme emergency is attested elsewhere (Šanda *II*, p.
24; Montgomery, p. *363*; Frazer, *The Golden Bough III*, ch. 13;
Derchain, *VT* 20 [1970], pp. 351–5). See also on 2 Kg. 16:3. **And
there came great wrath upon Israel**: As shown by Montgomery
(*ibid.*), early translations and commentaries avoided the implication
of this phrase, for it refers not to any action taken by Moab but to
divine wrath against Israel. It has to be asked, however, whether it
was wrath executed by Yahweh or by Chemosh; this question is
avoided by those who explain the wrath as a plague (Šanda II,
p. 24), or else explain the word **anger** as 'dismay', referring to
Israel's commiseration with the Moabites (cf. the Gk.; Josephus,
Ant. IX.3.2; Schmitt, *op. cit.*, p. 35; Gray, pp. 490f.). On balance,
it seems that the implication here is that the wrath of Chemosh
drove out the Israelites. It was Chemosh that had control over the
land of Moab, and the supposition behind the extreme act of sacrifice
was that he could be roused to action. Although it is not explicitly
stated, v. 27*b* contains the immediate result of the action taken in
v. 27*a*; in other words Chemosh caused panic among the Israelites,
cf. the *Mesha Inscription*, 'he . . . let me see my desire upon my
adversaries' (l.4). The acceptance of this interpretation does not
imply (as has been argued by Kittel, p. 196, and Šanda II, p. 24)
that the original reference to Chemosh has been deleted.

(iii) Elisha the wonder worker **4:1–44**
Four incidents depicting Elisha as a worker of miracles are reported
in this chapter: the provision of oil for a widow (vv. 1–7), the
resuscitation of the Shunammite's son (vv. 8–37), Elisha and 'death
in the pot' (vv. 38–41), and the miraculous feeding of a hundred

men (vv. 42–44). The material contained here obviously belongs to the same collection of wonder narratives as 2 Kg. 6:1–23 and 8:1–6. In seeking to trace the history of this material before and after its inclusion in the narrative collection, the following factors have to be taken into consideration: the different modes of referring to Elisha, sometimes by his proper name and sometimes by the title 'man of God'; the possible signs that a secular narrative has acquired theological accretions; the evidence for suggesting that there has been a conflation of sources or subsequent revision of the narratives.

The narrative about the birth and later resuscitation of the Shunammite's son in vv. 8–37 constitutes the main body of the chapter, and Schmitt (*Elisa*, pp. 89ff.) seems to have drawn a valid distinction between narratives and anecdotes, finding the former in vv. 8–37 and 2 Kg. 6:8–23, and the latter in vv. 1–7, 38–41 and 2 Kg. 6:1–7. Based on the more detailed analysis offered by Schmitt (*op. cit.*, pp. 93–9), three stages in the development of the narrative can be traced: (i) At the latter end of the process, a narrative that lacked any theological interest whatsoever was theologised by means of three short additions. The reference in v. 33*b* to Elisha's prayer to the Lord has introduced a new element to the semi-magical practice of vv. 33–35; to appreciate the full significance of this addition it is to be noted that the verb for praying only occurs here and in a similar addition in 2 Kg. 6:8 within the Elisha complex. Another addition that introduces a mention of the Lord and of his power is found in v. 27*b*. Although the Lord is not mentioned in v. 17*b*, Schmitt finds an addition in the phrase 'as Elisha had said to her' (cf. 2 Kg. 6:18) and also accepts that the difficult 'about that time the following spring' came in with the addition to connect it more firmly with the narrative. (ii) Accepting that the narrative in vv. 8–37, without its theological accretions, is not in its original form, Schmitt rightly rejects the view that it is a conflation of two sources (as suggested by example by Benzinger, p. 137), and favours the idea that an original narrative has been later revised by the redactor of the wonder narratives collection (cf. Kilian, *BZ* 10 [1966], pp. 51–6, but with many modifications by Schmitt). Verses 29–33*a*, 35 are regarded as additional for the following reasons: they use the Heb. *na'ar* for 'child' (vv. 29, 30, 31, 32, 35) instead of *yeled*(vv. 18, 26); it is in these verses that the motif of Elisha's staff is introduced (vv. 29–32), and with it the personal intervention of Elisha is emphasized; the addition too gives Gehazi a more prominent place than hitherto (vv. 29–32); a confirmation of the child's death in v. 32 heightens the miraculous element; v. 35 unnecessarily repeats the act of synanachrosis, which has already been reported in v. 34. Some indications that they have been added are also found in vv. 13–15; v. 15 is a repetition of v. 12, and this is interpreted by Schmitt as a deliberate repetition to join an addition to the original narrative (cf. Kuhl, *ZAW* 64 [1952], pp. 1–11) and v. 16 can be read immediately after v. 12. (iii) Since vv. 17*b* and 32 have been designated as later additions, the only remaining reference to Elisha is found in v. 8; elsewhere he is called 'the man of God' (vv. 9, 16, 21, 22, 25, 27). This would suggest that originally this was a narrative about an unnamed 'man of God', who was later identified with Elisha by the addition of his name in v. 8. In v. 25 this man of God is located in Carmel, and so it can be accepted that an original tradition about an unnamed man of God from Carmel was secondarily connected with Elisha (cf. Schmitt, *op. cit.*, pp. 153ff.).

Two of the anecdotes, vv. 1–7 and vv. 38–41, may have been originally connected with Elisha, but they have been more firmly embedded in their present context by the addition of the term 'man of God', confirming the identification of vv. 8–37. The first anecdote names Elisha twice in the opening verses (vv. 1, 2), and only at the very end is the term 'man of God' introduced, obviously to achieve a smoother transfer to the terminology of the following verses. Similarly, the prophet Elisha is named at the beginning of the second anecdote (v. 38), and only later is the term 'man of God' used. There is also a further attempt to bind this anecdote more firmly to its present context by adding a reference to Gilgal in v. 38, which is necessary because of the note in v. 25 suggesting that Elisha was at Carmel. It is preferable to regard both anecdotes as having originated from Gilgal (Schmitt, *op. cit.*, p. 156); there is no adequate reason for connecting vv. 1–7 with vv. 8–37, and deriving both from Carmel (as suggested by Gray, p. 491).

The final section, vv. 42–44, is very mixed. Elisha's words in v. 42*b* repeat words found in v. 41, and they are again repeated in v. 43*b*. Such phrases as 'for thus says the LORD' (v. 43) and 'according to the word of the LORD' (v. 44) are exceptional, as is the term 'servant' (*mᵉšārē*ṯ) in v. 43. Redactional activity is evident, and it may be that the section has grown out of an original tradition preserved in v. 42*a* about providing for the man of God.

1–7. Elisha's miraculous provision of food for a prophet's widow is a parallel for 1 Kg. 17:8–16, where Elijah provided for the widow of Zarephath. As noted above under 1 Kg. 17:1–24, it is probable that the Elijah narrative is dependent upon the Elisha tradition (Fohrer, *Elia*, pp. 35ff.; Schmitt, *op. cit.*, p. 15). In common with the anecdotes in vv. 38–41 and in 2 Kg. 6:1–7, the background of this narrative is the connection between Elisha and a group of prophets (vv. 1, 38; 6:1). Although v. 25 locates Elisha in Carmel (cf. also 2:25) and the impression is given that the location is the same for vv. 1–7, it has to be admitted that there is no evidence of a group of prophets in Carmel, only a man of God operating on his own (Schmitt, *ibid.*). The links between vv. 1–7 and both the anecdotes in vv. 38–41 and 2 Kg. 6:1–7 indicate that they have originated from among the prophetic group at Gilgal.

1. **the wife of one of the sons of the prophets**: Members of prophetic communities were permitted to marry, but it is not clear how they shared their time and commitments between the prophetic community and their own family and home. It may well be that community customs varied, cf. Šanda II, p. 27, who thinks that celibacy was practised in the larger communities of Bethel and Jericho. **Your servant my husband is dead**: The Targ. and Josephus (*Ant.* IX.4.2) have 'your servant Obadiah', and contain an extended reference to him based on 1 Kg. 18:4. Luc. has 'the servant of the Lord'. **and you know that your servant feared the LORD**: This phrase, which is an unnecessary intrusion breaking the sequence of the sentence, is regarded by Schmitt (*op. cit.*, p. 99) as a theologising accretion, which must be attributed to a reviser. **the creditor has come to take my two children to be his slaves**: Hebrew law allowed the selling of wife and children into slavery to settle a debt (cf. Exod. 21:7; Am. 2:6; 8:6; Isa. 50:1; Neh. 5:5, 8). Whereas the Code of Hammurabi (§ 117) provided for the release of those sold into slavery after three years, Hebrew law permitted them freedom in the year of jubilee (Lev. 25:39ff.).

2. **a jar of oil**: The word for **jar** (Heb. *'āsûk*) is not found elsewhere. It is unnecessary to render it as 'an anointing of oil' (enough for one anointing, with Burney, p. 273; cf. Gray, p. 491), for the word probably refers to a small pot or jar (Honeyman, *PEQ* 71 [1939], p. 79).

3–4. The preparations for the miracle are clearly set out in these two verses. Ample provision of utensils for the oil was encouraged, **empty vessels and not too few**; the flow of oil cannot be anything but a miracle—the prophet himself was not even present, and all happened behind closed doors with only **yourself and your sons** present; the flow of oil was plentiful, each vessel being filled in turn and **set aside** when full. Luc. adds to this verse the words 'and it shall not stay' (cf. v. 6*b*).

5–6. The instructions outlined in vv. 3, 4 were followed, and it was only after every vessel had been filled that **the oil stopped flowing**.

7. **the man of God**: As noted above, this anecdote consistently names Elisha until the final verse, which omits his name and refers to him as **the man of God**. This was obviously intentional in order to connect vv. 1–7 with vv. 8–37 and thus to identify Elisha with

the man of God. sell the oil and pay your debts: This rendering
of the Heb. (cf. *K-B*) is preferable to the Syr. and Vulg., 'repay
your creditor'. Oil was apparently of high value (cf. Sanda II,
pp. 28ff.).

8–37. Although this narrative is mainly concerned with the resuscitation of a child, it also goes back some years to the time when
Elisha was a guest at his mother's house and in gratitude for his
hospitality promises her a child. Both themes are found elsewhere
in the *OT*, the birth of a child to an elderly parent in return for
hospitality in Gen. 18:1–15, and the resuscitation of a child by a
prophet in 1 Kg. 17:17–24. Both themes are also well attested in
other oriental sources (Bronner, *Elijah and Elisha*, pp. 86–99,
106–22). There is no need, however, to suppose that two distinct
traditions have been fused here (as argued by Gressmann, *Geschichtsschreibung*, p. 393, and rejected by Gray, p. 492). A reference to
the circumstances of the child's birth was an integral part of the
resuscitation narrative (v. 28), and it seems, on the analysis
presented above, that an originally brief introduction about the
child's birth has been extended by the addition of vv. 13–15.

8. Shunem was on the border of Issachar (Jos. 19:18), on the
south-westerly slope of the hill of Moreh (*Nebi Dahi*), slightly south
of Mount Tabor and north of Jezreel (cf. *BHH III*, col. 1895).
Gray (pp. 494ff.) suggests that it was the seat of an oracle and the
home of a prophetic community which Elisha had just visited, but
it is more probable that he was passing through Shunem on his way
from Mount Carmel to Abel-meholah, where he lived. **a wealthy
woman:** *NEB*, 'great lady', is nearer the Heb. The woman was the
mistress of her house, able to offer free hospitality, and proud of
her family connections (v. 13). This suggests that she was a woman
of noble birth (cf. Ugaritic *att adrt*, according to Bronner, *op. cit.*,
p. 97), and had an eminent place in society (see further, Montgomery, p. 367).

9. a holy man of God: As noted above (p. 402), the prophet is
known in this section as **man of God**, and only by the addition of
the proper name in v. 8 is he identified with Elisha. The addition
of the adjective **holy** in this verse is an indication of the sacrosanct
nature of the prophet's status, rather than a pronouncement bearing
a moral connotation. Gray (p. 495) bases the arrangements made by
the woman to accommodate the prophet on her desire to avoid
contact with the holy man, for it would be unsafe for the family to
have contact with him by entertaining him in their own quarters.
Other evidence from the *OT* to confirm that contact with the
prophets was avoided is not produced, and it would seem more
reasonable to suggest that she simply wished to offer permanent and

comfortable hospitality arrangements for the prophet because of her belief that he would bring a blessing to her house.

10. a small roof chamber with walls: Adding **with walls** (Heb. *qîr*) to the description of the chamber may suggest that the walls were built up to make a permanent dwelling on the roof, in contrast to temporary arbours erected on the roof to accommodate guests (cf. 1 Sam. 9:26; 2 Sam. 16:22). Montgomery (p. 368) proposes to read *qîr* as *qôr* and to translate as 'a cool upper chamber' (cf. Jg. 3:20ff.).

12. Gehazi his servant: The unsuitable meaning 'valley of vision' (*BDB*) proposed for Gehazi (cf. Isa. 22:5) must be rejected in favour of Gray's suggestion (p. 495) that it is connected with an Arab. root meaning 'to be avaricious'; cf. especially 2 Kg. 5:20ff. Gehazi here takes an intermediary position between the prophet and the Shunammite; cf. also vv. 29ff. But the prominence given to Gehazi is mostly derived from a later revision of the narrative (cf. vv. 13-15, 29-31), apart from this present verse where he is sent to call the woman. **she stood before him**: In view of a later reference to her standing 'in the doorway' (v. 15), it is assumed that on this first occasion she stood before Gehazi. In order to avoid this difficulty, the phrase 'she stood before him' is sometimes rendered as 'she presented herself' (Montgomery, p. 368), or else made to refer to both men (Šanda II, p. 30). If vv. 13-15 are secondary, as suggested above, the original narrative simply relates how the woman, after coming to Elisha's presence, was given the message of v. 16.

13. you have taken all this trouble for us: This is an adequate rendering of the Heb. and does not read too much into the text, as is the case with the suggestion to render as 'to show solicitous deference' and to relate the sentence to the fear of infringing the sanctity of the prophet (see Gray, p. 495). **to the king or to the commander of the army**: This verse thinks of the prophet as a man of some influence in court and military circles. Gray (*ibid.*) dates the incident at a later period when the prophet lived in Samaria. Accepting that this verse is part of a later addition, it can be suggested that it reflects possibly a later concept of the prophet's status. The meaning is that the prophet is offering to secure for her elderly husband some relief from providing and equipping men for military service; but the woman seems to have understood him to be offering further favours such as protection or perhaps more possessions. **I dwell among my own people**: The woman's refusal indicates that she lived among her own relations, who would be willing to protect her and look after her interests. Gray (p. 496) finds in this a reflection of the ready acceptance of social responsibilities among settlements of kin-groups.

14. According to the revised version of this narrative the proposal for an adequate reward comes from Gehazi. It is in this revised form too that reference is made to the fact that **her husband is old**, thus establishing a connection between this version and the narrative about the birth of a son to elderly parents in Gen. 18.

16. At this season, when the time comes round: cf. Gen. 18:10, 14. Both phrases appear in the birth of Isaac narrative, the former coming in Gen. 18:14 as a parallel to the latter. The meaning of the phrase translated in *RSV* as **when the time comes round** (Heb. *kāʿēt ḥayyāh*) is uncertain. *NEB* has 'this time next year' (cf. *NIV*). Burney (p. 274) takes it to indicate the time of reviving, which was the spring. Skinner (*Genesis*, p. 301) proposes to read *ḥayyāh* as a noun denoting the period of pregnancy; cf. its use in late Heb. to denote a pregnant woman. If this suggestion is accepted, the phrase can be rendered 'according to the time of pregnancy' (Montgomery, p. 369) or 'according to the time of gestation' (Gray, *ibid.*).

17. about that time the following spring: In Heb. the phrase is identical with the previously discussed one in v. 16, and is an unnecessary repetition. **as Elisha had said to her**: *RSV*'s **as** is based on the Gk., which is slightly different from the Heb. reading of 'which'. Schmitt (*op. cit.*, p. 94) attributes this phrase to a reviser; the use of the proper name **Elisha** was not part of the original narrative, and the claim that the prophet had foretold an event has been similarly added in 2 Kg. 6:18.

18. When the child had grown: Šanda (II, p. 31), taking into consideration the fact that the lad was placed on his mother's lap, estimates that he was five or six years old.

19. Oh, my head, my head!: The boy had probably been out in the extremely hot weather and suffered a sunstroke, which is a more plausible explanation than the suggestion that he suffered a sudden attack of typhoid fever, also common in the Orient (see Šanda, *ibid.*). A similar account is given of the death of Manasses in Jdt. 8:2, 3.

21. and shut the door upon him: Gray (*ibid.*), following Gressmann (*Geschichtsschreibung*, p. 293), attaches significance to the closing of the door, which is interpreted as a deliberate move to retain the *nepeš* or life essence; although the *nepeš* was dissociated from the body, death was not final until the burial of the body. There may, however, be a more practical reason for shutting the door, namely, that the woman wished to conceal her child's death until she had visited the prophet. This also explains why she moved the child to the guest-chamber reserved for the prophet, and did not mention his death even to her husband (cf. v. 23; see Šanda, *ibid.*).

22. that I may quickly go to the man of God, and come back again: Although the distance from Shunem to Carmel was about 25 km, it seems that the woman intended to travel there and back in the same day.

23. It is neither new moon nor sabbath: Both are linked together in Am. 8:5; Hos. 2:11; Isa. 1:13f. The **new moon**, the first day of the new moon, was celebrated from ancient times (cf. Isa. 1:13ff.; Num. 28:11-15) and was a day of rest (Am. 8:5). See further, de Vaux, *Ancient Israel*, pp. 469ff. Whatever the connection between the origin of the Israelite **sabbath** and the Babylonian *šappatu*, the day of the full moon, or the Canaanite seven-day periods, or the practice of Kenite blacksmiths of abstaining from gathering wood and making fire on their day of rest, it appears from the *OT* that the observance of the sabbath had a distinctive significance in the life of Israel (cf. Exod. 20:8; Dt. 5:12; Lev. 23:3); it was held regularly every seventh day and not according to lunar phases, and it retained the main characteristic of its early origin as a day of rest (de Vaux, *op. cit.*, pp. 475–83). Significantly the husband's reply in this verse assumes that the acceptable time for consulting a prophet was on these rest days, **new moon nor sabbath**. This is taken as evidence that a prophet was normally consulted for oracular guidance on festival days at the sanctuary to which he was attached (Johnson, *Cultic Prophet*, pp. 25ff.). In this case, the sanctuary was Carmel. **It will be well**: The woman's reply was brief, the single word of the Heb. (*šālôm*) being translated as 'All is well' (Gray, p. 497) or 'It's all right' (*NIV*). By being intentionally brief, she avoided telling her husband that the boy was dead, and thus, according to Gray (*ibid.*), prevented him from finalizing the boy's death by responding to the news with words of lamentation.

24. Urge the beast on: The servant travelled on foot, leading the ass on which the lady was seated.

25. The repetition of the phrase **the man of God** in this verse is superfluous. Luc. substitutes the prophet's name for the second occurrence. Schmitt (*op. cit.*, p. 204) omits the first, and reads v. 25a as 'so she set out towards Mount Carmel'. **Gehazi his servant**: The introduction of **Gehazi** is similar to that of v. 12, and on this occasion too he only played a minor role. But, exactly as the extension of vv. 13–15 gave him more prominence at the time of the child's birth, so the addition in vv. 29ff. attributes to him a more important part in the resuscitation drama.

26. It is well: With the same curt reply as she had given her husband in v. 23, the woman deliberately refuses to divulge the reason for her mission to Gehazi. She was determined not to mention the boy's death to anyone but the prophet, and so again avoided the condolences and lamentation that would make his death more conclusive.

27. she caught hold of his feet: This was a sign of obeisance and respect; cf. Jn. 11:32. **for she is in bitter distress**: lit. 'for her soul is bitter'. Gray (p. 494) has 'she is deeply embittered'. **and the LORD has hidden it from me, and has not told me**: The point made is that Elisha had not received a divine revelation concerning the boy's death, as he had, for instance, when he was able to follow Gehazi's moves as is reported in 2 Kg. 5:26. Schmitt (*op. cit.*, p. 93) thinks that this statement belongs to the same category as the reference in v. 17*b* to Elisha's ability to foretell the boy's birth, and so he attributes both to the same reviser of the original narrative. Admittedly, this sentence can be omitted without any substantial effect on the narrative.

28. Did I ask my lord for a son?: This sentence recalls the fact that Elisha had promised her a son unbidden, for the woman herself had not made this request of him. Her second question, **Did I not say, Do not deceive me?**, echoes the words of v. 16.

29. As noted above (p. 401), the mission of Gehazi with Elisha's staff in his hand is regarded as a secondary accretion. The introduction of the staff motif is unexpected, and its presence has been attributed to the conflation of sources, one suggesting that resuscitation was achieved through Elisha's staff, and the other claiming that Elisha himself was personally involved in the miracle (cf. Benzinger, p. 137; Kilian, *op. cit.*, pp. 51–6). Naturally, in conflating the sources, precedence was given to the latter, and the staff motif was degraded. But, Schmitt (*op. cit.*, pp. 93ff.), because of the coincidence of the staff motif with both the use of the word *na'ar* for the boy and the more significant role played by the servant Gehazi, rightly regards vv. 29ff. as a later revision of the original narrative.

It is not easy to understand the exact implication of the two instructions **take my staff in your hand** and then **lay my staff upon the face of the child**. Gray (p. 498), accepting that the staff was a vehicle of man's power and prestige, as in the case of Jacob (Gen. 38:18) and Moses (Exod. 4:1–4; 17:8–13), suggests that Gehazi preceded Elisha carrying his staff as a guarantee of the prophet's personal engagement in the affair. Bronner (*op. cit.*, p. 121), on the other hand, thinks that Gehazi went ahead to guard the child's body and to prevent it being buried before the prophet arrived; it is presumed that Elisha would not arrive until the following morning and that the boy's death would by then be known to his father. Whatever the reason for sending Gehazi in advance with the prophet's staff, the following points are evident: since Elisha himself was following with the mother, Gehazi was not sent to revive the child; in view of the comment in v. 31 that 'there was no sound or sign of life', it can be assumed that Gehazi attempted resuscitation; in the present form of the narrative a contrast is obviously intended between Gehazi's unsuccessful mission and Elisha's personal success. **If you meet anyone, do not salute him**: There is no need to restrict the application of this instruction to the mourners who would by now have gathered at the home (as suggested by Šanda II, p. 32). It must rather be taken as an instruction to make haste and to consider the errand as one of utmost urgency (cf. Lk. 10:4).

30. I will not leave you: As in v. 26, the woman does not put her trust in Gehazi, but attaches herself to the prophet himself.

31. The child was not awaked: With this phrase Gehazi is probably reporting his own furtive attempt to revive the child through the use of Elisha's staff; but, as noted above, it was not Elisha's intention that Gehazi should attempt to resuscitate the child.

32. he saw the child lying dead on his bed: This confirmation of the child's death serves to heighten the miraculous nature of Elisha's action.

33. Verse 33a, according to Schmitt (*ibid.*), continues the revision of the wonder narrative found in vv. 29-30a and 35, whilst v. 33b is attributed to a different revision, which has here and there added a more theological tone to the narrative. The statement that he **prayed to the LORD** has a parallel in the accretion to 2 Kg. 6:18; in this particular case, it adds a new dimension, namely, that of divine power, to a passage that described contactual magic.

34. The two foremost elements in the resuscitation of the child in 1 Kg. 17:21 are prayer and bodily contact. According to the details given here, there was contact of mouth, eyes and hands; because the child was considerably shorter, it was necessary for the prophet to take up a crouching position. Gray's translation (p. 494) 'he crouched over him' gives a better rendering of the Heb. verb *gāhar* (cf. 1 Kg. 18:42) than *RSV*'s 'stretched himself upon him' and *NEB*'s 'pressed upon him'. The prophet evidently practised a form of magic that aimed at transferring life to the organs of one party from another by bringing them into contact with each other. The result is expressed in the statement that **the flesh of the child became warm**.

35. Schmitt (*ibid.*) rightly regards this verse as an accretion from the hand of a reviser. A repetition of the synanachrosis is unnecessary in view of the signs of life mentioned at the end of v. 34; it was probably added under the influence of 1 Kg. 17:21, where the resuscitation rite is repeated three times. The prophet **walked once to and fro in the house** to relax himself after his physical and spiritual exertion (Montgomery, p. 369; Gray, p. 499). **the child sneezed seven times**: Sneezing was a proof that the child had breath; its occurrence **seven times** is obviously based on popular associations of perfection with the magical figure seven.

36–37. The narrative is suitably concluded, as in 1 Kg. 17:24, with returning the son to his mother (v. 36) and an acclamation of the prophet by the mother (v. 37).

38–41. As noted above (p. 402), this section relating the narrative of death in the pot is an independent wonder-narrative, and the only secondary material here is the introductory phrase recording Elisha's return to Gilgal. The fact that the narrative stands in its present position in this collection of wonder-narratives has made the addition necessary, for the previous section locates Elisha in Mount Carmel.

38. Gilgal: As seen under 2 Kg. 2:1, the identification of Gilgal with the sanctuary between Jericho and the Jordan mentioned in Jos. 4:19ff.; 5:8ff. has been disputed (especially by Thenius, p. 270). But there is no conclusive reason for rejecting the Jordanian sanctuary and its identification with *Khirbet el-Mafjar* (Schmitt, *op. cit.*, pp. 158–62). **when there was a famine in the land**: The Heb. refers to 'the famine', which may suggest that it was the seven-year famine of 2 Kg. 8:1ff. **as the sons of the prophets were sitting before him**: This phrase, which depicts a number of prophets **sitting before** a leader or teacher for instruction, is significant for reconstructing the life and customs of the early prophetic communities. Montgomery (p. 369) attaches some weight to the connection between the verb *yāšab*, 'to sit' and the noun *yᵉšîbāh*, 'session, school', which appears in Sir. 51:29 and has remained as a technical term in Judaism (Haldar, *Associations*, p. 143; Johnson, *Cultic Prophet*, p. 17). The suggestion that Elisha instructed the other members of the school, together with the fact that he assumed responsibility for preparing the meal, indicates that he was the leader of the Gilgal community.

39. herbs: The word is not found elsewhere, but *K-B* identifies the plants as 'dwarf mallows'. The **wild vine** was probably a twining plant growing out in the open fields. **a lap full**: lit. 'garment full'. The custom of folding upwards the skirt of a mantle to form a large bag is well known. **wild gourds**: These are usually identified with the *Citrullus colocynthus*, which produces greenish yellow fruit about the size of a large orange or small melon, and are also known as 'Sodom's apple' (cf. Harland, *BA* 6 [1943], pp. 49ff.; Dalman, *Sites and Ways*, pp. 81ff.). These gourds are described as pungent and possessing strong purgative properties (*K-B*). **not knowing what they were**: *RSV* follows the Vsns. in reading a singular verb and thus referring it back to the one who went out to gather herbs. The plural verb of MT would suggest that the whole community did not recognize the fruit.

40. there is death in the pot: The reaction of the community members to the food presented to them is probably due to the supposed connection between bitter or ill-seasoned food and poison. Taken in small dosage the gourds were not poisonous, but taken in large quantities they could prove fatal.

41. bring meal: Elisha's action was probably an act of imitative magic, whereby he introduces wholesome meal into the pot to counteract the poison. Possibly too, as he was throwing it into the pot, he spoke words that were meant to counteract the words 'there is death in the pot'. Gray (p. 500) refers to a more recent tradition of using meal as a charm against supernatural influence.

42-44. As already suggested (p. 402), this narrative, which is probably unconnected with the previous anecdote in vv. 38-41, may have grown out of a simple account in v. 42a of how provision was made for the man of God. The extension, which has been composed by means of repetition, has turned the account of providing for the prophet into a narrative of miraculous provision for a hundred men.

42. Baalshalishah: The Gk. reads Bethsareisa, which may be identified with *Khirbet Sarisiyeh*, about 22 km. north of Lydda, or perhaps with *Kefr Thilth* (Arab. *tult* = Heb. *šālîš*), a couple of kilometres further north. **bread of the first fruits**: *NEB*, 'new season's bread'. The reference probably is to bread baked from the first milling of the season, which was offered as first fruits to God (Lev. 23:20). It may be that Elisha had appropriated the first fruits to prepare a sacramental meal, or else the first fruits were brought to the prophets as well as the priests (cf. Schmitt, *op. cit.*, p. 100). **fresh ears of grain in his sack**: The two Heb. words *wᵉkarmel bᵉṣiqlônô* have been variously interpreted. The word *karmel* is used elsewhere of fresh corn; cf. Lev. 2:14, where it is mentioned as a cereal offering. *bᵉṣiqlônô*, 'in his sack', although not translated by the Gk., was understood traditionally as meaning some form of carrier for the grain offering, 'in his garment' (Syr., Targ.) or 'in his bag' (Vulg.). A new meaning has been proposed on the basis of Ugaritic texts, which use the word *bṣql* for a part of a plant (cf. Gordon, *Textbook III*, no. 499, p. 375; Aistleitner, *Wörterbuch*, no. 563; Cohen, *Hapaxlegomena*, pp. 112ff.). The translation 'fresh corn in its ears' has been proposed (Bronner, *op. cit.*, p. 84), or else 'plants of his orchard' (accepting a transposition of two words; Gray, p. 501). Because of difficulty in handling the meaning proposed on the basis of Ugaritic usage, there is much in favour of the traditional rendering (cf. Schmitt, *op. cit.*, p. 211). **Give them to the men, that they may eat**: These words echo vv. 41ff.

43. a hundred men: Elsewhere too the prophets are counted in convenient round figures of fifty or a hundred (1 Kg. 18:4). **for thus says the LORD**: This phrase is not found elsewhere in this collection of wonder-narratives, although it is found in the prophetic revision of war narratives (cf. 2 Kg. 3:16, 17; 7:1) and in the historical section covering the revolt of Jehu (cf. 2 Kg. 9:26; 10:17).

44. and had some left: The miracle here is that a hundred men were fed with twenty loaves and some fresh grain or fruit (depending on the translation of v. 42), and had some to spare. As Gray comments (p. 502), the figures are restrained in comparison with the figures given in the *NT* accounts of feeding multitudes (cf. Mt. 14:13–21; 15:32–39; Mk. 6:30–44; 8:1–10; Lk. 9:10–17).

(iv) The healing of Naaman from Syria 5:1–27
Superficially this narrative in its present form appears to possess unity; it progresses smoothly from the healing of Naaman to the greed of Gehazi and its punishment, and there seems to be a deliberate and dramatic contrast between Naaman being a leper at its beginning and Gehazi being a leper at the end (Gressmann, *Geschichtsschreibung*, p. 297). But on closer analysis, it can be suggested that the chapter is a combination of three independent sections, each with a different theme and a different aim (so Gunkel, *Elisa*, pp. 38, 42, followed now by Schmitt, *Elisa*, pp. 78–80).

This first section of the present narrative, vv. 1–14, gives an account of the healing of Naaman, the Syrian commander, and because it illustrates the power of Elisha to heal, has the character of a wonder-narrative. Its theme is brought out in v. 8, 'that they may know that there is a prophet in Israel'. It has been classified as a 'derision narrative' (*BHH II*, col. 1279), which by demonstrating the helplessness of Syrian religion emphasizes the superiority of Israelite faith. It is the final literary form of the narrative, especially the connection of vv. 1–14 with v. 15, that gives it this character; when separated and treated on its own it provides another example of the miraculous power of Elisha.

Although the close link between v. 15 and vv. 1–14 favours the treatment of vv. 1–19 as a unit (as is done by Gray, pp. 502ff.), there are reasons for treating vv. 15–19a as a separate section. The theme is different: whereas vv. 1–14 prove 'that there is a prophet in Israel', vv. 15–19a are concerned with the theme that there is no God 'but the LORD' and with the problem of acknowledging him by pagans living in a different environment. There is also a significant difference of terminology: whereas vv. 15–19a abstain from referring to Elisha by name, vv. 1–14 consistently use the proper name (vv. 8, 9, 10). Obviously, therefore, an appendix has been added to the healing of Naaman from the so-called 'man of God' tradition. Schmitt, however, believes that vv. 15b–16 belong to the following Gehazi episode (as is evident from the use of the phrase 'as the LORD lives' in vv. 16 and 20 and also the verb 'and he urged him' in vv. 16 and 23), and that the content of the original proselyte narrative is preserved in vv. 17–19a. A difficulty in Schmitt's thesis here is that the title 'man of God' is not used at all in vv. 17–19a, only in the section which he separates and attaches to the Gehazi episode. It must be assumed that the proselyte narrative was the last addition to the chapter, and that the reviser responsible for its addition inserted it in the middle of the Gehazi episode, which he revised by inserting the title 'man of god' at its beginning.

An expansion of the Naaman narrative appears in vv. 19b–27 (so Schmitt; but vv. 20–27, according to Gray, pp. 508ff.). Gehazi has now become the central character, although he was not even mentioned in the original narrative. In v. 10 it is a messenger that carries Elisha's message to Naaman, and Gehazi plays no part until vv. 19ff. The episode, which is found in vv. 15–16, 19b–27, has as its theme the severe criticism of a member of the prophetic guild for using his position to secure personal gain.

When these different narratives were joined together, some revision became necessary. The accretion of the Gehazi incident is probably responsible for the reference to Naaman's gifts inserted in v. 5b; the gift has no function in the original healing narrative and has probably been added to link the Gehazi addition to it. When the proselyte narrative of vv. 17–19a was added from 'the man of God' tradition, further revision became necessary. Because the original Naaman narrative and the later accretion in the Gehazi episode used the proper name Elisha, the reviser added to it the further title 'man of God' on two occasions (in v. 8 in the original narrative and in v. 20 in the additional incident), and thus created a double nomenclature, which has caused trouble for the Gk. in both instances. Furthermore, the phrase 'according to the word of the man of God' was added to v. 14, and only the title 'man of God' appears in v. 15. It is also probable that the proselyte narrative, with its acknowledgement of Yahweh as the only God, brought the phrase 'because by him the LORD had given victory to Syria', which was added to v. 1a.

Because of the picture given of Elisha as having a house in Samaria v. 9) and as being on friendly terms with the royal household (v.8), Schmitt (op. cit., p. 173) is of the opinion that the original narrative in vv. 1–14 contains some reliable information, which can be compared with the original Elisha narratives of the Gilgal tradition.

1. **Naaman**: The name, also found in the Arab. *Nu'man*, 'charming, pleasant', appears now in the Ras Shamra texts both as a proper name and as an epithet for royalty. **commander of the army of the king of Syria**: One MS and the Gk. omit **of the king**; but it makes no significant difference. **and in high favour**: *NEB*, 'highly esteemed'. The expression used here (Heb. *nᵉśû' pānîm*, 'lifted of face') denotes the king's act of raising the face of a petitioner as a sign of favour; it is found elsewhere (cf. Isa. 3:3; 9:15; Job 22:8; Est. 8:3f.). **because by him the LORD had given victory to Syria**: As noted by Šanda (II, p. 38), the universalistic conception given expression here is also found in vv. 17–18. The introduction of this idea into a narrative where it is completely incidental, together with the use of the name Yahweh, which is not found elsewhere in the narrative except in one dubious occurrence in v. 11, confirms the judgment that this phrase was added to vv. 1–14 when this section was joined by the proselyte narrative of vv. 17–19a. Attempts have been made to find a period for the incident by trying to establish when Syria gained a victory over Israel and also which Syrian king is being mentioned. Šanda suggests that the Syrian king must have reigned before Hazael, and thinks that the reign of Benhadad II (cf. 2 Kg. 8:7) is suitable. However, the incident cannot be dated with any certainty, nor is it possible to establish the historical reliability of the reference to Naaman, the Syrian commander, and of the tradition that he was healed by Elisha. **He was a mighty man of valour**: The phrase is omitted from Luc; it is superfluous and may have been a gloss on **great man. but he was a leper**: The root used for leprosy in the *OT* (Heb. *ṣr'*) refers to skin diseases in general and not to leprosy proper (*Elephantiasis graecorum*), which cannot be cured like the diseases described under the term leprosy in Lev. 13. A distinction is often drawn in Gk. between leprosy proper (*leprē*) and a white rash of the skin (*leukē*); cf. Herodotus 1.138; Hippocrates, *Progn.* 114; the former was especially prevalent in Syria. Naaman's access to the king would not have been permissible if he had leprosy proper, for those suffering from this disease were enforced into quarantine (cf. 2 Kg. 7:3; Num. 12:10ff.). See further, Köhler, *ZAW* 67 [1955], pp. 290f., and Hulse, *PEQ* 107 [1975], pp. 87–105, where leprosy is described as a scaly skin disease which did not call for segregation.

2. **on one of their raids**: The period was one of uneasy relationship between Syria and Israel; even when open warfare was checked, incursions over the border to seize property were frequent.

3. **the prophet who is in Samaria**: Significantly the word prophet

(*nābî'*) is used, and not 'man of God' as he is introduced elsewhere in the narrative. This corroborates the view that the man of God element belongs to a later revision. **He would cure him of his leprosy**: It is impossible to derive the meaning **cure** from the Heb. verb *'āsap*, 'to gather', which does not occur anywhere else with this meaning. A link is usually suggested between the Heb. *'āsap* and the Akkad. *ašāpu*, 'to practise exorcism, to exorcise' (Montgomery, p. 378; Gray, p. 505); admittedly it is not a straightforward connection, but the meaning 'healing' or 'curing' is demanded by the context.

5. I will send a letter to the king of Israel: Correspondence between kings seeking medical help was usual, as is testified by the many instances preserved in ancient texts. For instance, a letter sent from the Hittite king Hattusil to the king of Babylon *c.* 1275 BC shows that a Babylonian physician and exorcist had been sent to the Hittite court. Again there is a record of a prince sending a message to Rameses II of Egypt asking for help to cure his daughter Bentreseh (see the Bentreseh stele, *ANET*, pp. 29-31). The Amarna letters also report how Tušratta of Mitanni had sent a statue of Astarte of Nineveh to the sick Egyptian Pharaoh, Amenhotep III, because of its healing powers (cf. Knudtzon, *El-Amarna*, no. 23). **ten talents of silver, six thousand shekels of gold, and ten festal garments**: The exaggerated weight of silver and gold quoted here makes Naaman's gift to the Israelite king exorbitant; cf. also 1 Kg. 9:14. It is not necessary to take these figures seriously in view of the above suggestion that v. 5*b* was added to the original narrative when vv. 15-16, 19-27 were combined with it.

6. When this letter reaches you: The English translation misses the more formal introduction to the message of the letter with 'and now . . .' The preliminary greetings are omitted, and it is the business section that is opened with 'and now . . .', following the normal pattern of letter writing in the ancient East (Šanda II, p. 39; Gray, p. 505). **Naaman my servant**: Naaman's high office in the Syrian court is indicated by the fact that he was sent directly from the king to the Israelite king with a letter of introduction and request. **that you may cure him of his leprosy**: The king of Israel was not expected to act personally to heal him, despite some evidence that the king, according to an ancient tradition of kingship, possessed some healing powers (cf. Gray, *ibid.*). Addressing the request to the king merely subscribes to one of the fundamental principles of oriental society, namely that all subjects should obey any demands made by the king.

7. The Israelite king took the Syrian approach to be aimed directly at him personally, and interpreted it as an attempt to find an excuse for war. According to his presumed way of reasoning, a failure on his part to heal Naaman would lead to reprisals. In view of the custom noted above under v. 5, the king's reaction cannot be justified, even by noting (as is done by Gray) that the Syrian letter does not mention the prophet. This element has probably been introduced because of the author's wish to contrast the king's consternation with the prophet's confidence. **to kill and to make alive**: cf. Dt. 32:39; I Sam. 2:6. **seeking a quarrel with me**: *NEB*, 'he is picking a quarrel with me'.

8. Elisha the man of God: One element in this double reference to the prophet is superfluous, the proper name being omitted from Luc. and the title from the Codex Vaticanus. It has been suggested above that the original Naaman narrative referred to the prophet by his proper name, and that the title is an addition (cf. Schmitt, *op. cit.*, p. 212). **that he may know that there is a prophet in Israel**: In these words the prophet seems to be reproving the king for not directing Naaman to him for healing. In addition to the king's interpretation of the Syrian approach noted in v. 7, it is also possible that, because of prophetic criticism of the house of Ahab, he deliberately snubbed Elisha on this occasion and so prevented him from acquiring favour with the Syrian court. Elisha's message to the king may thus imply that Naaman, unlike the Israelite king, would recognize him as a prophet.

10. Elisha sent a messenger to him: Despite the appearance of Naaman with his horses and chariots at Elisha's door, an indication perhaps that he lived not far from the royal residence in Samaria rather than in the narrower and poorer quarters of the city (Gray, p. 506), Elisha did not come out to see him, but merely communicated through a messenger. Various motives have been found behind Elisha's detachment: he may have been demonstrating that he was not a wonder-worker who expected payment, or else indicating that he wished no political involvement with Syria, or again be deliberately testing Naaman's faith. **Go and wash in the Jordan seven times**: The number **seven** was a mysterious and potent number; it is used here symbolically, since restoration to perfect health is made dependent upon washing seven times in the Jordan.

11. he would surely come out to me: The emphasis of the sentence is on **to me**, suggesting that it was discourteous of the prophet not to come out to a person of such high status as Naaman (so Gray, *ibid.*). **and call on the name of the LORD his God**: The omission of the divine name, Yahweh with the support of some Gk. MSS, is certainly correct; the name is not used elsewhere in the narrative in vv. 1-14, and has probably been inserted under the influence of vv. 15-19a (so Schmitt, *op. cit.*, p. 79, against Šanda

II, p. 40 and Montgomery, p. 378, who argue for its retention on the basis of its appearance in v. 17). **and wave his hand**: Some form of magic rite was expected to play a part in the prophet's healing practice; cf. the potency of the outstretched hand in Exod. 8:5; 14:21; **over the place**: The allusion in this phrase, which is omitted from one Gk. Codex (see *BHS*), is not clear. Although there are arguments in favour of taking it to refer to the place where Naaman was standing (Šanda, *ibid.*), or to the place of the sanctuary from which divine help was expected (so Kittel, p. 205), it seems more natural to find here an allusion to the place on the body affected by leprosy, as was so clearly understood by Luc. and the Vulgate (cf. Lev. 13:19).

12. Abana and Pharpar: Reference is made here to two rivers known in the region, rather than the city **of Damascus**. There is strong textual evidence for reading **Abana** as 'Amana' (cf. *BHS*), and it is known that the mountain region of the anti-Lebanon was known as Amana (cf. Ca. 4:8, and see the annals of Tiglath-pileser IV, Luckenbill, *Records I*, §*f* 770). It is probable that the river, named here after the region of its source, is to be identified with *Nahr Barada*, known to the Greeks as Chrysoas. The **Pharpar** is usually identified with the *Nahr el-A'waj*, which flows from its source in mount Hermon to the marshland south-east of Damascus, and whose name is still preserved in one of the tributaries of the *Nahr el-A'waj* known as the Barbar.

13. My father: The Heb. *'ābî*, 'my father', is not represented in the Gk., although Luc., followed by the other Vsns. (cf. *BHS*), retains it and retains **if** after it (as in *RSV*). In favour of its retention it can be said that the Akkad. *abn* was used in address and also as a title; cf. *abn immāni*, 'father of the army'; possibly an Aramaic title has been preserved here. But, its omission from the Gk., and the need for a conditional particle in the sentence, have led to the suggestion that the Heb. *'ābî* here, as in few other occurrences, means if (Honeyman, *JAOS* 64 [1944], p. 82; Schmitt, *op. cit.*, p. 214; *K-B*), and so the beginning of the sentence can be translated 'If the prophet had . . .' (cf. *NEB*).

14. according to the word of the man of God: This is the only instance in the narrative in vv. 1-14 of Elisha being given the title **man of God**; it is replaced by Elisha in Luc. The whole phrase is unnecessary and has been denoted by Schmitt (*op. cit.*, p. 79) as a redactional addition that has been inserted under the influence of the following section in vv. 15-19*a*.

15. As noted above (p. 412), v. 15 introduces the second section (vv. 15-19*a*), which is different in content and purpose from vv. 1-14. The view taken here is that vv. 15-16 belong to the Gehazi episode in vv. 19b–27, and that vv. 17–19a preserve the original proselyte narrative. When the Gehazi episode and the proselyte narrative were combined, probably by the 'man of God' revisers, the phrase **the man of God** was inserted at the beginning of this verse. **I know that there is no God in all the earth but in Israel:** This acknowledgement of God by Naaman gives clear expression to a monotheistic faith, and is similar to the testimony of Islam that there is no god but Allah. Because of distinct tendencies towards monotheism in the Syrian cult of Baal-shamaim (so Eissfeldt, *ZAW* 57 [1939], pp. 1ff.; followed by Gray, pp. 507ff.), Naaman's mono-theistic confession need cause no difficulty. The theme is repeated in vv. 17–19a, but there are some significant differences: whereas vv. 17–19a expressly name Israel's God as Yahweh, no name is given in v. 15; and again, the categorical statement of monotheism in v. 15 is fundamentally qualified in vv. 17–19a. Although the proselyte section (vv. 17–19a) has been inserted in its present context because of its similarity to v. 15, the basic difference between them has to be recognized. Verse 15 contains a general statement, which has been introduced in the context of offering a present to Elisha, but vv. 17–19a deal with more specifically theo-logical implications of worshipping Yahweh. **a present:** The Heb. has *berākāh*, 'blessing', which must refer to the means whereby a blessing was received. The present was offered in gratitude for Elisha's healing; for other occasions on which gifts exchanged hands, cf. Gen. 33:11; 1 Sam. 30:26; Jg. 1:15.

17. If not: The meaning is: if he will not agree to accept the present, will he accede to a request that Naaman wishes to make? But there is no real connection between the two things, and it is better to read *lō'* ('not') as *lû'* ('O that', 'if only'; cf. Schmitt, *op. cit.*, p. 213). There seems to be a forced attempt here to link vv. 17–19a with the preceding verses. **two mules' burden of earth:** The purpose of taking the earth to Syria was to build an altar for Yahweh, to **offer burnt offering and sacrifice.** The custom is atte-sted elsewhere; Benjamin of Tudela reports that a synagogue built in Nehardea in Persia was completely constructed of earth and stone brought from Jerusalem (cf. Thenius, p. 295; Šanda II, p. 42), and the empress Helena transported holy soil to Rome (Montgomery, p. 377). It is inferred here that Naaman regarded soil from the prophet's land to be holy, and so wishes to transport some to Syria.

18. This verse is full of repetition: **in this matter** and also **may the LORD pardon** appear at the beginning and the end of the verse, and **to worship, and I bow myself** and **when I bow myself** represent a threefold repetition of the Heb. verb *hištaḥªweh*. Several changes have been proposed on the basis of the Vsns. (see *BHS*), but the verse is best retained as it stands, except for the deletion with many MSS of **when I bow myself in the house of Rimmon**, which is a dittography. **the house of Rimmon**: Rimmon is the *Ramānu* of the Assyrian-Babylonian pantheon, and the *Rammān* of Syria, who was identified with Hadad and whose name is preserved in Tabrimmon the father of Benhadad. Zech. 12:11 mentions Hadad-Rimmon, and the name Rimmon is also preserved in the name of the village Brummâna or Bet-Ramana near Beirut in Lebanon (Šanda II, p. 43). Rimmon was not a specifically Syrian deity, but was the Aramaean manifestation of the storm-god, the god of thunder and the clouds, for the name of the Assyrian Ramānu means 'the Thunderer'. Gray (p. 508) identifies Rimmon with Baal-shamaim. **leaning on my arm**: The picture of the king leaning on the arm of one of his officers is found also in 2 Kg. 7:2, 17. **the LORD pardon your servant in this matter**: Naaman's request is that he be granted pardon for bowing before Rimmon, for he does not acknowledge any God but Yahweh. This reaction, according to Schmitt (*op. cit.*, pp. 78ff.), is concerned with the interest of pagans in Israelite faith, and with the question of the possibility for pagans to promote the worship of Yahweh in their everyday life. Although Naaman is presented in this section and in v. 15 as a monotheist and the first proselyte to Jewish religion (Gunkel, *op. cit.*, p. 39), he is allowed a special dispensation. As noted by Gray (p. 507), he professed monotheism, but was in practice bound to monolatry.

19. Go in peace: This section of the narrative is concluded with what amounts to Elisha's consent to Naaman's request. The narrative concerning Gehazi in v. 19*b* is a continuation of vv. 15–16. **a short distance**: The expression *kibᵉrat 'ereṣ*, found also in Gen. 35:16; 48:7, denotes an undetermined distance; cf. the Arabic phrase for the distance a horse can gallop, and the rendering of the Targ. suggesting approximately one acre, which was the area that could be ploughed in a day. Reference to the Assyrian *kirbâtu* is not helpful, for it means a region or a quarter of the earth, as does the Phoenician parallel. Hoffmann (cited by Burney, p. 281, and Gray, p. 508) finds in the Phoenician parallel and the Heb. a reference to the distance visible towards the horizon, or as much as one can see.

20. Gehazi: Gray (p. 508) finds this narrative to be motivated by the object of explaining the name **Gehazi**, 'avaricious'. But the servant's name is not brought out for explanation in the narrative, and it is more reasonable to accept with Schmitt (*op. cit.*, pp. 78ff.) that its motivation lies in its desire to demonstrate that no member of the prophetic circle was to use his status for personal gain. **Elisha the man of God**: The Gk. omits **the man of God**, which is superfluous, and may have been added under the influence of v. 15; **the Syrian** is also superfluous after **Naaman**, although there is no textual support for its omission, nor for that matter for the omission of the proper name as a gloss (cf. Gray, p. 508; Schmitt, *op. cit.*, p. 214). **As the LORD lives**: The repetition of a phrase used already in v. 16 establishes a link between vv. 15–16 and vv. 19*b*–27.

21. he alighted from the chariot: lit. 'he fell from the chariot'; but cf. Gen. 24:64, where the same verb is used for alighting from a camel.

22. from the hill country of Ephraim: Possibly the reference here is to members of the prophetic community at Bethel, which was considered to be in the hill country of Ephraim (cf. Jg. 4:5). **two festal garments**: *NEB*, 'two changes of clothing'. Because the reference to **two festal garments** does not fit smoothly into the syntax of v. 23, it has been suggested that it is a later addition to that verse and under its influence to v. 22; it also appears in the long addition to v. 5 (Šanda II, p. 44; Schmitt, *ibid.*). There is, however, no textual evidence to support this suggestion, and the text is best retained as it stands, although Naaman's reply in v. 23*a* only mentions the two talents.

23. And he urged him: The use of the same verb in v. 16 forms another link between vv. 15–16 and vv. 19*b*–17. **in two bags**: The Heb. *ḥᵃrīṭîm*, 'bags', is only found here and in Isa. 3:22, where it stands in a list of feminine adornments and probably means bags or pouches for perfumes. The bags used on this occasion were much larger. **before Gehazi**: This is a correct and necessary interpretation of the Heb. 'before him'.

24. when he came to the hill: *NEB*, 'to the citadel'. Although the Heb. *'ōp̄el*, 'swelling', can denote a hill or a mound, its occurrence in the *OT* suggests that it denoted an artificial construction rather than a natural hillock. In connection with Jerusalem there are suggestions that the Ophel was fortified with walls and a tower (2 Chr. 27:3; Neh. 3:27; Mic. 4:8), and again in the Mesha inscription (l.21ff.) the Ophel had gates and towers. This confirms *NEB*'s translation and suggests that Gehazi, like his master, lived close to the royal residence in the fortified area of Samaria.

26. Did I not go with you in spirit?: The Heb. *lō'* suggests a statement, and not an interrogative (which would be *hᵃlō'*); or else it must be treated as a rare example of expressing the interrogative without a particle before the negative (cf. Am. 7:14; see also Driver, *ExpT* 67 [1955–6], pp. 91ff.). The Heb. does not have **with you**, which must be understood as in the Gk. **Was it a time to accept?** The point made by Elisha is that the time when God's power was made manifest was no occasion for such rapacious behaviour. It is not necessary to emend the Heb. on the basis of LXX and Vulg. from *ha'ēt lāqaḥat* to *'attāh lāqaḥtā*, 'you have now taken'; the latter is less forceful (with Burney, p. 284, against Gray, p. 509; Schmitt, *ibid.*). The Heb. repeats the verb **accept**; but this is unnecessary,), since the meaning is 'to accept money for clothes, olive orchards, etc.', i.e. to buy clothes, etc.

27. Like Naaman before him, Gehazi was not confined to quarantine by his **leprosy**; cf. 2 Kg. 8:4. **as white as snow**: For a similar description, cf. Exod. 4:6; Num. 12:10. It is possible that these other descriptions of leprosy have influenced the present account of what befell Gehazi.

(v) The floating axe-head **6:1–7**
This narrative attributing another miraculous occurrence to Elisha obviously belongs to the same collection of wonder-narratives as 4:1–44 and 8:1–6. There are reasons for supposing that this anecdote originally followed immediately after the one recorded in 4:38–41, for they both belong to the same locality (Schmitt, *Elisa*, p. 156). In 4:38 mention is made of Gilgal, *Khirbet el-Mafjar*, between Jericho and the Jordan; this anecdote too is connected with the river Jordan, and may, like 4:38–41, have originated from Gilgal. It is a popular tradition about Elisha, and has probably been included in the collection with little revision apart from the addition of the phrase 'man of God' in v. 6, which came from the hand of the reviser responsible for the collection (cf. also 4:1–7, 38–41).

1. the place where we dwell under your charge: The suggestion here is that the prophets lived together as a community and that Elisha lived among them and had charge over them; cf. Skinner, p. 303; *NEB*, 'this place where our community is living, under you as its head'. In the Gilgal tradition Elisha is presented as the head of a prophetic community in the area; it probably had some kind of attachment to the Gilgal sanctuary. It is unnecessary to interpret this verse as referring to an assembly room rather than living quarters, as in *NIV* 'the place where we meet with you', or else to take it as referring more generally to members living in the same area as Elisha under his auspices (Šanda II, p. 48). Although the Gilgal tradition preserves this concept of a community living together, it is known from other traditions that Elisha had a private dwelling in Samaria.

2. let us make a place for us to dwell there: MT, as correctly rendered by *RSV*, implies that the new quarters would be built by the Jordan. But the thick undergrowth by the Jordan, as well as the prevalence of malaria in the area, makes it unlikely that the prophets would move to live by the Jordan itself (Gray, p. 510).

Luc. and Syr. omit **there** (Heb. *šām*), thus permitting an explanation of this building project as an extension to their present quarters; cf. *NEB*, 'and each fetch a log, and make ourselves a place to live in' (Schmitt, *op. cit.*, p. 213).

4. they cut down trees: Although the word **trees** is used here, the prophets were cutting logs, or beams, and not heavy timber, which may suggest that the place they were building was more of a shelter than a permanent house. Among the trees growing on the banks of the Jordan that would be suitable for this purpose were the willow, tamarisk, acacia, poplar and plane (Šanda II, p. 49; Gray, p. 511).

5. his axe-head fell into the water: The Heb. states simply 'the iron fell into the water'. Although 'the iron' is a nominative and is unexpectedly preceded by *'eṯ*, the sign of the accusative, Klostermann's suggestion (p. 408) that the word *'eṯ*, 'blade', is intended cannot be right, since *'eṯ* in biblical Hebrew means a ploughshare (so Gray, p. 511; Schmitt, *op. cit.*, p. 215). It has to be accepted that an **axe-head** is implied by 'the iron' in the present context, and that the sentence provides an example of using *'eṯ* with a nominative (cf. G-K, 117m and Hoftijzer, *OSt* 14 [1965], p. 21, against Blau, *VT* 4 [1954], pp. 7–19; see also Saydon, *VT* 14 [1964], pp. 192–210).

6. the man of God: The proper name Elisha is used at the beginning of this narrative, but here it has given way to the title; cf. above on 4:1–7, 38–41. **he cut off a stick, and threw it in there, and made the iron float**: There has been some speculation about the exact procedure for retrieving the lost axe-head. Although the prophet's action has been described as imitative magic (Montgomery, p. 381; Fricke, p. 78), it seems that he had adopted a simple and practical method of fishing out the axe-head with a pole or stick. The water was probably deep, but he managed either to raise the axe-head by inserting the tip of his stick into it, or else by moving it along the river bed into a shallower part from which it could be lifted out by hand. Naturally the text does not give any help for deciding the method used by the prophet, because in the tradition about Elisha his action was considered to be a miracle.

(vi) Elisha deceiving the Syrians 6:8–23

Because Syrian attacks on Israel were foiled on account of Elisha's interference, the Syrians attempted to seize the prophet. When they went to Dothan, where he lived, he led them through deception to the Israelite king in Samaria. The incident of the horses and chariots of fire in vv. 15–17 seems to be an intrusion (Galling, *ZThK* 53 [1956], pp. 136ff.). There are several reasons for regarding it as secondary: it plays no part in the development of the narrative; only in this section is Elisha's servant mentioned; the reference to Elisha alone at the beginning of v. 18 implies that he was without a companion; the reference to Yahweh and to the special connection between the prophet and the heavenly chariotry (cf. ch. 2) suggests that this section is a theological elaboration of the original narrative.

Separating vv. 15–17 as a later addition does not exhaust the questions arising in connection with the development of this narrative. Schmitt (*Elisa*, pp. 91ff.) argues that the prayers in vv. 17, 18, 20 can be considered together; v. 20 repeats words from v. 17, and the requests in vv. 18 and 20 stand or fall together, for if one is secondary the same is true of the other. The occurrence of the name Yahweh in vv. 18, 20 is an indication that they belong to the same revision as vv. 15–17, since the name is not found elsewhere in the narrative. Schmitt designates vv. 15b–17, 18, 20 (but with the retention of the phrase 'and when they came down against him') as secondary additions from the so-called Yahweh reviser.

Both the name Elisha and the title 'man of God' are used in this narrative. In his reconstruction of the original, Schweizer (*Elischa*, pp. 222–5) takes out all the 'man of God' references, replacing them with the name Elisha. Schmitt (*op. cit.*, pp. 216ff.) takes the opposite view and regards all the references to Elisha as secondary. The crux is whether the narrative in vv. 8–23 was originally an Elisha narrative. Many analogies with the narrative in 4:8–37 are evident. The accretions to both contain a reference to Elisha's prayer (4:33b; cf. 6:18), and also to occurrences fulfilling the word of Elisha (4:17b; cf. 6:18). A similar analogy seems probable in the introduction of the proper name Elisha to what must have originally been 'man of God' narrative. Exactly as 4:8–37 secondarily connected a tradition about an anonymous man of God from Carmel with Elisha, so 6:8–23 secondarily connected a tradition about an anonymous man of God from Dothan with Elisha (cf. Schmitt, *op. cit.*, pp. 155ff.). For the importance of the statement that he was in Dothan, see below on v. 13.

Some additions are to be attributed to the final reviser and represent an attempt to connect together the various parts of the narrative. Schmitt (*ibid.*) regards vv. 23b, 24aa as belonging to this category. Verse 23b is conspicuous because of its reference to 'the land of Israel', which is only found elsewhere in the Elisha narrative in 5:2, 4, where another reference is made to Syrian raids; it is therefore regarded as a redactional gloss intended to identify the Syrian campaign of 6:8ff. with that of 5:2. The narrative in 6:8–23 was not originally connected with the Syrian siege of Samaria in 6:24–7:20, but they were joined by a redactor who deliberately inserted 'afterward' at the beginning of v. 24. If Schmitt's reconstruction is accepted, the original narrative is read in vv. 8–15a, 19, 21, 22–23a (with the inclusion of 'and when they came against him' in v. 18a, for which see below).

It is not easy to date the events described in vv. 8–23. Šanda (II, pp. 49ff.) favours the linking of vv. 8–23 with 6:24–7:20, and gives them a date soon after 797 BC; it was a period when Israel was restricted to Samaria and was without chariots. Gray (pp. 512ff.), whilst accepting Šanda's dating for 6:24–7:20, dissociates 6:8–23 from that section and proposes a date c. 839 BC in the reign of Jehu, when Hazael may have taken action against Israel after Jehu's submission to Assyria in 841 BC. The separation of 6:8–23 from 6:24–7:20 can be justified on account of the character of the two sections. In 6:8–23 there is only a vague allusion to the historical situation, and these verses are mainly concerned with the prophet's activity; they may have as their background the activities of border tribes rather than the official Syrian army. This section can be correctly designated as a popular tradition about an unnamed prophet on the occasion of one of the frequent infiltrations of marauding bands over the Syrian border. Any attempt to give it an exact date and to identify 'the king of Syria' (v. 8) or the 'king of Israel' (v. 9) is mere guess-work.

8. Once when the king of Syria: The narrative opens with a vague reference to the supposed historical circumstances of the incident. It sets out to show how the prophet was frustrating the plans of raiders into Israel because he had previous knowledge of their moves, and how, by deceiving a band of raiders, he led them into the hands of the Israelite king in Samaria. The tradition, which probably originated with help given by an unnamed prophet in discovering the intended movements of attackers and in trapping them, has in the course of time elevated a band of marauders to be the Syrian army and the prophet's knowledge of their movements to be a knowledge of what was decided in the Syrian court (cf. v. 12). **The king** may have been no more than the leader of a tribe (cf. 1 Kg. 20:1; Fricke, p. 81). **shall be my camp**: The Heb. noun taḥ^{a}nōṯi, 'my camp', is a rare form; it has long been recognized that probably a verbal form was intended and that the same root is found in v. 9 (where RSV translates 'are going down there'). Many commentators have followed the proposal of Thenius (p. 300), with some support from Luc., Syr. and Vulg., to read verbal forms from the root ḥb', 'hide oneself', in both verses and to find in them a clear allusion to an ambush (so Burney, p. 285). But it is not easy to see how the Heb. ḥb' could have been corrupted to the forms found in MT. It is more reasonable to find in both verses a corruption from the root nāḥaṯ, 'to go down', especially to go down in the military sense with the intention of attacking or setting an ambush (cf. Jer. 21:13; see also *BHS*; *K-B*; Schmitt, *op. cit.*, p. 216; *NEB*, 'I mean to attack').

9. the man of God: The Gk., both here and in v. 10, reads Elisha for the anonymous **man of God**, and is followed by Schweizer (*op. cit.*, pp. 222ff.) and Gray (p. 514). But, following the interpretation given above, the title **man of God** must be retained in both verses, and the reading of the Gk. regarded as an attempt to make clearer the identification of the anonymous prophet with Elisha. **do not pass this place**: The Israelite king is warned not to go near the place where the Syrians had set their ambush; cf. *NEB*, 'avoid this place'. It is possible to construe the warning as advice not to pass the place in the sense of ignoring it or leaving it unfortified; he could thus prevent the Syrians from setting an ambush.

10. sent to the place: The implication is that he took special precautions by sending an army to guard the place; this confirms the latter interpretation of 'do not pass this place' in v. 9. **Thus he used to warn him**: This is missing from the Gk., and seems to be an unnecessary repetition of part of the previous sentence. But there are no grounds for dismissing the whole of v. 10*b*, as suggested by Schweizer (*op. cit.*, p. 214). **so that he saved himself there**: The Heb. uses the same verb as for 'Beware' in v. 9, which is best translated as 'so that he was on his guard' (*NIV*), and 'took special precautions' (*NEB*); cf. also Schmitt, *op. cit.*, p. 216.

11. the mind of the king of Syria was greatly troubled: The Heb. uses a strong verb, which Gray (p. 515) translates as 'the king was in a whirl' and *NEB* as 'the king was greatly perturbed'. These are better than *NIV*'s 'this enraged the king'. **who of us is for the king of Israel?**: *RSV* faithfully renders MT, the Heb. *'el* being understood as **for**, meaning 'in support of' (cf. Hos. 3:3; Jer. 15:1; Ezek. 36:9; Hag. 2:17). The Vsns. presuppose a stronger verb, 'who has betrayed us to the king of Israel?'; so *NEB*. The Heb. text has been emended accordingly, some reading the same consonants to give *mašlēnû*, 'misleading us' (see Burney, p. 285), some reading a different verb. *meᵍgallēnû*, 'betrayed us' (cf. Klostermann, p. 409; Benzinger, p. 140), and some adding *meᵍgallēnû* to the existing text (Kittel, p. 211, followed by Gray, p. 514). But MT makes good sense and can be retained (cf. Schweizer, *op. cit.*, p. 215).

12. Elisha: The introduction of the proper name may be due to later tradition which identified the unnamed prophet with Elisha. **the words that you speak in your bedchamber**: These words are intended to demonstrate the parapsychological knowledge of the prophet; they obviously contain an exaggeration, and need not be justified by referring to the leakage of secrets through such persons as the maid of Naaman's wife or concubines (as by Gray, p. 515).

13. he is in Dothan: Nowhere else is Elisha connected with Dothan, and therefore this note has received much attention and various interpretations. **Dothan**, spelt Dothaim in the Gk. and Dothain in Gen. 37:17, has been identified with *Tell Duthan*; it commanded the pass that separated the southern end of the Carmel range from the hill country of Ephraim and led from the coastal plain to the plain of Jezreel. It thus controlled an important access to the hill country of Ephraim and to the south of Samaria from the coast and the valley of Jezreel. Elisha, according to some commentators, was present at Dothan because of its strategic location; from this position he was able to advise the Israelite king in Samaria of the movement of Syrian troops, which virtually makes Elisha a prophet moving from place to place and having many local contacts, and being the head of an efficient intelligence service (cf. Montgomery, p. 381; Gray, p. 513). Another explanation of his presence in Dothan accepts that it was a mere accident; it was on his route from Carmel to Samaria, and he happened to have stopped there (Šanda II, p. 50). Schmitt (*op. cit.*, p. 155) rightly dismisses the idea of Elisha being a secret agent, and also finds the accidental presence of Elisha in Dothan to be unsatisfactory. His suggestion that an ancient tradition about an unnamed prophet from Dothan has been later attached to the Elisha narratives, is acceptable.

14. he sent there horses and chariots and a great army: Because Syrian action in Israel is represented in this passage as being instigated by the Syrian king (cf. vv. 8, 11), a Syrian army is sent to seize the prophet. Assuming that this is a correct presentation, Šanda (II, pp. 49ff.) finds evidence here for dating the event; Syria could have marched unhindered as far as Dothan when Israel was more or less confined to Samaria after 797 BC. But as noted above, it is more likely that what lay originally behind this passage was an infiltration of a band of attackers into Israel; they crossed the frontier and penetrated stealthily inland. In tradition this attack became exaggerated and was presented as the movement of a Syrian army.

15. the servant of the man of God: The phrase is not without its difficulties; it uses a rare word (*mᵉšārēt*) for **servant**, and then changes the subject of the following verb, for it was presumably Elisha who went out. Klostermann (p. 409), followed by many others, avoided the difficulty by emending *mᵉšārēt* to *mimmoḥᵒrāt* (cf. *BHS*), which gives the translation 'And the man of God rose early in the morning . . .'. Schmitt (*op. cit.*, p. 217), accepting the emendation, retains v. 15a as part of the original narrative. It seems better, however, to take the whole of v. 15 as an addition (cf. Schweizer, *op. cit.*, pp. 224–5).

17. Then Elisha prayed: For a similar reference to prayer, with the use of the same verb, cf. 4:33. **open his eyes**: The repetition of this sentence in v. 20 is taken by Schmitt (*op. cit.*, pp. 91ff.) as a reason for regarding that verse too as secondary. **horses and chariots of fire**: Gray (pp. 512ff., 516) finds a historical basis for this tradition in an occasion when a Syrian ambush in the hills around the plain of Dothan was closed in by the chariots of Israel. The boy, who was under an emotional stress, had a psychological experience in which he saw the Israelite chariotry as **horses and chariots of fire**. It may well be based on the part played by Elisha in the Syrian wars, with the consequence that Elisha became known as 'the chariots of Israel and its horsemen' (cf. 13:14). Gray's suggestion that the concept had been originally connected with Elijah (cf. 2:11), and that the boy was on this occasion asserting that Elisha was the successor of Elijah, cannot be accepted. It is more probable that this was originally a tradition connected with Elisha, but that it became wrongly attached to Elijah in 2:11 (see above, p. 385).

18. And when the Syrians came down against him: According to Schmitt (*op. cit.*, pp. 9; 1ff.), this sentence, which refers to Elisha alone without any mention of the young lad, was part of the original narrative. It forms a link between vv. 14 and 19. But it is not necessary to regard it so, since v. 19 can be linked directly with v. 14 (Schweizer, *op. cit.*, p. 218). **Elisha prayed**: The repetition of this statement from v. 17 marks this section as part of the same revision as that verse; this is the case too with the final phrase, **in accordance with the prayer of Elisha** (cf. 4:17). **Strike this people, I pray thee, with blindness**: Gray (p. 513) understands this prayer again in a historical context. The Syrian raiders were shadowed by the Israelites while they were being led southwards by Elisha to another ambush near Samaria, where the main Israelite force was waiting for them. In his prayer he was asking that they be kept unaware that they were being shadowed. The rare Heb. word for blindness, *sanwērîm*, is found only here and in Gen. 19:11. It is usually explained as a causative form of *nwr*, 'to be bright', and thus means 'to dazzle' (cf. Akkad.; *K-B*), which may have been used for 'to blind', rather than as an euphemism for 'to make dark' (cf. Burney, p. 286).

19. Schmitt (*op. cit.*, pp. 91ff.) considers this verse to be from the original account containing the tradition about the unnamed man of God; therefore, the proper name Elisha is deleted as secondary. **to the man whom you seek**: According to v. 13, the Syrian raiders had come out to seize the prophet.

20. As noted, the repetition of words from v. 17 marks this verse as secondary; it is a continuation of the addition in vv. 15–17, 18.

21. This verse continues the narrative in vv. 8–14, 19; the raiders, after arriving in Dothan, were deceived and led to Samaria. This verse records the reaction of the Israelite king to their presence in Samaria. **to Elisha**: This is omitted from the Gk.; it has been added to the original narrative to identify Elisha with the unnamed prophet. **My father**: The Israelite king uses the same title of respect for the prophet as is used by Joash in 13:14. **Shall I slay them?**: The repetition in MT can be avoided by reading the first word as an infinitive absolute standing before the verb for emphasis, as in the Vsns. (see *BHS*). The question can thus be translated simply as 'am I to destroy them?' (*NEB*).

22. **Would you slay those whom you have taken captive with your sword and with your bow?**: The prohibition against killing captives implied by this question is difficult to reconcile with normal practice. As noted by Burney (p. 287), total devastation of captives was sanctioned and even enforced by the prophets (cf. 1 Sam. 15:3, 33; 1 Kg. 20:42). The difficulty was felt by Luc., which inserted a negative (*lō'*) to give the meaning 'Would you strike down whom you have not taken with sword or bow?', which is accepted by many commentators (cf. Gray, p. 515). The implication is that since the king had not captured these men in battle, he had no right to slaughter them. But the lack of support for Luc. from other Gk. versions can be taken as confirmation of MT (so Montgomery, p. 382). One possible explanation of MT is that **taken captive with your sword and with your bow** refers to a rule of war specifying that captives that had surrendered were not to be killed. *NEB* achieves a good contrast by deleting the interrogative and translating 'You may destroy those whom you have taken prisoner with your own sword and bow, but as for these men . . .'.

23. **he prepared for them a great feast**: Although the root *krh* found in the verb **prepared** and the noun **feast** does not occur elsewhere in the *OT*, the meaning given in *RSV* is confirmed by the Vsns. It is usually identified with the Akkad. *kirētu*, denoting a feast to which guests were brought (cf. Burney, p. 287; *K-B*). **the Syrians came no more on raids**: MT has 'and bands of Syrians came no more . . .'. Schmitt (*ibid.*) regards the last statement of v. 23 as a redactional gloss based on 5:2 and intended to identify the Syrian campaign of 6:8–23 with that of 5:2. The phrases **on raids** and **the land of Israel** provide clear links with 5:2, and it has to be admitted that a better historical perspective is obtained from v. 23*b* than from vv. 8–23*a*. Although the narrative refers to the Syrian king (vv. 8, 11) and the Syrian army (v. 14), v. 23*b* more realistically accepts

that it was 'bands of Syrians', probably semi-nomadic invaders, that came to Israel. Thus the climax provided for vv. 8–23a not only forms a link between this section and other narratives in Kings but reflects more correctly the historical circumstances.

(vii) The siege of Samaria by the Syrians 6:24–7:20

This is a complex narrative of many parts. It begins with an account of starvation in the city and resulting cannibalism, when it was under siege by Syria in the reign of Benhadad (6:24–30). The king blamed Elisha for what was happening in the city (6:31), but after Elisha's oracle that the period of starvation was coming to an end, four lepers, who had decided to defect to the Syrian camp, found that the Syrians had fled; when the Israelites were told, they plundered the Syrian camp (7:1–16). An army captain, who had dared to challenge Elisha's word, was killed by the people (7:17–20).

Different methods have been proposed for dealing with the complexity of the narrative and for explaining its construction. Benzinger (pp. 141ff.) found behind the narrative two sources giving parallel accounts of this period; one described the siege of Samaria and the starvation of its population, but the other referred to a more general famine and included the encounter between the prophet and the king and again between the prophet and the unbelieving captain. But this solution does not give an adequate account of the complexity of the narrative. Gray (p. 517; cf. Fricke, pp. 88ff.) finds in the section a collection of originally independent anecdotes (6:24–31, 31–33; 7:1–2, 3–16, 17–20), which have been selected from a fuller historical narrative and combined to give the basis for a prophetic biography which is connected with the siege of Samaria. This solution makes no attempt to trace stages in the compilation of the narrative.

A more satisfactory method is the attempt to find an original kernel and to trace the stages through which the original account passed, with revisions and expansions leading to its present form. Schweizer (Elischa, pp. 324ff.) found the original unit to be substantial, and to it were added two major glosses, namely the king's threat against Elisha and the sending of a messenger to him (6:31, 32b), and the repetition in 7:18–20, together with the note in v. 17b stating that the prophet's word had been fulfilled. Two minor glosses appear in 7:2, one defining the captain as the one 'on whose hand the king leaned' and the other calling Elisha 'the man of God'. Schmitt (Elisa, pp. 37ff.) in his analysis of the chapter, by separating stage by stage the subsequent revisions, attempts to recover the original form of the narrative and to offer an account of its literary history.

The easiest task of all is the separation of the redactional gloss in 7:17–20 from the remainder of the narrative (cf. also Reiser, *ThZ* 9 [1953], pp. 330ff.). The proper name Elisha, which was used in the original narrative, has been completely excluded from this addition in favour of the title 'man of God'. Indeed, the whole of the episode concerning the faithless captain can be easily extracted without causing any serious damage to the original narrative. Whether placed at this stage or earlier, the reference in 7:2 to the disbelieving captain also belongs to a revision rather than to the original. Although Schmitt attributes all allusions to a famine in Samaria to a so-called 'drought revision' (cf. 6:25a; 7:2, 16b), the view taken here is that 6:25a belonged to the original narrative, that 7:2 belongs with 7:17–20 to the late redactional gloss, and that 7:16b belongs to the so-called prophetic revision of the narrative.

Schmitt proposes that, as in 3:4–27, a narrative which originally described a war incident has been modified by attributing in 6:31–7:1 an important role to the prophet Elisha. Several reasons can be given for taking these verses as originating from a prophetic revision: the king of Israel, who is described in 6:30 as being full of grief and distress because of conditions in Samaria and is in no way criticized in 7:3–16a, is given an entirely different character as the opponent of Elisha in 6:31–7:1; the penitence of the king in 6:30, which may in folk tradition have resulted in salvation for the people, plays no real part in the narrative if 6:31–7:1 are retained; many similarities can be established between 6:31–7:1 and the prophetic revision of chapter 3, especially the reference to Elisha as 'the son of Shaphat' (6:31; cf. 3:11), the negative attitude towards the king (6:33; cf. 3:10, 13) and the prophet's capability of knowing the future (7:1; cf. 3:19, 25). For this reason Schmitt attributes the prophetic revision to the author of the prophetic revision of chapter 3. It is to the same revision that Schmitt attributes 6:27, with its second reply of the woman in addition to the one given in v. 28 and its emphasis (like 6:33) on lack of faith in God.

Schmitt's reconstruction of the narrative's history is accepted after the deletion of his so-called drought revision. The original narrative (in 6:24–26, 28–30; 7:13–16a) received some accretions through a prophetic revision (6:27, 31–7:1, 16b), and again through the addition of a later redactional gloss (7:2, 17–20).

Another central issue in considering this section is the identification of the war with Syria during which Samaria was besieged and then relieved through an unexpected Syrian retreat. The present position of the narrative in Kings suggests that the unnamed Israelite king was identified with Joram, and that therefore the Syrian campaign is to be dated during the Omride dynasty (cf. Unger,

Israel and the Aramaeans, pp. 62–74). But, as noted above in discussing I Kg. 20; 22 (see pp. 336ff), it is not easy to envisage Syrian oppression of Israel at the time of the Omride dynasty. The Syrian wars of I Kg. 20; 22 have consequently been dated in the period of the Jehu dynasty, and the indications are that this section too refers to a siege of Samaria in that period (so Gray, pp. 517ff.; Schmitt, *op. cit.*, pp. 52ff.). The coalition against the Syrians mentioned in 7:6 is usually taken to be a rallying together of the Hittites and Cilician Musri against Damascus, which cannot be earlier than 842 BC in view of their alliance with Damascus against Assyria between 853 and 846 BC (see below; cf. Šanda II, p. 61; Gray, p. 18). Benhadad, the son of Hazael, came to the throne during the reign of Jehoahaz (cf. 13:3, 24–25), and, according to the reconstruction of events by Miller (*JBL* 85 [1966], pp. 441–54; *ZAW* 80 [1968], pp. 337–42), Jehoahaz defeated Benhadad on three occasions. Others see in the defeat of the Syrians on this occasion a revival of Israelite activity in the reign of his son Joash (Gray, *ibid.*). Whichever of the two suggestions is accepted, the Syrian suspicion of a coalition against them dates this incident early in the eighth century, for before long Benhadad was in coalition with other Syro-Hittite states against Zakir of Hamath (see the Zakir inscription, *ANET*, p. 501).

24. Afterward: *NEB*, 'later'; *NIV*, 'Some time later'. This is an editorial link to join this account of the Syrian siege of Samaria to the narrative in 6:8–23. **Benhadad, king of Syria**: On the use of the name **Benhadad** for several Syrian rulers and the suggestion that it was a throne-name rather than a proper name, see on I Kg. 20:1. As noted above, this verse does not refer to one of the kings of this name preceding Hazael, but to Benhadad the son of Hazael.

25. there was a great famine in Samaria: The implication is that the siege of Samaria caused **famine** in the city, although some commentators (Burney, p. 288; van den Born, p. 151) assume that this was the famine mentioned in 2 Kg. 8:1ff., which may have been the occasion of the Syrian attack on Samaria and not the result of it. Schmitt's proposal (*op. cit.*, pp. 37ff.) that the original narrative only referred to scarcity in the city due to the siege, and that the exact reference to the great famine in v. 25*a* came from a later drought revision, is unnecessary. The whole verse can be accepted as a description of the dire conditions in Samaria as a result of the siege. **an ass's head was sold for eighty shekels of silver**: The scarcity of food in the city raised the prices of even inferior foods to exorbitant levels; the price paid for a 'donkey's head' (so *NEB*, *NIV*) was equivalent to the weight of approximately a kilogram of silver. Plutarch (*Artaxerxes* 24) also refers to an ass's head being sold for a high price (60 drachmae), and Pliny (*Hist.* 8.82) records a siege in the time of Hannibal rocketing the price of a mouse to 200 denarii. The proposal to read **an ass's head** (*rō'š ḥᵃmôr*) as 'a homer of new wine' (*hōmer tīrôš*) has no foundation. **the fourth part of a kab of dove's dung for five shekels of silver**: The Heb. *hiryyōwnîm* (*Kᵉtîb*) is usually divided into two words, *ḥᵃrē yônîm*, which can be translated as in the *EVV*; *diḇyōnîm* (*Qᵉrē*) may also denote 'dove's droppings'. The literal meaning of the Heb. receives some support from similar references to parallel desperate measures in times of need, such as eating cow's dung when Jerusalem was besieged (Josephus, *War* v.13.7) and eating pigeon's dung during the great famine of 1316 (*HDB* i, p. 629). On the basis of Josephus, *Ant.* IX.4.4 it is suggested that doves' dung was used instead of salt. Among the suggestions to emend the text are 'sour wine' (*ḥarṣannîm*, Klostermann, p. 410), 'white meal' (*hōrî*, Winckler, cited by Šanda II, p. 54) and 'carob pods' (*ḥᵃrûḇîm*, Cheyne, *Exp* 10 [1899], p. 32; cf. 2 Kg. 18:27; Isa. 1:20; Lk. 15:16). Another possibility is that **dove's dung** was a popular name for a vegetable, such as roasted chickpeas, and has an analogy in the use of the Arab. for 'sparrow's dung' to denote a certain herb (cf. Gesenius, *Thesaurus*, p. 516*a*). This latter suggestion allows a retention of the Heb. text and a translation such as 'locust-beans' (*NEB*) or 'seed pods' (*NIV*). See further, Schweizer, *op. cit.*, pp. 311–13; **a kab**: This measure is not mentioned elsewhere in the *OT*, but is known in later Heb. as a capacity measure. The equivalence found in the Talmud makes **a kab** a sixth of a seah, and thus a measure of about two litres; the **fourth part** comes to about half a litre (Jastrow, *Dictionary II*, p. 1307*a*).

26. the king of Israel: Whereas the Syrian king is named in v. 25, the Israelite king remains unnamed throughout the narrative. See above for his identification.

27. As noted above, Schmitt (*op. cit.*, p. 41) attributes this verse to the prophetic revision of the original narrative. The presence of a double reply to the woman, one in this verse and another following in v. 28, has aroused suspicion. The proposal to delete v. 28*a* as secondary (Gunkel, *Elisa*, p. 97) must be rejected in favour of Schmitt's suggestion, which has the support of convincing arguments: 'and the king asked her' at the beginning of v. 28 provides a better link than the beginning of v. 27; the question 'what is your trouble?' in v. 28 is a better response to the cry of v. 26 (cf. 2 Sam. 14:4ff.); the incredulity of the king in v. 27 corresponds to his attitude in another part of the prophetic revision in 6:31–7:1. **If the LORD will not help you, whence shall I help you?**: MT (which uses *'al* for the more usual *'im lō'*) is correctly rendered in *RSV* as **If** (cf.

NEB), and it is unnecessary to translate as 'No! let Yahweh help you' (Montgomery, p. 385). The implication is that God is unable to save; therefore, the king has little chance of providing wheat or wine for the woman's needs.

28. Give your son, that we may eat him today: There are other instances in the *OT* of parents in exceptionally difficult circumstances being driven to eat their own children (cf. Dt. 28:56ff.; Ezek. 5:10; Lam. 2:20; 4:10). Josephus records another instance at the time of the Roman siege of Jerusalem (*War* VI.3.4), and there is evidence that this also happened when Ashurbanipal besieged Babylon (Luckenbill, *Records II*, p. 190; Oppenheim, *Iraq* 17 [1955], pp. 69ff.).

30. Both rending of clothes and wearing sackcloth, which were well known among the mourning customs of *OT* times (cf. 2 Sam. 1:2, 11; 3:31; 21:10), are also mentioned in connection with Ahab in 1 Kg. 21:27. In this way the king identified himself with his people in their distress. The **sackcloth** also symbolized penitence, and the king obviously identified himself with the people by taking part in such rites of penitence and prayer as were thought necessary to secure the removal of their troubles. By this means the king was seeking an act of divine salvation (cf. Schmitt, *op. cit.*, p. 39). This interpretation of v. 30 and its portrayal of the king is at variance with what is said about him in 6:31–7:1; the latter section is therefore attributed to a secondary revision.

31. The king's antagonism towards Elisha in 6:31–7:1 is out of character with the remainder of the narrative, which does not mention the king's lack of faith in God (except in v. 27, which is also regarded as secondary), nor his criticism of the prophet. As noted above, there are good reasons for attributing the prophetic revision of the war narrative through the addition of 6:27, 31–7:1 to the same hand as the revision in 3:4–27; both revisions are intended to portray the clash between the prophets and the representatives of the Omride dynasty. **May God do so to me, and more also**: For this form of an oath, by which the king declares his intention to kill the prophet, see 1 Kg. 2:23. Several causes have been found for the king's determination to be rid of Elisha. Some think that Elisha, by predicting a famine (2 Kg. 8:1ff.), was held responsible for the people's distress (cf. Burney, p. 288); but this transforms the crisis occasioned by the siege of Samaria to the more general famine of chapter 8. Another reason suggested is that Elisha by proclaiming Yahweh's oracles was extending the resistance of Samaria and thus causing more suffering than necessary (Skinner, p. 308); the prophet is thus being punished for his part as Yahweh's representative (cf. v. 33). The reason given by Gray (p. 523) is that

the king was directing attention from himself to the prophet because
he was apprehending riots. The narrative does not offer a reason,
and this may be due to the fact that this section is a later addition,
which does not relate specifically to the situation because its only
intention was to show how prophet and king stood in opposition to
each other.

32. To overcome the difficulties of this verse, *EVV* provide **the
king** as subject for the verb **dispatched** and also read 'the king' (for
MT's 'the messenger') in v. 33. The procedure envisaged is that the
king sent a messenger in advance, but followed him closely in
person. A more drastic treatment of the text would delete all reference to the messenger (Wellhausen, *Composition*, p. 360) and thus
read v. 33 immediately after the reference to the elders in v. 32*a*
(Schweizer, *op. cit.*, pp. 314ff.). Another possibility is to regard the
whole of this verse, with the exception of the opening in v. 32*a*, as
an interpolation referring to 'messenger' in v. 33*a* (Burney, p. 290),
thus supposing that it was only a messenger that came down to
deliver the word of the king recorded in v. 33*b*. Some uncertainty
about Elisha's visitor may have led to an extension of the original
text; but MT is satisfactorily rendered in *EVV*, which envisage a
visit from a messenger in advance of the king. **the elders**: The
presence of **the elders** with Elisha is interpreted by Gray (p. 523)
as an indication that he and his circle represented conservative
elements in Israel. They probably visited the prophet to consult
God through him and to receive a divine message (cf. Ezek. 8:1;
20:1). **the king had dispatched**: Luc. adds **the king**, and is followed
by *EVV* (cf. Schmitt, *op. cit.*, p. 219). **a man from his presence**:
NEB, 'one of his retinue'; *NIV*, 'a messenger ahead'. The latter
rendering, suggesting that he sent the messenger before him, is
preferable. **this murderer**: Although the Heb. has 'the son of a
murderer' (cf. *NEB*), it is not necessary to take this phrase as a
literal reference to either Ahab or Jehu. The phrase alludes to the
character of the king himself, and is correctly rendered as **murderer**
(cf. also *NIV*; 1 Sam. 20:30; Isa. 57:3). **hold the door fast against
him**: lit. 'press him with the door'.

33. **the king came down to him**: MT reads 'the messenger'
(*mal'āk*), which is usually corrected to **the king** (*melek*). *NIV*'s
retention of 'the messenger' here necessitates the insertion of 'the
king' before the direct speech at the end of the verse, and is more
cumbersome than the simple solution of *RSV* and *NEB*. Nevertheless, the direct speech is not suitable from the lips of a messenger,
and it is possible that 7:2 presupposes the king's presence. **Why
should I wait for the LORD any longer?**: The implication here is
that since the calamity has originated from God, it is in vain that

one turns to him for help. This is the usual interpretation and is preferable to the suggestion that the king is reflecting upon the question: if he pursues his threat against the prophet, what will God bring upon him?

7:1 Elisha's message to the king is introduced with two traditional formulae, a summons to listen (**Hear the word of the LORD**) and a messenger formula (**thus says the LORD**). The former, which is in the plural, is presumably addressed to the king and to the elders present as witnesses; the Gk., reading the singular, addresses it only to the king. The **measure** in this verse is *sᵉʾāh*, which was approximately 12 litres (cf. also 6:25). The **fine meal** was always double the worth of **barley**, according to Šanda (II, p. 59). The point made here is that **fine meal** and **barley** will be available once again in Samaria's market (**the gate of Samaria**), but at a high price. The Mishnah (*Erubin* 7.2) quotes the price of barley at 4 seahs for a shekel, which suggests that at this time it was sold for double the usual price (cf. Šanda II, p. 60).

2. For the word *šālîš*, translated **captain**, and its more general use for an 'aide-de-camp' (Gray, p. 524) or 'adjutant' (cf. Schmitt, *op. cit.*, p. 220), see on 1 Kg. 9:22. **on whose hand the king leaned**: cf. 2 Kg. 5:18; 9:25; 15:25. **if the LORD himself should make windows in heaven**: The windows (Heb. *ʾᵃrubbôṯ*, also translated 'roof-shutters' by Gray [p. 524], or 'sluices' by Burney [p. 290], or 'floodgates' [*NIV*]) were apparently openings in the heavens through which the rains were poured down (cf. Gen. 7:11; 8:2; Mal. 3:10; Isa. 24:18; Westermann, *Genesis*, p. 583). The same noun is also used in Ugaritic and appears in a description of the palace of Baal in Ras Shamra (Gordon, *Textbook* III, no. 329, p. 365). Gray's suggestion (*ibid.*) that a reference is made here to imitative magic, and that the officer is hinting that resorting to the cult of Baal might prove more effective, is unnecessary. The officer's meaning quite obviously is that even if God brought the famine to an immediate end by causing a downpour of rain, the prophet's claim that food would be available in Samaria 'tomorrow about this time' was totally unrealistic. **but you shall not eat of it**: This phrase announces punishment on the captain for his disbelief; although he will live to see the fulfilment of the prophet's prediction, he will not be permitted to partake of the food that will become available. This verse is to be taken with vv. 17–20, and must be attributed to the same reviser as that section.

3. This verse continues the narrative of the siege of Samaria begun in 6:24–30; it has been interrupted by the inclusion of a section recording the clash between king and prophet (6:31–7:1) and by a preamble to the episode concerning the king's adjutant (7:2). **four**

men who were lepers: For the nature of this disease, see above on
2 Kg. 5:1. Although it is stated that they were **at the entrance to
the gate**, and again later that they only came 'to the edge of the
camp' (v. 5) and 'to the gatekeepers of the city' (v. 10), it appears
that the four were free 'to enter the city' (v. 4). This suggests that
they were suffering from the same kind of skin disease as Naaman,
and so were not restricted to quarantine.

4. The position of the four men is soberly reviewed; whether they
remain at the gate or enter the city, they have no hope because of
the severity of the famine. They, therefore, decide to take the risk
of going out to the Syrians; if it came to the worse, they would be
killed, but there was a chance that **they spare our lives**. The verb
nāpal found in the phrase **let us go over to the camp of the Syrians**
is used elsewhere (cf. 1 Sam. 29:3) with the technical meaning of
desertion; they were willing to become deserters in order to snatch
the faint possibility of life that remained.

**6. the LORD had made the army of the Syrians hear the sound
of chariots**: The signs of panic are evident in vv. 6–7. But it is
unlikely that the Syrians would have abandoned camp at the sound
of an approaching army; more probable is the suggestion of the
second half of the verse that the Syrians became aware of suspicious
activities by Hittite kings in the northern region of their territory.
Gray (p. 524) suggests that the rumour was fermented by one of
the prophets and conveyed in a brief statement such as 'A sound of
chariots and horses and a great army!' **the king of Israel has hired
against us**: Hiring the help of allies was a well-known custom (cf.
2 Sam. 10:8; Hos. 8:9; Isa. 7:20), and the Syrians themselves had
become involved in such negotiations in the time of Asa (cf. 1 Kg.
15:18). Although knowledge of past history may have aroused
Syria's suspicion of Israel, on this occasion their interpretation of
events can be no more than a misguided rumour and possibly an
exaggeration belonging to Israelite tradition. **the kings of the
Hittites**: These kings, also mentioned in 1 Kg. 10:29, were Syrians
(Hoffner, *POTT*, p. 213), for the Hittites met so frequently in the
OT (Jos. 1:4; Jg. 1:26; 2 Sam. 24:6) were the inhabitants of Syrian
states, who had probably some connection through their ancestors
with the ancient city of Hattuša. In Assyrian documents too, Hatti-
land denoted Syria-Palestine (see Montgomery, p. 387). As noted
above, Hittite action against Damascus must be dated between the
time of their alliance against the Assyrians and their later alliance
against Zakir of Hamath. **and the kings of Egypt**: *EVV* have
retained 'the kings of Egypt' (*miṣrayim*) as in MT, against 'the kings
of Musri' (*muṣrîm*) accepted by most commentators. MT is dubious
because it uses the inappropriate term 'kings of Egypt' and suggests

an unlikely alliance between the Hittites and Egypt against Damascus. On the other hand, the Hittites would be more likely to contract an alliance with the inhabitants of Musri near the Taurus mountains, and it is possible that here, as in 1 Kg. 10:28f., *miṣrayim* is a corruption of *Musri*. An alliance on the northern borders of Syria between the Hittites and the Cilician Musri was considered a serious threat and called for the withdrawal of the Syrians from Samaria.

7. The Syrian camp was totally abandoned, but **their horses** has been omitted from some Vsns., and rightly so, for the fleeing Syrians would have made good use of their horses (Šanda II, p. 61). It is possible, of course, that reference is made to chariot-horses, which could not be mounted, and due to the haste of the Syrians could not be harnessed to the chariots.

9. After taking initial delight in the plunder discovered, the lepers had second thoughts and feared that they would be punished: **We are not doing right . . . punishment will overtake us**. The Heb. has 'the king's house' for *RSV*'s **the king's household**; the Heb., according to Šanda (*ibid.*), like a parallel Egyptian expression, refers to the king's palace euphemistically for the king himself.

10. to the gatekeepers: *RSV* rightly reads the plural, with some of the Vsns., for the singular of the Heb. Šanda, after deleting 'their horses' from v. 7, follows through by deleting **the horses tied** from this verse. But the deletions are not necessary.

13. After announcing the lepers' report to the king (v. 11) and having a guarded reaction to it based on the king's interpretation of the Syrian withdrawal as a plot (v. 12), a course of action is planned. Verse 13, however, is textually corrupt due to repetition, and is difficult to interpret. *RSV* has avoided obvious repetition, which is found in the more literal rendering of *NIV*: 'Make some men take five of the horses that are left in the city. Their plight will be like all the Israelites that are left here—yes, they will only be like all these Israelites who are doomed'. Two phrases are duplicated in MT—'those who are left in it' and 'see they will be like the whole multitude of Israel'. The Vsns. omit the second occurrence of both phrases as dittography (as in *RSV*; cf. Šanda II, p. 62; Montgomery, p. 388; Schmitt, *op. cit.*, pp. 221ff.); despite the attractiveness of other renderings made possible by varying the element omitted, as suggested by Gray (p. 521), the course taken by the Vsns. gives a satisfactory meaning. The proposal made to them is to launch a trial run by sending out five horsemen to the Syrian camp; the argument given is that if they remain in the city they will die of famine like the host of Israelites who have already perished. The risk of losing five more men to the Syrians is of no consequence in view of the probability that they will die if they remain in the city. A more drastic rewriting of the text, based on the Targ. and proposed by Burney (p. 292), is accepted by *NEB*; 'Send out a party of men with some of the horses that are left; if they live, they will be as well off as all the other Israelites who are still left; if they die, they will be no worse off than all those who have already perished'. This is far removed from MT, which, allowing for some duplication, can be satisfactorily rendered.

14. two mounted men: It was easier for mounted men to take the journey than for men in chariots.

15. Although the route taken **as far as the Jordan** is not specified, it is usually assumed that they went along the way of Bethshean and the military road through Bezek (1 Sam. 11:8). The **garments and equipment** littered along the route were probably the plunder taken by the Syrians, which may also be a confirmation that the famine experienced in Samaria was due to the siege of the city by a plundering army and not to any natural cause.

16. The statement in the first half of the verse that the Syrian camp was plundered provides a fitting climax to the narrative in vv. 3–16a. As noted above, v. 16b, which reports that the prophecy in v. 1 has been fulfilled, is to be taken as an addition made to the narrative when 6:31–7:1 were inserted to produce a prophetic revision.

17. Verses 17–20 recording the death of the faithless captain, together with v. 2, which gives an account of a prophecy that is fulfilled in these verses, belong to a late redaction of the narrative. Some (cf. Šanda II, pp. 67–8) retain v. 17, and with it v. 2, as the original record of the faithless captain incident, and delete vv. 18–20 as a secondary gloss, thus avoiding the double reference to the fulfilment of the prophet's word (i.e. **as the man of God had said when the king came down to him** in v. 17 and again **For when the man of God had said to the king** in v. 18). The view taken here is that the whole incident (vv. 2, 17–20) is additional; the moral of the addition is to prove once again the power of the prophetic word; cf. 1 Kg. 20:36; 2 Kg. 1:10ff.; 2:3ff.

(viii) *The return of the Shunammite* **8:1–6**

Another incident involving the Shunammite lady of 2 Kg. 4:8–37 is recorded in this section. Elisha is now dead, and the section is probably an appendix to the Elisha narrative. The tradition about the prophet is transmitted orally through his servant Gehazi, and this incident belongs to that strand of oral tradition that preserved, in addition to reminiscences about the prophets, references to events validating the prophet's ministry. This section, with 4:1–44 and

6:1-23, belongs to a collection of narratives depicting Elisha's power as a wonder worker (cf. Schmitt, *Elisa*, pp. 89ff.).

Although the indirect connection of this narrative with Elisha makes it different from the other narratives and anecdotes belonging to the wonder-working cycle, there are a few suggestions that it has undergone the same process of revision as the other sections of the Elisha cycle. The proper name Elisha is used in the opening verse and again in vv. 4, 5; but the introduction of the title 'man of God' in vv. 2, 4 is rightly interpreted by Schmitt (*ibid.*) as an indication of later revision. The phrase 'and did according to the word of the man of God' in v. 2a breaks the sequence of vv. 1, 2, which record the command of Elisha in v. 1b followed immediately by the statement that the woman arose and went. Again the description of Gehazi in v. 4a as 'the servant of the man of God' is unnecessary. These accretions were probably made when this anecdote was included in the collection of wonder narratives, where Elisha sections were combined with anecdotes about a 'man of God'.

Šanda's attempt (II, p. 66) to give a date to the Shunammite's seven-year sojourn in the land of the Philistines, beginning from the birth of the child in the reign of Joram (4:13), and suggesting that she returned *c.* 838 BC in the reign of Jehu, is unnecessary. Both anecdotes concerning the Shunammite woman belong to popular tradition, which cannot be precisely dated, and were only secondarily attached to the Elisha tradition.

1. **the woman whose son he had restored to life**: A reference is made to 4:8-37, where, according to Šanda (*ibid.*), this section is to be placed as an appropriate conclusion to the whole Shunammite narrative. A link is provided by the anomalous form of the pronoun *'attî* in the phrase **with your household**, which is also used in 4:16, 23. **sojourn wherever you can**: Literally translated the Heb. says 'sojourn where you sojourn', a common form to denote the inexplicit (cf. Dt. 1:46; 1 Sam. 23:13), which must be translated **wherever you can**. Although the verb *gûr* is used technically for a protected resident alien, it denotes more generally here 'living temporarily abroad' (so Gray, p. 524). **it will come upon the land for seven years**: Although the Egyptian famine of Gen. 41:30 lasted seven years, it is likely that the mention of a seven-year period in this instance was dictated by the law for the recovery of property (see on v. 3).

2. **and did according to the word of the man of God**: As noted above, the use of the title man of God and the interrupted sequence of vv. 1-2 marks out this phrase as an addition by a later reviser. **sojourned in the land of the Philistines**: The text does not specify

the area where she lived, and Šanda's suggestion (II, p. 66) that she went to the Gaza region is no more than conjecture.

3. she went forth to appeal to the king for her house and for her land: MT, which literally rendered has 'she went out to cry to the king', is supported by 6QK against the use of a different verb in some of the Vsns. Montgomery (p. 391) makes a valid suggestion that legal terminology is used here, cf. *NEB*, 'she sought an audience of the king to appeal'. The woman's legal position had to be settled. Property left temporarily was taken over by the crown and was held in trust until reclaimed by the legal owner. The Shunammite's right to the property was complicated by the fact that her husband, the legal owner, had probably died during their absence, and so she had to establish her claim upon the land. It was customary in Israel to restore property at the end of a seven-year period (cf. Exod. 21:2; 23:10ff.; Dt. 15:1ff.).

4. the king: No name is mentioned here, and the identification with Jehu on the grounds that he was more likely than Joram to ask for an account of **the great things that Elisha has done** (Šanda, *ibid.*) is possible, but not certain. **Gehazi**, although struck by leprosy (5:27), was not restricted in his movements (see above on 2 Kg. 5:1). **the servant of the man of God**: This phrase is a secondary addition.

5. while he was telling the king: This introduces a dramatic element into the narrative, for it is obvious that in recording how **he restored the dead to life** Gehazi was referring specifically to the Shunammite's son. Although **her son whom Elisha restored to life** accompanied his mother, it was the woman herself who **appealed to the king for her house and her land**; since the son was still a minor, claim on the property had to be lodged by the widow.

6. the king appointed an official for her: The title *sārîs*, translated **official** in *RSV*, is used elsewhere for the highest official of the kingdom, and sometimes for an official of a lower rank (cf. 1 Kg. 22:9). Because this particular official was accompanying a lady, it is thought that the original sense of 'eunuch' is intended here (so Montgomery, p. 391; Gray, p. 529; cf. *NEB*). But this is unnecessary, as the meaning is 'he assigned an official to her case' (*NIV*). **all the produce of the fields from the day that she left the land until now**: It is unlikely that **the produce of the fields** is to be taken literally here; the meaning is 'all the income from her land' (*NIV*) or 'all the revenues from her land' (*NEB*); cf. also *K-B*.

(ix) Elisha and Hazael of Damascus 8:7–15
This account of Elisha's interference in Syrian affairs was probably derived, like the story of Naaman in 2 Kg. 5:1–27 and the narrative

in 2 Kg. 13:14–19, 20ff. recording further works of Elisha, from a
source covering Syrian affairs, but which is to be distinguished from
the accounts of Syrian wars in 2 Kg. 6:24–7:20 (Schmitt, *Elisa*,
pp. 77ff.).

As noted under 5:1–27, the Naaman narrative probably preserves
some sound historical information. Despite the judgment of
Gressmann (*Geschichtsschreibung*, p. 304) that Elisha's intervention
in Syrian affairs is improbable, and that the narrative itself lacks a
motive for his interference, it can again be asserted that this section
too contains a core of historically reliable material. An Akkad.
document confirms that Hazael was an usurper; an inscription on
the basalt statue of Shalmaneser states that Adad-idri was murdered
and that 'Hazael, the son of a nobody' set himself on the throne
(cf. *ANET*, p. 280). He probably came to the throne about the
same time as Jehu, another usurper (cf. 1 Kg. 19:15–17, where both
usurpers are mentioned together by Elijah). Admittedly the name
of Hazael's immediate predecessor causes difficulty (see below, on
v. 7), but on the whole the historicity of the event behind the
account in vv. 7–15 is confirmed. Whether Elisha was as closely
connected with the affair as to be an instigator of the death of the
Syrian king is another matter. As noted under 1 Kg. 19:15–17, the
succession of Hazael and Jehu was primarily connected with Elisha,
but the Elisha circle made a secondary connection with Elijah. Gray
(p. 470) argues that the restrained part played by the prophet,
together with the detailed knowledge of Hazael's *coup d'état*, indicates a near contemporary source, which may be designated as a
historical work. Elisha's interference in foreign affairs is claimed to
be anticipating Amos and his successors, and it is noted that both
Elijah and Elisha had very close relations with foreign states
(Montgomery, p. 392). It is possible that an oracle spoken by Elisha
concerning Syrian affairs became at an early stage of its transmission
an oracle spoken directly to Hazael, thus representing Elisha as
being responsible for the subsequent murder of the Syrian king.

Whatever form the original kernel was given in early prophetic
tradition, it was later revised and expanded. The addition of the
title 'man of God' (in vv. 7, 8, 11) to the proper name Elisha (in
vv. 7, 10, 13, 14) indicates possible revision. Schmitt (*op. cit.*,
pp. 82ff.) does not take each instance of the title 'man of God' as
an indication of secondary material. It is suggested that vv. 11*b*–13*a*
are secondary, for the narrative proceeds smoothly if v. 11*a* is
followed directly by v. 13*b*; it is also noted that vv. 11*b*–13*a* contain
many traditional formulae. Verse 9 contains a still later addition in
the words 'all kinds of goods of Damascus, forty camel loads'. As
recognised by Luc., the syntactical connection between these words

and the preceding clause is not firm. Attempts have been made to retain the whole of v. 9 on the grounds that a distinction is drawn between what Hazael took personally in his own hand and what followed on camels (Stade and Schwally, *Kings*, pp. 215ff.). Schmitt rightly rejects such a distinction as an unlikely one (cf. 2 Kg. 5:5), and agrees with Gressmann (*ibid.*) that these words are secondary. The additional colouring provided by these words, and the element of exaggeration they introduce, take us to the realm of saga.

7. **Now Elisha came to Damascus**: The text offers no reason for the prophet's journey. It is unlikely that he went there subconsciously aware of a mission to anoint Hazael, as he had been commissioned by Elijah (1 Kg. 19:15), as suggested by Šanda (II, p. 67); the anointing of Hazael is not even mentioned in the narrative. It is unlikely too that he had been summoned to Damascus on account of his reputation as a healer (cf. chapter 5), for it is only after his arrival that the king sent Hazael to consult him (v. 8). There is no reason for assuming that he went there for refuge from the wrath of Jehoram (as suggested by Gray, p. 530). The text gives the impression that it was mere coincidence that brought him there at the time of Benhadad's ill-health; but the reason may by now be lost because the narrative has been extracted from its original context. **Benhadad, the king of Syria**: Because Shalmaneser's inscription names Hazael's predecessor as Adad-idri, i.e. Hadadeser, some account must be given of the use of the name **Benhadad** in this report. The view that Benhadad and Hadadeser can, by resorting to the Aramaic form Bar-adar, be regarded as equivalent (as argued by Kittel, p. 126), is no longer tenable. Other solutions have been proposed. Some have accepted the biblical account as correct by supposing that Hadadeser had an unknown son called Benhadad, who is to be distinguished from Benhadad I (1 Kg. 15:18). He reigned only for a very short period, from the autumn of 845 to the spring of 844 BC, when he was murdered and his throne was usurped by Hazael (Jepsen, *AfO* 14 [1942], p. 158; but later Jepsen revised his view and seems to make Hazael the successor of Hadadeser; cf. *VT* 20 [1970], pp. 359–61). Gray (p. 528) accepts this proposal, assuming that events have been telescoped in the Assyrian records relating to this period and that the brief reign of Benhadad the predecessor of Hazael and assassin of Hadadeser has gone unmentioned. Noth (*History*, p. 245), on the other hand, dismisses the biblical account and favours the Assyrian account that Hadadeser (Adad-idri of the cuneiform inscription) was replaced by Hazael. The name Benhadad was later added to the biblical text on the supposition that 'the king of Syria' was always named Benhadad. The possibility that Benhadad was a throne-name and Hadadeser a

personal name was also favoured by Albright (*BASOR* 87 [1942],
p. 28); but he, followed by others (like Montgomery, p. 277; Bright,
History, p. 224), maintained that Benhadad I of 1 Kg. 15:18 was
not yet dead and that this verse refers to the same monarch. Of the
many solutions advocated it is reasonable to assume that after the
death of Benhadad I the king of Syria was Hadadeser (Adad-idri),
whose throne was usurped by Hazael. The biblical account, working
on a mistaken assumption, gave Hadadeser the throne name
Benhadad.

8. Hazael: Šanda (II, p. 67) describes Hazael as a court-official
or a general who had no legitimate claim to the throne. Two different
spellings of his name occur, *hᵃzāh'ēl* (in vv. 8, 13, 15; cf. 2 Chr.
22:6) and *hᵃzā'ēl* (in vv. 9, 12; cf. 2 Chr. 22:13 and the Zakir
inscription), but there is no significance in the variation. It is to be
understood from the technical terms used in the instructions given
to Hazael to **take a present** and **go to meet** the prophet **and inquire
of the LORD through him**, that he made preparations to seek an
oracle from Yahweh. **Shall I recover from this sickness?**: The verb
used here, *ḥayah*, 'to live', probably denotes recovery from sickness.
The Vsns. read 'from this *my* sickness'.

9. all kinds of goods of Damascus, forty camel loads: This later
addition, drawing attention to both the quality and quantity of the
presents taken by Hazael, contains the magical number **forty** to
denote the exaggerated amount of Damascene goods presented. The
goods of Damascus are not specified, but Šanda (II, pp. 67ff.) lists
industrial products, arms, costly furniture and natural products,
especially apricots and wine, whilst Gray (p. 530) calls them varied
merchandise that would be expected from a caravan-city. **Your son**:
cf. 2 Kg. 6:21.

10. say to him, You shall certainly recover: MT's reading 'No!'
(*lō'*) for 'to him' (*lô*), which is the reading of the Qᵉrē, many MSS
and all the Vsns., is obviously an attempt to avoid the impression
that Elisha had given a false oracle. The meaning of MT is ' "You
shall not recover", for the LORD has shown me that he shall certainly
die'. It is usually regarded as a pre-Massoretic alteration of the text
to exonerate the prophet, but the reading of the Qᵉrē, although
raising a difficult theological problem, must be accepted. Commentators have striven hard to explain or to avoid the implication in v. 10
that Elisha deliberately lied to the king. Among the less convincing
proposals are Labuschagne's reading of 'You shall certainly recover'
as referring to Hazael himself (*ZAW* 77 [1965], pp. 327ff.), Gray's
suggestion that the first words represent loyal greeting to the king
and are to be translated 'Life to the king!' (pp. 529ff.), and Montgomery's attempt (p. 393) to distinguish between the spontaneous

response of the prophet in the first half of the verse and the more considered reply, probably granted through second-sight, contained in the second half. A more satisfactory explanation is to refer the first half of the reply to the king's enquiry concerning his disease, and the second to an unrelated cause of death. The prophet rightly assures the king that his illness was not serious; but he also knows that the king will die from another cause (cf. Skinner, p. 315; Fricke, p. 103).

11. **And he fixed his gaze and stared at him**: Because the Heb. is so concise and does not specify the subject of each verb used in this sentence, there has been considerable disagreement about the rendering. The possibilities are: (i) to take Hazael as the subject of the verbs until the final statement about Elisha weeping. MT, 'he set' (*wayyāśem*), is read as 'he stared' (*wayyiššōm*); cf. Rudolph, *ZAW* 63 [1951], pp. 211f.; *K-B*; *BHS*. In favour of this interpretation is that some reaction from Hazael to the words of v. 10 is expected. (ii) to assume that Elisha is the subject of all the verbs in the verse, cf. *NEB* 'The man of God stood (with the Gk.) there with set face like a man stunned, until he could bear it no longer; then he wept'. In favour of this reading is the fact that the verse is presented as a continuation of v. 10 without any indication of a change of subject. (iii) to assume a change of subject within the verse, as is clearly brought out in *NIV*, 'He stared at him with a fixed gaze until Hazael felt ashamed' (cf. Burney, pp. 293ff.; Gray, p. 529). In favour of this view is that by naming Hazael as the subject of the final clause of the sentence a contrast is implied with the previous subject, who must be Elisha. Accepting the latter suggestion, the view taken here is that Elisha stared at Hazael because he could, in an ecstatic trance, see the murder of king Benhadad; thus Hazael became embarrassed at the prophet's gaze because of his own guilt, for the usurpation of the throne had probably already been planned. **And the man of God wept**: the prophet's reaction is due to the atrocities foreseen in the reign of Hazael and described in v. 12. As noted above, vv. 11b–13a are a later expansion and interrupt the further prophecy of Elisha which is continued in v. 13b.

12. The prophet's concern with **the evil that you will do to the people of Israel** falls outside the interest of the narrative as a whole, and the listing of evils in this verse is foreign to its style. It seems that the composer of this addition has fallen back on traditional formulae; for **dash their little ones**, cf. Isa. 13:16; Hos. 13:16, and for **rip up their women with child**, cf. 2 Kg. 15:16; Am. 1:13; Hos. 13:16 (see Schmitt, *op. cit.*, p. 82; Steck, *Überlieferung*, p. 95). Probably some of Israel's experiences in the time of Hazael have

been inserted at a later date, for, as suggested by Gray (p. 531), the cruelties experienced by Gilead at the hands of Damascus, and described in Am. 1:3, included the severities of Hazael.

13. What is your servant, who is but a dog?: The Gk. reads 'a dead dog', which is used also in 1 Sam. 24:14; 2 Sam. 9:8; 16:9 for contempt. It is, however, an unnecessary reading, for the term 'dog' is well attested in this kind of interrogative phrase, with a clearly derogatory nuance, in the Lachish ostraca (Torczyner, *Lachish* ii, v, vi) and in the Amarna letters (Knudtzon, *El-Amarna*, nos. 60, 71 202). **The LORD has shown me that you are to be king over Syria**: Elisha prophesies that Hazael will be king over Syria, but does not anoint him as foretold in 1 Kg. 19:15. These words can hardly be interpreted as a sign of Elisha's involvement in the moves to take the throne from Benhadad; it may, however, be conceded that such a message from the prophet would have given Hazael confirmation in his resolve to take the throne. These words are a continuation of v. 11*a*.

14. He told me that you would certainly recover: Hazael faithfully repeats Elisha's answer to the king's enquiry about his illness (cf. v. 10) but tactfully omits the second part of the prophet's word, which envisages death from other causes.

15. he took the coverlet: The circumstances of Benhadad's death are by no means clear; the subject of the verb is not specified, and the nature and purpose of **the coverlet** is not stated. The word *makḇēr*, 'coverlet', is unknown, but may be related to the word translated 'pillow' (*RSV*) in 1 Sam. 19:13, 16 or to the word translated 'sieve' (*RSV*) in Am. 9:9. It is unclear why the item was **dipped in water** before suffocating the king with it. The possibilities here are: (i) that the king died from natural causes and not from suffocation. According to Gray (p. 532), a mosquito-net was soaked with water so that it would act as an air-conditioner; when it was removed in the morning to be freshly soaked, it was noticed that the king had died; (ii) that an unknown person suffocated the king, the verbs being taken as impersonal and stating that someone took the coverlet for soaking; (iii) that Hazael, the natural subject of the verb, took some netting material, and to make it more effective soaked it in water and suffocated the king 'so that he died' (*NIV*). This latter explanation is to be accepted, especially in view of the Assyrian reference to Hazael as 'the son of a nobody', which is interpreted as a designation of an usurper, and also in view of the pssibility that the Assyrian record too refers to Benhadad's violent death (Gray, p. 528). Undoubtedly Benhadad's passing away was reported as a natural death in the Syrian court; but the biblical narrative has attempted to provide additional information. **And**

Hazael became king in his stead: The year of Hazael's accession and the length of his reign are not given. It has been suggested above (see under v. 7) that he took the throne in 844 BC. Shalmaneser III mentions his name in connection with two of his campaigns one in the eighteenth year of his reign 841–840 BC and the other in his twenty-first year (837 BC); cf. the Black Obelisk, *DOTT*, p. 48.

(x) Summary notices relating to Jehoram and Ahazaiah, kings of Judah
8:16–29
The reigns of Jehoram of Judah (850–843 BC) and Ahaziah of Judah (843–842 BC) are covered in vv. 16–29. Some annalistic material, especially vv. 20–22, is embodied within the usual formulae for presenting kings from the Judaean province.

16. In the fifth year of Joram the son of Ahab: Joram of Israel succeeded Ahab in 854 BC, and his **fifth year**, 850 BC, was the year of Jehoram's accession in Judah (see Table, p. 28). Although the form **Joram** is reserved in this verse for the Israelite king, and the form **Jehoram** for the Judaean king, it appears that the two spellings are variants, and this can cause some confusion (cf. vv. 21, 23, 24). **king of Israel**: *RSV* rightly follows the Gk. and Syr. in omitting the superfluous phrase 'Jehoshaphat being king of Judah', which is found in MT. There is no need to follow the drastic suggestion that there was only one king of the name, Jehoram of Judah, and that an Israelite Joram never existed (Cook, *CAH* III, p. 367; Strange, *VT* 25 [1975], pp. 191–201).

17. and he reigned eight years in Jerusalem: The figure varies in the Vsns., the Gk. giving forty years and Luc. ten years. MT is accepted here, despite the tendency of some chronological schemes to make it a short reign of about three years. The formula is incomplete in that it does not record the name of Jehoram's mother. Sanda's suggestion (II, p. 71; cf. Gray, p. 534) is that his mother is not named because she had died before his accession; the mother was named when she was alive and became the first lady of the land.

18. he walked in the way of the kings of Israel, as the house of Ahab had done: The reason for this judgment appears in the next clause, which notes that Jehoram of Judah had married into the Israelite line of king Ahab. Under the influence of Athaliah presumably, a temple of Baal had been built in Jerusalem (2 Kg. 11:18); thus Jehoram of Judah was as evil in his ways, if not worse, than Joram of Israel (2 Kg. 3:1ff.). More details about the evils of Jehoram's reign are recorded in 2 Chr. 21:12ff., where it is claimed that he killed his six brothers (21:2), who were better men than he was. **the daughter of Ahab was his wife**: She is named as Athaliah in v. 26, where she is called 'a daughter of Omri' (although Luc. harmonises by reading 'daughter of Ahab'). The two verses ar not necessarily contradictory, for the word *baṯ*, 'daughter', may denote more generally a female descendant (cf. 2 Chr. 21:6, which reads 'sister of Ahab'). *RSV*, *NEB* and *NIV* translate 'granddaughter' in v. 26, and thus make Athaliah, as this verse claims, the daughter of Ahab and Jezebel. But, it has been maintained that genealogically the designation of Athaliah as 'a daughter of Omri' (v. 26) is correct, and that the tradition in the present verse can be dismissed (cf. Begrich, *ZAW* [1935], pp. 78ff.; Montgomery, p. 396). A more complex solution (cf. Katzenstein, *IEJ* 5 [1955], pp. 194–7; Miller, *VT* 17 [1967], p. 307; Gray, p. 534) is to accept that she was a daughter of Omri, born only shortly before his death, and brought up in Ahab's court under the influence of Jezebel, with the impression being given that she was Ahab's daughter. On the whole it is more feasible to take her, as the present text records, to be the daughter of Ahab (cf. Herrmann, *History*, p. 226). Because of Jehoram's alliance with the house of Ahab, the Chronicler introduces a word of rebuke through the prophet Elijah, who is claimed to have sent a letter to the king (2 Chr. 21:12–15). But obviously the letter was composed by the Chronicler himself (Williamson, *Chronicles*, pp. 306ff.).

19. for the sake of David his servant: God's promise to the house of David (cf. 2 Sam. 7:12–17) is clearly echoed here. **since he promised to give a lamp to him and to his sons for ever**: As noted under 1 Kg. 11:36, **lamp** is used in these particular instances as a symbol of life with reference to a representative of the house of David, or else to denote 'dominion'. MT's literal meaning that God had promised 'to give to him a lamp for his sons for ever' is awkward, for the real implication of the verse is that David's sons or descendants were the lamp. One possibility is to read 'for his sons' (*lᵉbānāw*) as 'before him' (*lᵉpānāw*); cf. 1 Kg. 11:36, 'before me' (Burney, p. 295; Gray, p. 533). But 2 Chr. 21:7 together with some MSS and Vsns. adds a conjunction and reads 'and to his sons' which is accepted by *RSV*, *NEB* and *NIV*; cf. *BHS*; this slight change gives a good meaning.

20. In his days here and 'at the same time' (v. 22) are taken by Montgomery (p. 395) as linking phrases to connect material derived from archival sources. **Edom revolted from the rule of Judah and set up a king of their own**: This statement seems to contradict 1 Kg. 22:47, which states that even before, in the time of Joram of Israel and Jehoshaphat, a deputy acted as king in Edom. 2 Kg. 3:9 too maintains that the king of Edom was in alliance with Joram and Jehoshaphat against Moab. Gray (p. 535) suggests that the failure of the joint campaign against Moab and the activity of Assyria in the west encouraged Edom to revolt against Judah. 2 Chr. 20:1ff. possibly mentions a revolt of Edom against Jehoshaphat.

21. Joram passed over to Zair: The shortened form **Joram** here and in vv. 23–24 denotes the king of Judah. **Zair** has been identified with Zoar (cf. Gen. 13:10) at the southern end of the Dead Sea (Montgomery, p. 396). But the Gk. took it to be another place, for it gives the name a different form from that used normally for Zoar. That seems preferable, for Zoar was in Moabite territory. **Zair** is thus identified with Zior (*Si'ir*), a village to the North-east of Hebron and mentioned in Jos. 15:54. This place not far from the Edomite border would have served as a suitable centre for Jehoram's action against Edom (Šanda II, p. 73; Gray, p. 535). **and he and his chariot commanders smote the Edomites who had surrounded him**: The Heb. is very unsatisfactory, since it makes Jehoram's chariot commanders a parallel object to the **Edomites**. There are two possibilitis here: (i) Šanda (*ibid.*) proposed to take Edom as the subject of the main clause, and Jehoram **and his chariot commanders** as the object; cf. *NEB*, 'but they were surrounded by the Edomites and defeated, whereupon the people fled to their tents'. (ii) It is possible, as in *RSV*, to take Jehoram **and his chariot commanders** as the subject of the verb, which is preferably translated as 'attacked' (Gray, p. 533) or 'broke through' (*NIV*). Although Jehoram and his troops were surrounded by the Edomites, a night attack gave him and his chariot-commanders a chance to break out. However, 'the people' (**his army**, according to *RSV*, or perhaps his infantry) was left to escape as best it could. This second solution does not call for a change of subject in the middle of the verse and is preferred.

22. to this day: Jehoram's escape did not alter the outcome of the revolt; Edom had been absolutely successful and was never again subject to Judah. According to 2 Kg. 14:22 Elath in Edomite territory was still in Judaean hands; the meaning of this statement must be that Edom was never after the days of Jehoram totally in Judaean hands. **Libnah revolted**: The position of **Libnah** is uncertain. Whether identified with *Tell es-Safi* in the western foothills of the Shephelah (Abel, *Géographie II*, pp. 369ff.) or with *Tell Burnat*, a few miles further south (Albright, *BASOR* 15 [1924], p. 9), it appears to have been a frontier town in the Philistine plain. Šanda (II, p. 74) finds significance in the suggestion of Chronicles that, when Edom was under Judaean control, there was peace with the Arabs and Philistines (cf. 2 Chr. 17:11, suggesting peace in the time of Jehoshaphat, but 2 Chr. 21:16; 26:7 connecting the Edomite revolt with hostility from the Arabs and Philistines). The significant

link here was the trade route to the Red Sea; when Israel had control
over Edom it had economic independence, and the Philistines and
Arabs had to assume a more subdued trading position. But, when
Edom revolted, the others were in a position to do likewise.

24. and was buried with his fathers in the city of David: 2 Chr.
21:20, whilst agreeing that Jehoram was buried in David's city,
adds the statement that he was not buried 'in the tombs of the
kings'. The Chronicler too provides details of the king's disease (2
Chr. 21:18–19), and it is possible that this notice was not his own
invention (Williamson, *Chronicles*, p. 308).

25–26. In the twelfth year of Joram: The synchronization here
causes some difficulty since Ahaziah's reign lasted only **one year**,
according to v. 26.The two kings died at the same time, and to
avoid confusion some have read **twelfth year** as 'eleventh year'
(following some of the Versions.; cf. 9:29) or else take **one year** to
mean a few months, which is more probable. Ahaziah may have
succeeded to the throne after the New Year Festival at which
Jehoram had begun his eighth year, but Ahaziah's own first year
was reckoned after the following New Year (Šanda II, p. 75).
Athaliah: There is uncertainty about the meaning of her name,
Noth (*Personennamen*, p. 191) connecing it with the Akkad. *etēlu*,
'to be manly', and Gray (p. 536) with the Arab. *'atala*, 'to be
abundant, bulky'. **a granddaughter of Omri**: See above, on v. 18.

27. he was son-in-law to the house of Ahab: The phrase is
omitted from the Gk. If it is retained, the term **son-in-law** has to
be taken as a general reference to relationship by marriage (cf. Gray,
p. 536, with reference to Arab. usage).

**28. he went with Joram the son of Ahab to make war against
Hazael**: The weight to be given to the phrase **went with . . . to
make war** has been debated; it is to be noted that v. 29, whilst
recording the fate of Joram of Israel in the battle, has nothing to
say about Ahaziah except that he went to visit his ally. Possibly
personal participation in the battle by the Judaean king is not
implied; it may be that he supported Israel only in its war against
Syria, as is implied in *NEB*, 'he allied himself with Jehoram the
son of Ahab to fight against Hazael' (cf. Donner, *IJH*, p. 391). His
presence at Ramoth-gilead cannot be pressed on the analogy that
the kings of Israel and Judah are elsewhere mentioned fighting side
by side at Ramoth (1 Kg. 22). The slaughter of his six brothers by
Jehoram (2 Chr. 21:4) can be interpreted as a move to suppress a
protest against the pro-Israelite policy of the Judaean kings; it was
a policy that was cemented, and probably directed, by Athaliah,
because of her position in the Judaean court, and was still being
pursued during the short reign of Ahaziah (cf. Šanda II, p. 72;

Gray, p. 536). **the Syrians wounded Joram**: Gray (p. 533), with some support from the Gk. translation of 2 Chr. 22:5, reads **Syrians** (*'arammîm*) as 'archers' (*hārōmîm*). It makes no difference to the meaning of the verse, and is an unnecessary emendation.

29. The content of this verse is given again in 2 Kg. 9:14*b*–15*a*, 16*b*, and because of its repetitive nature that version may be secondary (cf. Montgomery, p. 396). To distinguish between two kings bearing the name Jehoram, this verse defines one as **Jehoram the king of Judah** (the qualifying phrase is omitted from the Gk.) and the other as **Jehoram the son of Ahab**. This may be a sign of the difficulties of revising an original account.

(c) The revolt of Jehu
9:1–10:36

The detailed account of chapters 9–10, which outline step by step Jehu's *coup d'état*, was readily accepted into the deuteronomistic redaction of the books of Kings, because the zeal shown by Jehu against the Baal-worshippers of Samaria met with the approval of the deuteronomic school. It is an account that stresses the religious motives behind Jehu's action: he is presented as one designated by Yahweh to be king, one that fulfilled prophetic predictions, one that was briefed to take vengeance on Jezebel and the house of Ahab, and one that wiped out the house of Baal from Israel. Undoubtedly some aspects of the account have been overworked, especially the picture of Jehu as the champion of Yahwism in his determined attack on Baalism. This raises the question of the narrative's development into its present form, and the probability that through annotations and accretions some aspects of the events were deliberately brought into prominence.

The narrative in its present form is a deuteronomistic revision; but there is no agreement on the specific verses to be attributed to the deuteronomistic revisers. Noth (*ÜSt.*, p. 84, followed mostly by Plein, *ZAW* 78 [1966], p. 15) confined the deuteronomistic accretions to repetitions: 9:8*b*, 9, which are taken from 1 Kg. 21:21, 22*a*; 9:36, which is a repetition of 2 Kg. 9:10*a*; 10:10*b*, which is a doublet of 10:10*a*. But more recently the tendency is to consider more extensive sections as originating from the revisers. Schmitt (*Elisa*, pp. 19ff.) accepts basically the previously proposed analysis of Smend (*Zeugnisse*, pp. 168–71; cf. also Steck, *Überlieferung*, pp. 89ff.), who, on stylistic grounds as well as on considerations of content, regarded several verses as secondary; attributed to the deuteronomistic revisers are: 9:7–10*a*, which are additional to the orders given by Elisha in v. 3 and to their fulfilment in vv. 6, 10*b*,

and are deuteronomistic in style; 9:36ff., which digress from the
narrative and are again easily recognised on stylistic grounds;
10:10ff. are also the product of the deuteronomistic revisers, as is
10:17abb, which interrupts the sequence of vv. 16, 17aa, 18. See
further, Timm, *Die Dynastie*, pp. 136–42.

The present narrative also contains annalistic notices, which are
not deuteronomistic in style, but repeat material that is already
included in deuteronomistic sections of Kings. The notice of Jehu's
conspiracy and the whereabouts of Joram at that time (9:14, 15a)
not only interrupts the narrative in vv. 13, 15b, but contains material
that is also given in the deuteronomistic notice of 2 Kg. 8:28ff.
Again the report of Ahaziah's burial and the notice of the length of
his reign in 9:28ff. are derived from an annalistic source, but the
latter element contradicts what is stated in the deuteronomistic
summary in 8:25. Both notices (9:14, 15a and 9:28ff.) are attributed
by Schmitt (*op. cit.*, pp. 23ff.) to an annalistic reviser who obtained
his material from annals and added them at a later date than the
deuteronomistic revision.

A still further revision, which Schmitt (*op. cit.*, pp. 24ff.) calls
an 'apologetic revision', is seen in short accretions which are directly
aimed at justifying the actions of Jehu. The statement in 10:19b
that Jehu acted 'to destroy the worshippers of Baal' is different in
style from the remainder of the narrative and seeks to justify his
action. A similar motive lies behind 10:23, which, by recording that
Jehonadab the Rechabite went with Jehu to the temple, emphasizes
that Jehu's action was inspired by the loyalty of Yahweh-worship-
pers in opposition to the worshippers of Baal. It is under this
category too that Schmitt deals with the allusion to prophecy in
9:25ff., and with it 9:21bbcd. The question of the historical reliability of 9:25f. in relation to 1 Kg. 21, arises in this connection;
but it appears that it has been included to give a motive for the
murder of Joram. It is true that the narrative views Jehu's revolution
as motivated by Baal worship which had been introduced by Jezebel,
but the reference to the Naboth incident brings in a new dimension
and sees in the royal authority exercised by the Omrides another
justification for the course of events.

Schmitt (*op. cit.*, pp. 27ff.) rightly claims that such a presentation
of the narrative's growth through subsequent annotations deals
adequately with the content of these two chapters, and that without
resorting to the concept of an extensive and complex literary activity.
He, therefore, dismisses the suggestion (cf. Benzinger, p. 145; Gray,
p. 484) that the narrative betrays a combination of sources, one
prophetical (9:1–14a) and the other secular (containing the
remainder of the material). Another suggestion that can be dismissed

is that the episode of the murder of the Jewish princes and the meeting of Jehu and Jehonadab are to be deleted as secondary (Stade and Schwally, *Kings*, pp. 40, 228). Schmitt accepts that the two chapters present a sound chronological scheme: after his anointing (9:1–13), Jehu advanced against the kings of Israel and Judah, Joram and Ahaziah, and against Jezebel (9:15b–35). Then, after exterminating the remaining members of the two royal households (10:1–14), he proceeded with his attack against the worshippers of Baal (10:15–27), which is fittingly introduced with an account of Jehu's meeting with Jehonadab.

Accepting basically the account given in chapters 9–10, together with Elisha's participation in Jehu's revolt, the motive for these events connected with Jehu must be considered. According to the presentation in 9:1–10:27 the climax of the revolt and its ultimate aim was the removal of Baal worship from the northern kingdom (cf. especially 9:22). 'Zeal for the LORD' (10:16) is brought out in the narrative, and the motive for Jehu's revolt is provided in his anointing by a prophet sent by Elisha and his liaison with Jehonadab, i.e. by the prophetic movement and the Rechabites. It is also presented as an act of vengeance upon the house of Ahab, and especially upon the atrocities of Jezebel; it was thus brought about by the politico-religious policy of the Omrides.

Attempts have been made to delve deeper than the present form of the narrative in search for other motives. Alt's thesis (*Kleine Schriften II*, pp. 116–34) that this revolt, like other cases in the books of Kings (notably Jeroboam in 1 Kg. 11:29; 12:20 and Baasha in 1 Kg. 14:14; 15:27), was another stand for the charismatic ideal of kingship in the northern kingdom, has found much support. Admittedly, there are difficulties in establishing that Jehu's installation in 9:1–13 includes the classical ingredients of the charismatic ideal, namely, designation by a prophet and acclamation by the people (see especially the criticisms of Schmitt, *op. cit.*, pp. 141ff.). It has also been claimed that the *OT* texts on which Alt depends do not provide a basis for supposing that a charismatic ideal existed in the north and from time to time erupted in opposition to the dynastic principles introduced by some of the kings (cf. Soggin, *Königtum*, p. 99). Schmitt, in arguing for the total exclusion of the charismatic ideal motive from the Jehu revolt, explains the difference between the kingship in the north and the south as a difference of practice rather than of ideal (cf. also Würthwein, *Der 'amm ha'arez*, pp. 19–32; Soggin, *VT* 13 [1963], pp. 187–95). It may well be that the two interpretations of the motives of Jehu's revolt, on the one hand as a protest against the religio-political policy of the Omrides, and on the other as a renewal of the charismatic ideal of the kingship in opposition to the dynastic concept, both present too simplified a view of the monarchy, and are not to be regarded as mutually exclusive. Both aspects are basically closely related (cf. Miller, *VT* 17 [1967], pp. 320–4); the principle of dynastic succession was native to the Canaanites, who were Baal-worshippers, whereas the charismatic ideal belonged to the amphictyonic tradition of Yahwism. These two aspects are presented in the account of Jehu's revolt; the charismatic-dynastic controversy appears in the deliberate reference to 'the house of Ahab' (9:7) in preference to 'the house of Omri', for it was Ahab who achieved dynastic succession; the Yahwistic-Baalistic controversy appears in the attack on Baal worship which obviously dominates the present form of the narrative.

Another aspect of Jehu's revolt which has recently been explored is its relationship to the international situation, especially to the presence of Assyria in the Near East. The fact that Jehu was a military commander (9:5) is taken as a significant clue and it may well be that basically Jehu's reform was a political *putsch* by a junta of officers who were determined to make a king of their commander (cf. Hoffmann, *Reform*, pp. 97–104). Astour's novel interpretation of international events (*JAOS* 91 [1971], pp. 383–9; cf. Donner, *IJH*, p. 412) provides a possible background. The reference to destruction by Shalman in Hos. 10:14 is identified with a defeat of the Israelites in Transjordan by Shalmaneser III in 841 BC. It is further claimed, mainly on the grounds that Shalmaneser's march 'as far as the mountains of Ba'li-ra'si' refers to a march as far as Mount Carmel, that Shalmaneser followed up his Transjordan victory by marching across Israel. Consequently, Jehu's revolt is interpreted as an attempt to placate the Assyrians by taking steps to remove anti-Assyrian factions. Unquestionably political factors did contribute to Jehu's actions, whether they arose from a dynastic controversy in Israel or from a peculiar situation created by an Assyrian threat; but in the biblical presentation these factors have been ignored in the interests of the religious theme which dominates the narrative.

Despite the narrative's clear aim of showing that Jehu's revolt was legitimate (cf. Miller, *op. cit.*, pp. 321ff.), and too the fact that it is pro-Jehu in the satisfaction that it derives from the vengeance executed on the house of Ahab (cf. Benzinger, pp. 148ff.), these two chapters present what may be correctly called 'a historical narrative'. The composition is obviously derived from a time when the individual episodes belonging to the revolt were known and remembered. It is, therefore, accepted that this narrative originated, if not from the time of Jehu himself (as proposed by Šanda II, pp.

123ff.; Montgomery, p. 399), certainly from the time of the first kings of his dynasty (Schmitt, *op. cit.*, p. 30). It came from a circle that took a positive attitude towards this new dynasty, but it is difficult to be more specific and attribute it definitely to a military circle around Jehu (Steck, *op. cit.*, p. 47) or to a prophetic circle around Elisha (Montgomery, *ibid.*).

(i) *Jehu's coup d'état and the killing of Joram, Ahaziah and Jezebel*
9:1-37

As noted above, the account of the first stage of the revolt recorded in chapter 9 has been annotated by the insertion of two deuteronomistic accretions (9:7–10*a* and 9:36ff.), two annalistic notices (9:14, 15*a* and 9:28ff.) and two short apologetic additions (9:25ff. and 9:21*bbcd*). The major problem of the chapter, however, lies in the report of Jehu's anointing in vv. 1–13, since the historicity of the basic material in these verses has been doubted and their relationship to the other actions in the remainder of these two chapters has been debated. As noted above, the suggestion that this section originated from a different source, which is usually designated as 'prophetic', and that it therefore stands apart from the remainder of the narrative, is not acceptable.

Schmitt (*Elisa*, pp. 139ff.) defends the historicity of the section on the grounds that it refers to a concrete historical situation and lacks the characteristics of other legendary accounts of anointing a king by a prophet (cf. 1 Sam. 10:1; 16:13). His examination of the two instances from 1 Samuel shows that the anointing occurred during the king's youth, was not publicly known and had no historical connection with the king's later accession to the throne. In contrast, the anointing of Jehu has a concrete historical *Sitz im Leben*; it signified a critical moment in the revolt and thus provided legitimation for all that followed. Unlike the other instances noted, it was not a well-known and named prophet that acted, but rather an unnamed member of 'the sons of the prophets'. For these reasons the anointing of Jehu is separated from these other legendary accounts, and the historicity of the act is taken seriously.

1. one of the sons of the prophets: The reference is to a member of a prophetic guild, cf. 1 Kg. 20:35. As noted, the fact that an unnamed prophet performs the anointing sets this narrative apart from other reports of anointing by prophets. The reference to a prophetic guild does not necessarily mean that we are dealing with a prophetic legend. **flask of oil**: The word is also found in 1 Sam. 10:1 in connection with an anointing, but is not the same word as is used in 2 Kg. 4:2. *K-B* explains the Heb. *pak̠* as an onomatopoeic word imitating the gurgling of liquid; see further, Honeyman, *PEQ* 71 [1939], p. 86. **go to Ramoth-gilead**: See 1 Kg. 22:3.

2. Jehu: The name is used of a prophet in 1 Kg. 16:1. It has the same form as Abihu and Elihu, the first element being probably a short form of the name Yahweh (Noth, *Personennamen*, p. 143). Gray (p. 540) finds in the name a recollection of Elijah's victory on Mount Carmel and of the people's acclamation 'Yahweh, he is God', and suggests that because the name commemorated that occasion it denotes the conservative circle from which Jehu originated. Jehu is said here to be **the son of Jehoshaphat** ('Yahweh will judge') and the grandson of **Nimshi**, but is called 'the son of Nimshi' in v. 20 and in 1 Kg. 19:16. But the term 'son of' may have been used loosely to denote a descendant; cf. also 8:18. The suggestion that Nimshi was the name of Jehu's clan (Šanda II, p. 93) is counterbalanced by the use of the name of individuals in ancient records (Gray, p. 540). Noth (*ibid.*, p. 230) has suggested that it originated as a nickname meaning 'the weasel'. **an inner chamber**: See on 1 Kg. 22:25.

3. I anoint you king over Israel: On the rite of anointing and its significance see on 1 Kg. 1:34. Solomon, however, was anointed by a priest and a prophet, and so the present narrative must be considered in conjunction with the anointing of Saul by Samuel (1 Sam. 9:16; 10:1; 15:1) and of David by Samuel (1 Sam. 16:12ff.). But it cannot be established on the basis of these three examples that there was a special form of anointing, whereby a king was anointed by a prophet. The historicity of the reports in 1 Sam. 16:1–13 and of the anointing of Saul is in doubt, thus leaving the present case as the only historical example (cf. Kutsch, *Salbung*, pp. 57–9; Schmitt, *op. cit.*, pp. 149ff.). This solitary incident must, therefore have been a special, prophetical act. Its intention was to give Jehu legitimation; the prophet Elisha took over the function of a priest in order to give this new kingship religious approval and make it legitimate.

4. the young man, the prophet: The Heb. has 'the young man, the young man, the prophet', but *RSV*, following many MSS, the Gk. and Syr., omits the first occurrence of 'the young man'; cf. also *NEB* 'the young prophet'. Other MSS, Targ. and Vulg. read 'the young man' in the construct, which may be translated 'the prophet's lad'. It is possible that the original read 'the lad' (cf. Montgomery, pp. 400ff.), and that the additional 'the prophet's lad' was intended to specify that he was a younger member of the prophetic guild (cf. also Schmitt, *ibid.*, p. 225).

5. were in council: The Heb. has 'sitting together' (cf. *NEB*; *NIV*), which makes the gathering less formal than is suggested by

RSV. It is possible, however, that they were in conference and at that very moment discussing a military plot.

6. over the people of the LORD, over Israel: The description of **Israel** here as **the people of the LORD** has been added to the anointing formula found in v. 3, as indeed is the further description of the Lord as **the God of Israel**. Both may be regarded as additions made during the deuteronomistic revision of the narrative (cf. Schmitt, op. cit.; p. 225).

7–10a. Following upon the minor deuteronomistic revision of v. 6, there follows in vv. 7–10*a* a section that is to be regarded as deuteronomistic both in style and content (cf. Schmitt, *op. cit.*, p. 21; Smend, *Zeugnisse*, p. 168; Dietrich, *Prophetie*, pp. 47ff.). Typical deuteronomistic phrases are found in the passage, such as 'strike down the house' in v. 7*a* and 'my servants the prophets' in v. 7*b*. Many of the words in vv. 8–10*a* are repetitions of phrases found elsewhere, notably 'every male', 'bond and free in Israel', 'make the house of . . . like the house of . . .' and 'the dogs shall eat Jezebel'. As regards content, vv. 7–10*a* add to Jehu's brief in v. 3 and its fulfilment in v. 6; an exact parallel to v. 3 is provided if v. 10*b* is read immediately following v. 6. The section is an elaboration of the prophetic word, and the addition in v. 6*b* comes from the same hand.

7. you shall strike down the house of Ahab: This phrase is deuteronomistic; it is also found in 1 Kg. 15:29; 16:11, two verses which may be attributed to the deuteronomistic redaction (cf. Schmitt, *op. cit.*, p. 20). As already noted the use of the term **the house of Ahab** may indicate that the dynastic-charismatic controversy was a factor in this revolt. If this interpretation is correct, this verse combines the dynastic controversy with the atrocities of Jezebel, who in her zeal for Baal worship had killed **my servants the prophets**. This latter phrase is a typically deuteronomistic one (Burney, p. xv).

8. In elaborating on the fate of the house of Ahab, two phrases found elsewhere in deuteronomistic verses are repeated. **every male**: The Heb. uses the phrase 'him who pisses against the wall' (cf. 1 Kg. 14:10; 16:11; 21:21). The phrase **bond** and **free** also appears in 1 Kg. 14:10; 21:21 (Burney, p. xv).

9. The formula **I will make the house of . . . like the house of . . .** is also found in 1 Kg. 16:7; 21:22.

10. And the dogs shall eat Jezebel: For the same phrase, cf. 1 Kg. 14:11; 16:4; 21:24. Elijah's prophecy in 1 Kg. 21:23 declared that Jezebel was to be eaten by dogs 'within the bounds of Jezreel'; cf. also v. 37, below. On the relationship of this chapter to the murder of Naboth in 1 Kg. 21, see above, p. 351, where it is maintained that in prophetical circles Jezebel was hated and held responsible for the death of Naboth; the prophecy in 1 Kg. 21:23 was probably added in the light of the events described in 2 Kg. 9. On the difference between the prediction that she would die 'within the bounds of Jezreel' and the present statement that she would die **in the territory of Jezreel**, see above, p. 359. The account of Jezebel's death given in this chapter does not mention any connection between her death and Naboth's murder, which has led Miller (*VT* 17 [1967], p. 316) to suggest that her fate in Jezreel had nothing at all to do with the Naboth incident. Jezreel appears in the narrative simply because it was a royal city at the time of the Omrides (cf. Napier, *VT* 9 [1959], pp. 366–78). **Then he opened the door and fled**: Ignoring the intrusion in vv. 7–10*a*, this sentence can be read immediately after v. 6 to give a satisfactory follow up of v. 3.

11. mad fellow: *NIV*, 'madman'; *NEB*, 'crazy fellow'. The same word occurs in Hos. 9:7 and Jer. 29:26 to describe a prophet seized by ecstasy, and elsewhere to refer to madness in general (Dt. 28:34), most notably David's feigned madness at Gath (1 Sam. 21:13ff.). The use and associations of the word are not certain. Possibly it had some connection with the Arab. *saja'a*, which refers to a particular style of prophetic utterance found in the oldest parts of the Koran, and implying comparison with the cooing of turtle doves, a symbol of the goddess Ishtar (Haldar, *Associations*, pp. 187ff.; cf. *K-B*). Another possible explanation lies in its connection with the Akkad. *sēgu*, 'to be furious, howl, rage' (Gray, p. 542; *K-B*). Whatever the exact origin of the word, it had been taken over at some stage to describe the ecstatic behaviour of some members of the prophetic community and had an unmistakable derogatory nuance. **and his talk**: Both *NEB*'s 'and the way his thoughts run' and *NIV*'s 'the sort of thing he says' offer a freer interpretation than the more literal rendering of *RSV*. Montgomery (p. 401) renders 'his prattle' (*K-B*, 'empty talk'). Gray (p. 542) takes the word to denote the muttering speech of a man talking to himself, and according to Mowinckel (*Psalms II*, p. 144) the word denotes something emotional and implies the concentration involved in ecstatic trance. Schmitt (*op. cit.*, p. 226) translates 'screaming'. Most translations accept that the verb possesses ecstatic overtones.

12. That is not true: The Heb. more directly says 'It's a lie' (cf. Gray, p. 541); *NEB* has 'Nonsense!'. For a similar usage of the word to denote a lie; cf. Jer. 37:14. In reply to his colleague Jehu repeats the prophet's words from vv. 3, 6, **I anoint you king over Israel**.

13. Alt (*op. cit.*, p. 125) finds the two main elements of the charismatic royal ideology in this narrative, as he does elsewhere.

The designation of the king by the prophet appears in vv. 6, 10*b* and the acclamation follows in vv. 11–13. The validity of Alt's pattern has been doubted. For example, Omri was not designated by a prophet, and his acclamation by the army (1 Kg. 16:15ff.) is not the same as acclamation by the people. Similarly, Jehu was not acclaimed by the people, nor indeed by the whole army, but by a small group of officers. The incident is thus given the character of a military coup, which is not the same by far as the charismatic ideal of kingship (Schmitt, *op. cit.*, pp. 142ff.). Whether the recognition of Jehu by the officers was valid or not, it cannot be disputed that the basic elements of an acclamation are present in v. 13. **every man took his garment, and put it under him**: On the analogy of Mt. 21:8, this act is taken as a recognition of Jehu's authority and submission to him. **on the bare steps**: The Heb. uses an exceptional word here, *gerem*, which may on the analogy of the Aramaic be translated 'on the steps *themselves*' meaning **on the bare steps** as in *RSV* (cf. Šanda II, pp. 94ff.). Another possibility is to emend *gerem* to *merôm*, 'height, top' and render 'on the top of the steps' (cf. Aquila); Gray (p. 543) obtains the same meaning by taking *gerem* to be an architectural term to denote where the steps finished, or the landing. *NEB* has 'on the stones of the steps'. **they blew the trumpet**: cf. also 1 Kg. 1:34; 11:14, where the blowing of a trumpet was part of the accession ceremony. See also Ps. 47:5; 98:6 (cf. Mowinckel, *Psalms I*, p. 122). **Jehu is king**: The same form of acclamation is found also in 1 Kg. 1:11; cf. also Ps. 97:1–4; 98:6, 9; see Mowinckel, *op. cit.*, p. 107.

14–15a. Although opinions vary, with some retaining both verses (Eissfeldt, p. 556), others deleting only v. 14*a* (Steck, *Überlieferung*, p. 32), and others regarding this as an introduction to the Jehu narrative misplaced from 8:28ff. (Gunkel, *Elisa*, pp. 68, 98; Gray, p. 543), there is a strong case for regarding the whole of vv. 14–15*a* as a secondary addition derived from an annalistic source (so Schmitt, *op. cit.*, pp. 23ff.). The main argument for this latter course is that the sequence between vv. 13 and 15*b* is broken by a note that differs in style from the Jehu narrative.

15. Joram with all Israel had been on guard at Ramoth-gilead: Many commentators (cf. Schmitt, *op. cit.*, p. 226, with a full list) follow Graetz (*Emendationes III*, p. 35) in reading 'Jehu' for Joram in this sentence. As noted above under 1 Kg. 22, the events at Ramoth-gilead dated in the reign of Ahab probably happened at a later time, most likely in the reign of Joram, king of Israel (Miller, *VT* 17 [1967], pp. 314ff.). The situation envisaged is that, when Joram withdrew to Jezreel, the defence of Ramoth-gilead was left in the hands of Jehu. So Gray (p. 544) translates 'was warden in

Ramoth-gilead'. He had with him the armed forces of Israel, which are denoted by the phrase **with all Israel**, and decided at this point to bid for the kingship. As noted above, it is possible that Assyrian activity in the area may have influenced the decision to stage a revolt. Verse 15*b* continues the narrative at the end of v. 13. **If this is your mind**: The meaning is 'if you are intent on making me king'. The slight change suggested by the Gk. to give 'if you are on my side' (*NEB*) or 'if you are truly with me' (Gray, p. 544) is not necessary.

16. The verse would suggest that Jehu drove alone to Jezreel, but it can be assumed on the basis of v. 25 that an aide accompanied him in his chariot. The circumstances described here have also been covered in the summary in 8:28ff.

17. the tower in Jezreel: This was on the edge of the city and may have been part of the city wall. Verse 30 suggests that the royal palace too was built near the wall, and it may be that the watch-tower was part of the wall within the palace complex. It was on the eastern side, and so movement along the valley and plain of Jezreel was easily observed. **the company of Jehu**: The word *šip'āh*, translated **company** (*NEB*, 'troop'), occurs elsewhere for a company or multitude (Isa. 60:6; Ezek. 26:10; cf. also Job 22:11; 38:34), and it is not necessary to follow the Gk. by translating 'dust'. This verse again confirms the above comment that Jehu did not travel alone.

18. a man on horseback: The implication here is that action had to be taken quickly, and therefore a single rider was sent to meet the company and find out the nature of their visit by asking **Is it peace?** Jehu's reply **What have you to do with peace?**, if interpreted in the light of v. 22, means that peace cannot exist as long as the practices of Jezebel are tolerated by the house of Ahab. **Turn round and ride behind me**: The messenger was not allowed to return, but was forced to ride with Jehu's entourage.

20. After a second rider had been sent out and had received similar treatment to the first, the watchman in reporting back adds the significant information **and the driving is like the driving of Jehu,** which indicates that he has been recognised. **for he drives furiously**: *NIV* translates 'he drives like a madman', which correctly brings out the fact that the Heb. uses the same word for 'mad fellow' in v. 11. A different meaning appears in the Targ. 'quietly', which is also echoed in the leisurely driving described by Josephus (*Ant.* IX.6.3). Gray's 'with abandon' (pp. 545ff.) also weakens the implication of the Heb.

21. Jehoram gave orders to 'harness' his chariot (cf. *NEB*, which is better than *RSV*'s **made ready**), and he and Ahaziah met Jehu **at the property of Naboth**. Naboth's property or plot of ground is more specifically defined as a vineyard in 1 Kg. 21. As noted above, the sentence **and met him at the property of Naboth the Jezreelite** in this verse is to be taken in conjunction with the reference to Naboth in vv. 25ff. The religious motive of the revolt as outlined in v. 22 gives place in vv. 21, 25ff. to an impression that Jehu's action was a protest against the tyrannical aspect of the kingship as practised by the house of Ahab. Although the introduction of these verses is attributed by Schmitt (*op. cit.*, pp. 24ff.) to the so-called apologetic revision of the narrative, it represents an earlier version of the Naboth tradition than the deuteronomistic account given in 1 Kg. 21.

22. As in 10:17–27 below, the worship of Baal encouraged by Jezebel is given as the main reason for Jehu's revolt. **the harlotries and sorceries of your mother Jezebel**: cf. also 2 Kg. 17:17; 21:6; Dt. 18:10 for the use of similar terms. The word **harlotry** in referring to Jezebel's allegiance to Baal has been occasioned by the practice of prostitution in fertility rites. **sorceries**: The reference may be to evil arts associated with foreign cults (cf. Jer. 27:9). Gressmann (*Geschichtsschreibung*, p. 314) connects the term more specifically with the use of amulets of the fertility goddess and refers to the archaeological evidence provided by the discovery of many plaques of Astarte.

23. Joram reined about: *NEB*, 'wheeled about'; *NIV* 'turned about'; cf. also 1 Kg. 22:3ff. As noted by Šanda (II, p. 98), it appears that Joram suspected no evil and therefore drove out on his own to meet Jehu.

24. drew his bow with his full strength: The Heb. states literally that Jehu 'filled his hand with the bow', which, on the analogy of a similar phrase in 2 Sam. 23:7, means that 'he armed himself with a bow'; cf. *NEB* 'Jehu seized his bow'. *RSV* is based on Rashi's suggestion that he drew his bow with all his might, meaning that he drew it out to full stretch.

25. Bidkar his aide: Most translators take Bidkar to be a proper name, the most notable exception being the Syr., which translates it literally 'the son of stabbing'. Šanda (II, p. 98), accepting the Syr., suggests 'spear-boy'. But, as Gray rightly points out (p. 547), the description of this man as his **aide** (Heb. *šālîš*) means that his task was to hold the warrior's arms, without being involved himself in warfare. The rendering as a proper name must therefore be retained. On **his aide** see 1 Kg. 9:22. There are some differences between the allusion here to Naboth and his land and the narrative in 1 Kg. 21. Whereas the narrative describes it as a vineyard, the present verse refers to **the plot of ground**; whereas 1 Kg. 21 places the vineyard near Ahab's palace, this passage implies that it was outside the city. Moreover, 1 Kg. 21 does not mention the number of Naboth's sons as in this verse, and it has no parallel to the words of threat against Ahab in v. 26. Although this raises the question of the historical reliability of this account, Schmitt (*op. cit.*, p. 26) argues that it is historically acceptable; for one thing there was no room for a vineyard in the cities of ancient times, and again the concept of justice found in v. 26 is appropriate for the ninth century. Although belonging to an early period, when the events of the revolt were well known, vv. 25ff. are nevertheless regarded as an insertion into the narrative from an apologetic standpoint. Together with v. 21*b* they contain the only reference in the narrative to Naboth, and through their addition a new dimension has been added to the revolt, which now becomes a protest against the absolute power exercised by the Omride dynasty. Apart from introducing this new element to the revolt, these verses are also stylistically different from the narrative itself; they are more formal with their repetition of **says the LORD** and **in accordance with the word of the LORD**. **rode side by side**: The Heb. has *ṣᵉmāḏîm*, 'pairs', which is difficult to explain. Most translators take it as singular meaning 'as a pair', or a passive participle meaning 'paired'; both can be rendered by 'together' (*NIV*) or **side by side** (cf. *NEB*). If the form found in MT is retained, it can be taken to mean 'were driving chariot-teams' (Montgomery, p. 402; Gray, p. 545); but this is not very appropriate, since Jehu and Bidkar are made responsible for two different chariot-teams. **the LORD uttered this oracle against him**: The prophet is not named here, but it is assumed that it is Elijah; cf. 1 Kg. 21:17ff.

26. The oracle as reported here differs from the version given in 1 Kg. 21:19, which refers to the dogs licking the blood of Ahab. The form found in 1 Kg. 21:19 does not mention **yesterday, the blood of his sons**, nor does it use the term **requite**. The 'very place' of the other version is given here as **this plot of ground**.

27. No reason is given for Ahaziah's murder, but it is possible, as suggested by Gray (p. 548), that he was removed to avoid any revenge upon Jehu. **Beth-haggan**: This is En-gannim of Jos. 19:21; 21:29, and is to be identified with modern *Jenin* to the south of Jezreel (Abel, *Géographie II*, p. 317). **Ibleam**, mentioned further on in the verse, was also in the same direction and is identified with modern *Tell Belʿameh*, which is less than a kilometre south of Jenin. **and they shot him**: The Heb. 'Smite him too' is slightly emended by the Gk. to give 'And him too! and they wounded him in the chariot' (cf. Gray, p. 546; Schmitt, *op. cit.*, p. 229). **in the chariot**: This is misplaced in this verse, and is probably to be inserted after the verb 'carried him' in v. 28 (as is done in *RSV*, but it should be

omitted from v. 27); cf. Šanda II, p. 100; Montgomery, p. 402. **at the ascent of Gur**: This is probably to be identified with modern *Gurra* (Montgomery, *ibid.*). Ahaziah's decision to flee to Megiddo was, according to Gray (p. 548), due to: (a) his realization that he could move faster in the plain than in the mountainous region, and (b) his hope that at that great chariot centre he could still find loyalty to Joram. He managed to flee to Megiddo, but he **died there**. More details about the circumstances surrounding Ahaziah's death are given in 2 Chr. 22:7ff. (Williamson, *Chronicles*, p. 316).

28–29. Both verses are probably derived from annalistic material (cf. Schmitt, *op. cit.*, p. 24), but not necessarily from the same source (cf. Timm, *Die Dynastie*, pp. 138f.). The interest shown by v. 28 in the burial of the king in Jerusalem **in his tomb with his fathers** is quite unlike the interest of the account of Jehu's revolt in the north, and so can be regarded as an addition (so Smend, *Zeugnisse*, p. 169). It is similar to other annalistic material, especially 2 Kg. 23:20. The note in v. 29 that Ahaziah's reign began **in the eleventh year of Joram** contradicts 8:25, where it is said that he came to the throne in his twelfth year. There may be an attempt to correct the synchronisation of 8:25ff., possibly because Ahaziah's reign of 'one year' in 8:26 was taken too literally (see on 8:25; cf. Gray, p. 549; Schmitt, *op. cit.*, p. 24).

30. The narrative continues with an account of Jezebel's death. **she painted her eyes**: Literally 'she set her eyes in stibium' (so Burney, p. 300). The Heb. *pûḵ* is usually identified with kohl (Assyr. *quhlu*), sulphide of antimony, pulverised by the Arabs into a black powder, which was mixed with oil and used as an eye cosmetic (cf. *K-B*); see also Jer. 4:30; Ezek. 23:40; and further, Sommer, *JBL* 62 [1943], pp. 33ff. Gray (p. 550) proposes to connect the Heb. verb *śîm*, usually translated 'to set', with an Arab. root meaning 'to cover with dust', and so renders 'she blackened her eyes with kuhl'. But *RSV*'s rendering (cf. *NIV*, *NEB*) is adequate. **and looked out of the window**: There are instances from Egypt too of royal audiences being granted through the window (Montgomery, p. 403; cf. the ivory tablets from Samaria and Prov. 7:6ff.).

31. you Zimri, murderer of your master: Jezebel's greeting is full of sarcasm for she asks **is it peace?** to the man whom she compares with a murderer. The comparison with **Zimri** is a telling one; after killing Elah and those that remained of the house of Baasha, he only managed to retain the throne for a few days (1 Kg. 16:9–15). Jezebel caustically reminds him of Zimri's fate, and was perhaps indirectly threatening Jehu.

32. Who is on my side? The Gk. has 'Who are you? Come down with me', with a variant in Luc. 'Come down to me'. But *RSV*'s rendering of MT is possible and can stand. **Two or three eunuchs**: The term *sārîs* is taken here to denote eunuchs, who were attendants or chamberlains in the harem.

33. Jezebel's death, which is so vividly described in this verse, was caused by her being thrown down from her window and being trampled by horses. It seems that another cause of death is given in v. 36.

34. went in and ate and drank: Jehu behaves as if nothing out of the ordinary had happened. According to Gray (p. 551), Jehu's eating on this occasion was significant, for he interprets it as a communal meal in which Jehu and the community were bound together. It was intended to test the support of the local leaders to Jehu's revolt. Nevertheless, the text gives no hint that it was a communal meal, and it may be no more than an indication of Jehu's carefree attitude in that he gave Jezebel no further thought.

35. This verse does not give any explanation why no more than scant remains of Jezebel were found. A reason appears in v. 36.

36–37. These two verses, because of their content and on stylistic considerations, cannot be taken as an original part of the account of Jehu's revolution. According to vv. 30–35, Jezebel died within the precincts of the royal palace, but v. 36 locates her death **in the territory of Jezreel**. Again, whereas v. 33 says that she was trampled by horses, v. 36 suggests that the cause of her death was that she was eaten by dogs (cf. Steck, *op. cit.*, pp. 36ff.). Stylistically there are many connections between these verses and deuteronomistic material: the reference to Elijah as **servant** connects with 9:7 (see above), the motif of being eaten by dogs again connects with 9:10, the phrase **this is the word of the LORD** (cf. 2 Kg. 15:12), and the phrase **as dung upon the face of the field** (cf. Jer. 8:2; 16:4; 25:33). These two verses are, therefore, attributed to the deuteronomistic reviser (cf. Smend, *Zeugnisse*, p. 170; Schmitt, *op. cit.*, p. 22). **the dogs shall eat the flesh of Jezebel**: This prediction is also given in 1 Kg. 21:23, which may contain a secondary tradition based on this verse (see above on 1 Kg. 21). **as dung upon the face of the field**: Montgomery (pp. 291, 407) claims that there is a play here on the *zebel* element in the proper name Jezebel. The Arab. and Akkad. *zibl* means 'dung', which may have suggested the Heb. *dōmen*, 'dung'. See further, Held, *JAOS* 88 [1968], pp. 90–8.

(ii) The massacre of two royal houses and the worshippers of Baal
10:1–27
The account in this chapter of the killing of seventy sons of Ahab and forty-two kinsmen of Ahaziah (vv. 1–14) and of the slaughter of the worshippers of Baal in Samaria (vv. 15–27) has again received

some annotations. Two additions that can be easily attributed to the deuteronomistic reviser appear in vv. 10ff. and in v. 17*abb*, and notes of an apologetic nature are found in v. 19*b* and in v. 23.

Two passages calling for special comment here, because of their deletion by some commentators, are vv. 12–14, giving an account of the slaughter of the Judaean kinsmen of Ahaziah, and vv. 15–16, recording Jehu's meeting with Jehonadab. The first section does not connect smoothly with what precedes, and it is thought to be most unlikely that the kinsmen of Ahaziah would travel to and from Samaria after the massacre there of the royal household. Thus, commentators regard these verses as fictitious (Stade, *ZAW* 5 [1885], pp. 276ff.) or, to say the least, as chronological misplacements (de Vaux, p. 161). Gray (p. 556), whilst agreeing with the latter view, finds some support for the former in the conventional number forty-two, which is well known in legends and mythology. On the other hand, it is quite possible that they had visited Samaria before the massacre and were now on their way back from Jezreel (Skinner, p. 330; Schmitt, *Elisa*, p. 28), and that the account can be accepted (cf. Šanda II, p. 110). The meeting with Jehonadab is also regarded as dubious, since his presence in Samaria with Jehu would inevitably arouse suspicion of the latter's attempt to give an impression that he was professing allegiance to Baal. Moreover, after the deletion of v. 23 as an 'apologetic' accretion, the meeting with Jehonadab has no connection with the remainder of the narrative. Again the passage has been treated as secondary (Stade, *ibid.*, p. 666) or as a misplacement (de Vaux, p. 162). But Schmitt (*ibid.*) again retains the passage on the grounds that it belongs stylistically to the rest of the narrative, which probably contained a report of a number of episodes that were only loosely connected with each other. The author probably regarded the meeting of Jehu and Jehonadab as a fitting introduction to his account of the massacre of the Baal worshippers of Samaria.

1. **Ahab had seventy sons in Samaria**: Because vv. 2, 3 imply that Jehu was dealing with the sons of Joram ('your master's sons'), it has been suggested that this sentence is a later gloss (cf. Stade, *op. cit.*, p. 275). It can, however, be retained if the term **sons** is understood as referring broadly to the royal family, or more specifically to all the male descendants of the royal house of Ahab (cf. Schmitt, *op. cit.*, p. 230). As Šanda comments (II, pp. 104ff.), Ahab's male descendants, including grandsons and great grandsons, could well have reached a high figure by this time, but the number **seventy** is a round number to denote many; cf. also the number descending to Egypt (Gen. 46:27) and the family of Gideon (Jg. 8:30; 9:2), as well as extra-biblical examples in Aramaean inscriptions (Cooke,

Inscriptions, p. 62) and in Ras Shamra mythology (Gray, p. 553).
sent them to Samaria: The success of Jehu's revolt depended to a
large measure on his ability to take **Samaria**, which was the crown
possession of the Omride dynasty, and therefore, the base of its
power. As emphasised by Alt (*Kleine Shriften III*, pp. 285–8),
Samaria in the northern kingdom, like Jerusalem in the south, was
an independent city-state; it was a private possession of the Omrides
and had become the administrative centre of their kingdom. **to the
rulers of the city**: *RSV*'s rendering of MT's 'Jezreel' as **the city** is
based on Luc. and the Vulg. It is preferred because Jehu himself
was in Jezreel and was sending a communication to Samaria. **to the
guardians of the sons of Ahab**: MT's 'to the guardians Ahab' is
syntactically impossible, and instead of deleting Ahab (with Schmitt,
op. cit., p. 230) it is better to follow the Gk. and to render like
RSV. Although the term *'omᵉnîm* can denote **guardians** or foster-
parents (Ru. 4:16; Est. 2:7), it is possible that here those entrusted
with the education of the royal household are denoted (cf. Prov.
8:30). Hence *NEB* renders 'tutors' (cf. Schmitt, *op. cit.*, p. 230).
Gray (*ibid.*) notes the three categories of leaders who received Jehu's
letters: **the rulers of the city** were the professional soldiers who
were in command of the city and dependent on the king for their
status (cf. Montgomery, p. 408); **the elders** were the representatives
of the people (the 'Senators', according to Montgomery, *ibid.*) and
the **guardians** were the educators of potential rulers.

2. Now then, as soon as this letter comes to you: It was usual
in business letters to include such a formal statement in transferring
from the introductory formalities and the greetings to the business
section. The same form occurs in Naaman's letters in 2 Kg. 5:6, in
the Lachish letters, in Aramaic in Ezr. 4:8 and also in letters from
Elephantiné (for references, see Montgomery, p. 408). Jehu's challenge is directed specifically here at the soldiers whose position was
dependent on their allegiance to the king, who is called **your master**
several times in vv. 2, 3. *RSV* rightly follows MSS and Vsns. in
reading **cities** for the singular 'city' of MT, although the latter is
retained by some on the ground that the reference is a specific one
to the city of Samaria (cf. Montgomery, p. 413; Alt, *op. cit.*, p.
287).

3. fight for your master's house: Jehu craftily did not call upon
the officials of Samaria to surrender, but challenges them to appoint
a successor to Joram who would then put up a fight for them. As
is seen from the next verse, this proved itself an effective challenge,
for they realized the futility of any attempt to fight Jehu.

5. This list of officials is the same as in v. 1, with the difference
that 'rulers of the city' is now more carefully defined as **he who was**

over the palace, i.e. the commander or head of the palace (see on 1 Kg. 4:6), and **he who was over the city**, or city commandant. **sent to Jehu**: On the basis of the reference in v. 6 to a 'second letter', it can be assumed that the message was sent in the form of an official correspondence.

6. a second letter: So MSS and Gk. for MT's a 'second time' (cf. *BHS*). **take the heads of your master's sons**: The Heb. literally has 'the heads of the men of the sons of your master'. Many MSS and Vsns. omit 'the men' as a gloss (cf. *BHS*); some MSS too read **sons** (*beˈnē*) as 'house' (*bēṯ*), probably indicating the family. Variant textual traditions probably arose here because of the ambiguity of the Heb. term *rāšē*, which may denote 'heads' or 'chiefs'. The glossator may have wished to suggest that Jehu asked for the men, not their heads. But as the narrative develops there is no ambiguity (v. 8). **who were bringing them up**: This rendering (cf. *NIV*, *NEB*) is somewhat ambiguous; but Gray's translation (p. 552), 'whom the notables of the city are rearing', makes the meaning quite clear.

7. and sent them to him at Jezreel: Šanda (II, p. 106) unnecessarily labours the point that, by sending the heads to Jezreel and remaining in Samaria themselves, the tutors were dissociating themselves from the usurper. The point cannot be pressed in view of the possibility that they too were included in the verb 'They have brought . . .' in v. 8 (cf. Fricke, pp. 131ff.).

8. Lay them in two heaps at the entrance of the gate until the morning: The heads of the princes were left on purpose by the gate to be seen by all the inhabitants as they were leaving the city in the morning to work in the fields. It was to serve as a warning to them and also to coerce them to submit to the new regime. As Šanda (II, p. 107) notes, Assyrian kings, especially Ashurbanipal and Shalmaneser III, left pyramids of heads by city gates as a warning of the revenge that would follow any act of rebellion.

9. You are innocent: Jehu's statement is usually taken to be an exoneration of the people from the massacre of the royal family. He accepts that he himself was responsible for the murder of Joram (**my master**), and seems to attribute the death of the descendants of Ahab to the train of events that brought judgment on the house of Ahab, and which, according to v. 10, were in fulfilment of God's word. Another possibility here is to render *ṣaddîqîm* (**innocent**) as 'fair' or 'impartial' (so Šanda II, p. 107) and to interpret Jehu's words as an appeal for a fair judgment from the people. He invites them to judge impartially who was really responsible for the death of the princes, with the implication that a fair judgment would lay the responsibility on the people of Samaria themselves (cf. Gray, p. 555). *NEB* renders 'You are fair judges. If I conspired against my

master and killed him, who put all these to death?'. The question
who struck down all these? is not answered, but the implication is
that the policy of the house of Ahab in Samaria has led inevitably
to this slaughter and that it has brought this fate upon itself. Verse
10, however, adds another aspect to the issue by implying that it
was the result of divine judgment.

10. Like 9:36ff., this verse contains an allusion to a prophetic
pronouncement against the Omride dynasty, and specifically
mentions Elijah. Noth (*ÜSt*, p. 84) regards only the sentence **for
the LORD has done what he said by his servant Elijah** as deuteronomistic, but the phrase **there shall fall to the earth nothing of the
word of the LORD** is also so typically deuteronomistic that it cannot
be separated from it (cf. Burney, p. xiv). The whole verse is best
attributed to a deuteronomistic reviser (cf. Schmitt, *op. cit.*, p. 22),
who, by adding it, has given one possible interpretation of Jehu's
question in v. 9; it gives a more religious tone to Jehu's actions.

11. Schmitt (*op. cit.*, p. 23) argues that this verse too is a
deuteronomistic addition; the phrase **all that remained of the house
of Ahab** is found again in v. 17, which is also regarded as deuteronomistic, and likewise **until he left him none remaining** is a phrase
that belongs to deuteronomistic circles (cf. Num. 21:35; Dt. 3:3).
What is implied here is that all the Omri clan that remained in the
ancestral home in Jezreel was also exterminated. **all his great men**:
NEB, 'all his nobles' reading *gᵉdōlāw* as *gô'ᵃlāw* (cf. *BHS* and also 1
Kg. 16:11), which is preferred also by some commentators (Burney,
p. 303; Gray, p. 553).

12. As noted above (p. 464), it is preferable not to question the
originality of vv. 12–14 and to treat them as secondary; the view
taken is that the passage can be retained as an account of a connected
episode, which may have occurred on the return journey of the
Judaean princes from Jezreel (cf. Schmitt, *op. cit.*, pp. 27ff.). **Beth-
eked of the Shepherds**: *NEB*, 'a shepherd's shelter'. The Heb.
root *'ākad* means 'to bind' (cf. Gen. 22:9), but the Arab. root also
has the meaning 'to meet together'; cf. Targ., 'the house of
gathering'. It has therefore been suggested that it was a well-known
gathering place for **the Shepherds** as they were moving their flocks
to pasture on arable land. There is no need to seek another philolog-
ical connection, as is done by Gray (p. 556), who thinks that it
may have been a market centre. Following Eusebius (*Onomasticon*
56.26–58.2) the place is usually identified with *Beit Qad* to the
north-east of Jenin (cf. Montgomery, p. 409), although Alt identifies
it with *Kufr Rāʻi* because Beit Qad is too far from the main road
between Samaria and Jezreel (*PJB* 27 [1931], pp. 32ff.).

13. we came down to visit the royal princes and the sons of

the queen mother: As noted above, it is unlikely that the kinsmen of Ahaziah would visit Samaria, or indeed would have been permitted to leave the city, after the massacre of its royal household. It has therefore to be assumed that they had left Samaria before the killings and were now on their way back.

14. slew them at the pit of Beth-eked: cf. Jer. 41:7. **forty-two persons**: For the use of the same round figure, cf. 2 Kg. 2:24.

15. As noted above (p. 464), the account of Jehu's meeting with Jehonadab is not without its difficulties, but it can be retained as an episode that may have been connected with the attack on Baal worship in the following verses. **the son of Rechab**: This is a general reference to Jehonadab's clan; according to Jer. 35, he was the founder of the order known as 'Rechabites', an ascetic group which championed the nomadic and simple life as true Yahwism. They did not cultivate the land, or plant a garden or vineyards; they refrained from drinking wine and they lived in tents in preference to houses. The Rechabite movement is usually interpreted as a protest against settled life and its accompanying evils. Baalism provided a constant proof of the dangers that were emerging from too close a link with Canaanite ideas and from the influence of agricultural life. The clan is connected in 1 Chr. 2:55 with the Kenites (cf. 1 Chr. 4:11, 12, where Rechab is to be read with LXX); this suggests the origin of their primitive Yahwism. Their Kenite ancestry also gives a basis to the suggestion that they were craftsmen, and more specifically metal-workers, who, because they were making chariots and other weapons, were unable to adopt a settled way of life. In the light of this connection, and the lack of evidence that they were consciously staging a religious protest like the Nazirites, it has been suggested that it was their occupation rather than their religion that was responsible for their way of life (Frick, *JBL* 90 [1971], pp. 279–87). The alliance between Jehu and Jehonadab in this narrative is certainly intended to show that his revolt was more than a personal bid for the throne; it had the support of the more conservative factions in Israel. **Is your heart true to my heart as mine is to yours?**: This rendering is based on the Gk., which gives a more balanced sentence than the more clumsy Heb. 'Is it right with your heart, as my heart is with your heart?' *NEB* has 'Are you with me heart and soul, as I am with you?' **give me your hand**: A hand-clasp denoted friendship, confirmation of a promise or an oath of allegiance to a new king (cf. Fricke, p. 134). The latter meaning is understood here, for Jehonadab in associating himself with Jehu was giving a sign of his allegiance to the one who had established himself on the throne; cf. 1 Chr. 29:24; 2 Chr. 30:8; Ezra 10:19; Ezek. 17:18; Pedersen, *Der Eid*, pp. 32ff.

16. see my zeal for the LORD: The same word, *qin'āh*, **zeal**, is used by Elijah in his affirmation that he had 'been jealous for the LORD' (1 Kg. 19:10, 14). As rightly pointed out by Gray (p. 560), the word in these contexts denotes fanaticism. **So he had him ride in his chariots**: *RSV* reads a singular verb with the Vsns. (see *BHS*) in preference to the Heb. 'and they made him ride . . .'

17. Because of its deuteronomistic phraseology (cf. 1 Kg. 15:29), and its intrusion between vv. 16 and 18, most of this verse is regarded as an addition (cf. Schmitt, *op. cit.*, pp. 22ff.). The first phrase, **And when he came to Samaria**, may be retained and then followed immediately by 'Jehu assembled all the people' (v. 18).

18. The destruction of Samaria's Baal-worshippers was the result of Jehu's trickery; he gave the impression that he was going to worship Baal and to offer a great sacrifice to which all the other worshippers of Baal were summoned; but he took advantage of the gathering to slaughter them. **Ahab served Baal a little** may be a correct assessment (Gray, p. 560). He had obviously provided a Baal-cult in Samaria for Jezebel and her Phoenician followers and guests, exactly as Solomon had done in Jerusalem for his foreign wives; but, as shown by the names of his children, Ahaziah and Joram, he was a Yahweh worshipper. **Jehu will serve him much**: Gray's suggestion (p. 560) that Jehu for his own satisfaction, and that of his associates, intended a word-play on *'ābad*, 'to worship', and *'ibbad*, 'to destroy', is without foundation in this verse, although it is present in v. 19. The Baal-worshippers probably thought that Jehu, having achieved his political aims, would follow the Omrides in his religious policy and was now at the beginning of his reign turning to Baal for his consecration as king of Samaria.

19. all the prophets of Baal, all his worshippers and all his priests: On **the prophets of Baal**, see 1 Kg. 18:19. Many commentators (Burney, p. 304; Schmitt, *op. cit.*, p. 233) omit the reference to **all his worshippers** on the grounds that in the first instance Jehu summoned the **prophets** and **priests**, who were then responsible for proclaiming an assembly (vv. 20ff.). Two MSS and Luc. read **all his worshippers** after **his priests**, which may suggest that it was inserted later from the margin. **for I have a great sacrifice to offer**: As noted by Gray (p. 560), there is probably a play here on the double meaning of the word *zebah*, which in Arab. primarily means 'slaughter', and secondarily, 'sacrifice'. **with cunning**: The Heb. *'oqbāh* is derived from the root *'āqab*, which is so prominent in the narrative of Jacob and provides a popular etymology of the patriarch's name (Gen. 25:26; 27:35ff.). It is perhaps better translated as 'in guile' (Gray, p. 557), or 'Jehu outwitted' (*NEB*) or 'deceptively' (*NIV*).

20. Sanctify a solemn assembly: One MS, Syr. and Targ. deliberately extracted the element of holiness from the assembly summoned to Samaria by giving 'Call' instead of **Sanctify**. The solemn assembly was probably an occasion when work was stopped and the people thus precluded from contact with the profane (Gray, p. 561); cf. also Jl 1:14, where it stands parallel to a fast. **So they proclaimed it**: The Gk. and Vulg. read the singular; but, in view of the suggestion above that the cultic officials were responsible for calling an assembly, it is better to retain MT.

21. from one end to the other: cf. also 2 Kg. 21:16. The temple in Samaria, like the Jerusalem Temple, probably had an extensive open court, which could accommodate a large gathering of people.

22. who was in charge of the wardrobe: Although the Heb. *meltāḥāh* is only found here, the meaning **wardrobe** is obvious from the context. Similar words are found in other languages. Gray (p. 561) thinks that the Ugaritic *'ilh*, which is similar in meaning, lies behind the reference in Jer. 38:11 to rags taken from 'the vestment department of the store'. **Bring out the vestments**: The reference is to garments usually worn on festal occasions, which were to be clean (cf. Exod. 19:10; Gen. 35:2) and may have been white (cf. Lucian, *De Dea Syra* 42; according to Josephus (*War* II.8.3) the Essenes also put on white clothes for some of their religious services).

23. The allusion to **Jehonadab the son of Rechab** is usually taken to be a gloss; he does not play any part in the action described. Schmitt (*op. cit.*, p. 25) regards the whole verse as coming from the so-called 'apologetic' revision; nowhere else is it said that Jehonadab entered the Temple, for in v. 25 it is only Jehu alone who offers sacrifice; the retention of this verse makes Jehu enter the sanctuary twice (vv. 23 and 24). **there is no servant of the LORD among you, but only the worshippers of Baal**: The use of two words which only differ slightly from each other in Heb. (*'abᵉdē*, 'servant' and *'ōbᵉdē*, 'worshippers') is intentional. The term **worshippers of Baal**, which is consistently used in this section, is preferred to *NEB*'s 'the ministers of Baal'.

24. Then he went in: MT reads the plural; cf. *NEB*, which, if retained, must refer to Jehu and the worshippers of Baal, and not Jehu and Jehonadab. The singular of the Gk., which has been accepted in *RSV*, is more consistent with v. 25. **eighty men**: Although the figures vary in the Vsns. (the Syr. giving 380 and Luc. 3,000), MT seems a reasonable number, since their task was to block exits from the temple. *RSV*'s **the man who allows . . . to escape** is based on a very slight emendation of the Heb. vowels (reading *yᵉmallēṭ* and avoiding the very difficult *yimmālēṭ*). **shall**

forfeit his life: *NEB* has 'shall answer for it with his life', for a very brief Heb. original.

25. as soon as he had made an end of offering: Since this verse uses a singular verb it implies that Jehu himself was responsible for the sacrifice; cf. also Solomon at the dedication of the Temple in 1 Kg. 8:5. **Jehu said to the guard and to the officers**: The *raṣîm* (plural), **guard**, were literally those running in front (cf. 1 Kg. 1:5), and the *šālîšîm*, **officers**, were the lieutenants or adjutants (cf. 2 Kg. 7:2; 9:25). **the guard and the officers cast them out**: MT has no object for the verb, but *RSV* provides one. Klostermann (p. 426) found an object in the two words 'the guard and the officers' which he emended to give 'and they cast the Asherim down to the ground' (reading *'arṣāh hā'ašērîm*); but it is not an entirely satisfactory emendation, since there is the possibility of another reference to the Asherah in v. 26 (so Burney, pp. 305ff.). Gray too (p. 558) finds an object in the same phrase, which he emends to 'into the third court', suggesting that the bodies were thrown out from the second court to the outer, public court. Admittedly these emendations are guesswork, and we do not know the original object of the verb. **into the inner room**: MT's 'to the city of the house of Baal' is incorrect, and many have accepted Klostermann's emendation (*ibid.*) to 'inmost shrine' (reading *'îr*, 'city', as *dᵉbîr*; cf. 1 Kg. 6:5). Šanda (II, p. 117) reads 'the portico' (accepting a Phoenician equivalent), whilst Montgomery (p. 411) renders 'citadel'. Gray (p. 562) retains *'îr*, but takes it, like the Ugaritic cognate *gr*, to mean the innermost recesses or shrine of a temple.

26. the pillar that was in the house of Baal: The Heb. reads 'pillars' here, but in view of **burned it** at the end of the verse, MSS and Vsns. are correct in reading the singular. Because a stone pillar cannot be burned, Stade (*ZAW* 5 [1885], p. 278) read 'asherah' here; cf. 1 Kg. 16:33. But Gray (p. 558) argues for the retention of **the pillar** on the grounds that the most effective way of destroying a standing stone was to heat it and throw cold water over it (cf. the Moabite stone).

27. The duplication in this verse makes it dubious. **And they demolished the pillar of Baal**: This is an unnecessary repetition of what has already been recorded in the previous verse, and also resembles too closely the phrase that follows. It is to be deleted or else slightly emended to read 'and they pulled down the altar of Baal' (cf. Exod. 34:13; Dt. 7:5; 12:3; Burney, p. 306; Gray, p. 558). The second clause, **and demolished the house of Baal**, is omitted from the Codex Vaticanus; it is therefore better to emend the previous clause and to delete the second one. **and made it a latrine**: The Heb. means literally 'the places of dung' (see 6:25 for the same word). The Massoretes tried to avoid the indelicacy by reading 'excrement'.

(iii) Editorial comments on the reign of Jehu 10:28–36

The miscellaneous material relating to the reign of Jehu that has been brought together here contains: (i) an assessment of his reign, partly favourable, and explaining why his dynasty enjoyed such a long period in authority (v. 30), and partly condemning him for following the example of Jeroboam (vv. 29, 31); (ii) a general account of the defeat of Israel by the Syrians in areas to the east of the Jordan (vv. 32ff.); (iii) a formal notice of death, burial, sources and length of reign (vv. 34–36).

Noth (ÜSt, p. 84) ascribes the whole section to the deuteronomistic editor, who has used material from older sources and revised it. But the revision of the material may have been a more complex process than envisaged by Noth. Some suggest two deuteronomistic editors, one responsible for vv. 28–29 and the other for vv. 30–31 (Gray, p. 562); others take v. 29 to be a later addition (Šanda II, p. 118). Jepsen, in his reconstruction of the matter relating directly to Jehu (Die Quellen, tables), attributes the oldest component in vv. 35–36 to the synchronistic chronicle; the reference to source in v. 34 and the criticism of Jehu in vv. 28–29 come from a priestly reviser, and the remaining two verses (vv. 30–31) have originated from the deuteronomistic editor. The view taken here is that the tradition of an oracle to Jehu, preserved in v. 30 and explaining the extended life of the Jehu dynasty, was modified by the deuteronomistic editors in two stages—firstly, by a group interested in the law (v. 31), and later by another reviser who inserted v. 29 with its reference to Bethel and Dan. Of course the whole section is set in a deuteronomistic framework (vv. 34–36).

28. The summary of Jehu's reign opens naturally with a statement that gives a brief resumé of the main contribution of his reign. This is taken up by v. 30.

29. The last phrase, **the golden calves that were in Bethel, and in Dan**, is far removed from **the sins of Jeroboam**, to which it stands in apposition. The verse breaks the sequence of vv. 28 to 30, seems to give a further exposition of the content of v. 31, and is syntactically awkward. Because of this, the whole verse is best regarded as a later addition (Šanda, ibid.), and not simply the last phrase as suggested by BHS (cf. Montgomery, p. 412; Gray, p. 562). On the worship of **the golden calves**, see on 1 Kg. 12:28. Although the golden calves were originally intended to be used symbolically in connection with the worship of Yahweh, here, as in

the account of their installation in 1 Kg. 12, they are severely
condemned by the deuteronomistic redactor.

30. An oracle to Jehu gives divine approval to all that he had
done. The original form may have been expanded by inserting the
phrase **and have done to the house of Ahab according to all that
was in my heart**; it is tautologous; in MT it is not joined to the
remainder of the verse by means of a conjunction, and it may have
been added on the basis of 9:7ff. (see further on this verse, Dietrich,
Prophetie, p. 34). The approval given in the statement that **you have
done well in carrying out what is right in my eyes** is confirmed by
the support given to the dynasty of Jehu elsewhere in the book of
Kings (cf. 13:4ff., 14ff.). A more critical attitude appears in Hos.
1:4, where, according to Šanda (*ibid.*), 'the blood of Jezreel' implies
a specific condemnation of the slaughter of Ahaziah and the princes
of Judah. **your sons of the fourth generation shall sit on the throne
of Israel**: The fulfilment of this prophecy is noted in 15:12. The
dynasty of Jehu reached its climax in the reign of Jeroboam II, and
it came to an end when his son Zechariah was killed and his throne
seized.

31. The formula used here for stating the verdict upon Jehu, with
its affirmation that he **was not careful to walk in the law of the
LORD**, is rather exceptional. The second half, confirming that **he
did not turn from the sins of Jeroboam**, is more familiar in content
and form (cf. 13:6, 11; 14:24).

32. the LORD began to cut off parts of Israel: cf. a similar
expression in Hab. 2:10. It is not necessary to accept the rendering
of some Vsns. which have taken the verb to mean 'to loathe' or 'to
be angry with'. The meaning is clear in *RSV*, or in *NEB*, 'began
to work havoc on Israel', or in Gray, 'began to dock Israel' (p. 563).
Hazael defeated them: Hazael's attack on Israel's Transjordanian
territory has to be understood against the background of Assyrian
presence in the Near East. When Shalmaneser III invaded Syria in
841 BC, he received tribute from 'Jehu, the son of Omri' (*Ya-ú-a
mār Hu-um-ri-i*; cf. Black Obelisk, *ANET*, p. 280; and further,
McCarter, *BASOR* 216 [1974], pp. 5–7; Thiele, *BASOR* 222
[1976], pp. 19–23), but failed to conquer the city of Damascus.
During the years 841–838 BC, when Shalmaneser was harassing
Damascus, gaining some victories in the regions of Hermon and
Hauran, and devastating the country, Jehu was enjoying a period
of peace, and was not very active in foreign affairs. After 838 BC,
however, Assyria eased its pressure on Syria, and did not make real
advance against it until 805 BC, when Adad-nirari III (810–783 BC)
was on the Assyrian throne. It is this period of Assyrian withdrawal
that gives the setting for Hazael's campaigns in Transjordania; they

are dated *c*. 824–815 BC (cf. Šanda II, p. 120; Gray, p. 564). Hazael had been opposing Assyria on his own (cf. Jepsen, *AfO* 14 [1942], p. 159), and when the lull came he attacked Israel's Transjordanian territory in order to strengthen his rear. Israel as a result lost most of its territory in the area, and Syria gained control over lands to the south of Damascus, and even advanced as far as the Philistine coastal plain (cf. 12:17ff.; 13). It is probable that Israel's army suffered severe losses and was greatly reduced (cf. 13:7).

33. from the Jordan eastward: The historical reliability of this description, and especially the further definition, **from Aroer, which is by the valley of the Arnon**, has been questioned. It is known from the Mesha inscription that much of the territory north of the Arnon had already been lost to Moab. Consequently, the claim of v. 33 has been regarded as an exaggeration (Donner, *IJH*, p. 413), and either the whole verse (so Stade, *op. cit.*, p. 279), or at least parts of it (Burney, p. 307; Montgomery, p. 412), deleted as unhistorical. But it may be possible to argue for the retention of the verse on the grounds that some of Israel's Transjordanian territory had been returned before it was lost again to Hazael. Šanda (II, pp. 119ff.) suggested that Syria returned Ramoth-gilead to Israel in the hope that she might be induced to join forces with Syria against Assyria. As far as the Aroer region is concerned, it may be that Jehu had recovered it during his early years, when Hazael was engaged against the Assyrians (Šanda, *ibid.*), or else that Hazael had seized it from Moab and handed it over to Israel as a further inducement to help Syria against Assyria (Gray, p. 565). Whatever the exact course of events may have been, it is clear that Israel had lost its Transjordanian territory until it was later recored by Jeroboam II (2 Kg. 14:25). **Aroer, which is by the valley of the Arnon**: cf. also Dt. 2:36. It is mentioned elsewhere as the southern limit of Israelite territory (Jos. 12:2; 13:9, 16), and is usually identified with *'Ara'ir* to the north of the river **Arnon** (*Wadi Mojib*); see further, Glueck, *AASOR* [1934], pp. 49ff.

34. and all his might: cf. also 1 Kg. 5:23. Šanda (II, p. 120) interprets the phrase in this instance as a reference to Jehu's success in achieving the return of lost territory in Moab. The Gk. adds 'and the conspiracy which he made' on the analogy of the references to Zimri (1 Kg. 16:20) and Shallum (1 Kg. 15:15), but it is probably secondary.

35–36. It is unusual to record the length of a king's reign at the end of the account. Jehu's reign of **twenty-eight years** extended from 842 to 815 BC. At the end of these biographical notes, the Gk. adds material from 8:25ff.; 9 relating to the reign of Ahaziah.

4. A HISTORY OF THE TWO KINGDOMS TO THE FALL OF SAMARIA

2 Kg. 11:1–17:41

(a) Athaliah and the conspiracy of Jehoiada

11:1–20

Jehu's *coup d'état* in the northern kingdom had its counterpart in the southern kingdom when Athaliah, who had usurped the throne after Ahaziah's death, was deposed in favour of the boy-king Jehoash in a *coup* master-minded by Jehoiada the priest. The connection between these two revolts is that they were both directed against the influence of the house of Omri upon the two kingdoms. As a result of Jehu's revolt the Omride dynasty was overthrown, and, as Gray (p. 566) rightly remarks, Jehu ventured to kill Ahaziah because he knew that a strong conservative element in the southern kingdom was opposed to the liaison between the royal house of Judah and the house of Omri. Athaliah, who was herself from the house of Ahab and Jezebel, had anticipated opposition from conservative and nationalistic factions, and by killing the heirs to the throne had removed the persons most likely to be made the centre of such opposition. In this she followed the pattern set by Jehoram, who faced a similar situation on the death of Jehoshaphat (cf. 2 Chr. 21:4). The measures taken by Athaliah, together with the success of the *coup* in the north, strengthened the determination of the opposition in the south. However, some factors peculiar to the southern situation must be noted. The murder of the heirs-apparent by Athaliah, followed by a six-year reign by this queen of alien descent, constituted a real threat to the Davidic dynasty. The possibility that the Davidic line was becoming extinct aroused a strong feeling among the people and their leaders, with the result that when the time for revolt came it was a highly successful one. Whereas the revolt in the north was led by Jehu, a soldier, who took advantage of the opposition to the Omride dynasty fanned by the prophetic movement, the *coup d'état* in the south was a combined effort by the people, the priesthood and the palace guards. The movement in the north although inspired by the prophets, failed but the movement in the south, because it had been organized by the priesthood and involved military personnel and the populace, and was to a large degree a movement supported by the religious establishment, had a more permanent success (so Montgomery, p. 417).

The account as it appears in chapter 11 is not a unity (as recognised by Stade, *ZAW* 5 [1885], pp. 275–97), and vv. 13–18a are usually separated from vv. 1–12, 18b–20. The reasons given are as follows: (a) Athaliah's death seems to be reported twice (v. 16 and

20), and there are some differences of detail. Verses 13–18a report that Athaliah was killed in the palace after she had been moved from the Temple deliberately to avoid killing her in the holy precinct; but in v. 20 it is simply stated that she was killed in the palace without any mention of her presence in the Temple. Gray (p. 566) doubts the importance of this point, since both sections agree that she was murdered in the palace; but he attaches more weight to the actual timing of the death since vv. 13–18a place it before the covenant with God and the people, and v. 20 following he *coup* when calm had been restored. (b) In vv. 13–18a the queen's name is given as *Athalyāh*, but in vv. 4–12, 18b–20 the form is *Athalyāhû*. Gray (*ibid.*) does not find this a convincing argument because of the occurrence of both forms in vv. 1–3. (c) The comparative import- ance of priests and the people also deserves consideration. The main narrative relates how the priest Jehoiada planned the revolt, and after rallying the support of military personnel executed it successfully. Not until v. 13 are the people mentioned, but in vv. 13–18a they have a significant role in the procedure, despite Rudolph's attempt (*Fest. Bertholet*, pp. 473–8) to reduce the number of references to the people of the land in this section. On the basis of this distinction, the main narrative (vv 1–12, 18b–20) has been labelled as priestly and the minor section (vv. 13–18a) attributed to a popular source (cf. Šanda II, p. 135; Gray, pp. 565ff.). But this is not an entirely satisfactory designation, for vv. 1–12, 18b–20 also mention the people (vv. 19, 20), and vv. 13–18a picture the priest as taking the initiative and show respect to the Temple. So prominent is the religious aspect in vv. 13–18a that Montgomery (p. 418) regards it as a section underlining the religious motive behind the revolt in contrast to the political motives stressed in the main narrative. Even if the two traditions are separated, they are to be regarded as complementary rather than divergent; they depict the same historical situation, and are both reporting true history.

There is no agreement on the exact definition of the relationship between these two sections. From the time of Stade (*ibid.*) vv. 13–18a have been called an interpolation. Montgomery (*ibid.*) assumes that both sections came from contemporary writers, the main story being, like 2 Kg. 22–23, attributed to an official scribe and ignoring the more violent aspects of Athaliah's overthrow, and the interpolation, also historically reliable, having the vivid style of the northern raconteurs. Gray (*ibid.*) affirms Wellhausen's postul- ation (*Composition*, p. 293ff.) that the main narrative belongs to the same priestly source as chapters 12; 6:10ff.; 22; but, after the Josianic reformation, vv. 13–18a were added to give 'the people of the land' the same important role as they had in that later reform (see chapter

23). By adding these verses, what was implicit in the main narrative
is made explicit. The view taken here is that vv. 1–12, 18*b*–20
constitute the original historical narrative giving an account of the
coup d'état in the southern kingdom. It was a simple and straightforward narrative that lacked detail in comparison with the account in
chapter 9–10 of similar events in the north. A later editor revised
the original by adding a section giving more details of Athaliah's
death, emphasizing more clearly the religious, anti-Baal motives of
the revolt and showing too the extent of the popular support gained
by the leaders (Hoffmann, *Reform*, pp. 104–13).

1. **Athaliah the mother of Ahaziah**: Athaliah is also called the
daughter of Ahab, which, as noted under 2 Kg. 8:18, is acceptable.
There is uncertainty about the meaning of her name (see under
8:26), which in this narrative appears in two forms, the *Athalyāh* of
this verse being commonly retained, but vv. 2 and 20 giving the
alternative *Athalyāhû*. **she arose and destroyed all the royal family**:
Athaliah's massacre was directed specifically at the heirs-apparent;
cf. *NEB* 'all the royal line'; Gray (p. 569) 'all the seed royal'.
Jehu had slaughtered forty-two members of the royal family (2 Kg.
10–14), and it would appear that Athaliah moved with speed to
execute all that remained in Jerusalem. As noted by Gray (p. 569),
the absence of the usual editorial formulae for introducing Athaliah's
reign and for recording its conclusion indicates that it was regarded
as an usurpation.

2. **Jehosheba**: According to 2 Chr. 22:11, which may contain a
reliable tradition (Williamson, *Chronicles*, p. 315), she was the wife
of Jehoiada the priest, which explains how she was in a position
to hide the child in the Temple chambers. Her name, which contains
a combination of the divine name and *šeba'*, 'oath', has a different
form 'Jehoshabeath', in Chronicles. **sister of Ahaziah**: She was
probably a half-sister, and therefore not a daughter of Athaliah
(Šanda II, p. 127; Gray, p. 570). **Joash, the son of Ahaziah**: A
variant form of the name is Jehoash (cf. 12:1), and the same variation
occurs in reference to the northern king with an identical name (cf.
2 Kg. 13:9, 10). The name Joash is found in the Lachish letters
and the Elephantiné papyri; the verbal element also appears as *'ws*
in Aramaic names and corresponds to the Arab. *'ws*, 'to give' (so
Montgomery, p. 431); cf. also Josiah, which is from the same origin
and stole him: The verb *gānab* is used here to denote kidnapping
(cf. Gen. 40:15; Dt. 24:7), and may also have the same meaning in
the Decalogue (Exod. 20:15; cf. Gray, p. 570; Alt, *Kleine Schriften
I*, pp. 333–40).

3. **and he remained with her six years, hid in the house of the
LORD**: The ease with which Jehosheba's plan was executed can be

understood if two factors are borne in mind: first, since royal children were given out to foster mothers, Athaliah could be totally unaware of Joash's existence; second, the boy could easily be brought up in the priests' quarters in the Temple as one of the priests' children or as a young devotee (cf. Gray, p. 570). There is no need to doubt the historicity of this statement.

4. Jehoiada: Since this is the first mention of the main character in the drama, it is better to add 'the priest' with some Gk. MSS; cf. v. 9. **captains of the Carites**: The word **captains** in this instance translates the Heb. 'captains of the hundreds'; cf. *NEB*, 'captains of units of hundreds'. **the Carites**: They are only mentioned elsewhere in the *OT* in the *Kᵉtîb* of 2 Sam. 20:23. But Herodotus II.154 mentions Carians from Cilicia as the bodyguard of Psammeticus of Egypt (664–610 BC), and it is possible that they had also been employed for such a task by Judaean kings (so Šanda II, p. 127; Gray, p. 571). However, the *Qᵉrē* of 2 Sam. 20:23 reads Cherethites, who are frequently mentioned with the Pelethites as the royal bodyguard (see on 1 Kg. 1:38), and it is possible that this verse refers to the same group of mercenaries. **the guards**: The same word occurs in 1 Kg. 1:5 for those running before the king. **he made a covenant with them**: This is best translated as 'he made an agreement with them' (*NEB*).

5–8. Although the organizer of the *coup* issued detailed instructions, the meaning is by no means clear. It is generally accepted that v. 6 is a gloss (cf. Wellhausen, *Composition*, p. 361), originating from a person who was well informed about the position of troops. This addition, called a pre-redactional gloss by Šanda (II, p. 128), tried to explain the reference to **one third** in v. 5 by adding information about the other two thirds in v. 6. But, the whole issue becomes confused because v. 7 also refers to **two divisions** and provides a continuation of v. 5. If v. 6 is ignored, the position becomes clearer. On the sabbath there was a change in the pattern of guard duty, because on this day two companies were posted in the Temple and one in the palace instead of the normal weekday routine when only one company was on guard in the Temple and two in the palace. When the change was made on the sabbath, the two companies in the palace came up to the Temple to relieve the company on duty there. Jehoiada's plan was to take advantage of this change-over by retaining the three companies in the Temple (cf. Skinner, p. 338). It was a plan that was bound to succeed, because its timing to coincide with the movement of troops would not arouse suspicion; by retaining the three companies in the Temple to guard the newly acclaimed king, Athaliah and the palace were denuded of military personnel.

5. those who come off duty on the sabbath and guard the king's house: The first company was to **come off duty** in the Temple, and to return to quarters in the palace and there **guard the king's house**.

6. This intrusion contains many difficulties. **the gate Sur** is difficult to identify because the meaning of the term is unclear. 2 Chr. 23:5 has 'the Gate of the Foundation', and the Vsns. have obviosuly tried to guess the meaning. Galling (*PJB* 27 [1931], pp. 51ff.), followed by Rudolph (*op. cit.*, pp. 474ff.), takes **Sur** to be a corruption of *sûs*, 'horse', and thus finds a reference here to 'the horses' entrance' of vv. 16, 19. **the gate behind the guards**: According to Šanda (II, p. 128), the gate of the guards stood between the Temple and the palace (cf. v. 19). After the phrase **shall guard the palace** the Heb. reads an unknown word, *massāḥ*, which is omitted from the Gk. (cf. *RSV*, *NEB*). Many suggestions have been made to overcome the difficulty. Some ignore the word altogether, and either accept the remaining text (as in *RSV*) or else emend it slightly, as is done by Rudolph (*ibid.*), who reads 'at the other gate' and omits 'the guards' as a gloss. Others read it as a proper name, 'behind the house of Massach' (Šanda I, p. 125), whilst others again try to interpret the Heb., giving the meaning 'from destruction' (Syr.; Rashi) or 'and be a barrier' (RV) or 'relieving one another' (a cognate of the Arab. *nasaḥa*, 'to replace'; so Montgomery, p. 424; Gray, *ibid.*). Unfortunately there can be no certainty about any of these possibilities.

7. which come on duty in force on the sabbath: This refers to those coming **on duty**, in other words those coming out of their quarters in the palace and taking over guard at the Temple. MT adds 'to the king' at the end of the verse; it is omitted from the *RSV* (cf. *BHS*), but retained in *NEB*, 'shall be on duty for the king'.

8. shall surround the king: This applies to all three companies, the one of v. 5 and the two of v. 7. **the ranks**: *RSV* takes the Heb. *šᵉdērôṯ* (cf. Akkad. *sidirtu*) to be a military term denoting the ranks of the guardsmen. Šanda (II, p. 129) takes it to be the ranks of pillars or colonnades standing between the Temple and the palace (cf. v. 11, and also Aquila and Symmachus 'the precincts').

9. The three companies of guards mentioned in vv. 5, 7 are now brought together under two categories, namely, those going **off duty on the sabbath** and due to return to their palace quarters and those coming **on duty on the sabbath** and moving from their palace quarters to the Temple.

10. the spears and shields that had been King David's: 2 Sam. 8:7 refers to David's dedication of gold shields taken from the servants of Hadadeser; these were later replaced by bronze shields

(1 Kg. 14:26ff.), which were carried by the guards during royal visitations. A difficulty is raised by the fact that neither 2 Sam. 8:7 nor 1 Kg. 14:26–28 mention **spears** with the **shields**. *RSV* has followed the Vsns. and 2 Chr. 23:9 in reading the plural instead of MT's 'spear', and so assumes that **spears and shields** specially consecrated for use in the holy precincts were handed over to the guards when they reported for duty in the Temple (cf. Gray, p. 573). This explanation goes a long way to meet the objection to the idea that the guards came to the Temple unarmed. But, if the singular of MT is retained, it may be suggested that David's own spear and shield had been preserved in the Temple and were brought out for the coronation of a new king. As noted by Gray, the spear was a symbol of royal authority (cf. 1 Sam. 26:7) and may have been handed over by the commander to the king on this important ceremonial occasion. This gives a satisfactory explanation of the handing over by the priest, and renders unnecessary the suggestion that this verse is a gloss introduced from 2 Chr. 23:9 (as suggested by Skinner, p. 339; Montgomery, p. 420).

11. **from the south side of the house to the north side**: The guards probably formed a semi-circle around the altar and the house and extending from the south corner to the north corner of the Temple (so Burney, p. 310; Šanda II, p. 130); they thus enclosed the space between the porch and the altar. The second half of this verse is difficult to follow in MT, which can be translated 'by the altar and the house, by the king round about'; cf. *NEB*, 'surrounding the king'. Many commentators omit the reference to the king (Skinner, *ibid*.; Šanda, *ibid*.), arguing that it is premature, as the king had not yet been brought into the Temple. If retained, it can be justified on the grounds that the arrangements made anticipated the king's presence, and guards took up their positions to surround and protect the place where he would be standing. Burney (*ibid*.; followed by Gray, p. 571, and *RSV*) assumed that 'round about' was misplaced in MT and then later explained by adding a reference to the king. Despite the difficulty of the text, its meaning is clear—a semi-circle was formed to guard the area where the king's coronation was to be performed.

12. **and put the crown upon him**: The word *nēzer* is usually translated 'crown' or 'diadem', and there is no need to resort to such a cumbersome translation as 'symbol of dedication' in order to leave open the identity of the *nēzer* and to allow for its identification with the golden flower on the turban of the high priest (Exod. 29:6, 7; 39:30; Lev. 8:9, 10; cf. Gray, p. 573). 2 Sam. 1:10 suggests that the king wore some symbol on his headgear or over his helmet when he went out to war. Here, however, **the crown** may have been

a special headgear used on ceremonial occasions; cf. the pictures from Assyria and Egypt; see Šanda, *ibid*. **and gave him the testimony**: Since the time of Wellhausen (*Composition*, p. 361) an emendation of **testimony** ('*ēdût*) to 'bracelets' (*se'ādôt*) has found favour among commentators (Burney, p. 311; Skinner, p. 340; cf. Driver, *JTS* [1953], pp. 293ff.). In support of this change it can be noted that MT's 'put the crown and the testimony' (avoided by *RSV*) is awkward, and again that a crown and bracelets are mentioned together in 2 Sam. 1:10. Another emendation connected with 2 Sam. 1:10 is to read '*es'ādôt*, 'armlet', which is rejected by Yeivin (*IEJ* 24 [1974], pp. 17–20) in favour of a proposed Semitic root behind '*ēdût* denoting a piece of jewellery or decoration in the shape of a tailed and winged sun disk worn under the diadem. But recent reconstructions of the enthronement ritual envisage the handing over of a special document to the king, and the terms '*ēdût* here and *hōq* in Ps. 2:7ff. are taken to refer to such a document. The contents of such a document have been much debated, some implying that the law was handed over to the king (Widengren, *JSS* 2 [1957], pp. 2ff.), others thinking of a formal protocol giving the king's title deeds, his throne names and the conditions of his office (von Rad, *TLZ* [1947], col. 211–16; Falk, *VT* 11 [1961], p. 91; cf. *NEB*, 'handed him the warrant', with the emphasis on the conditions in relation to the people, not to God as by Fohrer, *ZAW* 71 [1959], p. 3), and yet others, working on the concept of a covenant between God and the Davidic king (2 Sam. 7:12–16), assume that the document contained either the promises of the covenant (von Rad, *ibid*.; Press, *ThZ* 13 [1957], p. 325) or its obligations (Johnson, *Sacral Kingship*, p. 21; Gray, pp. 573ff.). It is accepted here that, since the king's authority was based on God's covenant, the document handed over to the king during the enthronement ritual contained both the promises of the covenant and its obligations, or more specifically a declaration of the king's adoption by God and the demands made upon him in his new office (Jones, *VT* 15 [1965], pp. 336–44). **they proclaimed him king and anointed him**: The plural verbs are unnatural since the proclamation and anointing were probably undertaken, along with the crowning and handing over the testimony, by Jehoiada the priest. The Gk. rightly reads the two verbs in the singular (cf. *NEB*). MT may have been influenced by 2 Chr. 23:11, where the anointing was performed by 'Jehoiada and his sons'. On the anointing, see 1 Kg. 1:34; and on **Long live the king**, 1 Kg. 1:25. Šanda (II, p. 131) finds a parallel to the procedure here in the anointing of Aaron (Exod. 29:6, 7; Lev. 8:9, 10), where crowning preceded anointing.

13. the noise of the guard and of the people: The conjunction joining **the guard** to **the people** is not found in MT, although some MSS have inserted it. Many commentators favour the retention of **the people**, but the deletion of **the guard** on the grounds that it is an intrusion intended to connect a report that recognizes the part of the people in the revolt (vv. 13–18*a*) and the remainder of the narrative, which attributes the *coup* to the priesthood and the palace guard (cf. Burney, p. 311; Gray, p. 575). Although the priest and military personnel are also present in vv. 13–18*a*, the awkward grammatical construction of the sentence supports the omission of **the guard**. The meaning of **the people** is not easy to decide. Admittedly **the people** can in some instances denote 'the army' (Burney, *ibid.*; Montgomery, p. 421, who assumes that the patriots had been fully armed), but that does not seem to suit the context (Šanda, *ibid.*). Another possibility is to identify **the people** of this verse with 'the people of the land' in vv. 14, 18, 19, 20 (cf. Gray, p. 577, where it is argued against discriminating between them). But, because 'the people of the land' is a technical term for a specific class or faction of the population, it is preferable to retain **the people** here as a general designation of the assembled crowd which faced the queen as she walked into the Temple. On closer analysis it was an assembly of 'the people of the land', but initially it appeared to have been a common assembly of people; cf. *NEB*, which uses 'the people' in v. 13, but 'the populace' elsewhere.

14. the king standing by the pillar, according to the custom: There is no agreement on the translation of the Heb. *'ammûd*, rendered **pillar** in *RSV*; cf. also 2 Kg. 23:3. The parallel of 2 Kg. 23:3 in 2 Chr. 34:31 merely has 'in his place' (*'ōmᵉdô*); cf. also Neh. 8:7. It must be granted, however, that MT here, as in 2 Kg. 23:3, seems to identify a particular location in the Temple more specifically than is conveyed by the translation 'in his place'. The correction of *'ammûd* to *'ōmēd*, 'platform', thus giving 'on the platform' or 'on the dais' (*NEB*; cf. Thenius, p. 335; North, *ZAW* 50 [1932], pp. 19ff.), is made unlikely by the absence of other evidence of the use of a platform, in contrast to the many other references to the pillar. Montgomery (p. 421) refers to the Old Babylonian custom of holding legal procedures 'by the pillar of Shamash', and it is known that Thothmes II mentions 'the station of the king' in the Temple of Amon (cf. Šanda II, p. 131). Two references imply that **the pillar** was near the entrance of the Temple; cf. the parallel passage in 2 Chr. 23:13, which refers to 'his pillar by the entrance' and Ezek. 46:2 referring to 'the post of the gate'. This seems to confirm the view that he stood by one of the pillars Jachin and Boaz, which may have been symbols of the covenant between God and the Davidic dynasty (see on 1 Kg. 7:20). **the captains and the**

trumpeters beside the king: The Heb. has 'trumpets' (*ḥªṣōṣªrôṯ*) here, as it does later in the verse; but the appropriateness of the word has been questioned on the grounds that an impersonal noun is not expected here as a complement of **captains**. One way of avoiding the difficulty is followed by *RSV* in rendering 'trumpets' as **trumpeters**, and another by Gray (p. 576) in omitting it altogether because it is a dittograph of its later occurrence. Another entirely different solution is found by reading **captains** (*śārîm*) as 'singers' (*šārîm*); cf. Gk. and Vulg. (see *BHS*) and also 2 Chr. 23:13, which retains **captains** but characteristically adds another sentence giving prominence to 'singers' (Williamson, *Chronicles*, p. 316). *NEB* has changed the text slightly to give 'outbursts of song and fanfares of trumpets'. The **trumpets** were in this instance blown by the people, as a sign of rejoicing, exactly as pipes or flutes were played on Solomon's accession (cf. 1 Kg. 1:40); reference is not made here to the *šôp̄ār*, which had distinctly cultic associations; cf. Num. 10:1ff.

all the people of the land: This phrase is not precisely defined in the *OT*, and has therefore been open to various interpretations (for a survey, see Talmon, *Jewish Studies I*, pp. 71–6), which at times become confused, because the term is used in different periods, and sufficient allowance has not been made for the possibility of a change in its political and social, as well as religious, connotation. Its use in post-Exilic times to denote simple, provincial people in contrast to the spiritual leaders of Jerusalem, who were under the influence of the Babylonian Jewish community, marks a development in the concept. Some advocate such a distinction between the simple people and the leaders even in pre-Exilic times; **the people of the land** are thought to have been the proletariat robbed of their land and rights, and therefore, standing in contrast to the nobility (Galling, *AO* 28 [1929], pp. 5–64); cf. *NEB* 'the populace'. Others take a different view and explain **the people of the land** as property owners, who because of their position had certain privileges, but also some obligations (cf. de Vaux, *RA* 58 [1964], pp. 167–72). Alt (*Essays*, pp. 239–59) gave the term a political interpretation by finding in it a reference to the population of the provincial towns of Judah, especially the farmers, in contrast to the residents of Jerusalem; these were two distinct political and social classes (cf. 2 Kg. 23:2; Isa. 5:3), and it is claimed that, whenever the Jerusalem group plotted against the house of David, the people of Judah (called **the people of the land**) would enter Jerusalem and forcibly seize the throne to install upon it a descendant of the house of David. Whatever the difficulties of Alt's hypothesis, he was right in emphasizing the part played by **the people of the land** on occasions when support was needed for the Davidic claimant to the throne against plots among those around the court in Jerusalem and their desire to take the throne for a rival claimant; they are mentioned in connection with Joash, Amaziah, Uzziah and Josiah. Accepting this as his starting point, Soggin (*VT* 13 [1963], pp. 187–95) gives the term **the people of the land** a wider definition than is found among those who support an identification with the landowners of Judah (cf. Würthwein, *Der 'amm ha'arez*, pp. 19–22). According to Soggin, it denoted a large section of the population, not restricted to a special class nor having particular social affiliations, which was faithful to the Yahwistic tradition. They represented the sacral community which was loyal to the covenant tradition of Israel (cf. Gray, p. 578). The group had other interests in addition to its allegiance to the covenant tradition as expressed in its support for the Davidic dynasty. Added to the fact that the concept is always mentioned in pre-Exilic times in connection with Judaean affairs, but never in connection with the northern kingdom, are such factors as the possession of judicial authority by the group (Jer. 36; 2 Kg. 21:9), its military power (2 Kg. 25:19) and its ability to take action in dynastic matters (cf. 2 Kg. 14:21; 21:24; Daiches, *JTS* 30 [1929], pp. 245–9; Gordis, *JQR* 25 [1934–5], pp. 237–59). Whether the body was a national council representing the people and a development out of the older institution of the elders (as argued by Sulzberger, *'Am-ha-aretz*, pp. 72–8 and Auerbach, *Jewish Studies*, pp. 362–6) is far from certain. A still wider meaning is proposed by Halpern (*The Constitution*, pp. 190–5), who takes the term to refer to the enfranchised citizenry of Judah. In view of the varied and at times inconsistent use of the term, Nicholson (*JSS* 10 [1965], pp. 59–66) reaches a correct conclusion in saying that the term has no precise and set definition, cf. also Ihromi, *VT* 24 [1974], pp. 421–439, where it is argued that the term is used sometimes for a group in Judah, and sometimes for a group in Jerusalem. On the evidence of the present context, it seems that the group at this time represented a political element in Judah that showed loyalty to the house of David and to the principle of hereditary succession.

15. **the captains who were set over the army**: The Heb. has 'the captains of hundreds, the musterers (with a slight emendation) of the army'. Placing the two descriptions side by side is unnecessary, and it is plausible to suggest that 'the captains of hundreds' is a gloss added from vv. 4, 9, 10 in order to identify 'those set over the army' of this later addition (cf. Burney, pp. 311ff.). **Bring her out between the ranks**: The reference here to **the ranks** mentioned in v. 8 causes some difficulty, and it has been suggested that this phrase too is a secondary addition intended to bring together the

two sources found in the same chapter (Burney, p. 312; Šanda II,
p. 132). There is no textual support for its omission, but it is
difficult to conceive that Athaliah had gone inside the ranks which
were so carefully planned to protect the king. *NEB* translates 'bring
her outside the precincts', which gives a good sense, especially in
view of the latter half of the verse. **Let her not be slain in the
house of the LORD**: As noted above, a distinction between the two
accounts of Athaliah's overthrow that designates one as priestly and
the other as secular, is not entirely satisfactory. It is the priest that
takes the initiative in this verse, which is in the middle of the so-
called secular or popular account, and he characteristically shows
concern for the Temple.

16. So they laid hands on her: This is LXX's translation, and it
has been accepted by *AV*, *RSV* and *NEB*. The reading of the Targ.
and Syr., 'and they made way for her' (so *RV*), is doubtful, and
the adduced parallel usage in Jos. 8:12 is uncertain (Burney, p. 312).
Attempts have been made to avoid the impression of violence in
this connection, so that the statement that **she was slain** at the end
of the verse can be interpreted as a reference to the later occurrence
reported in v. 20. Thus Gray (pp. 576, 579) proposes 'she was
escorted'. Although the death of Athaliah is recorded twice, the
reports agree that she was murdered in the palace; the additional
detail supplied by this verse is that it happened immediately after
she had been escorted there from the Temple. **through the horses'
entrance**: Reference is made elsewhere to one of the entrances to
the Temple known as the Horse Gate (cf. 2 Kg. 23:11; Jer. 31:40;
Neh. 3:28). The **horses' entrance** of this verse, however, belongs
to the royal palace and not the Temple (cf. Fricke, p. 151), although
it is logical to assume that both were in some way related (Gray,
pp. 578ff.).

17. Jehoiada made a covenant: Despite the fact that this reference to covenant making belongs to the revised form of the narrative, considerable importance is attached to this verse. Gray (pp.
579ff.) rightly abandons the traditional description of the covenant
as possessing a religious and political aspect (cf. Skinner, p. 341;
Montgomery, p. 422) in order to bring out three phases in the
covenant transaction, namely the covenant between God and the
king, between God and the people and between the king and the
people. Whether these three aspects of covenant making were
customary, as is suggested by the use of the article in Heb., 'made
the covenant', is uncertain. A kingship based on a covenant relationship seems to emerge from *OT* texts describing David's covenant
with Israel at Hebron (2 Sam. 5:3), Nathan's oracle (2 Sam. 7:8–16),
the covenant with Joash in the present section and the covenant

made by Josiah (2 Kg. 23:3). Although these passages emphasize
the importance of a kingship based on a covenant relationship, with
the king being a custodian of the covenant law (Widengren, *op. cit.*,
pp. 1–32), appearing as the vassal of Yahweh because of the vassal-
treaty form of the covenant (de Vaux, *Fest. Tisserant*, pp. 119–23)
and being regarded as the earthly representative of God (Thornton,
JTS 14 [1963], pp. 1–11; Clements, *God and Temple*, pp. 60ff.), it
has to be admitted that the texts admit a number of variations and
that it is impossible to think of a uniform pattern for the royal
covenant (cf. Fohrer, *op. cit.*, pp. 1–22). Gray's distinction between
God's covenant with the king and his covenant with the people
seems in this particular case to be justified. The **covenant between
the LORD and the king** was the customary renewal of the Davidic
covenant, but the covenant between him and the people was the
renewal of the Sinai covenant, emphasizing a rededication of the
people, which of course had become necessary because of the introduction of foreign practices by Athaliah. The suggestion that the
covenant was made during the New Year Festival, the most suitable
practical occasion for staging a revolution because it was the usual
time for the enthronement of a new king, together with the hint
that there was some significance in the timing of the revolt in
Athaliah's seventh year, may be likely, but is by no means certain.
The more political aspect of the covenant, **also between the king
and the people**, is regarded by many commentators as suspect
because of its omission from 2 Chr. 23:16 and from some Gk. texts
(see *BHS*). But in view of other instances in the *OT* of a covenant
between king and people (2 Sam. 5:3; 1 Kg. 12:2ff.; 2 Kg. 23:3),
MT should be retained, and the omission of this element from later
tradition can be regarded as an attempt to simplify the text (Montgomery, p. 422; Gray, p. 580; Williamson, *Chronicles*, p. 317).
Montgomery (*ibid.*) found a parallel for this covenant involving
God, the king and the people in a South Arabian inscription giving
a constitution for the state of Kataban.

18. The final part of the revision in vv. 13–18*a*, which emphasizes
the religious motive of the revolt by referring to the removal of all
traces of the foreign cult supported by Athaliah, gives the Judaean
revolt the same character as the Samaritan uprising under Jehu.
went to the house of Baal: It is now impossible to locate the shrine
of Baal. Šanda (II, p. 137) suggests that it may have been situated
in the royal palace rather than in the Temple, whereas Gray (p. 580)
describes it as a sacred enclosure that was open to the sky, except
for a small inner shrine, and may have stood in the court of the
Temple. **and his images**: Whereas the account of the revolt in the
north describes how pillars (*maṣṣēḇôṯ*) were brought out and burnt

(see above, on 10:26ff.), the present reference to images gives a more explicit definition of the character of the *maṣṣēbôt*. Some of the stone pillars were images of foreign deities (cf. Am. 5:26; Ezek. 16:17). **Mattan the priest of Baal**: The priest's name, it has been claimed, is peculiarly Phoenician (Skinner, p. 341; Montgomery, p. 581), and is a contraction of Mattan-Baal (gift of Baal); cf. *KAT*, p. 104; Šanda II, p. 134. But Gray (p. 581) claims that it is related to very common Semitic names, especially the name Mattaniah (2 Kg. 24:17; 1 Chr. 25:4; Neh. 11:17, 22). It is also found on a seal from Lachish (Thompson, *BASOR* 86 [1942], pp. 24ff.). **the priest posted watchmen**: With this last sentence of v. 18 the narrative broken off at v. 12 is continued. Possibly a minority had not joined in the revolt, and to avoid any counter-action the Temple had to be guarded.

19. The mention of **all the people of the land** in this verse and in v. 20, the only two instances in the original narrative (vv. 1–12, 18b–20), need not necessarily be taken as harmonizing additions (as by Gray, p. 581). **the gate of the guards**: cf. v. 6, and obviously not the one used by Athaliah in v. 16.

20. the city was quiet after Athaliah had been slain: As noted above (p. 485), whilst the reference here to Athaliah's death agrees basically with v. 16 in placing the occurrence in the place and not the Temple, the account in v. 16 is more detailed and places the slaughter of Athaliah before the covenant of v. 17. Gray (*ibid.*) finds the original narrative more seemly in that the murder of Athaliah was postponed until after the ceremonies, which were, therefore, not marred by bloodshed.

(b) *Jehoash of Judah*
II:21–12:21 (MT 12:1–22)

The account of Jehoash's reign has been set within the usual deuteronomistic formulae, which in the introduction (11:21–12:3) record his accession, synchronistic material, the length of his reign, the name of his mother and a deuteronomistic assessment, and in the conclusion (12:19–21) mention sources and give notice of his obituary.

The main interest of the chapter naturally lies in the material inserted within these deuteronomistic formulae and containing arrangements made by the priests for keeping the Temple in repair (vv. 4–16) and also details of the financing of Jehoash's tribute to Hazael (vv. 17–18). There is no agreement about the origin of this middle section of the account. Wellhausen (*Composition*, pp. 293ff.) proposed an independent Temple history as the source from which this and other sections sharing the same interest in the Temple were derived. This continuous narrative of the Temple contained reports of the cleansing of the Temple (11:1–12, 18b–20), the changes made by Ahaz (16:10ff.), the reform of Josiah (2 Kg. 22–23), the final plundering of the Temple (25:13ff.), and possibly some of the details about its construction in 1 Kg. 6ff. Wellhausen's suggestion has not found favour, mainly because some of the passages attributed to this source have wider political and constitutional interests (especially 11:1–12, 18b–20; 22–23) and the Temple was only of incidental significance as the scene of the events (cf. Skinner, p. 343; Gray, p. 583).

Although it may be difficult to establish that a Temple history was in existence, it seems likely that vv. 4–16 in this chapter constituted an independent history which was then used by the deuteronomistic compiler. According to Noth (*ÜSt*, pp. 75ff.) it originated from a literary history of the kingdom of Judah based on state archives and then used by the deuteronomistic compiler, who was prompted to include it by his own interest in the Temple. Accepting this suggestion, Gray (pp. 522ff.) argues that this work came from the hands of priestly authors, which of course explains its interest in the Temple and related events. Thus v. 19 contains reliable information that the source used was 'the Book of the Chronicles of the Kings of Judah' (Skinner, p. 343; Smend, *Entstehung*, p. 138), which was itself probably dependent on state annals and temple archives. Rendtorff (*Opfers*, p. 54) rightly notes the similarity between these verses and 2 Kg. 16:10–18. The present section owes its origin to temple archives.

Its interest in the Temple naturally raises the question of attributing the present section to priestly circles, possibly at the earliest stage when temple archives were being composed, or else when the history of Judah was compiled by priestly circles (Gray), or at some stage when Kings were being revised by a priestly redactor. Šanda (II, pp. 148ff.; cf. Montgomery, p. 426) rejects the idea of a priestly connection; the narrative, it is claimed, is not favourable towards the priesthood (especially vv. 6–8), and there is no trace in it of the religious emphasis that is found, for example, in 11:18. Gray (pp. 32ff.), on the other hand, does not find the critical attitude towards the priests insuperable, and suggests that it may have originated from a priest after the reformation of Josiah. It can be further suggested that this account of how the tax system was reformed, whilst criticizing the priests for not fulfilling their duties with regard to the Temple fabric, is not basically hostile to the priesthood. The origin of the narrative in priestly circles can be accepted, with the proviso that v. 16 is a later expansion giving fuller information about the reformed system (cf. Šanda, *ibid.*, where it is called a pre-redactional gloss). The account given in 2 Chr. 24:4–14 differs from vv. 4–16 in this chapter, but the differences can be easily explained as having originated from the Chronicler's particular interests and as reflecting his method of rewriting what he found in Kings (Williamson, *Chronicles*, pp. 318ff.). Verses 17–18 are also derived from Temple archives (Hoffmann, *Reform*, pp. 118–25).

The record of Jehoash's reign in chapter 11–12 is not without parallel. Montgomery (p. 427) refers to the many Babylonian and Assyrian inscriptions celebrating the restoration of ancient temples. Liverani (*VT* 24 [1974], pp. 438–53) finds a very close parallel in the Akkadian state of Idrimi, which is admittedly separated from the present narrative by a span of 650 years and a distance of 500 km.

11:21. This verse stands at the beginning of chapter 12 in MT. But *EVV* place it at the end of chapter 11, probably on the grounds that a synchronism such as is found in 12:1 normally opens a new section. Luc. preserves a different and probably an original order in reading this statement about the king's age at his accession immediately after the synchronizing clause of the next verse. **seven years old when he began to reign:** Such a young boy required the help of a counsellor or agent, and although the text confines itself to the statement that Jehoiada was his tutor (v. 2) it seems probable that the priest played an active role in the government of Judah.

12:1. In the seventh year of Jehu: This synchronization with the reign of Jehu affirms that Jehoash was less than a year old when the great massacre of 11:1 occurred. **he reigned forty years in Jerusalem:** Montgomery (p. 427) regards this round figure of **forty** as suspicious, and claims that the length of Jehoash's reign should be reckoned from the year when he became heir and not from the year of his accession, thus excluding the illegal reign of Athaliah from the chronological scheme. But Gray (p. 583), on the basis of this synchronism with Jehu's reign, accepts that the reckoning is based on Jehoash's accession; cf. Table on p. 28, where Jehoash's years are given as 836–797 BC. **Zibiah of Beersheba:** The meaning of **Zibiah** is 'gazelle'; cf. the Aram. Tabitha in Ac. 9:36, 40. The use of animal names is not rare in the *OT*, e.g. Deborah ('bee'), Jonah ('dove'), Nun ('fish'); the name selected here is appropriate in view of the connection with Beersheba in the southern steppe (cf. Gray, *ibid.*). Marriage to Zibiah may be interpreted as a political move to secure support from Negeb tribes on the border of Edom (cf. Yeivin, *WHJP*, p. 150).

2. did what was right in the eyes of the LORD all his days: The Gk. has 'all the days', suggesting a connection with the following sentence; it can thus be rendered 'all the days wherein Jehoiada the priest instructed him' (cf. *AV*, *RV*, *NIV*). The effect of this connection is that it limits Jehoash's good behaviour to the life-time of Jehoiada, as is so clearly brought out by 2 Chr. 24:2 and the Chronicler's account of Jehoash's subsequent lapse into evil ways (24:15–22). But it is probable that the deuteronomistic work was unaware of Jehoash's defection, and that the Gk. presents a later attempt to harmonize the text with the Chronicler's account. The Heb. does not make clear the connection between the assessment of Jehoash and the statement about his instruction by Jehoiada. It is possible to render as **because** (*RSV*) or 'forasmuch' (Burney, p. 312), which forms a satisfactory link and makes it unnecessary to accept the suggestion that the phrase **because Jehoiada the priest instructed him** is a marginal gloss to qualify all his days in the light of 2 Chr. 24.

3. The favourable assessment of Jehoash is qualified, as was the judgment on Asa (1 Kg. 15:14) and on Jehoshaphat (1 Kg. 22:43). **the people continued to sacrifice and burn incense on the high places**: cf. 1 Kg. 3:2, 3.

4–16. It can be surmised from this passage that Solomon's Temple was by now ready for some repair and renovation. From the time of Solomon to the time of Jehoash the expense of keeping the Temple in good repair had presumably been met by the royal treasury. Jehoash, however, decided to transfer this expense on to the public and was moving decidedly towards making the Temple self-supporting (Skinner, p. 342). The first step, which is undated, was to entrust the collecting of taxes and voluntary gifts, as well as the responsibility for repairs, to the priests. The unsatisfactory outcome led the king in the twenty-third year of his reign to introduce a new system for collecting money for the upkeep of the fabric; at the same time he relieved the priests of their sole responsibility for the repairs.

4. All the money of the holy things: The term **money of holy things** (*NEB*, 'holy-gifts'; *NIV*, 'sacred offerings'), as this verse proceeds to explain, covers two main sources of income, namely, obligatory taxes and voluntary gifts. Tax-money is described as **the money for which each man is assessed**; *RSV* has followed Luc., which gives a sensible reading of a difficult Heb. text. MT is faithfully rendered by *RV* as 'in correct money' (cf. Gen. 23:16). The further definition of this income as **the money from the assessment of persons** is probably an explanatory gloss, which has found its way into the text and is similar to the legal terminology of Lev. 27:2ff. (cf. Stade, *ZAW* [1885], pp. 288ff.; Burney, pp. 313ff.). The gloss is probably due to the influence of later practice, for as later texts

show each Israelite was expected to pay a tax of half a shekel (cf.
Exod. 30:12–30). **the money which a man's heart prompts him to
bring**: Literally the Heb. has 'the money which comes upon a man's
heart to bring' (cf. Jer. 7:31). The meaning is well expressed in
NEB, 'which any man brought voluntarily' (cf. *NIV*).

   5. **each from his acquaintance**: The word translated **acquaintance** (*makkār*) is only found here, and is usually derived from *nākar*,
'to be familiar, to recognize'. It is difficult to think that a priest
collected money towards Temple repairs solely from among his own
acquaintances; such an understanding of this phrase is avoided by
Šanda's suggestion (II, p. 140) that each priest was allocated a
district where he became acquainted with the devout. A better
understanding of the word becomes possible by dissociating it from
the root *nākar* and connecting it possibly with the Assyrian *makâru*,
'to give abundantly', suggesting 'benefactor' (Šanda, *ibid.*); or preferably with the Ugar. *mkrm*, a class of persons listed with priests
and other temple personnel (Gordon, *Textbook*, II, texts 81, 82,
113, pp. 183ff., 188ff.). According to Gray (p. 586; cf. also *Legacy*,
p. 214) the *makārim* were business assessors responsible for fixing
the price of sacrificial animals, and also possibly for investing temple
moneys; cf. Montgomery (p. 432), 'trader, bargainer', and *NIV*,
'treasurers'. An explanation of the *makkār* as an official belonging
to the temple personnel is preferred to *NEB*'s 'for his own funds'.
let them repair the house: Literally 'let them strengthen the
breaches of the house'.

   6. **twenty-third year of King Jehoash**: Gray (*ibid.*) rightly takes
this to refer to the **twenty-third year** of his reign, when the king
was about thirty and Jehoiada, because of his old age, unable to
control the priests. As noted above, the Chronicler brings out more
prominently the breach between the king and the priesthood.

   7. **Jehoash summoned Jehoiada**: The preupposition here is that
the priesthood was responsible to the king, for the Temple was
fundamentally a royal chapel, cf. the position of the northern
sanctuary, Bethel, as is suggested in Am. 7:10–17. **take no more
money from your acquaintances**: Because the priests were **not
repairing the house**, the first stage in reforming the system was
to order them not to take money from the 'treasurers' or 'assessors'
for any purpose other than temple repairs.

   8. The agreement achieved with the priests seems to have gone a
step further than what was originally demanded in v 7. The implication of the two clauses of the agreement as recorded in this verse is
that the priests relinquished the two tasks involved in their responsibility for the Temple fabric, namely, the collecting of funds (**they**

should take no more money from the people) and the management
of repair work (they should not repair the house).

9. beside the altar on the right side as one entered the house:
This phrase seems to have combined two contradictory statements
about the location of the chest made by Jehoiada, one stating that
it was **beside the altar** and the other that it was near the entrance
of the Temple. Attempts have been made to avoid this difficulty.
A transliteration of the Heb. in the Gk. (Alexandrinus) gives the
reading 'beside the pillar' (reading *maṣṣēḇāh* for *mizbeaḥ*; see Stade,
ibid.); in support of this reading are the many references to the
pillar (cf. 2 Kg. 18:4; 23:14), but against it the suggestion that the
pillar was nearer the altar than the entrance (cf. Benzinger, p. 160).
Another possible solution is to accept a slight emendation of the
text to give 'beside the doorpost' (reading *mᵉzûzāh* for *maṣṣēḇāh*),
which agrees well with the following reference to the priests guar-
ding the threshold (Klostermann, p. 434; Skinner, p. 344; Gray, p.
584). However, modern translations (*RSV*, *NEB* and *NIV*) retain
the altar, which may be justified on the grounds that the term may
refer specifically to a threshold altar; the word *saḏ*, **threshold**, later
in the verse may denote an altar (cf. Honeyman, *JTS* 37 [1936],
pp. 56ff.; McKane, *ZAW* 71 [1959], pp. 260–5). **and the priests
who guarded the threshold**: The mention of this class of priests in
company with the chief priest and second priest in Jer. 52:24 indicates that they held a post of some importance among temple
personnel. Their task was to safeguard the Temple from contamination through the infiltration of unclean and alien elements.
According to 2 Kg. 25:18 this task was entrusted to three priests
(cf. also 2 Kg. 22:4; 23:4; Jer. 35:4).

10. **the king's secretary**: This represents another stage in the
transfer of responsibility for Temple collections and repairs from
the hands of the priests. A royal **secretary**, possibly a fiscal officer,
was in association with the chief priest to take charge of the operation of opening the chest and counting its contents. The use of the
term **high priest** causes some difficulty, for it is usually thought to
be of post-exilic origin, and its occurrence here and in a few other
places (cf. 2 Kg. 22:4, 8; 23:4) is explained as a reflection of later
usage (*BHH* II, cols. 737–40; Morgenstern, *AJSL* 55 [1938], pp.
1–24, 183–97, 360–77; Hoffmann, *op. cit.*, pp. 122ff.). Although
the actual term **high priest** may be late, there is evidence from
early times that one priest officiated as primate. A 'chief priest' is
mentioned in 2 Kg. 25:18, and the same term (*rb khnm*) is known
from Ugar. texts. **they counted and tied up in bags the money**:
RSV (cf. *NIV*), following some of the Vsns., has transposed the
order of the two verbs in MT to secure a better sequence. The first

verb in MT (ṣārar) means 'to wrap, tie up'. Some commentators emend the text slightly to read the verb found in the parallel passage in Chronicles, 'and they emptied it' (wayᵉʿārû; so Gray, p. 584), which does not necessitate the transposition of RSV. Others follow a suggestion made by Torrey (JBL 55 [1936], pp. 247-60) and argue for retaining the verb found in MT but deriving it from the root ṣûr, a by-form of yāṣar, 'to melt, mint' (K-B; cf. Jer. 18:11; Zech. 11:13). Behind the verb is envisaged a process of melting down contributions of precious metal, or even loose silver, into bullion, which was cast into ingots; cf. Herodotus III.96, where a similar process is connected with Darius I. Gray (p. 587) finds support for this suggestion in the listing of nsk ksp, 'casters of silver', with other temple personnel in the Ugar. texts (Gordon, Textbook, ibid.), and refers to the absence of coinage until the sixth century, with the result that weights of pure metal were stamped by private traders. Such a derivation of the verb gives a good meaning here; cf. NEB, 'and melted down the silver found in the house of the LORD and counted it'.

11. The money was then transferred to **the workmen who had oversight of the house**. These were the men appointed as foremen or masters of the work-force.

12. **to the masons and stone-cutters**: Although the emendation of **masons** (gôdᵉrîm) to 'carpenters' (gozᵉrîm) (Montgomery, p. 430; cf. BHS), provides a good parallel for the preceding 'carpenters and builders' and the following **timber and quarried stone**, it is an arbitrary change of the text.

13-14. According to these verses precious utensils were not to be made for use in the Temple, which implies that the priests had been over-spending on renewing valuable utensils rather than on the Temple fabric. For these items, cf. 1 Kg. 7:50. **for the house of the LORD**: Luc. omits this phrase, which some regard as an intentional gloss (Montgomery, ibid.; cf. NEB). Gray (p. 585) thinks that there is a point in retaining the phrase and rendering as 'in the house of the LORD', suggesting that utensils had previously been made privately by the priests within the Temple precincts so that they could avoid checks on the silver used. But the phrase is best omitted as a duplication of the original at the end of the verse. With this prohibition on the activity of the priests, the money spent on Temple vessels could now be counted as income towards repairs.

15. **they did not ask an accounting**: The subject of the verb (they) must refer back to the 'king's secretary and the high priest' (v. 10). They apparently made a block payment to the overseers or foremen, who in turn paid their craftsmen for the work done; no detailed accounting showing how the money had been spent was

necessary. The overseers **dealt honestly**, and the higher officials were satisfied that the work was carried out effectively.

16. This notice about the monies that were exempt from the arrangements outlined is probably a gloss. The distinction between **guilt offerings** (*'āšām*) and **sin offerings** (*ḥaṭṭā'ṯ*) is not made clear in *OT* texts, nor by early authors (de Vaux, *Ancient Israel*, pp. 420ff.). Although Lev. 4–5 suggest that *'āšām*, the sacrifice of reparation, was intended to cover cases in which God or fellow-man had been cheated of their rights, and that *ḥaṭṭā'ṯ* possibly covered a wider field, the examples given and the sacrifical code imply that both terms practically related to the same offences. Both sacrifices are said to be unknown until the period of the Exile, but de Vaux (*op. cit.*, pp. 429ff.) claims, mostly on the basis of the present text and his interpretation of Hos. 4:8, that **guilt offerings** and **sin offerings** were known before the Exile, and that the terms denote specific sacrifices. If this text is a late addition, de Vaux's argument is less convincing. On the basis of 1 Sam. 6:3, 8, Gray (p. 588) defines *'āšām* as a restitution offering equivalent to what we call damages, and suggests that the real difference between the two lies in the fact that *'āšām* relates to cases where restitution was possible. Lev. 5:16 stipulates that a fifth of the value of the offering was taken by the priests, which explains why this verse refers to **money**. See further, Rendtorff, *Opfers*, p. 54.

17–18. Material derived from the annals of Judah has been attached to its present setting by means of the linking phrase **at that time** (or 'then'), which does not offer an exact date for Hazael's expedition. It is a campaign that cannot be dated, because no account of Hazael's movements is given either in the annals of the northern kingdom or in extra-biblical sources. 2 Chr. 24:24ff. suggest a date towards the end of the reign of Jehoash, but Gray (p. 589) favours a date before 806 BC, when Adad-nirari III conquered Damascus and at the same time conducted campaigns in the Philistine plain (*ANET*, p. 282). It is possible that Hazael invaded the area soon after the Temple reform in the twenty-third year of Jehoash, which was also the first for Jehoahaz on the throne of Israel (2 Kg. 12:6; 13:1), i.e. after 815 BC, according to the Table on p. 28. Another possibility is that an opportunity for such a campaign occurred when Shamsi-adad V died in 811 BC. **and fought against Gath, and took it**: The identification of **Gath** is very much disputed. Aharoni (*Land*, p. 250) finds that the identification with *Tell el-'Areini* on the eastern edge of the coastal plain, between Lachish and Ashkelon (Albright, *AASOR* 2–3 [1923], pp. 11ff.), is discredited by archaeological excavations, as is the more recent identification with *Tell en-Nejileh*, a few miles further south (Bülow

and Mitchell, *IEJ* 11 [1961], pp. 101–10). Aharoni's own preference
is to identify it with *Tell es-Safi*, in the western foothills of the
Shephelah and commanding the passage through the Vale of Elah
(*Wadi es-Sant*). Although this latter identification agrees well with
the account of David's defeat of Goliath (1 Sam. 17:1), and with
the present text which pictures Gath having control over an
important pass leading to Jerusalem, others favour an identification
with *Tell esh-Sheri'ah* much further south (May, *Oxford Atlas*,
passim). It is more clear from this verse that it was because he had
gained control of Gath that Hazael was able to **set his face to go
up against Jerusalem**. Possibly the fall of Gath to Hazael is
mentioned in Am. 6:2, which may explain why Gath was omitted
from a list of Philistine towns in Am. 1:6–8. The statement of the
present verse can thus be accepted, and it is unnecessary to read
Gath as Gittaim, near Ramleh (as suggested by Mazar, *IEJ* 4 [1954],
pp. 230–5). Hazael's activities against Israel, which according to the
report in 2 Kg. 10:32ff. brought him as far down as the Arnon,
were now extended along the coastal plain to a position from which
he could threaten Jerusalem. He may, however, have been more
interested in gaining control over the main trade-routes than in
subduing Jerusalem (Montgomery, p. 430; Gray, p. 589). The
success of the measures taken by Jehoash to save Jerusalem seems
to confirm that the subjugation of the city was not Hazael's primary
aim. As had happened on other occasions (cf. 1 Kg. 15:18), treasures
from the Temple and the palace were sent to the aggressor. It may
come as a surprise to find the names of the evil **Jehoram and
Ahaziah** (cf. 2 Kg. 8:18, 27) listed alongside the pious **Jehoshaphat**
as kings who had made donations to the Temple.

20. **and made a conspiracy, and slew Joash**: The report of MT,
probably drawn from annals, is brief and does not speculate about
motives for this conspiracy against the king. 2 Chr. 24:20ff. has
elaborated, and claims that the king was responsible for stoning to
death Zechariah the son of Jehoiada the priest within the Temple
precincts (cf. Mt. 23:35). Zechariah had previously dared to criticize
the king (vv. 18ff.), and there was obviously a rift between the king
and the priesthood after Jehoiada's death. Gray (p. 590) accepts the
tradition preserved in Chronicles, but connects the antagonism of
the priesthood with the new financial arangements imposed by
Jehoash; he also accepts the report in 2 Chr. 24:2ff. of the humiliation of Jehoash by Syria, which provides an opportunity for the
priests to instigate action against the king (cf. also Williamson,
Chronicles, p. 232ff.). **in the house of Millo, on the way that goes
down to Silla**: The text here is very corrupt, and has been variously
rendered by the ancient Vsns. The Gk. omits **on the way that goes**

down (*NEB*, 'on the descent'), and it is thought that originally the Gk. read 'in the house of Maala which is in Gaala' (see Rahlfs, *Septuaginta*, p. 721). The possibilities here are: to treat **on the way that goes down to Silla** as a dittograph (Kittel, p. 256); to take it as a further geographical designation of the location of **the house of Millo**, as is done by *RSV*, *NEB*, *NV*; to construe it with Joash and read 'as he was going down to Sela' (Syr., Aquila, Symmachus); to emend the text by reading **Silla** as *mᵉsillāh*, and construing either 'as he was going down the ramp' (Gray, p. 590, also taking **the house of Millo** to mean 'barracks'; cf. Jg. 9:6), or 'as he was going down on the way to the house of Millo' (Thenius, p. 343; Sanda II, p. 148). These latter suggestions provide a good understanding of the text, although it is emended slightly.

21. **Jozacar the son of Shimeath and Jehozabad the son of Shomer**: MT gives identical names to the two assassins, which is taken as evidence by Begrich (*Die Chronologie*, p. 196) that two parallel sources can be traced in vv. 21, 22*a*. *RSV* follows many MSS by reading the first name as **Jozacar**. Nothing more is known about the two men, and it is feasible to suggest that they were professional soldiers who had been paid for their work. According to 2 Chr. 24:26, they were foreigners, the first being **the son of Shimeath**, an Ammonitess, and the second the son of Shimith, a Moabitess; but this tradition can be dismissed as a mistaken understanding of Shimeath as a feminine form. Other discrepancies also found in the Chronicler's report are the statements that he was killed in bed, and that he was not buried in the tombs of the kings (2 Chr. 24:25); the latter statement reflects the Chronicler's view that Jehoash was an apostate (cf. vv. 18ff.), see further, Williamson, *op. cit.*, pp. 325–6. On **Amaziah**, see below, on chapter 14.

(c) *Jehoahaz and Joash, kings of Israel*
13:1–25

The initial impression gained about this chapter is that it gives an account of two contemporaries of Jehoash of Judah within the usual framework, which in each case has an introductory formula, containing a synchronization (vv. 1–2, 10–11), and a concluding formula with details of sources, burial and accession of the king's successor (vv. 8f., 12ff.). However, when the chapter is analysed in detail, the order of events recorded presents a conundrum. Although the concluding formula for Joash appears in vv.12ff., it is followed by an account of the death of Elisha, dated in the reign of Joash (vv 14–19), and again by a report of the Syrian wars of the two kings, part of which is of course relevant to the reign of Joash (vv.

22–25). To complicate matters, another concluding formula appears
in 14:15ff. Another section that causes difficulty in its present position is found in vv. 4–6; it is obviously an intrusion into the account
of Syrian oppression started in v. 3 and continued in v. 7. These
verses anticipate the recovery of Israel, but their present location
dates the beginning of that recovery, which belongs to the reign of
Jeroboam, in the reign of Jehoahaz. In this connection too, it can
be stated that the relationship between vv. 22 and 23 is problematic.

Attempts have been made to reconstruct the original order of the
events by shifting verses and attributing them to different sources
(cf. Stade, *ZAW* 5 [1885], pp. 295ff.; Jepsen, *AfO* 14 [1942],
p. 158). Jepsen placed v. 22 in the period of Jehoahaz, but
connected vv. 3–6a with the time of Joash. His view of the chapter's
growth was as follows: the original account derived from the synchronistic Chronicle of the kings of Israel was constituted of vv. 1,
22, 7, 9, 10, 24, 25, 13; to this account the priestly redactor added
vv. 2, 8, 11, 12, and also possibly v. 6b; the final revision was made
by the deuteronomistic redactor, who added vv. 3, 4, 23, 5, 6a (see
also Fricke, pp. 166ff.). Jepsen's attempt to achieve the original
order of both the material derived from the Chronicles and what
was supplied later by redactors through an arbitrary shifting of
verses does not offer a satisfactory solution to the difficulties of this
chapter.

Obviously the first step in analysing the chapter is to separate the
deuteronomistic formulae relating to the reign of the two kings. The
introductory formulae are easily recognisable in vv. 1–2, 10–11, as
is the closing formula for the reign of Jehoahaz in vv. 8–9. But the
closing formula for Joash in vv. 12, 13, with its parallel version in
14:15, 16, causes a problem. The appropriate place for concluding
the reign of Joash is after 14:1–14, which, because they contain a
reference to the relations between Joash and Amaziah, belong as
much to the record of Joash as to that of Amaziah (Skinner, p. 349).
Moreover, v. 13 is very dubious because of its use of the exceptional
phrase 'and Jeroboam sat upon his throne'. Therefore, the formula
in 13:12, 13 must be regarded as a later insertion by someone who
found chapter 13 incomplete without such a conclusion, and who
mistakenly attached it to the introductory formula in vv. 10–11.

Within their own formulae the deuteronomistic editors included
some material derived from the royal annals of Israel, which gave
an outline of the relations between Israel and Syria during this
period. In the time of Jehoahaz, Israel was dominated by the Syrian
kings Hazael and Benhadad (v. 3), who had destroyed the effectiveness of the Israelite army (v. 7). After the death of Jehoahaz in
Israel and Hazael in Damascus, the Israelite Joash attempted a

recovery and had some success against Benhadad (vv. 22, 24–25). Joash conquered Transjordan and Northern Gilead, and his successful war against Aram was carried on by Jeroboam II (cf. Tadmor, *IEJ* 12 [1962], 114–19). Two later accretions have become attached to this material; vv. 4–6, which are of the same character as the deuteronomistic framework of the book of Judges, mistakenly trace the recovery of Israel under Joash, and more especially under Jeroboam II (cf. 14:27), as far back as the reign of Jehoahaz; v. 23 is a pious comment, which bears some relation to vv. 4–6 (cf. also Hoffmann, *Reform*, pp. 113–18).

The remainder of the chapter contains two traditions surrounding the death and burial of Elisha (vv. 14–19, 20–21). The two sections were not necessarily connected before their inclusion in the present complex, nor is it likely that they were introduced into the Kings narrative at the same time (so Schmitt, *Elisa*, pp. 8off.; against Galling, *ZThK* 53 [1956], pp. 13off.). The later accretion in vv. 20–21, with its pronounced miraculous element, was added after the inclusion of the Elisha narratives in the books of Kings. According to Schmitt's analysis, vv. 14–19 are not to be regarded as a literary unit; vv. 18–19 contain a 'man of God' revision of an earlier tradition which referred to the prophet by his name. Moreover, the isolated reference to Joash by name in v. 14 is a redactional gloss; thus the anecdote does not necessarily bring Elisha's activity as far down as the age of Joash. Schmitt attributes the narrative in vv. 14–17 to the same Aramaean corpus of tradition about Elisha as 5:1–27 and 8:7–15; the name Joash in v. 14 and the whole of vv. 18–19 belong to a later revision, and the supplement in vv. 20–21 was added still later.

1. **In the twenty-third year of Joash**: This figure is at variance with the chronology in 12:1, which states that Jehoash came to the throne in the seventh year of Jehu (836 BC), who reigned for twenty-eight years (i.e. to 815 BC). But the 23rd year of Jehoash would give the year 814 BC as the date for the accession of Jehoahaz. The discrepancy may be explained by the different custom of reckoning in the two kingdoms, and is not a serious one. In the Table on p. 28, Jehoash's years are given as 836–797 BC. **began to reign over Israel in Samaria**: Although the Gk. omits **over Israel**, it is best retained because it features regularly in the formula for the north (cf. v. 10; 3:1).

3. **he gave them continually into the hand of Hazael king of Syria and into the hand of Benhadad the son of Hazael**: Hazael probably died during the reign of Jehoahaz and was succeeded by his son Benhadad (see on 1 Kg. 20). As noted above, the Syrian wars of 1 Kg. 20; 22 are to be dated in the time of Benhadad the

son of Hazael, and so his opponent in Israel was either Jehoahaz or Joash.

4. Whereas the previous verse makes the point that Syria **continually** oppressed Israel (*NEB*, 'for some years'; Gray, 'without intermission'), vv. 4–6 mention a respite. However, a change in the fortunes of Israel in the time of Jehoahaz is questionable, for v. 22 states that Israel suffered Syrian oppression 'all the days of Jehoahaz'. Because v. 25 suggests a recovery in the time of Joash, it has been proposed that vv. 4–6 belong to his period; later they were misplaced, and Joash became Jehoahaz (so Gray, p. 594). Another suggestion is to read vv. 4–6 immediately after v. 7 (Montgomery, p. 433). The view taken here is that these verses are not a misplacement but an intrusion by a later editor, who was eager to demonstrate that the deuteronomistic principle established in the period of the judges was also operative at this time of Syrian oppression. Seeking the Lord led to some relief (v. 4) through the hands of a saviour (v. 5), but because of Israel's persistent unfaithfulness, the relief could only be temporary (v. 6). It may be that this later editor wished to qualify the harshness of the term 'continually' in v. 3, and did so by referring to a well-established deuteronomistic principle (cf. Skinner, p. 347).

5. The LORD gave Israel a saviour: The term **saviour** (*NEB*, 'deliverer') is used of Israel's deliverers in Jg. 3:9, 15, and if the parallel with that usage is pressed many of the attempts to identify the saviour prove unsatisfactory. Some support has been found for the identification of the saviour with Adad-nirari III, who invaded Syria in 806 BC (Hallo, *BA* 23 [1960], p. 42; Haran, *VT* 17 [1967], pp. 267ff.). Adad-nirari's expedition is described as being in the direction of Philistia and aimed at punishing the countries withholding their tribute to Assyria. He laid siege to Damascus, and imposed taxes upon its ruler, called Mar'i ('my lord'), presumably Benhadad. This action against Syria, it is claimed, brought relief to Israel. Another proposal is to identify the saviour with Zakir of Hamath, who resisted Syrian pressure aimed at forcing him into an alliance against Assyria (Cook, *CAH* III [1925], p. 367). Zakir's resistance is construed as an opportunity for Israel to seek some relief. It is doubtful, however, if the term **saviour** in this context denotes an easing of pressure upon Israel due to the intervention of a foreign power in Syrian affairs. On the basis of 2 Kg. 14:26ff., some suggest that Jeroboam II was the saviour of Israel (Skinner, p. 348; Montgomery, p. 433); but, if so, it has to be assumed that relief came later than expected, if it was in response to the supplication of Jehoahaz. Gray (p. 595) argues that the inclusion of the Elisha narrative (vv. 14–19) in the same context is a clear indication

that the deuteronomistic editor was thinking of Elisha's activity in
the same terms as that of charismatic leaders like Deborah in the
book of Judges. The separation of vv. 4–6 from vv. 14–19 does not
help Gray's argument. It would appear that the editor inserted these
verses to establish the general principle that, whereas unfaithfulness
brought oppression, turning to God brought a saviour; but he did
not give a hint of an identification. **dwelt in their homes as
formerly**: *NEB*, 'settled down again in their homes'. The Heb. has
'dwelt in their tents as hitherto', which is the basis of the interpretation favoured by Šanda (II, p. 153) and Gray (p. 594). It is assumed
that because of oppression the Israelites, not being able to settle in
the plains, were forced to live in villages on the hill-tops or in towns;
but, when relief from oppression came, they could live in open
settlements in their own ploughlands. The text may simply be
stating that no more battles were waged between Syria and Israel,
and that calmer and more settled conditions ensued. The suggestion
(Gray, pp. 595ff.) that dwelling in tents refers to the renewal of a
seven-year pilgrimage to a central sanctuary (such as Gilgal; Am.
4:4; 5:5) is unnecessary and too remote from the circumstances
described.

6. the sins of the house of Jeroboam: Some MSS and Syr. omit
the house of, and this is to be preferred. **but walked in them**: MT
reads the singular here, presumably referring back to Jehoahaz in
v. 4; but it is better to read the plural with the Vsns. and so take
the people of Israel as the subject of the verb. Šanda (*ibid.*) maintains
that the implied allusion to bull-worship is a proleptic reference to
conditions in the time of Jeroboam II, and suggests that Elisha's
influence prevented Jehoahaz and Joash from falling into such a
state of apostasy. But, in view of the possibility that Elisha did not
survive to the time of Joash, as suggested in vv. 14–21, his argument
is not valid. **and the Asherah also remained in Samaria**: It would
appear that this symbol was not removed during the purge of Jehu
(cf. 2 Kg. 10:26, 27).

7. The description of Syrian oppression begun in v. 3 continues
in this verse after the interruption in vv. 4–6. **there was not left**:
The Heb. has 'he did not leave', which, if taken as a continuation
of v. 3, must understand God as the subject of the verb. **an army**:
The Heb. has *'am*, people', which must here be understood to refer
to an army; cf. *NEB*, 'no armed force'. Gray's emendation (p. 596)
to *'ōṣem*, 'strength', on the assumption that ṣ was omitted through
haplography, is unnecessary. **fifty horsemen**: The word *pārāšîm* is
correctly rendered as **horsemen** rather than 'horses' (see on 1 Kg.
1:5). In recording the reduced military strength of Jehoahaz use is
made of round figures, **fifty, ten** and **ten thousand**. It is interesting

to compare the strength of his fighting forces with the figures given
for Ahab's army in the battle of Qarqar in 853 BC, as recorded in
the stele of Shalmanaser III. Ahab had 200 chariots and 10,000 men
(*DOTT*, p. 47), which suggests that it was only Israel's chariotry
that was drastically reduced during the Syrian opression.

8. The standard formula, coming immediately after a notice in
the previous verse that Jehoahaz's fighting force was reduced, introduces incongruously a reference to **his might** (cf. also 1 Kg. 15:23;
16:5, 27; 22:46; 2 Kg. 10:34; 14:15, 28; 20:20).

10. In the thirty-seventh year of Joash king of Judah: This
chronological detail is at variance with 2 Kg. 13:1 and 14:1, which
make Joash's accession to the throne of Israel in the thirty-ninth
year of Jehoash of Judah. Some MSS and the Gk. have noted the
error and read 'thirty-ninth' here (cf. *BHS*). It is better to accept
MT's reading as an error, and there is no need to assume a co-
regency of two years with his father (as by Gray, p. 597).

12–13. This concluding formula is also repeated in 2 Kg. 14:15,
16. The view taken here is that the version in chapter 14 is the
original one, and that the present version in chapter 13 is secondary;
an editor probably found that the conclusion to the reign of Joash
was inappropriately placed at the end of the Amaziah section of
chapter 14, and so located it elsewhere. But, it is even less appropriate standing immediately after the introductory formula to his
reign. Luc. read it at the end of the chapter, and this is accepted
by Šanda (II, p. 154). But Luc. is hardly to be followed here,
for it also omits 14:15, whilst retaining 14:16. The statement that
Jeroboam sat upon his throne is suspect because it is not found
elsewhere in these concluding formulae; the phrase is omitted from
Luc.

14. Elisha was on the scene when Hazael ascended the Syrian
throne in 840 BC, and his appearance again during the reign of
Joash, some forty years later, makes him an old man of 85 or 90
years old (so Šanda II, p. 155). On the other hand, if the name
Joash is omitted from this verse, and the title **king of Israel** retained
as in the remainder of the narrative (Schmitt, *op. cit.*, p. 234), the
death of Elisha can be dissociated from the reign of Joash. **went
down to him**: The place of Elisha's death is not exactly located,
and a clue is sought in this statement that the king **went down** to
the prophet. It is possible that the king visited Elisha in his own
house in Samaria (Šanda, *ibid.*), and that the prophet was later
buried in his ancestral home at Abel-meholah. The tradition in v.
20ff., connecting his grave with Moabite raids on Israel, gives
support to the suggestion that he was buried at Gilgal not far from
the Jordan. Gray (p. 598) presumes that he died at Gilgal on one

of his visits to the prophetic community there, and that the prophets, eager to have the honour of his tomb, buried him there rather than in Abel-meholah (cf. also Schmitt, *op. cit.*, pp. 174ff.). **My father, my father**: This title, when used by Elisha himself in 2 Kg. 2:12, indicated the position of reverence and authority held by Elijah in the eyes of his successor. It was also used by the king of Israel of Elisha in 2 Kg. 6:10. The implication is that the prophet was held in esteem by the king's court and that his word was considered authoritative. **The chariots of Israel and its horsemen**: The same phrase was again used by Elisha with reference to Elijah, where (see pp. 386f.) it appears to have been borrowed from the present context and is somewhat of a misfit. Elisha's participation in the Syrian wars makes the phrase an appropriate one to apply to him; he had inspired the defenders of Israel against Syrian attacks, and had foretold the relief of the siege (chapters 6–7). The king uses the phrase to acknowledge the part played by Elisha in Israel's life during those troubled years.

15–17. Elisha's command to the king to shoot arrows in the direction of the Syrians is usually described as an act of sympathetic magic. It is an action that probably contains more than divination to explore or to penetrate the future (as is suggested by Haldar, *Associations*, p. 153, where 1 Sam. 20:18ff. is quoted as a parallel). Obviously an attempt was made to influence future events. Other cases of creative or sympathetic magic similar in character to the present instance are: supporting the hands of Moses in the battle against Amalek (Exod. 17:8ff.), stretching a javelin towards Ai by Joshua (Jos. 8:18ff.) or breaking an earthen jar by Jeremiah (Jer. 18). Symbolic actions such as these were considered potent and contributed in some way towards bringing into effect the result that was portrayed in the symbolism. Originally they were considered potent because of their influence upon the deity; by auto-suggestion they secured the desired result. Many of these symbolic actions were consequently performed before military campaigns in an attempt to secure victory. With the course of time the thinking behind such actions was modified; instead of trying to implant an idea in the mind of the deity, they became for the prophets a means of impressing upon the people the certainty of the words they were proclaiming (cf. Gray, p. 599). Both aspects may have been implied in the present case; shooting arrows may have been an attempt on the one hand to secure divine victory against the Syrians, and on the other to stimulate the Israelite king into action by informing him that he would be victorious. For the thinking behind these actions and other Near Eastern parallels, see Lods, *Old Testament Essays*, pp. 55–76; Fohrer, *ZAW* 78 [1966], pp. 25–47.

16. Elisha laid his hands upon the king's hands: Elisha's action symbolizes prophetic support, and ultimately of course divine help. Basically it reaffirms what is evident from other narratives about Elisha, namely, that he supported the Jehu dynasty in its anti-Syrian operations. In this case the statement is clothed in a motif that is popular in legendary circles; extraordinary power is attributed to a dying man (cf. Gressmann, *Geschichtsschreibung*, pp. 185, 320). **The LORD'S arrow of victory, the arrow of victory over Syria!**: The potency of words spoken by a dying man are recognized elsewhere in the *OT*, cf. the words of Isaac (Gen. 27:1ff.), of Jacob (Gen. 48:10ff.), of Moses (Dt. 33:1ff.) and of David (2 Sam. 23:1–7).

17. you shall fight the Syrians in Aphek: The mention of Aphek is thought to be too precise, and is omitted as a gloss (so Šanda II, p. 156; Montgomery, p. 435; Gray, p. 598). The king is commanded to **open the window eastward**, i.e. in the direction of Syria, but Aphek (see 1 Kg. 20:36 for identification) was not to the east of Samaria or Gilgal. It is possible that **eastward** was used as a general designation of direction from which Syrian attacks were launched upon Israel, and that **Aphek** refers more specifically to the place where the Israelites on more than one occasion had attempted to block the Syrian drive against Israel. 1 Kg. 20:36 preserves one tradition of an Israelite triumph at Aphek.

18–19. As already noted, Schmitt separates vv. 18–19 from the narrative in vv. 14–17 and regards them as a later addition. His arguments in support are as follows: whereas vv. 14–17 envisage a devastating defeat of the Syrians (especially v. 17, 'until you have made an end of them'), these verses qualify the extent of Israel's success (contrast v. 19 with v. 17); the symbolism connected with the arrows is not the same in the two sections, the action in vv. 14–17 being aimed at influencing the future but that of vv. 18–19 simply foretelling the future; stylistic differences are evident, because the metrical incantation in v. 17 has no parallel in vv. 18–19; whereas vv. 14–17 use the proper name Elisha, vv. 18–19 refer to him as 'the man of God'.

18. Strike the ground with them: The procedure adopted here is intended to test the king, and from the result the prophet could draw his conclusions about the future destiny of his kingdom. Unlike the shooting of the arrows, the act of striking the ground had no magical influence on future events; but the forcefulness and determination with which the king operated gave the prophet some indication of the direction that future events would take.

19. you should have struck five or six times: The king is rebuked for having stopped after striking the ground three times, for it was interpreted as a proof of his lack of determination in tackling the enemy. More determination would secure the complete removal of this Syrian threat, as was promised at the end of v.17. But, in view of the lack of spirit and energy shown by Joash, that promise is now qualified; although Joash could have **struck down Syria until you had made an end of it**, he is now promised a more moderate success, **you will strike down Syria only three times**. The statement in v. 25 that Joash defeated the Syrian king three times and recovered some cities from him, had to be harmonized with the more glowing promise of v. 17. The reviser who added vv. 18–19 to vv. 14–17 attempted to reconcile the two verses, and attributed the change of fortune to a failure on the part of Joash, rather than to any error in the prophetic oracle of v. 17.

20–21. This section with its pronounced miraculous element is to be separated from vv. 14–19 and regarded as a later addition. Gray (p. 600) labels it as an anecdote derived from the Elisha hagiology of the prophetic community at Gilgal.

20. bands of Moabites used to invade the land: Raids across the Jordan upon the land of Israel were common, as it was vulnerable to Moabites (Am. 2:1ff.), Ammonites (Am. 1:13ff.) and Midianites (Jg. 6:11). It is more conceivable that the Moabites made raids on the area around Gilgal in the Jordan valley than on the area around the capital of Samaria or upon Elisha's home country in Abel-meholah. Gray (*ibid.*), seeking an occasion for the Moabite raid, suggests that the weakened state of Israel after the campaigns of Hazael and Benhadad provided an opportunity for the Moabites, or else that the Syrians, when engaged against Adad-nirari, safeguarded their rear by encouraging the Moabites to keep the Israelites occupied. But it is unnecessary to make the incident here more significant than one of the regular visits of marauders over the Jordan. **in the spring of the year**: The Heb. here does not make sense, but the Gk. suggests 'at the coming of the year', which is usually rendered 'when the new year came' (Burney, p. 317), or else as in *RSV*. Others read with a slight difference to give 'yearly' (Benzinger, pp. 146f.) or 'year by year' (*NEB*). Gray (*ibid.*), accepting the suggestion of the Gk., proposes 'at the going of the year' or 'at the end of the year', which was the best time for taking loot from the threshing floor (cf. Jg. 6:11). This is a plausible interpretation.

21. as soon as the man touched the bones of Elisha: *RSV* follows MT here and takes the Heb. idiom 'and he went and touched' to mean 'as soon as he touched'. *NEB* divides the verse differently, reading 'he went' in the plural with the preceding sentence and translating 'and (they) made off' (cf. Luc.; Skinner, p. 351; Schmitt, *op. cit.*, p. 235). **he revived and stood on his feet**: The prophet's dead body is reported to have the same miraculous power as Elisha

himself possessed when he was alive (cf. 2 Kg. 4:29ff.). This tradition is also preserved in Sir. 48:13–14, where it is claimed that 'his
body prophesied'.

22. oppressed Israel all the days of Jehoahaz: This verse belongs
to the annalistic material found in vv. 3, 7, 24ff., and it has been
variously transposed to follow v. 3 or to follow v. 7. It may have
been an intentional repetition of the material in vv. 3, 7 in order to
tie the Elisha insertion in vv. 14–19, 20–21 more closely to the
remainder of the chapter. The implication of the verse that Hazael
was still alive when Jehoahaz died in 799 BC is questioned; it is
thought to be unlikely, since Hazael had achieved some status when
he seized the throne in 841 BC. Although the last specific mention
of Hazael in Assyrian records appears in the account of Shalmaneser
III's campaign in 838 BC (*ANET*, p. 280), and the king of Damascus
at the time of Adad-nirari's campaign in 806 BC is only named *mar'i*,
'my lord', it is difficult to ascertain the year of Hazael's death. Gray
(p. 601) thinks that he died between 813 and 806 BC. Luc. adds a
sentence at the end of this verse suggesting that Hazael seized
Philistia from the western sea to Aphek from the hands of Joash,
but it is unreliable (Šanda II, p. 157; Montgomery, p. 438).

23. This is a pious comment based on vv. 4–6. It mentions God's
covenant with Abraham, Isaac and Jacob, and the statement that
God had not rejected his people **until now** marks the verse as a later
editorial composition.

24. As noted under v. 22, it is impossible to date the year of
Hazael's death and of Benhadad's accession. The year 806 BC has
some significance because of the record that Adad-nirari in that year
successfully laid siege to Damascus and 'shut up Mar'i, the king of
Damascus, in Damascus his royal city' and extracted a heavy indemnity from him (cf. Luckenbill, *Records I*, p. 739). The identity of
Mar'i is uncertain, and it is known that the Aramaic Zakir inscription refers to 'Bar-hadad bar Hazael king of Aram'. The best
solution here is to assume that Hazael had died before 806 BC and
was succeeded by Benhadad, who was given the title of respect
mar'i, 'my lord' (cf. Winckler, *Untersuchungen*, p. 66; de Vaux, *RB*
43 [1934], pp. 512ff.).

25. Israel took advantage of the pressures brought to bear upon
Syria by Adad-nirari III (810–783 BC). It was an opportunity to
seize from the hands of Benhadad **the cities which he had taken
from Jehoahaz**. This reversal of the fortunes of Israel is probably
described in 1 Kg. 20, which has been incorrectly modified after it
was connected with another era. **Three times Joash defeated him**:
Verse 25*b*, with its use of the form **Joash**, is often separated from
v. 25*a*, which uses the form **Jehoash**, and is attributed to a later

redactor who inserted it in order to provide fulfilment for the promise in vv. 18, 19 (Šanda II, p. 158; Montgomery, p. 437). But it is possible that both parts of v. 25 are derived from annals, but that vv. 18–19 were added by a later reviser to reconcile this record with v. 17.

(d) Amaziah of Judah and Jeroboam of Israel
14:1–29

(i) Amaziah 14:1–22

The introduction to the reign of Amaziah, the son of Jehoash of Judah, in vv. 1–6 contains the usual deuteronomistic data: a synchronization with the king of Israel, his age at accession, the length of his reign, the name of his mother and a deuteronomistic assessment. The phrase 'but not like David his father' in v. 3 is probably from a later hand, and the whole of v. 6, betraying an interest in 'the book of the law of Moses', may have originated from a nomistic reviser. Verse 18 contains a phrase belonging to the formal deuteronomistic conclusion to a reign, but it then gives way to another extract from the annals instead of continuing with the usual epilogue.

Within this deuteronomistic framework has been included material which has obviously been derived from the annals of the kings of Judah. The notice in v. 7 of a campaign against Edom, because of its brevity and its form, stands out as an annalistic report. Verses 19–22, reporting the death of Amaziah and his succession by Azariah, are also taken from an annalistic source, and have been appended to what appears to be a formal conclusion in v. 18.

The block of material found in vv. 8–14 does not belong to either the deuteronomistic reviser or the annals of the kings of Judah. Although the narrative gives an account of an incident involving both Amaziah of Judah and Joash of Israel the narrator's interest is attached to the latter. The critical attitude taken towards Amaziah and Judah (vv. 10f.) suggests that this material originated from the northern kingdom. The section possesses the character of a historical narrative, not unlike 1 Kg. 22 (cf. Gray, p. 603), and is not likely to have come from Israelite annals (cf. Šanda II, p. 174). It is possible that a historical narrative reporting incidents in the time of Joash was in circlation in the northern kingdom, and expressed the sentiments of the period of tension between the two kingdoms before 722 BC. Appended to this section is the deuteronomistic formula to conclude the reign of Joash (vv. 15–16). This Joash narrative (vv. 8–14) and its deuteronomistic notice (vv. 15–16) would be more appropriate immediately after 13:25, thus providing a fitting conclusion to the reign of Joash. A later redactor, realizing that vv. 8–16 belonged to the reign of Joash, attempted to connect them more closely with the reign of Amaziah by inserting the note found in v. 17. Additional information is provided in 2 Chr. 25:5–16, which is an expansion of 2 Kg. 14:7 and may contain some material from an earlier source (cf. Williamson, *Chronicles*, pp. 327ff.).

1–2. Three chronological statements are made about Amaziah: he came to the throne of Judah **in the second year of Joash the son of Jehoahaz**; he was **twenty-five years old when he began to reign**; his reign lasted **twenty-nine years**. Many studies of the chronological data have considered the figure **twenty-nine** years unrealistic and have reduced it to thirteen years (Lewy, *Die Chronologie*, pp. 1ff., assuming that after Amaziah's defeat by Joash his son Azariah became regent), sixteen years (Begrich, *Die Chronologie*, pp. 149ff.) or nineteen years (Fricke, p. 181). Others accept that Amaziah's reign lasted for **twenty-nine years**, some adding the proviso that Azariah acted as co-regent for the greater part of the time (Gray, pp. 65ff., 75), some making an adjustment to the figure given for Azariah's reign (Mowinckel, *ActOr* 10 [1932], pp. 240ff.) and some accepting the chronological notes of these verses as thoroughly reliable (Sanda II, p. 161). The chronological note is accepted in the table on p. 28 and a long reign from 797 to 769 BC credited to Amaziah. **His mother's name was Jehoaddin**: Whilst the form **Jehoaddin** of the K^{e}tîb has the support of the Gk., the Q^{e}rē, with the support of MSS, other Vsns., 2 Chr. 25:1 and Josephus, *Ant.* IX.9.1, gives 'Jehoaddan' as the queen-mother's name. The meaning is 'May Yahweh give pleasure'; cf. Gen. 18:12; see further, Noth, *Personennamen*, p. 267.

3. yet not like David his father: An excepting clause (introduced with *raq*, 'yet') is unnecessary here, especially in view of the more substantial excepting sentence in v. 4 (also introuced with *raq*). This clause must be regarded as a later interpolation (Šanda, *ibid.*; Montgomery, p. 439).

4. This verse betrays a deuteronomistic interest and is to be compared with 1 Kg. 3:2ff.

5. The phrase **as soon as the royal power was firmly in his hand** may suggest that it was with difficulty that Amaziah established himself on his father's throne. As recorded in 2 Kg. 12:20ff., Jehoash was put to death through a conspiracy among his courtiers, which may have been the result of antagonism between him and the priesthood. It is possible that the priesty hierachy preferred another of Jehoash's sons, younger than Amaziah, to succeed him on the throne; although there is no evidence of this, it would explain the hint of Amaziah's initial difficulties. His vengeance upon **his serv-**

ants who had slain the king strengthened his position and possibly reconciled the priestly party to him.

6. he did not put to death the children of the murderers: Conspiracies and assassinations were severely punished in the Ancient East in order to preserve the dynasty. According to the Sefire treaty, it was expected that action would be taken 'to avenge my blood from the hand of my enemies' (III.9–11; see Weinfeld, *Deuteronomy*, p. 89). Esarhaddon's vassal treaty, concluded at Ashurbanipal's enthronement, specifically states that the vassal was to 'seize and slay the perpetrators of rebellion. You will destroy their name and their seed from the land' (Weinfeld, *ibid*.). In contrast to Esarhaddon's treaty **the children of murderers** were not put to death by Amaziah. Although the concept of divine justice in the *OT* (Exod. 20:5; 34:7), together with instances of Israelite practice (Jos. 7:24ff.; 2 Sam. 21:1–9; 2 Kg. 9:26), suggests that the principle expressed by Esarhaddon's treaty was also acceptable in Israel, some caution is necessary here. Mayes (*Deuteronomy*, p. 326) finds that the form of the law cited in this passage from Dt. 24:16 indicates that it was an older law quoted by the legislator, and that the few instances in the *OT* of taking vengeance upon the children are not reflected in pre-deuteronomistic *OT* law. Amaziah's restraint was, therefore, not due to a new departure in jurisprudence (as suggested by Skinner, p. 354), but to the existence of an ancient law demanding such restraint (cf. Gray, p. 604). The orginal report of this statement probably contained the simple statement that Amaziah **did not put to death the children of murderers**, but of course a deuteronomistic editor could not miss the chance to link this statement with the formulation of this law in Dt. 24:16. For the phrase **according to what is written in the book of the law of Moses**, see on 1 Kg. 2:3.

7. This note is probably derived from annals; its peculiar Heb. form, comparable to the Mesha inscription, is a proof that it is a true archival item (cf. Montgomery, *ibid*.; and *JBL* 53 [1934], p. 50). **He killed ten thousand Edomites**: The figure **ten thousand** slain appears also in 2 Kg. 13:7. David is claimed to have killed 18,000 in the same region (2 Sam. 8:13; cf. Ps. 60). These figures are exaggerated round numbers to denote an extensive army; if they are recognized as such, it becomes unnecessary to suggest that they denote the whole defeated army and not the actual number slain (as suggested by Gray, p. 605). **in the Valley of Salt**: The identification of the valley where Amaziah was killed is debatable. A proposal to identify it with *Wadi el-Milḥ*, to the east of Beersheba, on the ancient highway down through the Arabah to Elath (Simons, *Texts*, p. 221), presupposes an incursion by Edom into Judaean territory, which may have been possible immediately after Judah had been conquered by Syria. Against this suggestion is the impression from 2 Chr. 25:5ff. that Judah was attacking Edom and not merely taking defensive action, and the probability that the valley was in Edomite territory. One possibility here is 'Ain Melihi, about 30 km west of Petra and on the route of a Judaean army making its way to Elath (Šanda II, p. 163; Montgomery, p. 439). In support of this identification is the tradition that the **Sela** occupied by Amaziah was the celebrated rock-city Petra. But, in view of the fact that Elath was not taken until its later conquest by Azariah (v. 22), it is unlikely that Amaziah had penetrated as far south as Petra. It is more plausible to identify **the Valley of Salt** with an area in the northern part of the Arabah, to the south of the Dead Sea, or possibly to the east of the Wadi Arabah (Noth, *History*, p. 196), and easily accessible to Amaziah along the Ascent of Akkrabim. **and took Sela by storm, and called it Jokthe-el**: Although more than one site may have borne the same name, (because they were built on isolated prominences; Glueck, *AASOR* 18–19 [1937–9], p. 26) **Sela**, 'rock', is a proper name (Jg. 1:36; Isa. 16:1) that is usually identified with Petra the capital of Edom, about 80 km south of the Dead Sea. The identification with Petra is impossible in Jg. 1:36 (cf. Moore, *Judges*, p. 55), which demands a site in the Arabah, and the same district is more likely here too (cf. Haran, *IEJ* 18 [1968], pp. 207–12). It can, therefore, be assumed that **Sela** refers to a site in the marshy Arabah district, possibly *es-Sela'* (Aharoni, *Land*, p. 37) or *Khirbet Sil'* a few km north-west of Buseirah (cf. Bartlett, *POTT*, p. 253). The renaming of **Sela** as **Jokthe-el** does not facilitate the identification. According to Jos. 15:38, there was a city of the name in Judah; but Eusebius (*Onomasticon* 36, 13; 142: 7; 144:7) preserves a tradition that identifies Sela with Petra and so locates Jokthe-el in that area. The probability that the **Valley of Salt** and **Sela** are to be identified with the Arabah in northern Edom defines the defeat of the Edomites by Amaziah as a successful incursion by the latter into the northern region of Edom, with Bozrah as its centre, and not into the southern region with Teman as its centre (Aharoni, *Land*, p. 37). Amaziah's success was not a lasting conquest of Edom (cf. Bartlett, *op. cit.*, p. 237).

8–14. A clash between Amaziah and Joash, resulting in a battle at Bethshemesh, is described with vivid details; after the defeat of Judaean troops and the capture of Amaziah, Joash marched against Jerusalem, broke down part of the city walls and plundered the city and Temple before returning with his troops to Samaria. This narrative is obscure and seems isolated, since no consequence of any significance is attached to the defeat of Judah. The view taken here is that the section is a historical narrative derived from the northern kingdom; its main interest is attached to Joash, and the mention of the Temple and its treasures in v. 14 does not provide sufficient grounds for ascribing it to the annals of the Judaean kings (as proposed by Noth, *ÜSt*, p. 76). In trying to decide what gave rise to this unique occasion when Israelite troops reached as far as Jerusalem, it may be suggested that this is an Israelite version of the disagreement between the two kings after Amaziah had sought help from the Israelite king to subdue Edom and gain control of the southern part of the King's Highway (cf. 2 Chr. 25:5–24; see also, Aharoni, *Land*, p. 313).

8. Come let us look one another in the face: Although v. 11 uses this expression for engaging in battle, it does not necessarily mean that the initial approach through Amaziah's messengers was a challenge to take up arms (as suggested by Gray, p. 607). Amaziah's first move was to seek agreement with Joash, and he probably suggested a meeting at which they could face each other to discuss matters of mutual concern; cf. *NEB*, 'to propose a meeting'. Possibly a marriage alliance was under consideration (cf. Yeivin, *WHJP*, p. 60), but Šanda's attempt (II, p. 165) to find a basis for this in v. 9 cannot be accepted. When the proposal failed and battle became inevitable, the phrase 'look one another in the face' acquired a different meaning.

9. A thistle on Lebanon sent to a cedar on Lebanon: The answer given by Joash is couched in the words of a fable, which, like Jotham's fable in Jg. 9:7–15, is concerned with trees. Judah's proposal to Israel, occasioned presumably by some success against Edom, is treated as an act of insolence, which is contemptuously described as an approach by the inferior **thistle** to the supreme **cedar on Lebanon**. Nothing better can come from such pride than the trampling of the thistle by a wild beast. Šanda's suggestion (*ibid.*; cf. also Gray, p. 606) that **on Lebanon** only appeared originally with **a cedar**, but was later mistakenly read with **a thistle** and again with **a wild beast**, is plausible.

10. your heart has lifted you up: Judah has now been seized by euphoria as a result of the success it enjoyed against Edom. *NEB*, 'it has gone to your head'. *NIV*, 'and now you are arrogant'. **Be content with your glory**: *NIV*, 'Glory in your victory', or better perhaps 'enjoy your triumph'. Amaziah's moment of glory is tolerated, provided that he remains at home and does not attempt further expansion. **why should you provoke trouble**: *RSV*'s translation, like *NEB*'s, 'why should you involve yourself in disaster?', is stronger than *EVV*'s, 'why shouldest thou meddle to thy hurt?',

and conveys more faithfully the meaning of the Heb. *gārāh*, 'to
contend, engage in battle or strife' (*K-B*).

11. **Beth-shemesh**: It is to be identified with *Tell er-Rumeileh* to
the west of Jerusalem (see on 1 Kg. 4:9), and is to be distinguished
from Beth-shemesh in Naphtali (*Khirbet Tell er-Ruweisi*, cf. Jg.
1:33; Jos. 19:38; see Aharoni, *Land*, pp. 200f.) and from modern
'*Ain es-Samsiyeh* south of Bethshean (Gray, p. 607), as is indicated
by the qualification **which belongs to Judah**. Although this latter
phrase is both necessary and correct, it may also be an indication
of the northern origin of the source. The advance of Joash to Beth-
shemesh on the west side of Jerusalem means that he was moving
towards the capital along the coastal plain. His choice of this route
in preference to attacking directly from Bethel in the north calls for
some explanation. Šanda (II, p. 166; followed by Gray. p. 608)
maintains that there was a border dispute between the two kingdoms
to the north of Beth-shemesh, after Judah, following the withdrawal
of Syria, had attempted to push its border further north (cf. 2 Chr.
25:13). Joash was eager, not only to protect his own frontier, but
also to gain control of the western terminal of the vital trade-route
to Elath. By moving along the coastal plain he gained access to
Jerusalem along the Vale of Sorek. See further on Beth-shemesh,
in Grant, *Beth Shemesh* and Emerton, *AOTS*, pp. 197–206.

12. **Judah was defeated by Israel**: No reason is given for the
superior strength of Israel on this occasion. Possibly it had acquired
strength and practice during its encounter with the Syrians. 2 Chr.
25:14, 20 brings a theological factor into the defeat of Amaziah by
interpreting it as divine punishment for introducing Edomite gods
to Jerusalem.

13. After capturing the Judaean king at Beth-shemesh, Joash
advanced against Jerusalem, and **broke down the wall of Jerusalem
for four hundred cubits, from the Ephraim Gate to the Corner
Gate**. Naturally the **Ephraim Gate** is taken to be located in the
north wall of the city; cf. also Neh. 12:39. The **Corner Gate** is also
mentioned elsewhere, cf. Jer. 31:38; Zech. 14:10, but there is no
certainty about its location. An earlier identification with a gate on
the north-eastern angle is not suitable in view of the attack coming
from the west. It is now thought to be at the north-western corner
of the city, although the location of the walls of Jerusalem in the
period of the monarchy is uncertain (Gray, pp. 803–13; and essays
in Yadin, *Jerusalem Revealed*). Possibly an early east-west wall ran
slightly south of the modern David Street (Ap-Thomas, *AOTS*,
p. 289), and thus **the Corner Gate** was on the western boundary
of Jerusalem (cf. also Simons, *Jerusalem*, pp. 231–4). It is unlikely
that the whole extent of the wall between the two gates was demoli-

shed, since Uzziah's subsequent restoration of the walls called only for repairing and refortifying towers (2 Chr. 26:9; see Montgomery, p. 441).

14. Joash took from Jerusalem **all the gold and silver, and all the vessels that were found in the house of the LORD and in the treasuries of the king's house**. The Temple and palace had been plundered on previous occasions by Shishak (1 Kg. 14:25ff.) and by Hazael (2 Kg. 12:19), and what happened here must be taken as a crude act of pillaging a sanctuary (see de Vaux, *Ancient Israel*, p. 322) **also hostages**: This term ($b^en\bar{e}$ $hatta^{ca}r\bar{u}b\hat{o}t$) appears only here and its parallel in 2 Chr. 25:24. Šanda (II, p. 168) suggests that the Temple and palace funds, recently depleted by Jehoash's payments to Hazael (12:18ff.), did not provide sufficient war indemnity for Joash, and that the **hostages** were in this case pledges for further war indemnity.

15-16. These verses contain the deuteronomistic formula for concluding the rule of Joash, and together with vv. 8-14 belong to the end of chapter 13. Another version of the concluding formula appears in 13:12, 13, but as noted the version found in the present verses is the original one. For some reason the whole of the section (vv. 8-16) was displaced and inserted in the account of the reign of Amaziah.

17. As noted above, this synchronistic note is an attempt to bring the reader back to the main subject of the section, namely the reign of Amaziah, following the digression in vv. 8-16, where the main interest lies in Joash. Although the statement that Amaziah **lived fifteen years after the death of Jehoash** is unique, it is not to be regarded as unhistorical, but contains reliable information.

18. Reference to the source of information about a king's reign begins the concluding formula and is generally followed by a notice of his death and burial. But in this case the formula is not pursued, and the usual formulaic statement is replaced by an account in vv. 19-22 of a conspiracy against Amaziah, which is probably derived from an annalistic source.

19. and they made a conspiracy against him in Jerusalem: No clue is given to help us to identify the perpetrators of this conspiracy. De Vaux (*Ancient Israel*, p. 377) thought that the plot was inspired by priests, who were annoyed because the Temple had been plundered as a result of the king's policies (cf. also 12:19). But Šanda (II, p. 169) takes the plot to be the work of a small military group in Jerusalem, and Gray (p. 613) finds support for this in the fact that the antagonists had influence in Lachish, a powerful fortress in the south-west of the kingdom. Whoever instigated the plot, its success was due to the general dissatisfaction among the people following

their humiliation at the hand of Joash. Possibly too Uzziah was
behind the plot, as is perhaps witnessed by the fact that he did not
bring the murderers to justice (cf. Yeivin, *WHJP*, p. 166). **he fled
to Lachish**: Former identifications of Lachish with *Umm Lakis* or
Tell el-Hesi (cf. Petrie, *Tell el Hesy*, p. 18) have by now been
abandoned in favour of *Tell ed-Duweir*. During the period 900–700
BC Lachish was one of the largest and most important cities in Judah
(Tufnell, *AOTS*, pp. 298–308).

20. And they brought him up on horses: There is no need to
read this sentence before 'and he fled' in v. 19; the reference here
is to a solemn funeral procession from Lachish to Jerusalem.

21. All the people of Judah: cf. a note on 'the people of the land'
in 2 Kg. 11:14. Here as elsewhere a group of people or a section of
the population, because of its faithfulness to the Yahwistic tradition
and its support for the Davidic dynasty, immediately took matters
into its own hands in order to install a descendant of David on the
throne. After the murder of Amaziah, probably by a military group
with the support of those dissatisfied after Amaziah's defeat in
battle, another group, **the people of Judah**, moved quickly to install
his successor. **Azariah**: A more frequently used variant is the name
Uzziah (see below, on 15:1). Gray's view (p. 614) of Azariah's reign
is that when he was sixteen years old he became co-regent with his
father, but that later he became sole king by popular acclaim. Such
a complicated view is unnecessary (see on Chronology, pp. 17ff),
and in the Table on p. 28 Azariah is given the years 769–741 BC.

22. He built Elath: This is probably an archival note, which is
similar in form to v. 7 (cf. Montgomery, p. 442). The present
location of the verse implies that Azariah conquered Elath after his
father's death. Amaziah had some measure of success south of the
Dead Sea (see v. 7), but it was his son who reached as far as Elath
on the Gulf of Aqaba (see 1 Kg. 9:26) and rebuilt it as a fortified
harbour, probably by refortifying Ezion-geber near Elath (see
Aharoni, *Land*, p. 313). A seal found there bearing the inscription
'(belonging) to Jotham' testifies to the presence of Azariah and his
son Jotham on the Gulf of Aqaba (Avigad, *BASOR* 163 [1961], pp.
18–22). But the harbour was lost again at a later date (see 2 Kg.
16:6).

(ii) Jeroboam 14:23–29

Jeroboam II's long and prosperous reign (784–753 BC) is not covered
in detail in the record given here in vv. 23–29. Of significance to
understand the background of Jeroboam's reign is the defeat of
Damascus by Adad-nirari III during one of his four thrusts to the
west between 805 and 796 BC. Assyrian expansion to the west was

continued under Shalmaneser IV (782–72 BC), who came against
Damascus in 773 BC and under Tiglath-Pileser III (743–726 BC),
who conducted military expeditions against Syria. This, and the
threat to the Aramaeans of Damascus from the rising kingdom of
Hamath on its northern frontier, made an end of Syrian oppression
in Israel (see Tadmor, *IEJ* 12 [1962], pp. 114–19). Jeroboam II
was thus enabled to expand his territory considerably to the east of
the Jordan (see on v. 25, below). Whether an exact date can be
given to Jeroboam's success, such as the reign of Ashur-dan III
(772–765 BC), as is proposed by Haran (*VT* 17 [1967], p. 279), is
uncertain and depends to some extent on the interpretation of his
activities in vv. 25, 28. Although vv. 23–29 make no mention of
the economic prosperity that came with the expansion and relative
calm of Jeroboam's reign, this aspect is covered to some extent in
the book of Amos, who prophesied at this time. Admittedly Amos
concentrated on the undesirable social consequences of the
prosperity of Israel, but his words do provide an interesting insight
into conditions in Israel under Jeroboam II. Possibly too ostraca
discovered in Samaria throw some light on the economic practices
of the period; but this depends on the date given to the texts
(see further, Herrmann, *History*, p. 238). Evidence of his building
activities may also be identified at Hazor and Megiddo (Yeivin,
WHJP, pp. 161ff.).

The account of Jeroboam's reign has the regular deuteronomistic
formulae to serve for an introduction (vv. 23–24) and a conclusion
(vv. 28–29). The material inserted between the formulae is not
uniform. Verse 25a contains annalistic material, which has probably
been derived from the annals of the kings of Israel and contains a
brief statement of the territory annexed by Jeroboam. The
deuteronomistic revisers, however, made two additions: (a) a statement in v. 25b that the expansion recorded in v. 25a was in fulfilment of a word from the prophet Jonah; (b) a comment on the
people's affliction and how God had made a promise to Israel and
had saved her through Jeroboam. These two additions have originated from different revisers; the former, because of its prophetic
interest, is designated as the product of DtrP and can be compared
with 1 Kg. 16:34 (so Dietrich, *Prophetie*, pp. 110ff.), and the latter,
being similar in thought to 2 Kg. 24:3ff., is connected with DtrN
(Dietrich, *op. cit.*, p. 35).

23. In the fifteenth year of Amaziah: The difficulties with regard
to chronology persist, for this verse, whilst compatible with vv. 1,
17, is at variance with 15:1, 8. Gray (p. 614) once again proposes a
period of co-regency for Jeroboam and his father Joash; this compli-

cates matters, and it is better to assign to Jeroboam II a reign from 784 to 753 BC (see Table, p. 28).

24. He did what was evil in the sight of the LORD: This is the usual judgment on the kings of the northern dynasty.

25. He restored the border of Israel from the entrance of Hamath as far as the Sea of the Arabah: The implication of this verse is that Jeroboam gained territory in Transjordan that had been disputed since the time of Solomon, which thus makes his kingdom in this region as extensive as the ideal Davidic kingdom. **The entrance of Hamath** is a term used to designate the northern frontier of Israelite territory in Transjordan; it does not refer to Hamath on the Orontes, but is most likely a place-name, 'Lebo-hamath' (so *NEB*), which stood on the border of the kingdom of Hamath (Herrmann, *History*, pp. 229ff.; Aharoni, *Land*, pp. 65–7; Haran, *op. cit.*, pp. 271ff.). This means that at one time Israelite territory had extended as far north as the Biqā' valley between Lebanon and Anti-Lebanon, which was well into the area north of Damascus. **The Sea of the Arabah** is to be located in the area of the Dead Sea, and may denote that an attempt was made to establish a border against the Moabites either at the northern end of the Dead Sea, which was the old Moabite-Israelite frontier, or else further south towards Arnon (Noth, *History*, p. 250). The emphasis of this verse is that Jeroboam did not conquer new territory in Transjordan, but restored what had been lost; in other words, he sought to regain the ideal borders of Israel as established in the time of David and Solomon. Jeroboam's success in Transjordan is confirmed in Am. 6:13, which refers to Lo-debar and Karnaim, two places in northern Gilead and Bashan, the former being identified with Lidbir in Gad or Lo-debar in Mahanaim and the latter with Sheikh Sa'ad in Bashan (Haran, *op. cit.*, p. 272). **according to the word of the LORD**: Because of the formula noting that Jeroboam's conquest was a fulfilment of a prophetic word, Dietrich (*op. cit.*, pp. 110ff.) rightly separates v. 25*b* from v. 25*a* and regards it as the work of the deuteronomistic 'prophetic' redactor (DtrP). The formula is found in the words **according to the word of the LORD . . . which he spoke by his servant Jonah, the son of Amittai, the prophet**: This prophet is otherwise unknown, except of course that later the Book of Jonah was connected with the same person. It is surprising that this passage mentions the unknown prophet Jonah, whilst the more significant prophet Amos is completely ignored. The reason is clear; he gave a prophetic word to encourage Jeroboam in his campaigns, and so belonged to the tradition of Elisha rather than Amos, who as seen from Am. 6:13 condemned the confidence encouraged by the conquest of Transjordan. The mention of Jonah and the promise of God to Israel in v. 27 have been construed as a polemic against Amos in the deuteronomistic history (see Crüsemann, *Fest. von Rad*, pp. 57–63). **who was from Gath-hepher**: The home of Jonah was in the territory of Zebulun, according to Jos. 19:13, and it is identified with *Khirbet ez-Zurra'*, not far from Nazareth.

26–27. These words, in which typical deuteronomistic terminology and concepts are employed, give an explanation of the preceding reference to fulfilling a prophetic word. An identical pattern is found in 2 Kg. 24:3ff., where another reference to the fulfilment of the words of the prophets is followed by a further elaboration similar to the one given here (Dietrich, *op. cit.*, p. 35). These verses are also to be compared with 2 Kg. 13:4ff. **the LORD had not said**: Montgomery (p. 443) argues that although the phrasing is inexact, a nationalistic oracle along these lines was originally spoken as a word of encouragement to Jeroboam. If so, it is not entirely correct to take this verse as a deliberate polemic against Amos; but admittedly, such a motive cannot be very far away.

28. how he recovered from Israel Damscus and Hamath, which had belonged to Judah: This part of the concluding formula given in vv. 28, 29 presents textual and historical problems. How to render the prepositions attached to Israel and Judah (literally 'to Judah for Israel') is uncertain, and *RSV*'s interpretation of **to** as meaning 'which had belonged to' (cf. *RV*) is not entirely satisfactory (Burney, p. 320). Moreover, the suggestion that **Damacus and Hamath** had been vassals is dubious, and their subjugation by Israel in Jeroboam's time is questionable. Various solutions have been proposed. Whilst MT has the support of most of the Vsns., the Syr., omitting the reference to Judah and simply reading 'to Israel', gives an easier text, but does not solve the historical difficulty. Burney (p. 320, followed by Šanda II, p. 173 and Gray, p. 616) proposed an emendation of the Heb. text (based mainly on reading the proper name Hamath as a noun, *ḥᵃmaṯ*, 'wrath') to give 'and how he fought with Damascus, and how he turned away the wrath of Yahweh from Israel'. But, as noted by Montgomery (p. 446), Jeroboam's role as the diverter of divine wrath is most improbable. Another possibility is that **Judah** is to be rendered as Jaudi, a state in north-west Syria, which is well known from the inscriptions of the kings of Sam'al (Herrmann, *History*, p. 246); cf. *NEB*, 'he recovered Damascus and Hamath in Jaudi for Israel'. The difficulties encountered by these proposed solutions have led to some readiness to accept the statement that there was a reassertion of Israelite power over Damascus and Hamath under Jeroboam. The control which he achieved over these lands can be interpreted as a modest success in recovering Israelite bazaars and markets in the two cities (Montgomery,

p. 444), or else that he annexed territories in these countries but not the cities themselves (Bright, *History* p. 232), or again that Jeroboam did actually make both kingdoms subservient to Israel in the sense that they paid taxes to Israel, but were not annexed as Israelite provinces (Haran, *op. cit.*, pp. 280ff.). The relationship between vv. 28 and 25 is significant; the annalistic report of v. 25 noting that the whole length of Israel's frontier was restored by Jeroboam was probably interpreted rather liberally by the deuteronomistic redactor, who found in the report's reference to Hamath a suggestion that both Damascus and Hamath had been annexed by Jeroboam, which made hs kingdom approximate to the ideal kingdom of David. His interpretation exaggerated Jeroboam's actual achievement.

(e) Two kings of Judah and five kings of Israel
15:1–38

Chapter 15 covers the reigns of seven kings and extends over the significant period of the rise of Assyria during the last years of the northern kingdom. The interest and bias of the record give an unmistakable indication that the chapter comes from the deuteronomistic compilers. The reign of each king is presented with the usual deuteronomistic formulae of introduction and conclusion, and there is an interest in assessing the king's work and pronouncing a judgment upon him (see vv. 3ff., 9, 18, 24, 28, 34ff.). For inclusion in their account the deuteronomists have selected material from older sources; this is easily recognised from its short annalistic style (see vv. 5, 10, 14, 16, 19ff., 25, 29ff., 35b and 37). The extracts are brief, and it is a fair comment on the redactors to draw attention to the disproportionate space given to summaries and judgments as compared with the scanty use of material from annals and archival sources (cf. Gray, p. 618). The reason for this imbalance is the theological bias of the compiler.

(i) Azariah of Judah 15:1–7
Azariah's long reign of fifty-two years is more significant than the impression gained from the few facts given in this record. The two pieces of information provided from the annals merely state that Azariah became a leper and that Jotham his son acted as co-regent (v. 5).

In attempting to assess the significance of Azariah's rule, consideration must be given to information that is found elsewhere. The notice of his accession in 2 Kg. 14:21, 22 is accompanied by a reliable archival note that it was he who 'built Elath and restored it to Judah'; in other words, he crowned his father's efforts to the south of the Dead Sea by restoring Judah's access to the Gulf of Aqaba (see above, on 14:22).

More details of Azariah's reign appear in the Chronicler's account (2 Chr. 26:6–15), which is difficult to assess historically. He is said to have successfully waged military campaigns against the Philistines, the Arabs, the Moabites and the Ammonites; he strengthened the fortifications of Jerusalem; he developed agriculture considerably; and he maintained a strong army and added to the effectiveness of his arms. The account in Kings finishes with the statement that 'his fame spread far'. Some of the material in 2 Chr. 26:6–15 comes from earlier sources, and must be regarded as historically reliable (cf. Williamson, *Chronicles*, pp. 333ff.). The account given of the king's foreign affairs (vv. 6–8) is basically accurate, as is the notice in v. 10, which has been confirmed by archaeological discoveries. Williamson further accepts the authenticity of the details about the king's army and its equipment (vv. 11–15). That Judah enjoyed a period of calm and prosperity during the long reign of Azariah is not to be doubted. Israel's experience under his contemporary Jeroboam II is likely to have been paralleled by similar developments in Judah. As the book of Amos reflects social and economic conditions in Israel in the time of Jeroboam, the book of Isaiah to some extent gives an insight into conditions in Judah in the period immediately after the reign of Azariah. It has been claimed that from the historical point of view he was one of the most important kings of Judah and that the province list of Jos. 19:40–46; 15; reflects the administrative reorganization of Judah under Azariah (Aharoni, *VT* [1959], pp. 245ff.).

The Chronicler also gives more details of Azariah's leprosy (26:16ff.). He attributes it to an act of sacrilege committed by the king, who in his pride dared to enter into the Temple to burn incense on the altar. The elaboration in Chronicles of the brief annalistic statement in 2 Kg. 15:5 is probably composed of legendary material to explain the king's leprosy; it may have arisen from a real controversy between Azariah and the priesthood (Curtis, *Chronicles*, p. 452; Morgenstern, *HUCA* 12–13 [1937–8], pp. 1ff.), but in its present context provides an example of the Chronicler's characteristic two-part structure for reporting a king's reign, with a favourable beginning giving way to a contrasting latter part (cf. Williamson, *op. cit.*, p. 332). On the Chronicler's report of the king's burial, see below, on v. 7.

The significance of references in Assyrian records to 'Azriyahu of Ja'udi' is debatable (Haran, *VT* 17 [1967], pp. 290ff.). In the two references to him Azriyahu is described as the leader of a coalition against which Tiglath-pileser III had to wage war (Luckenbill, *Records II*, p. 770). One body of opinion (cf. Herrmann, *History*, p. 246) dismisses this information as irrelevant, since it must refer to a king of the north-west Syrian state of Ja'udi, and therefore throws no light on Azariah's activities nor on his eminence among his compatriots. Others are not convinced by the Ja'udi connection nor by the implication that a 'Yahwistic' king ruled in that region, and argue that, despite the absence of biblical references to Azariah's Syrian activities, the leader of this coalition must have been Azariah of Judah (Luckenbill, *AJSL* 41 [1925], pp. 217–32; Tadmor, *ScrHier* 8 [1961], pp. 235–8; Haran, *op. cit.*, pp. 290–7). The proposed dating of this coalition between 743 and 738 BC makes the identification with Azariah feasible.

1. **the twenty-seventh year of Jeroboam**: This chronological note contradicts 14:2, 23 (see above), which imply that he came to the throne in Jeroboam's fifteenth year. Gray (p. 618) makes Azariah co-regent with his father, and takes this verse to refer to his accession as sole regent. Co-regency is not accepted in the Table on p. 28 and Azariah is assigned the years 769–741 BC. **Azariah**: The alternative name 'Uzziah', found in vv. 13, 20, 32, 34, is the usual one outside the books of Kings (except for 1 Chr. 3:12). The prophetical books only refer to Uzziah (Am. 1:1; Hos. 1:1; Is. 1:1; 6:1; 7:1). Both names are similar in meaning, Azariah being a combination of 'help' and Uzziah of 'strength' with the divine name; so they can be taken as variants and need not be explained as an example of a distinction between a throne name and the monarch's personal name (as argued by Honeyman, *JBL* 67 [1948], pp. 20–2).

2. **His mother's name was Jecoliah**: The meaning is 'Yahweh holds' (Šanda II, p. 178), although Noth (*Personennamen*, p. 190) takes the verb to be in the perfect tense.

3. **He did what was right in the eyes of the LORD**: Despite the favourable judgment passed on Azariah by the deuteronomistic historians, a qualifying statement is made in v. 4, and there is a reference to his leprosy in v. 5. When the Chronicler came to give his account of Azariah's reign, he thought it necessary to reconcile the deuteronomistic favourable judgment with the fact that the king was a leper; to achieve this he included legendary material describing the king's act of sacrilege.

4. **Nevertheless the high places were not taken away**: cf. also 1 Kg. 3:2ff.; 15:14; 2 Kg. 12:3; 14:4, where the same stricture appears in the deuteronomistic assessment of a king's reign.

5. This verse is the only one in this section that has been derived from the annals. **The LORD smote the king, so that he was a leper to the day of his death**: For the nature of this disease, see on 2

Kg. 5:1, and Hulse, *PEQ* 107 (1975), pp. 87–105. **and he dwelt in a separate house**: The significance of Azariah's confinement is uncertain because of the obscurity of the term **separate house**. The Gk. obviously did not understand the term and merely transliterated it; the Targ. paraphrased by offering 'outside Jerusalem' as an equivalent. The use of the word *hopší* for freedom from slavery (Exod. 21:2, 5; Dt 15:12ff. Jer. 34:9–11) and from civil obligations (1 Sam. 17:25) suggests that *hopšīṯ* in this verse means 'freedom' rather than 'separateness' (against Rudolph, *ZAW* 89 [1977], p. 418, who insists on the idea of isolation). Consequently many commentators read the adjective as an adverb here and render 'in his own house at freedom' (Burney, p. 321; Šanda II, pp. 178ff.; Gray, pp. 618ff.). This does not mean that he was not restrained or molested (as suggested by Klostermann, p. 444), but rather that he was exempt from performing royal functions; cf. *NEB*, 'he was relieved of all duties and lived in his own house'. Because Azariah had been relieved of his duties Jotham was acting for him, and appears to have had two spheres of responsibility: **he was over the household** (*NEB*, 'was comptroller of the household'; cf. 1 Kg. 4:6) and was **governing the people of the land** (*NEB*, 'and regent'). But the length of his period as co-regent is not specified (see below, on vv. 32–38).

7. **and they buried him with his fathers in the city of David**: An entirely contradictory report appears in 2 Chr. 26:23, where it is stated that he was buried 'with his fathers in the burial field which belonged to the kings, for they said "He is a leper" '. This suggests that he was buried apart from the tombs of the kings. An inscription in Aramaic discovered by Sukenik (*PEQ* 63 [1931], pp. 217ff.; see also Albright, *BASOR* 44 [1931], pp. 8–10), and reading 'Hither we brought the bones of Uzziah—do not open', can be construed as confirmation that Uzziah's remains were easily identifiable because they had been buried apart from those of the kings. Thus the version of Chronicles is preferred (Yeivin, *JNES* [1948], pp. 30–45).

(ii) *Zechariah of Israel* 15:8–12

Zechariah's short reign of six months is notable for two reasons: on the one hand, it marks the beginning of a series of conspiracies and assassinations that characterized the last years of the northern kingdom, and on the other, he was the last king from the dynasty of Jehu.

The usual deuteronomistic formulae are used to introduce and to conclude Zechariah's reign (vv. 8–9, 11). There is, however, one omission, for in common with all the kings from Zechariah to

Hoshea (with the exception of Menahem) the usual notice of burial is missing. The only annalistic material included in this report is found in the notice about Shallum's conspiracy in v. 10, which provides a good example of the standard annalistic pattern for reporting an uprising (cf. Dietrich, *Prophetie*, pp. 59ff., and above, on 1 Kg. 15:25–32). An unexpected addition to this section is the note in v. 12 (bracketed in *RSV*) stating that in the events of Zechariah's reign a divine oracle had been fulfilled. Dietrich (*op. cit.*, pp. 34ff.), commenting on the similarity between this verse and 2 Kg. 24:3ff., distinguishes between notices of the fulfilment of prophecy and these two examples of making effective God's word. This verse is attributed by Dietrich to DtrN.

8. In the thirty-eighth year of Azariah: A discrepancy in the chronology is evident when this verse is compared with 14:23 and 15:1, the former showing a difference of eleven years and the latter a difference of twenty-three years. Gray (p. 620) is able to accept the figure given in this verse because he maintains that Azariah was for a time acting as co-regent with his father. In the Table on p. 28, co-regency is not assumed, and after a substantial reduction in the figure given in this verse, Zechariah's reign is given as 753–752 BC, assuming that his six-month reign covered part of two years (cf. 1 Kg. 22:52).

9. This deuteronomistic verdict is what is expected for a king of the northern kingdom, and its allusion to **the sins of Jeroboam the son of Nebat** is typical. *NEB*'s 'who led Israel into sin', applying the relative to Jeroboam, is an easier reading of the Heb. than *RSV*'s **which he made Israel to sin**, with the relative being applied to **the sins of Jeroboam**.

10. The five basic statements of an uprising report are found here, namely a note of conspiracy, the naming of the conspirator and his father, a statement that the king was struck down, that he was killed and that the conspirator took his throne. The name **Shallum**, rendered 'requited' by Šanda (II, p. 181), does not contain an element of the divine name, and the description **son of Jabesh** is probably a reference to a clan or district rather than to his father, and may be rendered 'a man of Jabesh', possibly indicating that the reaction against Jehu's dynasty came from Jabesh-gilead in Transjordan. In the Assyrian records the usurper Shallum is called 'the son of a nobody'. **and struck him down at Ibleam:** If the rendering of the Syr., Targ. and Vulg. is accepted, MT means that he was struck down 'before the people'. It is not entirely satisfactory, since it assumes that an Aramaic word has been used (*qāḇāl*). Luc. read **at Ibleam**, which seems appropriate. Jehu's dynasty had been set up after the shooting of Ahaziah near Ibleam (2 Kg. 9:27), and now it was brought down with the killing of Shallum at Ibleam. Confirmation of this reading is obained again from an examination of the conspiracy reports, which, with the exception of v. 30, note the place of the assassination (see 1 Kg. 15:27; 16:9; 2 Kg. 15:14, 25).

12. This note confirming that God's promise to Jehu had been fulfilled refers the reader back to 2 Kg. 10:30. The original promise was given in two parts, with the reason for the promise (introduced with 'because') being followed by an announcement. The quotation in this verse omits the first element. The dynasty of Jehu had ruled the country successfully for almost a century, and the fall of the dynasty at the hands of Shallum marks the beginning of the end for the northern kingdom.

(iii) Shallum of Israel 15:13–16

Although the account of Shallum's short reign of one month is given within the usual deuteronomistic framework (vv.13, 15), there are some irregularities. As in the case of the other kings from Zechariah to Hoshea, no reference is made to his burial. Again like the account of Zechariah's reign in vv. 8–12 the deuteronomistic reference to sources is followed by additional material; but, whereas v. 12 is an insertion about the fulfilment of a divine promise, v. 16 contains further annalistic material concerning Menahem, who conspired against Shallum. The significance of the two annalistic notes in vv. 14 and 16 for the history of the period will be discussed below.

13. in the thirty-ninth year of Uzziah king of Judah: On the date, see above on v. 8. **he reigned one month**: the Heb. (*yeraḥ yāmîm*) means literally 'month of days', which is to be rendered 'one full month' (cf. *NEB*).

14. This verse is from the annals and is composed of the constituent elements of a conspiracy report (see above on v. 10). **Menahem, the son of Gadi**: It has been suggested that **Menahem**, 'comforter', was a name given to a child born to parents as a replacement of a dead child, and thus bringing them consolation (cf. Noth. *Personennamen*, p. 222). **the son of Gadi**: The name **Gadi** probably denotes the father's name, rather than Menahem's connection with the tribe of Gad or with the village of Baal Gad near Hermon. Šanda (II, p. 183) gives it the meaning 'my luck', a shortened form of Gadiyahu, 'Yahweh is my luck'. Although Menahem's place of origin is unknown, the seat of his power lay in **Tirzah** (*Tell el-Farʿah*), the capital of the northern province from the time of Baasha to the time of Omri (cf. 1 Kg. 15:21). The fact that Tirzah was in Manasseh's hands supports the view that Menahem was the leader of the Manasseh faction in the struggle for the throne after the collapse of the Jehu dynasty. For a discussion of the other parties involved, see below on v. 16.

15. This formulaic reference to sources has included an allusion to Shallum's conspiracy in the phrase **and the conspiracy which he made**; cf. 1 Kg. 16:20 for a similar allusion in the report of Zimri's reign.

16. At that time: The report from the annals in v. 16 is connected to the previous section in v. 1; by means of the linking phrase **at that time** (Heb. 'āz, 'then'). This is probably a correct reflection of the sequence of events; Menahem, after overpowering Shallum and establishing himself in Samaria, decided to move against **Tappuah**. There is no need to reverse the order of vv. 14 and 16, as once suggested (Skinner, p. 361). The crux of the verse, and a key to our understanding of the event, is the identificatiom of **Tappuah**, a name derived from Luc. for MT's *Tipsah*. The reliability of the Heb. *Tipsah*, identified with Thapsacus, an important caravan and military crossing on the Euphrates (cf. 1 Kg. 4:24), has not been without its defenders. It is argued that the reading of Luc. is a corruption, that it is unlikely that Menahem acted with such brutality against the neighbouring Tappuah, and that nothing in the political and military circumstances of the time prevented Israelite forces from marching through Damascus and Tadmor to Tipsah on the Euphrates (Haran, *VT* 17 [1967], pp. 284–90). Despite these arguments, no convincing motive for the penetration of an Israelite army as far as Thapsacus has been produced, and it is difficult, if not impossible, to believe that such a drive was made. Therefore, the reading of Luc. is accepted here. **Tappuah** was near the border between Ephraim and Manasseh (cf. Jos. 16:8; 17:7–8), and is identified as *Sheikh Abu Zarad* (Jenni, *ZDPV* 74 [1958], pp. 35–40). The reason for Menahem's brutality against Tappuah has to be sought in the struggle for the throne that followed the overthrow of the dynasty of Jehu. Gray's proposal (pp. 622ff.) is that two parties contended for the throne, an Ephraimite party represented by Shallum, who came from Tappuah, which was called Yasib, a name that may be concealed in the designation 'son of Jabesh', and a Manasseh party with its base at Tirzah and represented by Menahem. This ingenious suggestion suffers from the very dubious connection between Yasib and Jabesh. As noted above (under v. 10), Shallum probably came from Jabesh-gilead, and so the first reaction against the Jehu dynasty came from Transjordan. Menahem from Manasseh was unwilling to allow this move from Jabesh to go unchecked, and so conspired against Shallum. Realizing that an Ephraimite party was also organizing a drive for the throne, Menahem took quick and drastic action to subdue the rival uprising.

from Tirzah on: The Heb. for **from Tirzah** is capable of several interpretations. *RSV*'s rendering suggests that Menahem destroyed Tappuah **and its territory from Tirzah on**, giving the impression that the territory belonging to Tappuah was adjacent to Tirzah and that the whole area between Tirzah and Tappuah was conquered. But the two did not share a common boundary (Albright, *JPOS* 11 [1931], pp. 241–51). Another possibility is to omit from Tirzah as a duplication from v. 14 (Šanda II, p. 184); cf. *NEB*; it is argued that Menahem could not direct operations against Tipsah or Tappuah **from Tirzah** (Haran, *op. cit.*, p. 290). There is, however, no reason for doubting MT, as from Tirzah may simply mean that he set out against Tappuah, as indeed he had already done against Samaria, from his base at Tirzah; cf. *NIV*, 'starting out from Tirzah'. **because they did not open it to him, therefore he sacked it, and he ripped up all the women in it who were with child**: The Heb. is obscure, and *RSV*, like all other translators, has been dependent on the Gk. and Syr. to reconstruct a satisfactory text which can be meaningfully rendered. The atrocious behaviour of Menahem demands, according to Haran (*op. cit.*, pp. 287ff.), that it was directed against a foreign city. It was certainly no part of Israelite warfare; it belongs rather to the Assyrian period, and was directed against Israel on several occasions—by the Aramaeans (2 Kg. 8:12), the Ammonites (Am. 1:13) and the Assyrians (Hos. 14:1). It may be that Menahem emulated Assyrian practice in order to demonstrate his power and to stifle opposition.

(iv) Menahem of **15:17–22**

In addition to what has been stated about Menahem in the account of his conspiracy against Shallum, a suitable section covers his own reign. Within the usual deuteronomistic formulae, introducing (vv. 17–18) and concluding (vv. 21–22) the coverage of his reign, there comes from annalistic material a significant insertion (vv. 19–20) referring to the impact of Assyrian intervention on the Israelite kingdom.

17. In the thirty-ninth year: This is the same as v. 13, see above. **he reigned ten years in Samaria**: In this era of short reigns, Menahem succeeded in keeping his position for ten years, and, unlike his two predecessors and his two successors, he was not murdered by a conspirator. Verse 16 above provides one reason for his survival, namely that he held firmly to the throne through harsh and brutal measures; vv. 19–20 provide another reason, namely that he used the authority of the Assyrian overlord to consolidate his own position.

18. This repetition of the standard formula contains two slight

deviations. **all his days** is an unusual feature. Because the beginning
of v. 19 is also abrupt, it has been proposed to follow the Gk. and
read **all his days** as 'in his days' (a regular redactionary link) at the
beginning of v. 19 (Burney, p. 322; Montgomery, p. 450; cf. *NEB*).
Again the inclusion of **all** with **the sins of Jeroboam** is obtained by
accepting a slight emendation of the text with the Gk.

19–20. The background of these two verses is the renewal of the
Assyrian thrust westwards under Tiglath-pileser III (745–727 BC),
who was mainly responsible for the Assyrian policy of expansion
that led the Empire to the height of its power. Tiglath-pileser's
policy was one of increasing step by step Assyrian domination over
other states aiming ultimately at depriving them of their political
independence. Beginning with establishing a vassal relationship with
another state and the extraction of tribute from it, the pressure was
through different processes intensified and then military intervention occurred with the result that independence was lost when an
Assyrian governor assumed control. For a description of Assyrian
policy, see Donner, *VTS* 11 [1964], pp. 2ff.; *IJH*, pp. 415–21;
Herrmann, *History*, p. 244. Tiglath-pileser's first decisive success in
central Assyria was in 738 BC, when he conquered Hamath, and as
a result received submission as vassals from a number of states and
cities in Syria and Asia Minor, including Rasyan of Damascus (the
Resin of the *OT*; cf. 2 Kg. 15:37; 16:5ff.; Isa. 7:1–8) and Menih-
imme of Samaria (the Menahem of the *OT*). The reference in
Tiglath-pileser's annals to Menahem's tribute (*ANET*, pp. 282–4)
is also confirmed by a recently discovered stele from Iran (Levine,
BASOR [1972], pp. 40–2; Weippert, *ZDPV* [1973], pp. 26–53).

19. Pul the king of Assyria came against the land: The annals
from which vv. 19–20 are derived correctly use the name **Pul** for
Tiglath-pileser. When he ascended the Assyrian throne in 729 BC
he assumed the throne-name **Pul** (*ANET*, p. 272), which appears as
Porosid in the king-list of Ptolemy. **Menahem gave Pul a thousand
talents of silver**: Extracting a tribute and making a vassal of the
king was the first stage of Assyrian domination. It seems that for a
time Assyria was content to accept this stage of submission by
countries on the periphery of the Empire, but of course would take
further action at the first sign of unrest or dissatisfaction. The sum
of **a thousand talents** is less than the 2,300 demanded by Adad-
nirari III from Aram in 806 BC (*ANET*, pp. 281ff.), and can be
compared with the 30 gold talents and the 800 silver talents extracted
by Sennacherib from Zedekiah in 701 BC (*ANET*, p. 288). **that he
might help him to confirm his hold of the royal power**: *NEB*, 'to
obtain his help in strengthening his hold on the kingdom'. The
second part of the verse is missing from the Gk.; its omission makes

the first part ambiguous and capable of meaning that Menahem gave tribute to Tiglath-pileser either to help the Assyrian king or else to obtain help from him. The retention of the second part of the sentence makes it quite clear that the latter is the meaning; his position as vassal to Tiglath-pileser, and his authority to extract tax to pay the Assyrian king, contributed enormously to the consolidation of Menahem's power.

20. Menahem exacted the money from Israel, that is, from all the wealthy men: The verb translated **exacted** (Heb. Hip'îl of *yāṣā'*, 'to bring out') caused difficulty for older commentators who resorted to some emendation (Burney, pp. 322ff.). But Šanda's reference to a parallel Arab. usage (II, p. 186) for 'to impose a land-tax' makes the meaning of the verb quite clear; cf. *NEB*, 'Menahem laid a levy . . . .'. The **wealthy men** were the landowners who were liable to a levy; they may have also included royal officials and administrators in addition to the old established Israelite landowners (Herrmann, *History*, p. 245). **fifty shekels of silver from every man**: According to Galling's calculation (*BRL*, pp. 176, 185–8) a talent is worth 3,000 shekels; working on a rate of 50 shekels per person, it would appear that 60,000 persons had to be liable to tax to raise a national revenue of 1000 talents. The statement that the king of Assyria **turned back and did not stay there in the land** signifies that Tiglath-pileser was satisfied with the arrangements for the payment of tribute, thus reducing the kingdom to a state of vassalage. No further action was necessary as long as this position was maintained.

22. Menahem slept with his fathers: Since he was not assassinated by conspirators, Menahem is the only Israelite king of the five listed in chapter 15 who is reported to have **slept with his fathers**, i.e. who had a peaceful death and burial.

(v) Pekahiah of Israel **15:23–26**
Menahem's son, Pekahiah, was not as successful as his father in establishing himself firmly on the throne; in two years a conspiracy arose among military personnel, and Pekahiah was removed in favour of Pekah. The account of his reign is brief, and within the standard introductory (vv. 23–24) and closing (v. 26) formulae contains annalistic material in v. 25, which follows the set pattern of a conspiracy report (cf. vv. 10, 14, 30).

23. In the fiftieth year of Azariah: This chronological note is consistent with those provided for other reigns covered in this chapter; cf. vv. 8, 13, 17, 27. A period of **two years** for his reign is undoubtedly correct, despite the figure 'ten' given in Luc. His years are given as 753–752 BC in the Table on p. 28. The name **Pekahiah**, containing the root *pqḥ*, 'to open' (the eyes), can mean either 'Yahweh is open-eyed' (or 'alert'; so Gray, p. 625), or 'Yahweh has opened the eyes'; it corresponds to the form *Pkhj* found on a Palestinian seal (Diringer, *Le Iscrizioni*, p. 353).

25. The conspiracy report faithfully produces the name of the conspirator together with his father's name; he was **Pekah the son of Remaliah**. The name **Pekah** is an abbreviated form of Pekahiah, and corresponds to the Assyrian form *Paqaha*; it has also been found in the Lachish ostraca and on a jar in Hazor dated from the time of its destruction by Tiglath-pileser (Yadin, *Hazor II*, pp. 73ff.). The first component in the name **Remaliah** is probably the root *rml*, which is attested elsewhere (Ryckmans, *Les noms propres* I, p. 200), but whose meaning is obscure; this is preferred to Šanda's suggestion (II, p. 187) that it means 'God is exalted for me'. **his captain . . . with fifty men of the Gileadites**: Pekah was a military officer bearing the title of *šālîš* (see 1 Kg. 9:22), and the support given him by **Gileadites** suggests that he too originated from Gilead. His conspiracy probably reflects a resurgence of discontent in this area, for it was here too that opposition rose against the dynasty of Jehu. Possibly Menahem's succession by his son Pekahiah aroused the antipathy felt in some areas to a hereditary kingship, and the men of Gilead decided to strike again. **in the citadel of the king's house**: According to Gray (p. 625) he was killed in the residential quarters of the palace. The Heb. adds another phrase here, 'Argob and Arieh', which is omitted from *RSV*. Klostermann (pp. 446ff.) retained the two words in an emended form to give 'and his four hundred warriors', suggesting that Pekah with a small company organised a *coup* that annihilated the royal bodyguard. Others think that the king and 'Argob and Arieh', two units of his guards, were struck (Yeivin, *WHJP*, p. 174). On the basis of a new translation, 'near the eagle and near the lion', it has been suggested that Pekahiah, like Sennacherib, was murdered between the guardian figures of his palace (see Geller, *VT* 26 [1976], pp. 374–7). Much support has been found, however, for Stade's suggestion (*ZAW* 6 [1886], p. 160) that 'Argob and Arieh' were place-names that became displaced from the list of conquered districts in v. 29. The scribe's eye may have accidentally wandered from 'Gilead' in v. 25 to 'Gilead' in v. 29, with the result that these two place-names found with Gilead in v. 29 were also included in v. 25. Both were located in Transjordan, 'Argob' being a district in Bashan (1 Kg. 4:13) and 'Arieh' possibly the same as *Hawwôt-jair*, a group of settlements in the same area.

(vi) Pekah of Israel 15:27–31

Within the stereotyped framework (vv. 27–28 and v. 31) two annalistic notes relating to Pekah's rule have been inserted. The first (v.
29) records the appearance of Tiglath-pileser to conquer and
suppress districts in the north, and the second (v. 30) is yet again
a standard conspiracy report noting the overthrow of Pekah by
Hoshea the son of Elah.

27. **In the fifty-second year of Azariah**: The reckoning is
consistent with the other synchronisms with the reign of Azariah
found in this chapter (see above, on v. 23). **and reigned twenty
years**: The Heb. has in this instance omitted the verb **and reigned**.
A reign of **twenty years** by Pekah is impossible on comparison with
Assyrian records, unless it is assumed that he reigned elsewhere in
Israel before he came to Samaria (cf. Cook, *VT* 14 [1964], pp.
121–35). If Menahem lived to pay tribute to Tiglath-pileser in 738
BC and Pekah was replaced by Hoshea soon after Tiglath-pileser's
subjugation of northern territories in 732 BC, only seven years are
allowed for the reigns of Pekahiah and Pekah, which reduces the
latter's period to about five years. Even if Menahem had died before
738 BC, the maximum period that can be allowed for Pekah is ten
years (cf. Gray, p. 626; Herrmann, *History*, p. 228). In the Table
on p. 28 he is assigned the years 741–730 BC. See further, Thiele,
VT 16 [1966], pp. 83–103; McHugh, *VT*, 14 [1964], pp. 446–53.

29. Tiglath-pileser's appearance in the west must have been occasioned by activities which were anti-Assyrian, or at least could have
been so interpreted. It is known that Tiglath-pileser campaigned in
Philistia in 734 BC (*ANET*, p. 272; Wiseman, *Iraq* 13 [1951], pp.
21–6), and that he directed action against Gaza; he established a
military out-post on the *Wadi el-'Arish*, but it is not known if he
annexed some of Israel's eastern territory on this occasion (Donner,
IJH, p. 425). At the end of that year, or perhaps in 733 BC, Pekah
of Israel and Rasyan of Damascus formed a coalition, which must
be interpreted as an anti-Assyrian move. In what is known as the
Syro-Ephraimite war (see below on 2 Kg. 16:5ff.) they attempted
to coerce Ahaz of Judah to co-operate, but failed. A call by Ahaz
for help from Assyria brought Tiglath-pileser again to the west, and
he dealt with Pekah in 733 BC and with Damascus in the following
year. It is Tiglath-pileser's measures against Pekah that are described
in this verse.

The places mentioned indicate the extent of Israel's conquest by
Tiglath-pileser. **Ijon, Abel-beth-maacah . . . Kedesh, Hazor** were
in northern Galilee, as probably was **Janoah**, which is listed with
them; the area corresponds roughly with that ravaged by the Syrians
in 1 Kg. 15:20. He first of all conquered a chain of fortified towns

running from north to south, **Ijon** (*Tell ed-Dibbin*), **Abel-beth-maacah** (*Tell Abil*) and **Hazor** (*Tell el-Qebah*). which was destroyed at this time; cf. Yadin. *Hazor I*, pp. 22ff.; II, pp. 63ff.). This enabled Tiglath-pileser to gain the whole of Galilee, including **Kebesh** (*Tell Qadesh*) and **Janoah** (*Yamuh*). which show that he moved westwards towards the sea. He was also apparently able to move south, cross the Jordan and take possession of Gilead. With the Assyrian forces gaining domination over Galilee, Nephtali and Gilead, Pekah was isolated from Syria, and was confined to what is known as 'the rump state of Ephraim', which was the mountain area of Ephraim and Samaria.

Tiglath-pileser's conquest of Israel in 733 BC and of Damascus in 732 BC is well attested in Assyrian sources. In his annals (*ANET*, p. 283) he records how he added 'all the cities of Bit Humria' (the house of Omri) to his territory and had only left Samaria. Another fragmentary text (*ANET*, pp. 283ff.) refers to towns conquered in northern Syria and on the Phoenician coast, and more specifically to Gilead, Galilee and Abilakku (possibly Abel-beth-maacah) 'and the whole wide land of . . . li'. The land ending in '. . . li' was thought to be Naphtali, and therefore providing a parallel to the present verse; but on the basis of other inscriptions it must now be taken as 'Haza'ili', the land of the house of Hazael, or Aram-Damascus (cf. Wiseman, *Iraq* 18 [1956], pp. 117–29; Saggs, *Iraq* 17 [1955], pp. 131–3). At this time Tiglath-pileser formed three provinces in Israel and named them Megiddo (Magiddu), covering Galilee and the northern plains, Dor (Du'ru), including the plain of Sharon and extending as far as the Philistine border, and Gilead (Gal'aza), which was Israelite Transjordan (Alt, *Kleine Schriften II*, pp. 188–205). **and he carried the people captive to Assyria**: This was Israel's first taste of Assyria's method of reducing a district into an Assyrian province. When a state engaged in anti-Assyrian activities, the Assyrians deported the nation's upper class to another part of its empire and replaced it with a foreign one. This occurred during the more advanced stages of annexation (see now Oded, *Mass Deportations*). Tiglath-pileser's annals also confirm that he took all the inhabitants and their possessions to Assyria (*ANET*, pp. 283ff.).

30. In stereotyped form Hoshea's conspiracy against Pekah is recorded. According to the biblical report Hoshea ('saviour'), the son of Elah, was responsible for the overthrow of Pekah. But a slightly different version of the incident appears in Tiglath-pileser's annals, 'They overthrew their king Pa-qa-ha and I placed A-u- si' as king over them'. The two statements are not necessarily contradictory: the annals agree that the conspiracy originated among the

Israelites, but add information that is omitted from the biblical account, namely that the conspirator had the support of Assyria, which probably means that he was the nominee of the pro-Assyrian party. Taken with what is said about Menahem in v. 19, this verse throws interesting light on this period: Israel was probably divided into pro- and anti-Assyrian factions, with Menahem, his son Pekahiah and Hosea representing the former, and Pekah, the Gileadite conspirator, representing the latter. **in the twentieth year of Jotham the son of Uzziah**: This date for Hoshea's conspiracy is highly suspect. On the one hand, it is not usual to include a date in a conspiracy report (see on 1 Kg. 15:27), and on the other hand, it contradicts 2 Kg. 17:1, which dates Hoshea's accession 'in the twelfth year of Ahaz', and also 2 Kg. 15:33, which ascribes only sixteen years to Jotham. It is best regarded as an interpolation.

(vii) Jotham of Judah 15:32–38

Jotham, who is introduced with the standard details (vv. 32–33) was king in Judah for sixteen years, and receives from the deuteronomistic historians a favourable verdict (v. 34), but with the usual qualification (v. 35). The closing formula appears in vv. 36, 38. Two short statements, which are annalistic in character, have been inserted, but both are awkwardly placed. A statement at the end of v. 35 that he built 'the upper gate' of the Temple has become attached to the qualifying note that he did not remove the high places. Again v. 37, referring to the Syro-Ephraimite coalition, is an intrusion into the middle of the closing formula in vv. 36, 38. The Chronicler has added information about his buildings and his campaign against Ammon (2 Chr. 27:1–9; cf. Williamson, *Chronicles*, pp. 341ff.).

32. In the second year of Pekah: Reference is made here to Jotham's accession as sole ruler, and not to the time when he acted as co-regent with his father. His years were 741–734 BC, according to the Table on p. 28. **Jotham the son of Uzziah**: The name **Jotham** means 'Yahweh is perfect'. Excavations at *Tell el-Khaleifeh* (Eziongeber), which according to 14:22 had been restored to Judah by Jotham's father, brought to light a seal bearing the name Jotham. Whereas Glueck (*BASOR* [1940], p. 13; *Rivers*, p. 167) identified it as a seal of office belonging to Jotham or his representative, Gray (p. 629), because the seal bears the figure of a ram, maintains that it belonged to an official responsible for the royal flocks and for returning wool to Jotham (cf. Isa. 16:1). Whatever the purpose of the seal, it testifies to the extent of the area under Judaean control in the time of Uzziah and Jotham (Avigad, *BASOR* 163 [1961], pp. 18–22).

33. he reigned sixteen years in Jerusalem: The number **sixteen** is difficult to fit into the chronological scheme, and is probably a mistake for 'six'. His years in the Table on p. 28 are 741–734 BC. **Jerusha the daughter of Zadok**: His mother's name, if emended slightly to Jerushah, as in 2 Chr. 27:1, means 'possessed'. Gray (p. 629), proposing a connection with an Arab. root meaning 'to be firm', and assuming that Jerusha is an abbreviation of *yᵉrūšāʾēl*, gives it the meaning 'strengthened by God'. Her father cannot possibly have been the Zadok mentioned im 1 Chr. 5:38. Gray (p. 629) suggests that the name of Zadok designated the hereditary priest of Jerusalem; the fact that it was such a well-known family made it unnecessary to give Jerusha's home as is generally the case in these formulae.

35. He built the upper gate of the house of the LORD: This note, derived from the annals, is written in characteristic style, with the Heb. placing the emphatic **he** at the beginning. The **upper gate** is probably to be identified with 'the upper Benjamin Gate' of Jer. 20:2 and 'the upper gate, which faces north' of Ezek. 9:2. In 2 Chr. 27:3ff. a more extensive building programme is attributed to Jotham. He strengthened the wall of the Ophel and built other fortifications throughout the country; both activities were defence measures against the coming threat from the Syro-Ephraimite alliance (Gray, pp. 629ff.), but Williamson (*Chronicles*, p. 342) is dubious of the reliability of this information.

37. In those days the LORD began to send Rezin the king of Syria and Pekah the son of Remaliah against Judah: The information contained in this annalistic note is probably reliable, despite the fact that it is totally ignored in 2 Chr. 27. Admittedly the real danger from the Syro-Ephraimite alliance was only felt in the time of Ahaz (2 Kg. 16:5, 6), but, according to this note, movements had been initiated in the time of Jotham. That this note is a misplacement is obvious from the fact that it intrudes into the deuteronomistic closing formula (vv. 36, 38). The information derived from the annals has received from the editor the usual linking phrase **in those days**, and probably also the attribution of the Syro-Ephraimite alliance to **the LORD**.

(f) Ahaz of Judah
16:1–20

When Ahaz succeeded his father Jotham to the throne of Judah in 734 BC, he was facing perilous times. Tiglath-pileser had already marched against the Philistines, when he directed operations against Gaza in 734 and had penetrated as far south as the *Wadi el-ʿArish*

(Gray, *ExpT* 63 [1951–2], pp. 263–5; Saggs, *Iraq* 17 [1955], p. 152; Tadmor, *BA* 29 [1966], p. 86). The Assyrian army had been on an expedition that brought it very near to the kingdom of Judah. According to 2 Kg. 15:37 an alliance between Syria and Israel directed against Judah had been formed even before Ahaz had come to the throne. Although the report in chapter 16 of Ahaz's difficult reign is relatively short, it can be supplemented, not only from 2 Chr. 28, but also from the prophecies of Isaiah (especially Isa. 7:1–9; but not 10:27*b*–34, according to Wildberger, *Jesaja*, pp. 423–35; see further, Clements, *Isaiah*, pp. 117ff.), who was active at this time, from Hos. 5:8–6:6, which has the Syro-Ephraimite march against Judah as its background (cf. Alt, *Kleine Schriften II*, pp. 163–87) and from Assyrian records. The apostasy of Ahaz has been heightened in 2 Chr. 18:1–27, where the hand of the Chronicler is particularly evident (cf. Williamson, *Chronicles*, pp. 343ff.).

Literary analysis of the chapter has shown that it contains three elements. The easiest to separate is the deuteronomistic framework, which as usual contains an introductory section (vv. 1–4) and a concluding statement (vv. 19–20). Two distinct reports have been used for composing the material now standing between these intro-ductory and concluding sections. The first section (vv. 5–9) gives a brief report of the Syro-Ephraimite war against Judah and of the Assyrian response to Judah's plight. There are sufficient grounds for suggesting that this section only contains a résumé of a record of this period in the annals, and not an extract from those annals. Details of the Syro-Ephraimite war are lacking, and it is on the basis of Isa. 7:1–9 that a clearer picture of the situation is obtained (cf. also Oded, *CBQ* 34 [1972], pp. 153–65). It is perhaps surprising that no mention is made of Isaiah, who was so active during this crisis. But a likely explanation is that the deuteronomistic historian in his desire to condemn Ahaz for his cultic aberrations had no use for the Isaianic standpoint with its criticism of Ahaz for his lack of faith in God (Thompson, *Syro-Ephraimite War*, pp. 85ff.). Gray (pp. 630f.) rightly suggests that there has been a telescoping of history in vv. 5–9. The redactor responsible for the selection and compil-ation of material from the annals also provided a link with the phrase 'at that time', as well as the phrase 'to this day'; he also gave his own format and words for the message of Ahaz to Tiglath-pileser in v. 7 (so Šanda II, pp. 207f., where it is argued that the letter form was not derived from the annals).

The second section (vv. 10–18), which introduces changes made by Ahaz to the Temple and its furnishings, displays a unity of content. Unlike the simple reference to the regent as 'Ahaz' in the remainder of the chapter, this section consistently refers to him as

'King Ahaz' (see vv. 10, 11, 15, 16, 17), and is exclusively concerned
with matters of cultic interest. It has been proposed (Benzinger,
p. 170) that this material was derived from a source concerned with
the history of the Temple and that it is to be read in conjunction
with 2 Kg. 11; 12:5–17 and 22:3–23:25; the history may be reckoned
as the work of priests and derived from Temple archives. After a
careful analysis of the language and terminology in vv. 10–18, Rendtorff (*Opfers*, pp. 46–50) concludes that they are composed of two
smaller units, vv. 12ff. and 15ff., but he ascribes both to a tradition
connected with the Jerusalem Temple and finds in them affinity
with priestly texts. A forceful objection to the priestly origin of this
section is the absence of forthright criticism of Ahaz, as would be
expected from such quarters. For this reason Šanda (II, p. 207)
finds in this section material from a fragmentary history of the
reign of Ahaz which was non-priestly in origin and therefore more
objective. The other possible explanation, that the criticism of Ahaz
found in the original source was suppressed by the deuteronomistic
historian in view of his own criticism in vv. 1–4, is not very convincing. It may, therefore, be suggested that the compiler responsible
for this section used two sources: the annals of the kings of Judah
and an independent source displaying an interest in religious development. Because of his own bias, the compiler gave a short résumé
of the former in order to make more extensive use of the latter.

1. **In the seventeenth year of Pekah**: Because of the exaggeration
of Pekah's reign in MT (see above, on 15:27), the figure 'seventeen'
is impossible. A reckoning from an earlier bid for power *c*. 750 BC,
although offering support to MT (Gray, p. 631), is hypothetical. In
the Table on p. 28 Ahaz's accession is dated in 734 BC. **Ahaz**: This
abbreviated form of his name is found both in the Bible and on a
seal of 'Ašna, minister of Ahaz' (Torrey, *BASOR* [1940], pp. 27ff.).
It is thought to be an abbreviation of Jehoahaz, a name that is also
known from the list of Israelite kings (cf. 13:1; see Montgomery,
p. 456) and also given by Tiglath-pileser in the form Yauhazi (Luckenbill, *Records I*, p. 801; *ANET*, p. 282).

2. **He reigned sixteen years in Jerusalem**: Gray (p. 631) assumes
that Ahaz during the first few years acted as co-regent with his
father Jotham. His reign of **sixteen years** is probably calculated,
however, from the time of his recognition by Assyria *c*. 730 until
715 BC. The name of the king's mother is omitted, although it is
usual to include such information in the deuteronomistic formula
for introducing a Judaean king.

3. Ahaz is severely condemned by the deuteronomistic historian
because **he walked in the way of the kings of Israel**. One feature
that is noted in the apostasy of Ahaz is that he **burned his son as**

an offering or 'passed his son through the fire' (*NEB*), a reference
to child-sacrifice (Plataroti, *VT* 28 [1978], pp. 286–300). The Israelites had occasionally resorted to the practice in earlier times (Jg.
11:34ff.), but it became more widespread when national religion
was declining during the last years of the two kingdoms. It is
mentioned in connection with the fall of Israel (2 Kg. 17:17) and
again in connection with the reign of Manasseh in Judah (2 Kg.
21:6; 23:10). Sacrificing children is elsewhere associated with the
valley of the sons of Hinnom (see below, on 2 Kg. 23:10), and has
specific connections with the cult of the god Molech (see on 1 Kg.
11:5). It appears from 2 Kg. 3:27 that sacrifice of this kind was
offered in circumstances of extreme emergency; on this basis it can
be suggested that Ahaz resorted to child-sacrifice only because of
the imminent danger from the Syro-Ephraimite threat (cf. Šanda
II, pp. 195ff.). The introduction of child-sacrifice with the qualification that Ahaz was following **the abominable practices of the
nations whom the LORD drove out before the people of Israel**
clearly implies that Israel adopted this practice from its Canaanite
environment. Despite an apparent connection between sacrifice to
Molech and the Mesopotamian Malik, god of the underworld
(Albright, *Archaeology*, pp. 162–4), and also the possible significance
of the appearance of child-sacrifice in the Assyrian period, the Mesopotamian origin of the practice has been questioned. Saggs (*Assyriology*, p. 22), whilst claiming that the practice was unknown to the
Assyrians except through direct borrowing from Phoenicia, finds
that it is well attested in Phoenicia and its colonies, and so asserts
that it is of Phoenician rather than Assyrian origin. Indeed it is now
doubted if the Assyrians practised sacrifice through burning or
child-sacrifice in particular (McKay, *Religion*, pp. 39–41). On
evidence that the sacrificial term *mlk* appears in connection with
child-sacrifice in Phoenician sources, and on the suggestion of the
OT itself that the rites practised at Hinnom were Canaanite (Dt.
12:31; 18:9–10; cf. also 2 Chr. 28:3), it would seem that what was
practised by Ahaz was of Phoenicio-Canaanite origin and does not
display direct Assyrian influence (cf. Cogan, *Imperialism*, pp. 77–83,
where a distinction is drawn between a fire cult that did not involve
child sacrifice and a Canaanite cult of child-sacrifice).

4. The implication of this verse is that Ahaz was an apostate who
participated in Canaanite fertility rites **on the high places** (see on
1 Kg. 3:2). The practices in which they indulged at the high places
are characterised as fertility rites in the phrase **on the hills and
under every green tree** (see on 1 Kg. 14:23). Although **the high
places** (*bāmôt*) were initially local shrines at which worship of
Yahweh was legitimately practised, it appears that Canaanite fertility

rituals had infiltrated into these centres, especially in later monarchic times. High places in the north became associated with bull-cults (see on 1 Kg. 12:31–32; 13:32–33), and those in the southern kingdom saw the introduction of *'ašērîm* and *maṣṣēḇôṯ* (see on 1 Kg. 14:23); see further, Hoffmann, *Reform*, pp. 40–1. The implication behind the condemnation of these southern centres, which were situated **on the hills, and under every green tree**, is that sexual indulgence had become part of the fertility rites (de Vaux, *Ancient Israel*, pp. 284–6, and McKay, *op. cit.*, p. 90).

5. The account of Syro-Ephraimite activity against Ahaz, as it is presented here, opens with words which are almost identical with Isa. 7:1 and state that **Rezin the king of Syria and Pekah the son of Remaliah, king of Israel, came up to wage war.** The pressure exerted on Judah in the reign of Jotham (15:37) is now expressed more tangibly in an attack upon Jerusalem. Rasyan and Pekah, who had been Assyrian vassals since 738 BC, decided now to form an anti-Assyrian coalition, which had to be supported by Judah to achieve any success. When Ahaz refused to join, they decided to advance against Jerusalem; the additional information supplied by Isa. 7:6 shows that they intended to depose Ahaz and replace him with Tabe'el. In assessing the significance of the Syro-Ephraimite war, some caution is necessary, for it is now realised that in the past its place in international relationships was overestimated. According to more recent descriptions of it, the allies fought only a minor war, probably with only a part of their forces, and with the limited aim of deposing Ahaz rather than overrunning the whole of Judah and annihilating the Judaean army, which they obviously needed for their anti-Assyrian activities (Donner, *IJH*, p. 426; Herrmann, *History*, pp. 247ff.). The action of the allies was motivated by anti-Assyrian sentiments that had emerged in Syria and Israel, and is unlikely to have been occasioned by an expansionist policy in Damascus (as is argued by Oded, *CBQ* 34 [1972], pp. 153–65). **and they besieged Ahaz but could not conquer him**: Ahaz, because of his experience of Assyrian methods in Palestine, had decided not to involve Judah in the coalition; consequently the allies closed upon him. The literal meaning of MT here is that 'they were not able to fight', which according to *NEB* means that they 'could not bring him to battle', and according to *RSV* that they **could not conquer him**. Gray's emendation (p. 633), partially based on the Isaianic parallel and reading 'he could not fight for it', is unnecessary.

6. **At that time the king of Edom recovered Elath for Edom**: MT here reads 'At that time Rezin the king of Syria recovered Elath for Syria', but it is obvious from the pointing of the Massoretes that

they intended the latter half of the verse to refer to 'Edomites' coming to Elath. There are other instances of confusion between Edom and Aram (cf. 1 Kg. 9:26; 22:48ff.; 2 Kg. 14:7, 22), and it is understandable how the mistaken reading of Aram for Edom in the first half of the verse attracted to it the proper name 'Rezin'. Syria had never exercised control over Elath, and so it is obvious that this statement, which has to be read in parenthesis, refers to the recovery of Elath to Edom. The Edomites must have taken advantage of the Syro-Ephraimite pressure on Judah to regain control over the area which they had lost to Judah in the time of Azariah (2 Kg. 14:22). Glueck's excavations demonstrate that there was a change of occupation after the period of the seal of Jotham, and that jar-seals bearing the inscripion 'Belonging to Qausanal' refer to the Edomite god Qaus (*Rivers*, pp. 165–8).

7. **Ahaz sent messengers to Tiglath-pileser**: Ahaz's appeal for help is related to v. 5 rather than v. 6. The tense situation in Judah is vividly reflected in the account of Isaiah's encounter with Ahaz, who was probably at the time inspecting the city's fortifications (Isa. 7). Isaiah advocated a policy of non-participation in anti-Assyrian activities, and, although his advice was based on his religious stance, it was undoubtedly sound politically, for any alliance against Assyria would be instantly dissolved. Ahaz could not fully accept the prophet's challenge to exercise faith, but took action by submitting himself voluntarily to Assyria. He approached the Assyrian king by sending **messengers. I am your servant and your son**: The message sent to Tiglath-pileser cannot mean less than a voluntary acceptance of vassalage, and is probably to be dated after the Assyrian campaign in Philistia in 734 BC (Tadmor, *BA* 29 [1966], pp. 86–102). This is clearly denoted by the use of the term **servant**, which appears frequently in the Amarna letters (Montgomery, p. 348), and is also present in the use of the term **son**, which also belongs to the terminology of treaty making (cf. McCarthy, *CBQ* 27 [1965], pp. 144–7). **Come up and rescue me**: It cannot be ascertained whether Tiglath-pileser's subsequent action against Israel (733 BC) and Damascus (732 BC) was undertaken on his own initiative or came as a result of Ahaz's message. It is also uncertain if v. 7 reproduces faithfully the message sent by Ahaz and was totally dependent on state archives. A possible interpretation of the message sent by Ahaz is that he merely sent word to Tiglath-pileser that he was voluntarily submitting himself as a vassal; it was a declaration that he was not involved in anti-Assyrian activities and was a precautionary measure against Assyrian reprisals in Syria-Palestine. It was a short message faithfully reproduced in the phrase **I am your servant and your son**. But in summarizing the annals, the deuteronomistic historians

interpreted Ahab's message as a call for help against the Syro-
Ephraimite coalition by adding the words in v. 7*b*, **Come up . . .
attacking me.**

8. Ahaz also took the silver and the gold: cf. also 1 Kg. 14:18,
where Asa took silver and gold from the Temple and the treasury
to send to Syria. **and sent a present to the king of Assyria**: The
Heb. uses a word for **present** (*šōḥaḏ*) that is also used for 'a bribe'
(*NEB*). But in this case it was a 'tribute'. Tiglath-pileser recorded
that he took tribute from 'Yauhazi of Yaudea', but he makes no
distinction between Judah and its tribute and the twenty or so other
tribute-paying states that he lists in the same context (Luckenbill,
Records I, p. 801). For the Assyrians Ahaz's present was simply a
submission to vassalage, and not payment for Tiglath-pileser's help.
2 Chr. 28:20–21 may contain some truth in its suggestion that the
initiative came from Tiglath-pileser and that Judah was forced to
pay tribute (Williamson, *Chronicles*, pp. 347ff.).

9. the king of Assyria marched up against Damascus: Tiglath-
pileser's action against Israel in 733 BC is not recorded in this
account; but cf. 15:29. Damascus was not conquered until 732 BC,
after a two-year siege; Assyrian lists record the campaign against
Damascus for two successive years, 733 and 732 BC, which implies
that it was not taken without some effort. **carrying its people
captive to Kir**: Mention of **Kir** is also found in Am. 9:7; Isa. 22:5,
6, the former referring to it as the original home of the Aramaeans
and the latter mentioning it in the same context as Elam. Gray (p.
633) may be correct in suggesting that it is a common noun, 'the
city', referring to the Assyrian capital (Nineveh), but his attempt to
separate the Kir of Amos and make it a different place is
unnecessary. The Assyrian annals confirm that the land of Damascus
was depopulated (Luckenbill, *op. cit.*, pp. 777–9), but contain no
reference to Rezin's death. Because the Gk. omits **to Kir** from this
verse it can be suggested that it is a gloss from Amos to prove that
his prophecy was fulfilled.

10. This verse gives an account of Ahaz's visit to Damascus, and
the verses that follow refer to the consequent cultic changes in
Jerusalem (see Rendtorff, *Opfers*, pp. 46–50. **King Ahaz went to
Damascus to meet Tiglath-pileser**: As noted above, vv. 10–18
consistently refer to the Judaean king as **King Ahaz**, which probably
indicates the use of a different source from the one behind vv. 5–9.
Ahaz probably went to Damascus to pay homage to Tiglath-pileser
after his conquest of the city in 732 BC; his going was an affirmation
of his submission to Assyria. **he saw the altar that was at Damascus**: Although the text does not specify its origin, it has for a long
time been assumed that this was an Assyrian altar and that a change

of altar symbolized the replacement of Yahweh by Ashur in the Jerusalem cult (Östreicher, *Grundgesetz*, pp. 38, 55–6; cf. Olmstead, *History*, p. 452; Montgomery, p. 460). The incident is said to be one example of the Assyrians imposing the worship of their own gods on conquered peoples. In recent investigations, however, the weight of opinion is in favour of accepting that Ahaz's altar was Syro-Phoenician rather than Assyrian in origin (for a full discussion, see McKay, *op. cit.*, pp. 5–12; Cogan, *op. cit.*, pp. 73–7 and for a criticism of their interpretation see Spieckermann, *Sargonidenzeit*, pp. 318ff.). Among the reasons against Assyrian identification are: whereas this altar was used for burnt offerings (vv. 13, 15), the Assyrians did not have altars for offering burnt animal sacrifices; Galling's study of Near Eastern altars confirms that it was a Syrian model (*Der Altar*, pp. 43, 45, 54ff.); the statement in 2 Chr. 28:23 that Ahaz worshipped the gods of Aram may reflect the Chronicler's interpretation of a trustworthy tradition that the Jerusalem altar was a copy of Hadad's altar in Damascus (see Williamson, *Chronicles*, p. 349). Th circumstances surrounding the adoption of this new altar are not clear. One suggestion that may be dismissed as unlikely is that a Phoenician altar was introduced as part of an attempt to strengthen trading links with Phoenicia, which had become particularly urgent because of the tribute that was demanded by Tiglath-pileser (McKay, *op. cit.*, pp. 7ff.; Saggs, *Assyriology*, pp. 19–22). Separating the erection of a new altar from the Syro-Ephraimite war (cf. Ackroyd, *SEÅ* 33 [1968], pp. 18–54) tends to revive the suggestion that Ahaz introduced changes in the cultus for aesthetic reasons (Šanda II, p. 201; Skinner, pp. 369ff.), which must be rejected (Gray, p. 639; McKay, *op. cit.*, p. 7). The erection of this altar must be linked with Ahaz's subservient status *vi-à-vis* Tiglath-pileser, and it must have been introduced under obligation. A fresh assessment of Assyrian policy is presented by Spieckermann *op. cit*, pp. 227ff.). McKay's suggestion (*op. cit.*, p. 8) that worship on the old altar, which symbolised Yahweh's unique supremacy, had to be discontinued, and that the new altar reflected the nation's vassal status, is plausible. Because the treaty sealing the vassalage agreement between Tiglath-pileser and Ahaz was accompanied by the offering of sacrifice on a Syro-Phoenician altar in Damascus, this altar became the model for the Jerusalem Temple, where it served as a reminder of the people's new status as vassals of Assyria. **Uriah the priest**: The priest named here was one of Isaiah's 'reliable witnesses' when he wrote the name of his son on a tablet (Isa. 8:1). One argument adduced against interpreting this incident as introducing a foreign cult into the Jerusalem Temple is that the same priest served at the new altar. The interpretation offered above

allows for the worship of Yahweh at the new altar, which naturally
presupposes a continuation of the rites and priesthood that had been
associated with Yahweh. According to these verses, Ahaz by his
submission to Assyria was guilty of accepting the demotion of
Yahweh, which is not identical with the sin of apostasy for which
he is condemned in vv. 3ff. **a model of the altar, and its pattern,
exact in all its details**: The meaning is well expressed in *NEB*; 'he
sent a sketch and a detailed plan to Uriah the priest'.

11. The king had apparently been delayed in Damascus, and the
altar was made ready for his return. The Gk. omits the second half
of the verse, from **so Uriah . .** to **. . . from Damascus**, presumably
through homoioteleuton. The shorter text reads smoothly, but Luc.
agrees with MT.

12. Then the king drew near the altar, and went up on it: The
meaning of MT is made clear in *NEB*: 'approached it, and mounted
its steps'. The king presumably took charge of the sacrifices listed
in v. 13, which were intended as sacrifices to dedicate the new altar,
a rite that became complete when blood was sprinkled on the altar
to consecrate it. The king himself exercised his cultic privileges on
this occasion, exactly as Solomon had officiated at the dedication of
the Temple (cf. 1 Kg. 8:62ff.).

13. Exactly as 1 Kg. 8:62–64 specify the sacrifices offered by
Solomon, so this verse gives details of the sacrifices offered by Ahaz
to dedicate his new altar. They are the **burnt offering** (*'ōlāh*) or
holocaust, which was totally burnt on the altar, **the cereal offering**
(*minḥāh*), consisting of produce of the land, the **drink offering**
(*neseḵ*) or libation of wine and oil, and the **peace offerings** (*šelāmîm*)
or communion sacrifices, which were partly consumed on the altar
and partly eaten by the worshippers. When the king **threw the
blood of his peace offerings upon the altar**, it was duly consecrated
as a place of communion between God and his people. Nowhere is
it suggested in this verse that these sacrifices were directed towards
an alien god, such as Ashur. If this had been the case, the deuteronomistic compiler would not have missed the opportunity to castigate
Ahaz.

**14. And the bronze altar which was before the LORD he
removed**: According to MT's account, Ahaz removed **the bronze
altar** (1 Kg. 8:64) from its former position in the Temple and
replaced it with **his altar**, which then in v. 15 becomes 'the great
altar'. Luc., however, omits **altar** from this phrase and presumably
reads **bronze** with the altar at the end of v. 13 to give 'and sprinkled
upon the altar of bronze that was before the Lord'; thus the reference to removing a bronze altar is deleted. The ritual envisaged is
the sprinkling of blood first on the original altar and then to follow

on the new altar, thus ensuring the transfer of potency from one to the other. Ahaz did not remove the bronze altar, but built another permanent one for the sacrifices (Skinner, pp. 370ff.). However, there is no reason for abandoning MT here; despite the absence of the bronze altar from the list of bronze work in 1 Kg. 7:15–46, it is reasonable to accept the tradition that a bronze altar had been erected in Solomon's Temple (cf. 2 Chr. 4:1). Ahaz, however, removed the old bronze altar from its position between the new altar and the Temple and placed it on the north side of the new altar (McKay, op. cit., pp. 79ff.). This new altar may have been constructed of stone (Šanda II, p. 202).

15. The regulations proposed to the priest by the king provide for all ordinary sacrifices to be offered on the new altar, and the old one was reserved for the private use of the king himself. These directions undoubtedly reflect the cultic practices of pre-exilic times and are probably dependent on some written instructions. Four main categories are listed: **the morning burnt offering and the evening cereal offering** were the two basic sacrifices, the former ('ōlāh) being the morning blood sacrifice and the latter (minḥāh) the produce offering for the evening (cf. also Exod. 29:38–42); **the king's burnt offering and his cereal offering**, according to Ezek. 46, were offered on sabbaths and the new moon, whilst the communal sacrifices were offered on other days; **the burnt offering of all the people of the land, and their drink offering** were the daily offerings of the whole community; the blood of **the burnt offering** and of **the sacrifice** was to be sprinkled over the altar. The old altar was now reserved for the king's private use, which is defined as **for me to inquire by**. The meaning of this phrase is by no means clear, and several explanations have been offered. The least convincing solution is to render the Pi'el verb (lebaqqēr) as 'to ponder over' (i.e. to think what to do with it); cf. Benzinger, p. 171; Kittel, p. 271. The attempt to connect the verb with the word 'morning' (Heb. bōqēr), translating as 'to officiate at dawn' (Morgenstern, Fire, p. 36) or 'to offer morning sacrifice' (NEB), also seems unnecessary. Most commentators see in the word lebaqqēr (meaning 'to examine', Lev. 13:36; 'to discriminate', Lev. 27:33) a reference to taking omens, more specifically of opening the sacrificial victim and examining its entrails in search of omens. This practice does not necessarily point to Assyrian influence upon Ahaz, for there is evidence that it was not unknown in Palestine at an earlier period. McKay (op. cit., p. 81) refers to examples from Gezer, Hazor and Ras Shamra. Although the term was in use for a specific means of obtaining an omen, it is possible that here it was used in a more general sense of preparing a cultic act to obtain an oracle (McKay, op. cit., p. 8). This latter

suggestion confirms the translation **for me to inquire by**; cf. *NIV*, 'for seeking guidance'.

17. The reason for removing the objects listed here from the Temple is much more practical than Olmstead's complicated explanation (*History*, p. 452) that Yahweh was now being replaced by Ashur, and that the oxen no longer stood for the might of Yahweh. Ahaz stripped the Temple of some of its furnishings because he needed the valuable metals to pay his tribute-money to Tiglath-pileser. There is much in favour of Šanda's suggestion (II, pp. 203ff.) that the difficult 'because of the king of Assyria' should be transferred from v. 18 to the end of v. 17, thus implying that the objects were dismantled because of the pressure to find tribute money. **the frames of the stands**: cf. 1 Kg. 7:27f., where it is suggested that these were horizontal panels on the wheeled stands supporting the lavers in the Temple. Ahaz also removed **the sea** and reset it **upon a pediment of stone** (or 'on a stone base', *NEB*), so that he could use the metal from the bronze oxen that were under it; see on 1 Kg. 7:23ff.

18. This verse deals with the minor building reconstructions effected in the Temple by Ahaz. **the covered way for the sabbath**: This has been variously rendered by the Vsns. and commentators. The rendering of the Gk. 'the dais of his throne' (suggesting *haššebet* for *haššabbāt*) does not enhance the meaning, and MT is best retained. Ezek. 46:1ff. refers to a Temple gate which was only opened on the sabbaths and the new moon to allow the king into the Temple. Gray (pp. 635ff.) thinks that this reference in Ezek. reflects the practice of pre-Exilic times and renders as 'the barrier of the sabbath'. This rendering, or that of *RSV*, is preferable to *NEB*'s more cumbersome translation 'the structure they had erected for use on the sabbath'. **the outer entrance for the king**: The Heb. has *haḥîṣônāh*, 'to the outside', 'outwards', which may be rendered as an adjective 'the outer' (as in *RSV*). **he removed from the house of the LORD**: *RSV* has accepted slight emendations here in reading **he removed** (*hēsîr*) for 'he turned about' (*hēsēb*), and **from the house** (*mibbēt*) for 'the house' (*bēt*); cf. *BHK*. MT is preferable here; cf. *NEB*, 'in the house of the LORD he turned round'. **because of the king of Assyria**: This phrase causes difficulty. It has been rendered more literally, 'from before the face of the king of Assyria', implying that a statue of the Assyrian king had been erected in the Jerusalem Temple (Olmstead, *op. cit.*, p. 452). But this interpretation suffers from lack of evidence that the Assyrian kings erected statues or stelae in sanctuaries other than Assyrian ones. A closer link with v. 17 is possible if the emendation above to *hēsîr*, 'he removed', is accepted; the suggestion is that all alterations were made because of Israel's subservience to Assyria. It may be that the changes described in v. 18 also released some gold ornamentation for this use; another possibility is that v. 17 refers to removals from the Temple to pay the tribute, but that v. 18 lists alterations made in the connection between the Temple and the palace in order to suggest some demotion of the Judaean king, or at least to avoid emphasizing his status and dignity. As noted above, preference is given to Šanda's proposal to read **because of the king of Assyria** with v. 17, which deals with the tribute money. Verse 18 lists other minor works that may have been undertaken at the same time, but were not in any way connected with Ahaz's position *vis-à-vis* Assyria.

19–20. The standard concluding formula appears here without modification.

(g) Hoshea of Israel and the fall of the Northern Kingdom

17:1–41

On first appearance this account of the fall of the Northern Kingdom in the time of Hoshea is in three main sections: the reign of Hoshea and the fall of Samaria (vv. 1–6), a commentary on the events in the form of a review of Israel's history, which gives adequate reasons for the fall (vv. 7–23) and an account of the reoccupation of Samaria by foreigners (vv. 24–31). On closer analysis, however, the narrative is far more complex than the impression gained from such a simple division, and the analyses of the narrative's growth and compilation, which have been proposed by commentators, suggest a long and tortuous process.

The first section (vv. 1–6), after the normal deuteronomistic formula to introduce the king (vv. 1f.), gives a historical account of the main events surrounding the capitulation of Hoshea to Shalmaneser and the fall of the Northern Kingdom (vv. 3–6). However, these verses present several difficulties: (i) they imply that the Assyrian king undertook two or three campaigns against Israel, which is not confirmed by Assyrian sources; (ii) they present Samaria as holding out against Assyria for three years after the king had been captured by the Assyrians. For a long time, therefore, it has been held that these verses contain two different accounts of the same event (cf. Winckler, *Untersuchungen*, pp. 15ff.; Albright, *BASOR* 174 [1964], pp. 66–7). These strands can be traced back to different sources: vv. 3ff. are derived from the chronicles of Israel, and vv. 5ff. (which are parallel to 18:9–11 from Judaean annals) from the chronicles of Judah (so Noth, *ÜSt*, p. 78, and accepted by Gray, p. 638). Material derived from the chronicles or annals of the two kingdoms, although reflecting a difference of interest and emphasis, forms naturally the basis of the whole chapter and is the oldest of its various parts.

The second section (vv. 7-23) is a long deuteronomistic comment in which the downfall of Samaria is presented as divine retribution for Israel's long record of apostasy and her obstinate disregard of all the warnings that she had been given. Here again a process of annotation and expansion can be traced. Verses 21-23 are to be separated from vv. 7-20: *kî* at the beginning of v. 21 denotes a new beginning; the destruction of Israel is reported twice (in v. 20 and in v. 23); the prophets assume different roles in vv. 13 and 23*a*, in the former as preachers of the law and in the latter as announcing disaster (Noth, *op. cit.*, p. 85; Dietrich, *Prophetie*, p. 41). Literary analyses of this section have produced contradictory assessments of vv. 21-23. On the one hand they have been listed as constituting the compiler's own contribution to the structure of the chapter (Šanda II, p. 235) and therefore as belonging to the same stratum of tradition as the deuteronomistic formula in vv. 1f. (Gray, p. 638, where v. 18 is also taken with vv. 21-23). On the other hand, Noth (*op. cit.*, p. 85) regards vv. 21-23, like vv. 34*b*-41 as later glosses. Further complication is introduced by the inclusion of references to Judah in vv. 13 and 19, which have again been variously resolved. One solution is to divide the section into two, vv. 7-17 originating from one deuteronomistic redactor, and vv. 19, 20 from a later deuteronomistic redactor (Burney, pp. 330ff.). Another proposes to take vv. 7-18 as a unit, and vv. 19-20 as later glosses (Šanda, *ibid.*). Yet another considers vv. 7-17, 19-20 as a unit, the only extraction being v. 18, which belongs to an earlier stratum (Gray, pp. 638ff.). There can be no denying that vv. 7-23 throughout are deuteronomistic in language and thought (Burney, *ibid.*; cf. Hoffmann, *Reform*, pp. 127-39); disagreement becomes apparent in the attempt to trace stages in the deuteronomistic expansion of the material. Recent analyses of deuteronomistic revisions, each reflecting different emphases and interests on the part of the redactors, help our understanding of this passage. Dietrich's proposal (*op. cit.*, p. 42) to take vv. 7-11, 20 as the basic deuteronomistic material (DtrG), and to attribute vv. 12-19 to the nomistic redactor (DtrN) and vv. 21-23 to the prophetic redactor (DtrP), is accepted here as a working basis.

The third section (vv. 24-41) again contains a fusion of different elements, varying from a historical statement of the Assyrian settlement of Samaria (vv. 24-28) to a thoroughly deuteronomistic exposure of the apostasy of the colonists in that they did not fear the God of Israel (vv. 34-40). The composite nature of the material is well illustrated by the contradiction between the description of the foreign settlers fearing Yahweh, whilst still worshipping their own gods (vv. 32, 33, 41), and the categorical assertion elsewhere that they did not fear Yahweh (v. 34). Disagreement is evident among commentators both in their demarcation of the units within this section and in their views of the provenance. Burney pp. 333ff.), working on a division proposed earlier by Stade (ZAW 6 [1886], pp. 167ff.), ascribes vv. 24–34a, 41 to an older narrative accepted by the deuteronomistic compiler, with vv. 24–28, 41 forming the original kernel and vv. 29–34a being a later extension; a later addition, probably referring to the Samaritans of post-Exilic times, is found in vv. 34b–40. Sanda's formula (ibid.) is approximately the same; he was of the opinion that vv. 24–28 came from an older Israelite source, that vv. 29–33 were from a post-exilic redactor and that vv. 34–40 are a later gloss. Gray (p. 640) finds that the unit in vv. 24–28 originated from a historical source, which he connects with a priestly historian from Bethel; vv. 29–34a come from the same author, rather than a deuteronomistic redactor. Gray concedes that it was the deuteronomistic redactor who selected material from the original source; thus, whilst v. 41 is earlier than vv. 29–34a, vv. 34b–40 are a later redactional comment modifying v. 33. These proposed analyses have one feature in common: whilst recognizing that some of these sections contain older material which has been selected and annotated by the deuteronomistic redactor, they have not been very successful in defining the relationship between the redactor and his sources. In this, Noth's analysis (ibid.) is more satisfactory, and is thus accepted as a working basis. Basic historical material derived from the annals of Israel and found in vv. 24, 29–31 was annotated by the deuteronomistic compiler, who combined with it a local tradition from Bethel (vv. 25–28) and his own comment (vv. 32–34a). A later redactor added vv. 34b–40, and it may well be that he too was responsible for v. 41, which he composed on the basis of vv. 33, 34a in an attempt to give the passage a unity and to conceal the material which he added in vv. 34b–40. A similar, but not identical, analysis is accepted by Cogan (JBL 97 [1978], pp. 40–4), noting that the repetition of 'until this day' from v. 23 in v. 34 characteristically denotes vv. 24–34a as an interruption, and suggesting that vv. 34b–40, 41 with its attention to Israelites in exile belongs to the age of Josiah.

Although the literary analysis, especially in the case of vv. 3–6, resolves some of the historical problems raised by this chapter, one connected problem remains to be discussed. According to vv. 3–6 (cf. 18:9ff.), Shalmaneser was the Assyrian king responsible for the capture of Hoshea and taking Samaria; but in Assyrian inscriptions

Sargon claims that he, in his first year, conquered Samaria (*ANET*, pp. 284ff.). Because of doubts about the historical reliability of Assyrian display inscriptions, and indeed of Sargon's Khorsabad Annals (Olmstead, *AJSL* 21 [1906], pp. 179–82), and also because of the possibility that details of Samaria's downfall in 722/1 and Sargon's later campaigns in 720 and 716 BC have been telescoped (Tadmor, *JCS* [1958], pp. 33–9), the biblical ascription of the conquest to Shalmaneser can be taken as reliable. The so-called 'Babylonian Chronicle' also attributes the conquest to Shalmaneser V (Galling, *Textbuch*, p. 60). However, Sargon's details about the treatment of Samaria and its inhabitants are significant (Herrmann, *History*, pp. 250ff.), for he gives information about the people deported and refers to people from other countries that he had settled there (cf. *ANET*, p. 284; Gadd, *Iraq* 16 [1954], pp. 173ff.). The possibility that the naming of Hamath (conquered in 720 BC) in v. 24 indicates progressive resettlement, provides an important clue; whereas Shalmaneser conquered Samaria at the very end of his reign, the further implications of the conquest were worked out by Sargon in the first years of his reign. The fact that he was engaged in the aftermath and had to implement the deportation and resettlement programme gave him sufficient basis for telescoping the events and taking credit for the conquest of the city.

1. **In the twelfth year of Ahaz**: The synchronism again causes difficulty, for Hoshea's accession in Ahaz's twelfth year assumes that the reign of Pekahiah lasted for ten years (cf. Luc. in 16:23). It is more likely, however, that **twelve** here is a mistake for 'two', and that Hoshea came to the throne in 'the second year of Ahaz'. It may be that he was appointed vassal-king of Samaria in 732 BC, but that owing to anti-Assyrian feelings in Samaria he had some difficulty in establishing himself on the throne and was not recognized until *c*. 730 BC. Possibly Hoshea paid tribute to Tiglath-pileser III in 731 BC, when he was at the time besieging Barrabanu in Southern Babylon (see Borger and Tadmor, *ZAW* 94 [1982], pp. 244–9). **he reigned nine years**: If vv. 4, 5 are accepted as a reliable historical account, Hoshea was deposed three years before the fall of Samaria in 722/1 BC. But if vv. 4 and 5 are separated (as suggested above) and the arrest of Hoshea is dated at the end of the three-year siege, the statement that he reigned nine years needs some justification. Either the length of his reign has to be extended to eleven or twelve years (Šanda II, p. 212) or else it can be accepted that he was unable to take the throne until 730 BC. In the Table on p. 28, Hoshea's reign is given as 730–722 BC.

2. The deuteronomistic verdict that **he did what was evil** is exceptionally qualified in the sentence **yet not as the kings of Israel**

who were before him. No reason is given. But, it seems likely that, because of the political situation during his comparatively short and troublesome reign, he was unable to give attention to religious matters, and therefore escaped the more severe condemnation of the deuteronomistic editors.

3–4. Although the first account of Assyrian action against Samaria and its king reveals the intrigue of Hoshea, it refrains from referring specifically to the collapse of Samaria. The punishment falls upon Hoshea himself; he was bound and imprisoned, but reference to the fall of Samaria and the deportation of its inhabitants is discreetly avoided. This can be taken as a clear indication that the source behind these verses was the chronicles of Israel; the unpalatable facts of the siege and deportation are derived from the annals of Judah (vv. 5ff.; 18:9–11).

3. Shalmaneser king of Assyria: In 727 BC Tiglath-pileser III was succeeded by Shalmaneser V (Assyr. *Sulman asāridu*). Very few records of his reign are available, but it may be assumed that a change of ruler led to unrest and possibly to an attempt to form a coalition among western satellites. The affirmation that Shalmaneser came **against him** can be taken as a reference to Shalmaneser's visit to the west in 725 BC to reaffirm his control over these states; cf. Josephus's reference to his expedition at this time against Phoenician cities (*Ant.* IX.14.2; cf. Montgomery, p. 465; Gray, pp. 642ff., but not Donner, *IJH*, p. 432). The expedition was successful, and **Hoshea became his vassal and paid him tribute**.

4. Although Shalmaneser regained his hold over the west in 725 BC, a more determined effort to overthrow Assyrian domination, with Egypt leading a coalition of the western vassals, was staged in the following year. This was the **treachery** that the Assyrian king found in Hoshea. **he had sent messengers to So, king of Egypt**: Uncertainty over the identification of **So** is caused by the absence of the name from the known lists of Egyptian rulers and the many changes in the accepted identification over the years. Earlier proposals to read **Egypt** (*miṣrayim*) as the land of Musri, a north Arabian kingdom, and to identify its king possibly with the Silhu named in a report of one of Sargon's campaigns (Šanda II, pp. 214ff.; Weidner, *AfO* [1941], pp. 43ff.), have been abandoned because Egypt would be a more likely ally against Assyria than an Arabian ruler. The identification of **So** (= Sewe) with 'Sib'e, general of Egypt' mentioned in the annals of Sargon (*ANET*, p. 185) found much favour until it was shown to be philologically inadmissible (Borger, *JNES* 19 [1960], pp. 49–53). In more recent studies it has been accepted that **So** refers to Sais (*s'w*), the name of a place in the Nile Delta. The Egyptian ruler in the Delta at this time was

Tefnakhte (726–716 BC) and it is thought that the name of his capital (not his 'Horus name' as suggested by Sayed, *VT* 20 [1970], pp. 116–18) was mistakenly taken to be the king's name (see Goedicke, *BASOR* 171 [1963], pp. 64–5). This mistaken reading probably led to the omission of 'to' (*'el*) from the Heb., and it must be restored to give the reading 'to Sais, to the king of Egypt' (cf. *NEB*; Albright, *BASOR* 171 [1963], p. 66). Although Egypt itself was unsettled at this time because of the rise of the 25th Egyptian dynasty, which did not gain domination until 712 BC, it would obviously have been willing to take what action was possible against Assyria. The punishment executed on Hoshea for withholding his tribute was that the Assyrian king **shut him up, and bound him in prison**. Although *RSV* translates the verb *'āsar* as **shut up**, it obviously means that 'he arrested him' (*NEB*); cf. also Jer. 33:1; 36:5. When vv. 4 and 5 are read together, it is suggested that the city held out against Assyria for three years after Hoshea's arrest. Gray (pp. 639ff.; cf. Donner, *IJH*, p. 433) finds no insuperable difficulty in the king's captivity, and proposes that Hoshea had gone out of the city to meet Shalmaneser hoping that the Assyrian king would accept his explanation why tribute had been withheld, but that he was arrested. The inhabitants of Samaria were determined to defend their city without Hoshea. However, it is more reasonable, after separating vv. 3ff. from vv. 5ff., to assume that the arrest of Hoshea did not occur at the beginning of the siege of Samaria. The Israelite annals behind vv. 3ff., giving a restrained report of the conquest of Samaria, only mention the capture of its king.

5. Whereas **the king of Assyria** is not named in this version of the Judaean annals, he is specifically called Shalmaneser in 18:9. **and for three years he besieged it**: The city that had been so adequately fortified by Ahab and Omri held out for three years against the Assyrian onslaught. Naturally, this does not mean that Shalmaneser's army was kept there permanently (Herrmann, *History*, p. 250), but that it took him from 724 until 722 BC to conquer the city.

6. the king of Assyria captured Samaria: Like the previous verse, the Assyrian king is not named; but 18:9–11 attribute the final overthrow of the city to Shalmaneser. On the basis of Sargon's claims (*ANET*, p. 284), some have assumed that Shalmaneser died shortly before the collapse of the city and that Sargon, in his first year, was responsible for the final stages to its conquest (Skinner, p. 372; Montgomery, p. 466). But, in view of the preference given now to the claim of the Babylonian Chronicles that Shalmaneser broke the resistance of Samaria (see above), and the possibility that Sargon telescoped the capture of the city into later events for which he was responsible, it can be accepted that Shalmaneser took

Samaria shortly before he died (Herrmann, *History*, p. 250; Donner, *IJH*, p. 433). **he carried the Israelites away to Assyria**: It is possible that the people's deportation and the resettlement of Samaria were the stages for which Sargon became responsible after Shalmaneser's death. Sargon's own claim (*ANET*, p. 284; *DOTT*, p. 59) is that he carried away 27,290 inhabitants from Samaria. As noted by Montgomery (pp. 466ff.), the figure given by Sargon is modest in comparison with the statement in v. 18 that all but the tribe of Judah had been removed. The Judaean annals specify the areas in Assyria to which the deportees were transported. **Halah** is usually identified with Chalchitis on the west bank of the Tigris, which is mentioned by Ptolemy (5.18.4). Chalchitis was not far from **Gozan**, which is the Akkad. Guzana and which corresponds to Ptolemy's Gausanitis; the area is now identified with Tell Halaf (so von Oppenheim, *Tell Halaf* I, pp. 1–21). **Habor** was the district of Habūr, a great tributary of the river Euphrates. For **the cities of the Medes** Luc. suggests 'the mountains of the Medes', a mountain chain to the east of the Tigris; accepting this different reading, Gray (p. 644) considers that Israelites may have been used by Sargon as garrison troops in this area which he had recently conquered, exactly as they were used in Elephantiné by the Egyptians and in Libya by Ptolemy. The change of text is unnecessary, and 'the cities of Media' can be retained (cf. *NEB*).

7–11. These verses, giving a review of Israel's apostasy and its long record of sin against God, form the first unit in the longer section extending from v. 7 to v. 23. As noted above, Dietrich regards this smaller unit, together with v. 20 as the basic material originating from the deuteronomistic historian (DtrG). The tone of the passage is distinctly deuteronomistic, and Burney (p. 330) calls particular attention to 'other gods' (v. 7), 'drove out' (v. 8), 'on every high hill and under every green tree' (v. 10), 'provoking the LORD to anger' (v. 11). The opening phrase, 'and this was so, because . . .' summarizes the basic deuteronomistic theology of this passage; the downfall of Samaria and the deportation of its people was an act of divine retribution for Israel's unfaithfulness.

7. And this was so: cf. *NEB*, 'all this happened to the Israelites'. The Heb., although brief, links the deuteronomistic comment in vv. 7–23 decisively to the historical section in vv. 3–6. Luc., 'and Yahweh was angry with Israel, because . . .' (which is accepted by Burney, p. 331, followed by Gray, p. 645), makes the link more indirect and loses some of its force. **who had brought them up . . . of Egypt**: As noted by Gray (p. 646), the deuteronomistic commentator deliberately introduces Israel's sin in the context of *Heilsgeschichte*, referring here to the deliverance from Egypt (cf.

Exod. 20:2) and in v. 8 to the possession of the land (cf. also Jos. 24).

8. and in the customs which the kings of Israel had introduced: The sentence is ungrammatical in Heb., and *RSV* has linked it more smoothly to what precedes by repeating **and in the customs** from the previous phrase. Syr. omits this sentence, and that is acceptable (cf. *NEB*) on the grounds that it is probably an early gloss introduced to condemn the monarchy of the northern kingdom.

9. And the people of Israel did secretly: *EVV*, following the Gk., Rashi and Kimchi, derived the verb which is found only here in the *OT*, from the root *ḥāpā'*, 'to cover, conceal' (cf. *BDB*). But Driver (*People and the Book*, p. 89), following an earlier suggestion, takes the root to be *ḥāpā'* = Akkad. *hapu*, 'to utter'. Hence *NEB* has 'and uttered blasphemies against'. The Israelites built for themselves high places in all the towns, **from watch-tower to fortified city**; cf. 18:8, for this phrase denoting any kind of inhabited structure that could conceivably be called a town.

10. For **pillars and Asherim** see on 1 Kg. 14:23, and for **on every high hill and under every green tree**, see on 16:4; cf. also Jer. 2:20; 3:6, 13; 17:2.

11. there they burned incense on all the high places: **there** probably refers back to 'high places' in v. 9*b*, and so the introduction of **on all the high places** is tautologous; it is best to take this latter phrase as a gloss (cf. Šanda II, p. 221).

12–19. These verses are attributed by Dietrich to the nomistic redactor (DtrN). The character and origin of the section is clearly denoted by the nomistic content and terminology of v. 13. The theme is repeated in vv. 15, 16, 19.

12. Although this verse does not use the nomistic terminology found in v. 13, it evidently belongs to the same section because of its reference to the divine prohibition, **You shall not do this**, with regard to **idols** (cf. Exod. 20:4).

13. the LORD warned Israel and Judah: The two kingdoms, **Israel and Judah**, are coupled in this DtrN section; cf. vv. 18, 19. Although this has been construed as a proof of an exilic date (Gray, p. 647), or at least as indicating that a gloss was added after the fall of Jerusalem (Montgomery, p. 469), it has to be noted that these verses do not necessarily presuppose the fall of the southern kingdom. On the contrary, a distinction between the two kingdoms is drawn in v. 18. If v. 20 is separated from vv. 12–19 and is read with the basic material of vv. 7–11, it clearly refers to Israel. All that is said in v. 13 is that both kingdoms had been warned by the prophets. **Turn from your evil ways**: The nomistic redactor here emphasizes the kerygma that is basic to the deuteronomistic historical work (see above, pp. 77ff). **the law . . . which I sent to you by my servants the prophets**: The deuteronomistic conception of the prophetic office is made clear in this verse; they were regarded as preachers of the law and bearers of God's warning (**the LORD warned Israel**), his call for repentance (**Turn from . . .**) and his demand for obedience (**keep my . . .**); see further, von Rad, *Studies*, p. 83; Janssen, *Juda in der Exilszeit*, p. 74).

14. This verse continues the line of thought introduced in v. 13; despite all that God had mediated to his people through the prophets, they did **not listen**, but, like their fathers before them, were a **stubborn** (literally 'hardened their necks'; cf. Dt. 10:16; Jer. 7:26) and faithless people (who **did not believe**). The verb *he'ᵉmîn*, translated **believe**, has the meaning 'to rely on, trust in'; cf. *NEB* 'refused to put their trust in the LORD'; *NIV*, 'did not trust the LORD' (see also Isa. 7:9).

15. Whereas the former verse describes Israel's apostasy as lack of response to Yahweh, this verse concentrates on its infidelity to his covenant. They have **despised his statutes**, have ignored **the covenant** which he made and **the warnings** that he gave. Not unexpectedly **the covenant** in this nomistic addition has the meaning of law (cf. Dietrich, *op. cit.*, p. 43), and is associated with **the statutes**, denoting the stipulations or conditions that were laid down in the covenant, and **the warnings**, which were the solemn curses spoken on the occasion of sealing the covenant (cf. Dt. 27; see Gray, p. 647). **They went after false idols, and became false**: *RSV*, like the rendering of the earlier *EVV*, 'they went after vanity, and became vain', attempts to convey the use of a verb and its related noun in the Heb.; cf. *NEB* 'they followed worthless idols, and became worthless themselves'. The word *hebel*, translated 'vanity' elsewhere, means 'breath, air', and is often used to denote delusion or unreality (here and Ps. 94:11) and more specifically idols and foreign gods (Dt. 32:21; 1 Kg. 16:13, 26; Jer. 2:5; 8:19; 10:8; 14:22; 51:18). The word-play of this verse may have been borrowed from Jer. 2:5; cf. 51:18 (so Šanda, *ibid,*; Montgomery, *ibid.*).

16. Israel's infidelity in that **they made for themselves molten images** is made more specific by the addition of the phrase **two calves**, which may be an insertion from 1 Kg. 12. Because v. 10 only mentions the erection of Asherim, it has been suggested that the remainder of this verse, with its reference to **all the host of heaven** and **Baal**, is also an addition based on 21:3 (so Šanda, *ibid.*; Montgomery, *ibid.*). But it is quite probable that under Assyrian influence an astral cult had become known in Israel, as also it had been introduced in Judah during the reign of Manasseh (21:5; cf.

23:4, 5, 12). Am. 5:26 mentions the Mesopotamian astral deities,
Sakkuth and Kaiwan.

17. And they burned their sons and daughters: For this practice
and its emergence during the later monarchy, see on 16:3. **and used
divination and sorcery**: The different attempts to translate this
phrase, such as 'augury and divination' (*NEB*), 'divination and
prognostication' (Gray, p. 646), 'divination and enchantment'
(Montgomery, *ibid*.), demonstrate the difficulty of translating the
two Heb. terms and of distinguishing between them. The first word
(Heb. *qāsam*) is usually connected with an Arab. root meaning 'to
cut asunder, divide' (Gray, p. 648; *K-B*), and may denote hepato-
scopy, divination by gazing at entrails or a section of the liver. By
this method some guidance was expected with regard to the future.
Gray rejects Montgomery's suggestion on the basis of Ezek. 21:21
that the word refers primarily to divination by arrows; it is a wider
term that contains other forms of divination as well. The second
word, *niḥēš*, is used in Gen. 44:5 of hydromancy and in 1 Kg. 20:33
for listening for a portentous word. Montgomery suggests charm
practice, connecting it with the root *lāḥaš* which may mean 'charm'.
This association can be accepted; but it is not necessary to react
as negatively to a proposed connection with 'serpent', suggesting
'serpent-charmers', as is done by Gray, who favours a connection
with the word for 'copper', on the basis of the association of metal-
lurgy with the occult.

18. Gray (p. 649) separates this verse from the deuteronomistic
homily in vv. 7–17, 19–20 on the grounds that it only refers to the
fall of the northern kingdom, whereas the other verses refer to
Judah as well. But nowhere in vv. 7–17 or v. 19 is the fall of Judah
presupposed. Verse 18, stating that God was angry with Israel and
inflicted punishment upon it, forms a fitting conclusion in that it
recalls v. 7, where reference is made to the deportation of the people
because they had sinned. Dietrich's proposal (*op. cit.*, pp. 41ff.) to
attribute this verse to the nomistic redactor is accepted.

19. The deuteronomistic reviser (DtrN) immediately qualifies his
statement in v. 18*b* that only Judah was left by adding here a
comment that Judah too was guilty of the sins of Israel. Gray
(*ibid*.) suggests that it may be independent of vv. 7–17, and is a
qualification of v. 18 (cf. Skinner, p. 378, who takes both v. 19 and
v. 20 as later comments on v. 18). The view taken here is that v.
19 is not a later addition, but a qualification of v. 18 made by the
reviser himself (cf. Dietrich, *ibid*.).

20. According to the construction of vv. 7–20 accepted above,
this verse forms part of the basic DtrG material with vv. 7–11. It
does not, in connection with vv. 18*b*, 19, presuppose the punish-

ment of Judah as well. Separated from the specific allusion to Judah in vv. 18b, 19, it simply affirms in general that the descendants of the Israel that came out of Egypt (v. 7) were punished.

21–23. As noted above (p. 543), there are sufficient reasons for separating vv. 21–23 from vv. 7–20, and also for accepting Dietrich's suggestion (*ibid.*) that these verses are from the hand of his proposed DtrP redactor. The two main themes of this revision are: (a) that the essence of Israel's sin was that it followed the sin of Jeroboam the son of Nebat; (b) that punishment came in fulfilment of the words of the prophets, which therefore portrays the prophets as announcers of judgment and not as preachers of the law (v. 13).

21. The sin of Israel is now given a more political tone. Its roots are traced back to the division of the kingdom (**when Israel was torn . . . from the house of David**) and the choice of **Jeroboam the son of Nebat** as king over the northern tribes. Under his influence Israel turned **from following the LORD** and sinned.

22. This verse agrees essentially with the compiler's judgment of the Israelite kings. Like the basic deuteronomistic material (DtrG), this deuteronomistic redactor (DtrP) considers that Jeroboam had led Israel astray by deviating from the Jerusalem cult (Dietrich, *op. cit.*, pp. 105ff.).

23. until the LORD removed Israel out of his sight: cf. vv. 18, 20. **as he had spoken by all his servants the prophets**: The Exile is in this phrase interpreted as a fulfilment of announcements by the prophets. **Israel was exiled**: This refers back to vv. 3–6, but with the addition of **until this day**, which underlines the difference between the exile of Israel and the exile of Judah; whereas the Israelites went to exile never to return, there was a restoration of Judah and Jerusalem.

24. The third main section of this chapter (vv. 24–31) opens with an excerpt in v. 24 from an annalistic source ('chronicles of Israel', according to Noth, *ÜSt*, p. 78). It is concerned with the resettlement of Samaria, when people from other places were brought into the cities **instead of the people of Israel**. Only the upper classes had been deported from Samaria, for Sargon's figure of 27,290 could not have included the province's total population. The resettlement involved the bringing in of a foreign upper class, or 'governors' as they are called by Sargon (*ANET*, p. 284), and the evidence suggests that this happened in stages. Sargon had to suppress several revolts over the years—in 721 BC in Mesopotamia, with the movement of people to 'Hatti-land' (Syria and Palestine); cf. Luckenbill, *Records II*, p. 4; in 720 BC in Hamath, from where settlers were moved to Samaria, according to this verse; in 715 BC among the Arabs, with a movement of people again to Samaria (Luckenbill, *op. cit.*, pp.

17–18). **Cuthah** is usually identified with *Tell Ibrahim* to the northeast of Babylon. The name appears in Josephus, *Ant*, IX.14.3, and the form 'Kuthim' survived as a Jewish term of abuse for the Samaritans. **Avva**: Another form, Ivvah, appears in 18:34, where it is associated with other Syrian cities. But the identification is far from certain, since several places have been proposed, such as Imm, between Antioch and Aleppo, Ammia of the Amarna tablets, Tell Kefr 'Aya on the Orontes and 'Ama, an Elamite city conquered by Sargon in 710 BC. **Hamath** on the Orontes led a rebellion in the west in 720 BC, and was severely punished by Sargon, who killed its king, burnt its city and recruited 800 men for his chariotry (Luckenbill, *op. cit.*, p. 55). **Sepharvaim**: Another form, Sibraim, occurs in Ezek. 47:16. Its location is suggested by its listing among Syrian towns (cf. 18:34; 19:13), and it may be identified with Sabara'im of the Babylonian Chronicle (Rogers, *Parallels*, p. 210). This is preferable to an earlier identification with the Babylonian Sippar, despite the frequent reference to the rebellions of Sippar (Luckenbill, *op. cit.*, pp. 791, 796ff.).

25. As noted above (p. 544), vv. 25–28 contain a tradition associated with Bethel. Noth's analysis, with v. 24 being separated from vv. 25–28, is followed here. **the LORD sent lions among them**: A plague of **lions**, obviously encouraged by the many ruins left in the land by the Assyrians and possibly by unburied carcasses, is interpreted in this tradition as divine retribution for religious apostasy. Montgomery (p. 473) cites Ashurbanipal's reference to a plague of lions in the Babylonian marshes (cf. Luckenbill, *op. cit.*, p. 935) and the twelfth-century evidence of the Syrian Usāma ibn Munkidh.

26. the law of the god of the land: The word used here for **law** (Heb. *mišpāṭ*) means 'custom' or 'order'; cf. Gray (p. 650). 'the way of the god of the land'; *NEB*, 'the established usage of the god of the land'; *NIV*, 'what the god of the land requires'.

27. Send there one of the priests whom you carried thence: The Heb. here refers to **one of the priests**, whilst the verbs in the second half of the verse vary from plural (**let him go and dwell**) to singular (**let him teach**). Hardly any results could be expected after the commissioning of a single priest; but if a slight emendation is accepted to give 'certain of the priests', a more realistic attempt to instruct the people is envisaged. Because the words contained here are almost a verbatim reproduction of Sargon's instructions on an inscription commemorating the founding of Khorsabad, it has been suggested that it was part of his administrative policy to give deportees correct instruction in the cult of native gods (see Paul, *JBL* 88 [1969], pp. 73–4).

28. one of the priests: It is unnecessary to change the reading

here, since it is obvious that only one of the selected number sent
to Samaria came to work in Bethel. It may be assumed with Montgomery (*ibid.*) that these priests were encouraged and supported in
their work by Hezekiah of Jerusalem, and that his invitation to
people from the north to join his great Passover in Jerusalem (2
Chr. 30) is to be understood in this light.

29-34a. Instead of attributing these verses to one of the restored
priests or to a deuteronomistic redactor (Gray, p. 653), it is preferable
to divide the section into two units, vv. 29-31, containing annalistic
material derived from the chronicles of Israel, and vv. 32-34*a* being
the deuteronomistic redactor's own comment (cf. Noth, *USt.* pp.
78, 85).

29. every nation still made gods: Gray (*ibid.*) suggests that the
Heb. idiom here allows both for the recurrence of this practice and
for its existence in different localities. **put them in the shrines of
the high places**: *RSV* rightly reads the plural **shrines** with the
Vsns. for the singular of MT; cf. *NEB*, 'in niches at the shrines'.
For *RSV*'s 'put them', *NEB* has 'set them up'; cf. Gray, *ibid.*,
where it is suggested that the verb may denote setting up the idols
on pedestals or platforms.

30. Succoth-benoth: The second element of the name suggests a
connection with Zir-banitu ('seed creating'), which was a popular
twisted name for the goddess Sarpanitu, the consort of Marduk,
god of Babylon (Jastrow, *Religion I*, pp. 115ff.). The first element
has been identified with Sakkut, or Saturn, of the Babylonian
pantheon (cf. Am. 5:26). The suggestion to read the name of the
androgynous deity, Marduk-Banit, here has no conceivable basis in
the text. **Nergal**, the well-known city-god of Cuthah, was associated
with fire and destruction. He annihilated masses of men by means
of plague and war, and had the lion as his symbol (Jastrow, *op.
cit.*, pp. 157f.). **Ashima** is taken by Gray (p. 654) as a deliberate
misvocalisation of Asherah, the Canaanite mother-goddess. But,
there is evidence from Gk. tradition that Simi and Simios belonged
to a Syrian triad; the goddess Simi, daughter of Hadad, had a son
called Simios. The name also probably occurs in *'asmat* Samaria =
Ashmath Samaria in Am. 8:14 (Wolff, *Amos*, pp. 370ff.) and in
Ashem-bethel of the Elephantiné papyri (Montgomery. p. 475).
Macdonald (*Samaritans*, p. 95) thinks that the Assyrians called this
god 'Shemah' (= 'the Name'), which the Jews mistakenly took to
be a god called Ashima.

31. Nibhaz: No Babylonian or Syrian deity of this name is known,
and a proposed Elamite deity is not suitable. The name is, therefore,
considered to be a corruption or a deliberate Jewish distortion of
mizbeaḥ, 'altar'. Deification of an altar was not unknown; cf. the

possible deification of Bethel in the Elephantiné papyri (so Montgomery, p. 474; Gray, p. 654). **Tartak** is thought to be a shortened
form of Atargatis, the famous goddess Derceto. The deity, like her
name, was a composite figure, who combined the attributes of Attar
and his consort Anat. She was 'the Syrian goddess' of Lucian of
Samosata (Montgomery, *ibid.*). The people of Sepharvaim (see v. 2;)
practised child sacrifice to two deities, **Adram-melech** and **Anam-
melech**. Although **Adram-melech** appears also in 19:37 as the name
of one of Sennacherib's sons, and again as a Phoenician name
(Montgomery, p. 476), the occurrence of the name Adad-milki in
a Mesopotamian inscription favours a change of reading here to
Adad-melech, 'Adad is king' (cf. Albright, *Archaeology*, p. 163);
such sacrifices were offered to Adad. **Anam-melech** contains the
name Anu, the Sumerian god of heaven (cf. Albright, *AJSL* 42
[1925], pp. 73ff.); but, since this form of sacrifice is not mentioned
in connection with the god Anu, Gray suggests (*JNES* 8 [1949],
pp. 78-81) that *melek* refers to the Venus-god Attar, to whom
human sacrifice was made, and that there was a syncretism of the
Mesopotamian Anu and the West-Semitic Attar.

32. They also feared the LORD: The deuteronomistic comment
in vv. 32-34*a* describes the new settlers of Samaria attempting to
assimilate their own cults to that of the god of the land. This
was a natural development among people of mixed nationality and
culture, and a parallel may be usefully drawn with the Jews of
Elephantiné, who evidently practised a syncretistic form of religion
within which Yahweh, Anath and Bethel had been assimilated (cf.
Montgomery, p. 477). **appointed from among themselves all sorts
of peoples as priests**: The assimilation of deities was also accompanied by a deterioration of the priesthood, when any person could
be appointed for the office. Although this section is a condemnation
of the heathen Assyrians for introducing foreign cults, it was also
later interpreted as a condemnation of the Samaritan sect.

34b-40. A later redactor was responsible for this passage. It was
added to correct the impression of vv. 32-34*a* that the settlers of
Samaria worshipped Yahweh. The tone of the passage is distinctly
anti-Samaritan, especially in its affirmation that they did not follow
**the commandment which the LORD commanded the children of
Jacob, whom he named Israel**. Unlike vv. 21-23, the allegations
here are not specific, but contain a rambling, repetitive condemnation of the Samaritans, and by implication identify them with the
Assyrian settlers after the fall of Samaria. Three grounds are given
for this condemnation: **they do not fear the LORD** (vv. 34*b*, 36, 39);
they do not follow the ordinances, etc. (vv. 34*b*, 37); they were
unfaithful to **the covenant that I have made with you** (v. 38; cf.

v. 35). In language, concept and style the passage is thoroughly deuteronomistic.

41. This concluding verse affirms again what has been stated in vv. 32–34*a*, and is independent of vv. 34*b*–40. The view taken here is that the later glossator who introduced vv. 34*b*–40 also composed v. 41 in his attempt to conceal his insertion. For the same reason he concluded his insertion with a similar phrase as ends the former section (vv. 32–34*a*), namely, **they did according to their former manner.**

D. – THE KINGDOM OF JUDAH FROM THE FALL OF SAMARIA TO THE FALL OF JERUSALEM
2 Kg. 18:1–25:30

The fourth and last major section of the books of Kings covers the history of Judah alone and extends from the fall of the northern kingdom until 561 BC. It is a section in which three large narrative blocks stand out: narratives relating to the period of King Hezekiah but concentrating mainly on the prophet Isaiah (18:1–20:21); the account of Josiah's reform (chs. 22–23); and a report of the final collapse of Jerusalem in 587 BC (ch. 25). The composition and growth of these blocks will be discussed below.

I. HEZEKIAH AND HIS POLITICAL ACTIVITIES
2 Kg. 18:1–20:21

Although the account of Hezekiah's reign in chapters 18–20 contains a detailed coverage of his various activities, other additional material has to be taken into consideration before the course of events can be established and a balanced assessment of Hezekiah's true significance can be attained. 2 Chr. 29–32 supply more details of some aspects of Hezekiah's work, and an account that is parallel to 2 Kg. 18–20 appears in Isa. 36–39. Moreover, the description given in Assyrian royal inscriptions of Sennacherib's campaign against Judah during the reign of Hezekiah adds to our knowledge of the events and of the military situation in the west at the time. Further information comes from the unwritten evidence supplied by archaeological discoveries (Stern, *BA* 38 [1975], pp. 26–54).

Within the framework of the usual deuteronomistic formulae for introducing (18:1–8) and concluding (20:20ff.) Hezekiah's reign, the narrative introduces four elements: (i) From the annals of Judah there has come a report of the fall of Samaria (18:9–11, with an additional comment in v. 12). (ii) Another annalistic section in

18:13–16 describes Sennacherib's attack on Judah and the subsequent tribute imposed upon Hezekiah. (iii) A complex narrative in 18:17–19:37 describes in duplicate the visit of an emissary from Sennacherib to Jerusalem calling for the surrender of its king, and how the king, after receiving an oracle from Isaiah, refused to comply, and within a short time saw the retreat of Sennacherib from Jerusalem. (iv) A prophetic tradition, with Isaiah playing the leading role, reports the restoration of Hezekiah's health through the intervention of Isaiah (20:1–11) and again Isaiah's message to the king after the visit of envoys from Merodach-baladan of Babylon (20:12–19). Historical and literary problems connected with these various elements will be discussed under the individual sections below.

One general question that has to be raised is the relationship between some of the material in 2 Kg. 18–20 and parallel sections in Isa. 36–39. The repetition of 2 Kg. 18:17–20:19 almost word for word in Isa. 36–39, together with the close similarity of order between them, poses the question whether 2 Kg. has borrowed the material from a prophetic biographical source, or the Isaiah section has depended for this material on the historical source found in 2 Kg. Affirming Gray's opinion (p. 658) that one is dependent upon the other in preference to the idea that both had drawn on a common source, it seems reasonable to conclude that their setting in 2 Kg. is the original one and that they have been secondarily added to the book of Isaiah by a redactor (Clements, *Isaiah*, p. 277). Both sections begin with a common statement referring to the fourteenth year of Hezekiah (2 Kg. 18:13 = Isa. 35:1), and it is quite clear that this statement is most fittingly followed in 2 Kg. 18:13–16 by the annalistic record which is omitted from Isaiah; this is probably an indication that the original form in 2 Kg. has appeared in an abbreviated form in Isaiah. The actual positioning of this biographical material in the Book of Isaiah, namely, at the end of a compilation mainly composed of poetic oracles, is taken as a suggestion that it is a later addendum to the Isaianic tradition (cf. Šanda II, p. 315, followed by Gray, *ibid.*). According to Clements (*ibid.*) this material was deliberately inserted in the book of Isaiah to form a bridge between the 'Assyrian' background of chapters 1–35 and the 'Babylonian' background of chapters 40–66; thus a key to the understanding of the narratives is obtained from their setting in Kings rather than their setting in Isaiah. Such arguments are sufficiently convincing for us to accept that the narratives appear in their original setting in the book of Kings (against Norin, *VT* 32 [1982], pp. 337–8).

Another general aspect deserving brief attention is the historical background of the central events in these three chapters (see also Oded, *IJH*, pp. 435–41; Reviv, *WJHP*, pp. 193ff.). Judah, after escaping the catastrophe that had befallen Aram-Damascus in 732 BC and Samaria in 722 BC at the hands of the Assyrian kings, Tiglath-pileser III and Sargon II, had followed a policy of refraining from confrontation with Assyria. It had not intervened in the struggle that brought the downfall of the northern kingdom in 722 BC nor in the uprising against Sargon under the leadership of Hamath in 720 BC. Hezekiah, during the first years of his reign, probably followed a policy of strict non-intervention; there is no suggestion that he joined the Philistine uprising against Assyria which led to the subjugation of Ashdod in 712 BC (against Jenkins, *VT* 26 [1976], pp. 284–98); consequently no measures were taken against Judah. From 712 BC on, however, Sargon was engaged in subduing rebellions in Babylon and elsewhere, and when he was succeeded by Sennacherib in 705 BC the time appeared ripe for a Judaean revolt against Assyrian rule. Several factors made the circumstances full of promise from Hezekiah's standpoint and indicated that he was more likely to succeed than to fail (cf. Na'aman, *BASOR* 214 [1974], pp. 33–5; Oded, *IJH*, pp. 446ff.): (i) There was unrest in Assyria following Sargon's death in battle in 705 BC. (ii) Egypt, during the period of its recovery under the 25th Nubian dynasty, realised the danger of Assyrian power extending as far as its own border; it was willing to support any agitation against Assyria and to exert its influence in Palestine which stood between it and Assyria. (iii) The Assyrian army was kept occupied in the east by the appearance of Merodach-baladan in Babylon with Elamite and Arabian support. (iv) A rebellion against Assyria by Luli, king of Tyre and Sidon, had set a major obstacle on Assyria's path towards Judah, since Sidon controlled the main route between Syria and Palestine. (v) Hezekiah's position was strengthened through his alliance with Ṣidqa of Ashkelon and by his success in asserting his power over the Philistine rulers. When all these factors are taken into consideration, it is understandable that after 705 BC Hezekiah found an opportune moment for asserting his position against Assyria and embarking upon a policy that was distinctly anti-Assyrian.

(a) Introduction to Hezekiah's reign with annalistic reports

18:1–16

The deuteronomistic introduction to the reign of Hezekiah (vv. 1–8), in addition to the expected details, namely, synchronisation, age, length of reign, mother's name, and an assessment of his reign (vv. 1–3), contains some details about the king's activities (vv. 4–5,

7b–8). In the extension (vv. 6–7a) to the basic assessment (in v. 3), specific reference is made to obedience to God's commandments, which may suggest that the basic material (DtrG) has been revised by a nomistic redactor (DtrN; cf. Dietrich, *Prophetie*, p. 138). Among the details giving information about Hezekiah's activities there is a brief reference to his cultic reform in removing high places, breaking down the pillars and the Asherah and shattering in pieces the bronze serpent, Nehushtan (v. 4). A more detailed account of the reform in 2 Chr. 29–31 reports the sending of messengers 'throughout all Israel, from Beersheba to Dan' (29:5–11) as far as Zebulun, Asher and Issachar. Representatives from the northern province were present at the celebration of the Passover, a festival that lasted for a fortnight. Measures were taken to purify the Jerusalem cult (30:14), and this spread to Judah and Benjamin, and to Ephraim and Manasseh (31:1ff.); the people volunteered to raise contributions towards the Temple (30:21–27), and a thorough programme for organising the Temple, the priesthood and the Levites was undertaken (31:11–21). Admittedly, the Chronicler's account of the reform presents many difficulties (Williamson, *Chronicles*, pp. 350–88). The reliability of a report which is further removed from the actual events than the one presented in Kings is questioned; the Chronicler's dating of the reform in the first month of his reign, and the presentation of Hezekiah's revolt as a sequel of the reform is not convincing; the historicity of the inclusion of the northern kingdom in the reform has also been doubted (Rowley, *BJRL* 44 [1961–2], pp. 395–461; Moriarty, *CBQ* 27 [1965], pp. 399–406). Nevertheless, to appreciate the significance of the reform reported so briefly in v. 4 of this chapter some reference must be made to the Chronicler's version, for it is possible that the account in Kings has played down Hezekiah's reform in order to emphasize the significance of Josiah's later reform (cf. Rosenbaum, *HTR* 72 [1979], pp. 23–44). Taken together, the unmistakable implication of the two reports is that Hezekiah's reform did not simply arise from personal piety (vv. 3–6; cf. 2 Chr. 31:20ff.), but was politically motivated (cf. Todd, *SJTh* 4 [1956], pp. 288ff.; Weinfeld, *JNES* 23 [1964], pp. 202–12). As indicated in v. 22 there was a cessation of worship in the high places of Judah and concentration on the Jerusalem Temple; this can be interpreted as a move to increase the king's authority by strengthening the link between the king, the Temple and the provincial towns (Weinfeld, *op. cit.*, pp. 206ff.). Contacting Israelites living outside Judah, as reported in 2 Chr. 30:1, can be taken as an attempt to achieve national unity for all the children of Israel (Oded, *IJH*, p. 443) in preparation for open hostility against Assyria (Reviv, *WHJP*, p. 194). Despite the

doubtful connection between submission to Assyria and the introduction of foreign cults (see further, Cogan, *Imperialism*, pp. 110ff.,
and for a criticism of his standpoint, Spieckermann, *Sargonidenzeit*,
pp. 227ff.), it must be recognized that Hezekiah's religio-political
reform movement aimed at restoring the old kingdom of David
and Solomon (Nicholson, *VT* 13 [1963], pp. 383–9), and that any
strengthening of the Davidic dynasty at this time was an activity
that had anti-Assyrian implications. For the political implications
of the reform, see Welten, *Königs-Stempel*, pp. 156–61.

Another significant fact recorded in the deuteronomistic introduction is that Hezekiah 'smote the Philistines as far as Gaza' (v. 8), a
statement that is without parallel in 2 Chr. 29–32 and Isa. 36–39.
It is, however, a record that has to be taken seriously, for Hezekiah's
expansion in Philistia was again part of his anti-Assyrian policy
(Oded, *IJH*, pp. 444–6; Reviv, *WHJP*, pp. 195–6). Other references to Hezekiah's conquests in Philistia are available: according
to 1 Chr. 4:34–43 the Simeonites moved into Philistine territory in
the reign of Hezekiah and penetrated as far as Gerar (so the Gk.,
for the Heb. Gedor); the annals of Sennacherib (*ANET*, p. 287)
note that Ekron had no king because the people had handed over
Padi their king 'to Hezekiah, the Jew'; Sennacherib, in describing
his campaign in Judah in his 'Letter to God' (Na'aman, *op. cit.*, p.
27), refers to Hezekiah capturing and strengthening a royal city of
the Philistines. Hezekiah took advantage of Philistia's weakness due
to Assyrian campaigns against it in 734 BC and in 712 BC (cf.
Tadmor, *BA* 29 [1966], pp. 86–102), and regained Judaean territory
taken by the Philistines in the days of Ahaz. According to Assyrian
annals, Hezekiah was in alliance with Ṣidqa, king of Ashkelon
(*ANET*, pp. 287ff.), which must be interpreted as an anti-Assyrian
alliance that was active between 705 and 701 BC (cf. Reviv, *WHJP*,
p. 196). After the deuteronomistic introduction, there follows an
annalistic note recording the fall of Samaria (vv. 9–12), which is a
repetition of material included in 17:5f. The reference to 'the Israelites' in v. 11 gives a clear indication that this account of the fall of
Samaria and the exile of its people is written from a Judaean standpoint, and must, therefore, have been derived from the annals of
Judah (see above, on chapter 17). The appendix in v. 12, like vv.
5, 7a, comes from a nomistic redactor (DtrN) and so ties the section
more closely to the preceding verses (cf. Dietrich, *op. cit.*, p. 138).

The third element included in this first section is the annalistic
report in vv. 13–16 of Sennacherib's campaign against Jerusalem,
and of the tribute paid by Hezekiah to Assyria; although the information contained in v. 13 is repeated in 2 Chr. 32:1 and Isa.
36:1, these parallel texts do not refer to Hezekiah's subjugation and

payment of tribute to Sennacherib. Verses 13–16, however, agree basically with the Assyrian annalistic report, which states that Sennacherib laid siege to a number of Hezekiah's strong cities and small villages, imprisoned Hezekiah himself in Jerusalem 'like a bird in a cage', took a number of Judaean towns and gave them to the kings of Ashdod, Ekron and Gaza, and exacted from Hezekiah an increased tribute which was delivered to the Assyrian king in Nineveh (*ANET*, p. 288). That 2 Kg. 18:13–16 and the Sennacherib annals provide a parallel account of the same event, namely, the campaign of Sennacherib against Judah in 701 BC, is to be accepted without reservation. Moreover, it is clear that the biblical and Assyrian records are agreed in describing Hezekiah's subjugation in the terms of confinement to the city of Jerusalem, which remained unconquered, and also in referring to one campaign by Sennacherib in Judah. How to define the relationship between this agreed report of 18:13–16 and the Sennacherib annals and the more elaborate account in 18:17–19:37 is a problem that will be discussed below.

1. The synchronism of Hezekiah's accession with **the third year of Hoshea son of Elah** gives the beginning of Hezekiah's reign a date around 728 BC; cf. also vv. 9–10, where it is stated that he was in his sixth year when Samaria fell in 722 BC. But a different tradition in v. 13 below dates the Assyrian campaign of 701 BC in Hezekiah's 'fourteenth' year, thus making 715–714 BC the year of the accession. The suggestions that have been made to solve this discrepancy are discussed above (pp. 25ff; and by Thiele, *VT* 16 [1966], pp. 103–7); the conclusion reached is that the tradition preserved in the annalistic section in vv. 13–16 is to be preferred, and Hezekiah's dates are given as 715–697 BC. His mother's name **Abi** is an abbreviation of 'Abijah', the form found in 2 Chr. 29:1.

4. After the favourable verdict passed on Hezekiah in v. 3, where it is stated that he had acted **according to all that David his father had done** (cf. 22:2), there follows here an account of his cultic reform. Objections to the historicity of the reform on the grounds that v. 4 betrays late style, anticipates the Josianic reform, with the suggestion that v. 4*b* is authentic but that v. 4*a* is an expansion based on the later reform (Burney, pp. 337ff.) and is not included in Isa. 36–39, can be dismissed, despite Hoffmann's argument that vv. 1–6 are a deuteronomistic fiction (*Reform*, pp. 151–5). A movement towards a purification of the worship in Jerusalem is likely in view of Isaiah's frequent attacks on unacceptable practices (Isa. 1:29; 2:8, 18, 20; 8:19; 31:7) and the suggestion of Jer. 26:17–19 that Hezekiah had been influenced by the preaching of Micah. After comparing the two reforms, Haran (*Temples*, pp. 140ff.) distinguishes between them by proposing as a basis for Hezekiah's reform

an ideology that has found expression in priestly circles (P).
However, recent interpretations of the reformation (see above, p.
559) provide for it a motivation within the wider context of Assyrian
domination and a desire to consolidate the Judaean kingdom,
together with Israelite neighbours, in readiness for a drive towards
independence (Spieckermann, *op. cit.*, pp. 170ff.). Previous references have been made to the cult objects removed by Hezekiah, **the
high places** (see on 1 Kg. 3:2), **the pillars** (see on 1 Kg. 14:23) and
the Asherah (see on 1 Kg. 13:15). But it is here that we find the
only reference in Kings to **the bronze serpent that Moses had
made**. According to Num. 21:4–9, the bronze serpent was made by
Moses; but it is an aetiological narrative, and the connection with
Moses may be regarded as traditional and probably mythological.
More probable, however, is the suggestion that the serpent was an
old Jebusite symbol found in Jerusalem when it was taken over by
David; possibly Zadok, mentioned in the time of Solomon, was its
hereditary priest (cf. Rowley, *JBL* 58 [1939], pp. 113ff.; *BJRL* 44
[1961–2], pp. 395ff.). Archaeological discoveries bring evidence of
the very general use of the serpent as a cultic symbol in Palestine,
Egypt and Mesopotamia, sometimes having clear associations with
the fertility-cult and being associated with the mother-goddess
Asherah, and also having a widespread connection with healing.
(For a summary of the evidence from Ras Shamra, Tell Bet Mirsim,
Gezer and Hazor, see Gray, p. 670ff.) By the time of Hezekiah, the
serpent in the Temple was treated as an idol and had to be removed;
the Chronicler probably refrained from alluding to this historically
acceptable incident because he did not wish to make Moses responsible for the creation of an object of worship in the Temple. **it was
called Nehushtan**: The name is probably a mixed form from *nāḥāš*,
'serpent', and *neḥōšet*, 'bronze object' (*K-B*), with a determinative
ending '-an' (Montgomery, p. 501).

5. The favourable verdict of v. 3 is emphasized in v. 5 by means
of an extension, written probably under the influence of the reference to Hezekiah's cultic reform. In his enthusiasm the writer has
forgotten Hezekiah's exemplary predecessor, David, as well as his
successor, Josiah, who from the deuteronomistic standpoint, was
the ideal king (cf. 23:25). To redress this verse's oversight of David,
Gray (p. 671) omits the phrase **nor among those who were before
him**, which is in any case awkward and unsyntactic (cf. Šanda II,
p. 242; *BHS*); but Burney (p. 338) omits **after him**, which is placed
at the beginning of the sentence in Heb., thus reading 'there was
none like him among all the kings of Judah that were before him'.
The verse is obviously an exaggeration that is unsatisfactory in
content and syntax.

6. The comment of v. 5 is continued in vv. 6–7*a*, which, because of the phrase **kept the commandments which the LORD commanded Moses**, is designated by Dietrich (*op. cit.*, p. 138) as a nomistic revision (DtrN). Whether v. 5 comes from the same hand as vv. 6–7*a*, or is an earlier addition, we are clearly dealing here with extensions to the basic verdict on Hezekiah. Possibly some of the material was inserted as a direct result of the impression of Hezekiah's piety given in the 'Isaiah narratives' of 19:9*b*–35 and 20:1–11; it was finally revised by a nomistic redactor.

7. He rebelled against the king of Assyria: This short note in the introduction is further elaborated in vv. 13–16, and is to be taken as a reference to Hezekiah's aspirations before Sennacherib's attack in 701 BC. It is unnecessary to find in the phrase **and would not serve him** a reference to with-holding tribute after 701 BC; Hezekiah was probably compelled to pay suitable tribute to Assyria from 712 BC (Reviv, *WHJP*, p. 193).

8. He smote the Philistines as far as Gaza and its territory: As noted, this reference to Hezekiah's activities in Philistine country, although not given in the parallel accounts of 2 Chr. and Isa., is historically reliable and constitutes a significant element in his preparations for an anti-Assyrian thrust. Significantly the notice of his rebellion against Assyria and his conquest of Philistia appear as parallel activities in vv. 7*b*–8. It must be realised, however, that there were different aspects of Hezekiah's policy in Philistia. On the one hand, he was eager to engage in any activity that was directed at the weakening of Assyria's hold over Philistine territory, which was his own reason for deposing Padi the king of Ekron and for working in alliance with Ṣadqi of Ashkelon. On the other hand, he was ready to take advantage of the weakness and disunity of the Philistines in order to annex territories for Judah; it was whilst engaging in this activity that he penetrated **as far as Gaza**. Hezekiah was thus able to recover Judaean territory in southern Philistia, which, according to 2 Chr. 28:18–19, had been lost by Ahaz. His success, however, was only temporary, for when Sennacherib came against Hezekiah in 701 BC, **Gaza**, like Ashdod and Ekron, was given to loyal vassals of Assyria (Reviv, *WHJP*, p. 198).

9–12. Verses 9–11 repeat almost verbatim the material relating to the fall of Samaria in 17:–6; as already noted, this record was derived from the annals of Judah. The information has been included twice because the editor wished to place the fall of Samaria in its chronological setting in the reign of Hezekiah of Judah as well as in the history of the northern kingdom. The moralising note in v. 12 is from the hand of a later redactor, identified by Dietrich (*ibid.*) as the nomistic redactor (DtrN). It is a repetitive comment that states that **they did not obey . . . but transgressed . . . they neither listened nor obeyed.**

13. The annalistic report of Sennacherib's campaign against Judah opens with dating the event **in the fourteenth year of king Hezekiah,** cf. also Isa. 36:1. Assyrian records (*ANET*, pp. 287f.) confirm the date 701 BC for this, Sennacherib's third expedition, but there is some confusion in the biblical synchronisms. Despite the suggestion to read 'twenty-fourth' instead of **fourteenth** here, and to give Hezekiah's date of accession as 725 BC, with the suggestion that the error may have arisen due to a confusion with the expedition against Ashdod in 712 BC (Rowley, *BJRL* 44 [1961–2], pp. 411ff.; Clements, *Isaiah*, p. 280), it is preferred here to accept MT and to give Hezekiah's year of accession as 715 BC (see above, on vv. 1, 2). **Sennacherib king of Assyria:** He followed his father Sargon II, on his death in battle in 705 BC, and occupied the Assyrian throne until 681 BC. Details of his eight military expeditions are given in the annals of Sennacherib; and several copies are available of the annal referring to the third campaign in 701 BC (Luckenbill, *Annals*; Honor, *Invasion*; van Leeuwen, *OSt* 14 [1965], pp. 245–72). **came up against the fortified cities of Judah:** Sennacherib's annals give clearly the route which he followed until he eventually turned against Judah. Marching from Syria he turned in the direction of Phoenicia, and after forcing Luli the king of Sidon to flee to Cyprus he placed Ethbaal on the throne. Several small states, including Ashdod and rulers from Transjordan, pledged their loyalty to Sennacherib. He then turned south to Philistia, besieged a number of coastal cities and captured Ṣidqa of Ashkelon. When he concentrated on Ekron, Egyptian forces under the leadership of Tirhakah of Ethiopia came on the scene and a battle was fought at Eltekeh. The Assyrians gained victory, besieged Ekron, punished the rebels and restored Padi to the throne. It was then that Sennacherib directed his army against Hezekiah and all **the fortified cities of Judah.** The more detailed account in the Assyrian annals reports that Sennacherib: (i) besieged forty-six cities, walled forts and small villages; (ii) captured 200,150 people and much spoil; (iii) closed in upon Hezekiah in Jerusalem, where he was imprisoned 'like a bird in a cage', and built earthworks around the city, which ensured the capitulation of Hezekiah; (iv) reduced Judaean territory by dividing some of it between Ashdod, Ekron and Gaza; and (v) increased the annual tribute to be paid by Hezekiah. Although the report of the annals presents some problems (Childs, *Assyrian Crisis*, pp. 72ff.), it is not inconsistent with the biblical account of vv. 13–16, and some of the similarities are striking.

14. sent to the king of Assyria at Lachish: The Assyrian annals do not mention the capture of Lachish and, as suggested by this verse, the establishment of headquarters there for Sennacherib (cf. 2 Chr. 32:9; Mic. 1:13–15). However, an Assyrian relief depicting Sennacherib conquering the city of Lachish, receiving booty there and taking away prisoners, confirms the biblical record (*ANEP*, pp. 371–4). See further, Barnett, *IEJ* 8 [1958], pp. 161–4. **three hundred talents of silver and thirty talents of gold**: There is a discrepancy between the biblical and Assyrian records with regard to the tribute paid by Hezekiah, which, according to the annals amounted to '30 talents of gold, 800 talents of silver, precious stones, antimony, large cuts of red stone, couches inlaid with ivory, *nimedu*-chairs inlaid with ivory, elephant-hides, ebony-wood, boxwood, and all kinds of valuable treasures' (*ANET*, p. 288). Several proposals have been made to solve the difference between the 300 talents of the biblical record and the 800 talents of the Assyrian, such as the suggestion that heavy talents were the basis of the *OT* reckoning and light talents in the Assyrian system, or that the *OT* only refers to stamped ingots, whilst the Assyrian record takes into account the despoilation of the Temple and palace treasury, or again that the *OT* takes the figure paid from the Temple treasury without reckoning the amount taken from the palace, which has been included in the Assyrian figure (Childs, *op. cit.*, p. 72; Montgomery, p. 485; Gray, pp. 674ff.). It is not impossible that the Assyrian annals have at this point exaggerated; the high number of captives (given as 200,150) may also indicate a tendency to exaggerate, but its reduction to 2,150 (Ungnad, *ZAW* 59 [1942–3], pp. 199ff.) or even to 150 (Olmstead, *Historiography*, p. 8) is unrealistic (cf. Herrmann, *History*, p. 262). Attempts to explain the discrepancy between the two reports have also to take into account the exact agreement in the number of gold talents sent by Hezekiah.

15. Because of the basic agreement between vv. 13–16 and the Assyrian annals, it is obvious that the information contained in these verses has been derived from Judaean annals. References in this particular verse to the **house of the LORD** and **the treasuries of the king's house** and in v. 16 to 'the doors of the temple of the LORD' would suggest an archival source that was especially concerned with the Temple and the treasury.

16. At that time: The use of this linking phrase probably indicates that the information given here is derived from an archival note that was independent of that used for vv. 13–15 (cf. Montgomery, *JBL* 53 [1934], pp. 46–52). **and from the doorposts**: *NEB*, 'door-frames'. Although the Heb. *'ōmᵉnôt* is not found elsewhere, it is correctly taken to mean **doorposts**, and it is unnecessary to read 'shields' (cf. *BHS*) with reference to 1 Kg. 10:17. **which Hezekiah**

king of Judah had overlaid: If this information is correct, it suggests that Hezekiah renovated the Temple in conjunction with his cultic reform, which is probable. There is no foundation for changing the name to Solomon (Klostermann, p. 459; Skinner, p. 389) or Joash (Šanda II, p. 249). **and gave it to the king of Assyria:** Whereas the biblical record does not specify where the tribute was paid to Sennacherib, the Assyrian annals state that Hezekiah sent it later to Nineveh and that 'in order to deliver the tribute and to do obeisance as a slave he sent his personal messenger' (*ANET*, p. 288). In view of the tradition preserved in the Isaiah narratives and elsewhere (Herodotus II, p. 141), it is claimed that Sennacherib retreated suddenly from Jerusalem, making it necessary for the tribute to be sent to Nineveh. But, on account of the fact that Hezekiah paid an annual tribute to Assyria, there is no incongruity in the statement that he sent it 'later' (as emphasized in the annals) to Nineveh. On this occasion Jerusalem escaped and Hezekiah remained on the throne, two facts which gave rise to further theologising about the inviolability of the city and divine protection of the dynasty. As noted by Clements (*Deliverance of Jerusalem*, pp. 19ff.), the retention of the Jerusalem throne by Hezekiah does not necessarily prove leniency on the part of Assyria; after restricting Judah territorially, Assyria could perhaps secure stability by retaining the local leader as vassal king.

(b) Sennacherib's campaign and Hezekiah's response
18:17–19:37

Whereas the report in vv. 13–16 states only that Sennacherib campaigned against the cities of Judah with the result that Hezekiah was forced to submit and pay him tribute, the more extended narrative in 18:17–19:37 describes a visit to Jerusalem by Sennacherib's emissary, which called on Hezekiah to submit to the Assyrian king. Encouraged by an oracle from the prophet Isaiah, the Jerusalem king refused, and we are then informed that the Assyrians withdrew. This latter account (account B), which gives no suggestion that Hezekiah surrendered, stands in sharp contrast to both the brief report in vv. 13–16 (account A) and Sennacherib's own account in the Assyrian annals (*ANET*, p. 288). This discrepancy between the accounts poses a difficult problem for the literary critic and historian alike (see the detailed studies of Honor, *Invasion*; Childs, *Assyrian Crisis*; Clements, *Deliverance of Jerusalem*).

Although the historical problem seems more acute because of the scarcity of extra-biblical evidence (Childs, *op. cit.*, p. 120), as suggested by Clements (*op. cit.*, pp. 18ff.) a reasonably coherent picture of the events of 701 BC can be obtained. First of all, two attempts to reconcile the two reports have to be dismissed: (1) The longer narrative (account B), it has been claimed (cf. Rowley, *BJRL* 44 [1961–2], pp. 395–431), refers to a second stage in Sennacherib's dealings with Jerusalem in 701 BC. Initially Hezekiah surrendered (as reported in account A), and was leniently treated by Sennacherib, who took no further measures against Jerusalem. Later, for some unknown reason, Sennacherib regretted his leniency and proceeded to take Jerusalem; but for some unexplained reason he was forced to withdraw. Naturally, the Assyrian annals mention Hezekiah's surrender, but ignore Sennacherib's unsuccessful attempt to take Jerusalem. The biblical record has included both stages, the first in account A, the second in account B. (2) Another interpretation finds in account B a report of a later siege of Jerusalem during a subsequent Assyrian campaign under Sennacherib. Clues to a second Judaean campaign are provided by the reference to Tirhakah of Ethiopia (19:9), who could have been only a boy in 701 BC, and to Sennacherib's death (19:37), which occurred in 681 BC. It is therefore surmised that Sennacherib attempted to take Jerusalem during a second campaign, which is dated up to a decade after his first in 701 BC (Albright, *BASOR* 130 [1953], pp. 8ff.; van Leeuwen, *OSt* 14 [1965], pp. 264ff.; Horn, *AUSS* 4 [1966], pp. 1ff.). Again, it is assumed that the Bible reported both campaigns, whilst Assyrian annals conveniently ignored the second. Because both these solutions are based on the assumption of a second campaign by Sennacherib, their weakness is made apparent by the lack of evidence for such an Assyrian expedition to the west (Clements, *op. cit.*, p. 14; Reviv, *WHJP*, p. 197). The second interpretation noted above brings the second Assyrian expedition from the reign of Hezekiah to the reign of Manasseh, who was a faithful Assyrian vassal. Moreover, the naming of Tirhakah does not necessarily demand a date later than 701 BC, since he was probably 20–22 years old at that time (see below on 19:19). After denying the need to posit a second confrontation between Assyria and Hezekiah, Clements (*op. cit.*, p. 62) reconstructs the events of 701 BC as follows: Sennacherib, having destroyed Judaean towns, did not attack Jerusalem, but isolated it and forced Hezekiah to surrender; Hezekiah had to pay the Assyrians a substantial indemnity, but, in accordance with Assyrian policy, was confirmed on the throne; Sennacherib returned to Nineveh, where he died in 681 BC without having to launch a second campaign against Jerusalem.

Once account B is related to the events of 701 BC and thus becomes a parallel to account A, the need to define the nature of the narrative and to examine its historicity becomes apparent. This narrative, according to Clements, (i) comes from a time closely contemporaneous with the events it describes and is placed in the time of Josiah (*op. cit.*, p. 101); (ii) is to be defined as 'narrative theology' rather than a historical narrative proper (*op. cit.*, p. 21); (iii) gives expression to the concept of the inviolability of Jerusalem, a concept that is confirmed by the addition to it of the two narratives in chapter 20 (*op. cit.*, p. 63); (iv) belongs to the Deuteronomistic History (*op. cit.*, p. 101), not to prophetic circles (as argued by Dietrich, *Prophetie*, pp. 134ff.), and was included in the first draft of that work during Zedekiah's reign. Not all these conclusions can be considered in detail here, but the classification of the section as 'narrative theology' calls for comment. Clements correctly underlines the theological motivation of the narrative and categorizes it as a narrative that brings an insight into the way in which men viewed their historical experience (*op. cit.*, pp. 18ff.); but he at times seems to be denying this tradition any historical value. As a corrective it must be stated that, although it does not aim at describing the historical situation accurately, this narrative is not without its historical significance (cf. Gray, pp. 664ff.). Another point that has to be underlined is that the attribution of the narrative to the Deuteronomistic History and its dating during the Josianic period and definitely before the end of the reign of Zedekiah, is preferable to Gray's description of it as 'the Isaiah legend' (Gray, p. 659).

Since the time of Stade (*ZAW* 6 [1886], pp. 173ff.) it has been accepted that the section 18:17–19:37 consists of two versions, which are similar in theme and parallel in the sense that they describe the same incident (and not two delegations as suggested by Šanda II, pp. 289ff.). See further, Childs, *op. cit.*, pp. 69ff. The B1 account in 18:18–19:9a, 36–37 reports the appearance of Sennacherib's emissaries outside Jerusalem and the speech of Rabshakeh addressed to Hezekiah, which is followed by a second speech asserting that Hezekiah cannot save his people from the hand of Assyria. After initial signs of distress, there was a consultation with Isaiah the prophet, who delivers an oracle assuring them that the Assyrian king will return home (19:6–7). Sennacherib heard of a movement by Tirhakah of Ethiopia (v. 9a) and returned home to Nineveh (vv. 36f.), where at a later date presumably he was assassinated. It is to be noted that account B1 refers to Hezekiah's reforms (18:22) and to his dependence on Egypt for help (18:24), and that, because of its suggestion that Sennacherib returned to Nineveh on hearing a rumour of Tirhakah's move, it does not presuppose any supernatural divine intervention. As noted by Clements (*op. cit.*, p. 55), there is nothing in this account that cannot be reconciled with the Assyrian annals and account A. In the B2 account of 19:9b–35 the Assyrian

challenge to Hezekiah was delivered in a letter. Following Hezekiah's prayer in vv. 15–19, there is an extended message from Isaiah
(vv. 21–34), which can be divided into three independent sections,
one addressed to the king of Assyria (vv. 21–28), another addressed
to Hezekiah (vv. 29–31) and the third formulated in the third person
is concerned with the king of Assyria (vv. 32–34). This account is
concluded with a report that 'the angel of the LORD' slaughtered
185,000 men in the Assyrian camp (v. 35). The differences between
the two versions suggest that a more advanced theological interpretation lies behind the second account: Hezekiah, instead of merely
resorting to the house of the Lord, utters an extended prayer; Isaiah
turns from being a mouthpiece of God's message of reassurance to
appear as a prophet speaking a series of oracles; the theme of the
inviolability of Jerusalem is more developed and mature. The most
obvious difference between the two, however, appears in the reference to the slaughter of the Assyrians by 'the angel of the LORD' (v.
35), which constitutes the only real element in the biblical account B
that cannot be reconciled with the Assyrian annals and the biblical
account A. There is much to support the suggestion by Clements
(*op. cit.*, p. 59) that v. 35 is an intrusion that was added after
the combination of B1 and B2, which originally ran parallel. Both
accounts were intended to underline the theological significance of
the fact that Jerusalem was not taken by Assyria; B2 is more
advanced theologically than B1, but the climax of the theologizing
is found in v. 35, which heightens the manner in which God saved
Jerusalem.

17. The present version describes the sending of a three-man
envoy from Lachish to Jerusalem (cf. 'his servant' of 2 Chr. 32:9),
but Isa. 36:2 mentions only one of the three men, the Rabshakeh.
the Tartan, the Rabsaris and the Rabshakeh: These are three
titles, which are translated in *NEB* as 'the commander-in-chief, his
chief eunuch, and his chief officer' and in *NIV* as 'his supreme
commander, his chief officer and his field commander'. **the Tartan**
was a title for the chief commander of the Assyrian army (Isa. 20:1),
although *K-B* suggests that he was in effect a 'second commander'.
the Rabsaris, if a parallel is drawn with Heb. usage, was 'the chief
eunuch', but there is no proof that such an officer was known as a
member of staff at the Assyrian court. The title may be a corruption
of the Assyrian *rab ša rēsi*, who, as the head of the king's bodyguard,
held a senior military post (cf. Jer. 39:3, 13). The Heb. term
Rabshakeh means 'chief butler', but possibly the Assyrian title
denoted 'chief officer' or 'chieftain' (cf. Burney, p. 341). **with a
great army**: The first contact with Hezekiah was probably made
from Lachish by the three officers accompanied by an armed escort

rather by the whole army (cf. Gray, pp. 678f.). **they came and stood by the conduit of the upper pool, which is on the highway to the Fuller's Field**: The **upper pool** (cf. Isa. 7:3) has not been identified with any certainty; the two main difficulties are the connection between it and the lower pool of Isa. 22:9 and the desire to locate it too far from Hezekiah's palace. For discussions of the proposed identifications, see Šanda II, pp. 250–3; Gray, pp. 679–82. Although this remains an unsolved problem, it seems reasonable to suggest that the **upper pool** was the Pool of Siloam, or perhaps an earlier pool than Hezekiah's construction, and that the lower pool is to be identified with modern Birket el-Hamra (Ap-Thomas, *AOTS*, pp. 290ff.; Shaheen, *PEQ* [1977], pp. 107–12; Shiloh, *BA* [1979], pp. 165–71). **the highway**: In this connection it may denote the ramp or the embankment rather than the main north road coming in to Jerusalem (cf. Gray, p. 679). **the Fuller's Field**: This was near a good supply of water, for it was there that woollen cloth was stretched out for drying after being trodden down in water.

18. For the titles of the Judaean officers selected to represent the king, the one **over the household, the secretary** and **the recorder**, see on 1 Kg. 4:2. Both **Eliakim** and **Shebna** are mentioned in Isa. 22:15ff., where Shebna is denounced and Eliakim is named as the person to succeed him. But in view of the secondary nature of that passage, which took over the names from Isa. 36:3, and its concern with the kingship rather than with the officers named (Clements, *Isaiah*, pp. 187–91), it does not add any reliable information about these two men. A seal impression belonging to Jehoazarah, another son of Hilkiah, confirms that the latter was a servant of Hezekiah (Hestrin and Dayagi, *IEJ* 24 [1974], pp. 26–9). Nothing is known about **Joah the son of Asaph**.

19. The exact content and wording of the Rabshakeh's speeches in vv. 19–25, 28–35 are a free composition of the authors of the so-called 'Isaiah narratives', and who had knowledge of the content of Isaiah's prophecies (Clements, *op. cit.*, p. 281). Yet, these speeches cannot be dismissed as worthless. In their attempt to persuade the inhabitants of Jerusalem to surrender contrary to the will of their king, they seem to follow Assyrian practice, as seen from similar negotiations with the inhabitants of Babylon before the siege of their city in 731 BC (cf. Saggs, *Iraq* 17 [1955], pp. 23ff.). The Rabshakeh is a spokesman for the king of Assyria, whose self-designated title was **the great king** (*šarru rabū*).

20. The Rabshakeh sought to undermine the confidence of Jerusalem's inhabitants by (i) showing the futility of their dependence on Egypt (vv. 20ff.); (ii) challenging the idea that they were dependent on God (v. 22); (iii) demonstrating the inadequacy of their military skills (vv. 23f.) and (iv) asserting that the Assyrians themselves had been sent by God to destroy Judah (v. 25). **mere words are strategy and power for war**: Taken with the challenge in the question at the end of the verse, **on whom do you now rely?**, and the answer in v. 21, this verse obviously means that diplomatic negotiations with Egypt are not adequate substitute for military strategy and power, or 'skill and numbers' (*NEB*).

21. This denunciation of the people's trust in Egypt obviously reflects the standpoint expressed so often by Isaiah (cf. Isa. 28:14ff.; 29:13; 30:1ff.; 31:1ff.). **broken reed of staff**: *NEB*, 'splinted cane'; cf. also Ezek. 29:6, which Gray (p. 682) takes as an indication of dependence upon a popular proverb. The statement that the cane 'will run into a man's hand and pierce it if he leans upon it' conveys what Judah through bitter experience found was true; it was disappointed in its expectation of help from Egypt.

22. This verse, referring to Hezekiah's reforms of v. 4, presents an exceptional argument that the removal of his **high places and altars** was certainly no proof of trust in Yahweh. The argument is pointedly expressed in *NEB*, 'is he not the god whose hill-shrines and altars Hezekiah has suppressed?' Whether this verse can be taken as proof that the Assyrians had taken notice of Hezekiah's cultic reform because of its political implications (as suggested by Montgomery, p. 488, and Gray, p. 682) is far from certain.

23-24. make a wager with my master: *NEB*, 'make a bargain'. The Rabshakeh now taunts his opponents because of their military inadequacy, the implication being that they were totally dependent on militia men. The Assyrians were willing to bet that, even if Hezekiah were given the horses, he could not provide the trained cavalry men to ride them (cf. Šanda II, p. 256; Gray, p. 682). Judah's military deficiency could not be remedied by relying **on Egypt for chariots and for horsemen**.

25. The cruelest sting in Rabshakeh's taunt was the claim that the Assyrian king was acting on God's own command, **Go up against this land and destroy it**. Such a claim, although now placed in the mouth of the Assyrians, is probably based on Isa. 10:5ff. The arrogance displayed by the Assyrian spokesman here and in v. 27 is not exaggerated, for the same attitude is found in the Assyrian annals.

26. The implication of the Judaean deputation's request for the parley to be conducted in Aramaic, and of the Rabshakeh's insistence on speaking in Hebrew, is contained in the phrase **within the hearing of the people who are on the wall**. Hezekiah's negotiators, by using the language current in diplomatic circles, were anxious to keep the content of what was said to themselves; the Rabshakeh, by speaking in the native tongue, was aiming for a break-through to the people. **in the Aramaic language, for we understand it**: The language of diplomacy was **Aramaic**, which was used for conducting business between the Assyrian Empire and the Aramaean population, as it was later in the Babylonian period (cf. the bilingual Aramaic-Akkadian texts). The Rabshakeh's proficiency in Aramaic, therefore, causes no surprise. The point here is that this language, known to both sides in this parley, could not be understood by the common people. **do not speak to us in the language of Judah**: The **language of Judah** here denotes the Heb. language, rather than the Judaic in contrast to the Ephraimite dialect (Šanda II, p. 257). Most probably the Rabshakeh delivered his orations in Hebrew by means of an interpreter.

27. From his reply, the Rabshakeh obviously did not think of his task as that of conducting negotiations with Hezekiah and his representatives. His words were rather directed at the common citizens of Jerusalem, and his aim, as noted above under v. 19, was to persuade the people to come out of the city and to act contrary to official policy. The people are despicably described as those who, because of the siege of their city, are **to eat their own dung and drink their own urine**.

28–29. In his second speech the Rabshakeh once again attacks Hezekiah's leadership by claiming that the king is unable to deliver his people from Sennacherib's hand (v. 29), and is misconceived in persuading them to rely on the Lord (v. 30). His attempt to undermine Hezekiah is emphasized in these verses by using three negatives to follow each other—**Do not let Hezekiah deceive you** (v. 29); **Do not let Hezekiah make you rely** . . . (v. 30); **Do not listen to Hezekiah** (v. 31). In v. 29 *RSV* rightly follows the Vsns. in reading **from my hand** for MT's 'from his hand' (cf. *BHS*).

31. Make your peace with me: This translation (cf. *RV*, *NEB*, *NIV*) follows the Targ.; the Heb. literally means 'make blessing with me'. Burney (p. 342) thinks that 'blessing' in this context means 'mutual well wishing' and so denotes 'a treaty'. It is a better rendering than Montgomery's 'Salute me' (pp. 488ff.). Verse 31*b* promises well-being through the cultivation of fields and vineyards; but is followed immediately in v. 32 by the threat of deportation to another land, which is the ultimate aim of Assyria. There is, however, no contradiction between the promise of v. 31*b* and the threat of v. 32. Clements (*Isaiah*, p. 282) finds in it a reflection of the protracted deportation of the Israelites, who were still being deported as late as the reign of Esarhaddon (680–669 BC), although Samaria had fallen in 722 BC.

32. The picture given here of the land to which the people were to be deported, together with the emphasis on **that you may live and not die**, does not create an unfavourable impression of the deportation. This is confirmed by the Nimrud letters, which show how the Assyrians provided native wives for Aramaeans who were settled in Assyria (Saggs, *Iraq* 18 [1956], pp. 40ff.). Saggs suggests that the request for the parley to be conducted in Aramaic was an attempt to avoid the placing of such inducement before the people.

33. This verse introduces the theme of vv. 33–35, namely, the inability of national deities to save their people from the hands of the Assyrians. Clements (*ibid.*) traces this theme to Isa. 10:9 and finds in it the theological emphasis of the whole narrative complex in Isa. 36–37 (= 2 Kg. 18–20). These chapters demonstrate that Yahweh is superior to all other gods, including the Assyrian deity; the proof is Assyria's failure to take Jerusalem in 701 BC. The Rabshakeh's boast of the superiority of Assyria over all the gods serves to emphasise this theme.

34. the gods of Hamath and Arpad: The god of **Hamath** is named in 17:30. This verse adds **Arpad**, which is *Tell Erfad* near Aleppo. Both had already been conquered by Assyria in 720 BC. Of the next three names, **Sepharvaim, Hena and Ivvah**, the first and the last appear in the list of Syrian towns in 17:24, but nothing is known of **Hena**. The second and third names are omitted from some Gk. versions and from Isa. 36:19; since **Ivvah** and **Sepharvaim** are linked together in 17:24 and 19:13, MT may be retained. The attempt of the Targ. to render the nouns as verbs, giving 'he sent them wandering and caused them to stray', also misses the point. **Have they delivered Samaria out of my hand?**: This question stands in parenthesis to what precedes, and there is nothing to prevent **they** from being taken as the gods of the cities listed in v. 34*a*, which, of course, is not the meaning. Luc. inserts another question before it 'Where are the gods of the land of Samaria?', which safeguards the meaning, even if it is difficult to support textually (Rahlfs, *Studien III*, p. 378).

36. The people's silence in obedience to the king's command, **Do not answer him**, gives a brief but clear summary of the position: the arrogant and taunting pleas made to the people by the Rabshakeh made no impact, for they remained faithful to their king.

19:1. Hezekiah, adopting the traditional signs of mourning and distress by rending **his clothes** and covering **himself with sackcloth**, withdrew to the Temple to seek God's response to the crisis. The fact that Hezekiah himself and his servants (v. 2) were showing signs of humiliation is construed by Gray (p. 684) as the initiation of a public fast at which a prophet (in this case Isaiah) was expected to take part in the fast liturgy (cf. Jl. and Am. 7:1–6). The notice

of the king's retreat to **the house of the LORD** introduces a theme
that is developed in the trilogy of 'Isaianic narratives'. Hezekiah's
piety and submission to God are made more pronounced in the
second account by including his prayer in vv. 15–19, and again in
chapter 20 by giving it as the reason for his restoration to health
(20:2ff.).

2. to the prophet Isaiah, the son of Amoz: Isaiah, called to
prophesy in 736 BC, had been most critical of Hezekiah's rebellion
against Assyria in 705 BC (cf. Isa. 30:1–5; 31:1–3), had exposed the
false security of an alliance with Egypt and had emphasized that
Sennacherib's attack upon Judah and Jerusalem was an act of judgment upon Judah. Clements (*Deliverance of Jerusalem*, pp. 28–51)
has argued that Isaiah did not foretell the miraculous interruption
of Sennacherib's campaign against Jerusalem in 701 BC, and that
the passages quoted in support of such a contention are the work
of Josianic redactors of the book. The background of such passages
is the weakening of Assyrian power in Judah during Josiah's reign,
and therefore they do not apply retrospectively to 701 BC. Acceptance of this view calls into question the reliability of the words
attributed to Isaiah in vv. 6, 7. Moreover, the tradition that
Hezekiah sent a deputation to consult his critic Isaiah may reflect
the view of later interpolators, who wished to emphasize the king's
piety.

3. Jerusalem's distress is described briefly in what may be
arranged in two couplets. The latter, **children have come to the
birth, and there is no strength to bring them forth**, may contain
a popular proverb alluding generally to the weakened condition of
the people, or perhaps more specifically to their frustration at their
abortive rebellion against Assyria.

4. to mock the living God: The Rabshakeh, in his denigration
of national deities because of their inability to resist Assyrian power,
had implied that the God of Jerusalem was equally impotent. Such
words are clearly interpreted as mockery which God **will rebuke**.
In asking the prophet to pray for Jerusalem, it is called **the remnant
that is left**; although **the remnant** may have had other meanings in
this period (cf. Isa. 7:3; 37:30–32), there is no doubt that in this
particular context it can only refer to Jerusalem, the only city that
remained unconquered by Sennacherib.

**7. Behold, I will put a spirit in him, so that he shall hear a
rumour and return to his own land**: This verse merely states that
Sennacherib, because of some **rumour** that he heard, decided to
return home before accomplishing the conquest of Jerusalem;
although there is no suggestion here of a miraculous intervention,
it is claimed that God was responsible for putting **a spirit in him**,

which may simply refer to Sennacherib's presentiment (Montgomery, p. 491) rather than panic (Gray, p. 685). Various suggestions have been made: (1) On the basis of vv. 7*b*, 36ff. it has been
claimed that a rumour of domestic unrest reached Sennacherib's
camp; it was a serious unrest that ended with the king's assassination. Against this interpretation is the fact that Sennacherib
remained king of Assyria for another twenty years, and died in 681
BC. (2) On the basis of vv. 8–9 it has been assumed that he heard
of a movement against Assyria by Tirhakah of Ethiopia. This interpretation faces the historical difficulty that Tirhakah had already
been defeated at Eltekeh when the Assyrian army was on its way
to Judah (see on v. 9, below). It may well be that the simple reason
for Sennacherib's withdrawal was that Hezekiah submitted and
agreed to pay an indemnity, as reported in 18:13–16. The present
narrator, however, because he has decided to ignore Hezekiah's
surrender and the penalty imposed upon him, has given the rumour
of Tirhakah's movements as the reason for Assyria's withdrawal;
but in doing so he has confused the sequence of events (Clements,
op. cit., pp. 55f.). **and I will cause him to fall by the sword in his
own land**: This statement has to be taken in conjunction with vv.
36f., which contain the biblical tradition of a much later event.

8. fighting against Libnah: The identification of **Libnah** is uncertain (see under 8:22); it appears that Sennacherib had left Lachish,
probably moving his headquarters from that city (Reviv, *WHJP*,
p. 198), and was now concentrating upon **Libnah**.

9. The first 'Isaiah narrative', which is broken off abruptly at v.
9*a* for the introduction of the second narrative (vv. 9*b*–35), is
continued in vv. 36f. The statement that **Tirhakah king of Ethiopia
. . . has set out to fight against you** has been variously interpreted.
Those who take the view that Sennacherib undertook a second
campaign in Palestine later than 701 BC find supporting evidence in
this verse; Tirhakah did not become **king of Ethiopia** until 689 BC,
and it is claimed that he was too young to be in command of military
action against Assyria in 701 BC (Gray, pp. 660ff.). Others have
assumed that Tirhakah has been incorrectly named because he was
the best known ruler during this obscure period (Rowley, *BJRL*
44 [1961–2], pp. 420ff.). On the basis of recent investigations it can
be suggested that Tirhakah was active against Sennacherib in 701
BC, and that, although he was not king at the time, it is easy to see
how a later title became attached to his name (Kitchen, *Intermediate
Period*, pp. 154–72; 387–93; Janssen, *Bib* 34 [1953], pp. 23–43).
There is some confusion about the beginning of account B2 in v.
9*b*. *RSV*'s rendering, **he sent messengers again** (cf. *NEB*), is a
possible rendering of the two Heb. verbs (*wayyāšob̲ wayyišlaḥ*)

whose literal meaning 'and he returned and he sent' can be understood as 'and he sent again', thus taking both verbs as the beginning
of account B2. But if v. 9 is taken in close conjunction with vv.
7–8, *wayyāšob̲* may be the conclusion of the first account in v. 9*a*;
the brief statement 'and he returned' noted the fulfilment of the
prediction in v. 7. The parallel in Isa. 37:9 reads a different verb,
'and when he heard (*wayyišma'*) he sent'; but the Gk. and 1QIs^a
read both verbs 'and when he heard he sent again'. The reason for
this confusion is that at v. 9 two narratives have been combined;
possibly the phrase 'and he returned', which stood originally at the
end of account B1, was read at the beginning of account B2 and
construed differently (Childs, *Assyrian Crisis*, pp. 139ff.).

10. Despite the opening phrase **Thus shall you speak to
Hezekiah**, it is clear from v. 14 that this second message, unlike
the first one which had been delivered orally by the Rabshakeh,
was communicated in a letter. The point of this second message,
like the first, is that Yahweh cannot deliver Jerusalem from the
hands of the Assyrians. But, some variations are evident when the
two accounts are compared. Both agree that the Assyrians were
trying to invalidate the promise that Jerusalem will not be given
into the hand of the king of Assyria (cf. 18:30), and make the same
point 'Shall you be delivered?' (cf. 18:35). But, whereas the first
account attributes the promise to Hezekiah's deception (18:29f.),
this account says specifically **Do not let your God . . . deceive
you**. The change of emphasis may be due to further theological
reflection by the author, and need not be taken as an increase of
arrogance on the part of Sennacherib.

11–12. These words make the same point as 18:33, but with the
addition of a list of **the nations which my fathers destroyed**, which
is composed of nations which had long been incorporated in the
Assyrian Empire and had experienced transportations of their population. **Gozan**, also mentioned in 17:6 and identified with *Tell Halaf*,
had been subjected in 809 BC. **Haran** (cf. Gen. 11:31), situated on
a tributary of the Euphrates and an important trading centre on a
caravan route to Syria, had belonged to the Assyrian Empire since
1100 BC. **Rezeph** has been identified with *Rezzafeh* on the route
from Damascus through Palmyra; it had been incorporated in the
Empire possibly by Shalmaneser III in 856 BC, and at least before
804 BC. **the people of Eden**: They were the inhabitants of *Bit Adini*,
which was south of Haran and again on the Euphrates; its capital
was *Til Basir*, which is probably intended by the corrupt form **Tel-
assar**. Shalmaneser transported prisoners from this district.

13. For the names listed in this verse, see on 18:34 and 17:24,
31.

14. Hezekiah, after receiving the letter and reading it, **went up to the house of the LORD**. His reaction is identical to that described in v. 1, where it follows the reporting of the Rabshakeh's words by his envoys. It is envisaged that the letter was written in Aramaic on parchment, and could be **spread** out **before the LORD**.

15. Hezekiah prayed before the LORD: On the analogy of 2 Sam. 7:18ff., and in view of the reference to 'cherubim' in v. 16, it can be assumed that the king stood before the ark of Yahweh, and in accordance with his sacral status was acting as the people's representative. According to Childs (*op. cit.*, p. 100) there is a significant contrast between account B1 and account B2 in the role they attribute to Hezekiah. In the first account he requests Isaiah to offer an intercessory prayer (19:40), but here he has become the righteous king who approaches God himself in the tradition of David (2 Sam. 7:18ff.) and Solomon (1 Kg. 8:14ff.). This role fits into the framework of the deuteronomistic theology (Wolff, *ZAW* [1961], pp. 171ff.). The prayer attributed to Hezekiah here follows a traditional cultic pattern, with its invocation, complaint and plea. The detailed analysis given by Childs (*ibid.*) brings out these elements as follows: (i) The invocation enumerates the divine attributes in a style similar to a hymn—**God of Israel; enthroned above the cherubim; God, thou alone, of all the kingdoms; made heaven and earth.** (ii) The plea to attend leads on to the complaint (vv. 16–18). (iii) **So now** (Heb. *we'attāh*; see Brongers, *VT* 15 [1965], pp. 289ff.) introduces the plea for intervention (v. 19), which is followed by a motivation clause (**that all . . .**, v. 19b). The whole prayer is deuteronomistic in style (Weinfeld, *Deuteronomy*, p. 39).

16. which he has sent to mock the living God: The phrase **to mock the living God** has already appeared in the first account, but, as Childs rightly comments (*ibid.*), it is only now given an appropriate setting. There is a forceful contrast here between **the living God** and the 'no gods' of the nations (vv. 17–18).

17–18. Whether or not the Assyrians actually suppressed the cults of their subjects, this deuteronomistic prayer cannot resist a polemic against idolatry. It is a characteristic theme of Deuteronomy (Weinfeld, *op. cit.*, pp. 320ff.), as indeed is the phrase **the work of man's hands, wood and stone** (cf. Dt. 4:28) and the recollection of the deuteronomic command to burn idols (Dt. 7:5, 25).

19. The motivation phrase in v. 19b, **that all the kingdoms of the earth may know that thou, O LORD, art God alone,** is frequently used in the exilic period, especially by the prophet Ezekiel. It is also characteristic of the deuteronomistic tradition. For a study of this standard 'recognition formula', see Zimmerli, *Erkenntnis*, pp. 16ff.

20. The statement that God had heard Hezekiah's prayer introduces a lengthy reply in vv. 21–34. The original reply to the king's prayer is found in vv. 32–34, and the two oracles in vv. 21–31, one addressed to Sennacherib (vv. 21–28) and the other to Hezekiah (vv. 29–31) are probably later insertions. Clements (*Isaiah*, p. 285) suggests that they were added after the combination of the two accounts in 18:17–19:37, but not long after the composition of the narrative.

21. The oracle addressed to Sennacherib is poetic in form, and follows closely the elegaic 3:2 metre called *qînāh* (see especially, Montgomery, pp. 494ff., with reference to earlier literature). It has the character of a taunt-song, and by contrasting the earlier boasting of Sennacherib with his present humiliation it makes mockery of his defeat; cf. also Isaiah's taunt-song against Assyria in 10:5ff. Fundamentally the message is the same as Isaiah's message to Hezekiah in vv. 32–34, for the climax at the end of v. 28 is a repetition of v. 33. This opening verse describes the scorn with which Sennacherib is held by **the virgin daughter of Zion. She wags her head** behind him as a sign of her derision (cf. Ps. 22:7; 109:25; Job 16:4; Jer. 18:16; Lam. 2:15).

22. As in v. 4 Assyria's arrogant words, although directed against Israel, are virtually said to have **mocked and reviled** God himself. The designation of God as **the Holy One of Israel** is characteristic of Isaiah; he probably borrowed an ancient title from the cult and used it to emphasize God's holiness and also the fact that he was God of both kingdoms (so Clements, *op. cit.*, p. 31). The metre is disturbed in the line **against whom you have raised your voice**; possibly **against whom** is an unnecessary repetition.

23. Gray (p. 688) rightly takes the opening words **By your . . . said** as a prosaic gloss; the addition serves to connect the quoted words of Sennacherib in v. 23 with the question addressed to him in v. 22. The Assyrian kings often boasted of their ability to penetrate inaccessible areas: Sargon went up to mountain regions, and travelled over steep and terrifying paths (Luckenbill, *Records II*, p. 118); Sennacherib too went on horseback to high mountains, and when the terrain became steep he 'clambered up on foot like the wild-ox' (Luckenbill, *op. cit.*, p. 236); cf. also Ashurbanipal (Luckenbill, *op. cit.*, p. 823). **many chariots**: *RSV* here follows Q*erē*, MSS, Vsns. and Isa. 37:24 in reading **many. the far recesses of Lebanon**: Gray (pp. 689ff.), on the basis of Isa. 14:13–15, translates 'the utmost heights of Lebanon'. Both verbs **I felled** and **I entered** are correctly rendered by the past tense, following MSS and Vsns. **farthest retreat**: This is an attempt at rendering what stands literally in the Heb. 'farthest lodge'. Isa. 37:24 has 'its remotest height' (reading *merôm* for *melôn*).

24. The boast that he **dug wells** and **drank foreign waters** has a parallel in Ashurbanipal's account of how his soldiers after marching into distant lands 'dug for water to quench their thirst' (Luckenbill, *ibid.*). **all the streams of Egypt**: The Heb. has 'streams of a fortress' (*māṣôr*), which is rendered by the Vulg. as 'dammed rivers'. Most commentators and translators accept the reading 'streams of Egypt' (*miṣraim*), accepting that *māṣôr* was an intentional paronomasia on *miṣraim*, since Egypt was a fortified front against Asia (Montgomery, p. 504), or else reading the consonants of the Heb. as Missōr (cf. the Amarna tablets; see Burney, p. 346). Historically it is not correct, for Sennacherib did not conquer Egypt; but it can be readily accepted as presenting the typical exaggeration of Assyrian boasting. Because Tawil's attempt to defend the historicity of the reference by connecting it with Sennacherib's operations relating to his system of water supply in Mount Muṣri in the year 694 BC presupposes a later campaign against Jerusalem (*JNES* 41 [1982], pp. 195-206), it is not acceptable.

25. In his reply to Sennacherib's account of his accomplishments, God asserts that he himself has **determined it long ago**. Assyrian conquests were achieved because they were according to God's will and purpose, **planned from days of old**; cf. also the statement in Isa. 10:5 that Assyria was the rod of God's anger. MT's **heaps of ruins** may be rendered 'heaps of rubble' on the basis of the reading of 1QIsᵃ at Isa. 37:26; vf. *NEB*.

26. This verse contains the description of the Assyrian defeat of its enemies. **shorn of strength**: Literally 'short of hand', cf. Isa. 50:2. **blighted before it is grown**: The reading of 1QIsᵃ at Isa. 37:27 'blasted before the east wind' (cf. *NEB*) is an improvement of MT and only changes it slightly. It is interesting to note that the reading of 1QIsᵃ was proposed as an emendation by earlier commentators (cf. Thenius, pp. 409ff.; Kittel, p. 288; Skinner, p. 398). The image of grass withering before the wind occurs frequently in the OT; cf. Isa. 40:8; Ps. 102:4; and especially Ps. 129:6-8.

27. I know your sitting down: cf. Ps. 139:2, where sitting down is paralleled by 'rising up'. 1QIsᵃ adds 'your rising up' in Isa. 37:28. **and your raging against me**: Because these words are repeated in 'Because you have raged against me' in v. 28, they are usually left out of v. 27 as a dittograph (cf. Skinner, *ibid.*; Gray, p. 690; *BHS*). Stade, however, retains this line in v. 27, but omits its duplicate in v. 28, which is now confirmed by some MSS and 1QIsᵃ in Isa. 37:28-29.

28. I will put my hook in your nose: Although the idea may be connected with customs attached to the trapping of a wild beast, at which the animal was muzzled and led away with a hook in its nose (cf. Ezek. 19:4), in the present context it probably refers to an Assyrian practice to humiliate enemies (cf. Ezek. 38:4). Reference can be made to Esarhaddon's inscription at Senjirli on which Tirhakah of Egypt and Ballu of Tyre are bridled with a ring in the nose and led away by the conqueror (cited by Šanda II, p. 280; Montgomery, p. 496). **and I will turn you back on the way by which you came**: cf. v. 33.

29–31. These verses are addressed to Hezekiah, not Sennacherib as is the case in the preceding verses. They are not metrical in form (as proposed by Šanda II, pp. 280f.), although they are not without rhythm and parallelism of thought. Most probably we have here an original saying which has been expanded. The original saying referred to a sign that would be given and the application of its meaning (vv. 29–30); the 'remnant' concept connected with the sign is further expounded in v. 31 (cf. also Clements, *op. cit.*, pp. 286ff.). Although the saying in vv. 29–30 and its appendix in v. 31 contain characteristically Isaianic phraseology, Clements (*ibid.*) describes both as exegetical developments of Isaianic prophecies and attributes them to the years after 598 BC, but before 587 BC.

29. this shall be the sign for you: The sign (Heb. *'ôṯ*; cf. Isa. 7:11) was not necessarily a miraculous occurrence, but denotes a natural process that can be vested with symbolic meaning. In this particular case reference is made to the natural recovery of agriculture within a relatively short time following the devastation of the land by the Assyrian army; this is taken as a sign of the restoration of 'the remnant of the house of Judah'. Recovery is expected in the third year (cf. also Isa. 7:14; 20). For **this year** the people will be dependent on **what grows itself** (*NEB*. 'shed grain'), i.e. on grain growing from seed that had fallen the previous year from the ears of corn (cf. Lev. 25:5, 11, where *sāpîaḥ* denotes seed left undisturbed in the ground during the sabbatical year). **In the second year** they will live on **what springs of the same** (*NEB*, 'what is self-grown'); the term *sāḥîš* (*šāḥîs* in Isa. 37:30), unknown elsewhere, may denote what grows automatically in the second year (Montgomery. p. 497) or accidentally from seed that has fallen in waste places (Gray, p. 692). The third year sees a full recovery with sowing and reaping, planting vineyards and eating their fruit. Efforts have been made to apply this saying specifically to the Sennacherib invasion of 701 BC; it is implied that the Assyrians by remaining in the country from spring to autumn 701 BC prevented the harvest of that year, thus forcing the people to live on 'shed-grain', and also the autumn ploughing and sowing, which meant that there would be no harvest in 700 BC and that the people would have to live on 'what is self-grown'. Only in 699 BC would there be a full recovery (cf. Šanda II, pp. 280ff.; Skinner, p. 399). In view of our acceptance of the suggestion that this is a much later reflection on the 701 crisis and may have borrowed the concept of a three-year recovery from elsewhere, it is doubtful if an exact description of events was intended.

30. the surviving remnant of the house of Judah: The concept of a **surviving remnant** is characteristic of the collection of Isaianic prophecies. It is obvious, however, that the concept has been through various stages of development: (i) When Isaiah used the idea first in naming his son Shear-jashub during the Syro-Ephraimite crisis (7:3), he was announcing a message of assurance that opposing armies would be defeated by the Assyrians to the extent that only a remnant would be left. (ii) Accepting that the present text and its parallel in Isa. 37:30–32 give a later interpretation of the passing of the 701 crisis that originated from the period 598–587 BC, the 'remnant' is now applied specifically to **the house of Judah**. It had survived the onslaught of the Assyrians. (iii) After 587 BC the concept was applied to the exiles in Babylon, and several passages in the book of Isaiah reflect this further exegesis of the 'Shear-jashub' idea (Isa. 4:2–6; 6:13*c*; 10:20–23). See Clements, *Isaiah passim*; and for a full discussion of the concept, Hasel, *The Remnant*, especially pp. 330–9.

31. The statement that a **remnant** would recover is now suitably expanded by means of a complete parallelism, in which **a remnant** finds a parallel in **a band of survivors** and **Jerusalem** in **Mount Zion**. The final phrase, **The zeal of the LORD will do this**, is reminiscent of Isa. 9:6, where 'the LORD of hosts' is read. That is the reading here too according to the $Q^e r\bar{e}$, MSS and Vsns.; cf. also Isa. 37:32.

32. It is in vv. 32–34 that the reply to Hezekiah's prayer is given; it is probable that these verses followed v. 21 in the original account, before the oracles of vv. 22–31 were interpolated. In view of Sennacherib's account of how he 'surrounded him (Hezekiah) with earthwork' (*ANET*, p. 288), the assertion that the king of Assyria **shall not . . . come before it with a shield or cast up a siege mound against it** is somewhat exaggerated. On the other hand, because of the absence of any reference to the slaughter of Assyrian forces (as in v. 34), this later reflection on the events of 701 BC is relatively reliable.

33. The inserted oracle addressed to Sennacherib (vv. 22–28) has borrowed the basic content of this verse. The original oracle in vv. 32f. is concluded with the usual formula **thus says the LORD**. For a different view, making this verse a secondary addition, see Childs, *op. cit.*, pp. 75ff.

34. The author probably added this verse after the conclusion of the oracle reported in the previous two verses in order to emphasize the theological significance of its message. Two theological themes are underlined here: the inviolability of the city of Jerusalem, because of God's protection (**I will defend this city**), and God's special relationship with the Davidic dynasty (**for the sake of my servant David**).

35. that night the angel of the LORD went forth: The suggestion of a miraculous intervention compelling the Assyrians to retreat introduces at the very end of the B2 account an element that finds no place in the annals of Sennacherib nor in the B1 account of 18:17–19:9a, 36–37. Note has already been taken of the view that both accounts ran parallel before the addition of v. 35 to replace the original ending of account B2. Attempts have been made, however, to defend the historicity of v. 35, mainly because of the tradition that a plague forced the Assyrians to retreat. Herodotus (II.141) describes the sudden withdrawal of Sennacherib from Pelusium at the gates of Egypt because his camp was infested with a plague of mice which gnawed the leather on the weapons of his army. Although the possibility of such a plague outside the walls of Jerusalem has to be admitted (Gray, p. 694; von Soden, *Fest. Stier*, p. 45), the parallelism does not explain the death of a hundred and eighty-five thousand in the camp of the Assyrians. Moreover, the reliability of this tradition has been questioned (Baumgartner, *Aufsätze*, pp. 505–9; Montgomery, p. 498). A search for confirmation of this verse's historicity, suggesting a subsequent explanation of the occurrence as a natural catastrophe, is not necessary, according to Clements (*op. cit.*, pp. 287ff.). Rightly isolating v. 35 as a later addition, he proceeds to show that it is the result of later theological reflection on the statement in v. 34 that God was defending the city of Jerusalem. **the angel of the LORD** represents God's own activity on earth.

36. The first account of 18:17–19:9a is concluded with the simple statement that Sennacherib **departed, and went home, and dwelt at Nineveh**. Sennacherib's annals confirm this report in their reference to the payment of Hezekiah's indemnity directly to him at Nineveh (*ANET*, p. 288).

37. The tradition of Sennacherib's assassination by his two sons is not without some confirmation from extra-biblical sources. The evidence can be briefly summarized as follows (a) According to the annals of Ashburbanipal (*ANET*, p. 288), he was crushed by the statues of protective deities. (b) The Babylonian Chronicle (Rogers,

Parallels, p. 215) states that he 'was killed by his son'; this is confirmed by an inscription of Nabonidus, which refers to the assassin as 'the son, the issue of his inwards' (cf. 2 Chr. 32:21). See Montgomery, pp. 499. (c) Other documents refer to 'my brothers' as being responsible for his death (Luckenbill, *Records II*, pp. 500ff.; Meissner, *Preuss. Akad.*, pp. 252ff., the latter suggesting that the father and the son mentioned by Eusebius, *Chr.* 1.27.25–29 were brothers). For more details, cf. Montgomery, pp. 498–500. **he was worshipping in the house of Nisroch his god**: The identification of the god **Nisroch** and the location of Sennacherib's death present problems that have not been satisfactorily resolved. Gray (p. 695) identifies **Nisroch** with Nusku, who is mentioned in Assyrian inscriptions as an intermediary between the gods and men. His cult was known not only in Assyria but also in Harran (Dhorme, *Religions*, pp. 59, 111ff.; Cooke, *Inscriptions*, pp. 186–91). Others (such as Montgomery, p. 500) identify him with the Babylonian god Marduk, who had been moved to Ashur in 689 BC (Luckenbill, *op. cit.*, p. 712); possibly the name **Nisroch** (LXX, Esdrach, Asrach) is a shorter version of the compound name Ashur-Marduk (Lettinga, *VT* 7 [1957], pp. 105ff.). **Adrammelech and Sharezer**: Eusebius gives the names of the assassins as Adramelus and Nergilus, the former denoting **Adrammelech** and the other Nergal-sharezer (= **Sharezer**). See further, Montgomery, pp. 499f. **and escaped into the land of Ararat**: According to Assyrian records (*ANET*, p. 289) there was a civil war after Esarhaddon had come to power; he defeated his enemies and pursued them to Hanigalbat, which was in the direction of Urartu (= **Ararat**). **Esarhaddon his son**: He reigned from 681 to 668 BC. According to Ezr. 4:2, he brought alien elements into Israelite territory.

(c) Isaiah's intervention during Hezekiah's reign

20:1–21

The two incidents recorded in this section concentrate more on the prophet Isaiah than on king Hezekiah. In the first section (vv. 1–11) a brief notice of the king's illness is followed by the prophet's oracle (vv. 1–7) and the sign of a receding shadow (vv. 8–11). Similarly, the second section (vv. 12–19) opens with a report of envoys from Merodach-baladan visiting Jerusalem, and this is followed by Isaiah's intervention on that occasion (vv. 14–19). The last two verses in the chapter (vv. 20ff.) conclude Hezekiah's reign with the regular deuteronomistic formula. The account is repeated in Isa. 38–39, the most significant difference being the inclusion of a psalm of thanksgiving in Isa. 38:9–20.

The healing of Hezekiah (vv. 1–7) and the sign of the receding shadow (vv. 8–11) were probably independent traditions, which have been joined together by the composition of v. 8. The king's name is given as *ḥizqiyāhû* in vv. 1–7, 8, but as *yᵉḥizqiyāhû* in vv. 9–11 (cf. Šanda II, p. 311; Gray, p. 696). The two sections in their combined form give a narrative that belongs to the category of prophetic miracle-stories (cf. 2 Kg. 2:19–25; 4:1–44); possibly the second section was a popular prophetic legend that only secondarily became attached to Isaiah and the narrative about Hezekiah's sickness (so Clements, *Isaiah*, p. 289). The narrative portrays Hezekiah as a pious king (vv. 2, 5), and the restoration of his health is linked with the deliverance of the city 'out of the hand of the king of Assyria' and God's protection of the Davidic dynasty (v. 6).

Although the editorial link in v. 12 brings Merodach-baladan's envoys to Jerusalem on the occasion of Hezekiah's recovery from his illness, the visit is more probably to be connected with Hezekiah's anti-Assyrian activities. Merodach-baladan (Marduk-apla-Idinna), after a period of some years on the throne of Babylon (721–710 BC) had been expelled from the city, but after the death of Sargon in 705 BC he returned and had the support of the king of Elam and of Arab tribes. Merodach-baladan would naturally be willing to join and indeed to instigate rebellion against the Assyrian king, and the visit of his envoys to Jerusalem, which is not confirmed in extra-biblical sources, is to be understood against this background. Two features must be noted about the biblical account: (i) It has dated the visit of the envoys after the expedition of Sennacherib in 701 BC. Historically, however, this is impossible, and the visit has to be placed either during the anti-Assyrian activities of 713–711 BC, which came to an end with Sargon's expedition to Ashdod in 711 BC, or, more likely during the brief revival of Merodach-baladan's fortunes in 703–702 BC before he was finally expelled from Babylon. (ii) As seen from the reference in vv. 16–18 to carrying away the treasures of Jerusalem to Babylon, the events of 598 BC (but not of 587 BC, as rightly noted by Clements, *op. cit.*, p. 294) are presupposed. It must, therefore, be accepted that the narrative in vv. 12–19 was written after 598 BC and has dated an event that would be possible in 703 BC in an impossible period after 701 BC.

As shown by recent studies, the intention of the two narratives in chapter 20 can only be appreciated if they are taken in conjunction with 18:17–19:37 (see especially, Clements, *op. cit.*, pp. 277–97; *Deliverance of Jerusalem*, pp. 63ff.; Ackroyd, *SJTh* 27 [1974], pp. 329–52). Together they form a trilogy of 'Isaianic' narratives, which provide a series of theological reflections on the deliverance of Jeru-

salem from Sennacherib in 701 BC. The first theological reflection
on the event at which, according to the description of 18:13–16,
Hezekiah was forced to surrender, understands the deliverance of
the city of Jerusalem as an act of divine protection and as proof of
God's concern for the Davidic dynasty (see especially 19:34).
Clements places this retrospective theological understanding of the
event in the age of Josiah, when Assyrian influence in Judah was
weakening. Subsequent events, however, made it necessary to
modify this affirmation of God's protection of Jerusalem and of the
Davidic dynasty. The first was the death of Josiah at the hands of
Pharaoh Neco in 609 BC, which of course was a deep shock. At
this point was added the second narrative of the trilogy, namely,
Hezekiah's recovery from his illness, which is unquestionably
concerned with the theme of the protection of Jerusalem and of the
Davidic dynasty (20:6). It adds the qualification that it was an
exceptional protection granted to an exemplary king, and thus
depended on the fulfilment of certain conditions. Secondly, when
Jehoiachin surrendered to Babylon in 598 BC, which is reflected in
detail in 20:17–18, the confidence in Jerusalem's inviolability and
in the security of the Davidic dynasty engendered by the deliverance
of 701 BC was undermined. The third narrative in the trilogy,
therefore, makes it quite clear that Yahweh had determined as
far back as 701 BC that he would not protect Jerusalem from the
Babylonians as he had from the Assyrians (20:17–18). Because of
his success in connecting the whole of 18:17–20:19 with the historical report in 18:13–16, and in demonstrating the developing theologising of this trilogy of narratives, Clements has presented a
convincing analysis.

   1. **In those days**: This phrase does not give an exact dating, but
connects the narrative vaguely with what precedes. It is obvious
from v. 6 that the author intended this narrative to be connected
with the protection of Jerusalem during the crisis of 701 BC. The
introduction of Isaiah formally as **the prophet the son of Amoz** is
unnecessary after 18:17–19:37, and may be taken to indicate that
this section was an independent narrative. An intervention by a
prophet on such an occasion is by no means exceptional (cf. 1 Kg.
21:19, 21). **Set your house in order**: MT seemingly uses the verb
ṣiwwāh, 'to command, order'; but it is more likely that the verb is
used here and in 1 Kg. 2:1 like the Arab. waṣā, to denote 'making
a testament' (so Šanda II, p. 301). *NEB* has 'Give your last instructions'. Gray (p. 697) finds that this also called for the naming of a
successor, and suggests that the date was 695 BC, when Manasseh
was designated successor at the age of twelve. But in view of the
suggested interpretation of this narrative as a later reflection on the

protection of Jerusalem, it is precarious to take it as a basis for historical reconstruction. **for you shall die, you shall not recover**: Although the prophet presents this as the declared will of God, the king's prayer succeeds in changing God's will; thus the prophet announces a different verdict in v. 5. For a similar change of mind on God's part, see Am. 7:1–3, 4–6.

2. Hezekiah turned his face to the wall: Despite the more specific allusion in the Targ. 'to the wall of the Temple', the obvious meaning here is that he turned to the wall for private communion with God.

3. Hezekiah's prayer is exceptional in that he rehearses his merits before God with no suggestion whatsoever of penitence. According to Clements (*Isaiah*, p. 290), this is an intentional slant in order to bring out the author's emphasis on Hezekiah's piety and obedience. He had lived a perfect life, and had no need to repent of anything before coming to meet death. By emphasizing that the king's recovery was an exceptional act due to his exemplary life, the author makes the point that the deliverance of Jerusalem in 701 BC was also an exceptional act of divine protection; this qualifies the assurance of the previous narratives. Some of the expressions used in Hezekiah's prayer are found elsewhere in the books of Kings—**walked before thee in faithfulness, with a whole heart** and **done what is good in thy sight**; cf. 1 Kg. 2:4; 8:61; 11:38; 15:3, 14; but they have a different tone when they occur in the compiler's comment rather than in a quotation of the words of king Hezekiah himself.

4. before Isaiah had gone out of the middle court: These words are not found in Isa. 38:4. The $Q^e r\bar{e}$, **court** (*heḥāṣēr*), followed by MSS and Vsns., is preferred to the $K^e t\hat{\imath}\underline{b}$, 'the city' (*hā'îr*). The **middle court** is the same as 'the other court' of 1 Kg. 7:8; it was not in the Temple proper, but in the area between the Temple and the palace.

5. say to Hezekiah the prince of my people: The title **the prince of my people**, using the old title *nāgîd*, is omitted from Isa. 38:5. See on 1 Kg. 1:35. The title seems to have been used deliberately here because of the emphasis in this context on God's deliverance of Jerusalem for the sake of David. The title *nāgîd* suggests a parallelism between Hezekiah and David. **on the third day you shall go up to the house of the LORD**: The absence of this sentence from Isa. 38:5 has led to the suggestion that it is a secondary gloss (Šanda II, p. 302). But the presence of the latter half of the phrase in Isa. 38:22 confirms the priority of the present text. Presumably Hezekiah, because of his illness, had been barred from the Temple, but his immediate recovery means that he will be able to attend **on the third day**, the day after the morrow. The mention of **the third**

day here and in Hos. 6:2, and the occurrence of the same phrase in the Gospels with reference to the resurrection (Mt. 12:40; Mk 8:3; Lk. 13:32; 18:31), has naturally led to speculation concerning its significance. Even admitting that the third day may have a cultic background and has a loaded meaning in the context of agricultural cultic celebrations, in the present context the term can only denote a short interval, equivalent perhaps to 'soon' (Martin-Achard, *From Death to Life*, pp. 81ff.).

6. I will add fifteen years to your life: The figure has evidently been reached by calculating from the two dates given in 18:1–6; the first (18:2) ascribed to Hezekiah a reign of twenty-nine years, and the other (18:13) dated Sennacherib's campaigns in Hezekiah's fourteenth year. Although the latter is incorrect (see above, on 18:13), it has been accepted by the present narrator, who dated Hezekiah's illness at the time of Sennacherib's campaign and thus arrived at a figure of **fifteen**. It is a calculation based on previous data, and not a vague reference to the normal life of a man, as suggested by Gray (p. 698), nor a mistaken reading for 'ten years' as proposed by Šanda (II, p. 301), who argued for the placing of chapter 20 (referring to 704/3 BC) before 18:13ff. (covering the year 701 BC). **I will deliver you and this city out of the hand of the king of Assyria**: The author deliberately connects the recovery of the king with the deliverance of the city (Clements, *Deliverance of Jerusalem*, p. 65), and so the reference to the city is not to be deleted as a secondary addition from 19:34, as suggested by Montgomery (p. 597). The two significant points of 19:34 are repeated here, the inviolability of the city and God's care for the Davidic dynasty. However, the theological qualification proposed by the present narrative demands the association of these two factors with the healing of Hezekiah.

7. Bring a cake of figs: Isaiah's instructions follow Hezekiah's psalm of thanksgiving in Isa. 38. This difference of placing in Isa. 38 and its total omission from the account in 2 Chr. 32, have led Gray (*ibid.*) to suspect this verse and to describe it as an editorial gloss. He also argues that prescribing a cure for Hezekiah's ulcer was unnecessary after the promise of divine healing by the prophet in v. 6 (cf. also Montgomery, pp. 507ff.). But, as noted by Clements (*Isaiah*, p. 293ff.), the use of simple aids for healing is not contradictory to the belief that God was responsible for the recovery; the verse can be retained. Figs were used for the cure of ulcers (cf. Pliny, *Hist. Nat.* 23.7.122), and the word **cake** is used for 'plaster' in the Ras Shamra texts (Gordon, *Textbook* II, text 55 l.28; 56, l.33).

8. The sign of the receding shadow was probably only secondarily connected with Isaiah and the healing of Hezekiah. Although the request for a sign is not present in the version in Isa. 38, there is no need to take it as an editorial introduction, as proposed by Gray (*ibid.*). It was natural for the king, after receiving the oracle in v. 6 and seeing the prophet prescribing for his ulcer (v. 7), to ask for a sign (*'ôṯ*).

9. shall the shadow go forward ten steps, or go back ten steps?: MT reads the first half of the sentence as a statement and the second half as a question. But Hezekiah's reply in v. 10 implies that he had been given the choice of alternatives; most commentators and translators follow the Targ. and read an interrogative in both parts. The king was probably observing the sun's shadow stretching out in the late afternoon, and the sign to be given to him was connected with the movement of the shadow, either forwards or backwards.

10. It is an easy thing for the shadow to lengthen ten steps: It was natural (**an easy thing**; Heb. 'light') for the shadow to extend or go forward; as noted by Skinner (p. 402), a sign could only be derived from an acceleration of this natural process. Hezekiah, therefore, requested a contrary movement, **let the shadow go back ten steps**, which meant that he would receive a sign from a reversal of the natural process.

11. At Isaiah's request the shadow was then brought **back ten steps, by which the sun had declined.** *RSV* has added **the sun**, which is necessary because the feminine verb **had declined** cannot take the masculine **shadow** as its subject; thus the Syr., Targ. and Isa. 38:8 add **the sun** as a subject for the verb. **on the dial of Ahaz**: There is uncertainty about the meaning of the Heb. *ma'ᵃlôṯ*, which is translated **dial** here, although it is the word used also of 'steps': (i) To support the translation **dial** reference is made to the use of the dial in Babylon (Herodotus II.109); it is assumed that it was an innovation brought among many others from Assyria by Ahaz (Burney, pp. 349ff.; Montgomery, pp. 508ff.). If **dial** is accepted, it is more natural to translate *ma'ᵃlôṯ* elsewhere in these verses as 'degrees' instead of 'steps'. (ii) It is possible to take *ma'ᵃlôṯ* in this occurrence too as referring to steps and to translate as 'stairway'. This translation envisages the shadow falling on a flight of steps in the palace courtyard (Skinner, p. 403). (iii) 1QIsᵃ reads in Isa. 38:8 'the upper chamber of Ahaz' (reading *'ᵃlîyaṯ* for *ma'ᵃlôṯ*). On the basis of this reading it has been argued that Ahaz introduced a shrine for astral worship in the Temple precinct and probably erected it on a roof-top (Gray, p. 699, following Iwry, *BASOR* 147 [1957], pp. 27–33). But, as demonstrated by McKay (*Religion*, p. 10), the use of an upper chamber or roof altar does not of necessity indicate the worship of Assyrian astral deities. Assuming, therefore, that the word does not have to denote a **dial**, it is accepted that it refers to steps leading from a roof chamber (without necessarily implying

astral worship) or a balcony on which the late afternoon shadow
could be observed. The giving of a 'sign' ('*ôt*) to Hezekiah is probably to be understood in conjunction with such an incident as the
standing of the sun and the moon in Jos. 10:12–14. It is clearly
legendary in character, and any kernel of historical truth that may
have lain behind it has been distorted beyond recognition. Once
this definition of the narrative's character has been accepted, it
becomes unnecessary to take the '*ôt* as a natural phenomenon, as is
the case with some other 'signs', especially in the book of Isaiah
(7:11; 20:3ff.; 19:19–21). This approach has been attempted by
those who see in the incident an allusion to an eclipse of the sun on
11 January 689 BC, but this cannot be taken seriously. The exact
significance of the sign for Hezekiah is not stated; most probably,
what is denoted is that the fulfilment of the sign signifies God's
favour upon the king. It is easy to read too much into the incident
by finding an exact parallelism between the reversal of the shadow
on the stairs and the withdrawal of God's first oracle in v. 1 (as
suggested by Gray, p. 700).

12. **Merodach-baladan** is the usual spelling of the Heb. version
of the Babylonian Marduk-apal-Idinna (cf. MSS; Vsns.; Isa. 39:1),
and it is usually accepted here for MT's variant 'Berodach-baladan'
(Brinkman, *Fest. Oppenheim*, pp. 6ff.). His father's name, according
to the inscription of Tiglath-pileser, was Yakin (Luckenbill, *Records
I*, p. 794); he may have assumed **Baladan** as a patronymic to connect
with an earlier predecessor. **for he heard that Hezekiah had been
sick**: This links the third narrative of the trilogy with the account of
Hezekiah's sickness and so indirectly with the period of Jerusalem's
deliverance from Sennacherib. Merodach-baladan's envoys,
however, were not paying Hezekiah the courtesy visit suggested
here; they came to Jerusalem more probably to conduct negotiations
for an anti-Assyrian uprising. The visit must, therefore, be dated in
703 BC, before Merodach-baladan was finally overthrown by Assyria.

13. **Hezekiah welcomed them**: MT's 'listened to them' (using the
verb *yišma'*) has been changed to **welcomed them** (reading *yiśmaḥ*)
on the evidence of MSS, Vsns. and Isa. 39:2 (cf. *BHS*), and is a
more fitting introduction to the remainder of the verse. The account
of Hezekiah's welcome to the envoys, as a preparation for Isaiah's
oracle in vv. 16–17, emphasizes that he showed them all the treasures of Jerusalem. **his treasure house**: The Heb. *bēt nᵉkôt* is found
only here and in Isa. 39:2; it is usually thought to be equivalent
to the Akkad. *bīt nakkamāti*, 'treasure house' (cf. *K-B*; Cohen,
Hapaxlegomena, pp. 40, 113). The tradition of Hezekiah's wealth,
which is expanded in 2 Chr. 32:27ff., is confirmed by the inventory
in the Assyrian annals of the indemnity paid by him to Sennacherib

(*ANET*, p. 288). The inclusion of **spices** (also mentioned among the Queen of Sheba's gifts to Solomon, 1 Kg. 10:2, 10) and **precious oil** (or more correctly 'fragrant oil', *NEB*, or 'aromatic oil', reading the Heb. *ṭôḇ* as *ṭayḇ*, 'fragrant, sweet smelling'; cf. Akkad., Arab. and Ugaritic; Cohen, *op. cit.*, pp. 66ff.) suggests that good use had been made of trade with South Arabia. **His armoury** may have been the House of the Forest of Lebanon (cf. 1 Kg. 7:2ff.; Isa. 22:8; Skinner, p. 404). The list is concluded with the exaggerated claim that **there was nothing in his house or in all his realm that Hezekiah did not show them.**

14–15. Isaiah's courteous interview with Hezekiah merely establishes the position; it thus prepares the way for 'the word of the LORD' in v. 16.

17–18. Isaiah's prediction is twofold: (a) the treasures of the royal household (**all that is in your house**) will be taken to Babylon (v. 17); (b) some of the king's own dependents (taking **your own sons** to refer generally to descendants rather than more strictly the next generation) will be taken to **the palace of the king of Babylon.** Nowhere else in the prophecy of Isaiah is there a specific prediction of the Babylonian exile, and this narrative must be taken as a *post eventum* composition. The motives for tracing this prediction back to these particular circumstances are evidently theological. The fact that Jerusalem had been granted divine protection in 701 BC did not mean that the city was for ever inviolable; indeed in 701 BC it had been warned that things would not be the same under the Babylonians. The narrative, however, is to be dated after 598 BC, when the treasures of Jerusalem were taken to Babylon (see 2 Kg. 24:13) and king Jehoiachin became a prisoner there (2 Kg. 24:15); but this section is not aware of the more extensive exile of 587 BC. No reasons are given for the events of 598 BC. Isaiah himself does not pass judgment on Hezekiah, and there are no hints in the text to support the various proposed reasons for his prediction, such as Hezekiah's vanity and his pride in the treasures which he displayed (Skinner, p. 404), or his opposition to foreign alliances (Montgomery, p. 510), or even that it was bad policy to show the treasures to the Babylonian envoys because it led the Babylonians to covet them (Clements, *Isaiah*, p. 295). The author is merely concerned to make his point that Jerusalem did not enjoy protection from the Babylonians, and does not even hint at the reason why.

19. Hezekiah's initial response to the divine oracle was that of humble submission, **The word of the LORD which you have spoken is good.** By referring to it as **good** he does not mean that it is a 'favourable' oracle; he rather concedes that, even if adverse in its message, it is 'reliable'. The afterthought, **why not, if there will be**

peace and security in my days?, although absent from LXX and preserved in a slightly different form in Isa. 39:8, is not to be omitted. The meaning of the interrogative particle **why not?** (*hᵃlô'*), which is not in the Isaiah parallel, is problematic. Gray (p. 703) suggests that two different readings ('will not?' and 'if only') have been conflated, but understands the present reading as referring back to the king's initial response and meaning 'is it not so if . . .?'. The introduction of this second sentence does not intend to give the impression that the king was complacent and was not disturbed by the adverse oracle as long as all would be well during his own reign. He has to accept the oracle as a reliable message from God, but feels grateful that divine punishment has been postponed (cf. also 22:18ff.).

20–21. With the standard deuteronomistic formula this account of Hezekiah's reign is completed. To the usual reference to the king's **deeds** and **might**, there has been appended here the additional information that **he made the pool and the conduit and brought water into the city**; cf. also 2 Chr. 32:30; Sir. 48:17. Hezekiah was responsible for excavating the Siloam tunnel to bring the waters of the spring of Gihon on the east side of the city to the inner pool of Siloam. It appears that a conduit ran along the east side of Jerusalem's south-eastern hill from Gihon to Birket el-Hamra before the time of Hezekiah. It was an exposed canal that had been constructed for the purpose of irrigation, and was in use during the time of Ahaz (Isa. 7:3). Hezekiah, however, was more concerned with the defence of the city and dug a tunnel to bring the waters of Gihon to the west side of the Ophel. The so-called Siloam inscription, discovered on the wall of the tunnel, describes the engineering feat of its construction; the workmen had been digging from each end, and kept a record of how they eventually dug through and met with only a slight overlap, having constructed a tunnel of some 1200 cubits (*DOTT*, pp. 209–11; Ap-Thomas, *AOTS*, pp. 283ff.). The date of constructing the tunnel cannot be given precisely, some arguing that it had been completed before the crisis of 701 BC (*DOTT*, *ibid.*), and others, allowing for a longer project that could not have been completed during the hurried preparations before 701, date it later (Montgomery, p. 511). One estimate suggests a construction period of about nine months. (For other similar operations, see Montgomery, *ibid.*)

21. slept with his fathers: Further details about his burial are supplied in 2 Chr. 32:33 (Williamson, *Chronicles*, p. 388).

2.   THE REIGNS OF MANASSEH AND AMON
2 Kg. 21:1-26

Manasseh, whose reign of forty-five years (697–642 BC) was the longest in the history of the Davidic monarchy, and Amon, who was murdered in a conspiracy after a brief reign of two years (641–641 BC), are both severely condemned by the deuteronomistic historian. The fact that these two kings were placed between the most pious of kings, Hezekiah and Josiah, has coloured the presentation of their reigns. From the standpoint of the deuteronomistic historian, the exemplary reign of Josiah could only be portrayed in sharp contrast to whatever preceded it. Because of the desire to sharpen this contrast, the treatment of the reigns of Manasseh and Amon, especially the former, has to a large extent been distorted (Gray, p. 705; Dietrich, *Prophetie*, pp. 31ff.; Ackroyd, *Chronicler*, p. 45).

(a) Manasseh
21:1-18

Manasseh was king of Judah during the reign of Esarhaddon (681–669 BC) and Ashurbanipal (668–627 BC), when Assyrian domination reached a climax, as is demonstrated by the success of the latter in capturing the Egyptian city of No-Amon (Thebes). In the Assyrian annals Manasseh is described as a faithful vassal paying heavy tribute to Assyria (*ANET*, p. 294), helping Esarhaddon to build a new city in Phoenicia and supplying transport to convey building materials to Nineveh (*ANET*, p. 291; Wiseman, *Iraq* 20 [1958], pp. 1ff.). He also provided military and naval forces to assist Ashurbanipal in his campaign against Egypt (*ANET*, p. 294). Manasseh's vassalage is indeed well attested, and it may be that he was present at a gathering of vassals in 672 BC (Frankena, *OSt* 14 [1965], pp. 150–2). Nevertheless, within the terms of his vassalage, Manasseh was granted privileges by the Assyrian kings who were anxious to secure a peaceful relationship in Judah (Reviv, *WHJP*, p. 199).

Although the account of Manasseh's reign in Kings ignores entirely the implications of his relationship with Assyria, it has been argued that his religious policy reflects his submission to Assyria. In contrast to Hezekiah, whose purification of the cult has been interpreted as a step towards national independence, Manasseh's apostasy is thought by some to have been the result of Assyrian oppression (Weinfeld, *JNES* 23 [1964], pp. 202–12), although perhaps not the result of any direct enforcement by Assyria (so

Cogan, *Imperialism*, pp. 15ff.; but see now, Spieckermann, *Sargoni-denzeit*, pp. 227ff.). Moreover, it is possible that the reforms under-taken by Hezekiah and Josiah and the apostasy of the reigns of Manasseh and Amon reflect the conflict between two Judaean parties; one party wished to purify the cult, and had the support of prophets like Isaiah, Zephaniah and Jeremiah and the priests of the Jerusalem Temple, whilst the other sought reconciliation with the Assyrians and moved definitely towards a syncretistic culture with the support of members of the royal court and the priests of foreign gods (Smith, *Palestinian Parties*, pp. 15–16; Nielsen, *Jewish Studies I*, pp. 103–6).

The report in 2 Chr. 33:11–16 that Manasseh was taken prisoner to Babylon by an Assyrian commander, and then after his return to Jerusalem fortified parts of the city and strengthened the defences of Judaean cities, is not confirmed elsewhere. The emphasis of the narrative on Manasseh's repentance in Babylon raises the question of its authenticity, and it has been suggested that the Chronicler created the narrative to explain why Manasseh was permitted to rule for such a long time (Ehrlich, *ThZ* 21 [1965], pp. 281–6; Williamson, *Chronicles*, pp. 388–95). Other biblical texts give no indication that Manasseh repented (cf. 2 Kg. 23:12), and Assyrian annals do not know of his rebellion against either Esarhaddon or Ashurbanipal. It has been doubted too if Manasseh had been respon-sible for the strengthening of Jerusalem and other Judaean defences (Broshi, *IEJ* [1974], pp. 21–6). On the other hand it is clear from tablets found in Gezer that Assyrian captains were stationed in Judah at this time (Reviv, *WHJP*, p. 200), and it is possible that Manasseh did join one of the many uprisings against Assyria, the most likely being the rebellion of Shamash-shum-ukin against Ashurbanipal between 652 and 648 BC (Rudolph, *Chronikbücher*, pp. 316ff.; Oded, *IJH*, p. 455; Reviv, *ibid.*; Cogan, *op. cit.*, pp. 67ff.).

Ahlström (*Royal Administration*, pp. 75ff.), claiming that the bib-lical presentation of Manasseh as the promoter of foreign cults is misleading, finds that a closer analysis of 2 Chr. 33:14–17 provides a more realistic picture of the king. He recovered some of the territory lost by his father Hezekiah, and rebuilt and strengthened his defences. In order to incorporate these areas into his kingdom, he sent out troops and civil servants; he also sent out priests, and the high places in these areas became sanctuaries for the official religion of Judah. Manasseh's reorganization of the religious system to go hand in hand with territorial changes was not an attempt to introduce apostasy; the presentation of him as an apostate is rather the result of the deuteronomistic historian's personal view of his

cultic programme. Whether or not we accept Ahlström's novel interpretation and concede that the historian has given a completely
distorted picture of Manasseh, one thing is clear from an analysis
of the scheme in Kings: Manasseh is unfavourably evaluated as a
foil for the presentation of the narrator's ideal rulers, Hezekiah and
Josiah.

The deuteronomistic account in 2 Kg. 21:1-18 does not even
mention Assyria nor its rulers, but concentrates on Manasseh's cultic
aberrations. Within the standard deuteronomistic framework, with
its introductory (vv. 1-2) and concluding (vv. 17-18) formulae,
stands a report that is also thoroughly deuteronomistic. It cannot,
however, be attributed to a single narrator, because a detailed
analysis of its content betrays stages in the development of the
narrative. To he same basic material (DtrG) as the framework can
also be attributed the list of Manasseh's sins in vv. 3, 5-7a. The
list is specific in detail and mentions the worship of Baal, Asherah
and the host of heaven, with altars for the latter being built in the
two courts of the Temple. The sin is that of Manasseh, and in v. 3
he is compared to Ahab, king of Israel. The word against Judah
and Jerusalem in vv. 10-14 belongs to a later stage in the deuteronomistic tradition and because of its interest in prophecy must be
attributed to DtrP (Dietrich, *Prophetie*, p. 14). This prophetic
announcement, which is attributed to 'his servants the prophets'
and is directed against Manasseh, falls into the usual pattern of a
prophetic judgment speech, with an accusation ('because', ya'an
'*a*šer, v. 10) being followed by an announcement of judgment introduced with 'therefore thus says the LORD' and proceeding with
'Behold' (v. 12); see Westermann, *Forms*, pp. 148ff. At a later stage
in the tradition, the material was extended and an effort was made
to link it together to form a single narrative. The list of Manasseh's
sins in vv. 3, 5-7a is extended by the addition of vv. 4, 7b-9, which
refer in more general terms to Manasseh's altars, as is seen when v.
4 is compared with v. 5 and also in its deliberate shifting of the
emphasis from Manasseh's guilt to that of the whole people. Verses
15-16 also bring out the people's guilt. The fact that the former
adds a second accusation (with another ya'an '*a*šer) to the already
complete prophetic judgment saying indicates that it is an addition;
moreover, it modifies 'because Manasseh' in v. 11 to 'because they'.
The latter is an appendix to the list of sins in vv. 2-9, attached by
the use of 'moreover' (w*e*gam), giving a general reference to shedding
'innocent blood' and again emphasising the sin of Judah. Because
of the nomistic terminology of vv. 8f., this latter stage must be
attributed to DtrN (Dietrich, *op. cit.*, pp. 31ff.; cf. the analysis of
Hoffmann, *Reform* 155-63; Spieckermann, *op. cit.*, pp. 160ff.).

1. Manasseh was twelve years old when he began to reign: Manasseh's reign is reckoned to have extended from 697 to 642 BC, some assuming unnecessarily that in his early years he acted as co-regent (Gray, p. 706). His name, which appears as Menasi sar Iaudi or Minse sa Iaudi in the Assyrian annals, means 'he causes to forget', and may denote consolation for the loss of an earlier child (Noth, *Personennamen*, p. 222).

2. In passing judgment on Manasseh as an evil king, use is made of a typically deuteronomistic assertion that he followed **the abominable practices of the nations whom the LORD drove out before the people of Israel**, cf. Dt. 18:9; 1 Kg. 14:24; 2 Kg. 16:3, where the phrase 'abomination of the nations' clearly refers to idolatry. The term 'abominations' occurs again in the prophetic announcement of vv. 10–14, where it is the primary reason for the judgment that comes as punishment for Manasseh's sin.

3. The list of Manasseh's aberrations in vv. 3, 5–7a has been taken as an unmistakable proof that he introduced Assyrian cults into the Temple, and more especially Assyrian astral worship, which is designated by the term 'the host of heaven' (cf. v. 5). It has been assumed that Assyrian cultic practices were imposed on him because of his vassal status by his Assyrian overlords (cf. Östreicher, *Grundgesetz*, pp. 9ff.). But in view of the recent contention that Assyria did not suppress local cults by imposing Assyrian practices on their subjects (Cogan, *Imperialism*, pp. 15ff.) and the tendency to give the heathen practices of Judah, like those of its sister kingdom Israel, a Phoenician or Canaanite origin (cf. McKay, *Religion*), it seems more reasonable to accept that the age of Manasseh saw the resurgence of old Canaanite and Phoenician cults, and that possibly in the period of Assyrian domination some elements found special favour because of their predominance in Assyrian religion (McKay, *op. cit.*, p. 59). For **the high places which Hezekiah his father had destroyed**, see 18:4, and also on 16:4, where it is stated that **the high places** had become centres for the practice of Canaanite fertility rites. When Manasseh **erected altars for Baal** he was taking Judah back into a period of apostasy associated with the Canaanite deity well known from the Ras Shamra texts; there is no need to suppose that the use of the name Baal hides a reference to an Assyrian deity, although it is obvious from 1 Kg. 16:31–32 that for a time the name was applied to the Tyrian high-god Melqart. **and made an Asherah**: The cult of the mother-goddess had been introduced to Samaria when Ahab married Jezebel (1 Kg. 16:32–33; 18:19), and probably remained there until the fall of the Northern Kingdom (Patai, *JNES* 24 [1965], pp. 37–52). But very little is known of the Asherah cult in Jerusalem until the reign of Manasseh;

from a consideration of v. 7 below, it is likely that what was introduced by Manasseh at this point was the cult of the Phoenician
goddess and not the cult of the Assyrian Ishtar. The comparison
with Israel, conveyed in the words **as Ahab king of Israel had
done**, supports this conclusion. But, although Manasseh's sins
corresponded in many respects to those of Ahab, it has to be realized
that, whereas Ahab instituted an official central Phoenician cult in
Samaria, Manasseh introduced the cult in a more local and popular
form (cf. McKay, *op. cit.*, p. 91). Haran (*Temples*, p. 288) defines
Manasseh's sins as setting up vessels for Baal and Asherah in the
outer sanctuary, introducing the image of Asherah into the inner
sanctuary and removing the ark and cherubim. The final clause of
this verse, with its claim that Manasseh **worshipped all the host of
heaven and served them**, has the support of frequent references to
the same form of apostasy in Deuteronomy (4:19; 17:3, etc.) and
in the books of Zephaniah (1:5) and Jeremiah (8:2; 19:13). It is
Manasseh's worship of **the host of heaven** that has given rise to the
interpretation of his apostasy as betraying Assyrian influence, for it
has been claimed that **the host of heaven** refers to astral deities
derived from Assyria. McKay (*op. cit.*, pp. 45–59) in his study of
astral beliefs maintains that Israel's astral cults stood closer to the
cults of her immediate neighbours than to Mesopotamian religion,
and so places such a belief in a Canaanite-Phoenician milieu. He
further finds close links with Arabian astral religions (*op. cit.*, pp.
23ff.), proposing that Manasseh's wife was an Arabian woman and
that as a result of their marriage the cult of the Arabian astral god
Al-'Uzzā was introduced to Jerusalem. Nevertheless, it cannot be
denied that references to the worship of the host of heaven and of
the Queen of Heaven (Jer. 7:17–18; 44:16–19) belong to the
Assyrian period. Although the term **host of heaven** probably
denotes the heavenly court, and not specifically the heavenly bodies,
there can be little doubt that in this period of Assyrian domination
and influence Manasseh introduced Assyrian astral deities into
membership of the Israelite heavenly court. During this period of
apostasy there was, in addition to the resurgence of Canaanite and
Phoenician cults, an introduction of foreign cults from Assyria,
which may have come via the Aramaeans of Syria (Cogan, *Imperialism*, pp. 84–8).

4. This verse contains material that is found also in vv. 5 and 7*b*.
The view taken here is that together with vv. 7*b*–9 it belongs to a
later (nomistic) redaction. The statement in v. 5 that Manasseh 'built
altars for all the host of heaven' in the Temple defines specifically the
nature of his sin, whereas this verse is inexact in its assertion that
he built altars in the house of the LORD (Dietrich, *op. cit.*, pp.

31f.). By inserting this generalisation at this point, the redactor attempts to bind more closely his extension in vv. 7b–9 to the original list of Manasseh's sins. The homiletic nature of the verse (Montgomery, p. 519) and its grammatical construction (using the perfect with a conjunction, when the meaning is not frequentative; Gray, p. 705) are further indications that it is a later addition.

5. in the two courts of the house of the LORD: Because the specifications for the construction of the Temple in 1 Kg. 6ff. do not refer to two courts, this verse has been regarded as an interpolation (Skinner, p. 407; Gray, p. 707). The explanation given for its presence here is that the plan of the Second Temple, as is evident from Ezekiel's specifications, had an inner and outer court (Ezek. 40:19ff.), and that this latter plan has influenced the present interpolation. Another possible explanation is that the palace court, referred to as 'the middle court' in 20:4, because it was so close to the Temple, was virtually regarded as part of the Temple complex. This latter interpretation is preferred, and the verse is retained as part of the original account (Dietrich, *ibid.*; McKay, *op. cit.*, p. 98).

6. he burned his son as an offering: See on 2 Kg. 16:3. **he practiced soothsaying and augury**: *NEB*, 'soothsaying and divination'. Because of the possible connection between '*ōnēn*, 'to practise soothsaying', and '*ānān*, 'cloud', it is usually assumed that the word refers to soothsaying by observing the clouds (so Dhorme, *L'évolution*, pp. 229ff.), although other connections have been suggested (Gray, *ibid.*). For the word *niḥēš*, translated here **augury**, see on 17:17. **he dealt with mediums and wizards**: or 'with ghosts and spirits'. It is difficult to make a distinction between the two Heb. words used here for necromancy. Both '*ōb* and *yiddeʿōnîm* are found in connection with the appearance of the witch of Endor (1 Sam. 28:3ff.). Probably these words referred initially to ghosts and spirits, and secondarily came to denote their mediums. As noted by McKay (pp. 118ff.) these practices were widespread in the ancient Near East and were known in Israel before the Assyrian period.

7. the graven image of Asherah: The significance of this unique phrase has been variously interpreted. According to one suggestion it has been used here because reference is made to the Assyrian Ishtar and not the Canaanite Asherah. McKay (*op. cit.*, p. 23) thinks that the name represents an imported Phoenician goddess, and that the symbol used was different in appearance to the usual one for the Judaean mother-goddess. The fact that an image of the goddess was set up in the Temple was so objectionable to the Chronicler that he changed the phrase to 'the image of the idol' (2 Chr. 33:7). The basic account may have ended with the statement that Manasseh set the image 'in the house of the LORD'. When this account was extended, the redactor by inserting 'which' before the reference to the house managed to introduce a repetition of 'I will put my name' from v. 4, and thus linked vv. 7b–9 closely with the preceding verses. In reflecting upon the sins of Manasseh, it is implied that he was responsible for: (i) the fact that God's name was not in his Temple; (ii) the wandering of Israel from her land; (iii) the seduction of the people to incomparable evil.

8. if only they will be careful to do according to all that I have commanded them, and according to all the law that my servant Moses commanded them: These typical deuteronomistic phrases (Weinfeld, *Deuteronomy*, p. 336), with their emphasis on obedience to the commandments and to the law of Moses, designate this section as the work of the nomistic redactor (DtrN).

9. This verse combines Manasseh's own evil with the disobedience of the people who **did not listen. to do more evil**: The Gk. adds 'in the eyes of the LORD' as in vv. 2, 15.

10. As noted above, the prophetic condemnation of vv. 10–14 is not attributed to an individual prophet, but more generally to his servants the prophets.

11. The prophetic oracle is connected naturally with v. 2 by means of the word **abominations** (*tōʿēbōt*; cf. v. 2 'abominable practices'), and of the reference to Manasseh's sins being **more wicked than all that the Amorites did, who were before him**; cf. v. 2, 'the nations whom the LORD drove out before the people of Israel'. Obviously this prophecy is closely related to its fulfilment in 597 BC, for Nebuchadrezzar came against Jehoiakim 'according to the word of the LORD which he spoke by his servants the prophets' (2 Kg. 24:2). The statement of this verse that Manasseh **made Judah also to sin with his idols** provides another link with the Exile of 597 BC, for, according to 2 Kg. 24:3, 'this came upon Judah'. Both 21:11 and 24:3 stand in contrast to the oracle of Huldah in 2 Kg. 22:15ff., where punishment seems to be directed against Jerusalem, 'upon this place and upon its inhabitants'. Whereas Huldah's oracle has been influenced by the destruction of Jerusalem in 587 BC, the oracle in this verse has obviously been influenced by the Babylonian attack on Judah and Jerusalem in 597 BC.

12. Although the two formulae **therefore thus says the LORD, the God of Israel and Behold, I am bringing . . . evil** appear typical of prophetic utterances in general, there are grounds for establishing a very close relationship between this verse and the forms found in the book of Jeremiah (as established by Dietrich, *op. cit.*, pp. 70ff.). The use of the phrase **the God of Israel** in the first formula is typical of the book of Jeremiah, where the phrase occurs some 32 times. Likewise, the phrase **bringing . . . evil** occurs most frequently in the book of Jeremiah. **the ears of every one who hears of it will tingle**: Two parallel examples are found in Jer. 19:3 and I Sam. 3:11; since the Jeremianic passage (vv. 2b-9, 12) is a deuteronomistic interpolation, Dietrich (*op. cit.*, pp. 87ff.) is of the opinion that the prophetic redactor has borrowed it from I Sam. 3:11, but has replaced 'a thing' with **such evil**.

13. Stretching **the measuring line of Samaria and the plummet of the house of Ahab** over Jerusalem refers in the present context to its destruction. Admittedly the image is used elsewhere to refer to rebuilding or redistribution of the land (cf. Isa. 44:13; Zech. 1:16), as well as to destruction (cf. Isa. 34:11; Am. 7:8). For the combination of **measuring line** and **plummet**, the prophetic redactor is probably indebted to Isa. 28:17 (cf. Dietrich, *op. cit.*, p. 80). **I will wipe Jerusalem as one wipes a dish**: There is no evidence that this image has been borrowed from any other source. But, there can be no doubt regarding its meaning; it refers unmistakably to the punishment of Jerusalem, which will be wiped clean and turned upside down.

14. **I will cast off the remnant of my heritage**: The nearest parallel to this sentence is found in Jer. 12:7, 'I have abandoned my heritage'. In borrowing the sentence the prophetic redactor has only added **the remnant** to it; the reason for this addition was the Exile of 587 BC, for compared with the previous one of 597 BC this second exile could be described as a casting off of **the remnant** (Dietrich, *op. cit.*, pp. 74f.). It has also been claimed that the next sentence, **and give them into the hand of their enemies**, has been derived by this redactor from basic deuteronomistic material (DtrG; cf. Dt. 1:27; Jos. 7:7; Jg. 2:14; 6:1; 13:1; 2 Kg. 13:3; 17:20), which in turn had borrowed from Jeremianic thinking the application of the old holy war concept of Yahweh giving their enemies into the hands of Israel to the different situation where Yahweh gives Israel into the hands of her enemies (Dietrich, *op. cit.*, pp. 91ff.). **they shall become a prey and a spoil**: cf. Jer. 30:16; Isa. 42:22, with the present version being nearer to the form in Deutero-Isaiah (Dietrich, *op. cit.*, p. 79).

15. With the introductory **because** (*ya'an 'ašer*) this verse presents another reason for the announcement of punishment (vv. 12-14) in addition to the one already given in v. 11. This appendix to vv. 10-14 is connected to the preceding verses by the repetition of **done what is evil in my sight and have provoked me to anger** from v. 6, and is intended to emphasize that God's punishment has been occasioned not simply by the sins of Manasseh, but also because the whole people is guilty, **they have done what is evil**. This is

forcefully brought out by the use of the phrase **since the day their fathers came out of Egypt**. Dietrich (*op. cit.*, pp. 30ff.) labels this addition as a nomistic one (DtrN).

16. This verse again is from a later redactor: it is joined to the preceding by means of **Moreover** (Labuschagne, *Fest. Vriezen*, pp. 193–203). It again makes the point that Manasseh made **Judah to sin so that they did what was evil**; although its claim that **Manasseh shed very much innocent blood** appears to be specifying a particular sin, it is really very brief and unspecific, and belongs to the more general observations of the nomistic redactor (vv. 4, 7*b*–9; Dietrich, *op. cit.*, p. 30). The same point is made in 2 Kg. 24:4. Attempts to find a concrete situation behind the reference to shedding **innocent blood** by referring it to Manasseh's response when his pro-Assyrian policy was opposed (Reviv, *WHJP*, p. 199), or to child-sacrifice (Gray, p. 709) or to the slaughter of prophets (cf. Heb. 11:37), are difficult to substantiate; it is more feasible to take it as a general statement referring to domestic upheavals during his reign (Oded, *IJH*, p. 452).

17–18. The regular formula for concluding a reign has in the case of Manasseh the interesting note that he was **buried in the garden of his house, in the garden of Uzza**. Older commentators (Skinner, pp. 409ff.; Burney, p. 355) took **Uzza** to be a contraction of Uzziah, and suggested that, because there was no longer room in the royal necropolis, both Manasseh and Amon (v. 26) were buried in an extension to it that had been laid out in the palace court by Uzziah. Evidence that the royal necropolis was becoming full is found in the note in 2 Chr. 32:33 that Hezekiah was buried 'in the ascent of the sepulchres of the sons of David'. This explanation of Uzza as a contraction of Uzziah was abandoned after it was established that Uzza was an Arabic name for a deity. Al-'Uzzā was an astral deity usually identified with Venus (Gray, *JNES* 8 [1949], p. 80), and in view of the fact that Manasseh and Amon revived or introduced the worship of astral deities, and that possibly Manasseh's wife was an Arabian (McKay, *op. cit.*, pp. 24ff.), it has been suggested that **the garden of Uzza** (or 'enclosure of Uzza'; Gray, p. 709) was a precinct dedicated to this foreign deity. This is possibly the reason why the Chronicler deliberately omitted reference to **the garden of Uzza**, although he is usually precise and reliable in his notices of royal burials (Yeivin, *JNES* 7 [1948], pp. 30–45). If the burial ground of these apostates was **in the garden of his house** (although Luc. omits this phrase), it can be understood why the proximity of 'the dead bodies of the kings' (or 'the monuments of the kings') to the Temple was regarded by Ezekiel as a defilement of God's name (Ezek. 43:6–9).

(b) Amon
21:19–26

Amon's reign lasted for only a brief period of two years (641–640 BC) because of his assassination by conspirators. The account in these verses offers no reason for such a conspiracy (see below, on v. 23), nor again for the decision of 'the people of the land' to kill the conspirators (see below, on v. 24). Such omissions from the report, which are largely due to the deuteronomistic historian's sole aim of establishing that Amon fell into the same religious and cultic aberrations as his father (vv. 20–22), have led to speculation about the political and religious factions within the Judaean community at this time.

19. The information about Amon's mother, **Meshullemeth, the daughter of Haruz of Jotbah**, has aroused considerable interest because of its suggested Arabian associations. **Jotbah** appears from Num. 33:33 to have been two stages from Ezion-geber on Israel's sojourn in the wilderness, and is usually identified with *at-Taba* about twenty miles north of Aqaba (McKay, *op. cit.*, p. 24; Gray, p. 711). **Haruz** appears as a proper name in inscriptions from Sinai and Kihyani, although it is usually known in Philistia (Montgomery, pp. 521ff.). **Meshullemeth** is derived from the root *šlm*, which is frequently found in the formation of Arabian proper names (McKay, *op. cit.*, pp. 24, 95). The natural conclusion to be drawn from this evidence is that Amon's mother was an Arabian woman; the absence of her name from the Chronicler's account may be taken as confirmation of this (Mckay, *ibid.*).

20–22. The language is thoroughly deuteronomistic, and the content only states that Amon was totally devoted to following Manasseh in all his sins.

23. the servants of Amon conspired against him: Despite the placing of this verse immediately after a description of Amon's religious apostasy, the suggestion of a religious motive for his assassination by factions faithful to Israel's traditions is unrealistic (Oded, *IJH*, p. 456). There was more behind the murder than religious and cultic factors. Usually a deeper political unrest is found to be the cause; more specifically there was opposition to the pro-Assyrian policy of Amon, who was now following in the steps of his father. As for the general background, it has to be realised that the Assyrian Empire was now declining; on the one hand, Egypt was reviving and probably trying to assert its influence in Palestine (Gray, p. 712, following Nicolsky, *ZAW* 45 [1927], p. 184), and on the other hand, the Chaldaeans were ascending in power, and Ashburbanipal had to suppress a revolt by Elam in 642–639 BC. Whether Amon's retainers were influenced by Egyptian agents to remove the pro-Assyrian Amon, or were representing an emerging pro-Egyptian party in opposition to the pro-Assyrian policy of the king, remains unclear. It is not unlikely that some felt, in view of the rising power of Elam and Egypt, that the time was ripe for striking a blow against Assyria, and that the move was taken by court members who were in favour of alliance with Egypt. The action of 'the people of the land' (v. 24) placated the Assyrians, and there is no record of an expedition by Ashburbanipal against Judah (Malamat, *IEJ* 3 [1953], pp. 26–9).

24. The people of the land reacted against Amon's retainers, murdered them and placed the king's eight-year-old son, Josiah, on the throne. For a discussion of **the people of the land**, see above, on 2 Kg. 11:14; the general conclusion that this group represented a political element which showed loyalty to the house of David and to the hereditary principle can be affirmed by reference to the present instance, for after killing the conspirators the group made Josiah his son king in his stead. Whereas assassinations in many instances led to the overthrow of dynasties in Israel, it seems that in Judah there was an influential group that secured stability in dynastic succession (Oded, *IJH*, pp. 456ff.). This group acted quickly to secure the throne for Josiah the son of Amon, as it had acted before to secure it for Joash, the son of Ahaziah.

26. he was buried in his tomb in the garden of Uzza: See on v. 18 above.

3. JOSIAH AND THE DEUTERONOMIC REFORMATION
2 Kg. 22:1–23:30

Between the opening and closing deuteronomistic formulae (22:1–2; 23:28–30) for the reign of Josiah there stands an account of the discovery of 'the book of the law' in the Temple and the Josianic reform that followed. The report begins with a note of repair work in the Temple in the 'eighteenth year of King Josiah', during which the law book was discovered; it was handed over by Hilkiah the high priest to Shaphan the secretary, who read it to the king; the king was disturbed and decided to consult the Lord (22:3–13). The deputation that went to Huldah the prophetess received a twofold message: firstly, a proclamation of punishment upon Jerusalem, and to follow, a promise that Josiah himself would not see the evil that was to be brought upon the city (22:14–20). After reading the law book to an assembly of the people, Josiah made a covenant to obey the words written in the book and was joined by all the people (23:1–3). The so-called 'Josianic reform' followed: the Jerusalem

Temple was purified, priests were deposed from local sanctuaries
and their high-places were defiled, the altar at Bethel and the shrines
of the cities of Samaria were destroyed, the Passover was kept and
all abominations were removed from Judah and Jerusalem
(23:4–25). For a more detailed analysis, see Hoffmann, *Reform*, pp.
169–270; Spieckermann, *Sargonidenzeit*, pp. 41–170.

The two chapters devoted to Josiah appear to give a coherent
account of his activities and have been called a unified short story
constructed with care to explain the period 601–587 BC (Lohfink,
ZAW 90 [1978], pp. 319–47).

But the existence of a different version in 2 Chr. 34–35 brings
the reliability of the tradition in Kings into question. A different
sequence of events is given by the Chronicler; he dates the beginning
of Josiah's purification of the cult in Judah, Jerusalem and as far as
Naphtali in his twelfth year, six years before the discovery of the
law book (34:3–6). Following this purge, the law book was
discovered and the king sent a deputation to Huldah the prophetess;
in these details the Chronicler's account agrees with that in Kings.
Because the reform has been placed before the discovery of the
law book, the Chronicler confines Josiah's actions consequent upon
reading the law book to making a covenant and celebrating the
Passover; in this he is at variance with the account in Kings. Scholars
are far from agreement in deciding whether Josiah's reform was the
result of discovering the book, accepting the account of Kings, or
whether the discovery of the book followed the reform, giving
priority to the Chronicler. If an inseparable connection between the
newly discovered book of law and the consequent reforms of Josiah
is accepted, the report of Kings is naturally regarded as the more
reliable. In favour of the Kings report, it can be said that much of
the account has the flavour of a record derived from annals
(especially 22:3–23:3, as noted by Noth, *USt*, p. 92), and that,
because the Chronicler was dependent on Kings and did not have
any other source at his disposal, a rearrangement of the sequence
of the events was the Chronicler's own work (Williamson, *Chronicles*, pp. 397ff.). According to Mosis (*Untersuchungen*, pp. 195ff.),
the Chronicler was anxious to show that Josiah acted as soon as
possible to purify the cult, and so deliberately dated the reforms in
the king's twelfth year, which was the year of his majority; thus
priority is given to Kings (Mayes, *Deuteronomy*, p. 88).

Despite these arguments, a stronger case can be presented for
following the sequence of events suggested by the Chronicler. Östreicher (in his *Grundgesetz*), interpreting Josiah's reform as a bid for
independence from Assyria, finds the Chronicler's dating of the
reform in the twelfth year of Josiah reliable, for he takes it to be

the year of Ashurbanipal's death and thus the first opportunity for Josiah to take such action. Jerusalem was purged of Assyrian cults in 627 BC, and in 621 BC, when there were further disturbances in Nineveh, and with the incentive of a newly discovered law book, the reform was continued throughout Judah. The schematised account in Kings makes the law book of primary importance as the only incentive for the reform. A two-stage reform based on the sequence of events suggested by Chronicles is therefore accepted (Nicholson, *Deuteronomy*, pp. 12ff.; Oded, *IJH*, pp. 462ff.; Reviv, *WHJP*, pp. 201ff.); the first stage, possibly in 627 BC, and connected with a resurgence of nationalism and a drive for independence, saw the removal of foreign cults from Judah and Jerusalem; the second stage, following the discovery of the law book in 621 BC, was mainly, but not exclusively, aimed at purifying the Yahweh cult.

Various other considerations seem to confirm this conclusion: (i) The reference to Temple repairs in 2 Kg. 22:3–7 may be an allusion to the removal of cult emblems from the Jerusalem Temple before the discovery of the law book; if so, it provides a hint that the sequence of events accepted by the Chronicler was not unknown to the narrator of 2 Kg. 22–23 (Rowley, *From Moses*, p. 196). (ii) An anti-Assyrian party, which had been responsible for the death of Amon, was ready to take advantage of the first opportunity to break away from Assyria (Nicholson, *op. cit.*, p. 11; Malamat, *IEJ* 3 [1953], pp. 26–9), and so the political incentive was an important factor (Cross and Freedman, *JNES* 12 [1953], pp. 56–8). (iii) A closer analysis of the text shows that the account of the reform in 2 Kg. 23:4–20 makes no reference whatsoever to the law book, and that only its setting in its present context suggests its dependence on that book (Mayes, *op. cit.*, pp. 88ff.). Furthermore, an analysis of the narrative recording the discovery of the law book shows that it is a well-ordered entity of four parts constituting a covenant renewal ceremony (repentance, 22:3–11; oracle of salvation, 22:12–20; covenant renewal, 23:1–3; festival, 23:21–23. See further, Lohfink, *Bib* 44 [1963], pp. 261–88, 461–98; cf. the analysis of Hoffmann, *ibid.*, and Spieckermann, *ibid.*).

The Chronistic sequence of events, together with a consequential reassessment of the importance of the law book, is accepted as a basis for the analysis given below of chapters 22–23. Two strands of tradition have to be separated: (a) Narrative A relates how Josiah initiated a programme of minor works on the Jerusalem Temple, which constituted the first stage of his reform. After the discovery of a law book in the Temple he consulted Huldah the prophetess, read the book to an assembly of the people and made a covenant with God (22:3–2:3; see section (i) below). (b) Narrative B gives an account of Josiah's reforms without any reference to the law book (23:4–20). The difference between the two narratives, with the former being designated as a historical narrative compiled by the deuteronomist, and the latter being mostly material based on the annals of Judah (so Gray, pp. 714ff., following Östreicher, *ibid.*), will be discussed below.

The separation of the strands, with the implication that the law book was not the main incentive for the reform and also the designation of narrative A as a deuteronomistic 'historical narrative', raises the question of the historicity of the law book. An older view that has not gained much recent support is that the book of the law was prepared immediately before the reform by the Jerusalem priests, who fraudulently passed it on as a new discovery to the king through Hilkiah and his fellow priests (for a rejection of this view, see Rowley, *op. cit.*, pp. 195ff.; Nicholson, *op. cit.*, pp. 16ff.). Doubts concerning the historicity of the law book have appeared in another guise in the literary analysis that separates pre-deuteronomistic from deuteronomistic material, finds no reference to the law book in the pre-deuteronomistic tradition, and proposes that the deuteronomist added the reference to the book of law to provide a basis for Josiah's piety and to bring out an effective contrast between him and his predecessors, Manasseh and Amon (Mayes, *op. cit.*, pp. 100ff.). This recent proposal is open to the same basic objections as its earlier version: a fictitious account would be expected to make it clearer that the author was basing Josiah's reform on the book of Deuteronomy, and it is obvious that some aspects of the Josianic reform are unintelligible without reference to Deuteronomy (cf. 2 Kg. 23:9 with Dt. 18:6–8). It is, therefore, accepted that the second phase of Josiah's reforms in 621 BC did receive an impetus from the law book. (For a recent defence of the view that the finding of the law-book, the covenant and reform belong together logically and historically, see Spieckermann, *op. cit.*, pp. 153ff.)

An attempt can be made to reconstruct the sequence of events as follows: accepting that Deuteronomy was the product of a northern circle, presumably of prophets (Nicholson, *op. cit.*, pp. 58ff.), who, after fleeing to Judah when Samaria fell in 722 BC, drew up a programme of reform, it may be suggested that the reform envisaged was initially intended for the northern kingdom, with Shechem as the central sanctuary (Rowley, *op. cit.*, p. 198). By the time of Manasseh the deuteronomistic programme had been revised, with Jerusalem taking the place of Shechem. Undoubtedly, the Jerusalem cultic tradition contributed substantially to the concept of centralisation put forward in Deuteronomy (Nicholson, *op. cit.*, p. 95;

Clements, *VT* 15 [1965], pp. 300–12). Deuteronomy, on the other hand, made its contribution to the Jerusalemite tradition by giving it a basis in the law of Moses (Nicholson, *VT* 13 [1963], pp. 380–9). During the reign of Manasseh the supporters of the deuteronomistic reform programme waited patiently for an opportunity to sponsor a movement similar to that initiated earlier by Hezekiah. Neither the proposal that the book was a deposit of the reform and that the tradition of finding it was later imposed on the narrative (Mayes, *op. cit.*, pp. 100ff.), nor the suggestion that it was deposited in the Temple by the reformers in the hope that it would be discovered there (Nicholson, *Deuteronomy*, p. 102; cf. Lindblom, *Tempelur-kunde*, pp. 42ff., where it is ascribed to Levites who hid it in the Temple), is entirely satisfactory. The connection of the law book with the reform can be accepted without necessarily ascribing to the reliability of the tradition about its discovery in the Temple. It is proposed that these northern authors, when they realized that Josiah was intent on taking further action in 622 BC (possibly when Assyria was losing control of Babylon; Cross and Freedman, *op. cit.*, p. 56), decided, with the help of the Jerusalem priests, to press upon the king the advantage of their reform document as a confirmation and legitimisation of his programme.

Acceptance of the monarchy, even if reluctant (Dt. 17:14ff.), and the emphasis on centralisation, would give support to the national-istic aspirations of Josiah's moves to rid Judah of Assyrian domina-tion. Josiah accepted the programme. Because he did so, the deut-eronomistic historian wished to present him as a devout and ideal king, and in order to achieve this suppressed the idea that the king had been influenced into accepting *Urdeuteronomium* by writing in the story about discovering the law book in the Temple. This tradition supported the authenticity of the book and added to the picture of Josiah as the pious king. Non-deuteronomistic or pre-deuteronomistic sources did not possess the inside information of the deuteronomistic compilers about the influence of *Urdeuterono-mium* on Josiah's reform, and naturally do not mention it.

The generally accepted view, working on the basis of de Wette's identification of Josiah's law book with the book of Deuteronomy (in his *Dissertatio Critica* in 1805), is that the book of law contained an early version of Deuteronomy, a so-called *Urdeuteronomium*. For the difficulties of identifying the original book connected with Josiah's reformation, see Eissfeldt, *Introduction*, pp. 171–6; Nicholson, *op. cit.*, pp. 18–36.

(a) Temple repairs and discovering the law book
22:1–23:3

After the standard introduction in vv. 1–2, the narrative moves on
to the events of the eighteenth year of Josiah, when repairs of the
Temple were undertaken (vv. 3–7). A comparison of this account
with 2 Chr. 34–35 suggests that there has been some telescoping of
Josiah's reform movement in 2 Kg. 22–23, and that its initial stages
may be traced as far back as Josiah's twelfth year (2 Chr. 34:3).
Repairing the Temple in vv. 3–7 may be associated with its cleansing
of foreign cults, including some introduced under Assyrian
influence, in a bid for national independence. Cross and Freedman
(*JNES* 12 [1953], pp. 56–8) accept that Josiah began to repudiate
Assyrian influences (2 Chr. 34:3) after Ashurbanipal's death in 633
BC, and annexed Assyrian provinces in northern Israel after the
death of Ashur-etal-ilani in 629 BC. In recent studies Ashurbanipal's
death has been dated in 627 BC, which was Josiah's twelfth year
(Saggs, *Greatness*, pp. 134ff.; Reade, *JCS* 23 [1970], pp. 1ff.).
Despite the difficulties of finding an exact correlation between
Josiah's activities and the dates of Assyrian kings, it is right to
conclude that Josiah had begun his reform movement well before
621 BC, probably when there was a change of ruler in Assyria around
627 BC. In this context the reformation must be connected with an
assertion of independence. Associated with it was the geographical
expansion to Samaria (23:15), Megiddo (23:29) and possibly as far
as Gilead (Jos. 15; 18; 19). See further, Donner, *IJH*, pp. 463–6;
Cross and Wright, *JBL* 75 [1956], p. 222; Todd, *SJTh* 9 [1956],
pp. 288–93. There were also moves to reorganize the militia of
earlier days to meet the military challenge of this new situation
(Junge, *Der Wiederaufbau*, pp. 28–93; Sekine, *VT* 22 [1972], pp.
361–8). The acceptance of Cogan's contention that it was not
Assyrian policy to impose the worship of its own gods on conquered
peoples does not demand the acceptance of his further conclusion
that the reforms of Hezekiah and Josiah were not acts of rebellion
against Assyria (*Imperialism*, p. 113). Any move to centralize power
in the king and to assert his authority in Jerusalem had political
implications (Welten, *Königs-Stempel*, pp. 161–7).

The deliberate impression given by the author of vv. 3–7 is that
the first stage in Josiah's anti-Assyrian movement was connected
with repairing the Temple, and not with purifying the cult as in 2
Chr. 34. The wish of the deuteronomistic authors to show the
significance of the law book as the basis of the whole reform movement demanded the introduction of its discovery before any reform
measures were initiated. The suggestion above that the narrative

recording the discovery of the book was composed to conceal both
its origin and the hidden pressure upon Josiah to accept it, receives
some confirmation from the similarities between these verses and 2
Kg. 12:9–16. Following Dietrich's study of the two accounts (*VT*
27 [1977], pp. 18ff.), it seems likely that the deuteronomistic
historian based the introductory section of his narrative on 2 Kg.
12:9–16. To establish more firmly the link between discovering the
book (vv. 8–11) and repairing the Temple, v. 9 repeats material
from vv. 4–7 (cf. Dietrich, *op. cit.*, pp. 22–5).

Verses 3–11 need not be isolated from the remainder of the
complex, for the whole of vv. 3–20 and 23:1–3, 21–23 form a unit
that has been carefully constructed, as is shown by Lohfink (*Bib* 44
[1963], pp. 261–88, 461–98). Of the four sections into which the
narrative can be divided, two (22:3–11; 23:1–3) begin with 'the king
sent' and two (22:12–20; 23:21–23) with 'the king commanded',
thus establishing a pattern of alternating sections. All four sections
are concluded with a reference to the king. Lohfink finds that the
four sections correspond to the four acts of a covenant renewal:
repentance, oracle of salvation, covenant renewal and a festival, and
believes that the unit was constructed within the lifetime of Josiah,
as is indicated by the fact that it is unaware of his violent death.
Mayes (*Deuteronomy*, p. 90) adds a necessary corrective when he
states that the narrator does not describe a covenant renewal ceremony, but has adopted a covenant renewal pattern for describing
the actions of Josiah.

The four sections of the narrative will be analysed in more detail
below, but it must be emphasized here that all sections bear marks of
their deuteronomistic composition, and that this gives the narrative a
unity. One section, the oracle of Huldah (vv. 15–20), calls for special
comment. It is a double oracle, one part announcing God's judgment
on Jerusalem (vv. 15–17) and the other containing a promise to
king Josiah (vv. 18–20). Despite the claim that the original oracle
contained only the threat in v. 16, and was later modified through
the addition of a promise to Josiah in v. 18 (as, for instance, by
Gray, p. 727), it is now generally recognized that the first oracle
(vv. 16–17), which is general and formulaic, was a deuteronomistic
composition, and that the second (vv. 18–20), which is more specifically and personally directed at Josiah, is an older composition,
which the deuteronomist included in his narrative and suitably
modified by working over the original and adding deuteronomistic
phrases (see further discussion in Dietrich, *op. cit.*, pp. 25ff.;
Würthwein, *SThK* 73 [1976], pp. 404ff.; Rose, *ZAW* 89 [1977],
pp. 52ff.). Whereas the original oracle contains no reference to
the law book, the deuteronomistic composition in vv. 16–17 refers

specifically to the book and to Josiah's reading from it (Mayes, *op. cit.*, pp. 94ff.). This particular section shows how the deuteronomistic narrator, using earlier material, brought it into line with the remainder of the narrative, which was mainly concerned with the discovery of the law book.

1. Josiah was eight years old when he began to reign, and he reigned thirty-one years in Jerusalem: The Babylonian Chronicle of Nabopolassar dates Josiah's death in 609 BC, which then gives us the date of accession as 639 BC. The statement that he was **eight years old** at accession has been treated as suspect for two reasons: (a) the grammatical construction of the Heb. leads us to expect a numeral higher than ten, and there are two Gk. MSS which read 'eighteen' instead of 'eight'; (b) the fact that Jehoiakim his son came to the throne at the age of twenty-five means that Josiah was a father at the age of fourteen or fifteen. The first reason falls because there are other instances of exception to the grammatical rule (Gray, p. 720; *G-K*, p. 134,e,g) and the second because not all cases of early paternity are to be dismissed as impossible (Gray, *ibid.*). The name of **Josiah**, like the name of Joash (cf. 12:1), contains the element '*ws*, found also in Aram. and Arab., meaning 'to give' (Montgomery, p. 431; Noth, *Personennamen*, p. 212). His mother's name **Jedidah** means 'beloved' (*K-B*); his maternal grandfather's name **Adidah** is also found in Palestinian and South-Arabian inscriptions (Montgomery, p. 527). **Bozkath** is listed in Jos. 15:39 between Lachish and Eglon.

2. Josiah, like Hezekiah, receives unqualified commendation; the attitude of both kings to foreign cults, and their attempts to purify the worship, won for them approval in the deuteronomistic assessment of their reigns.

3. In the eighteenth year: Although this verse dates the beginning of Josiah's reform in 621 BC, the evidence of the Chronicler that 'he began to purge Judah and Jerusalem in his twelfth year' (2 Chr. 34:3) is accepted, and the temple works described in these verses are taken in conjunction with the first stages of Josiah's reform in 627 BC (see above, p. 603). **the king sent**: This is one of the key phrases used to introduce a major section in the alternating pattern that Lohfink finds in the complex in 22:3–23:13, 21–23, with the first section being designated as the one representing the 'repentance' element in the covenant renewal scheme. Although such an interpretation brings this passage into very close relationship with the remainder of the narrative, it provides no basis for dismissing the suggestion made above that the compiler modelled vv. 3–7 on 2 Kg. 12:9–16 in order to give a setting for the discovery of the law book during the temple repairs; in other words he wished to date the discovery of the book before the reform began, and not at a later stage in its progress. **Shaphan the son of Azaliah, son of Meshullam, the secretary**: The name **Shaphan**, meaning 'rock-badger' (*K-B*), appears in lists in 2 Kg. 25:22 and Jer. 36:11f.; but whether there is any relationship between them cannot be established. Others accompanied Shaphan, according to 2 Chr. 34:8.

4. Hilkiah the high priest: **Hilkiah**, meaning 'Yahweh is my portion', was the grandfather of Seraiah, the last high priest before the Exile (2 Kg. 25:18; cf. 1 Chr. 5:39, 40). He is not to be identified with Jeremiah's father, who was also called by the same name (Jer. 1:1); the high priest Hilkiah was a Zadokite, but the priests of Anathoth came from the line of Abiathar (cf. Šanda II, p. 329). **that he may reckon the amount of money**: It is assumed that the verb *tmm* has the meaning of 'summing up' the money, which can be derived from the literal meaning 'to make complete', although such usage is without parallel. The primary account in 2 Kg. 12:10 describes what happened in more detail: they 'counted and tied up in bags the money'. The more concise version in this verse should perhaps be translated as 'get ready the money' (Dietrich, *op. cit.*, p. 19; cf. *NIV*). If this verb is an attempt to represent in one word the process described in 12:10, the emendation to read it as *yattek* (from *nātak*, 'to smelt') with the Vsns. (cf. *NEB*, 'melt down the silver') becomes unnecessary. **which the keepers of the threshold have collected from the people**: cf. 12:9.

5-7. These verses are based on 12:11-12, 15. Montgomery (p. 524) eliminates the whole of vv. 4b-7 as secondary; it is taken to be an expansion of what is reported to the king in v. 9. Gray (p. 714) too discusses the passage with secondary sections and thinks that it has been worked over under the influence of 12:12ff. Agreeing with the view that this is a secondary section based on chapter 12, it is claimed here that the deuteronomistic historian, in his desire to connect the reform movement specifically with discovering the law book, avoided reference to the first stages of the reform by replacing it with this account of temple repairs. This had the advantage of providing a setting for the discovery of the law book, a link that is strengthened by repeating some of the material again in v. 9 (Dietrich, *op. cit.*, pp. 122ff.).

8. The introduction of this brief account of discovering the law book so abruptly into the narrative may be taken as an indication that the passage is not homogeneous. Once the discovery of the law book is dissociated from the verses dealing with temple repairs (vv. 4-7, 9), a more satisfactory account of finding the book is obtained from the basic material behind vv. 3, 8, 10, which relate briefly how Shaphan was sent to the Temple and, after being told of the law book by Hilkiah, read it and brought it to the king (Dietrich, *ibid.*). The basic material in vv. 3, 8, 10 may have been expanded, with the result that Shaphan is reported to have read the book twice, on the first occasion privately, and on the second loudly to the king. Although a variant spelling of the name Hilkiah occurs in v. 8*b*, it does not necessarily prove that the second half of this verse is from a later redactor (cf. 22:14; 23:4). But it is a more straightforward account if it merely states that, when Shaphan received the book from Hilkiah, he immediately brought it to the king and read it in the king's presence (Horst, *ZDMG* 2 [1923], p. 232). **I have found the book of the law**: The significance of using the definite article, *the* law book, has been variously interpreted. One possibility is that the book was a very familiar document, which had been lost for some time, and now rediscovered; because the book and its history was so well known, it is natural to use the definite article. Lohfink (*op. cit.*, pp. 28off.), accepting this interpretation, identifies the law book with the old covenant document of the Jerusalem Temple. On the other hand, it must be recognized that the narrative is presented by the deuteronomistic historian, who viewed the course of Israel's history in the light of the law of Moses in Deuteronomy, and so naturally referred to Deuteronomy as *the* law book (Skinner, p. 413; Mayes, *op. cit.*, pp. 91ff.).

9. This verse is obviously a link between the account of temple repairs (vv. 4–7) and the narrative about finding the law book (vv. 3, 8, 10); as such it repeats material from both sections. The opening sentence is another version of v. 10*a* (Dietrich, *op. cit.*, p. 23), and the remainder is a summary of vv. 4–7.

11. Many commentators find in this verse an introduction to the next section (so Dietrich, *op. cit.*, p. 25; cf. *BHS*, *RSV* and *NIV*). Accepting Lohfink's division of these chapters and his insistence on an alternating pattern in the introductory words and on the conclusion of each section with a reference to the king, v. 11 becomes the conclusion of the first section in vv. 3–11 and v. 12 the opening of the second section in vv. 12 20. **he rent his clothes**: The reaction of the king, with its clear signs of contrition and distress, is often linked with the curses that form a constituent part of the deuteronomic law (cf. Dt. 28:15ff.; 29:21ff.); so Skinner, p. 414; Montgomery, p. 525.

12. The second section, opening with **the king commanded** (cf. 23:21) deals with the king's deputation to Huldah the prophetess and her oracle. The members of the deputation were: **Hilkiah the priest**, who is credited with finding the book, and naturally as chief priest heads the deputation; **Ahikam, the son of Shaphan**, who is mentioned in 2 Kg. 25:22ff. as the father of Gedaliah, belonged to

the priestly party and helped Jeremiah (Jer. 26:24), but his father
was not **Shaphan the secretary**, who also appears in the list; cf. v.
3; **Achbor the son of Micaiah**, whose name means 'mouse', is also
named by Jeremiah (Jer. 26:22; 36:12); **Asaiah**, 'God made', whose
father is not named, bears the title **the king's servant** (*NEB*; *NIV*,
'king's attendant'; Gray, 'king's minister'), which denotes some
special responsibility, and is found on official seals from the period
(Albright, *JBL* 51 [1932], pp. 79ff.).

13. **inquire of the LORD for me**: This phrase is a technical expression for seeking a divine oracle; cf. 2 Kg. 1:2. **and for all Judah**:
The inclusion of this phrase is superfluous, since the previous reference to **for me, and for the people** includes all (so Šanda II, p.
334; Montgomery, *ibid.*). It is unnecessary to expand it further on
the basis of 2 Chr. 34:21 and to read 'and on behalf of the people
who are left in Israel and in Judah' (as proposed by Gray, p. 724).
to do according to all that is written concerning us: Some MSS and
Luc. here read 'all that is written in it'. If MT is retained, it can be
rendered either as in *RSV* **concerning us**, or as in *NEB*, 'that is
laid upon us'; or perhaps 'against us' (in the sense of a written
injunction, as is suggested by Kopf, *VT* 8 [1958], p. 180).

14. **Huldah the prophetess**: The choice of **Huldah** in preference
to the two well-known prophets of the time, Zephaniah and Jeremiah, has led to speculation. It has been suggested for instance that
Jeremiah was not in the city at that time (Montgomery, *ibid.*), that
the priests were more likely to obtain an oracle along the lines
desired from the wife of a Temple official than from prophets of an
independent spirit (Gray, p. 726), or that the king was more likely
to receive a favourable oracle from a woman who was free from the
pessimistic outlook of some of the prophets (Šanda II, p. 334).
Although her name is unknown, **a prophetess** was by no means
exceptional (cf. Miriam, Deborah, Noadiah and Anna). Her
husband, **Shallum the son of Tikvah, son of Harhas**, is unknown,
and there is no certainty, whether as **keeper of the wardrobe**, he
was employed at the palace or the Temple. The latter seems more
probable; cf. 2 Kg. 10:22 for a similar official in the temple of Baal.
the Second Quarter: This is usually taken to refer to the expansion
of Jerusalem towards the north (cf. also Neh. 3:9, 10). This occurred
after the building of the Temple, and accommodated personnel
employed at the palace and Temple (Gray, pp. 726ff.). Possibly too
refugees from the northern kingdom had settled in the northern
part of the city, and Cazelles (*TI*, p. 314) finds significant confirmation for the northern origin of Deuteronomy in the fact that a
prophetess from the refugee quarter was consulted.

15. When Huldah replies, beginning with the standard formula

Thus says the LORD, she has a double message, the first half containing words of threat against Jerusalem, and the second words of promise addressed personally to Josiah. Although there are difficulties in distinguishing the original oracle, it seems improbable that it contained a double message of threat and promise in its original form, and likely, therefore, that the two elements have to be separated. As noted above, it is accepted that the first oracle in vv. 16–17 is a deuteronomistic composition, but that vv. 18–20 contain an older composition, which in being worked over has received a number of deuteronomistic phrases. Dietrich (*op. cit.*, p. 27) finds that the double message of the oracle is now reflected in the exceptional use of 'for me and for the people' in v. 13, the former referring to vv. 18–20 and the latter to vv. 16f.; of the two elements in v. 13, the latter is probably a secondary addition (Spieckermann, *Sargonidenzeit*, pp. 58–71).

16–17. The first oracle has been described as general and formulaic (Mayes, *op. cit.*, p. 92). Many of these general, formulaic phrases are common to the deuteronomistic literature and Jeremiah: **have burned incense to other gods** (cf. Jer. 1:16; 19:4; 44:5, 8); **I will bring evil upon this place** (cf. Jer. 19:3, 15; 32:42); **that they might provoke me to anger** (cf. Jer. 7:18; 25:7; 32:29) and **my wrath will be kindled** (cf. Jer. 4:4; 21:12). This may indicate that this first oracle was a late composition, probably originating from a prophetic redactor (DtrP; so Dietrich, *ibid.*).

18–19. Whereas the previous oracle was general and formulaic, the words of the second are concrete and specific. Although it contains some deuteronomistic phrases, such as **that they should become a desolation and a curse** and **the evil which I shall bring**, the basic oracle probably originated from the time of Josiah himself and was later modified by the deuteronomistic redactor. Other expansions were made to connect it more closely to the preceding narrative: (i) the initial phrase, **regarding the words which you have heard**, is a linking phrase; (ii) **and you have rent your clothes and wept before me** is an expansion of the previous **and you humbled yourself before the LORD**, and obviously intends to establish a link with v. 11. The linkage, however, is not entirely satisfactory; the inclusion of the phrase **and wept before me** has no basis in v. 11, and the reason for Josiah's contrition, **when you heard how I spoke against this place**, is not as specific as the reason given in v. 11, the hearing of 'the words of the book of the law'. The most satisfactory approach to vv. 18–20 is to find in them a basically pre-deuteronomistic favourable oracle, which was then adapted to the narrative in 2 Kg. 22 by the deuteronomistic redactors, although they were not always successful in their adaptation (Mayes, *ibid.*).

20. I will gather you to your fathers, and you shall be gathered to your grave in peace: This phrase provides further confirmation of the oracle's origin from the time of Josiah (Priest, *VT* 30 [1980], pp. 366–8); such an assertion could not have originated after Josiah's death, which occurred in battle at Megiddo (23:29). At attempt to interpret the phrase **gathered to your grave in peace** as a reference to Josiah's death before the ruin of Jerusalem (Würthwein, *op. cit.*, pp. 404ff.) is not satisfactory, since the phrase usually refers to natural death (Rose, *op. cit.*, p. 59). The original oracle, coming from the time of Josiah himself, only contained this promise; but the later addition of **and your eyes shall not see all the evil which I will bring upon this place** after Josiah's death and possibly after 597 BC served two purposes: on the one hand, it gave a different interpretation of the promise that he would be gathered **in peace**, and on the other, by repeating the words **the evil which I will bring upon this place** from v. 16, it connects the oracle more closely with its immediate context. The last phrase, **and they brought back word to the king**, is not to be read with 23:1–3, as suggested by Gray (p. 728), since it provides a concluding reference to the king for the second of the main sections of the narrative (cf. vv. 11; 23:3, 23; Lohfink, *op. cit.*, pp. 469ff.).

23:1–3. This third unit of the narrative is devoted to the covenant which Josiah made with God, and in which the people joined. In many ways it is central to the narrative, and is thoroughly deuteronomistic, as is seen from the presence of the term 'the book of the covenant' and the phrase 'to keep his commandments and his testimonies and his statutes'.

1. the king sent: The opening of the section with these words conforms with the alternating pattern proposed by Lohfink (*ibid.*); cf. 22:3. **all the elders of Judah and Jerusalem were gathered**: Whereas this verse gives the impression that the people participated in the covenant ceremony through their representatives, v. 2 makes the occasion a popular one by insisting that 'all the people' were present. A parallel is found in Jos. 24:1ff., where there seems to be some confusion between the named representatives (in this case 'the elders, the heads, the judges and the officers') and 'all the people'.

2. and the priests and the prophets, all the people, both small and great: This list appears in 2 Chr. 34:20 with 'the Levites' replacing the prophets; it is obvious that the Chronicler's version has influenced the present text in some Heb. MSS (see *BHS*). But the whole sentence seems unnecessary after **all the men of Judah and all the inhabitants of Jerusalem** and may be omitted (cf. Gray, p. 728). It may also be suggested that **the men of Judah and the inhabitants of Jerusalem** are not to be taken too literally, for they

were spiritually present through the elders representing them,
although perhaps not physically present at the ceremony. **and he
read**: Whether it is implied that the king himself read from the book
is uncertain. The verb is capable of being rendered impersonally, or
it may be that the king, who was formally responsible for the
reading, was represented by a scribe (Montgomery, p. 528) or a
priest (Šanda II, p. 339). Gray (p. 729), with the support of the
Mishnah (*Sota* 7:8), believes that Josiah himself read aloud on this
solemn occasion. Whether he read it himself, or stood by whilst it
was being read in his name, Josiah on this occasion assumed the
role taken previously by Moses (Exod. 24:3–8) and Joshua (Jos.
8:34; 24) and later by Ezra (Neh. 8:2ff.). Possibly the present
narrative is dependent on earlier models. **the book of the covenant**:
'The book of the law' (v. 8) has now become **the book of the
covenant**, because it has been adopted as a basis for the covenant
which follows. Both the making of the covenant and the title given
to the book are eminently appropriate in view of the importance of
renewing the covenant, with a recital of the law and its acceptance,
in the book of Deuteronomy (cf. Dt. 27).

3. the king stood by the pillar: cf. 2 Kg. 11:14, where Joash on
his accession made a covenant with God, and was standing by the
pillar. **made a covenant**: The Heb. 'cut a covenant' was derived
from the custom of making the covenanting parties pass between
animals which had been cut to pieces (cf. Gen. 15:17). Josiah, in
making this covenant, was standing in the great tradition of Moses
and Joshua, and was acting as a mediator between God and the
people. Gray (p. 729), following Fohrer (*ZAW* 71 [1959], pp. 1–22),
emphasizes the difference between the older type of covenant with
its assembly of the sacral confederacy that was known in the north,
and the covenant with the dynasty of David known in the south.
Spieckermann (*op. cit.*, pp. 78ff.) believes that the three persons
that are connected in the deuteronomistic view of history are Moses,
David and Josiah. **before the LORD, to walk**: The emphasis of this
covenant, which was made in God's presence, lies on accepting the
standards given in the law book, which are defined in characteristic
deuteronomistic phrases. **all the people joined in the covenant**: or
'stood by the covenant'. *NEB*, *NIV*, 'pledged themselves to the
covenant'.

(b) Purification of the cult

23:4–20

The fact that this section has its own introduction (v. 4) and conclusion (v. 20, 'Then he returned to Jerusalem') enables it to stand

independently of the preceding narrative, which is also continued in 23:21–25. Its opening phrase ('and the king commanded', v. 4) is identical with that of two other sections (22:12; 23:21); but this is no reason for not separating this narrative from the deuteronomistic narrative in the preceding and following sections. Other characteristics which confirm that it was independent in origin are: (a) the total absence of any reference to the law book; (b) the short, abrupt style in the list of reform measures is more characteristic of annals than of historical narrative (Östreicher, *Grundgesetz*, pp. 13ff.; Mayes, *Deuteronomy*, p. 96; Gray, p. 715); (c) stylistically, the frequent use of '*wāw*-conjunctive' contrasts with the frequency of '*wāw*-consecutive' in the surrounding historical narrative (Östreicher, *ibid.*; Mayes, *ibid.*; Meyer, *Fest. Baumgärtel*, p. 122; Spieckermann, *Sargonidenzeit*, pp. 120ff.).

After separating the section and analysing it as a unit, different strands of tradition are noticeable. Some sections refer to reforms in Jerusalem itself (vv. 4, 66f., 8b, 10–12), others to reforms in the cities of Judah (vv. 5, 8a) and other sanctuaries (v. 13); some reforms were directed at the cult of Yahweh (vv. 6–8, 14–15), others at the cults of foreign gods (vv. 10–12); v. 4 refers to 'the temple of the LORD', whilst other verses refer to 'the house of the LORD' (vv. 6, 7, 12). There is also some repetition (cf. vv. 8, 13). On the basis of various analyses of this section (Würthwein, *ZThK* [1976], pp. 412ff.; Meyer, *op. cit.*, pp. 114ff.; Jepsen, *Fest. Baumgärtel*, pp. 97ff.; Hollenstein, *VT* 27 [1977], pp. 321–36) a development in four stages can be traced: (i) Possibly the deuteronomistic historian had access to a brief record of the Josianic reform measures. Hollenstein (*ibid.*) rightly isolates vv. 11–12, which concentrate on the removal of the more objectionable cultic practices from Jerusalem. It can be further suggested that this report was based on the first stage of Josiah's reform movement. (ii) The deuteronomistic historian composed his own basic account (DtrG) of Josiah's reform measures and incorporated into it the report of vv. 11–12 and also possibly other earlier material, which has left its traces in the exceptional use of the term 'the temple of the LORD' (instead of the more usual 'house of the LORD'), and of the unique reference to 'the vessels' in connection with the cult of foreign deities. The deuteronomistic material is found in vv. 4 (with the exception of the last phrase), 6–8a, 9. (iii) A later deuteronomistic redactor, known as DtrP (Dietrich, *Prophetie*, pp. 117ff.), added vv. 15–20, which are clearly interested in the fulfilment of prophecy and are closely linked with 1 Kg. 13. The words of 1 Kg. 13:3 are fulfilled in v. 15, the words of 13:2 in v. 20, the words of 13:32 in v. 19, and the tradition in 13:21 is echoed again in v. 17. This interpretation rejects the proposal (Lemke, *Magnalia Dei*, pp. 301–26) to take vv. 16–18 as a continuation of a pre-deuteronomistic narrative in 1 Kg. 13. (iv) From the hand of a later reviser too there came several insertions beginning with the '*wāw*-conjunctive' (vv. 4*c*, 5, 8*b*, 10, 13, 14). In these additions there is a polemic against Bethel (v. 4*c*) and an attempt to bring out more clearly an aspect of the Josianic reform that is not emphasized in the original report, namely, the centralization of the cult. Later revisers who wished to add again to the tradition of Josiah's piety, as the king who adopted unreservedly the deuteronomistic reform programme, brought out more emphatically his drive towards centralization. Hollenstein (*ibid.*) designates these additions as post-deuteronomistic, but it may be that this concern with the law of centralization, although lacking the characteristic phrases of the nomistic redactors (DtrN), may betray their interest in the fulfilment of the law and is to be attributed to their redactional work.

4. Although this verse, like 22:12 and 23:21, begins with **and the king commanded** and so belongs to the alternating pattern of these two chapters, it has to be separated in origin from the law book narrative. **the high priest, and the priests of the second order and the keepers of the threshold**: For a similar division of the priesthood into three orders, cf. 2 Kg. 25:18. Although the use of the term **high priest** is dubious here and in 22:4, 8, and is sometimes regarded as an exilic gloss, it is confirmed by the parallel term 'the chief priest' in 2 Kg. 25:18. Comparison with this latter verse and with Jer. 52:24 also suggests that **the priests of the second order** is to be read in the singular; cf. *NEB*, 'the deputy high priest'. For **the keepers of the threshold** (*NEB*, 'those on duty at the entrance'), see 2 Kg. 12:9. **the vessels made for Baal, for Asherah and for all the host of heaven**: The former identification of these deities with Assyrian gods is now abandoned in favour of an equation with Syro-Phoenician deities (Montgomery, p. 529; McKay, *Religion*, p. 30). The Ras Shamra texts refer to Baal and Asherah as Canaanite deities, and the Zakir inscription (*ANET*, p. 502) shows that even in the eighth century BC 'the gods of heaven' were associated with Baal. This verse indicates that cultic vessels were dedicated to the deities in the Temple itself. **he burned them outside Jerusalem in the fields of Kidron**: *RSV* translates the Heb. *šad^{e}môṯ* as **fields** (cf. *NIV*; *NEB* has 'open country'). New meanings have been proposed for the word with the support of Ugaritic parallels. A change to *š^{e}dēmôṯ* suggests *š^{e}dê môṯ*, 'fields of Mot' (the Canaanite god of drought), and the phrase is found in the Ras Shamra texts (Lehmann, *VT* 3 [1953], pp. 361–71; Croatta and Soggin, *ZAW* 74 [1962], pp. 46ff.). Another possibility is that *šad^{e}môṯ* is connected

with *šāḏam*, which refers to levelled land, and is to be translated
'terraces' (*K-B*). These attempts are not without their difficulties;
the former has to contend with the fact that the word for 'field' is
śᵉḏē not *śᵉḏē*, and the latter with the inappropriateness of suggesting
levelled terraces in the narrow Kidron ravine. Luc. suggests
miśrᵉp̄ôṯ, which has been interpreted as 'lime-kilns' and is accepted
by Burney (p. 357) and Gray (p. 730). It gives a good meaning. For
the geographical location, see Simons, *Jerusalem*, pp. 231ff. **and
carried their ashes to Bethel**: The introduction of this phrase with
a '*wāw*-conjunctive' denotes that it is one of the insertions made by
a later reviser. The probability is that it was suggested by the DtrP
redaction in vv. 15–20; but it is an absurd intrusion.

5. The reform of Jerusalem is described in vv. 4 and 6,
progressing from the burning of vessels in v. 4 to the removal of
'the Asherah' in v. 6. The reference of this verse to measures taken
in the provinces is obviously an intrusion; it begins with '*wāw*-
conjunctive' and comes from the same reviser as v. 4c. **he deposed
the idolatrous priests**: *NEB*, 'heathen priests'. The Heb. *kᵉmārîm*
appears to have been widely used in Semitic languages. In the *OT*
it is used invariably of the priests of pagan gods (cf. Zeph. 1:4;
Hos. 10:5) and bears a distinctly derogatory tone. The connection
envisaged in this verse between the *kᵉmārîm* and the **high places**
suggests that they were priests of the fertility cult, which has led
Albright to refer to them as 'eunuch priests' or 'male prostitutes'
(*From Stone Age*, pp. 234ff.; see further, Spieckermann, *op. cit.*,
pp. 85f.). **burned incense to Baal, to the sun, and the moon, and
the constellations and all the host of heaven**: The gods mentioned
here were Canaanite or Syro-Phoenician rather than Assyrian
(McKay, *Religion*, pp. 37ff.). The Zakir inscription (*ANET*, p. 502)
lists 'Baal of Heaven . . . the Sun and Moon and gods of heaven
and gods of earth'; an Aramaic inscription from Tarsus has 'the
Great Baal, Moon and Sun' (Montgomery, p. 530). *Šemeš* ('Sun')
and *Yareaḥ* ('Moon') were Semitic gods, and since both are
mentioned in the fertility myths of Ras Shamra (McKay, *op. cit.*,
pp. 38, 103), it can be suggested that they were local fertility deities.
There is considerable uncertainty about the meaning of the Heb.
mazzālôṯ, translated 'constellations' (see in detail, McKay, *op. cit.*,
pp. 38ff.). Its equation with the signs of the Zodiac (cf. Akkad.
manzaltu) is difficult to accept in view of the later origin of the
Zodiac and its twelve signs. A much more probable solution is that
the word refers to 'the planets' (cf. *NEB*), which were worshipped
throughout the Near East (Driver, *JTS* 4 [1953], pp. 208–11).

6. The account begun in v. 4 now proceeds with the removal of
the Asherah from the house of the LORD. the Asherah was the

image of the Canaanite mother-goddess; like other images
mentioned in the *OT* (Exod. 34:13; Dt. 12:3; Jg. 6:26; Mic. 5:13,
14; Patai, *JNES* 24 [1965], pp. 39–41) it was made of wood and
could therefore be carried out and burnt to dust, as described in
this verse.

7. **he broke down the houses of the cult prostitutes**: The masculine plural q*ᵉdēšîm* can either denote both sexes and be rendered **cult
prostitutes** as in *RSV* (Montgomery, p. 531; Gray, p. 734), or may
more specifically refer to 'male prostitutes' (*NEB*; cf. *NIV* 'male
shrine-prostitutes'). Whether employed in its general or specific
usage here, the term denotes cultic functionaries who practised
imitative magic in connection with the fertility cult (Brooks, *JBL*
60 [1941], pp. 227–53). **where the women wove hangings for the
Asherah**: The Heb. *bāṯîm*, 'houses', is wrong, and the translation
hangings cannot be justified (Burney, p. 359). Two other possibilities must be considered: (i) The transliteration of LXX and the
translation of Luc. both suggest the reading *kuttᵒnîm*, 'robes', which
is accepted by Burney (*ibid.*) and Gray (p. 730). (ii) The Heb.
consonants can be vocalised *battîm*, which may suggest the Arab.
battun, 'woven garment' (Šanda II, p. 344; Driver, *JBL* 55 [1936],
p. 107; *BHS*). This latter suggestion gives a satisfactory rendering
of the Heb., and may be taken with *NEB* to mean 'wove vestments
in honour of Asherah'; they were weaving ritual vestments (cf. 2
Kg. 10:21) rather than garments for the image (as suggested by
RSV and McKay, *op. cit.*, p. 31).

8. As noted above, v. 8*a* and v. 8*b* are attributed to different
hands, the first half having originated from the deuteronomistic
historian and continuing the account of vv. 6–7. Josiah **brought all
the priests out of the city of Judah**, and thus conformed in general
with the provision made in Dt. 18:6–8. The two main differences
between Josiah's measures and Deuteronomy's provision are: (a)
that Josiah seems to have compelled the priests to move to Jerusalem, which is not envisaged in Deuteronomy; (b) that the priests
did not serve at the altar (v. 9, contrary to Dt. 18:6ff.), although
they were given provisions as envisaged in Dt. 18:3–5. As noted by
Gray (pp. 734f.), Josiah found it necessary to modify some of the
prescriptions found in Deuteronomy. **from Geba to Beersheba**:
The name **Geba** was probably applied to more than one site (1 Kg.
15:22), and may here refer to *el-Jib* or *Tell el-Ful* or even *et-Tell*
(Reviv, *WHJP*, p. 347). **Beersheba** is known elsewhere as a shrine
to which pilgrimages were made (Am. 5:5). Although the intention
is to denote the northern and southern boundaries of Judah, **Geba**
and **Beersheba** were not strictly on the border, but were administra-

tive and cultic centres near the northern and southern borders of
Judah (Aharoni, *Land*, pp. 350ff.).

2 Chr. 34:6 has a different record and extends Josiah's activities
to 'the cities of Manasseh, Ephraim, and Simeon, and as far as
Naphtali'. Two interrelated problems arise in this connection, the
extent and the nature of the measures undertaken by Josiah. Josiah's
aim was to strengthen the relationship between the provincial cities
and his government in Jerusalem; and in seeking this consolidation
he did not restrict himself to the kingdom of Judah. His clash with
Pharaoh Neco at Megiddo suggests that he had asserted his power
as far as Galilee (Cross and Freedman, *JNES* 12 [1953], pp. 56–8),
but it is a debatable point whether or not Josiah held Megiddo. It
is probable that he enlarged his kingdom to the west, and the
inscription discovered at Mesad Hashavyahu (Naveh, *IEJ* 10 [1960],
pp. 129–30) as well as the evidence of settlement and building
fortifications along the Dead Sea, especially at Ein-Gedi (Mazar,
En-Gedi, p. 16), are taken as proof that Josiah had extended his
territory. Other proofs are found in the strengthening of the fortress
of Arad (Aharoni, *BA* 31 [1968], pp. 30–2) and in his marriage to
Zebidah from the family of Rumah in Galilee (v. 36) and to Hamutal
from the family of Libnah on the Philistine border (v. 31); Oded,
IJH, p. 464. It has been suggested too that Josiah's centralization
of the cult was accompanied by a fiscal reorganization of his
kingdom, and indeed facilitated the task of collecting taxes
(Claburn, *JBL* 92 [1973], pp. 11–22). Although there is considerable
uncertainty about the function of the so-called *lmlk* seal impressions,
their discovery at Mizpah, Gezer, Arad and Ein-Gedi gives an indication of the extent of the kingdom of Judah under Josiah (Oded,
ibid.; cf. Na'aman, *VT* 29 [1979], pp. 61–86, where it is maintained
that they cannot be used to deny Josianic expansion to the north).
No seals have been found in northern areas, but this may prove
only that Josiah had not fully organised the northern areas brought
under his power. The extent of his rule in the north is still debatable
(Cogan, *Imperialism*, p. 71; Lance, *HTR* 64 [1971], pp. 315–32;
Ogden, *ABR* 26 [1978], pp. 26–34). Some follow Alt, and find in
the town lists of Jos. 15:21–62; 19:2–7 a document related to Josiah's
administration of southern and northern tribes (Alt, *Kleine Schriften
II*, pp. 276–88), and it has even been claimed that Josiah was
attempting to restore the whole of the kingdom of David under his
rule and had subdued areas in Transjordan as well as the territories
of Israel and Judah (Ginsberg, *Fest. Marx*, pp. 355–63). Others take
a more cautious attitude and confine Josiah's rule to territories
forming the Assyrian province of Samaria, thus excluding Galilee
(Malamat, *Fest. Gaster*, p. 271). The texts are difficult to evaluate

and the question remains open. Nevertheless, it can be said that during the period of national revival under Josiah an attempt was made to reorganise the kingdom of Judah **from Geba to Beersheba** and to annex territories and strengthen fortresses outside Judah. Furthermore, the purification of the cult and its centralisation is to be understood against the background of Josiah's political reorganisation.

The second half of the verse is suspect because it is joined to the first half by means of a '*wāw*-conjunctive'. **he broke down the high places of the gates**: The phrase has been emended to read 'the high places of the Satyrs' (taking *haśśeʿārîm* as *haśśeʿîrîm*). The Satyrs were demonic creatures of the desert, and the suggestion is that Satyrs were worshipped in fear to ward off any danger. Such a cult is known from 2 Chr. 11:15; cf. Lev. 17:7. *NEB* translates, 'the hill-shrines of demons'. This understanding of the reference is preferred to Gray's emendation (p. 730) to *bēt haśśoʿārîm*, 'shrine of the gate-genii', with the suggestion that they corresponded to bull-colossi, which represented guardian genii of the entrance in Assyrian palaces (Snaith, *VT* 25 [1975], p. 116). Gray's suggestion has no support from other texts. The addition of v. 8*b* may have been a later aetiological note explaining some feature at the city gate that was associated with Josiah's reform. Yadin (*BASOR* 222 [1976], pp. 5–17) accepts that v. 8 is an interpolation, and argues that it refers to a high-place at Beersheba destroyed by Josiah, and that there never was such a high-place in Jerusalem.

9. Two comments are made here about the priests brought to Jerusalem from the cities of Judah: firstly, that they did not serve at the altar in Jerusalem, which seems to be contrary to the spirit of Dt. 18:6ff.; secondly, that they received the same subsistence allowance as the Jerusalem priests, **they ate unleavened bread among their brethren**. Although the significance of **unleavened bread** is not clarified in the text, it is generally assumed that the country priests had the same portion from sacrifices as the Temple priests. It is assumed that **unleavened bread** is mentioned either because reference is made to the Passover of vv. 21ff. (Šanda II, pp. 345f.), and by implication priests who shared the paschal food were allowed all sacred foods (Montgomery, p. 532), or else because of the connection between it and some sacrifices (Lev. 6:14–18), since the term can denote sacrificial portions. But there is no need to emend it (as suggested, for example, by Gray, *ibid.*).

10. This addition, introduced by the '*wāw*-conjunctive', refers to the cult of **Molech** in **the valley of the sons of Hinnom**, and is fraught with difficulties. Although **Topheth** is given as a proper name, the fact that it bears the vowels of *bōšet*, 'shame', and has the article in Heb. may indicate that it is a common noun with the meaning of 'fire-pit' or 'furnace' (Smith, *Religion*, p. 377; *BDB*; *K-B*). **the valley of the sons of Hinnom**: This place name (*ge-hinnom*) later became Gehenna; but there is insufficient evidence to support the suggestion that **the sons of Hinnom** were members of a sect gathering there to perform funerary rites (McKay, *op. cit.*, p. 105). The valley is not to be identified with the Kidron valley itself, but possibly with the place where the *Wadi er-Rababeh* turns to join the Kidron valley near *Bir Ayyub* (En Rogel). This broader space was more suitable for an assembly than the narrower ravines of the Kidron valley itself (Simons, *Jerusalem*, pp. 11ff.). Child-sacrifice was practised in the valley of Hinnom. Admittedly the Heb. for **might burn his son and daughter as an offering** is more correctly translated 'may make his son or daughter pass through the fire' (*NEB*), which has been interpreted as a ritual of initiation by passing the child over or through flames (Snaith, *VT* 16 [1966], pp. 123–4; Weinfeld, *Deuteronomy*, p. 216). But the use of the verb for 'burning' elsewhere (Dt. 12:31; 2 Kg. 17:31; Jer. 7:31; 19:5), together with evidence of child-sacrifice among the Phoenicians (McKay, *op. cit.*, p. 83) and more generally in the West Semitic world (Derchain, *VT* 20 [1970], pp. 351–5), is sufficient confirmation that child-sacrifice is meant here (but see Cogan, *op. cit.*, pp. 77–83). **to Molech**: Although there have been doubts if there ever was a god called **Molech**, Ugaritic literature gives confirmation of the use of *mlk* as a divine name in early Canaan (Cazelles, *DBS* 5, cols. 1337–46). The use of the term *mlk* in Israel may also betray some Phoenician influence; it may have initially denoted an 'offering', and Phoenician sources suggest some connection between child-sacrifices or fire offerings and the sacrificial term *mlk*. It can thus be argued (as is done by McKay, *op. cit.*, pp. 40ff.) that the deity honoured through the rites at Hinnom was of Canaanite-Phoenician origin, and not the underworld god Malik of Mesopotamia, who was identified with Nergal (as by Jensen, *ZA* 42 [1934], pp. 235–7). See further, Weinfeld, *UF* 4 [1972], pp. 133–54.

    11. the horses that the kings of Judah had dedicated to the sun: This is the only direct evidence from the *OT* that the horse was regarded as a sacred animal because of its dedication to the sun. But, there is evidence from many sources to confirm that both horses and chariots had a particularly close connection with solar religion (Weidner, *BibOr* 9 [1952], pp. 157–9). One Akkadian title used for the sun is *rākib narkabti*, 'chariot-rider' (Montgomery, p. 533; Gray, p. 736; but see Cogan, *op. cit.*, pp. 84–8, where it is argued that he is to be identified with 'charioteer', the adviser of Shamash). Again one of the deities of Zinjirli in the eighth century

BC, named along with Hadad, El, Reshep and Shamash, was *rk b'l*, a deity driving the royal chariot (Donner and Röllig, *KAI II*, p. 34). Models of horses and chariots add to the evidence. A model of a horse, chariot and two riders from Ras Shamra possibly exhibits a solar motif, with the Sun-god and his charioteer being the two riders (Schaeffer, *Texts*, plate xv, p. 2; McKay, *op. cit.*, p. 33). Model chariots with riders were also found at Gerar, and the many pottery models of chariot wheels excavated at Lachish, Megiddo and Bethshean were probably votive offerings, some no doubt the offerings of a solar cult (McKay, *ibid.*). Moreover, model horses with solar discs on their foreheads have been discovered at Jerusalem and Hazor (Kenyon, *PEQ* 100 [1968], pp. 97–109; Yadin, *BA* 21 [1958], pp. 30–47). To be added to this cumulative evidence of a solar cult in Palestine are the occasional suggestions in the *OT* itself that solar mythology was known (Hab. 3:3b–4; Isa. 66:15–16) and that there was sun-worship even in Jerusalem (Ezek. 8:6; 11:1; Job 31:26–27). It is, therefore, not surprising that **the kings of Judah** dedicated horses and chariots to the sun, and that in his attempt to purify the cult Josiah **removed the horses** and also **burned the chariots of the sun with fire**. This cult was located **by the chamber of Nathan-melech the chamberlain, which was in the precincts**. The word *sārîs*, translated **chamberlain**, means 'officer' in 1 Kg. 22:9 and can also denote an 'eunuch' (*NEB*). His **chamber** was located **in the precincts**, or 'colonnade' (*NEB*). The meaning and derivation of the Heb. *parwār*, translated **precincts**, are uncertain. Attempts have been made to find cognates in the Egyptian *pr wr*, 'Sun-chapel' or 'sun-barque' (Yahuda, *JBL* 66 [1947], p. 88), in the Persian *parwar*, 'an open kiosk' or 'summer house' (Gesenius-Buhl, *Handwörterbuch*, p. 598), or in the Sumerian *Ebabbar*, 'shining house', with reference to sun temples (Östreicher, *op. cit.*, p. 54). But the most probable connection is with the word *parbār* used in 1 Chr. 26:18 for 'the temple precinct' or 'forecourt' (cf. an Aramaic inscription, Donner and Röllig, *KAI I*, no. 260; *K-B*).

12. The original version probably referred to **the altars on the roof**, and a later gloss, based on 20:11, specified it as the roof of **the upper chamber of Ahaz** (see on 20:11 above). Other *OT* passages refer to the use of the roof to worship heavenly bodies (Jer. 19:13; Zeph. 1:5) and to offer sacrifices to Baal (Jer. 32:29); cf. also a Ras Shamra text, where the hero goes to the top of a tower to offer sacrifices to the bull and to Baal. **the altars which Manasseh had made in the two courts**: See on 2 Kg. 21:5. **and broke in pieces**: The Heb., 'and broke in pieces from there' (*wayyāroṣ miššām*), is impossible, and of the many emendations proposed the

best is to read *way^{e}diqqēm šām*, 'he beat them small there' (Gray, p. 731) or 'he pounded them to dust' (*NEB*).

13. to the south of the mount of corruption: The Heb. *har hammašhît* is a mistake for *har hammišhāh*, 'mountain of oil or of anointing', i.e. the Mount of Olives (so *NEB*); the argument for retaining MT (McKay, *op. cit.*, pp. 41ff.) is not convincing. **for Ashtoreth the abomination of the Sidonians, and for Chemosh the abomination of Moab and for Milcom the abomination of the Ammonites**: See 1 Kg. 11:5–7, where the founding of these cults is attributed to Solomon as a result of his foreign marriages. These cults probably shared a common sanctuary, for 1 Kg. 11:7 reads the singular 'high place', and the Gk. in this verse reads 'the house' for **high places**. Consequently it has been argued that the three deities mentioned were local manifestations of the same god, either Mars (Curtis, *HUCA* 28 [1957], pp. 137–80) or Attar-Venus (Gray, *JNES* 8 [1949], pp. 72–83).

14. This verse, beginning with a '*wāw*-conjunctive', is a general comment to conclude the additions made by the reviser.

15. With this verse is introduced the section (vv. 15–20) dealing with the altar at Bethel, which is attributed to the prophetic reviser (DtrP) and is mainly interested in the fulfilment of prophecy (see above, p. 616). Nevertheless, the verse has been taken as evidence that Josiah extended his rule over Bethel and other Samaritan towns (Cross and Wright, *JBL* 75 [1956], pp. 222ff.). A discrepancy is apparent between vv. 15 and 16; whereas v. 15 refers to the destruction of the altar, v. 16 presupposes that it is still standing. The reason for such contradiction is that the reviser has combined an account of the altar's destruction with his own fulfilment of prophecy theme, and it is unnecessary to separate v. 15 from vv. 16–20 (as done by Skinner, p. 422, and Gray, p. 738). This verse may also have been expanded, and there is a point in Montgomery's proposal (p. 534) to omit a whole section from **the high place . . . to . . . high place**, thus reading **the altar at Bethel, he pulled down**. If the present MT is retained, it is usually changed to avoid reference to burning the high place, and the reading accepted is **he broke in pieces its stones** (cf. *NEB*; *wayy^{e}šabbēr 'et '^{a}bānāw* is read for MT's *wayyiśrop 'et habbāmāh*). The final sentence, **also he burned the Asherah**, beginning with a '*wāw*-conjunctive', is a later addition.

16. This verse records the fulfilment of the prophecy in 1 Kg. 13:2ff. A longer text preserved in the Gk. contains a reference to the tomb of the man of God, which is a suitable preparation for Josiah's question in v. 17. *NEB* accepts the Gk. and reads 'thus fulfilling the word of the LORD announced by the man of God when

Jeroboam stood by the altar at the feast. But when he caught sight of the grave of the man of God who had foretold these things, he asked . . .' The probable explanation for the omission of this material from MT is that the scribe's eye ran on from the first occurrence of 'the man of God' to the second, and the words standing between them were omitted.

17. yonder monument: The **monument** (*ṣîyûn*) was a sign or a conspicuous mark; cf. the Arab. usage of the same word to denote a stoneheap used as a road-mark (so *K-B*), and also Jer. 31:21. It also denotes a place of burial in Ezek. 39:15, as does the word 'pillar' in Gen. 35:20. **It is the tomb**: The Heb. has 'The tomb!' as an exclamation and then proceeds clumsily with 'The man of God . . .'. Luc. reads 'This is the tomb of the man of God . . .'.

18. with the bones of the prophet who came out of Samaria: According to the narrative in 1 Kg. 13 the prophet 'came out of Judah', and the naming of Samaria here is anachronistic. Gray (p. 738) omits **who came** as a mistaken allusion under the influence of 1 Kg. 13:1, and interprets 'the prophet from Samaria' as a reference to the old prophet from Bethel, with 'Samaria' being used anachronistically of the northern kingdom. *BHS* suggests reading 'who was from Bethel'; it is possible that there was a mistake in copying under the influence of 'that were in the cities of Samaria' in v. 19.

19. The extension of Josiah's activities **to the cities of Samaria** had unmistakable anti-Assyrian overtones, for it is obvious that Josiah was now moving into territory belonging to the Assyrian province of Samaria (Malamat, *op. cit.*, p. 271). Understood against the background of Assyria's weakening power, Josiah's action must be interpreted as a positive step to take avantage of this opportunity to move into Assyrian held territory. (Ogden, *ABR* 26 [1978], pp. 26ff.; Spieckermann, *op. cit.*, pp. 117f.).

20. he slew all the priests of the high places: Nowhere else in the account of Josiah's reformation is there a reference to the slaughtering of priests on the altars of the high places destroyed. Although the slaughter of priests is not unknown (1 Kg. 18:40; 2 Kg. 10:18ff.), this verse is probably an exaggeration written under the direct influence of 1 Kg. 13:2.

(c) The Passover, further reforms and the end of Josiah's reign

23:21–30

Four independent elements have been brought together in this section: (i) vv. 21–23 contain a report that the Passover was kept in Jerusalem in Josiah's eighteenth year. The fact that it begins with the phrase 'and the king commanded' designates it as the fourth constituent element in the alternating cycle begun in 22:3–23:3; it belongs to that historical narrative rather than to the report of vv. 4–20. Despite some difficulties raised by the celebration of the Passover, which was a spring festival, there is no need to regard this passage as a later addition. In the tradition that brings out the significance of the law book for the Josianic reform, an important place was given to a centralised Passover. (ii) vv. 24–25 give an account of the removal of certain abominations from Judah and Jerusalem. These verses can be regarded as an appendix to the previous section. Although vv. 21–23, like the other sections in the alternating cycle established by Lohfink (*Bib* 44 [1963], pp. 261–88, 461–98), conclude with a reference to the king (cf. 22:11; 22:20; 23:3), v. 25 attempts to give the whole unit a more effective climax by providing a further assessment of Josiah's stature. (iii) vv. 26–27 are from the hand of a redactor and declare that despite Josiah's reforms God's wrath against Jerusalem because of the sins of Manasseh remained unabated. These verses are another version of the first oracle spoken by Huldah (22:16ff.), and may contain a redactor's version of that oracle which has been inserted here to emphasize again that the reformation did not cancel the threat contained in those words. (iv) vv. 28–30 conclude the account of Josiah's reign with the standard deuteronomistic formula and an annalistic note in vv. 29–30*a* reporting his clash with Pharaoh Neco at Megiddo. See also the analysis of Spieckermann, *Sargonidenzeit*, pp. 130–8.

21. Keep the passover: There is uncertainty about the etymology of the Heb. word for **passover**, *pesaḥ* (Gray, p. 740). Nevertheless, in origin the festival almost certainly came from a nomadic background and was connected with rites conducted by shepherds in the spring when they moved their flocks to new pastures (de Vaux, *Ancient Israel*, p. 489). Change of season and of locality called for the performance of these rites. In the *OT*, however, the Passover was invested with a historical significance and was connected with the deliverance of Israel from Egypt (cf. Exod. 12:21–27). The significance of this celebration cannot be missed, for a festival that recalled the deliverance from Egypt and the covenant with God was especially appropriate to express the nationalistic feeling that had emerged in Israel in this period of Assyrian decline. Nicolsky (*ZAW* 45 [1927], pp. 242–4) has read too much into the text in his suggestion that it had a particularly poignant message at a time when Israel was in danger of exchanging Assyrian for Egyptian vassalage.

2 Chr. 35:17 notes that on this occasion the people of Israel 'kept the Passover at that time, and the Feast of Unleavened Bread'. But the latter is not mentioned in this chapter, unless reference is made

to it in v. 9 above. The link between the Passover and the Feast of
Unleavened Bread is a complicated question. They were not
connected at the original celebration of the Passover in Exod.
12:21–27, and even when the connection is made in Dt. 16:1–8, it
can be argued that the account of the Passover (vv. 1, 2, 4b–7)
originally stood independently of the Feast of Unleavened Bread
(vv. 3, 4a, 8), the former being a one-day celebration and the latter
a seven-day festival (Mayes, *Deuteronomy*, pp. 254ff.; Segal, *The
Hebrew Passover*, pp. 226–8). Gray (pp. 741ff.) suggests that the
innovation introduced by Josiah was the transformation of the Passover, which was originally a family or a community feast, into a
national pilgrimage at a central shrine. This would suggest the
combination of the longer festival with the one-day celebration; but
whether this is to be attributed entirely to Josiah's celebration
remains an open question.

The Passover was a spring festival, but the emphasis of v. 23 that
it was celebrated in Josiah's eighteenth year after the discovery of
the law book has raised some doubts about the authenticity of the
account. It has been argued that a spring celebration does not allow
sufficient time for discovering the book and organizing a festival,
and that the account of the Passover is a later addition (Würthwein,
ZThK 73 [1976], pp. 407ff.). Several proposals have been made
here: Mowinckel, who gave the Covenant its *Sitz im Leben* in the
autumnal New Year Festival, maintains that the Passover was separated from its original spring *Sitz im Leben* and was joined to the
Covenant (*Le Décalogue*, pp. 119ff.); Gray (pp. 744ff.) thinks that
Josiah's reformation was inaugurated with a covenant in the autumn
and reached the end of its first phase with the Passover the following
spring. In support of Gray it must be emphasized again that the
reform tradition has been telescoped in the interest of dating it in
Josiah's eighteenth year. Verse 23, re-emphasizing the eighteenth
year at this particular point, is suspect, and it cannot be accepted
with any certainty that the Passover followed immediately after the
Covenant and was kept in the eighteenth year.

**22. For no such passover had been kept since the days of
the judges who judged Israel**: According to the Deuteronomistic
History, the only possible occasion for celebrating the Passover in
one place by Israel was after crossing the Jordan at Gilgal in the
time of Joshua (Jos. 5:10–12). If this is the case, there are doubts
about the validity of the report in 2 Chr. 30 that a Passover was
celebrated by King Hezekiah. The absence of any reference to
Hezekiah's Passover in 2 Kg., together with the categorical statement here that it had not been kept **during the days of the kings
of Israel or of the kings of Judah**, makes it unlikely that Hezekiah

kept a Passover as reported in 2 Chr. 30 (Rost, *VT* 19 [1969], pp. 113–20). On the possible connection between these verses and Jos. 5:10–12, see Spieckermann, *op. cit.*, pp. 132ff.

24. This verse may have been intended as an emphasis on Josiah's deliberate attempt to remove the evils of the reign of Manasseh. **the mediums and the wizards**: They are mentioned in connection with Manasseh in 2 Kg. 21:6. The **teraphim** were household gods (Gen. 31:19ff.), but were also used in divination (cf. Jg. 17:5; 18:14, 17), especially in imitative magic to promote fertility (so Gray, p. 745). There is no agreement about the derivation of the word **teraphim**, some taking it as meaning 'decaying ones' (cf. Preuss, *Verspottung*, p. 58), and others connecting it more specifically with interpreting dreams (Labuschagne *VT* [1966], pp. 115–17). Because of the reference to the **book that Hilkiah the priest found in the house of the Lord** this verse is best considered as an appendix to vv. 21–23 rather than a continuation of vv. 4–20.

25. In this evaluation of his work, Josiah is evidently considered to be the ideal king, despite the similar judgment of Hezekiah in 2 Kg. 18:5. This assessment of him is truly deuteronomistic: on the one hand, he had **turned to the Lord with all his heart, and with all his soul and with all his might**, cf. Dt. 6:4; on the other hand, he acted **according to all the law of Moses**.

26–27. These verses are based on 2 Kg. 21:10–15; 22:16ff., and emphasize that God's former pronouncements about the fate of Jerusalem and Judah still stand. Josiah may have acted in time to postpone the Exile, but not to avoid it. God's declaration about Jerusalem through his servants the prophets in the reign of Manasseh is confirmed in these verses, and the more recent announcement of judgment through Huldah the prophetess is affirmed. The reforms of Josiah will not turn away God's declared intention concerning Judah and Jerusalem.

28. This is the standard deuteronomistic concluding formula. It is unusual, however, to place it before the notice of the king's death.

29. Pharaoh Neco king of Egypt: The king in question was Pharaoh Neco II (610–595 BC), whose clash with Josiah must be understood in conjunction with the movements of contenders for power in the wake of Assyria's disintegration. With the weakening of Assyrian power, Babylon and Media had captured important Assyrian centres, including Nineveh in 612 BC. According to the Babylonian Chronicles, Egypt sent military assistance to the Euphrates region to support the Assyrian Ashuruballit in his struggle against Nabopolassar of Babylon (Wiseman, *Chronicles*, p. 19). Egypt had helped Assyria in 616 BC, and was obviously interested in gaining control over Syria and Palestine as a buffer against

Babylon. Psammeticus I (664–610 BC), Neco's father, had gained control over areas in Philistia and the Assyrian province of Maggidu, including Megiddo itself. Josiah was not unaware of the consequence for Judah in the event of Egyptian success against Babylon. In taking action against Neco in 609 BC, he was throwing his dice for Babylon against Egypt and Assyria, and may have hoped for control over Palestine after their defeat by Babylon (Malamat, *Fest. Gaster*, pp. 267–9; *WHJP*, pp. 205f.; Cross and Freedman, *JNES* 12 [1953], pp. 56–8). **went up to the king of Assyria**: As the Babylonian Chronicle makes clear, he went to support Ashuruballit (Hjelt, *Fest. Marti*, pp. 142–7); cf. *NEB*, 'to help the king of Assyria'. **King Josiah went to meet him**: The account of the encounter between Josiah and the Egyptian king is very brief, and the fuller version of 2 Chr. 35:20–24 does not offer a clearer picture of this incident. Although the version in 2 Chronicles does not answer the several questions that arise in connection with Josiah's death, it does contain some reflection on the problem of the contradiction between Huldah's prophecy and Josiah's fate. This has led to the suggestion that the Chronicles account was written by someone who was aware of the difficulties of the Kings narrative and had reflected upon them (Williamson, *VT* 32 [1982], pp. 242–7). Malamat (*WHJP*, pp. 205ff.) thinks that Josiah's move had been carefully calculated: the Egyptian king was new and inexperienced; the Egyptian army was in the plain of Megiddo, far from home and not within the safety of the stronghold Megiddo; Egypt had suffered earlier humiliation from the Scythians, and about six months previously the Egyptian army had been forced to abandon Haran. **and Pharaoh Neco slew him at Megiddo, when he saw him**: Unquestionably **Megiddo** was the capital of the Assyrian district of Maggidu in lower Galilee, despite the form Magdol given by Herodotus (II.159) and identified with Migdol on the Egyptian border. 2 Chr. 35:20–25 gives an account of a conversation between the two, and suggests that Neco did not plan to fight against Josiah (cf. Josephus, *Ant.* x.5.1). There is no reason for supposing that Josiah had been summoned to meet Neco (as proposed by Welch, *ZAW* 43 [1925], pp. 255f.), but it is possible that Neco sent a message to Josiah seeking safe passage through his country (Williamson, *op. cit.*, p. 410; Yadin, *IEJ* 26 [1976], pp. 9–14). Most probably there was a brief skirmish at Megiddo, possibly a surprise attack during which the Judaean king was killed (Herrmann, *History*, p. 272; Alfrink, *Bib* 15 [1937], pp. 173–84; Frost, *JBL* 87 [1968], pp. 369–82). Pharaoh Neco also captured Gaza or Kadytis (Herodotus II.159; Jer. 47:1) and probably destroyed Mesad Hashavyahu (Naveh, *IEJ* [1962], pp. 98f.).

30. the people of the land: As on previous occasions (see 2 Kg. 11:14; 21:24), this group acted to secure a successor on David's throne. They chose **Jehoahaz**, Josiah's second son, in preference to Eliakim, his eldest son. The reason for this choice is that they presumably thought that Jehoahaz was likely to follow in the steps of his father; this may also be the reason for his removal later by Pharaoh Neco.

4.   THE LAST KINGS OF JUDAH AND THE FALL OF JERUSALEM

2 Kg. 23:31–25:30

This final section of the narrative of Kings contains a mixture of material derived from a variety of sources. The deuteronomistic historian follows his normal procedure and attempts to give a record of the reigns of Jehoahaz, Jehoiakim, Jehoiachin and Zedekiah within his own standard formulae; but it is obvious that for the catastrophic last years of the kingdom of Judah this was becoming impossible. Whilst both the introductory and concluding formulae are supplied for the reign of Jehoiakim (23:36ff.; 24:5ff.), only the introductory formula is given in connection with Jehoahaz (23:31ff.), Jehoiachin (24:8ff.) and Zedekiah (24:18ff.). Each of these four kings, according to the introductory formulae, followed in the steps of his predecessors, as is denoted by the phrases 'according to all that his fathers had done' (23:32, 37), 'according to all that his father had done' (24:9) and 'according to all that Jehoiakim had done' (24:19). The presence of these formulae and the negative tone of the judgment have led Weippert (*Bib* 53 [1972], pp. 301–39) to suggest that a third redactor, R^{III}, was responsible for this section. Another suggestion (see above, p. 32) is that these formulae are carbon copies introduced by an exilic editor. Some of the material may have been derived from annalistic sources, but a substantial amount in this section has come from the personal experience of the deuteronomistic historian (especially 25:1–12, 18–21a; so Dietrich, *Prophetie*, p. 140). It is obvious that 25:22–26 are based on Jer. 40–41 and that 25:27–30 come from an early report of the fate of the exiles.

(a) Jehoahaz

23:31–35

The brief reign of Jehoahaz coincides with Pharaoh Neco's expedition to Haran. The Egyptian king, after defeating Josiah, went north and tried to establish Ashuruballit on the throne of Haran in a struggle that lasted from June/July to August/September 609 BC

(Wiseman, *Chronicles*, pp. 62ff.). Presumably it was because of his anti-Egyptian sentiments that Jehoahaz was chosen as Josiah's successor by 'the people of the land', who preferred him to his older brother Eliakim. Malamat has noted the anti-Egyptian attitude of this group during this period, and suggests that this is the reason why Jehoahaz, the son of Hamutal, 'the daughter of Jeremiah of Libnah', who traced her lineage to this group, was chosen king. It was the anti-Egyptian attitude of this group that later led the king of Babylon to place another of Hamutal's sons, Zedekiah, on the Judaean throne (Malamat, *WHJP*, p. 206; *VTS* 28 [1975], p. 126). After the failure of Ashuruballit's bid for the throne of Haran, Pharaoh Neco returned to Syria and Palestine, and now finally took possession of these countries from the hands of the Assyrians. It was in these circumstances that Pharaoh Neco summoned the anti-Egyptian Jehoahaz to his headquarters at Riblah.

31. Jehoahaz: The new king had perhaps significantly adopted **Jehoahaz,** 'Yahweh has seized', as his throne-name; his real name was Shallum (Jer. 22:11; 1 Chr. 3:15). **twenty-three years old when he began to reign:** His brother Eliakim was his senior by two years, but in their bid to continue the anti-Egyptian policy of Josiah, the people of the land by-passed the custom of primogeniture. **he reigned three months in Jerusalem:** As noted above, this period corresponds to Neco's abortive military expedition to Haran. **Hamutal the daughter of Jeremiah of Libnah:** In the reign of Jehoram **Libnah** had severed relations with Judah (cf. 2 Kg. 8:22); but by this time it is apparent that **Hamutal** or Hamital had established a connection with the Judaean people of the land. Josiah's marriage to Hamutal undoubtedly had political motives.

32. The judgment on Jehoahaz that **he did what was evil in the sight of the LORD** is the standard one and cannot be very meaningful with regard to the three-month reign of a new king. Gray (p. 749) appropriately thinks that it is deuteronomistic inference from the king's fate.

33. put him in bonds: *NEB* has 'removed him from the throne of Jerusalem', and omits all reference to Riblah. Reading the verb 'removed him' is confirmed by the Gk. and 2 Chr. 36:3. *BHS* suggests the omission of *RSV*'s **that he might not reign in Jerusalem**, and it may have been added to the present text under the influence of 2 Chr. 36:3; thus an unsuccessful attempt was made to combine the statements that Jehoahaz was put in custody at Riblah (Kings) and that he was deposed from the Jerusalem throne (Chronicles). **Riblah in the land of Hamath:** It is mentioned later as Nebuchadrezzar's headquarters (2 Kg. 25:6, 20). It was about 34 km south of Horus in the Orontes valley, and because it had access southwards via the Biqā' it was a suitable headquarters for an army proposing to invade Palestine. **laid upon the land a tribute of a hundred talents of silver and a talent of gold**: The war indemnity demanded from Judah was considerably lower than the levy of 300 talents of silver and 30 talents of gold that Sennacherib had imposed on Hezekiah a few years earlier (2 Kg. 18:14); both are much lower than the thousand talents demanded from Menahem of Israel (2 Kg. 15:19). The Gk. has raised **a talent of gold** to 'a hundred talents', and Luc. to 'ten talents'. Gray (p. 750) finds an explanation for Neco's lenient demand in the fact that he still faced a threat from Babylon.

34. made Eliakim the son of Josiah king . . . and changed his name to Jehoiakim: The change of name from **Eliakim**, 'God establishes', to **Jehoiakim**, 'Yahweh establishes', was only slight; some suggest that the use of Yahweh's name was a concession to Israelite feeling (Gray, p. 751) or else that it was given in satire suggesting that Yahweh was on Egypt's side. The real point of changing the name, however, was that it denoted the king's vassalage to Egypt; cf. also 2 Kg. 24:17, where Nebuchadrezzar changes the name of his vassal from Mattaniah to Zedekiah. **he came to Egypt and died there**: cf. the description of the fate of Jehoahaz in Jer. 22:10ff.

35. There is some obscurity in the details given of Jehoiakim's method of exacting taxation from the people. As in the days of Menahem (2 Kg. 15:19) a tax assessment was put in operation. Some argue for the omission of the phrase **the people of the land**, and contrast it to Menahem's taxation in that it was universally exacted, and not from the men of property alone (cf. Montgomery, p. 551; Gray, p. 751). Malamat (*WHJP*, p. 207) retains **the people of the land**, and thinks that the burden was laid on this group as a punishment for its anti-Egyptian feelings. Whoever paid the tax, the phrase **every one according to his assessment** may denote that every one who was taxed paid according to his ability (Herrmann, *History*, p. 274).

(b) Jehoiakim
23:36–24:7

Although Jehoiakim's taxation has already been noted in the context of his establishment on the throne by Pharaoh Neco, the account of his reign formally begins with the standard introductory formula in 23:36 and is concluded in 24:6ff.

The account of Jehoiakim's reign (609–598 BC) in 24:1–6 duly records the most significant event of the period, namely the appear-

ance of Nebuchadrezzar king of Babylon on the scene. Relevant
events in the early part of Nebuchadrezzar's reign must be briefly
summarized from the Babylonian Chronicles (Wiseman, *Chronicles*,
pp. 67ff.). After constant fighting between Egypt and Babylon in
Carchemish between 609 and 607 BC, and a further clash in 606 BC,
Nabopolassar handed over the command of his army to Nebuchadrezzar, who marched to Carchemish, crossed the river against the
Egyptians, defeated them absolutely and pursued them to Hamath.
The defeat of Neco at Carchemish occurred in 605 BC. Babylonian
forces moved to Syria and Palestine, and according to the Babylonian Chronicles they conquered 'the whole of the land of Hatti'
(i.e. northern Syria). The conquest of Syria-Palestine was interrupted by Nabopolassar's death and Nebuchadrezzar's return to
Babylon to be enthroned in September 605 BC. Nebuchadrezzar
returned again to Syria; Ashkelon fell in 604 BC and in the same
year 'all the kings of Hatti came before him and paid heavy tribute'.
It was after the fall of Ashkelon that Jehoiakim 'became his servant'
(24:1), either by submitting peacefully in 604 BC (as suggested by
Herrmann, *History*, p. 275) or else during Nebuchadrezzar's
campaign in the west in the autumn and winter of 603 BC (Malamat,
WHJP, p. 208). Judah's leaders held an emergency meeting after
the fall of Ashkelon in 604 BC and there was a day of fasting in
Jerusalem (Jer. 36:9ff.). Despite Jeremiah's shrewd assessment of
the situation and his firm belief that Nebuchadrezzar would rule
over Judah (Jer. 25:1–14), and despite his opinion that the authori-
ties would be well advised to submit voluntarily (Jer. 21:8–9;
38:2ff.), the king and his advisers were determined not to submit
to Babylon. But, when Nebuchadrezzar's army came to the west in
603 BC, Jehoiakim capitulated.

1. In his days Nebuchadrezzar king of Babylon came up: As
noted, it seems that Nebuchadrezzar sent an army to Syria and
Palestine in 603 BC, and that the verb **came up** is to be taken
literally. The Babylonian Chronicles describe his setting out with a
'mighty army' and the support of siege towers. Admittedly the
Babylonian record is incomplete (Wiseman, *Chronicles*, pp. 70ff.),
but Malamat rightly assumes (*WHJP*, p. 208; *IEJ* 18 [1968], pp.
141f.) that Nebuchadrezzar's intention was to subdue Philistia and
gain control over Judah and that the missing part of the record
referred to the conquest of a Philistine city and the surrender of
Jehoiakim. **Nebuchadrezzar** was now in the second year of his reign
that lasted nearly half a century (605–562 BC). The Babylonian
name *Nabū-kudurri-usur* would support the spelling Nebuchadrezzar
found in the *OT*. **Jehoiakim became his servant three years; then
he turned and rebelled against him**: Jehoiakim's rebellion is to be

understood in connection with Nebuchadrezzar's difficulties in Egypt and his subsequent defeat there. It may be assumed that Jehoiakim paid his first tribute to Nebuchadrezzar in the early winter of 603 BC, and that his third payment became due in the early winter of 601 BC. But in Kislev (November/December) of that year Nebuchadrezzar had marched at the head of his troops to Egypt. The Babylonian Chronicles describe how the Egyptians mustered a strong army and defeated the Babylonians and their king, who 'turned and went back to Babylon' (Wiseman, *op. cit.*, p. 70). At this moment of humiliation for Babylon, Jehoiakim withheld his tribute. Unquestionably, Jehoiakim saw in Egypt the hope of salvation for Judah, and it is known from an Aramaic letter from Saqqera (Memphis) that a ruler from Gaza, Ekron and Ashkelon thought likewise and approached Egypt for help against Babylon (Donner and Röllig, *KAI I*, no. 266).

2. Nebuchadrezzar was unable to reorganize his army for nearly two years following his Egyptian defeat. The fifth year of his reign (600–599 BC) was spent at home assembling his chariots and horses (Wiseman, *ibid.*), and even when he did set out again to 'the Hatti land' in the winter of 599–598 he only raided Arabian tribes who lived in the region to the east of Palestine (cf. Jer. 49:28–33). He kept check on the rebellious Jehoiakim by sending over some of his own garrisons to attack Judah; they were also helped by contingents sent by subject states to the east of Judah. Attacks by Chaldeans and Aramaeans are mentioned in Jer. 35:1, 11 and by Moab and Ammon in Zeph. 2:8–10. Malamat (*WHJP*, p. 209) suggests, on the basis of the Gk. version of 2 Chr. 36:5, that they were also joined by contingents from Samaria, which may have been cut off from Judah by the Babylonians. It is these attacks that are mentioned here in the reference to **bands of the Chaldeans, and bands of the Syrians, and bands of the Moabites and bands of the Ammonites** coming **against Judah to destroy it.** These activities against Judah were not haphazard attacks by marauding bands, but must have been punitive measures by military units taking orders from Nebuchadrezzar. This brief note has been expanded by two later additions: the subject of the sentence, **the LORD sent**, is an addition that is omitted from the Gk., which more naturally takes Nebuchadrezzar to be the subject as in v. 1; the fulfilment of prophecy formula, **according to the word of the LORD which he spoke by his servants the prophets**, is also a later annotation (Dietrich, *Prophetie*, pp. 22f., 60ff.).

3–4. The note about fulfilling the words of the prophets in v. 2 has been expanded in these two verses, which are based on 2 Kg. 21:1–18. They also take up the point made earlier in 23:26ff. that the reform measures undertaken by Josiah had not succeeded in cancelling the damage caused by Manasseh nor in turning back God's anger. These verses, therefore, interpret Nebuchadrezzar's attack on Jehoiakim as God's punishment on Judah for the sins of Manasseh. The addition has obviously introduced an interpretation of the events that is far removed from the historical situation, for Nebuchadrezzar was taking punitive action against Jehoiakim because of his rebellion against Babylon. These two verses are secondary (Dietrich, *op. cit.*, pp. 29ff.), and by the awkwardness and the repetitiveness of the phrase **for he filled Jerusalem with innocent blood** suggest that a further revision or addition occurred (Montgomery, pp. 552ff.; Gray, p. 757).

5–6. This standard formula offers no details of Jehoiakim's death. It is here suggested that he died of natural causes (**slept with his fathers**) during the siege of Jerusalem in Nebuchadrezzar's eighth year (598/7 BC), which is associated in the book of Kings with the reign of Jehoiachin (v. 10). The Babylonian Chronicles describe the siege of 'the city of Judah', which was taken in 'the month of Addaru' (March 598 BC), with Nebuchadrezzar appointing a new king 'to his liking' and carrying off the booty to Babylon (*ANET*, p. 564). Jehoiakim probably died in January, and his son in the third month of his reign decided not to offer further resistance but to surrender (cf. v. 12). See further, Herrmann, *History*, p. 278; Oded, *IJH*, pp. 470ff. The Gk. of 2 Chr. 36:8 and Luc. assert that 'he was buried in the garden of Uzza' (cf. 2 Kg. 21:26). The tradition preserved in the Gk. is in contradiction to Jer. 22:19 (cf. 36:10), which compares Jehoiakim's burial to that of an ass, and locates it outside the gates of Jerusalem. Although Jeremiah's reference to the king's burial may be a reflection of his antagonism towards Jehoiakim, it may nevertheless have been correctly based on the historical fact that under siege conditions the king was not given a proper burial.

7. This note, which is probably derived from an annalistic source, refers to a situation that had emerged before the siege of Jerusalem in 598 BC and should have been inserted at an earlier point in vv. 1–7. The Egyptians were forced back to their country when Nebuchadrezzar defeated Pharaoh Neco at Carchemish in 605 BC and marched his armies to Syria and Palestine. Although Egypt resisted the Babylonian attack of 605 and forced Nebuchadrezzar to return to Babylon, v. 7 gives a correct description of events after 605 BC. On **the Brook of Egypt**, *Wadi el'Arish*, see on 1 Kg. 8:65.

(c) Jehoiachin and the first deportation
24:8–17

As noted above (under vv. 5, 6), it is assumed that Jehoiachin succeeded his father when Jerusalem was under siege by Nebuchadrezzar. Some details of the siege are given in the Babylonian Chronicles, which state that 'in year 7, month Kislimu' (Kislev) the Babylonian king marched to 'Hatti land, laid siege to the city of Judah and the king took the city on the second day of the month Addaru' (*ANET*, p. 564). The second of Adar was March 16, and the year 598 BC.

8. Jehoiachin, 'Let Yahweh establish', is known by the name Jechoniah in Jer. 24:1; 28:4; 29:2, by the abbreviated form Coniah, 'Yahweh is firm', in Jer. 22:24, 28; 37:1, and by the variant Yochin on several jar handles (Albright, *JBL* 51 [1932], pp. 77ff.). The Akkad. form is Yakukina. **he reigned three months in Jerusalem**: The Babylonian record that Nebuchadrezzar set out in the month of Kislev (December/January) would suggest that the siege could not have begun before the end of January, and so lasted for only a few weeks. It may be, however, that the city was already under siege by Babylonian garrisons in the west (denoted as 'the servants of Nebuchadrezzar' in v. 10), helped by the subjects of Babylon (cf. v. 2), and that Nebuchadrezzar himself arrived only for the final surrender in March (Malamat, *WHJP*, p. 210). Gray (p. 752), assuming that an exilic deuteronomistic redactor was responsible for this section and that he was writing about events of which he had personal knowledge, maintains that the redactor composed the introductory formula in vv. 8ff. on the pattern used by the deuteronomistic compiler. But Dietrich (*Prophetie*, p. 143) more satisfactorily ascribes these verses to the basic deuteronomistic compiler (DtrG).

10–11. the servants of Nebuchadrezzar king of Babylon came up to Jerusalem: To co-ordinate this statement with v. 11 and the Babylonian Chronicles, it is assumed that Jerusalem was under siege by contingents of Babylonian garrisons in the West before Nebuchadrezzar set out from Babylon. When he arrived in Jerusalem, **while his servants were besieging it**, King Jehoiachin was on the point of surrender; as soon as Nebuchadrezzar himself, with a more powerful army from Babylon, came on the scene, he 'gave himself up' (v. 12). Jehoiachin presumably decided on this course in order to save Jerusalem from total destruction by Nebuchadrezzar's forces.

12. gave himself up to the king of Babylon: The Heb. has 'went out to', which is used elsewhere for surrendering (cf. 2 Kg. 18:31).

So *NEB*. **the king of Babylon took him prisoner in the eighth year of his reign**: There is a discrepancy between the eighth year of this verse and 'the seventh year' of Jer. 52:28 and the Babylonian Chronicles. Nebuchadrezzar's father died in 605 BC, and it is probable that he was enthroned in September of that year; his 'seventh' regnal year was 599/8 and his eighth was 598/7 BC. Gray (pp. 759ff.) accounts for the discrepancy by assuming two different systems of reckoning, a Judaean one (Jeremiah) reckoning from Nebuchadrezzar's formal accession at the following New Year Festival, and a Babylonian one (Kings) reckoning from the time when he assumed power. Malamat's explanation (*WHJP*, p. 211) is that Jeremiah's mention of the number of Jews carried away in the seventh year refers to captives taken from Judah in 598 BC and that this verse in Kings refers to captives taken from Jerusalem at the beginning of 597 BC. Whatever the reason for these discrepancies, it is accepted here that Jerusalem was besieged in 598 BC.

13–14. Because of the extensive repetition in vv. 13, 14, and also of the discrepancy between the 'ten thousand captives' on v. 14 and the reckoning given in v. 16, it is usually assumed that vv. 13, 14 are secondary additions (so Skinner, p. 430; Montgomery, pp. 555ff.; Gray, pp. 760ff.).

13. The fact that this verse is directly contradicted by Jer. 27:19ff., together with the presence of the fulfilment of prophecy theme in the last phrase, **as the LORD had foretold**, marks it as a secondary addition. In the account of the final collapse of Jerusalem in chapter 25, only the smaller Temple utensils are listed (especially v. 15). Gray (p. 760) rightly suggests that the material contained in v. 13 is derived from Jer. 27:22. It is obvious that this later addition incorrectly connects looting predicted in connection with the final fall of the city in 587 BC with the earlier surrender of 598 BC.

14. This verse clearly makes an exaggerated claim that **he carried away all Jerusalem**, which is modified at the end of the verse by the addition of **none remained, except the poorest people of the land**, which is also found in 2 Kg. 25:12. The list of those carried away from Jerusalem contains a repetition of v. 12 (**all the princes**) and of v. 16 (**all the men of valour . . . and the craftsmen and the smiths**). For the figure of **ten thousand captives** given in this verse, see on v. 16.

15. In addition to the king's family, **his officials** (*NEB*, 'his eunuchs'; Gray, 'his chamberlains') and **the chief men of the land**, probably landowners who had become community or provincial heads, were also taken into captivity. The significance of the first deportation was that the elite of Judah, its upper and ruling classes, had been removed. Jer. 29:21ff. adds to them religious leaders,

priests and prophets. The removal of these classes contributed significantly to the disintegration of the Judaean community. A blow
had been struck at the very foundations of the kingdom, for the
disappearance of experienced and acknowledged leaders led to the
prevalence of social and economic instability (Malamat, *WHJP*, pp.
211ff.).

16. all the men of valour: *NEB*, 'all the men of substance'. They
were the men of property who were liable either for military service
or for providing men and equipment for war (cf. 1 Kg. 1:8). **the
craftsmen and the smiths**: As noted by Montgomery (p. 552) and
Gray (p. 761) the Heb. nouns are in the singular to denote guilds;
a parallel is found in the Ras Shamra texts, where men are grouped
according to their craft for taxation and military service (Gordon,
Textbook II, texts 300, 400, pp. 203ff., 213ff.). The first group were
the craftsmen, or 'artisans', the second **smiths** rather than 'sappers'
(as suggested by Malamat, *WHJP*, p. 211). The grouping of
craftsmen for conscription is confirmed by the phrase **all of them
strong and fit for war**, or 'all of them able-bodied men and skilled
armourers' (*NEB*). The figures **seven thousand** and **one thousand**
are at variance with the 'ten thousand' of v. 14 and the 'three
thousand and twenty-three' of Jer. 52:28. Gray (pp. 761ff.) does
not find the figures of v. 16 convincing and accepts Jeremiah's
total as being more realistic than these approximations from a later
redactor. Montgomery (p. 556), on the other hand, finds 8,000 far
too modest a total, and suggests that if Jeremiah's 3,023 is the
number of men only, a much higher figure can be assumed for the
total deportation (cf. the 27,290 captives taken from Samaria by
Sargon). Malamat (*WHJP*, p. 211) has yet another solution, which
is based on his idea of a deportation in two stages; in the first phase,
3,023 Judaeans were taken, and in the second, 7,000 men (v. 16),
giving a total of 10,000 (v. 16). But the figure of 1,000 craftsmen
and smiths in v. 16 has still to be added to both totals; the isolation
of the figure **one thousand** is not entirely satisfactory. The suggestion of a combined figure of 10,000, with the 3,023 from Judah and
7,000 from Jerusalem, gives a reasonable total.

17. The Babylonian Chronicles confirm that Nebuchadrezzar
'appointed a king to his liking' over Jerusalem (*ANET*, p. 564), but
do not give names for the defeated king nor his replacement. As
noted in v. 18, **Mattaniah** was the son of 'Hamutal the daughter of
Jeremiah of Libnah', and like Jehoahaz his brother came from an
anti-Egyptian party, which explains why he was to Nebuchadrezzar's liking (Malamat, *WHJP*, p. 206). He is correctly designated
as **Jehoiachin's uncle**, and not his 'brother' as stated in 2 Chr.
36:10. A change of name by a foreign ruler denotes vassalage (see

under 2 Kg. 23:34). **Mattaniah**, also known from the Lachish letters
and appearing as Mattanjāma in Babylonian inscriptions (*K-B*),
meant 'gift of Yahweh'; he became **Zedekiah**, 'Yahweh is righteous'.

(d) Zedekiah and the fall of Jerusalem
24:18–25:21

Although Zedekiah retained the throne for eleven years (598–587
BC), his reign was by no means peaceful. His administration was
bereft of the upper ruling classes; possibly his kingdom was reduced
in size, if it is accepted that Jeremiah's references to 'the cities of
the Negeb' being 'shut up' (Jer. 13:18, 19) means that southern
Judah was lost in 598 BC (Alt, *Kleine Schriften II*, pp. 280ff.; Noth,
History, p. 283). Zedekiah's main problem, however, was dissension
within the Judaean community left. A strong pro-Egyptian faction,
which waited for the first opportunity to rebel against Babylon,
consisted of ministers and advisers (Jer. 38:5ff.), military personnel
and 'false prophets' (Jer. 28–29). Jeremiah, taking a pro-Babylonian
stance, advised against rebellion against the overlord (Jer. 27), and
had some sympathy from Zedekiah. Malamat (*WHJP*, pp. 213ff.)
finds that contention over the legitimacy of royal succession contributed to the controversy in Jerusalem. The pro-Egyptian faction
expected the return of the exiles and the reinstatement of Jehoiachin,
whom they presumably considered to be the legitimate king (cf.
Jer. 28:1–14); Jeremiah, on the other hand, rejected the legitimacy
of Jehoiachin's reign (Jer. 22:24ff.) and retained his allegiance to
Zedekiah (Jer. 38:14–26). In these difficult circumstances Zedekiah
proved himself to be a weak and vacillating character; basically he
belonged to the anti-Egyptian group, but he was so much afraid of
his pro-Egyptian advisers that he would not resist them (cf. Jer.
38:5).

International events encouraged the pro-Egyptian faction to put
added pressure on Zedekiah to rebel against Babylon. Although the
record in Kings proceeds immediately to Zedekiah's ninth year
(25:1), he took part in a conspiracy against Babylon in his fourth
year (595/4 BC). Envoys from a number of countries came to Jerusalem (Jer. 27:3) with the undoubted intention of forming an alliance
against Babylon. Psammeticus II of Egypt gave them some
encouragement, but the conspiracy was not successful, and it may
be that Zedekiah's visit to Babylon at this time (Jer. 51:59; cf. 29:3)
was intended to allay Babylon's suspicions.

When Zedekiah rebelled in his ninth year (590/89 BC), he was not
acting in isolation. A few years before (592 BC) Psammeticus II had
visited Palestine and the Phoenician coast, and his appearance in

the region, although arising from peaceful (Freedy and Redford, *JAOS* 90 [1970], pp. 479ff.) rather than military motives (Greenberg, *JBL* 76 [1957], pp. 304-9), gave Jerusalem's anti-Babylonian party renewed confidence. Jerusalem's rebellion, however, followed Pharaoh Hophra's accession early in 589 BC. Hophra was anxious to undermine Babylon's power in Palestine, and it is known from the Lachish letters that Judaean military commanders visited Egypt (*ANET*, p. 322). Tyre joined in the rebellion, and Nebuchadrezzar besieged it for thirteen years (cf. Ezek. 18:26-28; 29:17-20; Josephus, *Ap.* 1.21). Ammon also probably joined (Ezek. 21:23ff.; cf. Jer. 40:14; 41:15; see Ginsberg, *Fest. Marx*, pp. 365ff.). However, there was no effective anti-Babylonian block in the West, and although Jerusalem remarkably held out for at least a year and a half, the city fell to Nebuchadrezzar in the summer of 587 BC.

18. he reigned eleven years in Jerusalem: Zedekiah was installed king of Jerusalem as a Babylonian vassal. Nevertheless, Babylonian texts refer to Jehoiachin as the king of Judah, although he was residing in Babylon at the time. Malamat (*WHJP*, p. 213) does not think that Zedekiah was only a regent, but suggests that Jehoiachin was the titular head of the Jewish diaspora in Babylon. Undoubtedly, the removal of Jehoiachin in favour of Zedekiah played an important part in the controversy in Jerusalem during the last decade before the Exile. **Hamutal the daughter of Jeremiah of Libnah**: See under 2 Kg. 23:31.

19-20. The verdict on Zedekiah, set out according to the standard formula, that **he did what was evil in the sight of the LORD**, has been extended in v. 20*a* by an intrusion that resembles 24:3 very closely. Dietrich (*Prophetie*, pp. 139ff.) attributes this addition to the nomistic redactor (DtrN). Verse 20*b*, which continues the basic deuteronomistic report of vv. 18, 19, states briefly that **Zedekiah rebelled against the king of Babylon**. The date given in 25:1 shows that the author is moving directly to the rebellion of 589/8 BC, without giving any hint of the background, causes and prior build-up that have been outlined above. From this verse to 25:21 the narrator is mainly reporting what he himself had experienced; his account in 25:1-21*a* is introduced and concluded with two brief statements—24:20*b* sets the narrative in the context of Zedekiah's rebellion, and 25:2*b* states the ultimate result that Judah was taken to exile. The narrative falls into three sections: (a) vv. 1-12, the siege of the city and the exile of its population; (b) vv. 13-17, the plunder of the Temple; (c) vv. 18-21*a*, the execution of prominent Jerusalem leaders. The first and last sections have their origin in the author's own recollections, but the second is dependent upon 1

Kg. 7:15ff. (so Noth, *ÜSt*, p. 87; followed by Dietrich, *op. cit.*, p. 140).

2 Kg. 24:18–25 (except for vv. 22–26) appear again in Jer. 52, and 2 Kg. 25:1–12 are repeated in Jer. 39:1–10. The correspondence is striking, since Jer. 52:1–27 contain a repetition of the opening formula of the deuteronomistic account (cf. 24:18–20*a* with Jer. 52:1–3*a*) and its concluding statement (cf. 25:21*b* with Jer. 52:27*b*). Undoubtedly the version in 2 Kg. is the original: it is stylistically different from the prophecies of Jeremiah, and the inclusion of this section after the final statement of Jer. 51:64*b* ('thus far are the words of Jeremiah') marks it as a secondary appendix. Nevertheless the text of the secondary version in Jeremiah has been better preserved than the original version of Kings. The suggestion that 2 Kg. 25:1–12 is an excerpt from the Baruch narrative (Noth, *ÜSt*, pp. 86ff.) is refuted on the grounds that Jer. 39:1–10 appears to be a summary of either 2 Kg. 25:1–12 or Jer. 52; among the omissions are: 'on the tenth day of the month' (v. 1); the suggestion that famine made the breach possible (v. 3); the reference to a scattering of Zedekiah's soldiers (v. 5); the data in v. 8 and the listing of the Temple among the buildings burnt by the Babylonians (v. 9). Admittedly Jer. 39:3 contains some additional information, but the conclusion remains that Jer. 39:1–10 is based on 2 Kg. 25, probably via Jer. 52 (Rudolph, *Jeremia*, pp. 226ff.; Dietrich, *ibid.*).

25:1. in the ninth year of his reign, in the tenth month, on the tenth day of the month: If the reckoning is based on the Babylonian system, with the year commencing in the month of Nisan, the siege began early in 588 BC and lasted a year and a half until the middle of 587 BC; if a reckoning from Tishri is followed, it lasted until the summer of 586 BC. The former date is accepted here. **Nebuchadrezzar king of Babylon came**: Nebuchadrezzar himself remained at Riblah (cf. v. 6), and Jerusalem was expected to surrender to his 'princes' (Jer. 38:17ff.). Gray (p. 764) suggests that he was at the time dealing with a local rebellion in the Lebanon. Nebuchadrezzar's absence from the scene may have protracted Jerusalem's resistance; some temporary relief also possibly came with the interference of Egypt (Jer. 37:5, 11), but Egypt was too weak to offer Jerusalem any significant help (cf. Ezek. 17:17; 30:20, 26; Freedy and Redford, *op. cit.*, pp. 470ff., 481). **they built siegeworks against it round about**: Nebuchadrezzar, not only sent highly respected commanders to Jerusalem (Jer. 39:3), but he also used the most formidable techniques of siege warfare. He threw dikes around the city, raised ramps up to the walls and used battering rams against them (cf. also Jer. 32:24; 33:4; Ezek. 4:12; 17:17; 21:27).

2. the city was beseiged until the eleventh year of King Zede-

kiah: It fell in the summer of 587 BC or the summer of 586 BC, depending on the system of reckoning accepted (Kutsch, *Bib* 55 [1974], pp. 520–45; Larsson, *JTS* 18 [1967], pp. 417–23). Because the report in vv. 1–12 concentrates entirely on the siege of Jerusalem itself, it shows no interest in the country as a whole. There is evidence that the Babylonian forces spread throughout the land and captured other Judaean cities (cf. Jer. 34:7; 44:2; Lam. 2:2–5). The Lachish letters provide an insight into conditions in other Judaean cities and reflect the anxiety with which the progress of the Babylonians was followed (*ANET*, p. 322). Archaeological excavations also indicate that a number of sites in Judah had been completely destroyed during this period (Albright, *JBL* 51 [1932], pp. 103–6; Stern, *BA* 38 [1975], pp. 35ff.). The most notable exception was the land of Benjamin and its settlements, to the north of Jerusalem; it probably escaped destruction by surrendering to the Babylonians (Malamat, *WHJP*, pp. 217ff.).

3. The situation during the last month of the siege (**the fourth month**; cf. v. 8 for 'the fifth month') was that a severe famine had crippled the city and brought it to starvation point. With Babylonian siegeworks surrounding the city (v. 1), the harvest of one, if not two years had been prevented from reaching Jerusalem. Although no reference is made in this passage to deserters, it is probable that many of Jerusalem's inhabitants fled out and surrendered to Babylon during the last stages of the siege (Jer. 38:19), and that they were exiled while Jerusalem was still under siege (Jer. 52:29).

4. a breach was made in the city: The breach was probably made in the most vulnerable north wall of the city; this is confirmed, according to Malamat (*WHJP*, p. 220), by Zedekiah's position by the gate of Benjamin (Jer. 38:7), and by the gathering of Babylonian officers on the breach at the middle gate (Jer. 39:3). **the king with all the men of war fled**: The Heb. is impossible here, since it only has **all the men of war** without a verb. *RSV*'s reading is obtained from Jer. 39:4 and 52:7. **by the way of the gate between the two walls**: The reference here may be to a narrow corridor in the southeastern area of the city giving access to the Kidron valley (cf. Weill, *La Cité II*, pp. 36–39, 40ff., where a narrow corridor and stairs leading down from the city of David are described). Thus, when Nebuchadrezzar's men made an entrance through a breach in the north wall, the king and his retinue escaped through this corridor to the south-east of the city, and was obviously making for Transjordan, possibly to Baalis the king of Ammon. **by the king's garden**: The royal gardens were presumably in the fertile area near the pool of Siloam (cf. Neh. 3:15). **in the direction of the Arabah**: The king was aiming for the arid steppe region to the east of Jerusalem (cf.

v. 5 'the plains of Jericho'), which were to the south of Jericho in
a near desert area.

5. and all his army was scattered from him: The army disbanded
after reaching the open terrain of the Arabah, which offered the
men ample opportunity to hide and escape from their Babylonian
pursuers.

6. Nebuchadrezzar had remained at Riblah (cf. 23:33), and it was
there that Zedekiah was brought for judgment. The phrase **passed
sentence upon him** (*NEB*, 'where he pleaded his case before him')
suggests that he was granted a hearing. Montgomery (p. 562) finds
in the Heb. here a translation of the Babylonian legal phrase *dēna
dabābu* which is used in Jer. 12:1 for a legal argument. Zedekiah,
being a rebel against the Babylonian overlord, had not much of a
case to present.

7. After slaughtering Zedekiah's sons in front of him, the Babylonians **put out the eyes of Zedekiah**, which was a common punishment for captives. Montgomery (*ibid.*) finds such mutilation a deliberate destruction of the royal potency. Zedekiah disappears from
the scene when they **bound him in fetters** and taken **to Babylon**,
where according to Ezek. 12:12ff. he soon died.

8. In the fifth month, on the seventh day of the month: The
destruction of Jerusalem as outlined in vv. 8–12 occurred about a
month after the Babylonian army had gained entrance into the city.
It seems from this section that the destruction was systematically
executed and that a high ranking official was sent to accomplish the
task. Luc. and Syr. read the **seventh** as 'the ninth', obviously
thinking of the later destruction of Jerusalem on the 9th of Ab.
Nebuzaradan, Akkad. *Nabū-zār-iddina*, is called **captain of the
bodyguard**, which literally means 'chief of the slaughterers' (cf.
Gen. 37:36, 'chief cook'), and probably refers to 'the chief
executioner'.

9. The destruction of Jerusalem included burning the Temple,
the palace and **all the houses of Jerusalem**. The latter phrase has
been qualified by a secondary addition stating that **every great
house he burned down** and thus restricting the operation to every
'important' building (*NIV*) or to a 'magnate's house' (Montgomery,
p. 562; cf. Gray, p. 766, 'notable's house'). *NEB*'s reading of
the adjective *gādôl*, 'great', as a proper name, Gedaliah, has no
foundation. For other descriptions of the destruction of Jerusalem,
see Jer. 52:12–14; Ezek. 33:21; Neh. 2:13ff.

10. To complete the ravaging of the city, **the walls around Jerusalem** were broken down. Archaeological excavations have disclosed
the remains of demolished buildings both in the upper city and on
the eastern slopes of the south-eastern hill of Jerusalem. Burnt

remains and the number of arrowheads discovered in the upper city suggest that there was a fierce battle with the Babylonians (Avigad, *IEJ* 25 [1975], p. 261). The destruction of the south-eastern hill was so extensive that Nehemiah had to abandon the area and build his new wall on the inside (Kenyon, *Digging*, pp. 170f.; Malamat, *WHJP*, p. 220).

11. Three classes of people exiled are implied—those **who were left in the city, the deserters** and **the rest of the multitude**. There is uncertainty about the latter group, which is mentioned here and in Jer. 39:9; but it need not be omitted as a superfluous repetition of those **left in the city** (as suggested by Montgomery, p. 563, and Gray, p. 766). It may refer to 'any remaining artisans' (*NEB*) if *hehāmôn*, 'multitude', is read as *hā'āmôn*, 'artisans', on the basis of Jer. 52:15. **the captain of the guard carried into exile**: Oded (*IJH*, pp. 475f.) notes two differences between Babylonian and Assyrian practices with regard to deportation: (i) the Babylonians did not settle a new population in the areas from which people had been exiled; (ii) the Babylonians preferred a local governor to the appointment of a Babylonian to the post.

12. A clear picture of the deportation is not given. Verse 11 suggests that a large proportion of Jerusalem's population was carried away, and according to vv. 18ff. the leaders were executed at Riblah. However, a number of **the poorest of the land** (*NEB*, 'the weakest class of people') remained. Herrmann (*History*, pp. 284f.), accepting the reliability of the figure of 832 deportees in Jer. 52:28–30, suggests that interference with the native population was smaller than in the case of the northern kingdom and that a broad stratum of the native population was left in the land (Ackroyd, *Exile*, pp. 22ff.; Janssen, *Juda in der Exilszeit*, pp. 24–56). The ruling classes had undoubtedly been deported, and the natives left were **to be vinedressers and ploughmen**. The Heb. word translated **ploughmen** (*NEB*, 'labourers') is not easily explained. The word *yōgᵉbîm* appears here and in Jer. 52:16 with the meaning 'farmers' (Targ.); but Jer. 39:10 has *yᵉgēbîm*, 'fields', which is translated 'wells' by Jerome and Theodotion. The expected parallel for **vinedressers** is **ploughmen** or 'labourers'.

13–17. The details given here of the bronze furnishings, the vessels and the pillars of the Temple are based on 1 Kg. 7:15ff., and occur again in a fuller form in Jer. 52:17–23. It is a technical description which has probably been taken from an ancient inventory of the Temple.

13. Large items of bronze were broken in pieces and carried to Babylon. Among them were **the pillars** (1 Kg. 7:15–22), **the stands** (1 Kg. 7:27–37) and **the bronze sea** (1 Kg. 7:23–26). This verse

does not mention the bulls that supported the bronze sea, for they had been removed by Ahaz. They are included, however, in Jer. 52:20.

14. Small items of bronze, which are listed in 1 Kg. 7:40ff., were carried intact to Babylon.

15. What was of gold the captain of the guard took away as gold, and what was silver, as silver: This verse clearly means that the Babylonians were more interested in the material than in the actual vessels.

16–17. These verses contain a summary recapitulation of 1 Kg. 7:15ff., which describe the pillars. More detailed information appears in Jer. 52:20ff.

18–21. Some of the community leaders were taken by Nebuzaradan to Riblah, where they were executed by Nebuchadrezzar. According to Gray (p. 768), these were exemplary executions of notable leaders from among the nationalist resistance.

18. Seraiah the chief priest: Seraiah, who was the grandson of Hilkiah and the father of Jehozadak (1 Chr. 6:13–15), is the first to be given the title **the chief priest** (*kôhēn hārō'š*, in contrast to *hakkôhēn haggādôl* of 22:4; 23:4), which is commonly used in Chronicles and Ezra. **Zephaniah the second priest**: The Heb. may mean 'a priest of the second rank' (cf. 23:4); but, if changed slightly to conform with Jer. 52:24, the meaning is **the second priest. the three keepers of the threshold**: The figure **three** is missing from the parallel list in 2 Kg. 23:4. Members of the priestly hierarchy were the first group to be executed, for the list here corresponds to the three orders of the higher priesthood in 23:4.

19. The second group brought to Riblah consisted of three state officials. The **officer who had been in command of the men of war**, according to *NEB*, was 'a eunuch who was in charge of the fighting men'. *RSV*'s **five men of the king's council** is an attempt to render the Heb. 'five of them who saw the king's face'; cf. *NEB*, 'five of those with right of access to the king'. These were privy councillors, of whom only **five** ('seven' according to Jer. 52) had failed to escape and so **were found in the city**. The **secretary of the commander of the army** was probably an adjutant responsible for mobilising the army; cf. Jg. 5:14; he dealt with conscripts from among **the people of the land** as opposed to the professional army. **Sixty men of the people of the land** were in the city; they may have been provincial notables (Gray, p. 769; cf. Montgomery, p. 564) rather than simply 'the people' of *NEB*.

20–21. After reporting the execution of the Jerusalem religious and civil leaders at Nebuchadrezzar's headquarters **at Riblah in the land of Hamath**, the account of the fall of Jerusalem is fittingly concluded in v. 21*b* with the statement **So Judah was taken into exile out of its own land**. This is obviously the conclusion of the original version of the book (Montgomery, p. 546; Gray, *ibid*.), and is ascribed to DtrG by Dietrich (*op. cit.*, p. 142).

(e) Gedaliah, governor of Judah
25:22–26

This account of Gedaliah's period as governor of Judah is a shortened form of the more detailed account in Jer. 40:7–41:8. Gray (p. 770) supposes that the Jeremianic account originated from those actually involved, whereas the deuteronomistic redactor had definite reasons for giving a shortened form. Dietrich (*Prophetie*, p. 143) suggests that this brief account must be considered in conjunction with the release of Jehoiachin in vv. 27–30. He ascribes both to DtrN, and finds in the release of Jehoiachin, the representative of the Davidic dynasty, a more positive and optimistic ending to the book. The narrative of Gedaliah's murder contributes to that viewpoint by showing that there was no alternative to Jehoiachin on Judaean soil (Baltzer, *Fest. von Rad*, pp. 33–43).

22. he appointed Gedaliah the son of Ahikam, son of Shaphan, governor: The new governor came from a noble family, since his father **Ahikam** is mentioned in 2 Kg. 22:12, and had supported Jeremiah's policy (Jer. 26:24). He was probably chosen because of his known pro-Babylonian stance. A clay seal-impression discovered at Lachish is inscribed 'Belonging to Gedaliah who is over the household' (Hooke, *PEQ* 67 [1935], pp. 195–6), and is taken to imply that Gedaliah was previously a royal chamberlain under Zedekiah.

23. all the captains of the forces in the open country: The addition of **in the open country** from Jer. 40:7 designates these forces as armed bands, who went out in the open country around Jerusalem and had not surrendered to the Babylonians. It is not certain whether these were bands that had been engaged in guerilla warfare against the Babylonian forces during the siege of Jerusalem or bands that had, like Zedekiah, escaped from Jerusalem after the breaching of the northern wall. **at Mizpah**: cf. 1 Kg. 15:22, where it is identified with *Tell en-Nasbeh* to the north of Jerusalem. It is significant that this site is rather exceptional in that it shows no sign of destruction during the period when the Babylonians overran the whole of Judah (Albright, *Archaeology*, pp. 141ff.). **Ishmael the son of Nethaniah**: He is not known apart from this connection with the murder of Gedaliah. Verse 25 states that he was 'of the royal family', which is quite possible, for the name is known from two seals

(Diringer, *Le Iscrizioni*, pp. 203, 210). **Johanan the son of Kareah**: Details of Johanan's part in resisting Ishmael's activities are recorded in Jer. 41:11–18. **Seraiah the son of Tanhumeth the Netophathite**: Seraiah was probably from the Bethel area, if Netophah is identified with the area around the spring of '*Ain an-Natūf* to the south of Bethlehem (Kob, *PJB* 28 [1932], pp. 47–54); cf. also Ezr. 2:22; Neh. 7:26. **Jaazaniah the son of the Maacathite**: His father's name is not given, but Jaazaniah's name appears on a seal from Tell en-Nasbeh bearing the inscription 'Belonging to Ja'azaniah the servant of the king', which suggests that he was a high ranking officer (Badè, *ZAW* 51 [1933], pp. 150–6).

24. The pro-Babylonian policy of Gedaliah is clear from this verse; cf. the policy of co-operation with the Babylonians advocated by Jeremiah (Jer. 29:4–14). Presumably **Chaldean officials** helped the governor at Mizpah.

25. Ishmael's murder of Gedaliah and his supporters in Mizpah is reported in this verse. His further treachery against the men of Shechem, Shiloh and Samaria, which is reported in Jer. 41:4ff., is not mentioned in the version in Kings. This would seem to confirm Dietrich's suggestion (*ibid.*) that some details were left out by the deuteronomistic redactor because of his wish to make one point only, namely, that Gedaliah's murder meant that there was no rival for Jehoiachin in Judah.

26. Then all the people . . . arose and went to Egypt: According to Jer. 42–43, the prophet Jeremiah was reluctantly carried to Egypt with the people fleeing there for safety. The Jews settled in Tahpanhes, a border fortress near Pelusium, and other places in upper Egypt, Migdol, Noph (Memphis) and the land of Pathras (Jer. 44:1). There is evidence of Jewish settlers in the Delta region (cf. Isa. 19:18f.; Josephus, *Ant.* XIII.3.1–3), and also of an earlier colony of mercenaries at Yeb (Porten, *Archives*, *passim*).

(f) Jehoiachin's release in Babylon

25:27–30

This section again has a parallel in Jer. 52:31–34, which seems to have been based upon it (Noth, *ÜSt*, pp. 86ff.), although some take it to be an excerpt from Jer. 40:7–43:7 (Dietrich, *Prophetie*, pp. 140f.; Zenger, *BZ* 12 [1968], pp. 16ff.). A problem that arises in this connection is the lack of any reference to Jeremiah in these final chapters of Kings. Among the reasons that can be suggested are: (a) that, because Jeremiah had declared his solidarity with the people left in the land and had pinned his hopes to the community left under Gedaliah's rule, his standpoint was not acceptable to the deuteronomistic historian; (b) that vv. 27–30 originated from Babylon and that the author did not have access to the Jeremianic tradition (Pohlmann, *Fest. Würthwein*, pp. 94–109).

Behind the reference here to Jehoiachin's release there may be a more detailed report of the fate of the exiles (Dietrich, *Prophetie*, pp. 140ff.; Zenger, *BZ* 12 [1968], p. 17). The significance of the report in these verses is that in effect it asserts that Jehoiachin was now recognized as the official king of Judah and vassal of the Babylonian king (Zenger, *ibid.*). For the Babylonian Jews this was an important event and probably led to hopes for the restoration of the Davidic dynasty and a rebirth of the nation. The inclusion of the report at the end of the Deuteronomistic History suggests that the deuteronomists wished to hint that they saw in this event a possibility of a national revival under a Davidic king. It stands in marked contrast to the final section of the original work (DtrG), which ended on the pessimistic note of Jerusalem's fall and Judah's exile. Dietrich (*ibid.*) ascribes it to DtrN, and finds in it an assertion of a theme that recurs in the nomistic redactor's work, that Yahweh has established the Davidic dynasty and protects it even in Babylon. Von Rad (*Theology I*, p. 343) finds in the persistence of this hope what he calls a 'messianic' motif, even if he has to qualify that term. In view of the fact that the section is so brief and does not attempt to spell out the significance of the events described, there must be doubts about the validity of finding here a 'messianic' interpretation of these events. Nevertheless, it is obvious that the redactor DtrN saw some significance in the survival of the Davidic dynasty in Babylon, and inserted this section for a more profound reason than merely a wish to avoid closing the history on a despondent note (as is suggested by Gray, p. 773).

27. in the thirty seventh year of the exile: Jehoiachin had been held in captivity since 598 BC, and so his release came in 561 BC, which corresponds with the date of Evil-merodach's accession in the spring of that year, following the death of Nebuchadrezzar in 562 BC. **the year he began to reign**: This corresponds to the Akkad. expression 'the year of the start of the reign' (*šanat rēš šarrūti*), which did not count as a regnal year (see above, pp. 12ff.). The Heb. *šᵉnaṯ molkô* has a parallel in a Phoenician inscription from the Persian period (Cross, *Directions*, pp. 45ff.). According to Zenger (*ibid.*) this provided an opportunity for reaffirming the oath of vassaldom, and it is probable that Jehoiachin was released and recognised as a king for that purpose. **Evil-merodach king of Babylon**: Amelmarduk is reputed to have been an unrighteous king and enjoyed a reign of only two years, before he was assassinated by Nergal-sar-usur. **graciously freed Jehoiachin king of Judah from prison**: Presumably he was released as part of a general amnesty at the beginning of a new reign. Evidence from Mari and from an Assyrian letter to Esarhaddon suggests that this was a normal practice in Mesopotamia (Gray, p. 773; Zenger, *op. cit.*, pp. 18ff.). For the Heb. phrase ('lifted the head of Jehoiachin') behind the translation **graciously freed** (*NEB*, 'showed favour'), cf. Gen. 40:13. Zenger (*ibid.*) on the basis of his examination of the phrase in Heb. and Akkad. texts gives it the meaning 'summoned Jehoiachin from prison for an audience before the king'.

28. he spoke kindly to him: According to Zenger (*ibid.*) the phrase means more than what is implied in *RSV*; it refers specifically to friendship or good relations established through a treaty (Moran, *JNES* 22 [1963], p. 174). **the kings who were with him in Babylon**: The reference here is to other conquered kings, who were detained in political captivity in Babylon. It is suggested that vassal kings were present at the enthronement ritual to witness the accession of their new overlord (so Zenger, *ibid.*).

29–30. put off his prison garments: This suggests that he was rerobed in his royal garments. **he dined regularly at the king's table . . . a regular allowance was given him by the king**: Cuneiform tablets recording the rations allocated to foreigners, including Philistines and Jews, actually name Jehoiachin ('Jakukinu, the son of the king of Yakudu') and his five sons as recipients of rations. The tablets were discovered in small rooms, which were either storerooms or the apartments in which the exiles lived (Weidner, *Fest. Dussaud II*, pp. 933–5; *ANET*, p. 308). On this basis it has been suggested that Jehoiachin was a king-in-exile, who lived in comfortable conditions (Albright, *BA* 5 [1942], pp. 49–55). The book thus concludes on the fitting note that the Davidic king, even in exile, lived in dignity and honour.

GENERAL INDEX

INDEX OF AUTHORS